DATE DUE

MAR 21 1996			

POETRY

ITS APPRECIATION AND ENJOYMENT

POETRY

ITS APPRECIATION AND ENJOYMENT

by

LOUIS UNTERMEYER

Editor of Modern American Poetry, Modern British Poetry, The Book of Living Verse, Author of American Poetry since 1900, etc.

and

CARTER DAVIDSON

Knox College

HARCOURT, BRACE AND COMPANY

NEW YORK

5

Typography by Robert Josephy

PRINTED IN THE UNITED STATES OF AMERICA
BY QUINN & BODEN COMPANY, INC., RAHWAY, N. J.

The poet works with those dimensions of invisibility which exist at the opposite extreme from the microscopic dimensions which concern the scientist. He works with the over-obvious, the too-apparent, the phenomena which men cannot see because they are so close that vision blurs, the phenomena which approach the seeing eye so near that they become sometimes the seeing eye itself. It is for this reason that the true perceptions of the poet have such an overwhelming and instantaneous feel of truth. They require no demonstration because they were always true. They were merely never "seen" before. The poet, with the adjustment of a phrase, with the contrast of an image, with the rhythm of a line, has fixed a focus which all the talk and all the staring of the world has been unable to fix before him. His is a labor which is at all times necessary, for without it that sense of human reality which is the poet's greatest accomplishment is lost.

—ARCHIBALD MAC LEISH in *The Saturday Review of Literature*

PREFACE AND ACKNOWLEDGMENTS

To answer the question before it is put we, the authors, would like to define the purpose of the book. This is neither an advanced treatise for the scholar nor an analytical history of poetry, but an introduction to the poetic art and a study of its multiple forms.

To us the essence of poetry is not merely expression, but communion: a communication intended by a poet for a reader. This book is written that the communication may become more natural, pleasurable and profitable for students or general readers.

The division of the volume into two books is part of the plan. The first book is devoted to the appreciation of poetry as a record of experience, an outlet of emotion, a transcript of life and its various activities—in short, a consideration of poetry based on its subject-matter. The second book attempts to increase that enjoyment through an understanding of those devices by which poetry achieves its effects, through recognition of forms and patterns—a study of the structural element and the application of technique.

It is obvious that in anything short of a five-foot shelf of poetry many omissions must be made. It is impossible to include all the important poems which would serve to illumine the text; the lists of supplementary readings may be used partly to fill these gaps. We have tried to select representative poems which could be quoted in their entirety; in a few cases where complete quotation of a long poem was impossible, we have chosen self-sufficient units.

Whenever so complex a body is separated into a score of categorical chapters, all the categories immediately become suspect. We ourselves suspect them; several poems might be used to illustrate any one of a dozen aspects. In the text we have placed them so that they exemplify one element of poetry; it is for the reader to recognize the other values.

It should be said that the authors are not wedded to any one school of poetry, either classic or modern; in fact they have their doubts as to the authenticity, and even the very existence, of "schools." John Livingston Lowes has shown that the revolt of one age is the convention of the next and that the champion of "modernity" is likely to be defending an old tradition, of whose origins he may often be ignorant. All divisions into "periods" are dangerous and likely to be misleading. The truth is that each age is "modern" to itself, and the pendulum has always swung from one "influence" and "new movement" to another.

We also wish to declare that this book is a real collaboration, not a mere wedding of two names on the title-page. Most of the ideas expressed, most of the poems included, have come from a joint consideration of the material. This was made possible by our common conviction that a new approach for the reader of poetry is needed, and by a mutual agreement upon what that approach should be.

Our thanks are due various publishers and agents for their consent to reprint poems copyrighted and controlled by them; without their coöperation quotations of modern poetry would have been impossible. Our indebtedness is specifically acknowledged to:

THE BOOKFELLOWS, Chicago—for "Bees" from *A Tallow Dip* by Richard R. Kirk.

BRENTANO'S—for the selections from *The Complete Poems* of Francis Ledwidge.

BRANDT & BRANDT, INC.—as agents for Conrad Aiken, E. E. Cummings and Edna St. Vincent Millay.

THE BORZOI CHAPBOOKS (ALFRED A. KNOPF, INC.)—for "This Measure" by Léonie Adams, "Before March" by Archibald MacLeish and "Return at Night" by Sara Teasdale.

THE STEPHEN DAYE PRESS—for the selection from *Assent to Autumn* by Leila Jones.

DOUBLEDAY, DORAN AND COMPANY, INC.—for the selections from *Lincoln and Other Poems* by Edwin Markham, *Kensington Gardens* by Humbert Wolfe, and the authorized edition of *Leaves of Grass* by Walt Whitman, copyright, 1924, by Doubleday, Doran & Company, Inc.

DODD, MEAD AND COMPANY, INC.—for the selections from *The Collected Poems* of Rupert Brooke, copyright, 1915, by Dodd, Mead and Company, Inc.

FARRAR & RINEHART, INC.—for the selection from *City Child* by Selma Robinson.

THE FOUR SEAS COMPANY—for the selections from *Images Old and New* by Richard Aldington.

HARCOURT, BRACE AND COMPANY, INC.—for the selections from *Canzoni* by T. A. Daly, *Selected Poems* by W. H. Davies, *The Noise that Time Makes* by Merrill Moore, *Smoke and Steel* by Carl Sandburg, copyright, 1920, by Harcourt, Brace and Company, *Slabs of the Sunburnt West* by Carl Sandburg, copyright, 1922, by Harcourt, Brace and Company, *Food and Drink* by Louis Untermeyer, copyright, 1932, by Harcourt, Brace and Company, and *The Unknown Goddess* by Humbert Wolfe.

HARPER'S MAGAZINE—for "Epitaph for a Young Athlete" by Luella Boynton.

HARPER & BROTHERS—for the selections from *Mother Goose for Grown-Ups* by Guy Wetmore Carryl and *Wind in the Grass* by Christy MacKaye. "What lips my lips have kissed" and "Pity me not because the light of day," published by Harper & Brothers, are from *The Ballad of the Harp Weaver and Other Poems,* copyright, 1920, 1921, 1922, 1923, by Edna St. Vincent Millay. "Oh, sleep forever in the Latmian cave," is from *Fatal Interview,* published by Harper & Brothers, copyright, 1931, by Edna St. Vincent Millay.

THE HERALD TRIBUNE, INC.—for the selections from *The Conning Tower* by Franklin P. Adams and the poem by David McCord.

HENRY HOLT AND COMPANY—for the selections from *The Listeners* by Walter de la Mare, *North of Boston* by Robert Frost, *Mountain Interval* by Robert Frost and *New Hampshire* by Robert Frost, by permission of and by arrangement with Henry Holt and Company.

HOUGHTON MIFFLIN COMPANY—for the selections from *Complete Poems* by Thomas Bailey Aldrich, *Poems* by Ralph Waldo Emerson, *Pike County Ballads and Other Pieces* by John Hay, *The Complete Poetical Works* of Oliver Wendell Holmes, *The Complete Poetical Works* of Henry Wadsworth Longfellow, *The Complete*

Poetical Works of James Russell Lowell, *What's O'Clock* by Amy Lowell, *Poems: 1924-1933* by Archibald MacLeish, *Poems and Poetic Dramas* by William Vaughn Moody and *The Complete Poetical Works* of John Greenleaf Whittier, all of which are used by permission of and by arrangement with Houghton Mifflin Company.

WALTER KLINEFELTER, Glen Rock, Pennsylvania—for the selection from *First Editions* by Richard R. Kirk.

ALFRED A. KNOPF, INC.—for the selections from *Verse* by Adelaide Crapsey, *Theatre Guyed* by Newman Levy, *Unaccustomed As I Am* by Morrie Ryskind and *Collected Poems of Elinor Wylie,* all of which are used by permission of and by arrangement with Alfred A. Knopf, Inc.

LITTLE, BROWN & COMPANY—for the selections from *The Poems of Emily Dickinson,* Centenary Edition, Edited by Martha Dickinson Bianchi and Alfred Leete Hampson. Reprinted by permission of and by arrangement with Little, Brown & Company.

HORACE LIVERIGHT, INC.—for the selection from *Collected Poems by H. D.*

EDWIN MARKHAM—for "Lincoln, the Man of the People," copyright 1900, 1919, by Edwin Markham and reprinted with his special permission.

ROBERT M. MCBRIDE & COMPANY—for the selection from *Those Not Elect* by Léonie Adams.

THE MACMILLAN COMPANY—for "Crystal Moment" from *The Yoke of Thunder* by Robert P. T. Coffin, "Cargoes" from *Ballads and Poems* by John Masefield, "The Gale" from *Preludes and Symphonies* by John Gould Fletcher, one stanza from "The Wild Swans at Coole" from *The Wild Swans at Coole* by William Butler Yeats, and "Return at Night" and "In Memory of Vachel Lindsay" from *Strange Victory* by Sara Teasdale.

OXFORD UNIVERSITY PRESS—for the selections from *The Collected Poems of Robert Bridges* and *The Poems of Gerard Manley Hopkins.*

RANDOM HOUSE—for the selection from *Dear Judas* by Robinson Jeffers.

SIEGFRIED SASSOON and WILLIAM HEINEMANN, LTD.—for the selection from *Counter-Attack.*

THE SATURDAY REVIEW OF LITERATURE—for "The Love of Books" by James R. Clemens.

CHARLES SCRIBNER'S SONS—for the selections from *The Children of the Night* by Edwin Arlington Robinson, *The Town Down the River* by Edwin Arlington Robinson, *Dust and Light* by John Hall Wheelock and *Selected Poems* by Conrad Aiken, published by Charles Scribner's Sons, copyright, 1925, by Horace Liveright, Inc.

SMALL, MAYNARD & COMPANY—for the selections from *More Songs from Vagabondia* by Richard Hovey and Bliss Carman.

THOMAS SELTZER, INC.—for the selection from *Tulips and Chimneys* by E. E. Cummings.

THE VIKING PRESS, INC.—for the selections from *The Espalier* by Sylvia Townsend Warner and *Blossoming Antlers* by Winifred Welles, copyright, 1933; for "All Day I Hear" from *Chamber Music* by James Joyce; for "Strange Meeting" from *Poems* by Wilfred Owen; for "Epitaphs" from *Time Importuned* by Sylvia Townsend Warner—the poems being used by permission of and by arrangement with The Viking Press, Inc., New York.

The authors are also indebted to Julian R. Hovey, son of Richard Hovey, for permission to reprint two of his father's poems, to Margaret Conklin, as literary agent for the late Sara Teasdale, for two of Sara Teasdale's posthumous poems, and to

Archibald MacLeish, Selma Robinson, Franklin P. Adams, Richard R. Hoffmann, Merrill Moore, Melville Cane, David McCord, Luella Boynton, James R. Clemens, Marie Luhrs, Louis Ginsberg, Leila Jones and Michael Lewis for consent to quote certain poems not yet published in any of their volumes.

For critical examination of the manuscript as well as for suggestions toward its improvement and for checking the texts of various poems the authors are grateful to Tom Burns Haber, Ohio State University.

The first part of the chapter "The Rhythms of Poetry" was originally "A Note on Rhythm" by Louis Untermeyer in *The New Republic;* the analysis of rhyme appeared as an essay ("Rhyme and its Reasons" by Louis Untermeyer) in *The Saturday Review of Literature.*

CONTENTS

CONTENTS

POEMS QUOTED IN THE CHAPTERS

I. THE PREJUDICE AGAINST POETRY

II. THE DEFINITION OF POETRY

III. POETRY AND PROSE

IV. THE IMAGINATION OF POETRY

V. THE EXPERIENCES OF POETRY: I

VI. THE EXPERIENCES OF POETRY: 2

VII. THE EMOTIONS OF POETRY: I

VIII. THE EMOTIONS OF POETRY: 2

IX. THE THOUGHTS OF POETRY

X. SATIRE IN POETRY

XI. PLAY IN POETRY

XII. THE RHYTHMS OF POETRY

XIII. THE PATTERNS OF POETRY: I

XIV. THE PATTERNS OF POETRY: 2

XV. THE PATTERNS OF POETRY: 3

XVI. THE PATTERNS OF POETRY: 4

XVII. THE PATTERNS OF POETRY: 5

XVIII. THE WORDS OF POETRY

XIX. GOOD AND BAD POETRY

BOOK ONE

EXPERIENCE AND ENJOYMENT

CONTENTS FOR BOOK ONE

1

THE PREJUDICE AGAINST POETRY

No art is more closely related to man than poetry—and none has been so variously interpreted. It was regarded with reverence by primitive people, honored by the folk as well as by the sages throughout antiquity, quoted by peasants and beloved by the cultured in every civilization. It is only in our own time and in our own country that poetry is suspected. Lord Bacon considered the art nothing less than "divine" since "it raises the mind and hurries it into sublimity by conforming the show of things to the desires of the soul, instead of subjecting the soul to external things, as reason and history do." Yet the average man in America believes that poetry is not so much a sacred as a secret art, an abracadabra practiced and enjoyed only by the verbal magicians who are suspiciously expert in the craft. "Poetry is for poets," says the man in the street, with a sneer he does not trouble to disguise. "It has its place, I suppose, but personally," he adds, in cheerful dismissal, "I'm prejudiced against that sort of thing."

Although we do not need to justify poetry we must recognize such prejudice, the more so since it seems to be prevalent in these States. The prejudice is as paradoxical as it is inconsistent. It did not exist in Greece, where the poet was venerated as dramatist and spokesman-priest; nor in Rome, where the Caesars vied with the singers; nor in the Middle Ages, wherein no court was complete without its local laureate, no castle worthy of the name that did not house a troubadour or minnesinger. The prejudice is not native to the Orient, where people think the composing of poetry so natural an accomplishment that they improvise verses freely and seldom bother to sign their names to written poems; nor is it found in modern Europe, where the poems of Heine and Béranger and Carducci have become the folk-songs of unlettered multitudes. The prejudice against poetry is chiefly an Anglo-Saxon innovation, which appears most commonly in the form of three complaints: (1) Poetry is abnormal; (2) it is forbiddingly "highbrow" and "meaningless;" (3) it is effeminate. Let us examine these charges.

First prejudice: Poetry is abnormal. Of all the common misconceptions of poetry this is the most prevalent and the most discouraging: the notion that poetry is the creation of abnormal, neurotic or absurd creatures and requires similarly abnormal and neurotic natures to respond to it. The comic weekly cartoon indicates that the poet, next to the mother-in-law, is the surest material for a laugh: the poor fellow is usually shown long of hair and short of cash, hollow-eyed, unkempt, unaware of reality, gazing at the moon and jotting down precious phrases on a frayed cuff or in an equally shabby note-book. He is pictured wandering in space and time, oblivious to every ordinary activity, something like a fallen angel and something like a jackass. It has been remarked that a poet in the last century is picturesque, but a poet in the next apartment is a nuisance.

Undoubtedly there have been eccentrics in literature, but no profession is free of them. Emotional intensity and imaginative power sometimes set the poet apart from his fellow-man, but these gifts make him more, not less, able to feel, share, and express the common or unusual experiences of others. "There is no gap," says I. A. Richards, "between our everyday emotional life and the material of poetry. . . . We cannot avoid the material of poetry. If we do not live in consonance with good poetry, we must live in consonance with bad poetry. In fact, the idle hours of most lives are filled with reveries that are simply bad poetry." Man does not live by bread alone; Emerson went further than the Bible and maintained that he lived not only by poetry but through its agency. "See the power of national emblems. Some stars, lilies, leopards, a crescent, a lion, an eagle or other figure which came into credit God knows how, an old rag of bunting blowing in the wind . . . shall make the blood tingle under the rudest or most conventional exterior. The people fancy they hate poetry—and they are all poets and mystics! . . . For we are not pans and barrows, nor even porters of the fire and torch-bearers, but children of the fire, made of it, and only the same divinity transmuted."

Even the writing of poetry is by no means as uncommon as the prejudiced mind would have us believe. As an activity, far from being "abnormal," it is the most practiced of pursuits. It may be prompted by the stirrings of first love or by the shock of tragedy, or by the thrill of some unforeseen event, but the person whose pulse has never quickened into rapture and whose pen has never hurried into rhyme is the exception to the norm. An examination of the amount of verse printed in America alone in the twenty years between 1912 and 1932 reveals that approximately 40,000 poets have achieved publication and probably ten times that number have written without attaining the distinction of print—all within one generation. The prejudice against poetry in America is, therefore, doubly inconsistent since never before have the people of these States been so ready to express themselves in rhythm and adequate rhyme.

Second prejudice: Poetry is forbiddingly "highbrow" and often "meaningless." The charge, in other words, is (a) that poetry says too much, and (b) that it has nothing to say. Apart from the inconsistency of the complaint, the prejudice is stretched to include rhyme in all its manifestations. It is, according to certain detractors, a pleasant tinkle of pretty syllables, a kind of musical soothing-syrup, an erudite conjuring trick for the highly cultivated. Yet it is obvious that the lowest "lowbrow" enjoys rhyme for its own sake—as may be proved by the hundreds of thousands who have chuckled at the dexterity of the verses in the Gilbert and Sullivan operas. It is relished by all who have made up or memorized limericks—the very point of these being the oddity of the rhyming—by all who have repeated the words of the latest popular song. Poetry has always been the easiest, not the hardest, form to remember. Primitive legends and laws were transmitted in rhythmic form. Not only the Psalms but the Mosaic injunctions were written in Hebrew poetry. In childhood the memorization of names, dates, and other prosaic facts has commonly been speeded up and permanently retained by being cast in rhyme. Even the supposedly anti-poetic Puritans combined religion and verse; the very alphabet was rhymed in *The New England Primer*: "In *A*dam's fall We sinnéd all," "Thy life to mend This *B*ook attend," "The *C*at doth play And after slay" . . . and so on until "Youth forward slips Death soonest nips" and "Zaccheus he Did climb the tree His Lord to see." And who has not learned the days of the month by remembering that

Thirty days hath September,
April, June, and November . . . ?

The most casual reading of poetry will convince the skeptical that verse demands no special apparatus for its enjoyment and that in compensation for the occasional difficulties there are infinite rewards. Instead of being insufferably "intellectual" and incomprehensible, poetry has always expressed man's simplest as well as his most complicated emotions. William Hazlitt insists that "man is a poetical animal; and those of us who do not study the principles of poetry, act upon them all our lives—like Molière's *Bourgeois Gentilhomme,* who had always spoken prose 'without knowing it.' The child is a poet in fact when he first plays at hide-and-seek or repeats the story of Jack the Giant-killer; the shepherd-boy is a poet when he first crowns his mistress with a garland of flowers . . . the miser when he hugs his gold; the courtier who builds his hopes upon a smile; the slave who worships a tyrant, or the tyrant who fancies himself a god—the vain, the ambitious, the proud, the choleric, the hero and the coward, the rich and poor, the young and the old, all live in a world of their own making; and the poet does no more than describe what all the others think and act." Even though one might not be willing to be as inclusive as Hazlitt, one must recognize that poetry is not merely a "precious" speech confined to a few specialists, but a "universal language which the heart holds with nature and itself. He who has a contempt for poetry cannot have much respect for himself or anything else."

The "meaninglessness" of poetry is another false idea which has led thousands away from the perusal and appreciation of verse. Those prejudiced against it are willing to concede that poetry possesses a certain beauty of form, even a certain charm of music, but they contend it carries no significant message. "If I want to find facts I read the newspaper," says one. "I never look for truth in poetry; I consult the encyclopedia." This is to confuse the outer form with the inner spirit, to mistake the "fact" for the "truth." Data on unemployment may well be given in a statistical account; reaction of the heart to the terror and tragedy of unemployment is the material of poetry. To confuse "fact" and "truth" is to lose sight of the very function of poetry, for poetry has always sought to reach and reflect the deepest emotions, the intensities, the spiritual values, which the newspaper evades and the encyclopedia, for all its thoroughness, cannot express. The greatest truths of human existence have found their most powerful projections in poetry: the histories of great people in their epics and sagas; world religions in hymns and vedas, in a Dante's *Divine Comedy* and a Goethe's *Faust;* philosophic systems in Lucretius' *De Rerum Natura* and in the poems of Blake, Wordsworth, and Arnold. It must also be remembered that emotions are as "significant" as facts or ideas in determining human conduct—and poetry has proved itself to be, first of all, the language of the emotions.

Third prejudice: Poetry is effeminate. This is the commonest—and, seemingly, the most devastating—barrier erected between poetry and the average reader. It is an obstacle which is hard to overcome, for it has never been completely demolished since the time of the hardy men who hacked their way into the country. America was settled by those who sought freedom rather than beauty. Life on a savage continent demanded a communal purpose; conditions called for action, not for contemplative dreams. The pioneer had no time for art. His energies were consumed in clearing forests, fighting Indians, building stockades, and protecting his cabins. Isolation, lack of luxuries and distance from large centres stimulated the crafts, but crippled the creative impulses which depend on a measure of meditation. In a life struggling against difficulties, devoted to physical activity, poetry seemed an irrelevance, almost an impertinence.

Although there is little left to win from savagery, although the last frontier has been charted and the log cabin amplified to the one hundred and two stories of the Empire State Building, the pioneering impulse still persists, carrying with it a contempt for art. The prejudice against poetry, a prejudice both superficial and absurd, remains like a ghost which has never been laid.

The "feminine" aspect of poetry is part of this ghostlike past. The characterization was invented by the illiterate or merely muscular who thought all form of meditation was, somehow, effeminate. The application of the term is usually as foolish as it is false.

If poetry—and, for that matter, any of the creative arts—were not a masculine business, it would follow that Art has been practiced largely, if not chiefly, by women. But the opposite is the case. However one may explain it—on the basis of lack of opportunity or of economic necessity—the fact remains that, though woman may be fundamentally a creator, man has been the creative artist. With the rare exception of an occasional Sappho, an Emily Dickinson or an Emily Brontë, history shows an extraordinary lack of women as composers, sculptors, playwrights, painters or poets of the first rank. Even in the chief branch of literature in which they have attained excellence—the writing of love-lyrics—they have been surpassed and outnumbered by men in the proportion of a hundred to one. Poetry, then, is not only a masculine occupation, but an especially manly one.

Yet, as L. A. G. Strong points out,[1] "When a poet somehow becomes news, the papers are at pains to state that he wears his hair short and enjoys his beer. They would not feel the necessity of thus assuring their readers if he were a doctor or a chartered accountant." The real poets have always been real men, not falsetto posturers; they have been men of vigor and varied accomplish-

[1] In *Common Sense About Poetry.* Alfred A. Knopf, 1932.

ments. The roll-call of the greatest would include men who have shaped the world's affairs as well as its letters. David the Psalmist was no less a warrior for being a poet, greater even than the unpoetic and "practical" Saul. Solomon, reputed the author of the most passionate love-poem ever written, was also reputed the wisest of rulers. Plato was not only a philosopher but a lyric poet and an excellent amateur wrestler. When Caesar Augustus sought intelligent companions he invited the pastoral poet Virgil to grace his board and, during his campaigns, often sent couriers to the poet, imploring him to despatch another canto of the Æneid to cheer him during long sieges. The worldly Maecenas selected Horace, a writer of odes, for his closest associate. Dante was known to his fellows not only as the first poet of his times, but as an outstanding Florentine envoy. The turbulent Michelangelo hacked his way through stone, flung up cathedral domes, painted like a Titan, and composed sonnets as self-revealing as his sculpture. Chaucer, "the father of English poesy," acted as confidential ambassador and diplomat from England to France. Sir Walter Raleigh, courtier and soldier-of-fortune, never ceased to write poetry and chose that medium for his last message. Christopher Marlowe fulfilled the swashbuckler tradition of the Elizabethan period by his furious imagination and by "dying swearing," stabbed to death in a tavern brawl. Shakespeare, the world's incomparable poet-playwright, was in addition a shrewd enough business man to settle down in his home town at the height of his career, as Stratford-on-Avon's respectable landowner and distinguished citizen. Ben Jonson, a man's man to the last drop of his hot blood, spent his youth as a bricklayer, his young manhood as a swaggering duellist, and his old age in almost continuous talking and tippling. When Cromwell sought a Secretary of Foreign Affairs he found his man in the Puritan poet, John Milton. John Lyly, Henry Vaughan, George Crabbe, Mark Akenside, and Oliver Goldsmith were practicing physicians while at work upon their most memorable lines. Perhaps the most efficiently governed of German principalities in the early nineteenth century was the Duchy of Weimar, where the prime minister was Goethe. Robert Burns was a farmer. Whittier was, by turns, a chore-boy, cobbler, and a fiery anti-slavery pamphleteer. William Morris wrote his epical narratives while designing new fonts of type, making furniture, and revolutionizing interior decorating.

Thus the history of literature refutes the misconception of the poet as a feather-brained and unmanly incompetent. The present reinforces the past: John Masefield, poet laureate of England, spent his formative years as an able seaman with an episode as barkeeper's assistant in Greenwich Village. W. H. Davies, the most "bird-like" of living lyricists, was a cattleman, a berry-picker, a day-laborer, a "super-tramp," until his foot was cut off when he rode the rails in Canada. His compatriot, Ralph Hodgson, one of the purest voices of this age, is known as a writer to only a few, whereas every sportsman in England recognizes him as a famous dog-fancier and authority on boxing. Robert Frost was employed in the Massachusetts mills as a bobbin-boy and worked many years as a farmer in New Hampshire before his first book was published when he was nearly forty. Edgar Lee Masters, an Illinois lawyer, brought to his *Spoon River Anthology* a power of analysis rare even in the tensest courtroom. Carl Sandburg's illumination of industrial America came directly out of his experiences as harvest-hand, dish-washer, porter in a barber-shop and truck-handler. Siegfried Sassoon, Rupert Brooke, Wilfred Owen, Robert Graves, Alan Seeger, and Joyce Kilmer must be added to the great list of soldier-poets. . . . "I think," wrote Sir Philip Sidney, one of the bravest and most honorable fighters in the field, "and I think rightly, the laurel crown appointed for triumphant captains doth worthily, of all other learnings, honor the poet's triumph."

If poetry were the expression of abnormal, neurotic, and childish reflections of life, it could hardly appeal to those who have appreciated it most fervently: the highly civilized and mature Greeks of Periclean Athens; the old Scandinavian and Anglo-Saxon warriors who listened far into the night to the creations of their scops and gleemen; the world-conquerors of Queen Bess's England who were thrilled by a sonnet and excited by a poetic drama; the cowboys and lumberjacks of America who still spend the long watches of the dark singing ballads with plebeian pasts or royal pedigrees. The more richly human and experienced the reader, the more he will appreciate the work of his poetic fellows. For—and it cannot be repeated too often—poetry is a human activity, not only reflecting human activities, but powerfully affecting them.

THE POETS
(from "Ode")

We are the music-makers,
  And we are the dreamers of dreams,
Wandering by lone sea-breakers,
  And sitting by desolate streams;
World-losers and world-forsakers,
  On whom the pale moon gleams:
Yet we are the movers and shakers
  Of the world for ever, it seems.

With wonderful deathless ditties
We built up the world's great cities,
  And out of a fabulous story
  We fashion an empire's glory:
One man with a dream, at pleasure,
  Shall go forth and conquer a crown;
And three with a new song's measure
  Can trample an empire down.

We, in the ages lying
  In the buried past of the earth,
Built Nineveh with our sighing,
  And Babel itself with our mirth;
And o'erthrew them with prophesying
  To the old of the new world's worth;
For each age is a dream that is dying,
  Or one that is coming to birth.

—*Arthur O'Shaughnessy* (1844-1881)

PRECIOUS WORDS

He ate and drank the precious words.
His spirit grew robust;
He knew no more that he was poor,
Nor that his frame was dust.

He danced along the dingy days,
And this bequest of wings
Was but a book. What liberty
A loosened spirit brings!

—*Emily Dickinson* (1830-1886)

2

THE DEFINITION OF POETRY

Poetry (from poet, Greek *poietes,* a maker, from the verb *poieo,* I make). Without attempting to define poetry, it may be broadly stated as that form of expression which language takes when it consists of a definite number of measures in some fixed relation to each other and accompanied by a discernible and more or less definite rhythm.

—*The Encyclopedia Americana*

Poetry: The art of apprehending and interpreting ideas by the faculty of imagination; the art of idealizing in thought and expression.

—*Webster's International Dictionary*

THE DESIRE to capture and define the elusive spirit of poetry has hounded almost every writer. Yet, though countless definitions have been made, none has ever been comprehensive enough, none has proved conclusive or convincing to every other writer. "Definitions are for the most part unsatisfactory and treacherous; but definitions of poetry are proverbially so," wrote Theodore Watts-Dunton, who, nevertheless, ventured to say that poetry was "the concrete and artistic expression of the human mind in emotional and rhythmical language." Scientists, with all their graphs and recording-needles, have been no more successful than poets, aided by their more sensitive intuitions, in attempting to fix the essence of poetry in a few phrases. One might hazard another incomplete definition and say: "Poetry is the power to define the undefinable in terms of the unforgettable." Such a generalization is not as evasive as it seems. We can point to a poem for proof of poetry as we point to a sunset for a symbol of beauty, but we can no more translate the poem into other words—and maintain the quality of the poem—than we can translate a sunset. Similarly, since poetry is the most variable of the arts, one is tempted to agree with the statement which seems merely flippant: "Poetry is the thing which we immediately recognize as poetry!"

To show the divergence of opinion, here are twenty-seven statements from authorities—most of them poets—ranging from the sixteenth century to the present day. No effort has been made to impose an order or agreement upon these quotations, which are suggestive and sometimes contradictory; the arrangement is chronological. The interpretations are as diverse as the minds which determined what poetry may be and what it can do.

The poet's eye, in a fine frenzy rolling,
Doth glance from heaven to earth, from earth to heaven;
And as imagination 'bodies forth

The forms of things unknown, the poet's pen
Turns them to shapes, and gives to airy nothing
A local habitation and a name.
—*William Shakespeare* (1564-1616)

To which [the study of philosophy] poetry would be made subsequent—or indeed precedent—as being less subtile, but more *simple, sensuous and passionate.*
—*John Milton* (1608-1674)

Poetry is the music of the soul; and, above all, of great and feeling souls.
—*Voltaire* (1694-1778)

Poetry is the art of uniting pleasure with truth by calling imagination to the help of reason. . . . The essence of poetry is invention, such invention as, by producing something unexpected, surprises and delights. —*Samuel Johnson* (1709-1784)

Poetry ought not to take its course through the frigid region of the intellect; it ought never to force learning to be its interpreter. . . . It should go straight to the heart because it comes from the heart. —*Friedrich Schiller* (1759-1805)

Poetry is the spontaneous overflow of powerful feelings: it takes its origin from emotion recollected in tranquillity. —*William Wordsworth* (1770-1850)

The proper and immediate object of Science is the acquirement and communication of truth; the proper and immediate object of Poetry is the communication of immediate pleasure. . . . I wish our clever young poets would remember my homely definitions of prose and poetry; that is, prose = words in their best order; poetry = the *best* words in the best order. —*Samuel T. Coleridge* (1772-1834)

Poetry is the lava of the imagination whose eruption prevents an earthquake.
—*Lord Byron* (1788-1824)

Poetry is the record of the best and happiest moments of the best minds. . . . A poem is the very image of life expressed in its eternal truth.
—*Percy Bysshe Shelley* (1792-1822)

Poetry is that art which selects and arranges the symbols of thought in such a manner as to excite it the most powerfully and delightfully.
—*William Cullen Bryant* (1794-1878)

Poetry should surprise by a fine excess and not by singularity.
—*John Keats* (1795-1821)

By poetry we mean the art of employing words in such a manner as to produce an illusion on the imagination, the art of doing by means of words what the painter does by means of colours. —*T. B. Macaulay* (1800-1859)

Poetry is the only verity—the expression of a sound mind speaking after the ideal and not after the apparent. . . . The true poem is the poet's mind; the finest poetry was first experienced. —*Ralph Waldo Emerson* (1803-1882)

Poetry is simply the most beautiful, impressive, and widely effective mode of saying things.

—*Matthew Arnold* (1822-1888)

If I read a book and it makes my whole body so cold no fire can warm me, I know that is poetry. If I feel physically as if the top of my head were taken off, I know that is poetry. These are the only ways I know it. Is there any other way?

—*Emily Dickinson* (1830-1886)

I think that to transfuse emotion—not to transmit thought, but to set up in the reader's sense a vibration corresponding to what was felt by the writer—is the peculiar function of poetry.

—*A. E. Housman* (1859-)

The business of words in prose is primarily to *state;* in poetry, not only to state, but also—and sometimes primarily—to *suggest.*

—*John Livingston Lowes* (1867-)

Poetry is a language that tells us, through a more or less emotional reaction, something that cannot be said. All poetry, great or small, does this. And it seems to me that poetry has two outstanding characteristics: One is that it is, after all, undefinable. The other is that it is unmistakable.

—*Edwin Arlington Robinson* (1869-)

It is absurd to think that the only way to tell if a poem is lasting is to wait and see if it lasts. The right reader of a good poem can tell the moment it strikes him that he has taken an immortal wound—that he will never get over it. That is to say, permanence in poetry as in love is perceived instantly. It hasn't to await the test of time. . . . A living poem begins with a lump in the throat: a homesickness or a love-sickness. It is a reaching out toward expression, an effort to find fulfilment. A complete poem is one where an emotion has found its thought and the thought has found the words.

—*Robert Frost* (1875-)

Poetry is the opening and closing of a door, leaving those who look through to guess about what is seen during a moment. . . . Poetry is a series of explanations of life, fading off into horizons too swift for explanations. . . . Poetry is the paradox of earth cradling life and then entombing it. . . . Poetry is the synthesis of hyacinths and biscuits.

—*Carl Sandburg* (1878-)

Poetry is not greatly concerned with what a man thinks, but with what is so embedded in his nature that it never occurs to him to question it; not a matter of which idea he holds, but of the depth at which he holds it.

—*Ezra Pound* (1885-)

Poetry is founded on surprise: the surprise of recognizing something that was there but something we had failed to notice. It is the shock of finding the familiar in the strange, the strange in the familiar. . . . A poem does not state, it acts—and acts more swiftly than the liveliest prose. A poem is the shortest emotional distance between two points.

—*Louis Untermeyer* (1885-)

We must believe that "emotion recollected in tranquillity" is an inexact formula. For it [poetry] is neither emotion nor recollection nor, without a distortion of meaning, tranquillity. It is a *concentration,* and a new thing resulting from that concentration, of a great number of experiences—a concentration which does not happen consciously. . . . Poetry is not the assertion that something is true, but the making of that truth more fully real to us.

—*T. S. Eliot* (1888-)

A poem should be motionless in time . . .
A poem should not mean
But be.

—*Archibald MacLeish* (1892-)

There is no gap between our everyday emotional life and the material of poetry. The verbal expression of this life, at its finest, is forced to use the technique of poetry—that is the only essential difference. We cannot avoid the material of poetry.

—*I. A. Richards* (1893-)

There are two general kinds of statement about poetry. There is the metaphorical generalization of Wordsworth that "poetry is the breath and finer spirit of all knowledge." There is the practical "definition" by Aristotle, who first said that poetry is more philosophical than history. . . . There are thousands of possible deductions about poetry, but there is no possible way of saying *what* it is. The kind of statement which combines Aristotle's classification with Wordsworth's immediate insight is on the whole the best. . . . Poetry, of all the verbal arts, is the one most capable of setting up permanent human references and forms whose validity does not decrease with time.

—*Allen Tate* (1899-)

Poetry is an elemental kind of speech by means of which the poet manages to capture and record not only his thoughts and his emotions, but his intuitive mechanisms. It serves not only as his defense, but as his means of escape.

—*Merrill Moore* (1903-)

These definitions reveal distinct differences: each of them illustrates either the Age of the man defining it, or the particular problems confronting him, or his own highly individual art. The statements are illuminating and provocative, but they do not tell what poetry is. The suggestions are colorful, the implications are keen, the very contradictions are stimulating; but they do not satisfy us. We are thrown back upon the difficulty of discovering that poetry can be defined only by poetry. Who could describe the chord of C Major to a tone-deaf person or explain redness to a blind one? What poetry *is* is as "undefinable and as unmistakable" as a particular color or the odor of earth. It is unforgettably this, speaking clearly from the sixteenth century:

The cloud-capp'd towers, the gorgeous palaces,
The solemn temples, the great globe itself,
Yea, all which it inherit, shall dissolve,
And, like this insubstantial pageant faded,
Leave not a rack behind. We are such stuff
As dreams are made on; and our little life
Is rounded with a sleep. . . .

—*William Shakespeare* (The Tempest)

And poetry is breathlessly this, from an almost forgotten dramatist of the same period:

> O think upon the pleasures of the palace!
> Securéd ease and state! The stirring meats,
> Ready to move out of the dishes, that e'en now
> Quicken when they are eaten!
> Banquets abroad by torchlight! music! sports!
> Bareheaded vassals, that had ne'er the fortune
> To keep on their own hats, but let horns wear 'em!
> Nine coaches waiting—hurry, hurry, hurry—
> —*Cyril Tourneur* (The Revenger's Tragedy)

And it is lyrically this:

> Brightness falls from the air.
> Queens have died young and fair.
> Dust hath closed Helen's eyes. . . .
> —*Thomas Nashe* (In Time of Pestilence)

And it is no less this, from some ancient, anonymous balladist:

> This ae night, this ae night,
> —Every night and alle,
> Fire and sleet and candle-light,
> —And Christe receive thy saule.
> (A Lyke-Wake Dirge)

It is the compressed beauty and terror of this image from the great mystic of the eighteenth century:

> Tiger! Tiger! burning bright
> In the forests of the night,
> What immortal hand or eye
> Could frame thy fearful symmetry?
> —*William Blake* (The Tiger)

And it is this, from the most famous of modern ballads:

> The sun's rim dips; the stars rush out;
> At one stride comes the dark. . . .
> —*S. T. Coleridge* (The Rime of the Ancient Mariner)

Poetry is this, in the voice of one of the favorite lyricists of our own day:

> O God, I cried, no dark disguise
> Can e'er hereafter hide from me
> Thy radiant identity!
> Thou canst not move across the grass
> But my quick eyes will see Thee pass. . . .
> I know the path that tells thy way
> Through the cool eve of every day.
> God, I can push the grass apart
> And lay my finger on Thy heart.
> —*Edna St. Vincent Millay* (Renascence)

And it is equally recognizable in the work of one of the most daring of contemporary experimenters:

> yet they stand here enraptured, as among
> the slow deep trees perpetual of sleep
> some silver-fingered fountain steals the world.
>
> —*E. E. Cummings* (Sonnet: "This is the garden")

Quotation and the citing of authorities will not satisfy those eager for some simple finality. Perhaps a shift to the inductive experimental technique would bring us closer to an understanding. Let us examine an individual poem and find out what suggestions of a definition of poetry are contained therein. Few verses of recent times have attained the popularity of "Cargoes," by John Masefield, who was appointed British poet laureate in 1930.

CARGOES

> Quinquireme of Nineveh from distant Ophir,
> Rowing home to haven in sunny Palestine,
> With a cargo of ivory,
> And apes and peacocks,
> Sandalwood, cedarwood, and sweet white wine.
>
> Stately Spanish galleon coming from the Isthmus,
> Dipping through the Tropics by the palm-green shores,
> With a cargo of diamonds,
> Emeralds, amethysts,
> Topazes, and cinnamon, and gold moidores.
>
> Dirty British coaster with a salt-caked smoke-stack,
> Butting through the Channel in the mad March days,
> With a cargo of Tyne coal,
> Road-rails, pig-lead,
> Firewood, iron-ware, and cheap tin trays.
>
> —*John Masefield* (1878-)

When we read this poem our first impression is probably pictorial; three brilliantly vivid pictures of three ships flash upon our inward eye. But it is not merely to sight that they appeal. We can smell the sandalwood, taste the wine, receive the thrill of movement from the rowing-dipping-butting of the vessels. The poet possesses the image-making faculty, that ability to affect the senses and even to transcend them which we call imagination. We shall find that almost all great poetry contains it.

But even the first reading shows that there is more in Masefield's mind than mere representation. First, in his three scenes from three widely separated ages, he is drawing upon our whole social heritage, the experiences of the human race, the history of the Orient and the Spanish Main and modern commerce; here is a poem of our indirect knowledge, whereas the "dirty British coaster" is very much a matter of his own direct experience. Second, although examination reveals no finite form of a verb, the poet appears to be expressing an emotion—love of the sea, perhaps love of the romantic past—

at all events, a pronounced feeling. Third, the poem has meaning, significance; it is the embodiment of an idea which becomes clearer as we consider the poem: cargoes have changed from peacocks and jewels to coal and tin trays because life has changed from one social form to another, from oligarchy to democracy, and from the glamorous to the tawdry. This poem, therefore, has a quadruple content value—pictures, experiences, emotions, and ideas.

This much the reader's mind grasps easily. But his eyes and ears reveal other characteristics. He can see that the poem is written in units, here of five lines each, and that corresponding lines in these units are of approximately the same length; upon the printed page the shapes are suggestive. This perception of pattern is heightened by the fact that the first lines mention the ships, the second their location and manner of going, the last three lines "with a cargo" of one-two-three types. The idea is sharpened by the contrast of prosaic words ("smoke-stack," "pig-lead," "salt-caked") and exotic ones ("quinquireme," "moidores"), by the use of such luxurious words as "emeralds," "ivory," "peacocks," "sandalwood," and such richly associative words as "Nineveh," "Ophir," "Palestine," culminating in "cheap tin trays." Beneath the visual pattern the ear can detect a pulsation, a regulated movement of sound, a rhythm; in this poem it is subtler than in others, but perceptible. This musical quality is augmented by the flavor and sound of the words themselves, filled with flowing liquids and sliding sibilants in the first two stanzas and with a contrasting group of harsh stops and nasals in the last. The poet has chosen and combined his words with as much care as the composer of symphonies combines the notes of the scale and the *timbre* of the instruments.

The inductive method of study has furnished us with the materials of a working definition. Poetry, we now may venture to say, is *an imaginative medium of representation and communication of significant human experiences, emotions, and thoughts in rhythmic word-patterns.* This definition is not in conflict with most of the opinions expressed by the poets themselves, and is concretely applicable to the study of poems. It should also help us to decide what is best in the poetic art. It eliminates a large body of verse from the class of true poetry by insisting upon *imagination* and *significance,* for much that rhymes is prosaic in content and shallow in meaning. To establish its applicability to all poetry, try it at random upon the other poems of this volume. To begin, test it on Arthur Hugh Clough's simple but eloquent "Say Not the Struggle Nought Availeth:"

Say not the struggle nought availeth,
  The labor and the wounds are vain,
The enemy faints not, nor faileth,
  And as things have been they remain.

If hopes were dupes, fears may be liars;
  It may be, in yon smoke concealed,
Your comrades chase e'en now the fliers,
  And, but for you, possess the field.

For while the tired waves, vainly breaking,
  Seem here no painful inch to gain,

Far back, through creeks and inlets making,
  Comes silent, flooding in, the main.

And not by eastern windows only,
  When daylight comes, comes in the light,
In front, the sun climbs slow, how slowly,
  But westward, look, the land is bright.
    —*Arthur Hugh Clough* (1819-1861)

3

POETRY AND PROSE

But, it might be asked, cannot the definition of poetry offered in the preceding chapter be applied to the best prose? It is a natural inquiry, for it must be admitted that the line between prose and poetry cannot be drawn with sharpness or dogmatism. Much of good prose is undoubtedly poetic, whereas a great deal of writing in the *shape* of poetry is not poetic at all but prosy—sometimes prosier than prose. That a stanza has the proper amount of metrical feet, the correct rhythms, and perfect stresses is no assurance that the stanza is a piece of poetry. Witness:

A Mr. Wilkinson, a clergyman.

This line was invented by Tennyson to show that a line of technically flawless verse may be banal, the very opposite of poetry. Verse, which can be achieved mechanically, almost mathematically, verse as distinguished from poetry, has a place of its own—but this difference will be considered in a later chapter.

There is unquestionably a kinship between poetry and prose. But first a distinction must be made between the use of the word "poetry" in the vague and general sense and "poetry" as a specific art or craft. In the general sense of the word, poetry, or "poesy," the reactions of the human spirit to the meanings and beauty of nature, life, and art, is everywhere. It is best illustrated by Hazlitt's conclusion that "wherever there is a sense of beauty, or power, or harmony, as in the motion of a wave of the sea, or the growth of a flower that 'spreads its sweet leaves to the air and dedicates its beauty to the sun'—there is poetry." Using the word "poetry" in this sense, Shelley contended that "the distinction between poets and prose writers is a vulgar error."

But, considered as specific forms, as verbal designs, the distinction between poetry and prose exists and may be ascertained. Prose, in general, is a medium for statements of fact, for scientific account and analysis, and for a variety of rhetorical effects. The power of poetry, as Matthew Arnold has summarized it, "is its *interpretative* power; by which I mean not a power of drawing out in black and white an explanation of the universe, but the power of so dealing with things as to awaken in us a wonderfully full, new and intimate sense in them, and of our relations with them."

Sometimes the two mediums are so closely related as to be intermingled. The eloquent and uplifted passages in Herman Melville's *Moby Dick,* the magnificent jeremiads of Carlyle's *Sartor Resartus,* the highly colored descriptions in Ruskin's *Stones of Venice* are powerfully imaginative expressions of significant human experiences, emotions, and thoughts; one can even discover subtle rhythms, balanced repetitions and patterns in their prose. The great cadences of the *Psalms* and the *Song of Songs* are beyond comparison or category. Some critics have evaded the problem by calling these passages "poetic prose," but the term is a misnomer. Let us consider two examples:

Delight is to him—a far, far upward and inward delight—who against the proud gods and commodores of this earth, ever stands forth his own inexorable self. Delight is to him whose strong arms yet support him, when the ship of this base, treacherous world has gone down beneath him. Delight is to him, who gives no quarter in the truth, and kills, burns, and destroys all sin, though he pluck it out from under the robes of senators and judges. Delight—top-gallant delight—is to him who acknowledges no law or lord but the Lord his God, and is only a patriot to heaven. Delight is to him, whom all the waves of the billows of the seas of the boisterous mob can never shake from this sure Keel of the Ages. And eternal delight and deliciousness will be his, who, coming to lay him down, can say with his final breath—O Father!—chiefly known to me by thy Rod—mortal or immortal, here I die. I have striven to be Thine more than to be this world's or mine own. Yet this is nothing; I leave eternity to Thee; for what is man that he should live out the lifetime of his God?

—From *Moby Dick* (*Herman Melville*)

Oh, under that hideous coverlet of vapours, and putrefactions, and unimaginable gases, what a Fermenting-vat lies simmering and hid! The joyful and the sorrowful are there; men are dying there, men are being born; men are praying—on the other side of a brick partition, men are cursing; and around them all is the vast, void Night. The proud Grandee still lingers in his perfumed saloons, or reposes within damask curtains; Wretchedness cowers into truckle-beds, or shivers hunger-stricken into its lair of straw: while Councillors of State sit plotting, and playing their high chess-game, whereof the pawns are Men. The Lover whispers his mistress that the coach is ready; and she, full of hope and fear, glides down, to fly with him over the borders: the Thief, still more silently, sets-to his picklocks and crowbars, or lurks in wait till the watchmen first snore in their boxes. Gay mansions, with supper-rooms and dancing-rooms, are full of light and music and high-swelling hearts; but, in the Condemned Cells, the pulse of life beats tremulous and faint, and blood-shot eyes look out through the darkness, which is around and within, for the light of a stern last morning. Six men are to be hanged on the morrow: comes no hammering from the Rabenstein?—their gallows must even now be a-building. Upwards of five-hundred-thousand two-legged animals without feathers lie around us, in horizontal positions; their heads are all in nightcaps, and full of the foolishest dreams. Riot cries aloud, and staggers and swaggers in his rank dens of shame; and the Mother, with streaming hair, kneels over her pallid dying infant, whose cracked lips only her tears now moisten.—All these heaped and huddled together, with nothing but a little carpentry and masonry between them;—crammed in, like salt fish in their barrel;—or weltering, shall I say, like an Egyptian pitcher of tamed vipers, each struggling to get its head above the others: such work goes on under that smoke-counter-pane!—But I, *mein Werther,* sit above it all; I am alone with the Stars.

—From *Sartor Resartus* (*Thomas Carlyle*)

The eye perceives that the patterns of prose are those of the sentence and the paragraph, whereas poetry deals with the line and the stanza; the word and the phrase are common units, though poetry usually handles them more delicately than prose. The ear can ascertain that the rhythms of prose, when present, are more rapidly variable than those of most poetry; we must confess, however, that free-verse rhythms are frequently distinguishable from prose rhythms only with great difficulty. It would take little effort to rearrange these paragraphs from *Moby Dick* and *Sartor Resartus* into the line-patterns of free verse, though probably no two arrangers would agree on the same division of lines.

It is impossible to set up rigid rules for separating poetry from prose; perhaps a "misty mid-region" is necessary. Nevertheless, the reader will find some differing features usually applicable. As Robert Graves insists, "a poem is not an elaborate and arbitrary way of saying something which might have been said more simply and effectively in prose." There are basic differences in spirit which may be set up in two parallel columns:

PROSE	POETRY
1. Usually informative.	1. Usually suggestive.
2. Usually factual.	2. Usually imaginative.
3. Usually low-pitched and unemotional.	3. Usually tense and emotional.
4. Concerns judgments.	4. Concerns intuitions.
5. Irregular and expansive.	5. Formal and condensed.
6. Loosely rhythmic or not rhythmic at all.	6. Strict in rhythm or in pronounced rhythmic patterns.
7. Patterned by the sentence and paragraph.	7. The phrase, the line, and the stanza determine the pattern.

These categories apply to average prose and average poetry. They are, thus, *generally* true, although exceptions may be found, as in the two prose excerpts here reprinted. However, it is apparent that poetry, as a rule, is more imaginative, lifted to a higher plane of utterance, and far more powerfully concentrated than prose. "Translate" any poem in this volume into a paragraph of prose, and note how rapidly it loses its magic. One might test the difference by countless comparisons in theme and treatment, some of the simplest and most effective being a comparison of Emerson's essays with his odes, or Landor's classical "conversations" with his epigrammatic "Greek" quatrains, or any theological treatise upon death—even John Donne's thrilling sermon—with Tennyson's "Crossing the Bar."

CROSSING THE BAR

Sunset and evening star,
  And one clear call for me!
And may there be no moaning of the bar,
  When I put out to sea,

But such a tide as moving seems asleep,
  Too full for sound and foam,
When that which drew from out the boundless deep
  Turns again home.

Twilight and evening bell,
  And after that the dark!
And may there be no sadness of farewell,
  When I embark;

For though from out our bourne of Time and Place
  The flood may bear me far,
I hope to see my Pilot face to face
  When I have crossed the bar.

—*Alfred, Lord Tennyson* (1809-1892)

It is the pitch, the emotional tensity, which distinguishes poetry from prose. All the elements of a poem combine to lift the words beyond their ordinary meaning and project the idea into new dimensions. "To transfuse emotion," A. E. Housman wrote in *The Name and Nature of Poetry,* "not to transmit thought, but to set up in the reader's sense a vibration corresponding to what was felt by the writer is the peculiar function of poetry."

At first glance it appears that such a dictum tends to belittle the intellectual element of poetry and almost insists upon the omission of one of its chief attributes. But it is the fusion of thought and emotion, of music and meaning on a high plane, which is the chief distinction of poetry, the quality which lifts it above the other arts. To accomplish this fusion has been the aim of every poet. As Martin Armstrong recently put it in *The Week-End Review*: "In fine poetry words have been subdued to emotion and thought. The poet has selected them, consciously or unconsciously, with an eye to their fusibility in the fire of his imagination, and when the poem is complete the sharp individuality of its words has been dissolved into the larger individuality of the poem. The same is true of the details and images which make up the poem: these, too, if they are justified, are merged into the spirit of the whole. Words, images, details, all these different and separate crystals dissolve under the heat of the imagination into a single clear solution."

4

THE IMAGINATION OF POETRY: THE POEM AS PICTURE

THE GREAT critics from Aristotle through Lessing down to our own day have been concerned with setting the boundaries of the various arts. In the *Laokoön,* Lessing felt that he had made a lasting division into the time-arts and the space-arts. But since his day the tendency has been strong toward a "wedding of the arts," with the poet acting as matrimonial agent. Despite the fact that poetry when read is distinctly a time-art, when printed upon the page it becomes a space-art also. The poet has invaded the realm of the musician in his melodies and sound-effects; he has entered the field of the painter in his desire to picture life. Music at times must call poetry to its aid, and the portrait painter must frequently wish that his subject could move and speak. For the fullest appreciation of poetry and the other arts it is more important to realize their kinship than to emphasize their differences.

In all the arts the fundamental matter is the same. The intuitions and experiences giving rise to creation are common to all, but for the sculptor they come as shapes in bronze and marble, for the painter as color and composition on canvas, for the musician as sounds, and for the poet as words in poetic patterns. The imagination of all artists is likewise of one nature—Shakespeare has the level-minded Theseus, practical man of the world, liken it to the condition of the lunatic and the lover, who are also the victims of its tricks, for

> Such tricks hath strong imagination,
> That, if it would but apprehend some joy,
> It comprehends some bringer of that joy.

For the artist the essential element in the imagination is concreteness. Even "airy nothing" must have "a local habitation and a name." When Macbeth is brought face to face with the purposelessness of his life, he does not remark "Life is meaningless"; his creative, or poetic, imagination inspires him to say:

> "Out, out, brief candle!
> Life's but a walking shadow, a poor player
> That struts and frets his hour upon the stage
> And then is heard no more. It is a tale
> Told by an idiot, full of sound and fury,
> Signifying nothing."

Emerson, the great teacher of American youth, preaches a life of action, but he knows that a sermon falls flat without imagination, and so he writes:

DAYS

Daughters of Time, the hypocritic Days,
Muffled and dumb like barefoot dervishes,
And marching single in an endless file,
Bring diadems and fagots in their hands.
To each they offer gifts after his will,
Bread, kingdoms, stars, and sky that holds them all.
I, in my pleachéd garden, watched the pomp,
Forgot my morning wishes, hastily
Took a few herbs and apples, and the Day
Turned and departed silent. I, too late,
Under her solemn fillet saw the scorn.
—*Ralph Waldo Emerson* (1803-1882)

This pictorial creativeness, imagination, reproduces life as the poet sees it, romantically and realistically. It throws new light upon the commonplace by photographing it from a new angle, as Wordsworth attempted to do in his share of the *Lyrical Ballads;* it also gives to the unusual, even the unbelievable, as in Coleridge's *Rime of the Ancient Mariner,* the semblance of reality, even of actuality. John Livingston Lowes has shown in *The Road to Xanadu* how Coleridge's poetic imagination pieced together fragments of his own experience and of the experiences of hundreds of others to create what never was on sea nor land. The imagination passes beyond the fancy, with its quick perceptions of surface similarities, to a probing of the deepest spiritual truths and life's very essences.

This force of the imagination has impelled the poet and characterized him, made him not only a recorder of his age but kept him distinct from it. It will not be bound to a philosophy nor tied to a social theory; it escapes categories. The eighteenth century is usually considered an age of polish and pedantry. Yet two of the greatest poets of the period were the naïve Robert Burns and the mystic William Blake. Twentieth century literature has been characterized as highly nervous and complex; the modern world, according to some, is being mirrored in cerebral poetry of increasing sensibility, indecisive rhythms and obscure inner conflicts. Yet future historians will have to recognize, among the finest expressions of this age, the untroubled clarity of Robert Frost, the clean craftsmanship of Elinor Wylie, and the simple, straightforward lyricism of A. E. Housman. Revolting from the whole "intellectualist generation" that has been using poetry as a springboard for philosophical interpretation and an analysis of the world's psyche, Archibald MacLeish, one of the most eloquent of modern poets, has repudiated those critics who know more about the poet's mental processes than the poet himself and are too eager to "interpret" a poem in terms of neuroses and world movements. "As a spectator who loves poetry," he writes, "I listen only for that clean, sharp stroke which is heard when the axe goes into the living wood."

Because of its very power, imagination is dangerous when misused. The propagandist who uses a poem as a springboard or a soap-box is no less to be suspected than the "pure" poet who employs words only for their aesthetic and "abstract" values. A poem, no matter how vivid, which lines the path of virtue only with roses or paints modern war as "a glorious adventure," may be challenged as a perversion of imagination. Again, the imagination may become so confused that an impossible mixture of pictures results—not the exotically new or the grotesquely comic, but an incongruous "oil and water" combination. There is always the need of controlling the imagination and reducing it to order; it should never be forced and over-stimulated. The traditional hymns in the church hymnal are filled with mixed imagery, though the average singer never thinks of the words. The imagination may also grow so profuse that the subject is cluttered with details, made ugly by the thickness of the verbiage. A phrase of suggestion may be worth a volume of detail. Japanese flower-arrangers have taught the world that a few objects harmoniously arranged are more alluring than a piling up of effects. This is the poet's "economy of line."

In his search for the beautiful, the poet as well as the reader finds that the nature of beauty is art's great enigma. Socrates asked questions of the Athenian youths concerning it; Tolstoi preached it to czarist Russia. In the eighteenth century Mark Akenside, in *The Pleasures of the Imagination,* described the lover of beauty thus:

For him, the spring
Distills her dews, and from the silken hem
Its lucid leaves unfolds: for him, the hand
Of autumn tinges every fertile branch
With blooming gold and blushes like the morn,
Each passing hour sheds tribute from her wings;
And still new beauties meet his lonely walk;
And loves unfelt attract him. . . .
. . . Nor thence partakes
Fresh pleasure only: for th' attentive mind,
By this harmonious action on her powers,
Becomes herself harmonious.

—*Mark Akenside* (1721-1770)

Obviously our pleasure is increased by the presence of harmony in art. Beauty has a profound effect upon the emotions; when a subject is treated delicately but without emotional appeal we call it merely "pretty." Pope's *Rape of the Lock* is pretty, ironic, and fanciful; Keats's *Ode to a Nightingale* is imaginative, passionate, and beautiful. In poetry, therefore, the demand for harmony in the work of the imagination is a yearning for the beautiful, an attempt to fix the dissolving scene, to arrest the fading loveliness and keep it ever-present.

Though the writer most frequently calls imagination to the aid of his story or idea, at times he begins with the picture itself. Coleridge tells us that he had a kaleidoscopic dream and awoke to write "Kubla Khan," or as much of it as he could compose, until he was interrupted by the visit of "a man from

Porlock" who dispelled the half-conscious cluster of memories, impressions and associations which Coleridge could not again fuse. William Blake described in his prophetic verses the direct visions which had been granted to him by God. There are no abstractions in the land of sleep; ideas are translated into magnified shapes, problems in mathematics become fire-breathing monsters.

KUBLA KHAN

by Samuel Taylor Coleridge (1772-1834)

In Xanadu did Kubla Khan
  A stately pleasure-dome decree;
Where Alph, the sacred river, ran
  Through caverns measureless to man
Down to a sunless sea.
So twice five miles of fertile ground
With walls and towers were girdled round;
And there were gardens bright with sinuous rills
Where blossomed many an incense-bearing tree;
And here were forests ancient as the hills,
Enfolding sunny spots of greenery.

But O, that deep romantic chasm which slanted
Down the green hill athwart a cedarn cover!
A savage place! as holy and enchanted
As e'er beneath a waning moon was haunted
By woman wailing for her demon-lover!
And from this chasm, with ceaseless turmoil seething,
As if this earth in fast thick pants were breathing,
A mighty fountain momently was forced;
Amid whose swift, half-intermitted burst
Huge fragments vaulted like rebounding hail,
Or chaffy grain beneath the thresher's flail.
And 'mid these dancing rocks at once and ever
It flung up momently the sacred river.
Five miles meandering with a mazy motion
Through wood and dale the sacred river ran,
Then reached the caverns measureless to man,
And sank in tumult to a lifeless ocean;
And 'mid this tumult Kubla heard from far
Ancestral voices prophesying war!

  The shadow of the dome of pleasure
    Floated midway on the waves;
  Where was heard the mingled measure
    From the fountain and the caves.
It was a miracle of rare device,
A sunny pleasure-dome with caves of ice!

  A damsel with a dulcimer
    In a vision once I saw.

It was an Abyssinian maid,
And on her dulcimer she played,
Singing of Mount Abora.
Could I revive within me
Her symphony and song,
To such a deep delight 'twould win me,
That with music loud and long,
I would build that dome in air,
That sunny dome! those caves of ice!
And all who heard should see them there,
And all should cry, Beware! Beware!
His flashing eyes, his floating hair!
Weave a circle round him thrice,
And close your eyes with holy dread,
For he on honey-dew hath fed,
And drunk the milk of Paradise.

COLOR AND IMAGE

At times the author builds his whole poem around a fundamental image. Here the details of the picture are also the elements of the thought, as in George Herbert's "The Collar," Francis Thompson's "The Hound of Heaven," or William Drummond's "The Book of the World."

THE BOOK OF THE WORLD

Of this fair volume which we World do name
If we the sheets and leaves could turn with care,
Of Him who it corrects, and did it frame,
We clear might read the art and wisdom rare:
Find out His power which wildest powers doth tame,
His providence extending everywhere,
His justice which proud rebels doth not spare,
In every page, no period of the same.
But silly we, like foolish children, rest
Well pleased with colored vellum, leaves of gold,
Fair dangling ribbands, leaving what is best,
On the great Writer's sense ne'er taking hold;
Or if by chance we stay our minds on aught,
It is some picture on the margin wrought.

—*William Drummond* (1585-1649)

The pictures which the poet paints are usually not self-portraits, nor are they always pictures of life as he himself sees it. "A poet," said John Keats, perhaps the most pictorial of English poets, "is the most unpoetical of anything in existence, because he has no identity; he is continually in, for, and filling, some other body." This ability of the artist to identify himself with other human beings, with the objects of nature around him, and even with an impersonal spirit of the universe, is a function of the poetic imagination. The appreciative reader, in order to gain from a poem all which the poet has placed in it, should cultivate his own imagination—a reproductive rather than a productive process. He must be able momentarily to take the place of the artist, or with the latter to enter into the personalities of others.

The medium through which the poet's imagination must work is that of the senses—sight primarily, but also movement, hearing, touch, taste, and smell. Of all these, sight is the only one with a fully developed poetic vocabulary. Helen Keller has remarked that if we had but three hours in which we could see, color, light, shade, and line would be eagerly and carefully marked by all. Perhaps the commonness of color in the universe has made us careless of it; the various hues, their values and variations of intensity, slip by without notice. The inadequacy of our color vocabulary can be convincingly demonstrated by an attempt to describe a moonlit landscape with its delicate gradations or the changes which come over the sky at dawn; despite the fact that we may *see* something striking about the picture, we cannot convey it to the reader. The shapes of clouds or trees are as individual as human faces, but how often can we convey that individuality to others?

The power of visual description can and should be cultivated as a part of one's general education. The poets themselves must work to acquire a facility in it. Robert Graves remarks that "the inexperienced one drenches his poems in gold, silver, purple, scarlet, with the idea of giving them, in fact, 'colour.' The old hand almost never names a colour . . . he usually prefers to find a way round, for the appeal to the sense of colour alone is a most insecure way of creating an illusion; colours vary in mood by so very slight a change in shade or tone that pure colour named without qualification in a poem will seldom call up any precise image or mood." In 1913 a group of poets calling themselves "Imagists" organized to cultivate this very ability. In their creed they said: "We are not a school of painters, but we believe that poetry should render particulars exactly and not deal in vague generalities, however magnificent and sonorous." Amy Lowell, John Gould Fletcher, Richard Aldington, and H. D., all represented in this chapter, were members of this group. It is obvious that other poets felt the same without inventing a slogan or signing a manifesto to prove it. Keats was claimed by Miss Lowell as the master Imagist, which, in a broad sense, he was. Rossetti did not change his intuitions when he shifted from pigments to words. Shakespeare in his sonnets, Swinburne in "A Forsaken Garden," Richard Aldington in "Images," Francis Ledwidge in "An Evening in England," Elinor Wylie in "Velvet Shoes," and Leila Jones in her re-writing of the Circe story in "Unholy Garden," are Imagists in the sense that their images are evoked by the exact word and the fit phrase.

SONNET LXXIII

That time of year thou mayst in me behold
When yellow leaves, or none, or few, do hang
Upon those boughs which shake against the cold,
Bare ruined choirs, where late the sweet birds sang.
In me thou see'st the twilight of such day
As after sunset fadeth in the west,
Which by and by black night doth take away,

Death's second self, that seals up all in rest.
In me thou see'st the glowing of such fire
That on the ashes of his youth doth lie,
As the death-bed whereon it must expire
Consumed with that which it was nourished by.
This thou perceiv'st, which makes thy love more strong
To love that well which thou must leave ere long.
—*William Shakespeare* (1564-1616)

It is interesting to compare the inaccurate images of Swinburne with those of Aldington and Amy Lowell, which are almost always exact. The over-emphasizing of any one quality in verse always means the under-stressing of some other quality. By stressing music Swinburne surrendered the image-making particularity of poetry. "What we get in Swinburne," writes T. S. Eliot in a penetrating essay on his poetry, "is an expression by sound. . . . In Swinburne the meaning and the sound are one thing. He is concerned with the meaning of the word in a peculiar way: he employs, or rather 'works,' the word's meaning. And this is connected with an interesting fact about his vocabulary: he uses the most general word, because his emotion is never particular, never in direct line of vision, never focused; it is emotion reinforced, not by intensification, but by expansion."

A FORSAKEN GARDEN

by Algernon Charles Swinburne (1837-1909)

In the coign of the cliff between lowland and highland,
At the sea-down's edge between windward and lee,
Walled round with rocks as an inland island,
The ghost of a garden fronts the sea.
A girdle of brushwood and thorn encloses
The steep square slope of the blossomless bed
Where the weeds that grew green from the graves of its roses
Now lie dead.

The fields fall southward, abrupt and broken,
To the low last edge of the long lone land.
If a step should sound or a word be spoken,
Would a ghost not rise at the strange guest's hand?
So long have the gray bare walks lain guestless,
Through branches and briars if a man make way,
He shall find no life, but the sea-wind's, restless
Night and day.

The dense hard passage is blind and stifled
That crawls by a track none turn to climb
To the strait waste place that the years have rifled
Of all but the thorns that are touched not of time.
The thorns he spares when the rose is taken;
The rocks are left when he wastes the plain;
The wind that wanders, the weeds wind-shaken,
These remain.

Not a flower to be pressed of the foot that falls not;
  As the heart of a dead man the seed-plots are dry;
From the thicket of thorns whence the nightingale calls not,
  Could she call, there were never a rose to reply.
Over the meadows that blossom and wither,
  Rings but the note of a sea-bird's song;
Only the sun and the rain come hither
  All year long.

The sun burns sear, and the rain dishevels
  One gaunt bleak blossom of scentless breath.
Only the wind here hovers and revels
  In a round where life seems barren as death.
Here there was laughing of old, there was weeping,
  Haply, of lovers none ever will know,
Whose eyes went seaward a hundred sleeping
  Years ago.

Heart handfast in heart as they stood, "Look thither,"
  Did he whisper? "Look forth from the flowers to the sea;
For the foam-flowers endure when the rose-blossoms wither,
  And men that love lightly may die—but we?"
And the same wind sang, and the same waves whitened,
  And or ever the garden's last petals were shed,
In the lips that had whispered, the eyes that had lightened,
  Love was dead.

Or they loved their life through, and then went whither?
  And were one to the end—but what end who knows?
Love deep as the sea as a rose must wither,
  As the rose-red seaweed that mocks the rose.
Shall the dead take thought for the dead to love them?
  What love was ever as deep as a grave?
They are loveless now as the grass above them
  Or the wave.

All are at one now, roses and lovers,
  Not known of the cliffs and the fields and the sea.
Not a breath of the time that has been hovers
  In the air now soft with a summer to be.
Not a breath shall there sweeten the seasons hereafter
  Of the flowers or the lovers that laugh now or weep,
When, as they that are free now of weeping and laughter,
  We shall sleep.

Here death may deal not again forever;
  Here change may come not till all change end.
From the graves they have made they shall rise up never,
  Who have left naught living to ravage and rend.
Earth, stones, and thorns of the wild ground growing,
  While the sun and the rain live, these shall be;
Till a last wind's breath upon all these blowing
  Roll the sea.

Till the slow sea rise and the sheer cliff crumble,
  Till terrace and meadow the deep gulfs drink,
Till the strength of the waves of the high tides humble
  The fields that lessen, the rocks that shrink,
Here now in his triumph where all things falter,
  Stretched out on the spoils that his own hand spread,
As a god self-slain on his own strange altar,
  Death lies dead.

A TROPICAL MORNING AT SEA

by Edward Rowland Sill (1841-1887)

Sky in its lucent splendor lifted
  Higher than cloud can be;
Air with no breath of earth to stain it,
  Pure on the perfect sea.

Crests that touch and tilt each other,
  Jostling as they comb;
Delicate crash of tinkling water,
  Broken in pearling foam.

Plashings—or is it the pinewood's whispers,
  Babble of brooks unseen,
Laughter of winds when they find the blossoms,
  Brushing aside the green?

Waves that dip, and dash, and sparkle;
  Foam-wreaths slipping by,
Soft as a snow of broken roses
  Afloat over mirrored sky.

Off to the East the steady sun-track
  Golden meshes fill—
Webs of fire, that lace and tangle,
  Never a moment still,

Liquid palms but clap together,
  Fountains, flower-like, grow—
Limpid bells on stems of silver—
  Out of a slope of snow.

Sea-depths, blue as the blue of violets—
  Blue as a summer sky,
When you blink at its arch sprung over
  Where in the grass you lie.

Dimly an orange bit of rainbow
  Burns where the low west clears,
Broken in air, like a passionate promise
  Born of a moment's tears.

Thinned to amber, rimmed with silver,
  Clouds in the distance dwell,
Clouds that are cool, for all their color,
  Pure as a rose-lipped shell.

Fleets of wool in the upper heavens
  Gossamer wings unfurl;
Sailing so high they seem but sleeping
  Over yon bar of pearl.

What would the great world lose, I wonder—
  Would it be missed or no—
If we stayed in the opal morning,
  Floating forever so?

Swung to sleep by the swaying water,
  Only to dream all day—
Blow, salt wind from the north upstarting,
  Scatter such dreams away!

VELVET SHOES

Let us walk in the white snow
  In a soundless space;
With footsteps quiet and slow,
  At a tranquil pace,
  Under veils of white lace.

I shall go shod in silk,
  And you in wool,
White as a white cow's milk,
  More beautiful
  Than the breast of a gull.

We shall walk through the still town
  In a windless peace;
We shall step upon white down,
  Upon silver fleece,
  Upon softer than these.

We shall walk in velvet shoes:
  Wherever we go
Silence will fall like dews
  On white silence below.
  We shall walk in the snow.

—*Elinor Wylie* (1887-1928)

AN EVENING IN ENGLAND

From its blue vase the rose of evening drops;
Upon the streams its petals float away.
The hills all blue with distance hide their tops
In the dim silence falling on the gray.
A little wind said "Hush!" and shook a spray
Heavy with May's white crop of opening bloom;
A silent bat went dipping in the gloom.

Night tells her rosary of stars full soon,
They drop from out her dark hand to her knees.
Upon a silhouette of woods, the moon
Leans on one horn as if beseeching ease
From all her changes which have stirred the seas.
Across the ears of Toil, Rest throws her veil.
I and a marsh bird only make a wail.

—*Francis Ledwidge* (1891-1917)

UNHOLY GARDEN

All night the sinister moth has lain
Languid with feeding on the livid bud,
Polluted honey on his tongue, the stain
Upon his wing of blooms as dark as blood.

Eaters of lotus find herein no wine
To breed forgetfulness nor cleansing pardon;
Under the dreary hemlocks piteous swine
Grumble and grope in the unholy garden

For drowsy roots of a mandragora
Wherewith to ease the brain of memory
That turns with mortal tears to Ithaca
Washed clean by wind from the unsullied sea.

They lift lewd snouts to snuff the tang of pitch,
Or rimy wind or scent of hearth and home;
Here, drop by drop, the drug-enamoured witch
From tainted honey brews malignant foam.

She spins, or tends the tarnished buds at noon
That bees have harried, where the snail has clung,
But bares her white breast to the sultry moon,
Upon her heart a sprig of adder's tongue,

To weave a garland dark with noxious leaf
Of nightshade or a stalk of hellebore,
To listen for a keel upon the reef,
Or in the surf, the straining of an oar.

—*Leila Jones* (1889-   )

LILACS

by Amy Lowell (1874-1925)

Lilacs,
False blue,
White,
Purple,
Color of lilac,
Your great puffs of flowers
Are everywhere in this my New England.
Among your heart-shaped leaves
Orange orioles hop like music-box birds and sing
Their little weak soft songs;
In the crooks of your branches
The bright eyes of song sparrows sitting on spotted eggs
Peer restlessly through the light and shadow
Of all Springs.
Lilacs in dooryards
Holding quiet conversations with an early moon;
Lilacs watching a deserted house
Settling sideways into the grass of an old road;
Lilacs, wind-beaten, staggering under a lop-sided shock of bloom
Above a cellar dug into a hill.
You are everywhere.
You were everywhere.
You tapped the window when the preacher preached his sermon,
And ran along the road beside the boy going to school.
You stood by pasture-bars to give the cows good milking,
You persuaded the housewife that her dish-pan was of silver
And her husband an image of pure gold.
You flaunted the fragrance of your blossoms
Through the wide doors of Custom Houses—
You, and sandalwood, and tea,
Charging the noses of quill-driving clerks
When a ship was in from China.
You called to them: "Goose-quill men, goose-quill men,
May is a month for flitting,"
Until they writhed on their high stools
And wrote poetry on their letter-sheets behind the propped-up ledgers.
Paradoxical New England clerks,
Writing inventories in ledgers, reading the "Song of Solomon" at night,
So many verses before bedtime,
Because it was the Bible.
The dead fed you
Amid the slant stones of graveyards.
Pale ghosts who planted you
Came in the night time
And let their thin hair blow through your clustered stems.
You are of the green sea,
And of the stone hills which reach a long distance.
You are of elm-shaded streets with little shops where they sell kites and marbles,
You are of great parks where everyone walks and nobody is at home.
You cover the blind sides of greenhouses
And lean over the top to say a hurry-word through the glass
To your friends, the grapes, inside.

Lilacs,
False blue,
White,
Purple,
Color of lilac,
You have forgotten your Eastern origin,
The veiled women with eyes like panthers,
The swollen, aggressive turbans of jeweled Pashas.
Now you are a very decent flower,
A reticent flower,
A curiously clear-cut, candid flower,
Standing beside clean doorways,
Friendly to a house-cat and a pair of spectacles,
Making poetry out of a bit of moonlight
And a hundred or two sharp blossoms.

Maine knows you,
Has for years and years;
New Hampshire knows you,
And Massachusetts
And Vermont.
Cape Cod starts you along the beaches to Rhode Island;
Connecticut takes you from a river to the sea.
You are brighter than apples,

Sweeter than tulips,
You are the great flood of our souls
Bursting above the leaf-shapes of our hearts,
You are the smell of all Summers,
The love of wives and children,
The recollection of the gardens of little children,
You are State Houses and Charters
And the familiar treading of a foot to and fro on a road it knows.
May is lilac here in New England,
May is a thrush singing "Sun up!" on a tip-top ash-tree,
May is white clouds behind pine-trees
Puffed out and marching upon a blue sky.
May is a green as no other,
May is much sun through small leaves,
May is soft earth,
And apple-blossoms,
And windows open to a South wind.
May is a full light wind of lilac
From Canada to Narragansett Bay.

Lilacs,
False blue,
White,
Purple,
Color of lilac,
Heart-leaves of lilac all over New England,
Roots of lilac under all the soil of New England,
Lilac in me because I am New England,
Because my roots are in it,
Because my leaves are of it,
Because my flowers are for it,
Because it is my country
And I speak to it of itself
And sing of it with my own voice
Since certainly it is mine.

THE GALE
(from "Sand and Spray: A Sea Symphony")

by John Gould Fletcher (1886-)

Pale green-white, in a gallop across the sky,
The clouds retreating from a perilous affray
Carry the moon with them, a heavy sack of gold;
Sharp arrows, stars between them, shoot and play.
The wind, as it strikes the sand,
Clutches with rigid hands
And tears from them
Thin ribbons of pallid sleet,
Long stinging hissing drift,
Which it trails up inland.

I lean against the bitter wind;
My body plunges like a ship.
Out there I see gray breakers rise;
Their raveled beards are white,
And foam is in their eyes.
My heart is blown from me tonight
To be transfixed by all the stars.

Steadily the wind
Rages up the shore.
In the trees it roars and battles;
With rattling drums
And heavy spears,
Toward the house-fronts on it comes.

The village, a loose mass outflung,
Breaks its path.
Between the walls
It bounces, tosses in its wrath.
It is broken; it is lost.

With green-gray eyes,
With whirling arms,
With clashing feet,
With bellowing lungs,
Pale green-white in a gallop across the sky,
The wind comes.

The great gale of the winter flings himself flat upon earth.

He hurriedly scribbles on the sand
His transient tragic destiny.

IMAGES

by Richard Aldington (1892-)

I

Like a gondola of green scented fruits
Drifting along the dank canals of Venice,
You, O exquisite one,
Have entered into my desolate city.

II

The blue smoke leaps
Like swirling clouds of birds vanishing.
So my love leaps forth toward you,
Vanishes and is renewed.

III

A rose-yellow moon in a pale sky
When the sunset is faint vermilion
In the mist among the tree-boughs,
Art thou to me, my beloved.

IV

A young beech-tree on the edge of the forest
Stands still in the evening,
Yet shudders through all its leaves in the
light air
And seems to fear the stars—
So are you still and so tremble.

V

The red deer are high on the mountain,
They are beyond the last pine-trees.
And my desires have run with them.

VI

The flower which the wind has shaken
Is soon filled again with rain;
So does my heart fill slowly with tears,
O Foam-driver, Wind-of-the-vineyards,
Until you return.

SHAPE AND LINE

The likeness of the poet to the sculptor and landscape-artist is seen in the poems which follow. Edgar Allan Poe sees Helen as a statue never to be forgotten; John Keats describes a piece of pottery seen, perhaps, in the British Museum, and it becomes a symbol of eternal beauty. Robert Frost is first compelled by the shapes of bent birches though the memories they arouse finally compel the poem. Edwin Arlington Robinson uses the strict villanelle (see page 416) to picture the ruin and the very atmosphere of a deserted house; whereas Wordsworth, building a sonnet (see page 360), rouses us with the vision of a great metropolis sleeping in the dawn. "Grongar Hill," of John Dyer, is interesting because of its gradually changing point of view. The landscape poem reaches its highest expression in Milton's perfect companion-poems, "L'Allegro" and "Il Penseroso," which can be paralleled almost line by line to show how different aspects of the same thing appear under contrasting moods.

THE HOUSE ON THE HILL

They are all gone away,
  The House is shut and still,
There is nothing more to say.

Through broken walls and gray
  The winds blow bleak and shrill:
They are all gone away.

Nor is there one today
  To speak them good or ill:
There is nothing more to say.

Why is it then we stray
  Around that sunken sill?
They are all gone away.

And our poor fancy-play
  For them is wasted skill:
There is nothing more to say.

There is ruin and decay
  In the House on the Hill:
They are all gone away,
There is nothing more to say.

—*Edwin Arlington Robinson*
(1869-   )

TO HELEN

Helen, thy beauty is to me
  Like those Nicaean barks of yore,
That gently, o'er a perfumed sea,

The weary, wayworn wanderer bore
To his own native shore.

On desperate seas long wont to roam,
Thy hyacinth hair, thy classic face,
Thy Naiad airs have brought me home
To the glory that was Greece
And the grandeur that was Rome.

Lo! in yon brilliant window-niche
How statue-like I see thee stand,
The agate lamp within thy hand!
Ah, Psyche, from the regions which
Are Holy Land!

—*Edgar Allan Poe* (1809-1849)

ODE ON A GRECIAN URN

by John Keats (1795-1821)

Thou still unravished bride of quietness,
Thou foster-child of silence and slow time,
Sylvan historian, who canst thus express
A flowery tale more sweetly than our rhyme:
What leaf-fringed legend haunts about thy shape
Of deities or mortals, or of both,
In Tempe or the dales of Arcady?
What men or gods are these? What maidens loth?
What mad pursuit? What struggle to escape?
What pipes and timbrels? What wild ecstasy?

Heard melodies are sweet, but those unheard
Are sweeter; therefore, ye soft pipes, play on;
Not to the sensual ear, but, more endeared,
Pipe to the spirit ditties of no tone:
Fair youth, beneath the trees, thou canst not leave
Thy song, nor ever can those trees be bare;
Bold Lover, never, never canst thou kiss,
Though winning near the goal—yet, do not grieve;
She cannot fade, though thou hast not thy bliss,
For ever wilt thou love, and she be fair!

Ah, happy, happy boughs! that cannot shed
Your leaves, nor ever bid the Spring adieu;
And, happy melodist, unweariѐd,
For ever piping songs for ever new;
More happy love! more happy, happy love!
For ever warm and still to be enjoyed,
For ever panting, and for ever young;
All breathing human passion far above,
That leaves a heart high-sorrowful and cloyed,
A burning forehead, and a parching tongue.

Who are these coming to the sacrifice?
To what green altar, O mysterious priest,
Lead'st thou that heifer lowing at the skies,
And all her silken flanks with garlands dressed?
What little town by river or sea-shore,
Or mountain-built with peaceful citadel,

Is emptied of this folk, this pious morn?
And, little town, thy streets for evermore
Will silent be; and not a soul to tell
Why thou art desolate, can e'er return.

O Attic shape! Fair attitude! with brede
Of marble men and maidens overwrought,
With forest branches and the trodden weed;
Thou, silent form, dost tease us out of thought
As doth eternity: Cold Pastoral!
When old age shall this generation waste,
Thou shalt remain, in midst of other woe
Than ours, a friend to man, to whom thou say'st,
"Beauty is truth, truth beauty,—that is all
Ye know on earth, and all ye need to know."

BIRCHES

by Robert Frost (1875-   )

When I see birches bend to left and right
Across the line of straighter darker trees,
I like to think some boy's been swinging them.
But swinging doesn't bend them down to stay.
Ice-storms do that. Often you must have seen them
Loaded with ice a sunny winter morning
After a rain. They click upon themselves
As the breeze rises, and turn many-colored
As the stir cracks and crazes their enamel.
Soon the sun's warmth makes them shed crystal shells
Shattering and avalanching on the snow-crust—
Such heaps of broken glass to sweep away
You'd think the inner dome of heaven had fallen.
They are dragged to the withered bracken by the load,
And they seem not to break; though once they are bowed
So low for long, they never right themselves:
You may see their trunks arching in the woods
Years afterwards, trailing their leaves on the ground,
Like girls on hands and knees that throw their hair
Before them over their heads to dry in the sun.
But I was going to say when Truth broke in
With all her matter-of-fact about the ice-storm,
I should prefer to have some boy bend them
As he went out and in to fetch the cows—
Some boy too far from town to learn baseball,
Whose only play was what he found himself,
Summer or winter, and could play alone.
One by one he subdued his father's trees
By riding them down over and over again

Until he took the stiffness out of them,
And not one but hung limp, not one was left
For him to conquer. He learned all there was
To learn about not launching out too soon
And so not carrying the tree away
Clear to the ground. He always kept his poise
To the top branches, climbing carefully
With the same pains you use to fill a cup
Up to the brim, and even above the brim.
Then he flung outward, feet first, with a swish,
Kicking his way down through the air to the ground.
So was I once myself a swinger of birches.
And so I dream of going back to be.
It's when I'm weary of considerations,
And life is too much like a pathless wood
Where your face burns and tickles with the cobwebs
Broken across it, and one eye is weeping
From a twig's having lashed across it open.
I'd like to get away from earth awhile
And then come back to it and begin over.
May no fate wilfully misunderstand me
And half grant what I wish and snatch me away
Not to return. Earth's the right place for love.
I don't know where it's likely to go better.
I'd like to go by climbing a birch tree,
And climb black branches up a snow-white trunk
Toward heaven, till the tree could bear no more,
But dipped its top and set me down again.
That would be good both going and coming back.
One could do worse than be a swinger of birches.

COMPOSED UPON WESTMINSTER BRIDGE SEPTEMBER 3, 1802

Earth has not anything to show more fair:
Dull would he be of soul who could pass by
A sight so touching in its majesty:
This City now doth, like a garment, wear
The beauty of the morning; silent, bare,
Ships, towers, domes, theaters, and temples lie
Open unto the fields, and to the sky;
All bright and glittering in the smokeless air.
Never did sun more beautifully steep
In his first splendor, valley, rock, or hill;
Ne'er saw I, never felt, a calm so deep!
The river glideth at his own sweet will:
Dear God! the very houses seem asleep;
And all that mighty heart is lying still!

—*William Wordsworth* (1770-1850)

GRONGAR HILL

by John Dyer (1700-1758)

Silent Nymph, with curious eye!
Who, the purple evening, lie
On the mountain's lonely van,
Beyond the noise of busy man;
Painting fair the form of things,
While the yellow linnet sings;
Or the tuneful nightingale
Charms the forest with her tale;
Come, with all thy various hues,
Come, and aid thy sister Muse;
Now while Phoebus riding high
Gives lustre to the land and sky!
Grongar Hill invites my song,
Draw the landscape bright and strong;
Grongar, in whose mossy cells

Sweetly-musing Quiet dwells;
Grongar, in whose silent shade,
For the modest Muses made,
So oft I have, the even still,
At the fountain of a rill,
Sate upon a flowery bed,
With my hand beneath my head;
While strayed my eyes o'er Towy's flood,
Over mead, and over wood,
From house to house, from hill to hill,
Till Contemplation had her fill.
  About his chequered sides I wind,
And leave his brooks and meads behind,
And groves, and grottoes where I lay,
And vistas shooting beams of day:
Wider and wider spreads the vale,
As circles on a smooth canal:
The mountains round—unhappy fate!
Sooner or later, of all height,
Withdraw their summits from the skies,
And lessen as the others rise:
Still the prospect wider spreads,
Adds a thousand woods and meads;
Still it widens, widens still,
And sinks the newly-risen hill.
  Now I gain the mountain's brow,
What a landscape lies below!
No clouds, no vapors intervene,
But the gay, the open scene
Does the face of nature show,
In all the hues of heaven's bow!
And, swelling to embrace the light,
Spreads around beneath the sight.
  Old castles on the cliffs arise,
Proudly towering in the skies!
Rushing from the woods, the spires
Seem from hence ascending fires!
Half his beams Apollo sheds
On the yellow mountain-heads!
Gilds the fleeces of the flocks,
And glitters on the broken rocks!
  Below me trees unnumbered rise,
Beautiful in various dyes:
The gloomy pine, the poplar blue,
The yellow beech, the sable yew,
The slender fir, that taper grows,
The sturdy oak with broad-spread boughs;
And beyond the purple grove,
Haunt of Phyllis, queen of love!
Gaudy as the opening dawn,
Lies a long and level lawn
On which a dark hill, steep and high,
Holds and charms the wandering eye!
Deep are his feet in Towy's flood,
His sides are clothed with waving wood,
And ancient towers crown his brow,
That cast an awful look below;
Whose ragged walls the ivy creeps,
And with her arms from falling keeps;
So both a safety from the wind
On mutual dependence find.
  'Tis now the raven's bleak abode;
'Tis now th' apartment of the toad;
And there the fox securely feeds;
And there the poisonous adder breeds
Concealed in ruins, moss, and weeds;
While, ever and anon, there falls
Huge heaps of hoary mouldered walls.
Yet time has seen, that lifts the low,
And level lays the lofty brow,
Has seen this broken pile complete,
Big with the vanity of state;
But transient is the smile of fate!
A little rule, a little sway,
A sunbeam in a winter's day,
Is all the proud and mighty have
Between the cradle and the grave.
  And see the rivers how they run,
Through woods and meads, in shade and sun,
Sometimes swift, and sometimes slow,
Wave succeeding wave, they go
A various journey to the deep,
Like human life to endless sleep!
Thus is nature's vesture wrought,
To instruct our wandering thought;
Thus she dresses green and gay,
To disperse our cares away.
  Ever charming, ever new,
When will the landscape tire the view!
The fountain's fall, the river's flow,
The woody valleys, warm and low;
The windy summit, wild and high,
Roughly rushing on the sky;
The pleasant seat, the ruined tower,
The naked rock, the shady bower;
The town and village, dome and farm,
Each gives each a double charm,
As pearls upon an Aethiop's arm.
  See, on the mountain's southern side,
Where the prospect opens wide,

Where the evening gilds the tide;
How close and small the hedges lie!
What streaks of meadows cross the eye!
A step methinks may pass the stream,
So little distant dangers seem;
So we mistake the future's face,
Eyed through Hope's deluding glass;
As yon summits soft and fair,
Clad in colors of the air,
Which to those who journey near,
Barren, and brown, and rough appear;
Still we tread tired the same coarse way;
The present's still a cloudy day.
O may I with myself agree,
And never covet what I see:
Content me with an humble shade,
My passions tamed, my wishes laid;
For while our wishes wildly roll,
We banish quiet from the soul:
'Tis thus the busy beat the air,
And misers gather wealth and care.
Now, even now, my joy runs high,
As on the mountain-turf I lie;
While the wanton Zephyr sings,
And in the vale perfumes his wings;
While the waters murmur deep;
While the shepherd charms his sheep;
While the birds unbounded fly,
And with music fill the sky,
Now, even now, my joy runs high.
Be full, ye courts, be great who will;
Search for Peace with all your skill:
Open wide the lofty door,
Seek her on the marble floor,
In vain ye search, she is not there;
In vain ye search the domes of Care!
Grass and flowers Quiet treads,
On the meads and mountain-heads,
Along with Pleasure, close allied,
Ever by each other's side:
And often, by the murmuring rill,
Hears the thrush, while all is still,
Within the groves of Grongar Hill.

L'ALLEGRO

by John Milton (1608-1674)

Hence, loathéd Melancholy,
Of Cerberus and blackest Midnight born
In Stygian cave forlorn
'Mongst horrid shapes, and shrieks, and sights unholy!
Find out some uncouth cell,
Where brooding Darkness spreads his jealous wings,
And the night-raven sings;
There, under ebon shades and low-browed rocks,
As ragged as thy locks,
In dark Cimmerian desert ever dwell.
But come, thou Goddess fair and free,
In heaven yclept Euphrosyne,
And by men heart-easing Mirth,
Whom lovely Venus, at a birth,
With two sister Graces more,
To ivy-crownéd Bacchus bore;
Or whether—as some sager sing—
The frolic wind that breathes the spring,
Zephyr, with Aurora playing,
As he met her once a-Maying,
There, on beds of violets blue,
And fresh-blown roses washed in dew,
Filled her with thee, a daughter fair,
So buxom, blithe, and debonair.
Haste thee, Nymph, and bring with thee
Jest and youthful Jollity,
Quips and Cranks and wanton Wiles,
Nods and Becks and wreathéd Smiles,
Such as hang on Hebe's cheek,
And love to live in dimple sleek;
Sport that wrinkled Care derides,
And Laughter holding both his sides.
Come, and trip it, as you go,
On the light, fantastic toe;
And in thy right hand lead with thee
The mountain-nymph, sweet Liberty;
And, if I give thee honor due,
Mirth, admit me of thy crew,
To live with her, and live with thee,
In unreprovéd pleasures free:
To hear the lark begin his flight,
And, singing, startle the dull night,
From his watch-tower in the skies,
Till the dappled dawn doth rise;
Then to come, in spite of sorrow,
And at my window bid good-morrow,
Through the sweet-brier or the vine
Or the twisted eglantine;
While the cock, with lively din,
Scatters the rear of darkness thin,
And to the stack, or the barn-door,

Stoutly struts his dames before;
Oft listening how the hounds and horn
Cheerly rouse the slumbering morn,
From the side of some hoar hill,
Through the high wood echoing shrill;
Sometime walking, not unseen,
By hedgerow elms, on hillocks green,
Right against the eastern gate,
Where the great Sun begins his state,
Robed in flames and amber light,
The clouds in thousand liveries dight;
While the plowman, near at hand,
Whistles o'er the furrowed land,
And the milkmaid singeth blithe,
And the mower whets his scythe,
And every shepherd tells his tale
Under the hawthorn in the dale.
  Straight mine eye hath caught new pleasures,
Whilst the landscape round it measures:
Russet lawns, and fallows gray,
Where the nibbling flocks do stray;
Mountains on whose barren breast
The laboring clouds do often rest;
Meadows trim, with daisies pied;
Shallow brooks and rivers wide.
Towers and battlements it sees
Bosomed high in tufted trees,
Where perhaps some beauty lies,
The cynosure of neighboring eyes.
  Hard by, a cottage chimney smokes
From betwixt two aged oaks,
Where Corydon and Thyrsis met
Are at their savory dinner set
Of herbs and other country messes,
Which the neat-handed Phyllis dresses;
And then in haste her bower she leaves
With Thestylis to bind the sheaves;
Or, if the earlier season lead,
To the tanned haycock in the mead.
  Sometimes, with secure delight,
The upland hamlets will invite,
When the merry bells ring round,
And the jocund rebecks sound
To many a youth and many a maid
Dancing in the checkered shade;
And young and old come forth to play
On a sunshine holiday,
Till the livelong daylight fail;
Then to the spicy nut-brown ale,
With stories told of many a feat,
How Faëry Mab the junkets eat.
She was pinched and pulled, she said;
And he, by Friar's lantern led,
Tells how the drudging goblin sweat
To earn his cream-bowl duly set,
When in one night, ere glimpse of morn,
His shadowy flail hath threshed the corn
That ten day-laborers could not end;
Then lies him down, the lubber-fiend,
And, stretched out all the chimney's length,
Basks at the fire his hairy strength,
And crop-full out of doors he flings,
Ere the first cock his matin rings.
Thus done the tales, to bed they creep,
By whispering winds soon lulled asleep.
  Towered cities please us then,
And the busy hum of men,
Where throngs of knights and barons bold,
In weeds of peace, high triumphs hold,
With store of ladies, whose bright eyes
Rain influence, and judge the prize
Of wit or arms, while both contend
To win her grace whom all commend.
There let Hymen oft appear
In saffron robe, with taper clear,
And pomp, and feast, and revelry,
With masque and antique pageantry;
Such sights as youthful poets dream
On summer eves by haunted stream.
Then to the well-trod stage anon,
If Jonson's learnéd sock be on,
Or sweetest Shakespeare, Fancy's child,
Warble his native wood-notes wild.
  And ever, against eating cares,
Lap me in soft Lydian airs,
Married to immortal verse,
Such as the meeting soul may pierce,
In notes with many a winding bout
Of linkéd sweetness long drawn out
With wanton heed and giddy cunning,
The melting voice through mazes running,
Untwisting all the chains that tie
The hidden soul of harmony;
That Orpheus' self may heave his head
From golden slumber on a bed
Of heaped Elysian flowers, and hear
Such strains as would have won the ear
Of Pluto to have quite set free
His half-regained Eurydice.
  These delights if thou canst give,
  Mirth, with thee I mean to live.

IL PENSEROSO

by John Milton (1608-1674)

Hence, vain, deluding Joys,
The brood of Folly without father bred!
How little you bestead,
Or fill the fixéd mind with all your toys!
Dwell in some idle brain,
And fancies fond with gaudy shapes possess,
As thick and numberless
As the gay motes that people the sunbeams,
Or likest hovering dreams,
The fickle pensioners of Morpheus' train.
But, hail! thou Goddess, sage and holy!
Hail, divinest Melancholy!
Whose saintly visage is too bright
To hit the sense of human sight,
And therefore to our weaker view,
O'erlaid with black, staid Wisdom's hue;
Black, but such as in esteem
Prince Memnon's sister might beseem,
Or that starred Ethiop queen that strove
To set her beauty's praise above
The Sea-nymphs, and their powers offended.
Yet thou art higher far descended;
Thee bright-haired Vesta long of yore
To solitary Saturn bore;
His daughter she; in Saturn's reign
Such mixture was not held a stain.
Oft in glimmering bowers and glades
He met her, and in secret shades
Of woody Ida's inmost grove,
Whilst yet there was no fear of Jove.
Come, pensive Nun, devout and pure,
Sober, steadfast, and demure,
All in a robe of darkest grain,
Flowing with majestic train,
And sable stole of cypress lawn
Over thy decent shoulders drawn.
Come; but keep thy wonted state
With even step, and musing gait,
And looks commercing with the skies,
Thy rapt soul sitting in thine eyes;
There, held in holy passion still,
Forget thyself to marble, till
With a sad, leaden, downward cast
Thou fix them on the earth as fast.
And join with thee calm Peace and Quiet,
Spare Fast, that oft with gods doth diet,
And hears the Muses in a ring
Aye round about Jove's altar sing;
And add to these retiréd Leisure,
That in trim gardens takes his pleasure;
But, first and chiefest, with thee bring
Him that yon soars on golden wing,
Guiding the fiery-wheeléd throne,
The cherub Contemplatión;
And the mute Silence hist along,
'Less Philomel will deign a song,
In her sweetest, saddest plight,
Smoothing the rugged brow of Night,
While Cynthia checks her dragon yoke
Gently o'er the accustomed oak.
Sweet bird, that shunn'st the noise of folly,
Most musical, most melancholy!
Thee, chauntress, oft the woods among
I woo, to hear thy evensong;
And, missing thee, I walk unseen
On the dry, smooth-shaven green,
To behold the wandering moon
Riding near her highest noon,
Like one that had been led astray
Through the heaven's wide, pathless way,
And oft, as if her head she bowed,
Stooping through a fleecy cloud.
Oft, on a plat of rising ground,
I hear the far-off curfew sound,
Over some wide-watered shore,
Swinging slow with sullen roar;
Or, if the air will not permit,
Some still, removéd place will fit,
Where glowing embers through the room
Teach light to counterfeit a gloom,
Far from all resort of mirth,
Save the cricket on the hearth,
Or the bellman's drowsy charm
To bless the doors from nightly harm.
Or let my lamp, at midnight hour,
Be seen in some high, lonely tower,
Where I may oft outwatch the Bear,
With thrice-great Hermes, or unsphere
The spirit of Plato, to unfold
What worlds or what vast regions hold
The immortal mind that hath forsook
Her mansion in this fleshly nook;
And of those demons that are found
In fire, air, flood, or underground,
Whose power hath a true consent

With planet or with element.
Sometime let gorgeous Tragedy
In sceptered pall come sweeping by,
Presenting Thebes, or Pelops' line,
Or the tale of Troy divine,
Or what—though rare—of later age
Ennobled hath the buskined stage.
But, O sad Virgin! that thy power
Might raise Musaeus from his bower;
Or bid the soul of Orpheus sing
Such notes as, warbled to the string,
Drew iron tears down Pluto's cheek,
And made Hell grant what love did seek;
Or call up him that left half told
The story of Cambuscan bold,
Of Camball, and of Algarsife,
And who had Canace to wife,
That owned the virtuous ring and glass,
And of the wondrous horse of brass
On which the Tartar king did ride;
And if aught else great bards beside
In sage and solemn tunes have sung,
Of tourneys, and of trophies hung,
Of forests, and enchantments drear,
Where more is meant than meets the ear.
Thus, Night, oft see me in my pale career,
Till civil-suited Morn appear,
Not tricked and frounced, as she was wont
With the Attic boy to hunt,
But kerchiefed in a comely cloud,
While rocking winds are piping loud,
Or ushered with a shower still,
When the gust hath blown his fill,
Ending on the rustling leaves,
With minute drops from off the eaves.
And, when the sun begins to fling
His flaring beams, me, Goddess, bring
To archéd walks of twilight groves,
And shadows brown, that Sylvan loves.
Of pine, or monumental oak,
Where the rude ax with heavéd stroke
Was never heard the nymphs to daunt,
Or fright them from their hallowed haunt.
There in close covert, by some brook,
Where no profaner eye may look,
Hide me from day's garish eye,
While the bee with honeyed thigh,
That at her flowery work doth sing,
And the waters murmuring,
With such consort as they keep,
Entice the dewy-feathered Sleep.
And let some strange, mysterious dream
Wave at his wings, in airy stream
Of lively portraiture displayed,
Softly on my eyelids laid;
And, as I wake, sweet music breathe
Above, about, or underneath,
Sent by some Spirit to mortals good,
Or the unseen Genius of the wood.
But let my due feet never fail
To walk the studious cloister's pale,
And love the high embowéd roof,
With antique pillars massy proof,
And storied windows richly dight,
Casting a dim, religious light.
There let the pealing organ blow,
To the full-voiced choir below,
In service high and anthems clear,
As may with sweetness, through mine ear,
Dissolve me into ecstasies,
And bring all heaven before mine eyes.
And may at last my weary age
Find out the peaceful hermitage
The hairy gown and mossy cell,
Where I may sit and rightly spell
Of every star that heaven doth shew,
And every herb that sips the dew,
Till old experience do attain
To something like prophetic strain.
These pleasures, Melancholy, give,
And I with thee will choose to live.

MOVEMENT

The sense of movement, the kinaesthetic sense, is specially adaptable to poetry because of the movement of verse itself. The flight of birds, the swiftly flowing stream, the running of horses, dogs and deer, the graceful swaying of the dance, the straining of the muscles in physical combat—all have been the subjects of poetry. Browning loves to sing of marching men and galloping horses; Byron thrills to the surge of the sea in *Childe Harold:*

Roll on, thou deep and dark blue Ocean,—roll!
  Ten thousand fleets sweep over thee in vain;
Man marks the earth with ruin—his control
  Stops with the shore;—upon the watery plain
  The wrecks are all thy deed, nor doth remain
A shadow of man's ravage, save his own,
  When, for a moment, like a drop of rain,
He sinks into thy depths, with bubbling groan,
Without a grave, unknell'd, uncoffin'd, and unknown.

In the poems which follow, Whitman has recorded the movements of many objects as he sees them from the ferry, Shelley limits himself to the commotion created by one force, the west wind, Sorley has put into words the sheer joy of running, and Merrill Moore, combining motion and emotion, records a casual circling of swallows in terms of wonder.

FROM "CROSSING BROOKLYN FERRY"

by Walt Whitman (1819-1892)

It avails not, neither time or place—distance avails not;
I am with you, you men and women of a generation, or ever so many generations hence;
I project myself—also I return—I am with you, and know how it is.

Just as you feel when you look on the river and sky, so I felt;
Just as any of you is one of a living crowd, I was one of a crowd;
Just as you are refreshed by the gladness of the river and the bright flow, I was refresh'd;
Just as you stand and lean on the rail, yet hurry with the swift current, I stood, yet was hurried;
Just as you look on the numberless mass of ships, and the thick-stemm'd pipes of steamboats, I look'd.

I, too, many and many a time cross'd the river, the sun half an hour high;
I watched the Twelfth-month sea-gulls—I saw them high in the air, floating with motionless wings, oscillating their bodies,
I saw how the glistening yellow lit up parts of their bodies, and left the rest in strong shadow,
I saw the slow-wheeling circles, and the gradual edging toward the south.

I, too, saw the reflection of the summer sky in the water,
Had my eyes dazzled by the shimmering track of beams,
Look'd at the fine centrifugal spokes of light around the shape of my head in the sun-lit water,
Look'd on the haze on the hills southward and southwestward,
Look'd on the vapor as it flew in fleeces tinged with violet,
Look'd toward the lower bay to notice the arriving ships,
Saw their approach, saw aboard those that were near me,
Saw the white sails of schooners and sloops—saw the ships at anchor,
The sailors at work in the rigging, or out astride the spars,
The round masts, the swinging motion of the hulls, the slender serpentine pennants,

The large and small steamers in motion, the pilots in their pilot-houses,
The white wake left by the passage, the quick tremulous whirl of the wheels,
The flags of all nations, the falling of them at sun-set,
The scallop-edged waves in the twilight, the ladled cups, the frolicsome crests and glistening,
The stretch afar growing dimmer and dimmer, the gray walls of the granite storehouses by the docks,
On the river the shadowy group, the big steam-tug closely flanked on each side by the barges—the hay-boat, the belated lighter,
On the neighboring shore, the fires from the foundry chimneys burning high and glaringly into the night,
Casting their flicker of black, contrasted with wild red and yellow light, over the tops of houses, and down into the clefts of streets.

ODE TO THE WEST WIND

by Percy Bysshe Shelley (1792-1822)

I

O wild West Wind, thou breath of Autumn's being,
Thou, from whose unseen presence the leaves dead
Are driven, like ghosts from an enchanter fleeing,

Yellow, and black, and pale, and hectic red,
Pestilence-stricken multitudes: O thou,
Who chariotest to their dark wintry bed

The wingèd seeds, where they lie cold and low,
Each like a corpse within its grave, until
Thine azure sister of the Spring shall blow

Her clarion o'er the dreaming earth, and fill
(Driving sweet buds like flocks to feed in air)
With living hues and odors plain and hill:

Wild Spirit, which art moving everywhere;
Destroyer and preserver; hear, oh, hear!

II

Thou on whose stream, 'mid the steep sky's commotion,
Loose clouds like earth's decaying leaves are shed,
Shook from the tangled boughs of Heaven and Ocean,

Angels of rain and lightning: there are spread
On the blue surface of thine airy surge,
Like the bright hair uplifted from the head

Of some fierce Maenad, even from the dim verge
Of the horizon to the zenith's height,
The locks of the approaching storm. Thou dirge

Of the dying year, to which this closing night
Will be the dome of a vast sepulchre,
Vaulted with all thy congregated might

Of vapors, from whose solid atmosphere
Black rain, and fire, and hail will burst: oh, hear!

III

Thou who didst waken from his summer dreams
The blue Mediterranean, where he lay
Lulled by the coil of his cryståalline streams,

Beside a pumice isle in Baiae's bay,
And saw in sleep old palaces and towers
Quivering within the wave's intenser day,

All overgrown with azure moss and flowers
So sweet, the sense faints picturing them! Thou
For whose path the Atlantic's level powers

Cleave themselves into chasms, while far below
The sea-blooms and the oozy woods which wear
The sapless foliage of the ocean, know

Thy voice, and suddenly grow gray with fear,
And tremble and despoil themselves: oh, hear!

IV

If I were a dead leaf thou mightest bear;
If I were a swift cloud to fly with thee;
A wave to pant beneath thy power, and share

The impulse of thy strength, only less free
Than thou, O uncontrollable! If even
I were as in my boyhood, and could be

The comrade of thy wanderings over heaven,
As then, when to outstrip thy skiey speed
Seemed scarce a vision; I would ne'er have striven

As thus with thee in prayer in my sore need.
Oh, lift me as a wave, a leaf, a cloud!
I fall upon the thorns of life! I bleed!

A heavy weight of hours has chained and bowed
One too like thee: tameless, and swift, and proud.

V

Make me thy lyre, even as the forest is:
What if my leaves are falling like its own!
The tumult of thy mighty harmonies

Will take from both a deep, autumnal tone,
Sweet though in sadness. Be thou, Spirit fierce,
My spirit! Be thou me, impetuous one!

Drive my dead thoughts over the universe
Like withered leaves to quicken a new birth!
And, by the incantation of this verse,

Scatter, as from an unextinguished hearth
Ashes and sparks, my words among mankind!
Be through my lips to unawakened earth

The trumpet of a prophecy! O Wind,
If Winter comes, can Spring be far behind?

THE SONG OF THE UNGIRT RUNNERS

We swing ungirded hips,
And lightened are our eyes,
The rain is on our lips,
We do not run for prize.
We know not whom we trust
Nor whitherward we fare,
But we run because we must
  Through the great wide air.

The waters of the seas
Are troubled as by storm.
The tempest strips the trees
And does not leave them warm.
Does the tearing tempest pause?
Do the tree tops ask it why?
So we run without a cause
  'Neath the big bare sky.

The rain is on our lips,
We do not run for prize.
But the storm the water whips
And the waves howl to the skies.
The winds arise and strike it
And scatter it like sand,
And we run because we like it
  Through the broad bright land.

—*Charles Hamilton Sorley* (1895-1915)

TWITTER OF SWALLOWS

Even horses cocked an eye upward, passers-by
Stared and the street-car conductor stopped and stared.
A child said: "The swallows act as if they were scared;
Maybe it means someone is going to die."

The swallows indeed seemed much excited about
Something, something, something—what could it be?
Here was an ordinary park, an ordinary tree,
The day had been an ordinary day,
And twilight fell quite unexcitedly.

But here were the swallows twittering, milling about,
Screaming as if a vital wrong were done
To each and all of them, as if the sun
Were stolen, nevermore to grace their sky,
Or as if the sun had gone away to die!

—*Merrill Moore* (1903-   )

SOUND AND SILENCE

Poets have long tried in vain to reproduce the melodies of music in words. In a few cases, such as the songs of Burns, they have found words which enhance the beauty of the air, but never the air itself. There have been several attempts to suggest the sounds of various musical instruments, from Pope's "Ode for Music on St. Cecilia's Day," with

> In a sadly-pleasing strain
> Let the warbling lute complain:
>   Let the loud trumpet sound,
>   'Till the roofs all around
>   The shrill echoes rebound:
> While in more lengthened notes and slow,
> The deep, majestic, solemn organs blow . . .

down to Carl Sandburg's "Jan Kubelik," an interpretation of a great violinist, the same author's "Jazz Fantasia," Amy Lowell's "Stravinsky's Three Pieces, 'Grotesques,' for String Quartet," and Vachel Lindsay's "The Kallyope Yell." Bryant's "Robert of Lincoln," and Wordsworth's "To a Cuckoo" are among the poems that have tried to interpret the songs of birds. Unless we are trained musicians, our vocabulary of sounds is pitifully small; few of us have trained our ears even to the point where we can follow any part in a quartet except the one which sustains the melody, or pick out the second violins in a symphony. Yet sounds can vary in quality, volume, pitch, and duration in a myriad different ways. The conductor of a great chorus or orchestra must train his ear to detect one discord among a hundred sounds; in like manner the poet trains his ear to catch the sounds of life—the human voice, murmur of the night, the pulse of a machine—and reproduce them through the imagination.

The most astonishing *tour de force* in the field of sound-reproduction is Edgar Allan Poe's "The Bells," notable almost entirely for auditory effect. The other poems in this group, Browning's "Meeting at Night," De la Mare's "The Listeners," and Alfred Douglas's "The Green River," place as much emphasis upon the silence as upon the sound.

THE BELLS

by Edgar Allan Poe (1809-1849)

I

Hear the sledges with the bells—
Silver bells!
What a world of merriment their melody foretells!
How they tinkle, tinkle, tinkle,
In the icy air of night!
While the stars that oversprinkle
All the heavens, seem to twinkle
With a crystalline delight;
Keeping time, time, time,
In a sort of Runic rhyme,
To the tintinnabulation that so musically wells
From the bells, bells, bells, bells,
Bells, bells, bells—
From the jingling and the tinkling of the bells.

II

Hear the mellow wedding bells—
Golden bells!
What a world of happiness their harmony foretells!
Through the balmy air of night
How they ring out their delight!—
From the molten-golden notes,
And all in tune,
What a liquid ditty floats
To the turtle-dove that listens, while she gloats
On the moon!
Oh, from out the sounding cells,
What a gush of euphony voluminously wells!
How it swells!
How it dwells
On the Future!—how it tells
Of the rapture that impels
To the swinging and the ringing
Of the bells, bells, bells—
Of the bells, bells, bells, bells,
Bells, bells, bells—
To the rhyming and the chiming of the bells!

III

Hear the loud alarum bells—
Brazen bells!
What a tale of terror now their turbulency tells!
In the startled ear of night
How they scream out their affright!
Too much horrified to speak,
They can only shriek, shriek,
Out of tune,
In a clamorous appealing to the mercy of the fire,
In a mad expostulation with the deaf and frantic fire,
Leaping higher, higher, higher,
With a desperate desire,
And a resolute endeavor
Now—now to sit, or never,
By the side of the pale-faced moon.
Oh, the bells, bells, bells!
What a tale their terror tells
Of Despair!
How they clang, and clash, and roar!
What a horror they outpour
On the bosom of the palpitating air!
Yet the ear, it fully knows,
By the twanging
And the clanging,
How the danger ebbs and flows;
Yet the ear distinctly tells,

In the jangling
And the wrangling,
How the danger sinks and swells,
By the sinking or the swelling in the anger of the bells—
Of the bells,—
Of the bells, bells, bells, bells,
Bells, bells, bells—
In the clamor and the clangor of the bells!

IV

Hear the tolling of the bells—
Iron bells!
What a world of solemn thought their monody compels!
In the silence of the night,
How we shiver with affright
At the melancholy menace of their tone!
For every sound that floats
From the rust within their throats
Is a groan.
And the people—ah, the people—
They that dwell up in the steeple,
All alone,
And who tolling, tolling, tolling,
In that muffled monotone,
Feel a glory in so rolling
On the human heart a stone—
They are neither man nor woman—
They are neither brute nor human—
They are Ghouls:—
And their king it is who tolls:—
And he rolls, rolls, rolls,
Rolls
A paean from the bells!
And his merry bosom swells
With the paean of the bells!
And he dances, and he yells;
Keeping time, time, time,
In a sort of Runic rhyme,
To the paean of the bells—
Of the bells:
Keeping time, time, time,
In a sort of Runic rhyme,
To the throbbing of the bells—
Of the bells, bells, bells—
To the sobbing of the bells:—
Keeping time, time, time,
As he knells, knells, knells,
In a happy Runic rhyme,
To the rolling of the bells—
Of the bells, bells, bells:—
To the tolling of the bells—

Of the bells, bells, bells, bells,
Bells, bells, bells—
To the moaning and the groaning of the bells.

MEETING AT NIGHT

The gray sea and the long black land;
And the yellow half-moon large and low;
And the startled little waves that leap
In fiery ringlets from their sleep,
As I gain the cove with pushing prow,
And quench its speed i' the slushy sand.

Then a mile of warm sea-scented beach;
Three fields to cross till a farm appears;
A tap at the pane, the quick sharp scratch
And blue spurt of a lighted match,
And a voice less loud, through its joys and fears,
Than the two hearts beating each to each!

—*Robert Browning* (1812-1889)

THE LISTENERS

by Walter de la Mare (1873-)

"Is there anybody there?" said the Traveler,
Knocking on the moonlit door;
And his horse in the silence champed the grasses
Of the forest's ferny floor:
And a bird flew up out of the turret,
Above the Traveler's head:
And he smote upon the door again a second time;
"Is there anybody there?" he said.
But no one descended to the Traveler;
No head from the leaf-fringed sill
Leaned over and looked into his gray eyes,
Where he stood perplexed and still.
But only a host of phantom listeners
That dwelt in the lone house then
Stood listening in the quiet of the moonlight
To that voice from the world of men:
Stood thronging the faint moonbeams on the dark stair,
That goes down to the empty hall,
Hearkening in an air stirred and shaken
By the lonely Traveler's call.
And he felt in his heart their strangeness,
Their stillness answering his cry,
While his horse moved, cropping the dark turf,
'Neath the starred and leafy sky;
For he suddenly smote on the door, even
Louder, and lifted his head:—
"Tell them I came, and no one answered,

That I kept my word," he said.
Never the least stir made the listeners,
Though every word he spake
Fell echoing through the shadowiness of the still house
From the one man left awake:
Aye, they heard his foot upon the stirrup,
And the sound of iron on stone,
And how the silence surged softly backward,
When the plunging hoofs were gone.

THE GREEN RIVER

I know a green grass path that leaves the field
And, like a running river, winds along
Into a leafy wood, where is no throng
Of birds at noon-day; and no soft throats yield
Their music to the moon. The place is sealed,
An unclaimed sovereignty of voiceless song,
And all the unravished silences belong
To some sweet singer lost or unrevealed.

So is my soul become a silent place. . . .
Oh, may I wake from this uneasy night
To find some voice of music manifold.
Let it be shape of sorrow with wan face,
Or love that swoons on sleep, or else delight
That is as wide-eyed as a marigold.

—*Alfred Douglas* (1870-)

TOUCH, TASTE, AND SMELL

The senses of touch, taste, and smell, though highly important in daily life, are not sufficiently articulate to give rise to a large body of poetry exclusively devoted to them. They are, however, frequently introduced in connection with the others. It is odd that the poetry of physical pain does not loom large in the anthologies; even the strong sensations of heat and cold have given rise to but little poetry. H. D.'s "Heat" is one of the most graphic of "touch and feeling" poems.

HEAT

O wind, rend open the heat,
cut apart the heat,
rend it to tatters.

Fruit cannot drop
through this thick air—
fruit cannot fall into heat
that presses up and blunts
the points of pears
and rounds the grapes.

Cut through the heat—
plough through it,
turning it on either side
of your path.
—*H. D.* (1886-)

John Keats is the great genius of the gustatory sense. It is told of him that he used to pour red pepper down his throat in order that the cool wine which followed might be more thoroughly enjoyed. The glowing description of the meal set before his mistress by Porphyro in "The Eve of St. Agnes" is enough to set any mouth watering. One must read it "delicately, and at the tip-end, as it were, of one's tongue," gaily said Keats's friend, Leigh Hunt. To many people foods are either sweet or sour, salt or bitter; but this sense may likewise be cultivated—witness the tea-tasters, who can distinguish a hundred brands.

For most poets of the past, there was but one odor—sweet. Roses, perfumes, fair ladies—all smelt "sweet." Only rarely do we find such passages as this from John Gay's "Trivia:"

Here steams ascend
That, in mix'd fumes, the wrinkled nose offend.
Where chandlers' cauldrons boil; where fishy prey
Hide the wet stall, long absent from the sea;
And where the cleaver chops the heifer's spoil,
And where huge hogsheads sweat with trainy oil,
Thy breathing nostril hold; but how shall I
Pass, where in piles Cornavian cheeses lie?

The first two poems which follow use the cataloguing method of listing sensory appeals—the pleasant sensations in both Rupert Brooke's "The Great Lover" and Richard Le Gallienne's "A Ballade Catalogue of Lovely Things." Thoreau's "Smoke" and Sandburg's "Smoke and Steel" present startlingly different approaches. George Meredith's "Love in the Valley" is an exquisite series of pictures in which sight, sound and emotion are beautifully blended. Besides its pictorial and sensual appeal Sandburg's "Smoke and Steel" provokes a new awareness of human conduct; here imagery is fused with a definite social theory. The symbol of man and the background against which he works are integrated: smoke is the spirit and mind of man, steel the body.

THE GREAT LOVER

by Rupert Brooke (1887-1915)

I have been so great a lover: filled my days
So proudly with the splendour of Love's praise,
The pain, the calm, and the astonishment,
Desire illimitable, and still content,
And all dear names men use, to cheat despair,
For the perplexed and viewless streams that bear
Our hearts at random down the dark of life.
Now, ere the unthinking silence on that strife
Steals down, I would cheat drowsy Death so far,

My night shall be remembered for a star
That outshone all the suns of all men's days.
Shall I not crown them with immortal praise
Whom I have loved, who have given me, dared with me
High secrets, and in darkness knelt to see
The inenarrable godhead of delight?
Love is a flame;—we have beaconed the world's night.
A city:—and we have built it, these and I.
An emperor:—we have taught the world to die.
So, for their sakes I loved, ere I go hence,
And the high cause of Love's magnificence,
And to keep loyalties young, I'll write those names
Golden for ever, eagles, crying flames,
And set them as a banner, that men may know,
To dare the generations, burn, and blow
Out on the wind of Time, shining and streaming . . .

These I have loved:
        White plates and cups, clean-gleaming,
Ringed with blue lines; and feathery, faëry dust;
Wet roofs, beneath the lamp-light; the strong crust
Of friendly bread; and many-tasting food;
Rainbows; and the blue bitter smoke of wood;
And radiant raindrops couching in cool flowers;
And flowers themselves, that sway through sunny hours,
Dreaming of moths that drink them under the moon;
Then, the cool kindliness of sheets, that soon
Smooth away trouble; and the rough male kiss
Of blankets; grainy wood; live hair that is
Shining and free; blue-massing clouds; the keen
Unpassioned beauty of a great machine;
The benison of hot water; furs to touch;
The good smell of old clothes; and other such—
The comfortable smell of friendly fingers,
Hair's fragrance, and the musty reek that lingers
About dead leaves and last year's ferns . . .
                                        Dear names,
And thousand others throng to me! Royal flames;
Sweet water's dimpling laugh from tap or spring;
Holes in the ground; and voices that do sing:
Voices in laughter, too; and body's pain,
Soon turned to peace; and the deep-panting train;
Firm sands; the little dulling edge of foam
That browns and dwindles as the wave goes home;
And washen stones, gay for an hour; the cold
Graveness of iron; moist black earthen mould;
Sleep; and high places; footprints in the dew;
And oaks; and brown horse-chestnuts, glossy-new;
And new-peeled sticks; and shining pools on grass;—
All these have been my loves. And these shall pass,
Whatever passes not, in the great hour,
Nor all my passion, all my prayers, have power

To hold them with me through the gate of Death.
They'll play deserter, turn with the traitor breath,
Break the high bond we made, and sell Love's trust
And sacramented covenant to the dust.
—Oh, never a doubt but, somewhere, I shall wake,
And give what's left of love again, and make
New friends, now strangers . . .
                                        But the best I've known
Stays here, and changes, breaks, grows old, is blown
About the winds of the world, and fades from brains
Of living men, and dies.
                                        Nothing remains.

O dear my loves, O faithless, once again
This one last gift I give: that after men
Shall know, and later lovers, far-removed,
Praise you, "All these were lovely"; say, "He loved."

A BALLADE CATALOGUE OF LOVELY THINGS

by Richard Le Gallienne (1867-   )

I would make a list against the evil days
  Of lovely things to hold in memory:
First, I set down my lady's lovely face,
  For earth has no such lovely thing as she;
  And next I add, to bear her company,
The great-eyed virgin star that morning brings;
  Then the wild-rose upon its little tree—
So runs my catalogue of lovely things.

The enchanted dog-wood, with its ivory trays,
  The water-lily in its sanctuary
Of reeded pools, and dew-drenched lilac sprays,
  For these, of all fair flowers, the fairest be;
  Next I write down the great name of the sea,
Lonely in greatness as the names of kings;
  Then the young moon that hath us all in fee—
So runs my catalogue of lovely things.

Imperial sunsets that in crimson blaze
  Along the hills, and, fairer still to me,
The fireflies dancing in a netted maze
  Woven of twilight and tranquillity;
  Shakespeare and Virgil, their high poesy;
Then a great ship, splendid with snowy wings,
  Voyaging on into eternity—
So runs my catalogue of lovely things.

Envoi

Prince, not the gold bars of thy treasury,
  Not all thy jewelled sceptres, crowns, and rings,
Are worth the honeycomb of the wild bee—
  So runs my catalogue of lovely things.

SMOKE

Light-wingèd Smoke, Icarian bird,
Melting thy pinions in thy upward flight;
Lark without song, and messenger of dawn,
Circling above the hamlets as thy nest;
Or else, departing dream, and shadowy form
Of midnight vision, gathering up thy skirts;
By night star-veiling, and by day
Darkening the light and blotting out the sun;
Go thou, my incense, upward from this hearth,
And ask the gods to pardon this clear flame.
—*Henry David Thoreau* (1817-1862)

SMOKE AND STEEL

by Carl Sandburg (1878-)

Smoke of the fields in spring is one;
Smoke of the leaves in autumn another;
Smoke of a steel-mill roof or a battleship funnel—
They all go up in a line with a smoke-stack,
Or they twist . . . in the slow twist . . . of the wind.

If the north wind comes, they run to the south.
If the west wind comes, they run to the east.
By this sign
all smokes
know each other.
Smoke of the fields in spring and leaves in autumn,
Smoke of the finished steel, chilled and blue,
By the oath of work they swear: "I know you."

Hunted and hissed from the center
Deep down long ago when God made us over,
Deep down are the cinders we came from—
You and I and our heads of smoke.

✦

Some of the smokes God dropped on the job
Cross on the sky and count our years
And sing in the secrets of our numbers;
Sing their dawns and sing their evenings,
Sing an old log-fire song:
You may put the damper up,
You may put the damper down,
The smoke goes up the chimney just the same.

Smoke of a city sunset skyline;
Smoke of a country dusk horizon—
They cross on the sky and count our years.

✦

Smoke of a brick-red dust
        Winds on a spiral
        Out of the stacks
For a hidden and glimpsing moon.
This, said the bar-iron shed to the blooming mill,
This is the slang of coal and steel.
The day-gang hands it to the night-gang;
The night-gang hands it back.

Stammer at the slang of this—
Let us understand half of it.
        In the rolling mills and sheet mills,
        In the harr and boom of the blast fires,
        The smoke changes its shadow
        And men change their shadow;
        A nigger, a wop, a bohunk changes.

        A bar of steel—it is only
Smoke at the heart of it, smoke and the blood of a man.
A runner of fire ran in it, ran out, ran somewhere else,
And left—smoke and the blood of a man
And the finished steel, chilled and blue.

So fire runs in, runs out, runs somewhere else again,
And the bar of steel is a gun, a wheel, a nail, a shovel,
A rudder under the sea, a steering-gear in the sky;
And always dark in the heart and through it,
        Smoke and the blood of a man.
Pittsburgh, Youngstown, Gary—they make their steel with men.

In the blood of men and the ink of chimneys
The smoke nights write their oaths:
Smoke into steel and blood into steel;
Homestead, Braddock, Birmingham, they make their steel with men.
Smoke and blood is the mix of steel.

        The birdmen drone
        in the blue; it is steel.
        a motor sings and zooms.

✦

Steel barb-wire around the Works.
Steel guns in the holsters of the guards at the gates of the Works.
Steel ore-boats bring the loads clawed from the earth by steel, lifted and lugged by arms of steel, sung on its way by the clanking clam-shells.
The runners now, the handlers now, are steel; they dig and clutch and haul; they hoist their automatic knuckles from job to job; they are steel making steel.
Fire and dust and air fight in the furnaces; the pour is timed, the billets wriggle; the clinkers are dumped:
Liners on the sea, skyscrapers on the land; diving steel in the sea, climbing steel in the sky.

Finders in the dark, you, Steve, with a dinner bucket, you, Steve, clumping in the dusk on the sidewalks with an evening paper for the woman and kids, you, Steve, with your head wondering where we all end up—
Finders in the dark, Steve. I hook my arm in cinder sleeves; we go down the street together; it is all the same to us; you, Steve, and the rest of us end on the same stars; we all wear a hat in hell together, in hell or heaven.

Smoke nights now, Steve.
Smoke, smoke, lost in the sieves of yesterday;
Dumped again to the scoops and hooks today.
Smoke like the clocks and whistles, always.
    Smoke nights now.
    Tomorrow—something else.

Luck moons come and go;
Five men swim in a pot of red steel.
Their bones are kneaded into the bread of steel;
Their bones are knocked into coils and anvils
And the sucking plungers of sea-fighting turbines.
Look for them in the woven frame of a wireless station.
So ghosts hide in steel like heavy-armed men in mirrors.
Peepers, skulkers—they shadow-dance in laughing tombs.
They are always there and they never answer.

One of them said: "I like my job; the company is good to me; America is a wonderful country."
One: "Jesus, my bones ache; the company is a liar; this is a free country, like hell."
One: "I got a girl, a peach; we save up and go on a farm and raise pigs and be the boss ourselves."
And the others were roughneck singers a long ways from home.
Look for them back of a steel vault door.

    They laugh at the cost.
    They lift the birdmen into the blue.
    It is steel a motor sings and zooms.

In the subway plugs and drums,
In the slow hydraulic drills, in gumbo or gravel,
Under dynamo shafts in the webs of armature spiders,
They shadow-dance and laugh at the cost.

The ovens light a red dome.
Spools of fire wind and wind.
Quadrangles of crimson sputter.
The lashes of dying maroon let down.
Fire and wind wash out the slag.
Forever the slag gets washed in fire and wind.
The anthem learned by the steel is:
    Do this or go hungry.
Look for our rust on a plow.
Listen to us in a threshing-engine razz.
Look at our job in the running wagon wheat.

✦

Fire and wind wash at the slag.
Box-cars, clocks, steam-shovels, churns, pistons, boilers, scissors—
Oh, the sleeping slag from the mountains, the slag-heavy pig-iron will go down many roads.
Men will stab and shoot with it, and make butter and tunnel rivers, and mow hay in swaths, and slit hogs and skin beeves, and steer airplanes across North America, Europe, Asia, round the world.

Hacked from a hard rock country, broken and baked in mills and smelters, the rusty dust waits
Till the clean hard weave of its atoms cripples and blunts the drill chewing a hole in it.
The steel of its plinths and flanges is reckoned, O God, in one-millionth of an inch.

✦

Once when I saw the curves of fire, the rough scarf women dancing,
Dancing out of the flues and smoke-stacks—flying hair of fire, flying feet upside down;
Buckets and baskets of fire exploding and chortling, fire running wild out of the steady and fastened ovens;
Sparks cracking a harr-harr-huff from a solar-plexus of rock-ribs of the earth taking a laugh for themselves;
Ears and noses of fire, gibbering gorilla arms of fire, gold mud-pies, gold bird-wings, red jackets riding purple mules, scarlet autocrats tumbling from the humps of camels, assassinated czars straddling vermillion balloons;
I saw then the fires flash one by one: good-by: then smoke, smoke;
And in the screens the great sisters of night and cool stars, sitting women arranging their hair,
Waiting in the sky, waiting with slow easy eyes, waiting and half-murmuring:
"Since you know all
and I know nothing,
tell me what I dreamed last night."

✦

Pearl cobwebs in the windy rain,
in only a flicker of wind,
are caught and lost and never know again.

A pool of moonshine comes and waits,
but never waits long; the wind picks up
loose gold like this and is gone.

A bar of steel sleeps and looks slant-eyed
on the pearl cobwebs, the pools of moonshine;
sleeps slant-eyed a million years,
sleeps with a coat of rust, a vest of moths,
a shirt of gathering sod and loam.

The wind never bothers . . . a bar of steel.
The wind picks only . . . pearl cobwebs . . . pools of moonshine.

LOVE IN THE VALLEY

by George Meredith (1828-1909)

Under yonder beech-tree single on the greensward,
  Couched with her arms behind her golden head,
Knees and tresses folded to slip and ripple idly,
  Lies my young love sleeping in the shade.
Had I the heart to slide an arm beneath her,
  Press her parting lips as her waist I gather slow,
Waking in amazement she could not but embrace me—
  Then would she hold me and never let me go?

Shy as the squirrel and wayward as the swallow,
  Swift as the swallow along the river's light
Circleting the surface to meet his mirrored winglets,
  Fleeter she seems in her stay than in her flight.
Shy as the squirrel that leaps among the pine-tops,
  Wayward as the swallow overhead at set of sun,
She whom I love is hard to catch and conquer,
  Hard, but O the glory of the winning were she won!

When her mother tends her before the laughing mirror,
  Tying up her laces, looping up her hair,
Often she thinks, were this wild thing wedded,
  More love should I have, and much less care.
When her mother tends her before the lighted mirror,
  Loosening her laces, combing down her curls,
Often she thinks, were this wild thing wedded,
  I should miss but one for many boys and girls.

Heartless she is as the shadow in the meadows
  Flying to the hills on a blue and breezy noon.
No, she is athirst and drinking up her wonder;
  Earth to her is young as the slip of the new moon.
Deals she an unkindness, 'tis but her rapid measure,
  Even as in a dance; and her smile can heal no less:
Like the swinging May-cloud that pelts the flowers with hailstones
  Off a sunny border, she was made to bruise and bless.

Lovely are the curves of the white owl sweeping
  Wavy in the dusk lit by one large star.
Lone on the fir-branch, his rattle-note unvaried,
  Brooding o'er the gloom, spins the brown evejar.
Darker grows the valley, more and more forgetting;
  So were it with me if forgetting could be willed.
Tell the grassy hollow that holds the bubbling wellspring,
  Tell it to forget the source that keeps it filled.

Stepping down the hill with her fair companions,
  Arm in arm, all against the raying west,
Boldly she sings, to the merry tune she marches,

Brave is her shape, and sweeter unpossessed.
Sweeter, for she is what my heart first awaking
Whispered the world was; morning light is she.
Love that so desires would fain keep her changeless;
Fain would fling the net, and fain have her free.

Happy, happy time, when the white star hovers
Low over dim fields fresh with bloomy dew,
Near the face of dawn, that draws athwart the darkness,
Threading it with color, like yewberries the yew.
Thicker crowd the shades as the grave east deepens
Glowing, and with crimson a long cloud swells.
Maiden still the morn is; and strange she is, and secret;
Strange her eyes; her cheeks are cold as cold sea-shells.

Sunrays, leaning on our southern hills and lighting
Wild cloud-mountains that drag the hills along,
Oft ends the day of your shifting brilliant laughter
Chill as a dull face frowning on a song.
Aye, but shows the southwest a ripple-feathered bosom
Blown to silver while the clouds are shaken and ascend
Scaling the mid-heavens as they stream,—there comes a sunset
Rich, deep like love in beauty without end.

When at dawn she sighs, and like an infant to the window
Turns grave eyes craving light, released from dreams,
Beautiful she looks, like a white water-lily
Bursting out of bud in havens of the streams.
When from bed she rises clothed from neck to ankle
In her long nightgown sweet as boughs of May,
Beautiful she looks, like a tall garden-lily
Pure from the night, and splendid for the day.

Mother of the dews, dark eye-lashed twilight,
Low-lidded twilight, o'er the valley's brim,
Rounding on thy breast sings the dew-delighted skylark,
Clear as though the dewdrops had their voice in him.
Hidden where the rose-flush drinks the rayless planet,
Fountain-full he pours the spraying fountain showers.
Let me hear her laughter, I would have her ever
Cool as dew in twilight, the lark above the flowers.

All the girls are out with their baskets for the primrose;
Up lanes, woods through, they troop in joyful bands.
My sweet leads. She knows not why, but now she loiters,
Eyes the bent anemones, and hangs her hands.
Such a look will tell that the violets are peeping,
Coming the rose; and unaware a cry
Springs in her bosom for odors and for color,
Covert and the nightingale; she knows not why.

Kerchiefed head and chin she darts between her tulips,
Streaming like a willow gray in arrowy rain.

Some bend beaten cheek to gravel, and their angel
  She will be; she lifts them, and on she speeds again.
Black the driving rain-cloud breasts the iron gateway;
  She is forth to cheer a neighbor lacking mirth.
So when sky and grass met rolling dumb for thunder
  Saw I once a white dove, sole light of earth.

Prim little scholars are the flowers of her garden,
  Trained to stand in rows, and asking if they please.
I might love them well but for loving more the wild ones.
  O my wild ones! they tell me more than these.
You, my wild one, you tell of honeyed field-rose,
  Violet, blushing eglantine in life; and even as they,
They by the wayside are earnest of your goodness,
  You are of life's, on the banks that line the way.

Peering at her chamber the white crowns the red rose,
  Jasmine winds the porch with stars two and three.
Parted is the window; she sleeps; the starry jasmine
  Breathes a falling breath that carries thoughts of me.
Sweeter unpossessed, have I said of her my sweetest?
  Not while she sleeps. While she sleeps the jasmine breathes,
Luring her to love; she sleeps; the starry jasmine
  Bears me to her pillow under white rose-wreaths.

✦

O the golden sheaf, the rustling treasure-armful!
  O the nutbrown tresses nodding interlaced!
O the treasure-tresses one another over
  Nodding! O the girdle slack about the waist!
Slain are the poppies that shot their random scarlet
  Quick amid the wheat-ears. Wound about the waist,
Gathered, see these brides of Earth one blush of ripeness!
  O the nutbrown tresses nodding interlaced!

Large and smoky red the sun's cold disk drops,
  Clipped by naked hills, on violet-shaded snow.
Eastward large and still lights up a bower of moonrise,
  Whence at her leisure steps the moon aglow.
Nightlong on black print-branches our beech-tree
  Gazes in this whiteness; nightlong could I.
Here may life on death or death on life be painted.
  Let me clasp her soul to know she cannot die!

Gossips count her faults; they scour a narrow chamber
  Where there is no window, read not heaven or her.
"When she was a tiny," one aged woman quavers,
  Plucks at my heart and leads me by the ear.
Faults she had once as she learned to run and tumbled;
  Faults of feature some see, beauty not complete.
Yet, good gossips, beauty that makes holy
  Earth and air, may have faults from head to feet.

Hither she comes; she comes to me; she lingers,
  Deepens her brown eyebrows, while in new surprise
High rise the lashes in wonder of a stranger;
  Yet am I the light and living of her eyes.
Something friends have told her fills her heart to brimming,
  Nets her in her blushes, and wounds her, and tames.—
Sure of her haven, O like a dove alighting,
  Arms up, she dropped; our souls were in our names.

Soon will she lie like a white-frost sunrise.
  Yellow oats and brown wheat, barley pale as rye,
Long since your sheaves have yielded to the thresher,
  Felt the girdle loosened, seen the tresses fly.
Soon will she lie like a blood-red sunset,
  Swift with the tomorrow, green-winged Spring!
Sing from the southwest, bring her back the truants,
  Nightingale and swallow, song and dipping wing.

Soft new beech-leaves, up to beamy April
  Spreading bough on bough a primrose mountain, you
Lucid in the moon, raise lilies to the sky-fields,
  Youngest green transfused in silver shining through;
Fairer than the lily, than the wild white cherry;
  Fair as in image my seraph love appears
Borne to me by dreams when dawn is at my eyelids—
  Fair as in the flesh she swims to me on tears.

Could I find a place to be alone with heaven,
  I would speak my heart out; heaven is my need.
Every woodland tree is flushing like the dogwood,
  Flashing like the whitebeam, swaying like the reed.
Flushing like the dogwood crimson in October;
  Streaming like the flag-reed southwest blown;
Flashing as in gusts the sudden-lighted whitebeam:
  All seem to know what is for heaven alone.

SUGGESTIONS FOR ADDITIONAL READING

POEMS OF COLOR

Mary Coleridge, *L'Oiseau Bleu*
Amy Lowell, *The Garden by Moonlight*
Amy Lowell, *Towns in Color*
Amy Lowell, *Beech, Pine, and Sunlight*
Amy Lowell, *A Legend of Porcelain*
Walter de la Mare, *Silver*
Vachel Lindsay, *On the Garden Wall*
Conrad Aiken, *White Nocturne*
Conrad Aiken, *Variations*
Conrad Aiken, *Improvisations*
John Gould Fletcher, *Irradiations*
John Gould Fletcher, *Green Symphony*

POEMS OF SHAPE AND LINE

William Cowper, *A Rural Walk*
E. A. Poe, *The City in the Sea*
Vachel Lindsay, *Moon Poems*
John Gould Fletcher, *The Skaters*

POEMS OF MOVEMENT

Robert Browning, *Childe Roland to the Dark Tower Came*
Robert Browning, *Cavalier Tunes*
Robert Browning, *Through the Metidja to Abd-el-Kadr*
Vachel Lindsay, *The Santa Fé Trail*

John Gould Fletcher, *Arizona: The Windmills*

POEMS OF SOUND

John G. Whittier, *The Pipes at Lucknow*
T. B. Aldrich, *The Piazza of St. Mark at Midnight*
Richard W. Gilder, *The Night Pasture*
Arthur Symons, *During Music*
Amy Lowell, *The Bombardment*
Amy Lowell, *Stravinsky's Three Pieces, "Grotesques," for String Quartet*
Carl Sandburg, *Jan Kubelik*
Carl Sandburg, *Jazz Fantasia*
Vachel Lindsay, *The Kallyope Yell*
Vachel Lindsay, *The Congo*
G. K. Chesterton, *Lepanto*

POEMS OF TOUCH, TASTE, SMELL

William E. Henley, *In Hospital*
Christopher Morley, *Chimneysmoke*
William Cowper, *A Winter Evening*
Rupert Brooke, *The Old Vicarage, Grantchester*
Louis Untermeyer, *Food and Drink*
Léonie Adams, *Country Summer*

5

THE EXPERIENCES OF POETRY—1: THE POEM AS STORY

MAN's interest in story-telling is both pre-historic and ultra-modern; his passion for living is scarcely greater than his passion for shaping life to his fictions. Unable to think in the abstract about eternal truths, he has stated his religious beliefs in legends of the gods, Biblical narratives, Dante's tour through Hell and Heaven, Bunyan's allegory. The ardent speaker who cannot find an anecdote to enliven his address is less effective than the man without a message who can tell a story entertainingly. Crowds gather about the display in which there is visible movement; the static advertisement receives only a passing glimpse. The "talkies" are sufficient proof that what the average human being desires in entertainment must be filled with action and rapid dialogue.

In reading or listening to a story, we ask for the relation of action in fairly chronological order. We can be amused by either fact or fable, provided it is concrete, animated, unusual, and arranged to create suspense. We discover an added aesthetic pleasure if the story is ordered artistically and told beautifully. From the times of Homer and the gleemen the audience has found the story enhanced by the rhythms and melodies of poetry. Most poetry, ancient and modern, belongs in the realm of narrative, the poetry of human experiences.

The story in verse must meet the same tests as the story in prose; verse is no excuse for poor plotting or careless characterization. The reader should be able to follow the carefully ordered events from the exposition and inciting force through the climax to the dénouement. He should perceive the interweaving of the strands of the story, the handling of conflict—primitive physical struggles, battles of wits and wills, internal psychological upheavals. He should note the story-problem set by the author, and how he has solved it. The part played by the setting—the use of pictorial imagination in connection with the story—also merits observation.

Story-tellers in general follow one of two paths in their method and mood of narration: romance or realism. It becomes increasingly obvious that these terms are merely suggestive, but the controversy that still rages over the justice and significance of this differentiation has at least served to mark rough boundaries for the two fields. Romance must not be confused with Romanticism, an historical movement of the eighteenth and nineteenth centuries, though the spirit behind the two is probably the same. The "Romantic Movement," according to Heinrich Heine, was a "return to the mediaeval." Walter Pater found in it "strangeness, wonder, aspiration;" Victor Hugo held that Romanticism resided in *grotesquerie* and "liberalism in literature." To Ferdinand Brunetière it meant subjectivity and freedom from restraint; to George Saintsbury it was suggestion and symbolism. The neo-classic humanists, led by Professor Irving Babbitt, have branded Romanticism as "an escape from truth."

ROMANTIC ADVENTURE

Perhaps all of these characteristics can be found in romance also. Romance seems the expression of nostalgia, a mood of yearning for something different from that which life offers; in realism, the sense of fact prevails, and the idealistic imagination succumbs. This distinction implies that the romantic element in literature varies with the individual. To the disabled veteran there is but little romance in war and much in sailing the seas; but to the sailor, bored with the waste of ocean, the roar of artillery might well possess romantic glamor. Melville's realistic picture of life in the South Seas appeared highly romantic to New York and Boston; life in the great city seems thrillingly exotic to the dweller in lonely places. It might be said that romance is what the other man has, and the romantic land is the land where one does not happen to live.

It is therefore not necessarily the material which makes a story romantic or realistic, though certain subjects seem to fit one type better than another. The life of a stoker in an ocean vessel seems material for realism; yet Victor Hugo made romance live in the sewers of Paris. The distinction lies in the approach of the writer. Cervantes takes the material of mediaeval romance and makes realistic burlesque of it; Carl Sandburg transforms a puddle in a deserted brickyard into an object of delicate beauty. A realist in love might be irritated by Wordsworth, just as a lover of country life might revolt at Crabbe. When we try to place our finger on what is romantic or realistic in an individual poem, we find ourselves involved in controversy.

The typical romanticist sees life through the lens of his own hopes and ideals, and finds it colored to suit his taste; the realist, too often, photographs it through a keyhole or a microscope, and then enlarges the picture to discover the flaws in detail. Here the romanticist objects that mere photography is less revealing, and therefore less true than artistic portraiture. To the realist who boasts that he "refuses to shirk the commonplace and ugly" the romancer replies that life cannot refuse to include the beautiful and harmonious.

In "The Lady of Shalott" Tennyson presents a romanticist afraid to look at life except as a reflection and whose one glimpse of reality was fatal.

THE LADY OF SHALOTT

by Alfred, Lord Tennyson (1809-1892)

PART I

On either side the river lie
Long fields of barley and of rye,
That clothe the wold and meet the sky;
And through the field the road runs by
  To many-towered Camelot;
And up and down the people go,
Gazing where the lilies blow
Round an island there below,
  The island of Shalott.

Willows whiten, aspens quiver,
Little breezes dusk and shiver
Through the wave that runs forever
By the island in the river
  Flowing down to Camelot.
Four gray walls, and four gray towers,
Overlook a space of flowers,
And the silent isle imbowers
  The Lady of Shalott.

By the margin, willow-veiled
Slide the heavy barges trailed
By slow horses; and unhailed
The shallop flitteth silken-sailed
  Skimming down to Camelot.
But who hath seen her wave her hand?
Or at the casement seen her stand?
Or is she known in all the land,
  The Lady of Shalott?

Only reapers, reaping early
In among the bearded barley,
Hear a song that echoes cheerly
From the river winding clearly,
  Down to towered Camelot;
And by the moon the reaper weary,
Piling sheaves in uplands airy,
Listening, whispers " 'Tis the fairy
  Lady of Shalott."

PART II

There she weaves by night and day
A magic web with colors gay.
She has heard a whisper say
A curse is on her if she stay
  To look down to Camelot.
She knows not what the curse may be,
And so she weaveth steadily,
And little other care hath she,
  The Lady of Shalott.

And moving through a mirror clear
That hangs before her all the year,
Shadows of the world appear.
There she sees the highway near
  Winding down to Camelot;
There the river eddy whirls,
And there the surly village-churls,
And the red cloaks of market girls,
  Pass onward from Shalott.

Sometimes a troop of damsels glad,
An abbot on an ambling pad,
Sometimes a curly shepherd-lad,
Or long-haired page in crimson clad,
  Goes by to towered Camelot.
And sometimes through the mirror blue
The knights come riding two and two.
She hath no loyal knight and true,
  The Lady of Shalott.

But in her web she still delights
To weave the mirror's magic sights,
For often through the silent nights
A funeral, with plumes and lights
  And music, went to Camelot.
Or when the moon was overhead,
Came two young lovers lately wed;
"I am half sick of shadows," said
  The Lady of Shalott.

PART III

A bow-shot from her bower-eaves,
He rode between the barley-sheaves,
The sun came dazzling through the leaves,
And flamed upon the brazen greaves
  Of bold Sir Lancelot.
A red-cross knight forever kneeled
To a lady in his shield,
That sparkled on the yellow field,
  Beside remote Shalott.

The gemmy bridle glittered free,
Like to some branch of stars we see
Hung in the golden Galaxy.
The bridle bells rang merrily
  As he rode down to Camelot.
And from his blazoned baldric slung
A mighty silver bugle hung,
And as he rode his armor rung,
  Beside remote Shalott.

All in the blue unclouded weather
Thick-jeweled shone the saddle-leather;
The helmet and the helmet-feather
Burned like one burning flame together,
  As he rode down to Camelot;
As often through the purple night,
Below the starry clusters bright,
Some bearded meteor, trailing light,
  Moves over still Shalott.

His broad clear brow in sunlight glowed;
On burnished hooves his warhorse trode;
From underneath his helmet flowed

His coal-black curls as on he rode,
  As he rode down to Camelot.
From the bank and from the river
He flashed into the crystal mirror,
"Tirra lirra," by the river
  Sang Sir Lancelot.

She left the web, she left the loom,
She made three paces through the room,
She saw the water-lily bloom,
She saw the helmet and the plume,
  She looked down to Camelot.
Out flew the web and floated wide;
The mirror cracked from side to side;
"The curse is come upon me," cried
  The Lady of Shalott.

PART IV

In the stormy east-wind straining,
The pale yellow woods were waning,
The broad stream in his banks complaining,
Heavily the low sky raining
  Over towered Camelot;
Down she came and found a boat
Beneath a willow left afloat,
And round about the prow she wrote
  The Lady of Shalott.

And down the river's dim expanse
Like some bold seër in a trance,
Seeing all his own mischance—
With a glassy countenance
  Did she look to Camelot.
And at the closing of the day
She loosed the chain, and down she lay;
The broad stream bore her far away,
  The Lady of Shalott.

Lying, robed in snowy white
That loosely flew to left and right—
The leaves upon her falling light—
Through the noises of the night
  She floated down to Camelot;
And as the boat-head wound along
The willowy hills and fields among,
They heard her singing her last song,
  The Lady of Shalott.

Heard a carol, mournful, holy,
Chanted loudly, chanted lowly,
Till her blood was frozen slowly,
And her eyes were darkened wholly,
  Turned to towered Camelot.
For ere she reached upon the tide
The first house by the water side,
Singing in her song she died,
  The Lady of Shalott.

Under tower and balcony,
By garden-wall and gallery,
A gleaming shape she floated by,
Dead-pale between the houses high,
  Silent into Camelot.
Out upon the wharfs they came,
Knight and burgher, lord and dame,
And round the prow they read her name,
  The Lady of Shalott.

Who is this? and what is here?
And in the lighted palace near
Died the sound of royal cheer;
And they crossed themselves for fear,
  All the knights at Camelot.
But Lancelot mused a little space;
He said, "She has a lovely face;
God in his mercy lend her grace,
  The Lady of Shalott."

Here we find many of the qualities normally associated with romance: idealism, symbolism, and the worship of the beautiful. By placing the action in Arthurian Camelot, Tennyson has also satisfied the longing for the exotic, the far-away and long-ago. About it all there hovers an air of mystery and emotional refinement, remote and romantic.

The adventures of romantic poetry are usually brave, brisk and exciting, such as those in the familiar ballad "The Highwayman" by Alfred Noyes. The bravado of romantic love is well shown in the following poem by Sir Walter Scott. Scott belongs historically to the Romantic movement, and is perhaps better known for his prose romances of mediaeval England, *Ivanhoe* or *The Talisman,* than for his romantic poetry. Every schoolboy, however, has read the royal escapades of *The Lady of the Lake,* and probably has followed the thrilling adventures of *Marmion* and *The Lay of the Last Minstrel.*

LOCHINVAR

by Walter Scott (1771-1832)

Oh, young Lochinvar is come out of the west;
Through all the wide Border his steed was the best;
And save his good broadsword he weapons had none.
He rode all unarmed, and he rode all alone.
So faithful in love, and so dauntless in war,
There never was knight like the young Lochinvar.

He stayed not for brake, and he stopped not for stone;
He swam the Eske River where ford there was none;
But, ere he alighted at Netherby gate,
The bride had consented, the gallant came late;
For a laggard in love, and a dastard in war,
Was to wed the fair Ellen of brave Lochinvar.

So boldly he entered the Netherby hall,
'Mong bridesmen and kinsmen and brothers and all;
Then spoke the bride's father, his hand on his sword
(For the poor craven bridegroom said never a word),
"Oh, come ye in peace here, or come ye in war,
Or to dance at our bridal, young Lord Lochinvar?"

"I long wooed your daughter, my suit you denied—
Love swells like the Solway, but ebbs like its tide;
And now I am come, with this lost love of mine
To lead but one measure, drink one cup of wine.
There are maidens in Scotland more lovely by far
That would gladly be bride to thc young Lochinvar."

The bride kissed the goblet; the knight took it up;
He quaffed off the wine, and he threw down the cup.
She looked down to blush, and she looked up to sigh,
With a smile on her lips and a tear in her eye.
He took her soft hand ere her mother could bar—
"Now tread we a measure!" said young Lochinvar.

So stately his form, and so lovely her face,
That never a hall such a galliard did grace;
While her mother did fret, and her father did fume,
And the bridegroom stood dangling his bonnet and plume;
And the bride-maidens whispered, " 'Twere better by far
To have matched our fair cousin with young Lochinvar."

One touch to her hand, and one word in her ear,
When they reached the hall door and the charger stood near;
So light to the croup the fair lady he swung,

So light to the saddle before her he sprung!
"She is won! we are gone, over bank, bush, and scar!
They'll have fleet steeds that follow!" quoth young Lochinvar.

There was mounting 'mong Graemes of the Netherby clan;
Forsters, Fenwicks, and Musgraves, they rode and they ran;
There was racing and chasing on Cannobie Lee;
But the lost bride of Netherby ne'er did they see.
So daring in love, and so dauntless in war,
Have ye e'er heard of gallant like young Lochinvar?

Perhaps the paragon of romantic love-poems is John Keats's "The Eve of St. Agnes." Certainly the poem contains the highest qualities of historical Romanticism. A mediaeval setting, a perfect hero and heroine, beauty of sensory appeal, and high passion combine to make the poem one of the most colorful as well as one of the most graphic in all literature.

THE EVE OF ST. AGNES

by John Keats (1795-1821)

St. Agnes' Eve—ah, bitter chill it was!
The owl, for all his feathers, was a-cold;
The hare limp'd trembling through the frozen grass,
And silent was the flock in woolly fold:
Numb were the Beadsman's fingers while he told
His rosary, and while his frosted breath,
Like pious incense from a censer old,
Seem'd taking flight for heaven without a death,
Past the sweet Virgin's picture, while his prayer he saith.

His prayer he saith, this patient, holy man;
Then takes his lamp, and riseth from his knees,
And back returneth, meagre, barefoot, wan,
Along the chapel aisle by slow degrees:
The sculptured dead, on each side, seem to freeze,
Emprison'd in black, purgatorial rails:
Knights, ladies, praying in dumb orat'ries,
He passeth by, and his weak spirit fails
To think how they may ache in icy hoods and mails.

Northward he turneth through a little door,
And scarce three steps, ere Music's golden tongue
Flatter'd to tears this aged man and poor.
But no—already had his death-bell rung;
The joys of all his life were said and sung;
His was harsh penance on St. Agnes' Eve:
Another way he went, and soon among
Rough ashes sat he for his soul's reprieve,
And all night kept awake, for sinners' sake to grieve.

That ancient Beadsman heard the prelude soft;
And so it chanced, for many a door was wide,

From hurry to and fro. Soon, up aloft,
The silver, snarling trumpets 'gan to chide:
The level chambers, ready with their pride,
Were glowing to receive a thousand guests.
The carvèd angels, ever eager-eyed,
Stared, where upon their heads the cornice rests,
With hair blown back, and wings put crosswise on their breasts.

At length burst in the argent revelry,
With plume, tiara, and all rich array,
Numerous as shadows haunting faërily
The brain new-stuff'd, in youth, with triumphs gay
Of old romance. These let us wish away,
And turn, sole-thoughted, to one Lady there,
Whose heart had brooded, all that wintry day,
On love, and wing'd St. Agnes' saintly care,
As she had heard old dames full many times declare.

They told her how, upon St. Agnes' Eve,
Young virgins might have visions of delight,
And soft adorings from their loves receive
Upon the honey'd middle of the night,
If ceremonies due they did aright;
As, supperless to bed they must retire,
And couch supine their beauties, lily white;
Nor look behind, nor sideways, but require
Of Heaven with upward eyes for all that they desire.

Full of this whim was thoughtful Madeline:
The music, yearning like a God in pain,
She scarcely heard: her maiden eyes divine,
Fix'd on the floor, saw many a sweeping train
Pass by—she heeded not at all: in vain
Came many a tiptoe, amorous cavalier,
And back retired; not cool'd by high disdain,
But she saw not: her heart was otherwhere;
She sigh'd for Agnes' dreams, the sweetest of the year.

She danced along with vague, regardless eyes,
Anxious her lips, her breathing quick and short:
The hallow'd hour was near at hand: she sighs
Amid the timbrels, and the throng'd resort
Of whisperers in anger or in sport;
'Mid looks of love, defiance, hate, and scorn,
Hoodwink'd with faëry fancy; all amort,
Save to St. Agnes and her lambs unshorn,
And all the bliss to be before tomorrow morn.

So, purposing each moment to retire,
She linger'd still. Meantime, across the moors,
Had come young Porphyro, with heart on fire
For Madeline. Beside the portal doors,

Buttress'd from moonlight, stands he, and implores
All saints to give him sight of Madeline,
But for one moment in the tedious hours,
That he might gaze and worship all unseen;
Perchance speak, kneel, touch, kiss—in sooth such things have been.

He ventures in: let no buzz'd whisper tell,
All eyes be muffled, or a hundred swords
Will storm his heart, Love's fev'rous citadel:
For him, those chambers held barbarian hordes,
Hyena foemen, and hot-blooded lords,
Whose very dogs would execration howl
Against his lineage; not one breast affords
Him any mercy in that mansion foul,
Save one old beldame, weak in body and in soul.

Ah, happy chance! the aged creature came,
Shuffling along with ivory-headed wand,
To where he stood, hid from the torch's flame,
Behind a broad hall pillar, far beyond
The sound of merriment and chorus bland.
He startled her: but soon she knew his face,
And grasp'd his fingers in her palsied hand,
Saying, "Mercy, Porphyro! hie thee from this place;
They are all here tonight, the whole blood-thirsty race!

"Get hence! get hence! there's dwarfish Hildebrand:
He had a fever late, and in the fit
He cursèd thee and thine, both house and land:
Then there's that old Lord Maurice, not a whit
More tame for his grey hairs—Alas me! flit!
Flit like a ghost away."—"Ah, Gossip dear,
We're safe enough; here in this arm-chair sit,
And tell me how—" "Good saints! not here, not here!
Follow me, child, or else these stones will be thy bier."

He follow'd through a lowly archèd way,
Brushing the cobwebs with his lofty plume;
And as she mutter'd "Well-a—well-a-day!"
He found him in a little moonlight room,
Pale, latticed, chill, and silent as a tomb.
"Now tell me where is Madeline," said he,
"O tell me, Angela, by the holy loom
Which none but secret sisterhood may see,
When they St. Agnes' wool are weaving piously."

"St. Agnes! Ah! it is St. Agnes' Eve—
Yet men will murder upon holy days.
Thou must hold water in a witch's sieve,
And be liege-lord of all the Elves and Fays
To venture so: it fills me with amaze
To see thee, Porphyro!—St. Agnes' Eve!

God's help! my lady fair the conjurer plays
This very night: good angels her deceive!
But let me laugh awhile,—I've mickle time to grieve."

Feebly she laugheth in the languid moon,
While Porphyro upon her face doth look,
Like puzzled urchin on an aged crone
Who keepeth closed a wondrous riddle-book,
As spectacled she sits in chimney nook.
But soon his eyes grew brilliant, when she told
His lady's purpose; and he scarce could brook
Tears, at the thought of those enchantments cold,
And Madeline asleep in lap of legends old.

Sudden a thought came like a full-blown rose,
Flushing his brow, and in his painèd heart
Made purple riot: then doth he propose
A stratagem, that makes the beldame start:
"A cruel man and impious thou art!
Sweet lady, let her pray, and sleep and dream
Alone with her good angels, far apart
From wicked men like thee. Go, go!—I deem
Thou canst not surely be the same that thou didst seem."

"I will not harm her, by all saints I swear!"
Quoth Porphyro: "O may I ne'er find grace
When my weak voice shall whisper its last prayer,
If one of her soft ringlets I displace,
Or look with ruffian passion in her face.
Good Angela, believe me, by these tears;
Or I will, even in a moment's space,
Awake, with horrid shout, my foemen's ears,
And beard them, though they be more fang'd than wolves and bears."

"Ah! why wilt thou affright a feeble soul?
A poor, weak, palsy-stricken, churchyard thing,
Whose passing-bell may ere the midnight toll;
Whose prayers for thee, each morn and evening,
Were never miss'd." Thus plaining, doth she bring
A gentler speech from burning Porphyro;
So woeful, and of such deep sorrowing,
That Angela gives promise she will do
Whatever he shall wish, betide her weal or woe.

Which was, to lead him, in close secrecy,
Even to Madeline's chamber, and there hide
Him in a closet, of such privacy
That he might see her beauty unespied,
And win perhaps that night a peerless bride,
While legion'd faëries paced the coverlet,
And pale enchantment held her sleepy-eyed.
Never on such a night have lovers met,
Since Merlin paid his Demon all the monstrous debt.

"It shall be as thou wishest," said the Dame:
"All cates and dainties shall be storèd there
Quickly on this feast-night: by the tambour frame
Her own lute thou wilt see: no time to spare,
For I am slow and feeble, and scarce dare
On such a catering trust my dizzy head.
Wait here, my child, with patience; kneel in prayer
The while. Ah! thou must needs the lady wed,
Or may I never leave my grave among the dead."

So saying she hobbled off with busy fear.
The lover's endless minutes slowly pass'd;
The dame return'd, and whisper'd in his ear
To follow her; with agèd eyes aghast
From fright of dim espial. Safe at last
Through many a dusky gallery, they gain
The maiden's chamber, silken, hush'd, and chaste;
Where Porphyro took covert, pleased amain.
His poor guide hurried back with agues in her brain.

Her faltering hand upon the balustrade,
Old Angela was feeling for the stair,
When Madeline, St. Agnes' charmèd maid,
Rose, like a mission'd spirit, unaware:
With silver taper's light, and pious care,
She turn'd, and down the agèd gossip led
To a safe level matting. Now prepare,
Young Porphyro, for gazing on that bed;
She comes, she comes again, like ring-dove fray'd and fled.

Out went the taper as she hurried in;
Its little smoke, in pallid moonshine, died:
She closed the door, she panted, all akin
To spirits of the air, and visions wide:
No utter'd syllable, or, woe betide!
But to her heart, her heart was voluble,
Paining with eloquence her balmy side;
As though a tongueless nightingale should swell
Her throat in vain, and die, heart-stifled, in her dell.

A casement high and triple-arch'd there was,
All garlanded with carven imageries,
Of fruits and flowers, and bunches of knot-grass,
And diamonded with panes of quaint device,
Innumerable of stains and splendid dyes,
As are the tiger-moth's deep-damask'd wings;
And in the midst, 'mong thousand heraldries,
And twilight saints, and dim emblazonings,
A shielded scutcheon blush'd with blood of queens and kings.

Full on this casement shone the wintry moon,
And threw warm gules on Madeline's fair breast,

As down she knelt for Heaven's grace and boon;
Rose-bloom fell on her hands, together prest,
And on her silver cross soft amethyst,
And on her hair a glory, like a saint:
She seem'd a splendid angel, newly drest,
Save wings, for heaven:—Porphyro grew faint:
She knelt, so pure a thing, so free from mortal taint.

Anon his heart revives: her vespers done,
Of all its wreathèd pearls her hair she frees;
Unclasps her warmèd jewels one by one;
Loosens her fragrant bodice; by degrees
Her rich attire creeps rustling to her knees:
Half-hidden, like a mermaid in sea-weed,
Pensive awhile she dreams awake, and sees,
In fancy, fair St. Agnes in her bed,
But dares not look behind, or all the charm is fled.

Soon, trembling in her soft and chilly nest,
In sort of wakeful swoon, perplex'd she lay,
Until the poppied warmth of sleep oppress'd
Her soothèd limbs, and soul fatigued away;
Flown, like a thought, until the morrow-day;
Blissfully haven'd both from joy and pain;
Clasp'd like a missal where swart Paynims pray;
Blinded alike from sunshine and from rain,
As though a rose should shut, and be a bud again.

Stol'n to this paradise, and so entranced,
Porphyro gazed upon her empty dress,
And listen'd to her breathing, if it chanced
To wake into a slumberous tenderness;
Which when he heard, that minute did he bless,
And breath'd himself: then from the closet crept,
Noiseless as fear in a wide wilderness,
And over the hush'd carpet, silent, stept,
And 'tween the curtains peep'd, where, lo!—how fast she slept!

Then by the bed-side, where the faded moon
Made a dim, silver twilight, soft he set
A table, and, half anguish'd, threw thereon
A cloth of woven crimson, gold, and jet:—
O for some drowsy Morphean amulet!
The boisterous, midnight, festive clarion,
The kettle-drum, and far-heard clarionet,
Affray his ears, though but in dying tone:—
The hall-door shuts again, and all the noise is gone.

And still she slept an azure-lidded sleep,
In blanchèd linen, smooth, and lavender'd,
While he from forth the closet brought a heap
Of candied apple, quince, and plum, and gourd;

With jellies soother than the creamy curd,
And lucent syrops, tinct with cinnamon;
Manna and dates, in argosy transferr'd
From Fez; and spicèd dainties, every one,
From silken Samarcand to cedar'd Lebanon.

These delicates he heap'd with glowing hand
On golden dishes and in baskets bright
Of wreathèd silver: sumptuous they stand
In the retired quiet of the night,
Filling the chilly room with perfume light.—
"And now, my love, my seraph fair, awake!
Thou art my heaven, and I thine eremite:
Open thine eyes, for meek St. Agnes' sake,
Or I shall drowse beside thee, so my soul doth ache."

Thus whispering, his warm, unnervèd arm
Sank in her pillow. Shaded was her dream
By the dusk curtains:—'twas a midnight charm
Impossible to melt as icèd stream:
The lustrous salvers in the moonlight gleam;
Broad golden fringe upon the carpet lies:
It seem'd he never, never could redeem
From such a steadfast spell his lady's eyes;
So mused awhile, entoil'd in woofèd phantasies.

Awakening up, he took her hollow lute,—
Tumultuous,—and, in chords that tenderest be,
He play'd an ancient ditty, long since mute,
In Provence call'd "La belle dame sans mercy":
Close to her ear touching the melody;—
Wherewith disturb'd, she utter'd a soft moan:
He ceased—she panted quick—and suddenly
Her blue affrayèd eyes wide open shone:
Upon his knees he sank, pale as smooth-sculptured stone.

Her eyes were open, but she still beheld,
Now wide awake, the vision of her sleep:
There was a painful change, that nigh expell'd
The blisses of her dream so pure and deep.
At which fair Madeline began to weep,
And moan forth witless words with many a sigh,
While still her gaze on Porphyro would keep;
Who knelt, with joinèd hands and piteous eye,
Fearing to move or speak, she look'd so dreamingly.

"Ah, Porphyro!" said she, "but even now
Thy voice was at sweet tremble in mine ear,
Made tunable with every sweetest vow;
And those sad eyes were spiritual and clear:
How changed thou art! how pallid, chill, and drear!
Give me that voice again, my Porphyro,

Those looks immortal, those complainings dear!
Oh, leave me not in this eternal woe,
For if thou diest, my Love, I know not where to go."

Beyond a mortal man impassion'd far
At these voluptuous accents, he arose,
Ethereal, flush'd, and like a throbbing star
Seen 'mid the sapphire heaven's deep repose;
Into her dream he melted, as the rose
Blendeth its odour with the violet,—
Solution sweet: meantime the frost-wind blows
Like Love's alarum, pattering the sharp sleet
Against the window-panes; St. Agnes' moon hath set.

'Tis dark: quick pattereth the flaw-blown sleet.
"This is no dream, my bride, my Madeline!"
'Tis dark: the icèd gusts still rave and beat:
"No dream, alas! alas! and woe is mine!
Porphyro will leave me here to fade and pine.
Cruel! what traitor could thee hither bring?
I curse not, for my heart is lost in thine,
Though thou forsakest a deceivèd thing;—
A dove forlorn and lost with sick unprunèd wing."

"My Madeline! sweet dreamer! lovely bride!
Say, may I be for aye thy vassal blest?
Thy beauty's shield, heart-shaped and vermeil-dyed?
Ah, silver shrine, here will I take my rest
After so many hours of toil and quest,
A famish'd pilgrim,—saved by miracle.
Though I have found, I will not rob thy nest,
Saving of thy sweet self; if thou think'st well
To trust, fair Madeline, to no rude infidel.

"Hark! 'tis an elfin storm from faëry land,
Of haggard seeming, but a boon indeed:
Arise—arise! the morning is at hand;—
The bloated wassailers will never heed;—
Let us away, my love, with happy speed;
There are no ears to hear, or eyes to see,—
Drown'd all in Rhenish and the sleepy mead.
Awake! arise! my love, and fearless be,
For o'er the southern moors I have a home for thee."

She hurried at his words, beset with fears,
For there were sleeping dragons all around,
At glaring watch, perhaps, with ready spears.
Down the wide stairs a darkling way they found;
In all the house was heard no human sound.
A chain-droop'd lamp was flickering by each door;
The arras, rich with horseman, hawk, and hound,
Flutter'd in the besieging wind's uproar;
And the long carpets rose along the gusty floor.

They glide, like phantoms, into the wide hall;
Like phantoms to the iron porch they glide,
Where lay the Porter, in uneasy sprawl,
With a huge empty flaggon by his side:
The wakeful bloodhound rose, and shook his hide,
But his sagacious eye an inmate owns:
By one, and one, the bolts full easy slide:—
The chains lie silent on the footworn stones;
The key turns, and the door upon its hinges groans.

And they are gone: ay, ages long ago
These lovers fled away into the storm.
That night the Baron dreamt of many a woe,
And all his warrior-guests with shade and form
Of witch, and demon, and large coffin-worm,
Were long be-nightmared. Angela the old
Died palsy-twitch'd, with meagre face deform;
The Beadsman, after thousand aves told,
For aye unsought-for slept among his ashes cold.

MAGIC AND MYSTERY

Romance in its weird or otherworldly aspect was the province of Samuel Taylor Coleridge, the most scintillating of Romantic critics. By agreement with Wordsworth in the composition of the *Lyrical Ballads,* Coleridge was to attempt to make the impossible appear real—one of the functions of romance—while Wordsworth found significant romance in the commonplace. Coleridge created uncanny atmosphere in *Christabel,* but left it a puzzling fragment. *The Rime of the Ancient Mariner,* however, was completed and assumed its place as one of the great peaks of narrative poetry.

THE RIME OF THE ANCIENT MARINER

by Samuel Taylor Coleridge (1772-1834)

PART I

An ancient Mariner meeteth three Gallants bidden to a wedding-feast, and detaineth one.

It is an ancient Mariner,
And he stoppeth one of three.
"By thy long grey beard and glittering eye,
Now wherefore stopp'st thou me?

The Bridegroom's doors are opened wide,
And I am next of kin;
The guests are met, the feast is set:
May'st hear the merry din."

He holds him with his skinny hand,
"There was a ship," quoth he.
"Hold off! unhand me, grey-beard loon!"
Eftsoons his hand dropt he.

The Wedding-Guest is spell-bound by the eye of the old sea-faring man, and constrained to hear his tale.

He holds him with his glittering eye—
The Wedding-Guest stood still,
And listens like a three years' child:
The Mariner hath his will.

The Wedding-Guest sat on a stone:
He cannot choose but hear;
And thus spake on that ancient man,
The bright-eyed Mariner.

"The ship was cheered, the harbour cleared,
Merrily did we drop
Below the kirk, below the hill,
Below the lighthouse top.

The Mariner tells how the ship sailed southward with a good wind and fair weather, till it reached the line.

The sun came up upon the left,
Out of the sea came he!
And he shone bright, and on the right
Went down into the sea.

Higher and higher every day,
Till over the mast at noon—"
The Wedding-Guest here beat his breast,
For he heard the loud bassoon.

The Wedding-Guest heareth the bridal music; but the Mariner continueth his tale.

The bride hath paced into the hall,
Red as a rose is she;
Nodding their heads before her goes
The merry minstrelsy.

The Wedding-Guest he beat his breast,
Yet he cannot choose but hear;
And thus spake on that ancient man,
The bright-eyed Mariner.

The ship driven by a storm toward the south pole.

"And now the Storm-blast came, and he
Was tyrannous and strong:
He struck with his o'ertaking wings,
And chased us south along.

With sloping masts and dipping prow,
As who pursued with yell and blow
Still treads the shadow of his foe,
And forward bends his head,
The ship drove fast, loud roared the blast,
And southward aye we fled.

And now there came both mist and snow,
And it grew wondrous cold:
And ice, mast-high, came floating by,
As green as emerald.

The land of ice, and of fearful sounds where no living thing was to be seen.

And through the drifts the snowy clifts
Did send a dismal sheen:
Nor shapes of men nor beasts we ken—
The ice was all between.

The ice was here, the ice was there,
The ice was all around:
It cracked and growled, and roared and howled,
Like noises in a swound!

Till a great sea-bird, called the Albatross, came through the snow-fog, and was received with great joy and hospitality.

At length did cross an Albatross,
Thorough the fog it came;
As if it had been a Christian soul,
We hailed it in God's name.

It ate the food it ne'er had eat,
And round and round it flew.
The ice did split with a thunder-fit;
The helmsman steered us through!

And lo! the Albatross proveth a bird of good omen, and followeth the ship as it returned northward through fog and floating ice.

And a good south wind sprung up behind;
The Albatross did follow,
And every day, for food or play,
Came to the mariner's hollo!

In mist or cloud, on mast or shroud,
It perched for vespers nine;
Whiles all the night, through fog-smoke white,
Glimmered the white moon-shine."

The ancient Mariner inhospitably killeth the pious bird of good omen.

"God save thee, ancient Mariner!
From the fiends, that plague thee thus!—
Why look'st thou so?"—With my cross-bow
I shot the Albatross.

PART II

The Sun now rose upon the right:
Out of the sea came he,
Still hid in mist, and on the left
Went down into the sea.

And the good south wind still blew behind,
But no sweet bird did follow,
Nor any day for food or play
Came to the mariner's hollo!

His shipmates cry out against the ancient Mariner, for killing the bird of good luck.

And I had done a hellish thing,
And it would work 'em woe:
For all averred, I had killed the bird
That made the breeze to blow.
Ah wretch! said they, the bird to slay,
That made the breeze to blow!

But when the fog cleared off, they justify the same, and thus make themselves accomplices in the crime.

Nor dim nor red, like God's own head,
The glorious Sun uprist:
Then all averred, I had killed the bird
That brought the fog and mist.
'Twas right, said they, such birds to slay,
That bring the fog and mist.

The fair breeze continues; the ship enters the Pacific Ocean, and sails northward, even till it reaches the Line.

The fair breeze blew, the white foam flew,
The furrow followed free;
We were the first that ever burst
Into that silent sea.

The ship hath been suddenly becalmed.

Down dropt the breeze, the sails dropt down,
'Twas sad as sad could be;
And we did speak only to break
The silence of the sea!

All in a hot and copper sky,
The bloody Sun, at noon,
Right up above the mast did stand,
No bigger than the Moon.

Day after day, day after day,
We stuck, nor breath nor motion;
As idle as a painted ship
Upon a painted ocean.

And the Albatross begins to be avenged.

Water, water, every where,
And all the boards did shrink;
Water, water, every where
Nor any drop to drink.

The very deep did rot: O Christ!
That ever this should be!
Yea, slimy things did crawl with legs
Upon the slimy sea.

About, about, in reel and rout
The death-fires danced at night;
The water, like a witch's oils,
Burnt green, and blue and white.

A Spirit had followed them; one of the invisible inhabitants of this planet, neither departed souls nor angels; concerning whom the learned Jew, Josephus, and the Platonic Constantinopolitan, Michael Psellus, may be consulted. They are very numerous, and there is no climate or element without one or more.

And some in dreams assurèd were
Of the Spirit that plagued us so,
Nine fathom deep he had followed us
From the land of mist and snow.

And every tongue, through utter drought,
Was withered at the root;
We could not speak, no more than if
We had been choked with soot.

The ship-mates, in their sore distress, would fain throw the whole guilt on the ancient Mariner: in sign whereof they hang the dead sea-bird round his neck.

Ah! well a-day! what evil looks
Had I from old and young!
Instead of the cross, the Albatross
About my neck was hung.

PART III

There passed a weary time. Each throat
Was parched, and glazed each eye.

The Ancient Mariner beholdeth a sign in the element afar off.

A weary time! a weary time!
How glazed each weary eye,
When looking westward, I beheld
A something in the sky.

At first it seemed a little speck,
And then it seemed a mist;
It moved and moved, and took at last
A certain shape, I wist.

A speck, a mist, a shape, I wist!
And still it neared and neared:

At its nearer approach, it seemeth him to be a ship; and at a dear ransom he freeth his speech from the bonds of thirst.

As if it dodged a water-sprite,
It plunged and tacked and veered.

With throats unslaked, with black lips baked,
We could nor laugh nor wail;
Through utter drought all dumb we stood!
I bit my arm, I sucked the blood,
And cried, A sail! a sail!

A flash of joy;

With throats unslaked, with black lips baked,
Agape they heard me call;
Gramercy! they for joy did grin,
And all at once their breath drew in,

And horror follows. For can it be a ship that comes onward without wind or tide?

As they were drinking all.

See! see! (I cried) she tacks no more!
Hither to work us weal;
Without a breeze, without a tide,
She steadies with upright keel!

The western wave was all a-flame.
The day was well nigh done!
Almost upon the western wave
Rested the broad bright Sun;
When that strange shape drove suddenly
Betwixt us and the Sun.

It seemeth him but the skeleton of a ship.

And straight the Sun was flecked with bars,
(Heaven's Mother send us grace!)
As if through a dungeon-grate he peered
With broad and burning face.

Alas! (thought I, and my heart beat loud)
How fast she nears and nears!
Are those her sails that glance in the Sun,
Like restless gossameres?

And its ribs are seen as bars on the face of the setting Sun.

Are those her ribs through which the Sun
Did peer, as through a grate?
And is that Woman all her crew?
Is that a Death? and are there two?
Is Death that woman's mate?

The Spectre-Woman and her Death-mate, and no other on board the skeleton-ship. Like vessel, like crew!

Her lips were red, her looks were free,
Her locks were yellow as gold:
Her skin was as white as leprosy,
The nightmare Life-in-Death was she,
Who thicks man's blood with cold.

Death and Life-in-Death have diced for the ship's crew, and she (the latter) winneth the ancient Mariner.

The naked hulk alongside came,
And the twain were casting dice;
"The game is done! I've won! I've won!"
Quoth she, and whistles thrice.

No twilight within the courts of the Sun.

The Sun's rim dips; the stars rush out:
At one stride comes the dark;
With far-heard whisper, o'er the sea,
Off shot the spectre-bark.

At the rising of the Moon,

We listened and looked sideways up!
Fear at my heart, as at a cup,
My life-blood seemed to sip!
The stars were dim, and thick the night,
The steersman's face by his lamp gleamed white;
From the sails the dew did drip—
Till clomb above the eastern bar
The hornèd Moon, with one bright star
Within the nether tip.

One after another,

One after one, by the star-dogged Moon,
Too quick for groan or sigh,
Each turned his face with a ghastly pang,
And cursed me with his eye.

His ship-mates drop down dead.

Four times fifty living men,
(And I heard nor sigh nor groan)
With heavy thump, a lifeless lump,
They dropped down one by one.

But Life-in-Death begins her work on the ancient Mariner.

The souls did from their bodies fly,—
They fled to bliss or woe!
And every soul, it passed me by,
Like the whizz of my cross-bow!

PART IV

The Wedding-Guest feareth that a Spirit is talking to him;

"I fear thee, ancient Mariner!
I fear thy skinny hand!
And thou art long, and lank, and brown,
As is the ribbed sea-sand.

I fear thee and thy glittering eye,
And thy skinny hand, so brown."—

But the ancient Mariner assureth him of his bodily life, and proceedeth to relate his horrible penance.

Fear not, fear not, thou Wedding-Guest!
This body dropt not down.

Alone, alone, all, all alone,
Alone on a wide, wide sea!
And never a saint took pity on
My soul in agony.

He despiseth the creatures of the calm.

The many men, so beautiful!
And they all dead did lie:
And a thousand thousand slimy things
Lived on; and so did I.

And envieth that they should live, and so many lie dead.

I looked upon the rotting sea,
And drew my eyes away;
I looked upon the rotting deck,
And there the dead men lay.

I looked to heaven, and tried to pray;
But or ever a prayer had gusht,
A wicked whisper came, and made
My heart as dry as dust.

I closed my lids, and kept them close,
And the balls like pulses beat;
For the sky and the sea, and the sea and the sky
Lay like a load on my weary eye,
And the dead were at my feet.

But the curse liveth for him in the eye of the dead men.

The cold sweat melted from their limbs,
Nor rot nor reek did they:
The look with which they looked on me
Had never passed away.

An orphan's curse would drag to hell
A spirit from on high;
But oh! more horrible than that
Is the curse in a dead man's eye!
Seven days, seven nights, I saw that curse,
And yet I could not die.

In his loneliness and fixedness he yearneth towards the journeying Moon, and the stars that

The moving Moon went up the sky,
And nowhere did abide:

still sojourn, yet still move onward; and everywhere the blue sky belongs to them, and is their appointed rest, and their native country and their own natural homes, which they enter unannounced, as lords that are certainly expected and yet there is a silent joy at their arrival.

Softly she was going up,
And a star or two beside—

Her beams bemocked the sultry main,
Like April hoar-frost spread;
But where the ship's huge shadow lay,
The charmèd water burnt alway
A still and awful red.

By the light of the Moon he beholdeth God's creatures of the great calm.

Beyond the shadow of the ship,
I watched the water-snakes:
They moved in tracks of shining white,
And when they reared, the elfish light
Fell off in hoary flakes.

Within the shadow of the ship
I watched their rich attire:
Blue, glossy green, and velvet black,
They coiled and swam; and every track
Was a flash of golden fire.

Their beauty and their happiness.

O happy living things! no tongue
Their beauty might declare:
A spring of love gushed from my heart,
And I blessed them unaware:
Sure my kind saint took pity on me,
And I blessed them unaware.

He blesseth them in his heart.

The spell begins to break.

The selfsame moment I could pray;
And from my neck so free
The Albatross fell off, and sank
Like lead into the sea.

PART V

Oh sleep! it is a gentle thing,
Beloved from pole to pole!
To Mary Queen the praise be given!
She sent the gentle sleep from Heaven,
That slid into my soul.

By grace of the holy Mother, the ancient Mariner is refreshed with rain.

The silly buckets on the deck,
That had so long remained,
I dreamt that they were filled with dew;
And when I awoke, it rained.

My lips were wet, my throat was cold,
My garments all were dank;
Sure I had drunken in my dreams,
And still my body drank.

I moved, and could not feel my limbs;
I was so light—almost
I thought that I had died in sleep,
And was a blessèd ghost.

He heareth sounds and seeth strange sights and commotions in the sky and the element.

And soon I heard a roaring wind:
It did not come anear;
But with its sound it shook the sails,
That were so thin and sere.

The upper air burst into life!
And a hundred fire-flags sheen,
To and fro they were hurried about!
And to and fro, and in and out,
The wan stars danced between.

And the coming wind did roar more loud,
And the sails did sigh like sedge;
And the rain poured down from one black cloud;
The Moon was at its edge.

The thick black cloud was cleft, and still
The Moon was at its side:
Like waters shot from some high crag,
The lightning fell with never a jag,
A river steep and wide.

The loud wind never reached the ship,
Yet now the ship moved on!
Beneath the lightning and the Moon
The dead men gave a groan.

The bodies of the ship's crew are inspired, and the ship moves on;

They groaned, they stirred, they all uprose,
Nor spake, nor moved their eyes;
It had been strange, even in a dream,
To have seen those dead men rise.

The helmsman steered, the ship moved on;
Yet never a breeze up-blew;
The mariners all 'gan work the ropes,
Where they were wont to do;
They raised their limbs like lifeless tools—
We were a ghastly crew.

The body of my brother's son
Stood by me, knee to knee:
The body and I pulled at one rope
But he said nought to me.

But not by the souls of the men, nor by daemons of earth or middle air, but by a blessed troop of angelic spirits, sent down by the invocation of the guardian saint.

"I fear thee, ancient Mariner!"
Be calm, thou Wedding-Guest!
'Twas not those souls that fled in pain,
Which to their corses came again,
But a troop of spirits blest:

For when it dawned—they dropped their arms,
And clustered round the mast;
Sweet sounds rose slowly through their mouths,
And from their bodies passed.

Around, around, flew each sweet sound,
Then darted to the Sun;
Slowly the sounds came back again,
Now mixed, now one by one.

Sometimes a-dropping from the sky
I heard the sky-lark sing;
Sometimes all little birds that are,
How they seemed to fill the sea and air
With their sweet jargoning!

And now 'twas like all instruments,
Now like a lonely flute;
And now it is an angel's song,
That makes the heavens be mute.

It ceased; yet still the sails made on
A pleasant noise till noon,
A noise like of a hidden brook
In the leafy month of June,
That to the sleeping woods all night
Singeth a quiet tune.

Till noon we quietly sailed on,
Yet never a breeze did breathe:
Slowly and smoothly went the ship,
Moved onward from beneath.

The lonesome Spirit from the south-pole carries on the ship as far as the Line, in obedience to the angelic troop, but still requireth vengeance.

Under the keel nine fathom deep,
From the land of mist and snow,
The Spirit slid: and it was he
That made the ship to go.
The sails at noon left off their tune,
And the ship stood still also.

The Sun, right up above the mast,
Had fixed her to the ocean:
But in a minute she 'gan stir,
With a short uneasy motion—
Backwards and forwards half her length
With a short uneasy motion.

The Polar Spirit's fellow-daemons, the invisible inhabitants of the element, take part in his wrong; and two of them relate, one to the other, that penance long and heavy for the ancient Mariner hath been accorded to the Polar Spirit, who returneth southward.

Then like a pawing horse let go,
She made a sudden bound:
It flung the blood into my head,
And I fell down in a swound.

How long in that same fit I lay,
I have not to declare;
But ere my living life returned,
I heard and in my soul discerned
Two voices in the air.

"Is it he?" quoth one, "Is this the man?
By Him who died on cross,
With his cruel bow he laid full low
The harmless Albatross.

The Spirit who bideth by himself
In the land of mist and snow,
He loved the bird that loved the man
Who shot him with his bow."

The other was a softer voice,
As soft as honey-dew:
Quoth he, "The man hath penance done,
And penance more will do."

PART VI

First Voice

"But tell me, tell me! speak again,
Thy soft response renewing—
What makes that ship drive on so fast?
What is the ocean doing?"

Second Voice

"Still as a slave before his lord,
The ocean hath no blast;
His great bright eye most silently
Up to the moon is cast—

If he may know which way to go;
For she guides him smooth or grim.
See, brother, see! how graciously
She looketh down on him."

First Voice

The Mariner hath been cast into a trance; for the angelic power causeth the vessel to drive northward faster than human life could endure.

"But why drives on that ship so fast,
Without or wave or wind?"

Second Voice

"The air is cut away before,
And closes from behind.

Fly, brother, fly! more high, more high!
Or we shall be belated:
For slow and slow that ship will go,
When the Mariner's trance is abated."

The supernatural motion is retarded;

I woke, and we were sailing on
As in a gentle weather:
'Twas night, calm night, the moon was high,
The dead men stood together.

the Mariner awakes, and his penance begins anew.

All stood together on the deck,
For a charnel-dungeon fitter:
All fixed on me their stony eyes,
That in the moon did glitter.

The pang, the curse, with which they died,
Had never passed away:
I could not draw my eyes from theirs,
Nor turn them up to pray.

The curse is finally expiated.

And now this spell was snapt: once more
I viewed the ocean green,
And looked far forth, yet little saw
Of what had else been seen—

Like one, that on a lonesome road
Doth walk in fear and dread,
And having once turned round walks on,
And turns no more his head;
Because he knows, a frightful fiend
Doth close behind him tread.

But soon there breathed a wind on me,
Nor sound nor motion made:
Its path was not upon the sea,
In ripple or in shade.

It raised my hair, it fanned my cheek
Like a meadow-gale of spring—
It mingled strangely with my fears,
Yet it felt like a welcoming.

Swiftly, swiftly flew the ship,
Yet she sailed softly too:
Sweetly, sweetly blew the breeze—
On me alone it blew.

And the ancient Mariner beholdeth his native country.

Oh! dream of joy! is this indeed
The light-house top I see?
Is this the hill? is this the kirk?
Is this mine own countree?

We drifted o'er the harbour-bar,
And I with sobs did pray—
O let me be awake, my God!
Or let me sleep alway.

The harbour-bay was clear as glass,
So smoothly it was strewn!
And on the bay the moonlight lay,
And the shadow of the moon.

The rock shone bright, the kirk no less,
That stands above the rock:
The moonlight steeped in silentness
The steady weathercock.

And the bay was white with silent light
Till rising from the same,
Full many shapes, that shadows were,
In crimson colours came.

The Angelic spirits leave the dead bodies,

A little distance from the prow
Those crimson shadows were:
I turned my eyes upon the deck—
Oh, Christ! what saw I there!

And appear in their own forms of light.

Each corse lay flat, lifeless and flat,
And, by the holy rood!
A man all light, a seraph-man,
On every corse there stood.

This seraph-band, each waved his hand;
It was a heavenly sight!
They stood as signals to the land,
Each one a lovely light;

This seraph-band, each waved his hand,
No voice did they impart—
No voice; but oh! the silence sank
Like music on my heart.

But soon I heard the dash of oars,
I heard the Pilot's cheer;
My head was turned perforce away,
And I saw a boat appear.

The Pilot and the Pilot's boy,
I heard them coming fast:
Dear Lord in Heaven! it was a joy
The dead men could not blast.

I saw a third—I heard his voice:
It is the Hermit good!
He singeth loud his godly hymns
That he makes in the wood.
He'll shrieve my soul; he'll wash away
The Albatross's blood.

PART VII

The Hermit of the Wood.

This Hermit good lives in that wood
Which slopes down to the sea.
How loudly his sweet voice he rears!
He loves to talk with marineres
That come from a far countree.

He kneels at morn, and noon, and eve—
He hath a cushion plump:
It is the moss that wholly hides
The rotted old oak-stump.

The skiff-boat neared: I heard them talk,
"Why, this is strange, I trow!
Where are those lights so many and fair,
That signal made but now?"

Approacheth the ship with wonder.

"Strange, by my faith!" the Hermit said—
"And they answered not our cheer!
The planks look warped! and see those sails,
How thin they are and sere!
I never saw aught like to them,
Unless perchance it were

Brown skeletons of leaves that lag
My forest-brook along;
When the ivy-tod is heavy with snow,
And the owlet whoops to the wolf below,
That eats the she-wolf's young."

"Dear Lord! it hath a fiendish look—
(The Pilot made reply)
I am a-feared"—"Push on, push on!"
Said the Hermit cheerily.

The boat came closer to the ship,
But I nor spake nor stirred;
The boat came close beneath the ship,
And straight a sound was heard.

The ship suddenly sinketh.

Under the water it rumbled on,
Still louder and more dread:
It reached the ship, it split the bay;
The ship went down like lead.

The ancient Mariner is saved in the Pilot's boat.

Stunned by that loud and dreadful sound,
Which sky and ocean smote,
Like one that hath been seven days drowned
My body lay afloat;
But swift as dreams, myself I found
Within the Pilot's boat.

Upon the whirl, where sank the ship,
The boat spun round and round;
And all was still, save that the hill
Was telling of the sound.

I moved my lips—the Pilot shrieked
And fell down in a fit;
The holy Hermit raised his eyes,
And prayed where he did sit.

I took the oars: the Pilot's boy,
Who now doth crazy go,
Laughed loud and long, and all the while
His eyes went to and fro.
"Ha! ha!" quoth he, "full plain I see,
The Devil knows how to row."

And now, all in my own countree,
I stood on the firm land!
The Hermit stepped forth from the boat,
And scarcely he could stand.

The ancient Mariner earnestly entreateth the Hermit to shrieve him; and the penance of life falls on him.

"O shrieve me, shrieve me, holy man!"
The Hermit crossed his brow.
"Say quick," quoth he, "I bid thee say—
What manner of man art thou?"

Forthwith this frame of mine was wrenched
With a woful agony,
Which forced me to begin my tale;
And then it left me free.

And ever and anon throughout his future life an agony constraineth him to travel from land to land,

Since then, at an uncertain hour,
That agony returns:
And till my ghastly tale is told,
This heart within me burns.

I pass, like night, from land to land;
I have strange power of speech;
That moment that his face I see,
I know the man that must hear me:
To him my tale I teach.

What loud uproar bursts from that door!
The wedding-guests are there:
But in the garden-bower the bride
And bride-maids singing are:
And hark the little vesper bell
Which biddeth me to prayer!

O Wedding-Guest! this soul hath been
Alone on a wide, wide sea;
So lonely 'twas, that God himself
Scarce seemèd there to be.

O sweeter than the marriage-feast,
'Tis sweeter far to me,
To walk together to the kirk
With a goodly company!—

To walk together to the kirk,
And all together pray,

While each to his great Father bends,
Old men, and babes, and loving friends,
And youths and maidens gay!

And to teach, by his own example, love and reverence to all things that God made and loveth.

Farewell, farewell! but this I tell
To thee, thou Wedding-Guest!
He prayeth well, who loveth well
Both man and bird and beast.

He prayeth best, who loveth best
All things both great and small;
For the dear God who loveth us,
He made and loveth all.

The Mariner, whose eye is bright,
Whose beard with age is hoar,
Is gone: and now the Wedding-Guest
Turned from the bridegroom's door.

He went like one that hath been stunned,
And is of sense forlorn:
A sadder and a wiser man,
He rose the morrow morn.

The Romantic Movement did not die with Byron at Missolonghi, but, transmuted, continues to the present day. Tennyson carried its principles through the century, as did the leading Pre-Raphaelites, William Morris and Dante Gabriel Rossetti. In America, Joseph Rodman Drake's *Culprit Fay* expressed the delicacy of faëry-lore, heightened and made macabre by Poe. Algernon Charles Swinburne and Alfred Noyes bring the Romantic tradition down to the present day: "The Highwayman" of the latter contains distinct echoes of Scott's ballads. One of the almost perfect reproductions of the atmosphere of mediaeval magic and the form of the mediaeval dialogue-ballad is Rossetti's "Sister Helen."

SISTER HELEN

by Dante Gabriel Rossetti (1828-1882)

"Why did you melt your waxen man,
Sister Helen?
Today is the third since you began."
"The time was long, yet the time ran,
Little brother."
(*O Mother, Mary Mother,
Three days today, between Hell and Heaven!*)

"But if you have done your work aright,
Sister Helen,
You'll let me play, for you said I might."
"Be very still in your play tonight,
Little brother."
(*O Mother, Mary Mother,
Third night, tonight, between Hell and Heaven!*)

"You said it must melt ere vesper-bell,
Sister Helen;
If now it be molten, all is well."
"Even so,—nay, peace! you cannot tell,
Little brother."
(*O Mother, Mary Mother,
O what is this, between Hell and Heaven?*)

"Oh the waxen knave was plump today,
Sister Helen;
How like dead folk he has dropped away!"
"Nay now, of the dead what can you say,
Little brother?"
(*O Mother, Mary Mother,
What of the dead, between Hell and Heaven?*)

"See, see, the sunken pile of wood,
Sister Helen,

Shines through the thinned wax red as blood!"
"Nay now, when looked you yet on blood,
Little brother?"
(*O Mother, Mary Mother,*
How pale she is, between Hell and Heaven!)

"Now close your eyes, for they're sick and sore,
Sister Helen,
And I'll play without the gallery door."
"Aye, let me rest,—I'll lie on the floor,
Little brother."
(*O Mother, Mary Mother,*
What rest tonight, between Hell and Heaven?)

"Here high up in the balcony,
Sister Helen,
The moon flies face to face with me."
"Aye, look and say whatever you see,
Little brother."
(*O Mother, Mary Mother,*
What sight tonight, between Hell and Heaven?)

"Outside it's merry in the wind's wake,
Sister Helen;
In the shaken trees the chill stars shake."
"Hush, heard you a horse-tread, as you spake,
Little brother?"
(*O Mother, Mary Mother,*
What sound tonight, between Hell and Heaven?)

"I hear a horse-tread, and I see,
Sister Helen,
Three horsemen that ride terribly."
"Little brother, whence come the three,
Little brother?"
(*O Mother, Mary Mother,*
Whence should they come, between Hell and Heaven?)

"They come by the hill-verge from Boyne Bar,
Sister Helen,
And one draws nigh, but two are afar."
"Look, look, do you know them who they are,
Little brother?"
(*O Mother, Mary Mother,*
Who should they be, between Hell and Heaven?)

"Oh, it's Keith of Eastholm rides so fast,
Sister Helen,
For I know the white mane on the blast."
"The hour has come, has come at last,
Little brother!"
(*O Mother, Mary Mother,*
Her hour at last, between Hell and Heaven!)

"He has made a sign and called Halloo!
Sister Helen,
And he says that he would speak with you."
"Oh tell him I fear the frozen dew,
Little brother."
(*O Mother, Mary Mother,*
Why laughs she thus, between Hell and Heaven?)

"The wind is loud, but I hear him cry,
Sister Helen,
That Keith of Ewern's like to die."
"And he and thou, and thou and I,
Little brother."
(*O Mother, Mary Mother,*
And they and we, between Hell and Heaven!)

"Three days ago, on his marriage-morn,
Sister Helen,
He sickened, and lies since then forlorn."
"For bridegroom's side is the bride a thorn,
Little brother?"
(*O Mother, Mary Mother,*
Cold bridal cheer, between Hell and Heaven!)

"Three days and nights he has lain abed,
Sister Helen,
And he prays in torment to be dead."
"The thing may chance, if he have prayed,
Little brother!"
(*O Mother, Mary Mother,*
If he have prayed, between Hell and Heaven!)

"But he has not ceased to cry today,
Sister Helen,
That you should take your curse away."
"*My* prayer was heard,—he need but pray,
Little brother!"
(*O Mother, Mary Mother,*

Shall God not hear, between Hell and Heaven?)

"But he says, till you take back your ban,
Sister Helen,
His soul would pass, yet never can."
"Nay then, shall I slay a living man,
Little brother?"
(*O Mother, Mary Mother,*
A living soul, between Hell and Heaven!)

"But he calls for ever on your name,
Sister Helen,
And says that he melts before a flame."
"My heart for his pleasure fared the same,
Little brother."
(*O Mother, Mary Mother,*
Fire at the heart, between Hell and Heaven!)

"Here's Keith of Westholm riding fast,
Sister Helen,
For I know the white plume on the blast."
"The hour, the sweet hour I forecast,
Little brother!"
(*O Mother, Mary Mother,*
Is the hour sweet, between Hell and Heaven?)

"He stops to speak, and he stills his horse,
Sister Helen;
But his words are drowned in the wind's course."
"Nay hear, nay hear, you must hear perforce,
Little brother!"
(*O Mother, Mary Mother,*
What word now heard, between Hell and Heaven?)

"Oh he says that Keith of Ewern's cry,
Sister Helen,
Is ever to see you ere he die."
"In all that his soul sees, there am I,
Little brother!"
(*O Mother, Mary Mother,*
The soul's one sight, between Hell and Heaven!)

"He sends a ring and a broken coin,
Sister Helen,
And bids you mind the banks of Boyne."
"What else he broke will he ever join,
Little brother?"
(*O Mother, Mary Mother,*
No, never joined, between Hell and Heaven!)

"He yields you these and craves full fain,
Sister Helen,
You pardon him in his mortal pain."
"What else he took will he give again,
Little brother?"
(*O Mother, Mary Mother,*
Not twice to give, between Hell and Heaven!)

"He calls your name in an agony,
Sister Helen,
That even dead Love must weep to see."
"Hate, born of Love, is blind as he,
Little brother!"
(*O Mother, Mary Mother,*
Love turned to hate, between Hell and Heaven!)

"Oh it's Keith of Keith now that rides fast,
Sister Helen,
For I know the white hair on the blast."
"The short, short hour will soon be past,
Little brother!"
(*O Mother, Mary Mother,*
Will soon be past, between Hell and Heaven!)

"He looks at me and he tries to speak,
Sister Helen,
But oh! his voice is sad and weak!"
"What here should the mighty Baron seek,
Little brother?"
(*O Mother, Mary Mother,*
Is this the end, between Hell and Heaven?)

"Oh his son still cries, if you forgive,
Sister Helen,
The body dies but the soul shall live."
"Fire shall forgive me as I forgive,
Little brother!"
(*O Mother, Mary Mother,*
As she forgives, between Hell and Heaven!)

"Oh he prays you, as his heart would rive,
Sister Helen,
To save his dear son's soul alive."
"Fire cannot slay it, it shall thrive,
Little brother!"
(*O Mother, Mary Mother,*
Alas, alas, between Hell and Heaven!)

"He cries to you, kneeling in the road,
Sister Helen,
To go with him for the love of God!"

"The way is long to his son's abode,
Little brother."
(O Mother, Mary Mother,
The way is long, between Hell and Heaven!)

"A lady's here, by a dark steed brought,
Sister Helen,
So darkly clad, I saw her not."
"See her now or never see aught,
Little brother!"
(O Mother, Mary Mother,
What more to see, between Hell and Heaven?)

"Her hood falls back, and the moon shines fair,
Sister Helen,
On the Lady of Ewern's golden hair."
"Blest hour of my power and her despair,
Little brother!"
(O Mother, Mary Mother,
Hour blest and banned, between Hell and Heaven!)

"Pale, pale her cheeks, that in pride did glow,
Sister Helen,
'Neath the bridal-wreath three days ago."
"One morn for pride and three days for woe,
Little brother!"
(O Mother, Mary Mother,
Three days, three nights, between Hell and Heaven!)

"Her clasped hands stretch from her bending head,
Sister Helen;
With the loud wind's wail her sobs are wed."
"What wedding-strains hath her bridal-bed,
Little brother?"
(O Mother, Mary Mother,
What strain but death's, between Hell and Heaven!)

"She may not speak, she sinks in a swoon,
Sister Helen,—
She lifts her lips and gasps on the moon."
"Oh! might I but hear her soul's blithe tune,
Little brother!"
(O Mother, Mary Mother,
Her woe's dumb cry, between Hell and Heaven!)

"They've caught her to Westholm's saddle-bow,
Sister Helen,
And her moonlit hair gleams white in its flow."
"Let it turn whiter than winter snow,
Little brother!"
(O Mother, Mary Mother,
Woe-withered gold, between Hell and Heaven!)

"O Sister Helen, you heard the bell,
Sister Helen!
More loud than the vesper-chime it fell."
"No vesper-chime, but a dying knell,
Little brother!"
(O Mother, Mary Mother,
His dying knell, between Hell and Heaven!)

"Alas! but I fear the heavy sound,
Sister Helen;
Is it in the sky or in the ground?"
"Say, have they turned their horses round,
Little brother?"
(O Mother, Mary Mother,
What would she more, between Hell and Heaven?)

"They have raised the old man from his knee,
Sister Helen,
And they ride in silence hastily."
"More fast the naked soul doth flee,
Little brother!"
(O Mother, Mary Mother,
The naked soul, between Hell and Heaven!)

"Flank to flank are the three steeds gone,
Sister Helen,
But the lady's dark steed goes alone."
"And lonely her bridegroom's soul hath flown,
Little brother."
(O Mother, Mary Mother,
The lonely ghost, between Hell and Heaven!)

"Oh the wind is sad in the iron chill,
Sister Helen,
And weary sad they look by the hill."
"But he and I are sadder still,
Little brother!"
(O Mother, Mary Mother,
Most sad of all, between Hell and Heaven!)

"See, see, the wax has dropped from its place,
Sister Helen,
And the flames are winning up apace!"
"Yet here they burn but for a space,
Little brother!"
(O Mother, Mary Mother,
Here for a space, between Hell and Heaven!)

"Ah! what white thing at the door has crossed,
Sister Helen?
Ah! what is this that sighs in the frost?"
"A soul that's lost as mine is lost,
Little brother!"
(O Mother, Mary Mother,
Lost, lost, all lost, between Hell and Heaven!)

REALISM

It has been frequently asserted that the modern mood is realistic, without romantic illusion; we are led to believe that the fact is worshipped and imagination distrusted. The prevalence of realism is traced to the influence of modern science. Yet Chaucer, in 1380, was practicing the method of the modern realist; in Queen Elizabeth's day, Thomas Dekker wrote plays of an almost naturalistic cast, and Shakespeare moved easily out of the romantic mood of the fairy Titania to the unvarnished realism of Bottom the weaver. Our modern novelists have not yet exceeded Daniel Defoe in actualism, nor have O'Neill and other dramatists shown starker photographs of life than did the Restoration playwrights of two centuries ago. Realism, it is clear, is as vital as romance; the psychological milieu of our generation may be more friendly to the former than to the latter, but there is no precedence of age.

It has been argued that the natural form for realism is prose rather than poetry. This erroneously assumes that the subject-matter of poetry is restricted. All aspects of human life, as long as they are powerfully felt, vividly seen, and imaginatively expressed, belong to the realm of poetry. Comedy and tragedy, morality and frivolity, belong equally to the poet.

We have already seen how realism differs from romance in its point of view; the two also differ in method. The realist may tell his story about the everyday actions of middle-class characters in a normal setting, using a conversational manner of speech. If the characters belong by caste to the aristocracy, they are presented in their essentially human qualities. Because the actions are seemingly casual, the realistic poet centers his attention upon personality, and makes the characters live richly for the reader. This is the method of Edwin Arlington Robinson in *Children of the Night,* of Edgar Lee Masters in *The Spoon River Anthology,* of Robert Frost in *North of Boston.* John Masefield is a realist in *The Everlasting Mercy,* as is Thomas Hardy in *Satires of Circumstance,* and Siegfried Sassoon in *Picture-Show.* The two poems which follow must be combined with many poems in other chapters before and after to give a well-rounded idea of realism. Both draw a moral, but the forms and appeals are strikingly unlike. Browning makes his characters out of the past very normal in their procrastination; Whittier presents a telling picture of mob violence and a burning conscience.

It should be added that it is impossible to avoid some measure of romanticism; not even the most determined realist can be photographically or microscopically realistic. The romantic or realistic character of a work depends on the way in which these qualities are used; the very definition of the terms cannot be absolute, but is usually a matter of emphasis.

THE STATUE AND THE BUST

by Robert Browning (1812-1889)

There's a palace in Florence, the world knows well,
And a statue watches it from the square,
And this story of both do our townsmen tell.

Ages ago, a lady there,
At the farthest window facing the East
Asked, "Who rides by, with the royal air?"

The bridesmaids' prattle around her ceased;
She leaned forth, one on either hand;
They saw how the blush of the bride increased—

They felt by its beats her heart expand—
As one at each ear and both in a breath
Whispered, "The Great-Duke Ferdinand."

That selfsame instant, underneath,
The Duke rode past in his idle way,
Empty and fine like a swordless sheath.

Gay he rode, with a friend as gay,
Till he threw his head back—"Who is she?"
—"A bride the Riccardi brings home today."

Hair in heaps laid heavily
Over a pale brow spirit-pure—
Carved like the heart of the coal-black tree,

Crisped like a war-steed's encolure—
And vainly sought to dissemble her eyes
Of the blackest black our eyes endure.

And lo, a blade for a knight's emprise
Filled the fine empty sheath of a man—
The Duke grew straightway brave and wise.

He looked at her, as a lover can;
She looked at him, as one who awakes—
The past was a sleep, and her life began.

Now, love so ordered for both their sakes,
A feast was held that selfsame night
In the pile which the mighty shadow makes.

(For Via Larga is three-parts light,
But the Palace overshadows one,
Because of a crime which may God requite!
To Florence and God the wrong was done,
Through the first republic's murder there
By Cosimo and his cursed son.)

The Duke (with the statue's face in the square)
Turned in the midst of his multitude
At the bright approach of the bridal pair.

Face to face the lovers stood
A single minute and no more,
While the bridegroom bent as a man subdued—

Bowed till his bonnet brushed the floor—
For the Duke on the lady a kiss conferred,
As the courtly custom was of yore.

In a minute can lovers exchange a word?
If a word did pass, which I do not think,
Only one out of the thousand heard.

That was the bridegroom. At day's brink
He and his bride were alone at last
In a bed-chamber by a taper's blink.

Calmly he said that her lot was cast,
That the door she had passed was shut on her
Till the final catafalque repassed.

The world meanwhile, its noise and stir,
Through a certain window facing the East
She could watch like a convent's chronicler.

Since passing the door might lead to a feast,
And a feast might lead to so much beside,
He, of many evils, chose the least.

"Freely I choose, too," said the bride—
"Your window and its world suffice,"
Replied the tongue, while the heart replied—

"If I spend the night with that devil twice,
May his window serve as my loop of hell
Whence a damned soul looks on paradise!

"I fly to the Duke who loves me well,
Sit by his side and laugh at sorrow
Ere I count another ave-bell.

"'Tis only the coat of a page to borrow,
And tie my hair in a horse-boy's trim,
And I save my soul—but not tomorrow"—

(She checked herself and her eye grew dim)—
"My father tarries to bless my state;
I must keep it one day more for him.

"Is one day more so long to wait?
Moreover the Duke rides past, I know—
We shall see each other, sure as fate."

She turned on her side and slept. Just so!
So we resolve on a thing and sleep.
So did the lady, ages ago.

That night the Duke said, "Dear or cheap
As the cost of this cup of bliss may prove
To body or soul, I will drain it deep!"

And on the morrow, bold with love,
He beckoned the bridegroom (close on call,
As his duty bade, by the Duke's alcove)

And smiled, "'Twas a very funeral
Your lady will think, this feast of ours,
A shame to efface, whate'er befall!

"What if we break from the Arno bowers
And let Petraja, cool and green,
Cure last night's fault with this morning's flowers?"

The bridegroom, not a thought to be seen
On his steady brow and quiet mouth,
Said, "Too much favor for me so mean!

"But alas! my lady leaves the South.
Each wind that comes from the Apennine
Is a menace to her tender youth.

"Nor a way exists, the wise opine,
If she quits her palace twice this year,
To avert the flower of life's decline."

Quoth the Duke, "A sage and a kindly fear.
Moreover Petraja is cold this spring—
Be our feast tonight as usual here!"

And then to himself—"Which night shall bring
Thy bride to her lover's embraces, fool—
Or I am the fool, and thou art the king!

"Yet my passion must wait a night, nor cool—
For tonight the Envoy arrives from France,
Whose heart I unlock with thyself, my tool.

"I need thee still and might miss perchance.
Today is not wholly lost, beside,
With its hope of my lady's countenance—

"For I ride—what should I do but ride?
And passing her palace, if I list,
May glance at its window—well betide!"

So said, so done; nor the lady missed
One ray that broke from the ardent brow,
Nor a curl of the lips where the spirit kissed.

Be sure that each renewed the vow—
No morrow's sun should arise and set
And leave them then as it left them now.

But next day passed, and next day yet,
With still fresh cause to wait one day more
Ere each leaped over the parapet.

And still, as love's brief morning wore,
With a gentle start, half smile, half sigh,
They found love not as it seemed before.

They thought it would work infallibly,
But not in despite of heaven and earth—
The rose would blow when the storm passed by.

Meantime they could profit in winter's dearth
By store of fruits that supplant the rose—
The world and its ways have a certain worth!

And to press a point while these oppose
Were simple policy—better wait,
We lose no friends and we gain no foes.

Meanwhile, worse fates than a lover's fate,
Who daily may ride and pass and look
Where his lady watches behind the grate!

And she—she watched the square like a book,
Holding one picture and only one,
Which daily to find she undertook.

When the picture was reached, the book was done,
And she turned from the picture at night to scheme
Of tearing it out for herself next sun.

So weeks grew months, years; gleam by gleam
The glory dropped from their youth and love,
And both perceived they had dreamed a dream,

Which hovered as dreams do, still above;
But who can take a dream for a truth?
Oh, hide our eyes from the next remove!

One day as the lady saw her youth
Depart, and the silver thread that streaked
Her hair, and, worn by the serpent's tooth,

The brow so puckered, the chin so peaked—
And wondered who the woman was,
Hollow-eyed and haggard-cheeked,

Fronting her silent in the glass—
"Summon here," she suddenly said,
"Before the rest of my old self pass,

"Him, the Carver, a hand to aid,
Who fashions the clay no love will change,
And fixes a beauty never to fade.

"Let Robbia's[1] craft so apt and strange
Arrest the remains of young and fair,
And rivet them while the seasons range.

"Make me a face on the window there
Waiting as ever, mute the while,
My love to pass below in the square!

"And let me think that it may beguile
Dreary days which the dead must spend
Down in their darkness under the aisle—

"To say—'What matters it at the end?
I did no more while my heart was warm
Than does that image, my pale-faced friend.'

"Where is the use of the lip's red charm
The heaven of hair, the pride of the brow,
And the blood that blues the inside arm—

"Unless we turn, as the soul knows how,
The earthly gift to an end divine?
A lady of clay is as good, I trow."

But long ere Robbia's cornice, fine
With flowers and fruits which leaves enlace,
Was set where now is the empty shrine—

[1] Luca della Robbia, who developed the craft of terra cotta busts and bas-reliefs into a Florentine art.

(And, leaning out of a bright blue space,
As a ghost might lean from a chink of sky
The passionate pale lady's face—

Eying ever, with earnest eye
And quick-turned neck at its breathless stretch,
Someone who ever is passing by—)

The Duke sighed like the simplest wretch
In Florence, "Youth, my dream escapes!
Will its record stay?" And he bade them fetch

Some subtle molder of brazen shapes—
"Can the soul, the will, die out of a man
Ere his body find the grave that gapes?

"John of Douay shall effect my plan,
Set me on horseback here aloft,
Alive, as the crafty sculptor can,

"In the very square I have crossed so oft!
That men may admire, when future suns
Shall touch the eyes to a purpose soft,

"While the mouth and the brow stay brave in bronze—
Admire and say, 'When he was alive,
How he would take his pleasure once!'

"And it shall go hard but I contrive
To listen the while and laugh in my tomb
At idleness which aspires to strive."

✦

So! while these wait the trump of doom,
How do their spirits pass, I wonder,
Nights and days in the narrow room?

Still, I suppose, they sit and ponder
What a gift life was, ages ago,
Six steps out of the chapel yonder.

Surely they see not God, I know,
Nor all that chivalry of his,
The soldier-saints who, row on row,

Burn upward each to his point of bliss—
Since, the end of life being manifest,
He had burned his way through the world to this.

I hear your reproach—"But delay was best,
For their end was a crime!"—Oh, a crime
  will do
As well, I reply, to serve for a test,

As a virtue golden through and through,
Sufficient to vindicate itself
And prove its worth at a moment's view!

Must a game be played for the sake of pelf?
Where a button goes, 'twere an epigram
To offer the stamp of the very Guelph.

The true has no value beyond the sham.
As well the counter as coin, I submit,
When your table's a hat, and your prize a
  dram.

Stake your counter as boldly every whit,
Venture as warily, use the same skill,
Do your best, whether winning or losing it,

If you choose to play—is my principle!
Let a man contend to the uttermost
For his life's set prize, be it what it will!

The counter our lovers staked was lost
As surely as if it were lawful coin.
And the sin I impute to each frustrate ghost

Is—the unlit lamp and the ungirt loin,
Though the end in sight was a vice, I say.
You of the virtue (we issue join)
How strive you? *De te, fabula!* [2]

SKIPPER IRESON'S RIDE

by John Greenleaf Whittier (1807-1892)

Of all the rides since the birth of time,
Told in story or sung in rime,—
On Apuleius's Golden Ass,
Or one-eyed Calender's horse of brass,
Witch astride of a human back,
Islam's prophet on Al-Borák,—
The strangest ride that ever was sped
Was Ireson's, out from Marblehead!
  Old Floyd Ireson, for his hard heart,
  Tarred and feathered and carried in a cart
    By the women of Marblehead!

Body of turkey, head of owl,
Wings a-droop like a rained-on fowl,
Feathered and ruffled in every part,
Captain Ireson stood in the cart.
Scores of women, old and young,
Strong of muscle, and glib of tongue,
Pushed and pulled up the rocky lane,
Shouting and singing the shrill refrain:
  'Here's Flud Oirson, fur his horrd horrt,
  Torr'd an' futherr'd an' corr'd in a corrt
    By the women o' Morble'ead!'

Wrinkled scolds with hands on hips,
Girls in bloom of cheek and lips,
Wild-eyed, free-limbed, such as chase
Bacchus round some antique vase,
Brief of skirt, with ankles bare,
Loose of kerchief and loose of hair,
With conch-shells blowing and fish-horns'
    twang,
Over and over the Maenads sang:
  'Here's Flud Oirson, fur his horrd horrt,
  Torr'd an' futherr'd an' corr'd in a corrt
    By the women o' Morble'ead!'

Small pity for him!—He sailed away
From a leaking ship in Chaleur Bay,—
Sailed away from a sinking wreck,
With his own town's-people on her deck!
'Lay by! lay by!' they called to him.
Back he answered, 'Sink or swim!
Brag of your catch of fish again!'
And off he sailed through the fog and rain!
  Old Floyd Ireson, for his hard heart,
  Tarred and feathered and carried in a cart
    By the women of Marblehead!

Fathoms deep in dark Chaleur
That wreck shall lie forevermore.
Mother and sister, wife and maid,
Looked from the rocks of Marblehead
Over the moaning and rainy sea,—
Looked for the coming that might not be!
What did the winds and the sea-birds say
Of the cruel captain who sailed away?—
  Old Floyd Ireson, for his hard heart,
  Tarred and feathered and carried in a cart
    By the women of Marblehead!

Through the street, on either side,
Up flew windows, doors swung wide;
Sharp-tongued spinsters, old wives gray,
Treble lent the fish-horn's bray.

[2] This fable concerns you!

Sea-worn grandsires, cripple-bound,
Hulks of old sailors run aground,
Shook head, and fist, and hat, and cane,
And cracked with curses the hoarse refrain:
'Here's Flud Oirson, fur his horrd horrt,
Torr'd an' futherr'd an' corr'd in a corrt
By the women o' Morble'ead!'

Sweetly along the Salem road
Bloom of orchard and lilac showed.
Little the wicked skipper knew
Of the fields so green and the sky so blue.
Riding there in his sorry trim,
Like an Indian idol glum and trim,
Scarcely he seemed the sound to hear
Of voices shouting, far and near:
'Here's Flud Oirson, fur his horrd horrt,
Torr'd an' futherr'd an' corr'd in a corrt
By the women o' Morble'ead!'

'Hear me, neighbors!' at last he cried,—
'What to me is this noisy ride?
What is the shame that clothes the skin
To the nameless horror that lives within?
Waking or sleeping, I see a wreck,
And hear a cry from a reeling deck!
Hate me and curse me,—I only dread
The hand of God and the face of the dead!'
Said old Floyd Ireson, for his hard heart,
Tarred and feathered and carried in a cart
By the women of Marblehead!

Then the wife of the skipper lost at sea
Said, 'God has touched him! why should we!'
Said an old wife mourning her only son,
'Cut the rogue's tether and let him run!'
So with soft relentings and rude excuse,
Half scorn, half pity, they cut him loose,
And gave him a cloak to hide him in,
And left him alone with his shame and sin.
Poor Floyd Ireson, for his hard heart,
Tarred and feathered and carried in a cart
By the women of Marblehead!

SUGGESTIONS FOR ADDITIONAL READING

POEMS OF ROMANTIC ADVENTURE

Author unknown, *Sir Gawain and the Green Knight*
Sir Walter Scott, *Marmion*
Lord Byron, *The Corsair*
Alfred, Lord Tennyson, *The Revenge*
William Morris, *The Lady of the Land*
Edmund Clarence Stedman, *How Old Brown Took Harper's Ferry*
Dante Gabriel Rossetti, *The King's Tragedy*

POEMS OF ROMANTIC LOVE

Geoffrey Chaucer, *The Knight's Tale*
Christopher Marlowe, *Hero and Leander*
William Shakespeare, *Venus and Adonis*
Walter Savage Landor, *The Hamadryad*
William Morris, *Atalanta's Race*
Alfred Noyes, *The Highwayman*
Amy Lowell, *Patterns*

POEMS OF ROMANTIC FANTASY

Samuel Taylor Coleridge, *Christabel*
Joseph Rodman Drake, *The Culprit Fay*

POEMS OF REALISM

Geoffrey Chaucer, *The Pardoner's Tale*
Robert Browning, *Dramatis Personae*
Thomas Hardy, *Satires of Circumstance*
Edwin Arlington Robinson, *The Man Against the Sky*
Edgar Lee Masters, *Spoon River Anthology*
Robert Frost, *North of Boston*
John Masefield, *Dauber*
John Masefield, *The Everlasting Mercy*
Siegfried Sassoon, *Picture-Show*
Siegfried Sassoon, *Counter-Attack*
Wilfred Owen, *Poems*

STORIES WITH A MORAL

Robert Browning, *The Pied Piper of Hamelin*
Alfred, Lord Tennyson, *Morte D'Arthur*
James R. Lowell, *The Vision of Sir Launfal*
E. R. Sill, *Opportunity*
Rudyard Kipling, *The Explorer*

6

THE EXPERIENCES OF POETRY—2: COMEDY AND TRAGEDY

PLATO, who was very particular about what he admitted into his ideal republic, condescendingly allowed its inhabitants some little laughter now and then. Shakespeare towers above Milton and Wordsworth because, for one thing, he possessed a sense of humor which the other poets, for all their eloquence, lacked. What is this appreciation of the comedy of life? Upon what does it depend? Despite the warnings of Cazamian and Croce that humor cannot be defined, and despite the epigram of G. K. Chesterton that anyone who tries to define a sense of humor thereby acknowledges the lack of one, critics and psychologists are still delving to discover the sources of laughter.

Aristotle declared *ex cathedra* that comedy is "ugliness without pain," and deals with "ignoble characters in ignoble situations." This definition places all comedy upon a low level, and would forbid Charles II to sharpen his wit or Abraham Lincoln to point a story. Plato, Thomas Hobbes, Henri Bergson, and modern psychologists generally make laughter the product of primitive human cruelty, roused by a feeling of superiority to the person or action laughed at, and released as a shock-absorber. Humor is often a revulsion against the stiffness and pomposity of man. Puffed-up dignity is in constant need of deflation, as Chesterton has merrily shown in his essay "On Running After One's Hat."

This method of approach seems too deductive; perhaps the examination of some admittedly comic situations would reveal what makes us laugh. The "absent-minded professor" of the comic strip and the college joke-book—why is he admittedly a comic figure? Is he ugly without pain? An ignoble character in an ignoble situation? A symbol of rigidity who rouses a feeling of superiority in us? Is it not perhaps the paradoxical combination of theoretical wisdom and practical carelessness? The Connecticut Yankee in King Arthur's court goes through a series of admittedly comic situations. Are they laughable because they are ugly, ignoble, or rigid, or merely because they are unexpected and incongruous? The caricature-cartoon of the big head on the small body, the huge nose of a Cyrano, the big feet of a Chaplin are all incongruities and therefore comic. What is a pun but the sudden and surprising juxtaposition of words? This concept can be applied to dozens of situations from ordinary experience—a sneeze at a tense moment, a stout lady running to catch a train, a gentleman chasing his hat on a windy street, any pompous person made ridiculous, a Don Quixote, Bourgeois Gentilhomme, Bottom, Falstaff, Mrs. Malaprop, Perrichon, or Mr. Pickwick. Even death can be made comic, if it is treated incongruously by a burlesque Pyramus and Thisbe. The comedy's incongruity might be one of exaggeration, as in Rabelais and Mark Twain, or one of ironic understatement, as in Swift and Anatole France.

If a sense of humor, therefore, rises from an ability to gain enjoyment from a perception of disproportion and incongruity, it is not only definable but also measurable. Since such perceptions reside in the intellect, comedy is intellectual rather than emotional. Horace Walpole decided that "life is a comedy to a man who thinks, and a tragedy to a man who feels." This need not imply, however, that we cannot laugh and sympathize at the same time. Shelley knew that "our sincerest laughter with some pain is fraught." We should also guard against the idea that comedy cannot be serious; in satire it becomes a powerful social weapon. George Meredith felt that the chief function of comedy is the correction of folly; Aristotle and Freud have implied that comedy produces a catharsis similar to that of tragedy, a purging of anger and envy.

Since comedy is a by-product of the human intellect, it varies in nature with the types of human minds. Irish humor, French wit, and American jokes are often enigmas to the Englishman. "In the kingdoms of comedy," John Palmer remarks, "there are no papers of naturalization." The eighteenth century, "age of reason" and therefore age of wit, epigram, and comedy, lost prestige during the reign of the Romanticists and the Victorian sentimentalists; it is now apparently coming again into favor. Even the sexes differ in their appreciation of a joke.

THE COMIC SENSE

It is obvious, therefore, that there will be levels of comedy to correspond to stages of mental development. Low comedy of the slapstick, custard-pie-throwing type requires no great mental acuteness to appreciate. Much higher is the comedy of intrigue, in which ingenuity is employed to get the characters into an incongruous situation and then out of it, as in Cowper's "The Diverting History of John Gilpin." Comedy of character, of "humors," partly seen in Chaucer's "Nonne Preestes Tale" and in Burns' "Tam o' Shanter," requires more understanding of human nature. Comedy of manners, or "social comedy," treads on the toes of the reader through satire, as in Byron's *Don Juan,* and demands a quick and subtle mind. High comedy, or comedy of wit, reveals its chief cleverness in the expression, and therefore frequently flies over the heads of the multitude. Each reader will find a level of comedy to correspond to his stage of mental development.

The comedy of the Middle Ages could find no better poetic exemplar than Chaucer. After the reader has overcome the minor difficulties of the language, he enters upon the rich field of beast fable, allegorical satire, and social comedy. "The Nonne Preestes Tale" is one of the brightest, many-faceted gems of English comedy.

THE NONNE PREESTES TALE

by Geoffrey Chaucer (1340-1400)

A povre widwe, somdel stope in age,
Was whylom dwelling in a narwe cotage,
Bisyde a grove, stonding in a dale.
This widwe, of which I telle yow my tale,
Sin thilke day that she was last a wyf,
In pacience ladde a ful simple lyf,
For litel was hir catel and hir rente;
By housbondrye, of such as God hir sente,
She fond hir-self, and eek hir doghtren two.
Three large sowes hadde she, and namo,
Three kyn, and eek a sheep that highte Malle.
Ful sooty was hir bour,[1] and eek hir halle,
In which she eet ful many a sclendre meel.
Of poynaunt sauce hir neded never a deel.
No deyntee morsel passed thurgh hir throte;
Hir dyete was accordant to hir cote.
Repleccioun ne made hir never syk;
Attempree dyete was al hir phisyk,
And exercyse, and hertes suffisaunce.
The goute lette hir no-thing for to daunce,
N'apoplexye shente nat hir heed;
No wyn ne drank she, neither whyt ne reed;
Hir bord was served most with whyt and blak,
Milk and broun breed, in which she fond no lak,
Seynd bacoun, and somtyme an ey or tweye,
For she was as it were a maner deye.[2]
A yerd she hadde, enclosed al aboute
With stikkes, and a drye dich with-oute,
In which she hadde a cok, hight Chauntecleer,
In al the land of crowing nas his peer.
His vois was merier than the mery orgon
On messe-dayes that in the chirche gon;
Wel sikerer[3] was his crowing in his logge,
Than is a clokke, or an abbey orlogge.[4]
By nature knew he ech ascencioun
Of equinoxial in thilke toun;
For whan degrees fiftene were ascended,
Thanne crew he, that it mighte nat been amended.
His comb was redder than the fyn coral,
And batailed,[5] as it were a castel-wal.
His bile was blak, and as the jeet it shoon;
Lyk asur were his legges, and his toon;
His nayles whytter than the lilie flour,
And lyk the burned gold was his colour.
This gentil cok hadde in his governaunce
Sevene hennes, for to doon al his pleasaunce,
Whiche were his sustres and his paramours,
And wonder lyk to him, as of colours.
Of whiche the faireste hewed on hir throte
Was cleped faire damoysele Pertelote.
Curteys she was, discreet, and debonaire,
And compaignable, and bar hir-self so faire,
Sin thilke day that she was seven night old,
That trewely she hath the herte in hold
Of Chauntecleer loken in every lith;[6]
He loved hir so, that wel was him therwith.
But such a joye was it to here hem singe,
Whan that the brighte sonne gan to springe,
In swete accord, "my lief is faren in londe."
For thilke tyme, as I have understonde,
Bestes and briddes coude speke and singe.
And so bifel, that in a daweninge,
As Chauntecleer among his wyves alle
Sat on his perche, that was in the halle,
And next him sat this faire Pertelote,
This Chauntecleer gan gronen in his throte,
As man that in his dreem is drecched[7] sore.
And whan that Pertelote thus herde him rore,
She was agast, and seyde, "O herte dere,
What eyleth yow, to grone in this manere?
Ye been a verray sleper, fy for shame!"
And he answerde and seyde thus, "Madame,
I pray yow, that ye take it nat a-grief:
By God, me mette[8] I was in swich meschief
Right now, that yet myn herte is sore afright.
Now God," quod he, "my swevene recche aright,
And keep my body out of foul prisoun!
Me mette, how that I romed up and doun
Withinne our yerde, wher-as I saugh a beste,

[1] Room.
[2] A sort of dairy-woman.
[3] More certain.
[4] Church-clock.
[5] Indented.
[6] Locked in every limb.
[7] Troubled.
[8] I dreamed.

Was lyk an hound, and wolde han maad areste
Upon my body, and wolde han had me deed.
His colour was bitwixe yelwe and reed;
And tipped was his tail, and bothe his eres,
With blak, unlyk the remenant of his heres;
His snowte smal, with glowinge eyen tweye.
Yet of his look for fere almost I deye;
This caused me my groning, doutelees."
"Avoy!" quod she, "fy on yow, hertelees!
Allas!" quod she, "for, by that God above,
Now han ye lost myn herte and al my love;
I can nat love a coward, by my feith.
Fer certes, what so any womman seith,
We alle desyren, if it mighte be,
To han housbondes hardy, wyse, and free,
And secree, and no nigard, ne no fool,
Ne him that is agast of every tool,
Ne noon avauntour, by that God above!
How dorste ye seyn for shame unto your love,
That any thing mighte make yow aferd?
Have ye no mannes herte, and han a berd?
Allas! and conne ye been agast of swevenis? [9]
No-thing, God wot, but vanitee, in sweven is.
Swevenes engendren of replecciouns,
And ofte of fume, and of complecciouns,
Whan humours been to habundant in a wight,
Certes this dreem, which ye han met tonight,
Cometh of the grete superfluitee
Of youre rede *colera,* pardee,
Which causeth folk to dreden in here dremes
Of arwes, and of fyr with rede lemes,
Of grete bestes, that they wol hem byte,
Of contek,[10] and of whelpes grete and lyte;
Right as the humour of malencolye
Causeth ful many a man, in sleep, to crye,
For fere of blake beres, or boles blake,
Or elles, blake develes wole hem take.
Of othere humours coude I telle also,
That werken many a man in sleep ful wo;
But I wol passe as lightly as I can.
Lo Catoun; which that was so wys a man,
Seyde he nat thus, ne do no fors of dremes?
Now, sire," quod she, "whan we flee fro the bemes,
For Goddes love, as tak som laxatyf;
Up peril of my soule, and of my lyf,
I counseille yow the beste, I wol nat lye,
That bothe of colere and of malencolye
Ye purge yow; and for ye shul nat tarie,
Though in this toun is noon apotecarie,
I shal my-self to herbes techen yow,
That shul ben for your hele, and for your prow;
And in our yerd tho herbes shal I finde,
The whiche han of hir propretee, by kinde,
To purgen yow binethe, and eek above.
Forget not this, for Goddes owene love!
Ye been ful colerik of compleccioun.
Ware the sonne in his ascencioun
Ne fynde yow nat repleet of humours hote;
And if it do, I dar wel leye a grote,
That ye shul have a fevere terciane,
Or an agu, that may be youre bane.
A day or two ye shul have digestyves
Of wormes, er ye take your laxatyves,
Of lauriol, centaure, and fumetere,
Or elles of ellebor, that groweth there,
Of catapuce, or of gaytres beryis,
Of erbe yve, growing in our yerd, that mery is;
Pekke hem up right as they growe, and ete hem in.
Be mery, housbond, for your fader kin!
Dredeth no dreem; I can say yow namore."
"Madame," quod he, *"graunt mercy* of your lore.
But nathelees, as touching daun Catoun,
That hath of wisdom such a greet renoun,
Though that he had no dremes for to drede,
By God, men may in olde bokes rede
Of many a man, more of auctoritee
Than ever Catoun was, so mote I thee,
That al the revers seyn of his sentence,
And han wel founden by experience,
That dremes ben significaciouns,
As wel of joye as tribulaciouns
That folk enduren in this lyf present.
Ther nedeth make of this noon argument;
The verray preve sheweth it in dede.
Oon of the gretteste auctours that men rede
Seith thus, that whylom two felawes wente
On pilgrimage, in a ful good entente;
And happed so, thay come into a toun,
Wher-as ther was swich congregacioun
Of peple, and eek so streit of herbergage [11]
That they ne founde as muche as o cotage

9 Dreams.
10 Conflict.
11 So little room in the inns.

In which they bothe mighte y-logged be.
Wherfor thay mosten, of necessitee,
As for that night, departen compaignye;
And ech of hem goth to his hostelrye,
And took his logging as it wolde falle.
That oon of hem was logged in a stalle,
Fer in a yerd, with oxen of the plough;
That other man was logged wel y-nough,
As was his aventure, or his fortune,
That us governeth alle as in commune.
And so bifel, that, longe er it were day,
This man mette in his bed, ther-as he lay,
How that his felawe gan up-on him calle,
And seyde, 'allas! for in an oxes stalle
This night I shal be mordred ther I lye.
Now help me, dere brother, er I dye;
In alle haste com to me,' he sayde.
This man out of his sleep for fere abrayde;
But whan that he was wakned of his sleep,
He turned him, and took of this no keep;
Him thoughte his dreem nas but a vanitee.
Thus twyës in his sleping dremed he.
And atte thridde tyme yet his felawe
Cam, as him thoughte, and seide, 'I am now slawe;
Bihold my blody woundes, depe and wyde!
Arys up erly in the morwe-tyde,
And at the west gate of the toun,' quod he,
'A carte ful of dong ther shaltow see,
In which my body is hid ful prively;
Do thilke carte aresten boldely.
My gold caused my mordre, sooth to sayn;'
And tolde him every poynt how he was slayn,
With a ful pitous face, pale of hewe.
And truste wel, his dreem he fond ful trewe;
For on the morwe, as sone as it was day,
To his felawes in he took the way;
And whan that he cam to this oxes stalle,
After his felawe he bigan to calle.
The hostiler answered him anon,
And seyde, 'sire, your felawe is agon,
As sone as day he wente out of the toun.'
This man gan fallen in suspecioun,
Remembring on his dremes that he mette,
And forth he goth, no lenger wolde he lette,
Unto the west gate of the toun, and fond
A dong-carte, as it were to donge lond,
That was arrayed in the same wyse
As ye han herd the dede man devyse;
And with an hardy herte he gan to crye
Vengeaunce and justice of this felonye:—
'My felawe mordred is this same night,
And in this carte he lyth gapinge upright.
I crye out on the ministres,' quod he,
'That sholden kepe and reulen this citee;
Harrow! allas! her lyth my felawe slayn!'
What sholde I more un-to this tale sayn?
The peple out-sterte, and caste the cart to grounde,
And in the middel of the dong they founde
The dede man, that mordred was al newe.
O blisful God, that art so just and trewe!
Lo, how that thou biwreyest mordre alway!
Mordre wol out, that see we day by day.
Mordre is so wlatsom[12] and abhominable
To God, that is so just and resonable,
That he ne wol nat suffre it heled be;
Though it abyde a yeer, or two, or three,
Mordre wol out, this my conclusioun.
And right anoon, ministres of that toun
Han hent the carter, and so sore him pyned,
And eek the hostiler so sore engyned,
That thay biknewe[13] hir wikkednesse anoon,
And were an-hanged by the nekke-boon.
Here may men seen that dremes been to drede,
And certes, in the same book I rede,
Right in the nexte chapitre after this
(I gabbe nat, so have I joye or blis),
Two men that wolde han passed over see,
For certeyn cause, in-to a fer contree,
If that the wind ne hadde been contrarie,
That made hem in a citee for to tarie,
That stood ful mery upon an havensyde.
But on a day, agayn the even-tyde,
The wind gan chaunge, and blew right as hem leste,
Jolif and glad they wente un-to hir reste,
And casten hem ful erly for to saille;
But to that oo man fil a greet mervaille.
That oon of hem, in sleping as he lay,
Him mette a wonder dreem, agayn the day;
Him thoughte a man stood by his beddes syde,
And him comaunded, that he sholde abyde,
And seyde him thus, 'if thou to-morwe wende,
Thou shalt be dreynt; my tale is at an ende.'
He wook, and tolde his felawe what he mette,

[12] Heinous.
[13] Confessed.

And preyde him his viage for to lette;
As for that day, he preyde him to abyde.
His felawe, that lay by his beddes syde,
Gan for to laughe, and scorned him ful faste.
'No dreem,' quod he, 'may so myn herte agaste,
That I wol lette for to do my thinges.
I sette not a straw by thy dreminges,
For swevenes been but vanitees and japes.
Men dreme al-day of owles or of apes,
And eke of many a mase therwithal;
Men dreme of thing that never was ne shal
But sith I see that thou wolt heer abyde,
And thus for-sleuthen wilfully thy tyde,[14]
God wot it reweth me; and have good day.'
And thus he took his leve, and wente his way,
But er that he hadde halfe his cours y-seyled,
Noot I nat why, ne what mischaunce it eyled,
But casuelly the shippes botme rente,
And ship and man under the water wente
In sighte of othere shippes it byside,
That with hem seyled at the same tyde.
And therfor, faire Pertelote so dere,
By swiche ensamples olde maistow lere,
That no man sholde been to recchelees
Of dremes, for I sey thee, doutelees,
That many a dreem ful sore is for to drede.
  Lo, in the lyf of seint Kenelm, I rede,
That was Kenulphus sone, the noble king
Of Mercenrike, how Kenelm mette a thing;
A lyte er he was mordred, on a day,
His mordre in his avisioun he say.
His norice him expouned every del
His sweven, and bad him for to kepe him wel
For traisoun; but he nas but seven yeer old,
And therfore litel tale hath he told
Of any dreem, so holy was his herte.
By God, I hadde lever than my shert
That ye had rad his legende, as have I.
Dame Pertelote, I sey yow trewely,
Macrobeus, that writ th'avisioun
In Affrike of the worthy Cipioun,
Affermeth dremes, and seith that they been
Warning of thinges that men after seen.
  And forther-more, I pray yow loketh wel
In th'olde testament, of Daniel,
If he held dremes any vanitee.
Reed eek of Joseph, and ther shul ye see
Wher dremes ben somtyme (I sey nat alle)
Warning of thinges that shul after falle.
Loke of Egipt the king, daun Pharao,
His bakere and his boteler also,
Wher they ne felte noon effect in dremes.
Who-so wol seken actes of sondry remes,
May rede of dremes many a wonder thing.
  Lo Cresus, which that was of Lyde king,
Mette he nat that he sat upon a tree,
Which signified he sholde anhanged be?
Lo heer Andromacha, Ectores wyf,
That day that Ector sholde lese his lyf,
She dremed on the same night biforn,
How that the lyf of Ector sholde be lorn,
If thilke day he wente in-to bataille;
She warned him, but it mighte nat availle;
He wente for to fighte nathelees,
But he was slayn anoon of Achilles.
But thilke tale is al to long to telle,
And eek it is ny day, I may nat dwelle.
Shortly I seye, as for conclusioun,
That I shal han of this avisioun
Adversitee; and I seye forther-more,
That I ne telle of laxatyves no store,
For they ben venimous, I woot it wel;
I hem defye, I love hem never a del.
  Now let us speke of mirthe, and stinte al this;
Madame Pertelote, so have I blis,
Of o thing God hath sent me large grace;
For whan I see the beautee of your face,
Ye ben so scarlet-reed about your yën,
It maketh al my drede for to dyen;
For, also siker as *In principio,*
Mulier est hominis confusio;[15]
Madame, the sentence of this Latin is—
Womman is mannes joye and al his blis.
For whan I fele a-night your softe syde,
Al-be-it that I may nat on you ryde,
For that our perche is maad so narwe, alas!
I am so ful of joye and of solas
That I defye bothe sweven and dreem."
And with that word he fley doun fro the beem,
For it was day, and eek his hennes alle;
And with a chuk he gan hem for to calle,
For he had founde a corn, lay in the yerd.
Royal he was, he was namore aferd;
He fethered Pertelote twenty tyme,
And trad as ofte, er that it was pryme

[14] Lose the tide because of sloth.

[15] In the beginning, woman is man's confusion.

He loketh as it were a grim leoun;
And on his toos he rometh up and doun,
Him deyned not to sette his foot to grounde.
He chukketh, whan he hath a corn y-founde,
And to him rennen thanne his wyves alle.
Thus royal, as a prince is in his halle,
Leve I this Chauntecleer in his pasture;
And after wol I telle his aventure.
  Whan that the month in which the world bigan,
That highte March, whan god first maked man,
Was complet, and y-passed were also,
Sin March bigan, thritty dayes and two,
Bifel that Chauntecleer, in al his pryde,
His seven wyves walking by his syde,
Caste up his eyen to the brighte sonne,
That in the signe of Taurus hadde y-ronne
Twenty degrees and oon, and somwhat more;
And knew by kynde, and by noon other lore,
That it was pryme, and crew with blisful stevene.
"The sonne," he sayde, "is clomben up on hevene
Fourty degrees and oon, and more, y-wis.
Madame Pertelote, my worldes blis,
Herkneth thise blisful briddes how they singe,
And see the fresshe floures how they springe;
Ful is myn herte of revel and solas."
But sodeinly him fil a sorweful cas;
For ever the latter ende of joye is wo.
God woot that worldly joye is sone ago;
And if a rethor coude faire endyte,
He in a cronique saufly mighte it wryte,
As for a sovereyn notabilitee.
Now every wys man, lat him herkne me;
This storie is al-so trewe, I undertake,
As is the book of Launcelot de Lake,
That wommen holde in ful gret reverence.
Now wol I torne agayn to my sentence.
  A col-fox, ful of sly iniquitee,
That in the grove hadde woned yeres three,
By heigh imaginacioun forn-cast,
The same night thurgh-out the hegges brast
Into the yerd, ther Chauntecleer the faire
Was wont, and eek his wyves, to repaire;
And in a bed of wortes stille he lay,
Til it was passed undern of the day,
Wayting his tyme on Chauntecleer to falle,
As gladly doon thise homicydes alle,
That in awayt liggen to mordre men.
O false mordrer, lurking in thy den!
O newe Scariot, newe Genilon! [16]
False dissimilour, O Greek Sinon,
That broghtest Troye al outrely to sorwe!
O Chauntecleer, acursed be that morwe,
That thou into that yerd flough fro the bemes!
Thou were ful wel y-warned by thy dremes,
That thilke day was perilous to thee.
But what that god forwoot mot nedes be,
After the opinioun of certeyn clerkis.
Witnesse on him, that any perfit clerk is,
That in scole is gret altercacioun
In this matere, and greet disputisoun,
And hath ben of an hundred thousand men.
But I ne can not bulte it to the bren,
As can the holy doctour Augustyn,
Or Boëce, or the bishop Bradwardyn,
Whether that Goddes worthy forwiting
Streyneth me nedely for to doon a thing,
(Nedely clepe I simple necessitee);
Or elles, if free choys be graunted me
To do that same thing, or do it noght,
Though God forwoot it, er that it was wroght;
Or if his writing streyneth nevere a del
But by necessitee condicionel.
I wol not han to do of swich matere;
My tale is of a cok, as ye may here,
That took his counseil of his wyf, with sorwe,
To walken in the yerd upon that morwe
That he had met the dreem, that I yow tolde.
Wommennes counseils been ful ofte colde;
Wommannes counseil broghte us first to wo,
And made Adam fro paradys to go,
Ther-as he was ful mery, and wel at ese.—
But for I noot, to whom it mighte displese,
If I counseil of wommen wolde blame,
Passe over, for I seyde it in my game.
Rede auctours, wher they trete of swich matere,
And what thay seyn of wommen ye may here.
Thise been the cokkes wordes, and nat myne;
I can noon harm of no womman divyne.—
  Faire in the sond, to bathe hir merily,
Lyth Pertelote, and alle hir sustres by,

[16] Scariot: Iscariot; Genilon: the betrayer of Roland.

Agayn the sonne; and Chauntecleer so free
Song merier than the mermayde in the see;
For Phisiologus seith sikerly,
How that they singen wel and merily.
And so bifel that, as he caste his yë,
Among the wortes, on a boterflye,
He was war of this fox that lay ful lowe.
No-thing ne liste him thanne for to crowe,
But cryde anon, "cok, cok," and up he sterte,
As man that was affrayed in his herte.
For naturelly a beest desyreth flee
Fro his contrarie, if he may it see,
Though he never erst had seyn it with his yë.
  This Chauntecleer, whan he gan him espye,
He wolde han fled, but that the fox anon
Seyde, "Gentil sire, allas! wher wol ye gon?
Be ye affrayed of me that am your freend?
Now certes, I were worse than a feend,
If I to yow wolde harm or vileinye.
I am nat come your counseil for t'espye;
But trewely, the cause of my cominge
Was only for to herkne how that ye singe.
For trewely ye have as mery a stevene
As eny aungel hath, that is in hevene;
Therwith ye han in musik more felinge
Than hadde Boëce, or any that can singe.
My lord your fader (God his soule blesse!)
And eek your moder, of hir gentilesse,
Han in myn hous y-been, to my gret ese;
And certes, sire, ful fayn wolde I yow plese.
But for men speke of singing, I wol saye,
So mote I brouke wel myn eyen tweye,
Save yow, I herde never man so singe,
As dide your fader in the morweninge;
Certes, it was of herte, al that he song.
And for to make his voys the more strong,
He wolde so peyne him, that with bothe his yën
He moste winke, so loude he wolde cryen,
And stonden on his tiptoon ther-with-al,
And strecche forth his nekke long and smal.
And eek he was of swich discrecioun,
That ther nas no man in no regioun
That him in song or wisdom mighte passe.
I have wel rad in daun Burnel the Asse,
Among his vers, how that ther was a cok,
For that a preestes sone yaf him a knok
Upon his leg, whyl he was yong and nyce,
He made him for to lese his benefyce.
But certeyn, ther nis no comparisoun
Bitwix the wisdom and discrecioun
Of youre fader, and of his subtiltee.
Now singeth, sire, for seinte Charitee,
Let see, conne ye your fader countrefete?"
This Chauntecleer his winges gan to bete,
As man that coude his tresoun nat espye,
So was he ravisshed with his flaterye.
  Allas! ye lordes, many a fals flatour
Is in your courtes, and many a losengeour,[17]
That plesen yow wel more, by my feith,
Than he that soothfastnesse unto yow seith.
Redeth Ecclesiaste of flaterye;
Beth war, ye lordes, of hir trecherye.
  This Chauntecleer stood hye up-on his toos,
Strecching his nekke, and heeld his eyen cloos,
And gan to crowe loude for the nones;
And daun Russel the fox sterte up at ones
And by the gargat hente[18] Chauntecleer,
And on his bak toward the wode him beer,
For yet ne was ther no man that him sewed.
O destinee, that mayst nat been eschewed!
Allas, that Chauntecleer fleigh fro the bemes!
Allas, his wyf ne roghte nat of dremes!
And on a Friday fil al this meschaunce.
O Venus, that art goddesse of plesaunce,
Sin that thy servant was this Chauntecleer,
And in thy service dide al his poweer,
More for delyt, than world to multiplye,
Why woldestow suffre him on thy day to dye?
O Gaufred, dere mayster soverayn,
That, whan thy worthy king Richard was slayn
With shot, compleynedest his deth so sore,
Why ne hadde I now thy sentence and thy lore,
The Friday for to chyde, as diden ye?
(For on a Friday soothly slayn was he.)
Than wolde I shewe yow how that I coude pleyne
For Chauntecleres drede, and for his peyne.
  Certes, swich cry ne lamentacioun
Was never of ladies maad, whan Ilioun
Was wonne, and Pirrus with his streite swerd,
Whan he hadde hent king Priam by the berd,

17 Flatterer.
18 Siezed by the throat.

And slayn him (as saith us *Eneydos*),[19]
As maden alle the hennes in the clos,
Whan they had seyn of Chauntecleer the sighte.
But sovereynly dame Pertelote shrighte,
Ful louder than dide Hasdrubales wyf,
Whan that hir housbond hadde lost his lyf,
And that the Romayns hadde brend Cartage;
She was so ful of torment and of rage,
That wilfully into the fyr she sterte,
And brende hir-selven with a stedfast herte.
O woful hennes, right so cryden ye,
As, whan that Nero brende the citee
Of Rome, cryden senatoures wyves,
For that hir housbondes losten alle hir lyves;
Withouten gilt this Nero hath hem slayn.
Now wol I torne to my tale agayn:—
  This sely widwe, and eek hir doghtres two,
Herden thise hennes crye and maken wo,
And out at dores sterten they anoon,
And syen the fox toward the grove goon,
And bar upon his bak the cok away;
And cryden, "Out! harrow! and weylaway!
Ha, ha, the fox!" and after him they ran,
And eek with staves many another man;
Ran Colle our dogge, and Talbot, and Gerland,
And Malkin, with a distaf in hir hand;
Ran cow and calf, and eek the verray hogges
So were they fered for berking of the dogges
And shouting of the men and wimmen eke,
They ronne so, hem thoughte hir herte breke.
They yelleden as feendes doon in helle;
The dokes cryden as men wolde hem quelle;
The gees for fere flowen over the trees;
Out of the hyve cam the swarm of bees;
So hidous was the noyse, a! *benedicite!*
Certes, he Jakke Straw, and his meynee,
Ne made never shoutes half so shrille,
Whan that they wolden any Fleming kille,
As thilke day was maad upon the fox.
Of bras thay broghten bemes, and of box,
Of horn, of boon, in whiche they blewe and pouped,
And therwithal thay shryked and they houped;
It semed as that heven sholde falle.
Now, gode men, I pray yow herkneth alle!
  Lo, how fortune turneth sodeinly

[19] *Eneydos:* the Aeneid.

The hope and pryde eek of hir enemy!
This cok, that lay upon the foxes bak,
In al his drede, un-to the fox he spak,
And seyde, "sire, if that I were as ye,
Yet sholde I seyn (as wis God helpe me),
Turneth agayn, ye proude cherles alle!
A verray pestilence up-on yow falle!
Now am I come un-to this wodes syde,
Maugree your heed, the cok shal heer abyde;
I wol him ete in feith, and that anon."—
The fox answerde, "in feith, it shal be don,"—
And as he spak that word, al sodeinly
This cok brak from his mouth deliverly,
And heighe up-on a tree he fleigh anon.
And whan the fox saugh that he was y-gon,
"Allas!" quod he, "O Chauntecleer, allas!
I have to yow," quod he, "y-doon trespas,
In-as-muche as I maked yow aferd,
Whan I yow hente, and broghte out of the yerd;
But, sire, I dide it in no wikke entente;
Com doun, and I shal telle yow what I mente.
I shal seye sooth to yow, God help me so."
"Nay than," quod he, "I shrewe us bothe two,
And first I shrewe my-self, bothe blood and bones,
If thou bigyle me ofter than ones.
Thou shalt na-more, thurgh thy flaterye,
Do me to singe and winke with myn yë.
For he that winketh, whan he sholde see,
Al wilfully, God lat him never thee!"[20]
"Nay," quod the fox, "but God yeve him meschaunce,
That is so undiscreet of governaunce,
That jangleth whan he sholde holde his pees."
  Lo, swich it is for to be recchelees,
And necligent, and truste on flaterye.
But ye that holden this tale a folye,
As of a fox, or of a cok and hen,
Taketh the moralitee, good men.
For seint Paul seith, that al that writen is,
To our doctryne it is y-write, y-wis.
Taketh the fruyt, and lat the chaf be stille.
  Now, gode God, if that it be thy wille,
As seith my lord, so make us alle good men;
And bringe us to his heighe blisse. Amen.

[20] Thrive.

Max Eastman, in *The Sense of Humor,* has set forth standards upon which to judge a humorous story. It must, he says, deal with really interesting, rich, living material, chiefly on the surface of life, so that it may not arouse feelings too deep. It must be natural, not forced; pointedly brief, not explained. These are aims difficult to achieve, but Robert Burns has come near to attaining them all. In "Tam o' Shanter" the broad Scotch dialect does not hinder, but adds spice to the comedy of Tam's character and the situation in which he finds himself. The undercurrent of satire gives the poem additional point.

TAM O' SHANTER

A Tale

by Robert Burns (1759-1796)

"Of Brownyis and of Bogillis full is this Buke."
GAWIN DOUGLAS.

When chapman billies [1] leave the street,
And drouthy neibors neibors meet;
As market days are wearing late,
And folk begin to tak the gate,
While we sit bousing at the nappy,[2]
An' getting fou and unco happy,
We think na on the lang Scots miles,
The mosses, waters, slaps [3] and stiles,
That lie between us and our hame,
Where sits our sulky, sullen dame,
Gathering her brows like gathering storm,
Nursing her wrath to keep it warm.

This truth fand honest Tam o' Shanter,
As he frae Ayr ae night did canter
(Auld Ayr, wham ne'er a town surpasses,
For honest men and bonie lasses).

O Tam! had'st thou but been sae wise,
As taen thy ain wife Kate's advice!
She tauld thee weel thou was a skellum,[4]
A blethering, blustering, drunken blellum; [5]
That frae November till October,
Ae market-day thou was no sober;
That ilka melder [6] wi' the Miller,
Thou sat as lang as thou had siller; [7]
That ev'ry naig was ca'd a shoe on [8]
The Smith and thee gat roarin fou on;
That at the Lord's house, ev'n on Sunday,
Thou drank wi' Kirkton Jean till Monday;
She prophesied that late or soon,
Thou wad be found, deep drown'd in Doon,
Or catch'd wi' warlocks [9] in the mirk,
By Alloway's auld, haunted kirk.

Ah, gentle dames! it gars me greet,[10]
To think how mony counsels sweet,
How mony lengthen'd, sage advices,
The husband frae the wife despises!

But to our tale:—Ae market night,
Tam had got planted unco right,
Fast by an ingle,[11] bleezing finely,
Wi' reaming swats [12] that drank divinely;
And at his elbow, Souter Johnie,
His ancient, trusty, drouthy crony:
Tam lo'ed him like a very brither; [13]
They had been fou for weeks thegither.
The night drave on wi' sangs an' clatter;
And aye the ale was growing better:
The Landlady and Tam grew gracious,
Wi' favours secret, sweet and precious:
The Souter tauld his queerest stories;
The Landlord's laugh was ready chorus:
The storm without might rair and rustle,
Tam did na mind the storm a whistle.

Care, mad to see a man sae happy,
E'en drown'd himsel amang the nappy.
As bees flee hame wi' lades [14] o' treasure,
The minutes wing'd their way wi' pleasure:
Kings may be blest, but Tam was glorious,
O'er a' the ills o' life victorious!

1 Peddlers.
2 Drinking ale.
3 Gaps.
4 Rogue.
5 Babbler.
6 Corn-grinding.
7 (Silver) Money.
8 Every nag had a shoe driven on.
9 Male witches.
10 Makes me weep.
11 A fireplace.
12 New ale.
13 Brother.
14 Loads.

But pleasures are like poppies spread,
You seize the flow'r, its bloom is shed;
Or like the snow falls in the river,
A moment white—then melts for ever;
Or like the borealis race,
That flit ere you can point their place;
Or like the rainbow's lovely form
Evanishing amid the storm.
Nae man can tether time or tide;—
The hour approaches Tam maun ride;
That hour, o' night's black arch the key-
stane,
That dreary hour he mounts his beast in;
And sic a night he taks the road in,
As ne'er poor sinner was abroad in.

The wind blew as 'twad blawn its last;
The rattling showers rose on the blast;
The speedy gleams the darkness swallowed;
Loud, deep, and lang, the thunder bellowed:
That night, a child might understand,
The Deil [15] had business on his hand.

Weel mounted on his gray mare, Meg,
A better never lifted leg,
Tam skelpit [16] on through dub [17] and mire,
Despising wind, and rain, and fire;
Whiles holding fast his guid blue bonnet;
Whiles crooning o'er some auld Scots sonnet;
Whiles glowering round wi' prudent cares,
Lest bogles [18] catch him unawares;
Kirk Alloway was drawing nigh,
Whare ghaists and houlets [19] nightly cry.

By this time he was cross the ford,
Whare in the snaw the chapman smoored,[20]
And past the birks and meikle-stane,[21]
Whare drunken Charlie brak's neckbane;
And through the whins, and by the cairn,[22]
Whare hunters fand the murdered bairn:
And near the thorn, aboon the well,
Whare Mungo's mither hanged hersel.
Before him Doon pours all his floods;
The doubling storm roars through the woods;
The lightnings flash from pole to pole;
Near and more near the thunders roll:
When, glimmering thro' the groaning trees,
Kirk Alloway seemed in a bleeze;
Through ilka bore [23] the beams were glanc-
ing;
And loud resounded mirth and dancing.

Inspiring bold John Barleycorn!
What dangers thou canst make us scorn!
Wi' tippenny,[24] we fear nae evil;
Wi' usquebae,[25] we'll face the Devil!
The swats sae reamed in Tammie's noddle,
Fair play, he cared na deils a boddle.[26]
But Maggie stood right sair astonished,
Till, by the heel and hand admonished,
She ventured forward on the light;
And, wow! Tam saw an unco sight!
Warlocks and witches in a dance;
Nae cotillion brent-new frae France,
But hornpipes, jigs, strathspeys, and reels,
Put life and mettle in their heels.
At winnock-bunker [27] in the east,
There sat auld Nick, in shape o' beast;
A towzie tyke,[28] black, grim, and large,
To gie them music was his charge:
He screwed the pipes and gart them skirl,[29]
Till roof and rafters a' did dirl.[30]—
Coffins stood round, like open presses,
That shawed the dead in their last dresses;
And by some devilish cantrip [31] sleight,
Each in its cauld hand held a light,—
By which heroic Tam was able
To note upon the haly table
A murderer's banes in gibbet-airns; [32]
Two span-lang, wee, unchristened bairns;
A thief, new-cutted frae a rape,[33]
Wi' his last gasp his gab [34] did gape;
Five tomahawks wi' blude red-rusted;
Five scimitars wi' murder crusted;
A garter which a babe had strangled;
A knife a father's throat had mangled,
Whom his ain son of life bereft,

[15] Devil.
[16] Splashed.
[17] Puddle.
[18] Goblins.
[19] Ghosts and owls.
[20] Smothered.
[21] The large stone.
[22] Through brush by the stone-pile
[23] Every chink.
[24] Twopenny ale.
[25] Whiskey.
[26] Cared not a copper for devils.
[27] Window-seat.
[28] Shaggy cur.
[29] Played the bag-pipes and made them scream.
[30] Rattle.
[31] Magic.
[32] Gallows-irons.
[33] Rope.
[34] Mouth.

The grey hairs sticking to the heft;
Wi' mair of horrible and awfu',
Which even to name wad be unlawfu'.

As Tammie glowr'd, amaz'd and curious,
The mirth and fun grew fast and furious;
The Piper loud and louder blew,
The dancers quick and quicker flew,
They reel'd, they set, they cross'd, they cleekit,[35]
Till ilka carlin swat and reekit,[36]
And coost her duddies to the wark,[37]
And linkit at it in her sark![38]

But Tam kent what was what fu' brawlie:[39]
There was ae winsome wench and waulie[40]
That night enlisted in the core,[41]
Lang after ken'd on Carrick shore
(For mony a beast to dead she shot,
And perish'd mony a bonie boat,
And shook baith meikle corn and bear,
And kept the country-side in fear);
Her cutty sark,[42] o' Paisley harn,[43]
That while a lassie she had worn,
In longitude tho' sorely scanty,
It was her best, and she was vauntie.[44]
Ah! little ken'd thy reverend grannie,
That sark she coft[45] for her wee Nannie,
Wi' twa pund Scots ('twas a' her riches),
Wad ever grac'd a dance of witches!

But here my Muse her wing maun cower,
Sic flights are far beyond her power,
To sing how Nannie lap and flang
(A souple jade she was and strang),
And how Tam stood, like ane bewitch'd,
And thought his very een enrich'd:
Even Satan glowr'd, and fidg'd fu' fain,[46]
And hotch'd[47] and blew wi' might and main:

[35] Joined hands.
[36] Till every old woman sweat and reeked.
[37] And cast off her clothes in the excitement.
[38] And danced in her shirt.
[39] Fine.
[40] Jolly.
[41] Corps, company.
[42] Short shirt.
[43] Linen.
[44] Vain, proud of it.
[45] Bought.

Till first ae caper, syne anither,
Tam tint[48] his reason a' thegither,
And roars out, "Weel done, Cutty-sark!"
And in an instant all was dark:
And scarcely had he Maggie rallied,
When out the hellish legion sallied.

As bees bizz out wi' angry fyke,[49]
When plundering herds assail their byke;[50]
As open pussie's[51] mortal foes,
When, pop! she starts before their nose;
As eager runs the market-crowd
When "Catch the thief!" resounds aloud;
So Maggie runs, the witches follow,
Wi' mony an eldritch[52] skreich and hollo.

Ah, Tam! Ah, Tam! thou'll get thy fairin![53]
In hell they'll roast thee like a herrin!
In vain thy Kate awaits thy comin!
Kate soon will be a woefu' woman!
Now, do thy speedy utmost, Meg,
And win the key-stane o' the brig;[54]
There, at them thou thy tail may toss,
A running stream they dare na cross;
But ere the key-stane she could make,
The fiend a tail she had to shake!
For Nannie, far before the rest,
Hard upon noble Maggie prest,
And flew at Tam wi' furious ettle;[55]
But little wist she Maggie's mettle!
Ae spring brought off her master hale,
But left behind her ain grey tail:
The carlin claught her by the rump,
And left poor Maggie scarce a stump.

Now wha this tale o' truth shall read,
Ilk' man and mother's son, take heed,
Whene'er to drink you are inclined,
Or cutty-sarks run in your mind,
Think, ye may buy the joys o'er dear:
Remember Tam o' Shanter's mare!

[46] Fidgeted eagerly.
[47] Squirmed.
[48] Lost.
[49] Fuss.
[50] Hive.
[51] The hare's.
[52] Unearthly.
[53] Reward.
[54] Bridge.
[55] Aim, intent.

MORALS IN FOOLSCAP

The moral tale which is clad in fool's motley has often proved more effective than the serious call to duty. The satirist who wishes to sting must first put his reader in a receptive mood of tolerant humor; he must tickle his victim's fancy with one hand while he pierces with the other. John Hay has done precisely that in the mock antiquity of "The Enchanted Shirt."

THE ENCHANTED SHIRT

by John Hay (1838-1905)

Fytte ye Firste: wherein it shall be shown how ye Truth is too mightie a Drugge for such as be of feeble temper.

The King was sick. His cheek was red
And his eye was clear and bright;
He ate and drank with a kingly zest,
And peacefully snored at night.

But he said he was sick, and a king should know,
And doctors came by the score.
They did not cure him. He cut off their heads
And sent to the schools for more.

At last two famous doctors came,
And one was as poor as a rat,—
He had passed his life in studious toil,
And never found time to grow fat.

The other had never looked in a book;
His patients gave him no trouble.
If they recovered they paid him well,
If they died their heirs paid double.

Together they looked at the royal tongue,
As the King on his couch reclined;
In succession they thumped his august chest,
But no trace of disease could find.

The old sage said, "You're as sound as a nut."
"Hang him up!" roared the King in a gale,
In a ten-knot gale of royal rage.
The other leech grew a shade pale;

But he pensively rubbed his sagacious nose,
And thus his prescription ran—
The King will be well, if he sleeps one night
In the Shirt of a Happy Man.

Fytte ye Seconde: telleth of ye search for ye Shirte and how it was nighe founde but was notte, for reasons which are sayd or sung.

Wide o'er the realm the couriers rode,
And fast their horses ran,
And many they saw, and to many they spoke,
But they found no Happy Man.

They found poor men who would fain be rich,
And rich who thought they were poor;
And men who twisted their waists in stays,
And women that short hose wore.

They saw two men by the roadside sit,
And both bemoaned their lot;
For one had buried his wife, he said,
And the other one had not.

At last they came to a village gate,
A beggar lay whistling there;
He whistled and sang and laughed and rolled
On the grass in the soft June air.

The weary couriers paused and looked
At the scamp so blithe and gay;
And one of them said, "Heaven save you, friend!
You seem to be happy today."

"O yes, fair sirs," the rascal laughed,
And his voice rang free and glad,
"An idle man has so much to do
That he never has time to be sad."

"This is our man," the courier said;
"Our luck has led us aright.
I will give you a hundred ducats, friend,
For the loan of your shirt tonight."

The merry blackguard lay back on the grass,
And laughed till his face was black;

"I would do it, God wot," and he roared with the fun,
"But I haven't a shirt to my back."

Fytte ye Thirde: Shewing how Hys Majestie ye King came at last to sleepe in a Happie Man hys Shirte.

Each day to the King the reports came in
Of his unsuccessful spies,
And the sad panorama of human woes
Passed daily under his eyes.

And he grew ashamed of his useless life,
And his maladies hatched in gloom;
He opened his windows and let the air
Of the free heaven into his room.

And out he went in the world and toiled
In his own appointed way;
And the people blessed him, the land was glad,
And the King was well and gay.

THE TRAGIC SPIRIT

It is impossible to be unaffected by tragedy in life or in art. The great poets have always had a tragic sense of life, seeing man battle against overwhelming odds, caught in the maelstrom of uncontrollable emotions, baffled by nature and an elemental cruelty, aspiring to the heights and doomed to defeat. Aristotle revealed this when he prescribed tragic drama as a catharsis, a purgative of hate and fear. His theory of catharsis rested on man's willingness to witness tragedy and his natural desire to escape it; beholding and sharing the pain of others, man is enlarged and, at the same time, liberated, released by suffering.

The same conflict and release is true today; man is no longer in conflict with the gods, but with himself. Observing the struggles of his fellowmen, he is able to face life more calmly and courageously. He regards the misfortunes of others with a peculiar combination of understanding sympathy and that form of pleasure which the Germans call *Schadenfreude,* pleasure in someone else's pain. We see in the suffering hero a projection of our own personalities—a procrastinating Hamlet, a jealousy-frustrated Othello, a destiny-tortured Oedipus—and while we share their pain we are pleased that it is they and not ourselves who suffer in such heroic proportions. Their tragedies harden us for our own.

In the conflict of purposes out of which human tragedy rises, it is rare that the reader's sympathies are evenly divided; he sides with good against evil, with man against fate. If he can attain an Olympian calm and perceive the inevitable outcome against the indifference of the universe, he may raise tragedy to the level of philosophy, as fatalists, from the Greeks to Thomas Hardy, have done. Tragedy is profoundly serious; if there is comedy, as in the drunken porter episode in *Macbeth,* it must heighten the tragic irony, serve as a mental relief in order that the emotions should not be overstrained. Tragedy probes deeper than comedy into character and motives; it rises to bolder heights, propelled by greater intensity and a correspondingly richer style. The permeating emotional effect of great tragedy should not be depressing, but elevating; it should not follow the road suggested by Schopenhauer, "to make us despise life," but it should rather conform to Hegel's suggestion, "to make us tolerant."

Narrative poetry of tragedy is a rich field. From Chaucer's "Pardoner's

Tale" to Ralph Hodgson's "The Bull" it deals chiefly with death—the son killed by the father in Matthew Arnold's Oriental tapestry-poem, "Sohrab and Rustum;" the father killed in spirit by his son in Wordsworth's "Michael;" the child hurled to its death over a precipice in Sidney Lanier's "Revenge of Hamish;" the daughter dying by the side of her father in Longfellow's "Wreck of the Hesperus;" the mother and child dying together in Jean Ingelow's "High Tide on the Coast of Lincolnshire."

In the two poems which follow, death is found by different paths. In Robert Frost's "Death of the Hired Man" the dark angel comes serenely to relieve an unwanted old man of life's frustrations; in Siegfried Sassoon's "Counter-Attack" it destroys youth and its hopes in a violent and purposeless conflict. In the first poem there is a play of sentiment and understanding; in the other there is only bitter disillusionment. The first gives the reader suggestions enough to build a whole life-history; the second offers only a nightmare glimpse.

THE DEATH OF THE HIRED MAN

by Robert Frost (1875-   )

Mary sat musing on the lamp-flame at the table
Waiting for Warren. When she heard his step
She ran on tip-toe down the darkened passage
To meet him in the doorway with the news
And put him on his guard. "Silas is back."
She pushed him outward with her through the door
And shut it after her. "Be kind," she said.
She took the market things from Warren's arms
And set them on the porch, then drew him down
To sit beside her on the wooden steps.

"When was I ever anything but kind to him?
But I'll not have the fellow back," he said.
"I told him so last haying, didn't I?
'If he left then,' I said, 'that ended it.'
What good is he? Who else will harbour him
At his age for the little he can do?
What help he is there's no depending on.
Off he goes always when I need him most.
'He thinks he ought to earn a little pay,
Enough at least to buy tobacco with,
So he won't have to beg and be beholden.'
'All right,' I say, 'I can't afford to pay
Any fixed wages, though I wish I could.'
'Someone else can.' 'Then someone else will have to.'
I shouldn't mind his bettering himself
If that was what it was. You can be certain,
When he begins like that, there's someone at him
Trying to coax him off with pocket-money,—
In haying time, when any help is scarce.
In winter he comes back to us. I'm done."

"Sh! not so loud: he'll hear you," Mary said.

"I want him to: he'll have to soon or late."

"He's worn out. He's asleep beside the stove.
When I came up from Rowe's I found him here,
Huddled against the barn-door fast asleep,
A miserable sight, and frightening, too—
You needn't smile—I didn't recognize him—
I wasn't looking for him—and he's changed.
Wait till you see."

"Where did you say he'd been?"

"He didn't say. I dragged him to the house,
And gave him tea and tried to make him smoke.
I tried to make him talk about his travels,
Nothing would do: he just kept nodding off."

"What did he say? Did he say anything?"

"But little."

"Anything? Mary, confess

He said he'd come to ditch the meadow for me."

"Warren!"

"But did he? I just want to know."

"Of course he did. What would you have him say?
Surely you wouldn't grudge the poor old man
Some humble way to save his self-respect.
He added, if you really care to know,
He meant to clear the upper pasture, too.
That sounds like something you have heard before?
Warren, I wish you could have heard the way
He jumbled everything. I stopped to look
Two or three times—he made me feel so queer—
To see if he was talking in his sleep.
He ran on Harold Wilson—you remember—
The boy you had in haying four years since.
He's finished school, and teaching in his college.
Silas declares you'll have to get him back.
He says they two will make a team for work:
Between them they will lay this farm as smooth!
The way he mixed that in with other things.
He thinks young Wilson a likely lad, though daft
On education—you know how they fought
All through July under the blazing sun,
Silas up on the cart to build the load,
Harold along beside to pitch it on."

"Yes, I took care to keep well out of earshot."

"Well, those days trouble Silas like a dream.
You wouldn't think they would. How some things linger!
Harold's young college boy's assurance piqued him.
After so many years he still keeps finding
Good arguments he sees he might have used.
I sympathise. I know just how it feels
To think of the right thing to say too late.
Harold's associated in his mind with Latin.
He asked me what I thought of Harold's saying
He studied Latin like the violin
Because he liked it—that an argument!
He said he couldn't make the boy believe
He could find water with a hazel prong—
Which showed how much good school had ever done him.
He wanted to go over that. But most of all
He thinks if he could have another chance
To teach him how to build a load of hay—"

"I know, that's Silas' one accomplishment.
He bundles every forkful in its place,
And tags and numbers it for future reference,
So he can find and easily dislodge it
In the unloading. Silas does that well.
He takes it out in bunches like birds' nests.
You never see him standing on the hay
He's trying to lift, straining to lift himself."
"He thinks if he could teach him that, he'd be
Some good perhaps to someone in the world.
He hates to see a boy the fool of books.
Poor Silas, so concerned for other folk,
And nothing to look backward to with pride,
And nothing to look forward to with hope,
So now and never any different."

Part of a moon was falling down the west,
Dragging the whole sky with it to the hills.
Its light poured softly in her lap. She saw
And spread her apron to it. She put out her hand
Among the harp-like morning-glory strings,
Taut with the dew from garden bed to eaves,
As if she played unheard the tenderness
That wrought on him beside her in the night.
"Warren," she said, "he has come home to die:
You needn't be afraid he'll leave you this time."

"Home," he mocked gently.

"Yes, what else but home?
It all depends on what you mean by home.
Of course he's nothing to us, any more
Than was the hound that came a stranger to us
Out of the woods, worn out upon the trail."

"Home is the place where, when you have to go there,
They have to take you in."

"I should have called it
Something you somehow haven't to deserve."

Warren leaned out and took a step or two,
Picked up a little stick, and brought it back
And broke it in his hand and tossed it by.
"Silas has better claim on us, you think,
Than on his brother? Thirteen little miles
As the road winds would bring him to his door.
Silas has walked that far no doubt today.
Why didn't he go there? His brother's rich,
A somebody—director in the bank."

"He never told us that."

"We know it though."

"I think his brother ought to help, of course.
I'll see to that if there is need. He ought of right
To take him in, and might be willing to—
He may be better than appearances.
But have some pity on Silas. Do you think
If he'd had any pride in claiming kin
Or anything he looked for from his brother,
He'd keep so still about him all this time?"

"I wonder what's between them."

"I can tell you.
Silas is what he is—we wouldn't mind him—
But just the kind that kinsfolk can't abide.
He never did a thing so very bad.
He don't know why he isn't quite as good
As anyone. He won't be made ashamed
To please his brother, worthless though he is."

"I can't think Si ever hurt anyone."

"No, but he hurt my heart the way he lay
And rolled his old head on that sharp-edged chair-back.
He wouldn't let me put him on the lounge.
You must go in and see what you can do.
I made the bed up for him there tonight.
You'll be surprised at him—how much he's broken.
His working days are done; I'm sure of it."

"I'd not be in a hurry to say that."

"I haven't been. Go, look, see for yourself.
But, Warren, please remember how it is:
He's come to help you ditch the meadow.
He has a plan. You mustn't laugh at him.
He may not speak of it, and then he may.
I'll sit and see if that small sailing cloud
Will hit or miss the moon."

It hit the moon.
Then there were three there, making a dim row,
The moon, the little silver cloud, and she.

Warren returned—too soon, it seemed to her,
Slipped to her side, caught up her hand and waited.

"Warren?" she questioned.

"Dead," was all he answered.

COUNTER-ATTACK

by Siegfried Sassoon (1886-)

We'd gained our first objective hours before
While dawn broke like a face with blinking eyes,
Pallid, unshaved and thirsty, blind with smoke.
Things seemed all right at first. We held their line,
With bombers posted, Lewis guns well placed,
And clink of shovels deepening the shallow trench.
The place was rotten with dead; green clumsy legs
High-booted, sprawled and groveled along the saps;[1]
And trunks, face downward, in the sucking mud,
Wallowed like trodden sand-bags loosely filled;

[1] Saps: temporary, approach trenches.

And naked sodden buttocks, mats of hair,
Bulged, clotted heads slept in the plastering slime.
And then the rain began—the jolly old rain!
A yawning soldier knelt against the bank,
Staring across the morning blear with fog;
He wondered when the Allemands would get busy;
And then, of course, they started with five-nines
Traversing, sure as fate, and never a dud.
Mute in the clamor of shells he watched them burst
Spouting dark earth and wire with gusts from hell,
While posturing giants dissolved in drifts of smoke.
He crouched and flinched, dizzy with galloping fear,
Sick for escape—loathing the strangled horror
And butchered, frantic gestures of the dead.

An officer came blundering down the trench:
"Stand-to and man the fire-step!" On he went . . .
Gasping and bawling, "Fire-step . . . counter-attack!"
Then the haze lifted. Bombing on the right
Down the old sap; machine-guns on the left;
And stumbling figures looming out in front.
"O Christ, they're coming at us!" Bullets spat,
And he remembered his rifle . . . rapid fire . . .
And started blazing wildly . . . then a bang
Crumpled and spun him sideways, knocked him out
To grunt and wriggle. None heeded him; he choked
And fought the flapping veils of smothering gloom,
Lost in a blurred confusion of yells and groans . . .
Down, and down, and down, he sank and drowned,
Bleeding to death. The counter-attack had failed.

THE DRAMATIC MONOLOGUE

The line between poetic drama and dramatic poetry becomes thin indeed when the poet permits a character to tell his own story. Yet this method of relation, this change in the angle of narration, gives added interest to the tale itself. For now the reader is interested not only in the story itself, but also in the self-revelation of the teller. The drunken visitor to the Zoo in William Vaughn Moody's "The Menagerie" is totally unconscious of his own failings; Tennyson's "Northern Farmer" speaks in a dialect that is strange and rude, but forceful with individuality.

The reader's imagination is exercised fully to gain all the values from a dramatic monologue. The setting, the accompanying actions and gestures, the implied dialogue, and the appearance of the speaker must all be supplied by the reader with the aid of a few hints. In Tennyson's "Rizpah" all these details must be furnished. Byron's "Prisoner of Chillon" gains immensely in poignancy by being told in the first person, though all the descriptive details are included by the speaker.

RIZPAH

17—

by Alfred, Lord Tennyson (1809-1892)

Wailing, wailing, wailing, the wind over land and sea—
And Willy's voice in the wind, "O mother, come out to me!"
Why should he call me tonight, when he knows that I cannot go?
For the downs are as bright as day, and the full moon stares at the snow.

We should be seen, my dear; they would spy us out of the town.
The loud black nights for us, and the storm rushing over the down,
When I cannot see my own hand, but am led by the creak of the chain,
And grovel and grope for my son till I find myself drenched with the rain.

Anything fallen again? nay—what was there left to fall?
I have taken them home, I have numbered the bones, I have hidden them all.
What am I saying? and what are *you?* do you come as a spy?
Falls? what falls? who knows? As the tree falls so must it lie.

Who let her in? how long has she been? you—what have you heard?
Why did you sit so quiet? you never have spoken a word.
O—to pray with me—yes—a lady—none of their spies—
But the night has crept into my heart, and begun to darken my eyes.

Ah—you, that have lived so soft, what should *you* know of the night,
The blast and the burning shame and the bitter frost and the fright?
I have done it, while you were asleep—you were only made for the day.
I have gathered my baby together—and now you may go your way.

Nay—for it's kind of you, madam, to sit by an old dying wife.
But say nothing hard of my boy, I have only an hour of life.
I kissed my boy in the prison, before he went out to die.
"They dared me to do it," he said, and he never has told me a lie.
I whipped him for robbing an orchard once when he was but a child—
"The farmer dared me to do it," he said; he was always so wild—
And idle—and couldn't be idle—my Willy—he never could rest.
The King should have made him a soldier, he would have been one of his best.

But he lived with a lot of wild mates, and they never would let him be good;
They swore that he dare not rob the mail, and he swore that he would;
And he took no life, but he took one purse, and when all was done
He flung it among his fellows—"I'll none of it," said my son.

I came into court to the judge and the lawyers. I told them my tale,
God's own truth—but they killed him, they killed him for robbing the mail.
They hanged him in chains for a show—we had always borne a good name—
To be hanged for a thief—and then put away—isn't that enough shame?
Dust to dust—low down—let us hide! but they set him so high
That all the ships of the world could stare at him, passing by.
God 'ill pardon the hell-black raven and horrible fowls of the air,
But not the black heart of the lawyer who killed him and hanged him there.

And the jailer forced me away. I had bid him my last good-bye:
They had fastened the door of his cell. "O mother!" I heard him cry.
I couldn't get back though I tried, he had something further to say,
And now I never shall know it. The jailer forced me away.

Then since I couldn't but hear that cry of my boy that was dead,
They seized me and shut me up: they fastened me down on my bed.
"Mother, O mother!"—he called in the dark to me year after year—
They beat me for that, they beat me—you know that I couldn't but hear;
And then at the last they found I had grown so stupid and still
They let me abroad again—but the creatures had worked their will.

Flesh of my flesh was gone, but bone of my bone was left—
I stole them all from the lawyers—and you, will you call it a theft?—
My baby, the bones that had sucked me, the bones that had laughed and had cried—
Theirs? O, no! they are mine—not theirs—they had moved in my side.

Do you think I was scared by the bones? I kissed 'em, I buried 'em all—
I can't dig deep, I am old—in the night by the churchyard wall.
My Willy 'ill rise up whole when the trumpet of judgment 'ill sound,
But I charge you never to say that I laid him in holy ground.

They would scratch him up—they would hang him again on the cursèd tree.
Sin? O, yes, we are sinners, I know—let all that be,
And read me a Bible verse of the Lord's good-will toward men—
"Full of compassion and mercy, the Lord"—let me hear it again;
"Full of compassion and mercy—long-suffering." Yes, O, yes!
For the lawyer is born but to murder—the Savior lives but to bless.
He'll never put on the black cap except for the worst of the worst,
And the first may be last—I have heard it in church—and the last may be first.
Suffering—O, long-suffering—yes, as the Lord must know,
Year after year in the mist and the wind and the shower and the snow.

Heard, have you? what? they have told you he never repented his sin.
How do they know it? are *they* his mother? are *you* of his kin?
Heard! have you ever heard, when the storm on the downs began,
The wind that 'ill wail like a child and the sea that 'ill moan like a man?

Election, Election, and Reprobation [1]—it's all very well.
But I go tonight to my boy, and I shall not find him in hell.
For I cared so much for my boy that the Lord has looked into my care,
And He means me I'm sure to be happy with Willy, I know not where.

And if *he* be lost—but to save *my* soul, that is all your desire—
Do you think I care for *my* soul if my boy be gone to the fire?
I have been with God in the dark—go, go, you may leave me alone—
You never have borne a child—you are just as hard as a stone.

Madam, I beg your pardon! I think that you mean to be kind,
But I cannot hear what you say for my Willy's voice in the wind—
The snow and the sky so bright—he used but to call in the dark,

[1] Terms connected with the Calvinistic doctrine of grace and foreordination.

And he calls to me now from the church and not from the gibbet—for hark!
Nay—you can hear it yourself—it is coming—shaking the walls—
Willy—the moon's in a cloud— Good-night. I am going. He calls.

THE PRISONER OF CHILLON

by Lord Byron (1788-1824)

My hair is gray, but not with years,
  Nor grew it white
  In a single night,
As men's have grown from sudden fears:
My limbs are bowed, though not with toil,
  But rusted with a vile repose,
For they have been a dungeon's spoil,
  And mine has been the fate of those
To whom the goodly earth and air
Are banned, and barred—forbidden fare;
But this was for my father's faith
I suffered chains and courted death:
That father perished at the stake
For tenets he would not forsake;
And for the same his lineal race
In darkness found a dwelling-place;
We were seven—who now are one,
  Six in youth, and one in age,
Finished as they had begun,
  Proud of Persecution's rage;
One in fire, and two in field,
Their belief with blood have sealed,
Dying as their father died,
For the God their foes denied;
Three were in a dungeon cast,
Of whom this wreck is left the last.

There are seven pillars of Gothic mould,
In Chillon's dungeons deep and old,
There are seven columns, massy and gray,
Dim with a dull imprisoned ray,
A sunbeam which hath lost its way
And through the crevice and the cleft
Of the thick wall is fallen and left;
Creeping o'er the floor so damp,
Like a marsh's meteor lamp:
And in each pillar there is a ring,
And in each ring there is a chain;
That iron is a cankering thing,
  For in these limbs its teeth remain,
With marks that will not wear away,
Till I have done with this new day,
Which now is painful to these eyes,
Which have not seen the sun so rise
For years—I cannot count them o'er,
I lost their long and heavy score,
When my last brother drooped and died,
And I lay living by his side.

They chained us each to a column stone,
And we were three—yet, each alone;
We could not move a single pace,
We could not see each other's face,
But with that pale and livid light
That made us strangers in our sight:
And thus together—yet apart,
Fettered in hand, but joined in heart,
'Twas still some solace, in the dearth
Of the pure elements of earth,
To hearken to each other's speech,
And each turn comforter to each
With some new hope, or legend old,
Or song heroically bold;
But even these at length grew cold.
Our voices took a dreary tone,
An echo of the dungeon stone,
  A grating sound, not full and free,
  As they of yore were wont to be;
  It might be fancy, but to me
They never sounded like our own.

I was the eldest of the three,
  And to uphold and cheer the rest
  I ought to do—and did my best—
And each did well in his degree.
  The youngest, whom my father loved,
Because our mother's brow was given
To him, with eyes as blue as heaven—
  For him my soul was sorely moved;
And truly might it be distressed
To see such bird in such a nest;
For he was beautiful as day—
  (When day was beautiful to me
  As to young eagles, being free)—
  A polar day, which will not see
A sunset till its summer's gone,
  Its sleepless summer of long light,
The snow-clad offspring of the sun:
  And thus he was as pure and bright,
And in his natural spirit gay,
With tears for nought but others' ills,
And then they flowed like mountain rills,

Unless he could assuage the woe
Which he abhorred to view below.

The other was as pure of mind,
But formed to combat with his kind;
Strong in his frame, and of a mood
Which 'gainst the world in war had stood,
And perished in the foremost rank
With joy:—but not in chains to pine:
His spirit withered with their clank,
I saw it silently decline—
And so perchance in sooth did mine:
But yet I forced it on to cheer
Those relics of a home so dear.
He was a hunter of the hills,
Had followed there the deer and wolf;
To him this dungeon was a gulf,
And fettered feet the worst of ills.

Lake Leman lies by Chillon's walls:
A thousand feet in depth below
Its massy waters meet and flow;
Thus much the fathom-line was sent
From Chillon's snow-white battlement,
Which round about the wave enthralls:
A double dungeon wall and wave
Have made—and like a living grave.
Below the surface of the lake
The dark vault lies wherein we lay:
We heard it ripple night and day;
Sounding o'er our heads it knocked;
And I have felt the winter's spray
Wash through the bars when winds were high
And wanton in the happy sky;
And then the very rock hath rocked,
And I have felt it shake, unshocked,
Because I could have smiled to see
The death that would have set me free.

I said my nearer brother pined,
I said his mighty heart declined,
He loathed and put away his food;
It was not that 'twas coarse and rude,
For we were used to hunter's fare,
And for the like had little care:
The milk drawn from the mountain goat
Was changed for water from the moat;
Our bread was such as captives' tears
Have moistened many a thousand years,
Since man first pent his fellow-men
Like brutes within an iron den;
But what were these to us or him?
These wasted not his heart or limb;
My brother's soul was of that mould
Which in a palace had grown cold,
Had his free breathing been denied
The range of the steep mountain's side.
But why delay the truth?—he died.
I saw, and could not hold his head,
Nor reach his dying hand—nor dead—
Though hard I strove, but strove in vain,
To rend and gnash my bonds in twain.
He died—and they unlocked his chain
And scooped for him a shallow grave
Even from the cold earth of our cave.
I begged them, as a boon, to lay
His corse in dust whereon the day
Might shine—it was a foolish thought,
But then within my brain it wrought,
That even in death his free-born breast
In such a dungeon could not rest.
I might have spared my idle prayer—
They coldly laughed—and laid him there:
The flat and turfless earth above
The being we so much did love;
His empty chain above it leant,
Such murder's fitting monument!

But he, the favorite and the flower,
Most cherished since his natal hour,
His mother's image in fair face,
The infant love of all his race,
His martyred father's dearest thought,
My latest care, for whom I sought
To hoard my life, that his might be
Less wretched now, and one day free;
He, too, who yet had held untired
A spirit natural or inspired—
He, too, was struck, and day by day
Was withered on the stalk away.
O God! it is a fearful thing
To see the human soul take wing
In any shape, in any mood:—
I've seen it rushing forth in blood,
I've seen it on the breaking ocean
Strive with a swollen convulsive motion,
I've seen the sick and ghastly bed
Of Sin delirious with its dread:
But these were horrors—this was woe
Unmixed with such,—but sure and slow:
He faded, and so calm and meek,
So softly worn, so sweetly weak,

So tearless, yet so tender, kind,
And grieved for those he left behind;
With all the while a cheek whose bloom
Was as a mockery of the tomb,
Whose tints as gently sunk away
As a departing rainbow's ray—
An eye of most transparent light,
That almost made the dungeon bright,
And not a word of murmur, not
A groan o'er his untimely lot,
A little talk of better days,
A little hope my own to raise,
For I was sunk in silence—lost
In this last loss, of all the most:
And then the sighs he would suppress
Of fainting nature's feebleness,
More slowly drawn, grew less and less.
I listened, but I could not hear;
I called, for I was wild with fear;
I knew 'twas hopeless, but my dread
Would not be thus admonishèd;
I called, and thought I heard a sound—
I burst my chain with one strong bound,
And rushed to him: I found him not;
I only stirred in this black spot,
I only lived—*I* only drew
The accursed breath of dungeon-dew;
The last, the sole, the dearest link
Between me and the eternal brink
Which bound me to my failing race,
Was broken in this fatal place.
One on the earth, and one beneath—
My brothers—both had ceased to breathe:
I took that hand which lay so still;
Alas, my own was full as chill;
I had not strength to stir, or strive,
But felt that I was still alive—
A frantic feeling, when we know
That what we love shall ne'er be so.
I know not why
I could not die;
I had no earthly hope but faith,
And that forbade a selfish death.
What next befell me then and there
I know not well—I never knew:—
First came the loss of light, and air,
And then of darkness too:
I had no thought, no feeling—none—
Among the stones I stood a stone,
And was, scarce conscious what I wist,
As shrubless crags within the mist;
For all was blank, and bleak, and gray;
It was not night, it was not day;
It was not even the dungeon-light,
So hateful to my heavy sight,
But vacancy absorbing space,
And fixedness, without a place;
There were no stars, no earth, no time,
No check, no change, no good, no crime,
But silence, and a stirless breath
Which neither was of life nor death;
A sea of stagnant idleness,
Blind, boundless, mute, and motionless!

A light broke in upon my brain,—
It was the carol of a bird;
It ceased, and then it came again,
The sweetest song ear ever heard;
And mine was thankful, till my eyes
Ran over with the glad surprise,
And they that moment could not see
I was the mate of misery;
But then by dull degrees came back
My senses to their wonted track,
I saw the dungeon walls and floor
Close slowly round me as before,
I saw the glimmer of the sun
Creeping as it before had done,
But through the crevice where it came
That bird was perched, as fond and tame,
And tamer than upon the tree;
A lovely bird, with azure wings,
And song that said a thousand things,
And seemed to say them all for me!

I never saw its like before.
I ne'er shall see its likeness more!
It seemed, like me, to want a mate,
But was not half so desolate,
And it was come to love me when
None lived to love me so again,
And cheering from my dungeon's brink,
Had brought me back to feel and think.
I know not if it late were free,
Or broke its cage to perch on mine,
But knowing well captivity,
Sweet bird, I could not wish for thine!
Or if it were, in wingèd guise,
A visitant from Paradise;
For—Heaven forgive that thought! the while
Which made me both to weep and smile—
I sometimes deemed that it might be
My brother's soul come down to me;

But then at last away it flew,
And then 'twas mortal well I knew,
For he would never thus have flown,
And left me twice so doubly lone,
Lone as the corse within its shroud;
Lone as a solitary cloud,—
A single cloud on a sunny day,
While all the rest of heaven is clear,
A frown upon the atmosphere,
That hath no business to appear
When skies are blue and earth is gay.

A kind of change came in my fate,
My keepers grew compassionate;
I know not what had made them so,
They were inured to sights of woe;
But so it was:—my broken chain
With links unfastened did remain,
And it was liberty to stride
Along my cell from side to side,
And up and down, and then athwart,
And tread it over every part;
And round the pillars one by one,
Returning where my walk begun,
Avoiding only, as I trod,
My brothers' graves without a sod;
For if I thought with heedless tread
My step profaned their lowly bed,
My breath came gaspingly and thick,
And my crushed heart fell blind and sick.

I made a footing in the wall,
It was not therefrom to escape,
For I had buried one and all
Who loved me in a human shape;
And the whole earth would henceforth be
A wider prison unto me:
No child, no sire, no kin had I,
No partner in my misery;
I thought of this, and I was glad,
For thought of them had made me mad;
But I was curious to ascend
To my barred windows, and to bend
Once more, upon the mountains high,
The quiet of a loving eye.

I saw them, and they were the same,
They were not changed like me in frame;
I saw their thousand years of snow
On high—their wide long lake below,
And the blue Rhone in fullest flow;
I heard the torrents leap and gush
O'er channelled rock and broken bush;
I saw the white-walled distant town,
And whiter sails go skimming down;
And then there was a little isle,
Which in my very face did smile,
The only one in view;
A small green isle, it seemed no more,
Scarce broader than my dungeon floor,
But in it there were three tall trees,
And o'er it blew the mountain breeze,
And by it there were waters flowing,
And on it there were young flowers growing,
Of gentle breath and hue.
The fish swam by the castle wall,
And they seemed joyous each and all;
The eagle rode the rising blast,
Methought he never flew so fast
As then to me he seemed to fly;
And then new tears came in my eye,
And I felt troubled—and would fain
I had not left my recent chain;
And when I did descend again,
The darkness of my dim abode
Fell on me as a heavy load;
It was as is a new-dug grave,
Closing o'er one we sought to save,—
And yet my glance, too much opprest,
Had almost need of such a rest.

It might be months, or years, or days,
I kept no count, I took no note,
I had no hope my eyes to raise,
And clear them of their dreary mote;
At last men came to set me free;
I asked not why, and recked not where;
It was at length the same to me,
Fettered or fetterless to be,
I learned to love despair.
And thus when they appeared at last,
And all my bonds aside were cast,
These heavy walls to me had grown
A hermitage—and all my own!
And half I felt as they were come
To tear me from a second home:
With spiders I had friendship made,
And watched them in their sullen trade,
Had seen the mice by moonlight play,
And why should I feel less than they?
We were all inmates of one place,
And I, the monarch of each race,

Had power to kill—yet, strange to tell!
In quiet we had learned to dwell;
My very chains and I grew friends,
So much a long communion tends
To make us what we are:—even I
Regained my freedom with a sigh.

Frequently the age, and not the poet alone, fashions the poem. It determines not only the kind of imagery, the way in which things are seen and attitudes taken, but shapes the form in which a poem, play or novel is written. If Chaucer had lived in the Renaissance, he might have written plays; if Shakespeare were alive today, he would perhaps be writing novels. Robert Browning's personal tastes were all for dramatization, and he tried again and again to write a play which would catch the fancy of the theatre-going public. The taste of Victorian audiences, however, was not for poetic drama, and Browning was not interested in stage mechanics, so none of his plays was successful. His genius found its expression in fragments rather than in wholes, in suggestion rather than representation, in dramatic monologues rather than five-act plays. The powerful soliloquies in the plays of Shakespeare and Marlowe were noble predecessors; Browning brought the monologue to the highest point of development as a self-contained expression. It is perhaps significant dramatic irony that *Caponsacchi,* one of the most successful stage productions of a recent New York season, is the "dramatization" of Browning's most ambitious dramatic monologue, *The Ring and the Book.*

Two of Browning's best monologues are here. The first, *My Last Duchess,* is a complete novel in fifty-six lines, a miracle of condensation; the other, *Andrea Del Sarto,* is crammed with suggestions of the Renaissance ideal, the painter's personality, and the tragic story of his life and love.

MY LAST DUCHESS

Ferrara

by Robert Browning (1812-1889)

That's my last Duchess painted on the wall,
Looking as if she were alive. I call
That piece a wonder, now: Frà Pandolf's hands
Worked busily a day, and there she stands.
Will't please you sit and look at her? I said
"Frà Pandolf" by design, for never read
Strangers like you that pictured countenance,
The depth and passion of its earnest glance,
But to myself they turned (since none puts by
The curtain I have drawn for you, but I)
And seemed as they would ask me, if they durst,
How such a glance came there; so, not the first
Are you to turn and ask thus. Sir, 'twas not
Her husband's presence only, called that spot
Of joy into the Duchess' cheek: perhaps
Frà Pandolf chanced to say "Her mantle laps
Over my Lady's wrist too much," or "Paint
Must never hope to reproduce the faint
Half-flush that dies along her throat"; such stuff

Was courtesy, she thought, and cause enough
For calling up that spot of joy. She had
A heart . . . how shall I say? . . . too soon made glad,
Too easily impressed; she liked whate'er
She looked on, and her looks went everywhere.
Sir, 'twas all one! My favour at her breast,
The drooping of the daylight in the West,
The bough of cherries some officious fool
Broke in the orchard for her, the white mule
She rode with round the terrace—all and each
Would draw from her alike the approving speech,
Or blush, at least. She thanked men,—good; but thanked
Somehow . . . I know not how . . . as if she ranked
My gift of a nine hundred years' old name
With anybody's gift. Who'd stoop to blame
This sort of trifling? Even had you skill
In speech—(which I have not)—to make your will
Quite clear to such an one, and say "Just this
Or that in you disgusts me; here you miss,
Or there exceed the mark"—and if she let
Herself be lessoned so, nor plainly set
Her wits to yours, forsooth, and made excuse,
—E'en then would be some stooping, and I choose
Never to stoop. Oh, Sir, she smiled, no doubt,
Whene'er I passed her; but who passed without
Much the same smile? This grew; I gave commands;
Then all smiles stopped together. There she stands
As if alive. Will't please you rise? We'll meet
The company below, then. I repeat,
The Count your master's known munificence
Is ample warrant that no just pretence
Of mine for dowry will be disallowed;
Though his fair daughter's self, as I avowed
At starting, is my object. Nay, we'll go
Together down, sir. Notice Neptune, though,
Taming a sea-horse, thought a rarity,
Which Claus of Innsbruck cast in bronze for me!

ANDREA DEL SARTO

Called "The Faultless Painter"

by Robert Browning (1812-1889)

But do not let us quarrel any more,
No, my Lucrezia; bear with me for once.
Sit down and all shall happen as you wish.
You turn your face, but does it bring your heart?
I'll work then for your friend's friend, never fear,
Treat his own subject after his own way,
Fix his own time, accept, too, his own price,
And shut the money into this small hand

When next it takes mine. Will it? tenderly?
Oh, I'll content him—but tomorrow, Love!
I often am much wearier than you think,
This evening more than usual, and it seems
As if—forgive now—should you let me sit
Here by the window with your hand in mine
And look a half hour forth on Fiesole,
Both of one mind, as married people use,
Quietly, quietly, the evening through,
I might get up tomorrow to my work
Cheerful and fresh as ever. Let us try.
Tomorrow, how you shall be glad for this!
Your soft hand is a woman of itself,
And mine the man's bared breast she curls inside.
Don't count the time lost, neither; you must serve
For each of the five pictures we require—
It saves a model. So! keep looking so—
My serpentining beauty, rounds on rounds!
—How could you ever prick those perfect ears,
Even to put the pearl there! oh, so sweet—
My face, my moon, my everybody's moon,
Which everybody looks on and calls his,
And, I suppose, is looked on by in turn,
While she looks—no one's; very dear, no less!
You smile? why, there's my picture ready made.
There's what we painters call our harmony!
A common grayness silvers everything—
All in a twilight, you and I alike
—You, at the point of your first pride in me
(That's gone you know), but I, at every point;
My youth, my hope, my art, being all toned down
To yonder sober pleasant Fiesole.
There's the bell clinking from the chapel-top;
That length of convent-wall across the way
Holds the trees safer, huddled more inside;
The last monk leaves the garden; days decrease
And autumn grows, autumn in everything.
Eh? the whole seems to fall into a shape
As if I saw alike my work and self
And all that I was born to be and do,
A twilight-piece. Love, we are in God's hand.
How strange now looks the life he makes us lead;
So free we seem, so fettered fast we are!
I feel he laid the fetter; let it lie!
This chamber, for example—turn your head—
All that's behind us! You don't understand
Nor care to understand about my art,
But you can hear at least when people speak;
And that cartoon, the second from the door
—It is the thing, Love! so such things should be—
Behold Madonna! I am bold to say.

I can do with my pencil what I know,
What I see, what at bottom of my heart
I wish for, if I ever wish so deep—
Do easily, too—when I say, perfectly,
I do not boast, perhaps. Yourself are judge
Who listened to the Legate's talk last week,
And just as much they used to say in France.
At any rate 'tis easy, all of it!
No sketches first, no studies, that's long past—
I do what many dream of all their lives—
Dream? strive to do, and agonize to do,
And fail in doing. I could count twenty such
On twice your fingers, and not leave this town,
Who strive—you don't know how the others strive
To paint a little thing like that you smeared
Carelessly passing with your robes afloat,
Yet do much less, so much less, someone says,
(I know his name, no matter) so much less!
Well, less is more, Lucrezia! I am judged.
There burns a truer light of God in them,
In their vexed, beating, stuffed, and stopped-up brain,
Heart, or whate'er else, than goes on to prompt
This low-pulsed forthright craftsman's hand of mine.
Their works drop groundward, but themselves, I know,
Reach many a time a heaven that's shut to me,
Enter and take their place there sure enough,
Though they come back and cannot tell the world.
My works are nearer heaven, but I sit here.
The sudden blood of these men! at a word—
Praise them, it boils, or blame them, it boils, too.
I, painting from myself and to myself,
Know what I do, am unmoved by men's blame
Or their praise either. Somebody remarks
Morello's outline there is wrongly traced,
His hue mistaken—what of that? or else,
Rightly traced and well ordered—what of that?
Speak as they please, what does the mountain care?
Ah, but a man's reach should exceed his grasp,
Or what's a heaven for? All is silver-gray
Placid and perfect with my art—the worse!
I know both what I want and what might gain—
And yet how profitless to know, to sigh
"Had I been two, another and myself,
Our head would have o'erlooked the world!" No doubt.
Yonder's a work, now, of that famous youth,
The Urbinate who died five years ago.
('Tis copied, George Vasari sent it me.)
Well, I can fancy how he did it all,
Pouring his soul, with kings and popes to see,
Reaching, that Heaven might so replenish him,
Above and through his art—for it gives way;

That arm is wrongly put—and there again—
A fault to pardon in the drawing's lines,
Its body, so to speak! its soul is right,
He means right—that a child may understand.
Still, what an arm! and I could alter it.
But all the play, the insight, and the stretch—
Out of me! out of me! And wherefore out?
Had you enjoined them on me, given me soul,
We might have risen to Rafael, I and you.
Nay, Love, you did give all I asked, I think—
More than I merit, yes, by many times.
But had you—oh, with the same perfect brow,
And perfect eyes, and more than perfect mouth,
And the low voice my soul hears, as a bird
The fowler's pipe, and follows to the snare—
Had you, with these the same, but brought a mind!
Some women do so. Had the mouth there urged
"God and the glory! never care for gain.
The present by the future, what is that?
Live for fame, side by side with Agnolo!
Rafael is waiting. Up to God all three!"
I might have done it for you. So it seems—
Perhaps not. All is as God overrules.
Beside, incentives come from the soul's self;
The rest avail not. Why do I need you?
What wife had Rafael, or has Agnolo?
In this world, who can do a thing, will not—
And who would do it, cannot, I perceive.
Yet the will's somewhat—somewhat, too, the power—
And thus we half-men struggle. At the end,
God, I conclude, compensates, punishes.
'Tis safer for me, if the award be strict,
That I am something underrated here,
Poor this long while, despised, to speak the truth.
I dared not, do you know, leave home all day,
For fear of chancing on the Paris lords.
The best is when they pass and look aside;
But they speak sometimes; I must bear it all.
Well may they speak! That Francis, that first time,
And that long festal year at Fontainebleau!
I surely then could sometimes leave the ground,
Put on the glory, Rafael's daily wear,
In that humane great monarch's golden look—
One finger in his beard or twisted curl
Over his mouth's good mark that made the smile,
One arm about my shoulder, round my neck,
The jingle of his gold chain in my ear,
I painting proudly with his breath on me,
All his court round him, seeing with his eyes,
Such frank French eyes, and such a fire of souls
Profuse, my hand kept plying by those hearts—

And, best of all, this, this, this face beyond,
This in the background, waiting on my work,
To crown the issue with a last reward!
A good time, was it not, my kingly days?
And had you not grown restless—but I know—
'Tis done and past; 'twas right, my instinct said;
Too live the life grew, golden and not gray—
And I'm the weak-eyed bat no sun should tempt
Out of the grange whose four walls make his world.
How could it end in any other way?
You called me, and I came home to your heart.
The triumph was—to reach and stay there; since
I reached it ere the triumph, what is lost?
Let my hands frame your face in your hair's gold,
You beautiful Lucrezia that are mine!
"Rafael did this, Andrea painted that—
The Roman's[1] is the better when you pray,
But still the other's Virgin was his wife—"
Men will excuse me. I am glad to judge
Both pictures in your presence; clearer grows
My better fortune, I resolve to think.
For, do you know, Lucrezia, as God lives,
Said one day Agnolo, his very self,
To Rafael . . . I have known it all these years . . .
(When the young man was flaming out his thoughts
Upon a palace-wall for Rome to see,
Too lifted up in heart because of it)
"Friend, there's a certain sorry little scrub
Goes up and down our Florence, none cares how,
Who, were he set to plan and execute
As you are pricked on by your popes and kings,
Would bring the sweat into that brow of yours!"
To Rafael's!—And indeed the arm is wrong.
I hardly dare—yet, only you to see,
Give the chalk here—quick, thus the line should go!
Ay, but the soul! he's Rafael! rub it out!
Still, all I care for, if he spoke the truth,
(What he? why, who but Michel Agnolo?
Do you forget already words like those?)
If really there was such a chance, so lost,
Is, whether you're—not grateful—but more pleased.
Well, let me think so. And you smile indeed!
This hour has been an hour! Another smile?
If you would sit thus by me every night,
I should work better, do you comprehend?
I mean that I should earn more, give you more.
See, it is settled dusk now; there's a star;
Morello's gone, the watch-lights show the wall,
The cue-owls[2] speak the name we call them by.

[1] Rafael's, because Rafael painted mostly in Rome.
[2] Almost a pun, for the Italian word for the owl's call is "chiu!"

Come from the window, Love—come in, at last,
Inside the melancholy little house
We built to be so gay with. God is just.
King Francis may forgive me. Oft at nights
When I look up from painting, eyes tired out,
The walls become illumined, brick from brick
Distinct, instead of mortar, fierce bright gold,
That gold of his I did cement them with!
Let us but love each other. Must you go?
That Cousin here again? he waits outside?
Must see you—you, and not with me? Those loans!
More gaming debts to pay? you smiled for that?
Well, let smiles buy me! have you more to spend?
While hand and eye and something of a heart
Are left me, work's my ware, and what's it worth?
I'll pay my fancy. Only let me sit
The gray remainder of the evening out,
Idle, you call it, and muse perfectly
How I could paint were I but back in France,
One picture, just one more—the Virgin's face,
Not yours this time! I want you at my side
To hear them—that is, Michel Agnolo—
Judge all I do and tell you of its worth.
Will you? Tomorrow, satisfy your friend.
I take the subjects for his corridor,
Finish the portrait out of hand—there, there,
And throw him in another thing or two
If he demurs; the whole should prove enough
To pay for this same Cousin's freak. Beside,
What's better and what's all I care about,
Get you the thirteen scudi for the ruff.
Love, does that please you? Ah, but what does he,
The Cousin, what does he to please you more?

I am grown peaceful as old age tonight.
I regret little, I would change still less.
Since there my past life lies, why alter it?
The very wrong to Francis! it is true
I took his coin, was tempted and complied,
And built this house and sinned, and all is said.
My father and my mother died of want—
Well, had I riches of my own? you see
How one gets rich! Let each one bear his lot.
They were born poor, lived poor, and poor they died;
And I have labored somewhat in my time
And not been paid profusely. Some good son
Paint my two hundred pictures—let him try!
No doubt there's something strikes a balance. Yes,
You loved me quite enough, it seems tonight.
This must suffice me here. What would one have?
In heaven, perhaps, new chances, one more chance—

Four great walls in the New Jerusalem,
Meted on each side by the angel's reed,
For Leonard, Rafael, Agnolo, and me
To cover—the three first without a wife,
While I have mine! So—still they overcome
Because there's still Lucrezia—as I choose.

Again the Cousin's whistle! Go, my Love.

THE POETIC PORTRAIT

On the border-line between narrative and pictorial verse is the poetic portrait. The painter of portraits of the highest quality must be an expert in human nature as well as in oils. The "characters" which amused the prose-writers of seventeenth-century England and France find here their counterpart in verse. If, as Pope suggests, "the proper study of mankind is man," then the portrait galleries of John Masefield's *Reynard the Fox* and Edgar Lee Masters' *Spoon River Anthology* deserve our careful scrutiny. The great prototype of all English poetic photograph-albums is the Prologue to Chaucer's *Canterbury Tales,* which furnishes material for a study of civilization of an entire period.

PROLOGUE
(from "The Canterbury Tales")

by Geoffrey Chaucer (1340-1400)

Whan that Aprille with his shoures sote
The droghte of Marche hath perced to the rote,
And bathed every veyne in swich licour,
Of which vertu engendred is the flour;
Whan Zephirus eek with his swete breeth
Inspired hath in every holt and heeth
The tendre croppes, and the yonge sonne
Hath in the Ram his halfe cours y-ronne,
And smale fowles maken melodye,
That slepen al the night with open yë,
(So priketh hem nature in hir corages): [1]
Than longen folk to goon on pilgrimages
(And palmers for to seken straunge strondes)
To ferne halwes,[2] couthe in sondry londes;
And specially, from every shires ende
Of Engelond, to Caunterbury they wende,
The holy blisful martir for to seke,
That hem hath holpen, whan that they were seke.
Bifel that, in that seson on a day,
In Southwerk at the Tabard as I lay
Redy to wenden on my pilgrimage
To Caunterbury with ful devout corage,
At night was come in-to that hostelrye
Wel nyne and twenty in a companye,
Of sondry folk, by aventure y-falle
In felawshipe, and pilgrims were they alle,
That toward Caunterbury wolden ryde;
The chambres and the stables weren wyde,
And wel we weren esed atte beste.
And shortly, whan the sonne was to reste,
So hadde I spoken with hem everichon,
That I was of hir felawshipe anon,
And made forward erly for to ryse,
To take our wey, ther as I yow devyse.
But natheles, whyl I have tyme and space,
Er that I ferther in this tale pace,
Me thinketh it acordaunt to resoun,
To telle yow al the condicioun
Of ech of hem, so as it semed me,
And whiche they weren, and of what degree;
And eek in what array that they were inne:
And at a knight than wol I first biginne.
A KNIGHT ther was, and that a worthy man,
That fro the tyme that he first bigan
To ryden out, he loved chivalrye,
Trouthe and honour, fredom and curteisye.
Ful worthy was he in his lordes werre,
And therto hadde he riden (no man ferre)
As wel in Cristendom as hethenesse,

[1] Hearts.
[2] Distant shrines.

And ever honoured for his worthinesse.
At Alisaundre he was, whan it was wonne;
Ful ofte tyme he hadde the bord bigonne
Aboven alle naciouns in Pruce.
In Lettow hadde he reysed and in Ruce,
No Cristen man so ofte of his degree.
In Gernade at the sege eek hadde he be
Of Algezir, and riden in Belmarye.
At Lyeys was he, and at Satalye,
Whan they were wonne; and in the Grete See
At many a noble aryve hadde he be.
At mortal batailles hadde he been fiftene,
And foughten for our feith at Tramissene
In listes thryes, and ay slayn his fo.
This ilke worthy knight had been also
Somtyme with the lord of Palatye,
Ageyn another hethen in Turkye:
And evermore he hadde a sovereyn prys.
And though that he were worthy, he was wys,
And of his port as meke as is a mayde.
He never yet no vileinye ne sayde
In al his lyf, un-to no maner wight.
He was a verray parfit gentil knight.
But for to tellen yow of his array,
His hors were gode, but he was nat gay.
Of fustian he wered a gipoun
Al bismotered with his habergeoun; [3]
For he was late y-come from his viage,
And wente for to doon his pilgrimage.
With him ther was his sone, a yong SQUYER,
A lovyere, and a lusty bacheler,
With lokkes crulle, as they were leyd in presse.
Of twenty yeer of age he was, I gesse.
Of his stature he was of evene lengthe,
And wonderly deliver, and greet of strengthe.
And he had been somtyme in chivachye,
In Flaundres, in Artoys, and Picardye,
And born him wel, as of so litel space,
In hope to stonden in his lady grace.
Embrouded was he, as it were a mede
Al ful of fresshe floures, whyte and rede.
Singinge he was, or floytinge, al the day;
He was as fresh as is the month of May.
Short was his goune, with sleves longe and wyde.
Wel coude he sitte on hors, and faire ryde.
He coude songes make and wel endyte,
Juste and eek daunce, and wel purtreye and wryte.
So hote he lovede that by nightertale
He sleep namore than dooth a nightingale.
Curteys he was, lowly and servisable,
And carf biforn his fader at the table.

Ther was also a Nonne, a PRIORESSE,
That of hir smyling was ful simple and coy;
Hir gretteste ooth was but by sëynt Loy;
And she was cleped madame Eglentyne.
Ful wel she song the service divyne,
Entunéd in hir nose ful semely;
And Frensh she spak ful faire and fetisly,
After the scole of Stratford atte Bowe,
For Frensh of Paris was to hir unknowe.
At mete wel y-taught was she with-alle;
She leet no morsel from hir lippes falle,
Ne wette hir fingres in hir sauce depe.
Wel coude she carie a morsel, and wel kepe,
That no drope ne fille up-on hir brest.
In curteisye was set ful muche hir lest.
Hir over lippe wyped she so clene
That in hir coppe was no ferthing sene
Of grece, whan she dronken hadde hir draughte.
Ful semely after hir mete she raughte,
And sikerly she was of greet disport,
And ful plesaunt, and amiable of port,
And peyned hir to countrefete chere
Of court, and been estatlich of manere,
And to ben holden digne of reverence.
But, for to speken of hir conscience,
She was so charitable and so pitous,
She wolde wepe if that she sawe a mous
Caught in a trappe, if it were deed or bledde.
Of smale houndes had she, that she fedde
With rosted flesh, or milk and wastel-breed.
But sore weep she if oon of hem were deed,
Or if men smoot it with a yerde smerte:
And al was conscience and tendre herte.
Ful semely hir wimpel pinched was;
Hir nose tretys; [4] hir eyen greye as glas;
Hir mouth ful smal, and ther-to softe and reed;
But sikerly she hadde a fair forheed;

[3] *He wore a short coat of coarse material soiled with his chain-armor.*

[4] Well-shaped.

It was almost a spanne brood, I trowe;
For, hardily, she was nat undergrowe.
Ful fetis was hir cloke, as I was war.
Of smal coral aboute hir arm she bar
A peire of bedes gauded al with grene;
And ther-on heng a broche of gold ful shene,
On which there was first write a crowned A,
And after, *Amor vincit omnia.*

✦

A Monk ther was, a fair for the maistrye,
An out-rydere, that lovede venerye; [5]
A manly man, to been an abbot able.
Ful many a deyntee hors hadde he in stable:
And whan he rood men mighte his brydel here
Ginglen in a whistling wind as clere,
And eek as loude as dooth the chapel-belle,
Ther-as this lord was keper of the celle.
The reule of seint Maure or of seint Beneit,
By-cause that it was old and som-del streit,
This ilke monk leet olde thinges pace,
And held after the newe world the space.
He yaf nat of that text a pulled hen,
That seith that hunters been nat holy men;
Ne that a monk, whan he is recchelees,
Is lykned til a fish that is waterlees;
This is to seyn, a monk out of his cloistre.
But thilke text held he nat worth an oistre.
And I seyde his opinioun was good.
What sholde he studie, and make him-selven wood,
Upon a book in cloistre alwey to poure,
Or swinken with his handes, and laboure,
As Austin bit? How shal the world be served?
Lat Austin have his swink to him reserved.
Therfore he was a pricasour [6] aright;
Grehoundes he hadde, as swifte as fowel in flight;
Of priking and of hunting for the hare
Was al his lust, for no cost wolde he spare.
I seigh his sleves purfiléd at the hond
With grys, and that the fyneste of a lond;
And, for to festne his hood under his chin,
He hadde of gold y-wroght a curious pin:
A love-knotte in the gretter ende ther was.
His heed was balled, that shoon as any glas,
And eek his face, as he had been anoint.
He was a lord ful fat and in good point;
His eyen stepe, and rollinge in his heed,
That stemed as a forneys of a leed;
His botes souple, his hors in greet estat.
Now certeinly he was a fair prelat;
He was nat pale as a for-pyned goost.
A fat swan loved he best of any roost.
His palfrey was as broun as is a berye.

A Frere ther was, a wantown and a merye,
A limitour, a ful solempne man.
In alle the ordres foure is noon that can
So muche of daliaunce and fair langage.
He hadde maad ful many a mariage
Of yonge wommen, at his owne cost.
Un-to his ordre he was a noble post.
Ful wel biloved and famulier was he
With frankeleyns over-al in his contree,
And eek with worthy wommen of the toun:
For he had power of confessioun,
As seyde him-self, more than a curat,
For of his ordre he was licentiat.
Ful swetely herde he confessioun,
And plesaunt was his absolucioun;
He was an esy man to yeve penaunce
Ther as he wiste to han a good pitaunce;
For unto a povre ordre for to yive
Is signe that a man is wel y-shrive.
For if he yaf, he dorste make avaunt,
He wiste that a man was repentaunt.
For many a man so hard is of his herte,
He may nat wepe al-thogh him sore smerte.
Therfore, in stede of weping and preyeres,
Men moot yeve silver to the povre freres.
His tipet was ay farsed ful of knyves
And pinnes, for to yeven faire wyves.
And certeinly he hadde a mery note;
Wel coude he singe and pleyen on a rote.[7]
Of yeddinges [8] he bar utterly the prys.
His nekke whyt was as the flour-de-lys;
Ther-to he strong was as a champioun.
He knew the tavernes wel in every toun,
And everich hostiler and tappestere
Bet than a lazar or a beggestere,
For un-to swich a worthy man as he
Acorded nat, as by his facultee,
To have with seke lazars aqueyntaunce.
It is nat honest, it may nat avaunce
For to delen with no swich poraille,
But al with riche and sellers of vitaille.

[5] Hunting.
[6] Hard rider.
[7] Fiddle.
[8] Proverbs.

And over-al, ther as profit sholde aryse,
Curteys he was, and lowly of servyse.
Ther nas no man no-where so vertuous.
He was the beste beggere in his hous;
And yaf a certeyn ferme for the graunt;
Noon of his bretheren cam ther in his haunt;
For thogh a widwe hadde noght a sho,
So plesaunt was his *"In principio,"*
Yet wolde he have a ferthing, er he wente.
His purchas was wel bettre than his rente.
And rage he coude, as it were right a whelpe.
In love-dayes ther coude he muchel helpe.
For there he was nat lyk a cloisterer,
With a thredbar cope, as is a povre scoler,
But he was lyk a maister or a pope.
Of double worsted was his semi-cope,
That rounded as a belle out of the presse.
Somwhat he lipsed, for his wantownesse,
To make his English swete up-on his tonge;
And in his harping, whan that he had songe,
His eyen twinkled in his heed aright,
As doon the sterres in the frosty night.
This worthy limitour was cleped Huberd.
  A MARCHANT was ther with a forked berd,
In mottelee, and hye on horse he sat,
Up-on his heed a Flaundrish bever hat;
His botes clasped faire and fetisly.
His resons he spak ful solempnely,
Souninge alway th'encrees of his winning.
He wolde the see were kept for any thing
Bitwixe Middelburgh and Orewelle.
Wel coude he in eschaunge sheeldes selle.
This worthy man ful wel his wit bisette;
Ther wiste no wight that he was in dette,
So estatly was he of his governaunce,
With his bargaynes, and with his chevisaunce.[9]
For sothe he was a worthy man with-alle,
But sooth to seyn, I noot how men him calle.
  A CLERK ther was of Oxenford also,
That un-to logik hadde longe y-go.
As lene was his hors as is a rake,
And he nas nat right fat, I undertake;
But loked holwe, and ther-to soberly.
Ful thredbar was his overest courtepy;
For he had geten him yet no benefyce,
Ne was so worldly for to have offyce.
For him was lever have at his beddes heed
Twenty bokes, clad in blak or reed,
Of Aristotle and his philosophye,
Than robes riche, or fithele, or gay sautrye.
But al be that he was a philosophre,
Yet hadde he but litel gold in cofre;
But al that he mighte of his freendes hente,
On bokes and on lerninge he it spente,
And bisily gan for the soules preye
Of hem that yaf him wher-with to scoleye.
Of studie took he most cure and most hede.
Noght o word spak he more than was nede,
And that was seyd in forme and reverence,
And short and quik, and ful of hy sentence.
Souninge in moral vertu was his speche,
And gladly wolde he learne, and glady teche.

✦

  With us ther was a DOCTOUR OF PHISYK,
In al this world ne was ther noon him lyk
To speke of phisik and of surgerye;
For he was grounded in astronomye.
He kepte his pacient a ful greet del
In houres, by his magik naturel.
Wel coude he fortunen the ascendent
Of his images for his pacient.
He knew the cause of everich maladye,
Were it of hoot or cold, or moiste, or drye,
And where engendred, and of what humour;
He was a verrey parfit practisour.
The cause y-knowe, and of his harm the rote,
Anon he yaf the seke man his bote.
Ful redy hadde he his apothecaries,
To sende him drogges and his letuaries,[10]
For ech of hem made other for to winne;
Hir frendschipe nas nat newe to biginne.
Wel knew he th'olde Esculapius,
And Deiscorides, and eek Rufus,
Old Ypocras, Haly, and Galien;
Serapion, Razis, and Avicen;
Averrois, Damascien, and Constantyn;
Bernard, and Gatesden, and Gilbertyn.
Of his diete mesurable was he,
For it was of no superfluitee,
But of greet norissing and digestible.
His studie was but litel on the Bible.
In sangwin and in pers he clad was al,
Lyned with taffata and with sendal;
And yet he was but esy of dispence;
He kepte that he wan in pestilence.
For gold in phisik is a cordial,
Therfore he lovede gold in special.
  A good WYF was ther of bisyde BATHE,

[9] Borrowings.

[10] Medical syrups.

But she was som-del deef, and that was scathe.
Of clooth-making she hadde swiche an haunt,
She passed hem of Ypres and of Gaunt.
In all the parisshe wyf ne was ther noon
That to th' offring bifore hir sholde goon;
And if ther dide, certeyn, so wrooth was she,
That she was out of alle charitee.
Hir coverchiefs ful fyne were of ground;
I dorste swere they weyeden ten pound
That on a Sonday were upon hir heed.
Hir hosen weren of fyn scarlet reed,
Ful streite y-teyd, and shoos ful moiste and newe.
Bold was hir face, and fair, and reed of hewe.
She was a worthy womman al hir lyve,
Housbondes at chirche-dore she hadde fyve,
Withouten other companye in youthe;
But therof nedeth nat to speke as nouthe.
And thryes hadde she been at Jerusalem;
She hadde passed many a straunge streem;
At Rome she hadde been, and at Boloigne,
In Galice at seint Jame, and at Coloigne.
She coude muche of wandring by the weye:
Gat-tothed was she, soothly for to seye.
Up-on an amblere esily she sat,
Y-wimpled wel, and on hir heed an hat
As brood as is a bokeler or a targe;
A foot-mantel aboute hir hipes large,
And on hir feet a paire of spores sharpe.
In felawschip wel coude she laughe and carpe.
Of remedyes of love she knew perchaunce,
For she coude of that art the olde daunce.

A good man was ther of religioun,
And was a povre Persoun of a toun;
But riche he was of holy thoght and werk.
He was also a lerned man, a clerk,
That Cristes gospel trewely wolde preche;
His parisshens devoutly wolde he teche.
Benigne he was, and wonder diligent,
And in adversitee ful pacient;
And swich he was y-preved ofte sythes.
Ful looth were him to cursen for his tythes,
But rather wolde he yeven, out of doute,
Un-to his povre parisshens aboute
Of his offring, and eek of his substaunce.
He coude in litel thing han suffisaunce.
Wyd was his parisshe, and houses fer asonder,
But he ne lafte nat, for reyn ne thonder,
In siknes nor in meschief, to visyte
The ferreste in his parisshe, muche and lyte,[11]
Up-on his feet, and in his hand a staf.
This noble ensample to his sheep he yaf,
That first he wroghte, and afterward he taughte;
Out of the gospel he tho wordes caughte;
And this figure he added eek ther-to,
That if gold ruste, what shal iren do?
For if a preest be foul, on whom we truste,
No wonder is a lewed man to ruste;
And shame it is, if a preest take keep,
A shiten shepherde and a clene sheep.
Wel oghte a preest ensample for to yive,
By his clennesse, how that his sheep shold live.
He sette nat his benefice to hyre,
And leet his sheep encombred in the myre,
And ran to London, un-to sëynt Poules,
To seken him a chaunterie for soules,
Or with a bretherhed to been withholde;
But dwelte at hoom, and kepte wel his folde,
So that the wolf ne made it nat miscarie;
He was a shepherde and no mercenarie.
And though he holy were, and vertuous,
He was to sinful man nat despitous,
Ne of his speche daungerous ne digne,
But in his teching discreet and benigne.
To drawen folk to heven by fairnesse
By good ensample, was his bisinesse:
But it were any persone obstinat,
What-so he were, of heigh or lowe estat,
Him wolde he snibben sharply for the nones.
A bettre preest, I trowe that nowher noon is.
He wayted after no pompe and reverence,
Ne maked him a spyced conscience,
But Cristes lore, and his apostles twelve,
He taughte, and first he folwed it him-selve.

✦

With him ther rood a gentil Pardoner
Of Rouncival, his freend and his compeer,
That streight was comen fro the court of Rome.
Ful loude he song, "Com hider, love, to me."
This somnour bar to him a stif burdoun,
Was never trompe of half so greet a soun.
This pardoner hadde heer as yelow as wex,
But smothe it heng, as dooth a strike of flex;

[11] Great and small.

By ounces [12] henge his lokkes that he hadde,
And ther-with he his shuldres over-spradde;
But thinne it lay, by colpons [12] oon and oon;
But hood, for jolitee, ne wered he noon,
For it was trussed up in his walet.
Him thoughte, he rood al of the newe jet;
Dischevele, save his cappe, he rood al bare.
Swiche glaringe eyen hadde he as an hare.
A vernicle hadde he sowed on his cappe.
His walet lay biforn him in his lappe,
Bret-ful of pardoun come from Rome al hoot.
A voys he hadde as smal as hath a goot.
No berd hadde he, ne never sholde have,
As smothe it was as it were late y-shave;
I trowe he were a gelding or a mare.
But of his craft, fro Berwik into Ware,
Ne was ther swich another pardoner.
For in his male he hadde a pilwe-beer,
Which that, he seyde, was our lady veyl:
He seyde, he hadde a gobet of the seyl
That sëynt Peter hadde, whan that he wente
Up-on the see, til Jesu Crist him hente.
He hadde a croys of latoun, ful of stones,
And in a glas he hadde pigges bones.
But with thise relikes, whan that he fond
A povre person dwelling up-on lond,
Up-on a day he gat him more moneye
Than that the person gat in monthes tweye.
And thus, with feyned flaterye and japes,
He made the person and the peple his apes.
But trewely to tellen, atte laste,
He was in chirche a noble ecclesiaste.
Wel coude he rede a lessoun or a storie,
But alderbest he song an offertorie;
For wel he wiste, whan that song was songe,
He moste preche, and wel affyle his tonge,
To winne silver, as he ful wel coude;
Therefore he song so meriely and loude.

[12] Small bunches.

In the gallery of poetic portraits, some are studies of types, some are creatures of the imagination, some are taken from people seen in daily life; others are actual historical personages interpreted through the eye of the imagination. In our own day two poets have perfected two memorable—and two utterly different—portraits of the ineffectual dreamer: the half-humorous, half-pathetic failure in E. A. Robinson's "Miniver Cheevy" and the maladjusted escapist in T. S. Eliot's "The Love Song of J. Alfred Prufrock." Their affirmative opposites may be found in the pages of poets not usually accused of undue optimism; notably in Edgar Lee Masters' "Lucinda Matlock" and Robert Frost's "A Hundred Collars."

W. E. Henley's "In Hospital" is a set of sharp and delicate etchings, realistic and illuminating in intimate detail. "Visitor" and "Staff-Nurse: Old Style" depict the bearing and background of two opposed types of hospital women and, in their very contrast, present a skillfully balanced pair of sonnets. "Apparition" in the same sequence is a better portrait of Robert Louis Stevenson than any of the familiar photographs; his character as well as his lineaments are revealed in such lines as

> Most vain, most generous, sternly critical,
> Buffoon and poet, lover and sensualist:
> A deal of Ariel, just a streak of Puck,
> Much Antony, of Hamlet most of all,
> And something of the Shorter-Catechist.

VISITOR

Her little face is like a walnut shell
With wrinkling lines; her soft, white hair adorns
Her withered brows in quaint, straight curls, like horns;

And all about her clings an old, sweet smell.
Prim is her gown and quakerlike her shawl.
Well might her bonnets have been born on her.
Can you conceive a Fairy Godmother
The subject of a strong religious call?
In snow or shine, from bed to bed she runs,
All twinkling smiles and texts and pious tales,
Her mittened hands, that ever give or pray,
Bearing a sheaf of tracts, a bag of buns;
A wee old maid that sweeps the Bridegroom's way,
Strong in a cheerful trust that never fails.
—*William Ernest Henley* (1849-1903)

STAFF-NURSE: OLD STYLE

The greater masters of the commonplace,
Rembrandt and good Sir Walter—only these
Could paint her all to you: experienced ease
And antique liveliness and ponderous grace;
The sweet old roses of her sunken face;
The depth and malice of her sly, grey eyes;
The broad Scots tongue that flatters, scolds, defies;
The thick Scots wit that fells you like a mace.
These thirty years has she been nursing here,
Some of them under Syme, her hero still.
Much is she worth, and even more is made of her.
Patients and students hold her very dear.
The doctors love her, tease her, use her skill.
They say 'The Chief' himself is half-afraid of her.
—*William Ernest Henley* (1849-1903)

Among the figures in American history, none has inspired the poets more than Lincoln; in the personality poems of the past, Jesus has been the central figure. The two poetic sketches of Lincoln which follow are congruous though different.

LINCOLN, THE MAN OF THE PEOPLE

by Edwin Markham (1852-)

When the Norn Mother saw the Whirlwind Hour
Greatening and darkening as it hurried on,
She left the Heaven of Heroes and came down
To make a man to meet the mortal need.
She took the tried clay of the common road—
Clay warm yet with the genial heat of Earth,
Dasht through it all a strain of prophecy,
Tempered the heap with thrill of human tears,
Then mixt a laughter with the serious stuff.
Into the shape she breathed a flame to light
That tender, tragic, ever-changing face;
And laid on him a sense of the Mystic Powers,
Moving—all husht—behind the mortal veil.

Here was a man to hold against the world,
A man to match the mountains and the sea.

The color of the ground was in him, the red earth;
The smack and tang of elemental things:
The rectitude and patience of the cliff,
The good-will of the rain that loves all leaves,
The friendly welcome of the wayside well,
The courage of the bird that dares the sea,
The gladness of the wind that shakes the corn,
The pity of the snow that hides all scars,
The secrecy of streams that make their way
Under the mountain to the rifted rock,
The tolerance and equity of light
That gives as freely to the shrinking flower
As to the great oak flaring to the wind—
To the grave's low hill as to the Matterhorn
That shoulders out the sky. Sprung from the West,
He drank the valorous youth of a new world.
The strength of virgin forests braced his mind,
The hush of spacious prairies stilled his soul.
His words were oaks in acorns; and his thoughts
Were roots that firmly gript the granite truth.

Up from log cabin to the Capitol,
One fire was on his spirit, one resolve—
To send the keen ax to the root of wrong,
Clearing a free way for the feet of God,
The eyes of conscience testing every stroke,
To make his deed the measure of a man.
He built the rail-pile as he built the State,
Pouring his splendid strength through every blow:
The grip that swung the ax in Illinois
Was on the pen that set a people free.

So came the Captain with the mighty heart;
And when the judgment thunders split the house,
Wrenching the rafters from their ancient rest,
He held the ridgepole up, and spikt again
The rafters of the Home. He held his place—
Held the long purpose like a growing tree—
Held on through blame and faltered not at praise—
Towering in calm rough-hewn sublimity.
And when he fell in whirlwind, he went down
As when a lordly cedar, green with boughs,
Goes down with a great shout upon the hills,
And leaves a lonesome place against the sky.

THE MASTER

Lincoln as He Appeared to One Soon After the Civil War

by Edwin Arlington Robinson (1869-)

A flying word from here and there
Had sown the name at which we sneered,
But soon the name was everywhere,
To be reviled and then revered—
A presence to be loved and feared,
We cannot hide it, or deny
That we, the gentlemen who jeered,
May be forgotten by and by.

He came when days were perilous
And hearts of men were sore beguiled;
And having made his note of us,
He pondered and was reconciled.
Was ever master yet so mild
As he, and so untamable?
We doubted, even when he smiled,
Not knowing what he knew so well.

He knew that undeceiving fate
Would shame us whom he served unsought;
He knew that he must wince and wait—
The jest of those for whom he fought;
He knew devoutly what he thought
Of us and of our ridicule;
He knew that we must all be taught
Like little children in a school.

We gave a glamour to the task
That he encountered and saw through;
But little of us did he ask,
And little did we ever do.
And what appears if we review
The season when we railed and chaffed?—
It is the face of one who knew
That we were learning while we laughed.

The face that in our vision feels
Again the venom that we flung.
Transfigured, to the world reveals
The vigilance to which we clung.
Shrewd, hallowed, harassed, and among
The mysteries that are untold—
The face we see was never young,
Nor could it wholly have been old.

For he, to whom we had applied
Our shopman's test of age and worth,
Was elemental when he died,
As he was ancient at his birth.
The saddest among kings of earth,
Bowed with a galling crown, this man
Met rancor with a cryptic mirth,
Laconic—and Olympian.

The love, the grandeur, and the fame
Are bounded by the world alone;
The calm, the smoldering, and the flame
Of awful patience were his own;
With him they are forever flown
Past all our fond self-shadowings,
Wherewith we cumber the Unknown
As with inept, Icarian wings.

For we were not as other men;
'Twas ours to soar and his to see.
But we are coming down again,
And we shall come down pleasantly;
Nor shall we longer disagree
On what it is to be sublime,
But flourish in our perigee
And have one Titan at a time.

Poetic portraits, especially portraits of the spirit, are revealed more swiftly by suggestion than by direct delineation. The naïve wonder and divine irreverence which characterize America's greatest woman poet are suggested in the following poem which depicts Emily Dickinson's entrance into Heaven.

FOR EMILY DICKINSON

by Hortense Landauer (1911-)

The gates were triple adamant,
The sapphire walls were seven,
Where I saw Emily's lightfoot ghost
Slip into Milton's heaven.

On the dimity apron round her waist
Were folded her narrow hands,
The Cherubim and the Seraphim stood
In massy luminous bands.

The Principalities and the Powers,
Dominions, Virtues, Thrones,

The Angels and Archangels viewed
Her small and spectral bones.

As she cast one look at the far-below world
Swung on a golden chain,
And over her valorous brow there passed
An unimmortal pain.

The Powers and Dominions flew
In cautious orbits round
The throne where their Creator sat
With flame excessive crowned;

The Cherubim and the Seraphim
Veiled their celestial gaze,
With both their wings they shunned the sight
Of His effulgent blaze.

But plucking her dimity apron straight
And setting her collar right,
Emily took three confident steps
Up to the Core of Light.

Through the terrible nimbus of His throne
Three confident steps she trod,
Till sheer in His presence Emily stood,
Framed in the Glory of God,

And where the Angels were bowing blind
She widened imperative eyes
That made beyond predestined bliss
Insatiable surmise.

SUGGESTIONS FOR ADDITIONAL READING

POEMS OF COMEDY AND SATIRE

Alexander Pope, *The Rape of the Lock*
William Cowper, *The Diverting History of John Gilpin*
Robert Burns, *Holy Willie's Prayer*
Robert Burns, *Death and Doctor Hornbook*
Lord Byron, *Don Juan*
Bret Harte, *Plain Language from Truthful James*
Lewis Carroll, *The Hunting of the Snark*
James Laver, *A Stitch in Time*

POEMS OF TRAGEDY

Geoffrey Chaucer, *The Pardoner's Tale*
William Wordsworth, *Michael*
Walter Scott, *Rosabelle*
Matthew Arnold, *Sohrab and Rustum*
Jean Ingelow, *High Tide on the Coast of Lincolnshire*
H. W. Longfellow, *The Wreck of the Hesperus*
Sidney Lanier, *The Revenge of Hamish*
Bayard Taylor, *The Fight of Paso Del Mar*
William Vaughn Moody, *The Death of Eve*
Ralph Hodgson, *The Bull*
Stephen Vincent Benét, *John Brown's Body*
E. A. Robinson, *Tristram*
John G. Neihardt, *The Song of Three Friends*
Robinson Jeffers, *Cawdor*

DRAMATIC MONOLOGUES

Alfred, Lord Tennyson, *Northern Farmer, Old Style*
Matthew Arnold, *The Forsaken Merman*
Dante Gabriel Rossetti, *The King's Tragedy*
Robert Browning, *Abt Vogler*
Robert Browning, *Fra Lippo Lippi*
Robert Browning, *The Bishop Orders His Tomb in St. Praxed's Church*
George Meredith, *Last Words of Juggling Jerry*
Edgar Allan Poe, *The Raven*
Edgar Allan Poe, *For Annie*
Amy Lowell, *Patterns*
Amy Lowell, *Number 3 on the Docket*
Charlotte Mew, *Madeleine in Church*
John Masefield, *The Everlasting Mercy*
Sara Teasdale, *Helen of Troy*
E. A. Robinson, *Poor Relation*

PORTRAIT POEMS

Robert Burns, *The Cotter's Saturday Night*
Mackworth Praed, *The Vicar*
Robert Browning, *The Grammarian's Funeral*

W. E. Henley, *House-Surgeon*
W. E. Henley, *Etching*
W. E. Henley, *Back-View*
James Russell Lowell, *The Courtin'*
Thomas Hardy, *In the Servants' Quarters*
Walter de la Mare, *Old Susan*
William Vaughn Moody, *The Daguerreotype*
Witter Bynner, *A Farmer Remembers Lincoln*
E. A. Robinson, *Ben Jonson Entertains a Man from Stratford*
E. A. Robinson, *Richard Cory*
E. A. Robinson, *Miniver Cheevy*
E. A. Robinson, *Flammonde*
E. L. Masters, *Spoon River Anthology*
Robert Frost, *Mending Wall*
Robert Frost, *An Old Man's Winter Night*
Robert Frost, *Home Burial*
John Masefield, *Reynard the Fox*
John Masefield, *The Everlasting Mercy*
T. S. Eliot, *The Love Song of J. Alfred Prufrock*
T. S. Eliot, *Portrait of a Lady*

7

THE EMOTIONS OF POETRY—1: THE HUMAN PROBLEMS

TOLSTOI once remarked that art was at its highest when it produced the greatest effect with the least apparent effort. The effect of which he was thinking was chiefly emotional; throughout the ages man has measured art by its power to arouse the feelings. Aristotle and Quintilian, those ancient and dependable authorities on writing, state that the purpose of writing is to inform, to please, to move. If we consider pleasure a form of emotion, this might be simplified to a dual purpose: to inform or to arouse. Thomas De Quincey distinguishes the two types as the "literature of knowledge" and the "literature of power." If we ask ourselves which of the two constitutes the greater literature, we should agree that a scientific treatise has very little chance of becoming "literature," since it makes little or no appeal to the emotions. There are, of course, exceptions, such as Charles Darwin's *Origin of Species* and Sir Isaac Newton's *Principia,* but they are none too frequent.

Since the emotional content of literature is all-important, it is essential that we, as readers or creators, should appraise the kinds of emotion we are likely to meet. Fortunately for the reader, the emotions of literature are not the same as those of life; that is, they are not as real, not, let us hope, as poignant. For in reading the bitterest tragedy of broken hearts and ruined lives there is the possibility of great pleasure. This ability to gain pleasure from the contemplation of pain is bound up in the very nature of poetry; the poet must separate himself from his emotion in order that he may express it, must view it objectively, must depersonalize it. In this process there is no need that the reality of the emotion should disappear; the poet merely turns from feeling to expression, from experience to communication, in order that even life's most unpleasant moments can be transmuted into pleasant form. It is what the psychologists have termed "sublimation." William Wordsworth has said this very effectively:

> I have said that poetry is the spontaneous overflow of powerful feelings: it takes its origin from emotion recollected in tranquillity: the emotion is contemplated till, by a species of reaction, the tranquillity gradually disappears, and an emotion, kindred to that which was before the subject of contemplation, is gradually produced, and does itself actually exist in the mind. In this mood successful composition generally begins, and in a mood similar to this it is carried on; but the emotion, of whatever kind, and in whatever degree, from various causes, is qualified by various

pleasures, so that in describing any passions whatsoever, which are voluntarily described, the mind will, upon the whole, be in a state of enjoyment.

We have so far been considering the emotions as those of the author and the reader. What of the emotions of the characters in literature? Shakespeare, the most varied of emotional poets, a writer who peopled a universe, rarely, except possibly in his sonnets, expressed an emotion which can be labeled his own. Herein lies the difference between lyric and dramatic poetry, and out of it grow two sets of standards by which we may judge poetic emotions. If the poet is expressing his own emotions, we may justly demand of him sincerity, true emotion rather than the pose and exaggeration of sentimentality. We find this false emotion, this debasing and distortion of sentiment in Pollyanna, the "glad girl," or in the youth who is "in love with love." In life it may have some place, but in art it has none. The only safe standard in dramatic poetry is that of consistency—the emotions should fit the character to whom they are given; if the character dissembles emotion, as Iago does, we must know it.

The range of human emotions is seemingly illimitable. Man goes from the lighter sentiments of Burns's "Cotter's Saturday Night" and Longfellow's "Children's Hour" through the shaken grief of Tennyson's "Break, break, break," or the proud power of Carl Sandburg's "Chicago" to the towering passions of Shelley's "Adonais" or Shakespeare's tempestuous climaxes in *Othello* and *Macbeth.* The poet rises in the scale from the physical reactions to bodily stimuli, through the individualized, personal desires, to the joys of contemplating the ideal, the whole process being clearly revealed in Browning's "Saul," as David mounts a ladder of music to the skies.

In attempting to classify emotions, psychologists and critics have met with the inevitable difficulty of fitting names to the inner states of a billion individuals, no two of them precisely alike. John Ruskin said that the great writer deals only with the "noble" emotions of Love, Veneration, Admiration, and Joy, with their counterparts, Hate, Indignation, Horror, and Grief. But between and beyond these limits are a hundred or more shades and variations, all of them legitimate material for the poet. A man's feelings for a woman may grow from indifference through attraction, geniality, sympathy or pity, to approval, trust and liking, whence they may develop through tenderness, affection, devotion and desire into love and passionate attachment—or back again to indifference. A man's attitude toward his enemies can change from apathy to annoyance, and thence through distrust, dislike, envy, disdain, rebellion, disgust, loathing and execration, to hate, vituperation, and terrible revenge.

It is with our other emotions as with these two: we may run the gamut from top to bottom. Our emotions toward divinity may develop from unconcern through gratitude and reverence, to complete adoration; or, in the other direction from the mid-point of lack of interest, we may view the world and its ways with distaste and irritation, finally to arrive at the extremes of anger or a completely negative pessimism. Our reactions toward the beauties of nature may rise from complacency through appreciation and excitement to wonder; toward some of nature's cruelties we may rise from this same complacency through alarm and agony to the limit of horror. In our search for success our feelings may grow from carelessness to courage and joy to the very peak of exultation; or, if our security fails and evil days come upon us, we may ascend past uncertainty and disappointment to stoicism, or we may continue downward through defeat, desperation and, at last, black despair. Some psychologists would confine emotions to love and fear, but even the differentiations made here do not account for pride, gluttony, the lusts of the flesh, which Ruskin would eliminate from the realm of art as ignoble. From Aeschylus to O'Neill, however, the drama has been filled with evocations of these very "ignoble" emotions.

The mathematical mind might enjoy contemplating the endless permutations and combinations of these emotions open to the creative artist. For the artist and reader, however, the major problem is: How can these emotions be expressed? The dramatist can leave much to the facial expression and gestures of the actors. The novelist can analyze at length every indecision, every emotional disturbance. But the poet, except in narrative poetry, has only three ways of communicating his emotion to the reader. The first method is by direct statement. The second is by the use of sensory images; emotions are more powerfully transmitted by pictures than by abstract concepts. Wordsworth's

> And then my heart with pleasure fills
> And dances with the daffodils,

is infinitely more stimulating than "A sense of exaltation has taken possession of me." For a third method, the poet can use associations. Emotions cluster about symbols—a spire, a bird, a banner, a cross, a work of art—and can be evoked by their allusions. Because the poet's first duty is to clarify his emotion, he must be painstaking in his choice of words; Wordsworth felt that the simpler the language, the more universal and enduring the appeal. The involved emotional conceits of Donne and "the metaphysical school" have never won great audiences because their complexities are unrelated to the lives and longings of most readers.

Poets are not only the recorders of their Age, but the reflectors of the feelings which dominate it; nothing is more illuminating than the intensity and range of their emotions. Some, we find, harp upon the same string; others, like Browning, seem never to repeat a note. Poe tells us we cannot sustain strong emotions for more than a hundred lines; Milton piles them up throughout a whole epic.

For ease of study, let us consider the emotions of poetry under the headings of Love and Hate, Joy and Sorrow, Admiration of Nature and Art. Awe of the Universe and the Adoration of God, as well as the fear of Death, come so close to philosophy that they may well be treated in another chapter; Anger and Condemnation will be found in the section on Satire.

LOVE

The love of one human being for another has probably brought forth more lyric verse than all other emotions combined. "The way of a man with a maid" is poetry's most ardent theme—a theme with countless burning variations. It is interesting to speculate upon how many of these passionate terms were genuinely felt and how many were merely conventions and affectations. The differences between the sensuous love of Rossetti and the idealized love of Wordsworth, between the light lyricism of Philip Sidney or the polished compliments of Ben Jonson and the intense devotion of Elizabeth Barrett Browning or the impassioned suffering of Emily Dickinson, between the romantic treatment of Tennyson and the rebellious realism of Donne, make this a theme of unlimited possibilities. Many poets are unable to express their feelings for their beloved without revealing their attitude toward the rest of the world. The poems which follow in this group are arranged in general chronological order. Though the expression has altered, though fashions in form have changed, the language of love is much the same now as it was three centuries ago.

EPITHALAMION

by Edmund Spenser (1552-1599)

Ye learnéd sisters, which have oftentimes
Beene to me ayding, others to adorne,
Whom ye thought worthy of your gracefull rymes,
That even the greatest did not greatly scorne
To heare theyr names sung in your simple layes,
But joyéd in theyr praise;
And when ye list your owne mishaps to mourne,
Which death, or love, or fortunes wreck did rayse,
Your string could soone to sadder tenor turne,
And teach the woods and waters to lament
Your dolefull dreriment:
Now lay those sorrowful complaints aside,
And having all your heads with girlands crownd,
Helpe me mine owne loves prayses to resound;
Ne let the same of any be envide:
So Orpheus did for his owne bride:
So I unto my selfe alone will sing;
The woods shall to me answer, and my eccho ring.

Early, before the worlds light-giving lampe
His golden beame upon the hils doth spred,
Having disperst the nights unchearefull dampe,
Doe ye awake, and, with fresh lustyhed,
Go to the bowre of my belovéd love,
My truest turtle dove:
Bid her awake; for Hymen is awake,
And long since ready forth his maske to move,
With his bright tead [1] that flames with many a flake,
And many a bachelor to waite on him,
In theyr fresh garments trim.
Bid her awake therefore, and soone her dight,
For lo! the wishéd day is come at last,
That shall, for al the paynes and sorrowes past,
Pay to her usury of long delight:
And whylest she doth her dight,
Doe ye to her of joy and solace sing,
That all the woods may answer, and your eccho ring.

Bring with you all the nymphes that you can heare,
Both of the rivers and the forrests greene,
And of the sea that neighbours to her neare.
Al with gay girlands goodly wel beseene.
And let them also with them bring in hand
Another gay girland,
For my fayre love, of lillyes and of roses,
Bound truelove wize with a blew silke riband.
And let them make great store of bridale poses,
And let them eeke bring store of other flowers,
To deck the bridale bowers.
And let the ground whereas her foot shall tread,
For feare the stones her tender foot should wrong,
Be strewed with fragrant flowers all along,

[1] Torch.

And diapred lyke the discolored mead.
Which done, doe at her chamber dore awayt,
For she will waken strayt;
The whiles doe ye this song unto her sing,
The woods shall to you answer, and your eccho ring.

Ye nymphes of Mulla, which with carefull heed
The silver scaly trouts doe tend full well,
And greedy pikes which use therein to feed,
(Those trouts and pikes all others doo excell)
And ye likewise which keepe the rushy lake,
Where none doo fishes take,
Bynd up the locks the which hang scatterd light,
And in his waters, which your mirror make,
Behold your faces as the christall bright,
That when you come whereas my love doth lie,
No blemish she may spie.
And eke ye lightfoot mayds which keepe the dere
That on the hoary mountayne used to towre,
And the wylde wolves, which seeke them to devoure,
With your steele darts doo chace from comming neer,
Be also present heere,
To helpe to decke her, and to help to sing,
That all the woods may answer, and your eccho ring.

Wake now, my love, awake! for it is time:
The rosy Morne long since left Tithones bed,
All ready to her silver coche to clyme,
And Phoebus gins to shew his glorious hed.
Hark! how the cheerefull birds do chaunt theyr laies,
And carroll of loves praise!
The merry larke hir mattins sings aloft,
The thrush replyes, the mavis descant playes,
The ouzell shrills, the ruddock [2] warbles soft,
So goodly all agree, with sweet consent,
To this dayes merriment.
Ah! my deere love, why doe ye sleepe thus long,
When meeter were that ye should now awake,
T'awayt the comming of your joyous make,
And hearken to the birds love-learnéd song,
The deawy leaves among?
For they of joy and pleasance to you sing,
That all the woods them answer, and theyr eccho ring.

My love is now awake out of her dreams,
And her fayre eyes, like stars that dimméd were
With darksome cloud, now shew theyr goodly beams
More bright then Hesperus his head doth rere.
Come now, ye damzels, daughters of delight,
Helpe quickly her to dight.
But first come ye, fayre Houres, which were begot,
In Joves sweet paradice, of Day and Night,
Which doe the seasons of the year allot,
And al that ever in this world is fayre
Do make and still repayre.
And ye three handmayds of the Cyprian Queene,
The which doe still addorne her beauties pride,
Helpe to addorne my beautifullest bride:
And as ye her array, still throw betweene
Some graces to be seene:
And as ye use to Venus, to her sing,
The whiles the woods shal answer, and your eccho ring.

Now is my love all ready forth to come:
Let all the virgins therefore well awayt,
And ye fresh boyes, that tend upon her groome,
Prepare your selves, for he is comming strayt.
Set all your things in seemely good aray,
Fit for so joyfull day,
The joyfulst day that ever sunne did see.
Faire Sun, shew forth thy favourable ray,
And let thy lifull heat not fervent be,
For feare of burning her sunshyny face,
Her beauty to disgrace.
O fayrest Phoebus, father of the Muse,
If ever I did honour thee aright,
Or sing the thing that mote [3] thy mind delight,
Doe not thy servants simple boone refuse,
But let this day, let this one day be myne,

[2] Redbreast.

[3] Might.

Let all the rest be thine.
Then I thy soverayne prayses loud wil sing,
That all the woods shal answer, and theyr eccho ring.

Harke how the minstrels gin to shrill aloud
Their merry musick that resounds from far,
The pipe, the tabor, and the trembling croud,[4]
That well agree withouten breach or jar,
But most of all the damzels doe delite,
When they their tymbrels smyte,
And thereunto doe daunce and carrol sweet,
That all the sences they doe ravish quite,
The whyles the boyes run up and downe the street,
Crying aloud with strong confuséd noyce,
As if it were one voyce.
'Hymen, Iö Hymen, Hymen,' they do shout,
That even to the heavens theyr shouting shrill
Doth reach, and all the firmament doth fill;
To which the people, standing all about,
As in approvance doe thereto applaud,
And loud advaunce her laud,
And evermore they 'Hymen, Hymen' sing,
That al the woods them answer, and theyr eccho ring.

Loe! where she comes along with portly pace,
Lyke Phoebe, from her chamber of the east,
Arysing forth to run her mighty race,
Clad all in white, that seemes a virgin best.
So well it her beseemes, that ye would weene
Some angell she had beene.
Her long loose yellow locks lyke golden wyre,
Sprinckled with perle, and perling flowres atweene,
Doe lyke a golden mantle her attyre,
And being crownéd with a girland greene,
Seeme lyke some mayden queene.
Her modest eyes, abashéd to behold
So many gazers as on her do stare,
Upon the lowly ground affixéd are;
Ne dare lift up her countenance too bold,
But blush to heare her prayses sung so loud,
So farre from being proud.
Nathlesse doe ye still loud her prayses sing,
That all the woods may answer, and your eccho ring.

Tell me, ye merchants daughters, did ye see
So fayre a creature in your towne before,
So sweet, so lovely, and so mild as she,
Adornd with beautyes grace and vertues store?
Her goodly eyes lyke saphyres shining bright,
Her forehead yvory white,
Her cheekes lyke apples which the sun hath rudded,
Her lips lyke cherryes charming men to byte,
Her brest like to a bowle of creame uncrudded,[5]
Her paps lyke lyllies budded,
Her snowie necke lyke to a marble towre,
And all her body like a pallace fayre,
Ascending uppe, with many a stately stayre,
To honours seat and chastities sweet bowre.
Why stand ye still, ye virgins, in amaze,
Upon her so to gaze,
Whiles ye forget your former lay to sing,
To which the woods did answer, and your eccho ring?

But if ye saw that which no eyes can see,
The inward beauty of her lively spright,
Garnisht with heavenly guifts of high degree,
Much more then would ye wonder at that sight,
And stand astonisht lyke to those which red
Medusaes mazeful hed.
There dwels sweet Love and constant Chastity,
Unspotted Fayth, and comely Womanhood,
Regard of Honour, and mild Modesty;
There Vertue raynes as queene in royal throne,
And giveth lawes alone,
The which the base affections doe obay,
And yeeld theyr services unto her will;
Ne thought of thing uncomely ever may
Thereto approch to tempt her mind to ill.
Had ye once seene these her celestial threasures,
And unrevealéd pleasures,
Then would ye wonder, and her prayses sing,
That al the woods should answer, and your eccho ring.

Open the temple gates unto my love,
Open them wide that she may enter in,

[4] Violin.

[5] Fresh, unchurned.

And all the postes adorne as doth behove,
And all the pillours deck with girlands trim,
For to receyve this saynt with honour dew,
That commeth in to you.
With trembling steps and humble reverence,
She commeth in before th' Almighties vew:
Of her, ye virgins, learne obedience,
When so ye come into those holy places,
To humble your proud faces.
Bring her up to th' high altar, that she may
The sacred ceremonies there partake,
The which do endlesse matrimony make;
And let the roring organs loudly play
The praises of the Lord in lively notes,
The whiles with hollow throates
The choristers the joyous antheme sing,
That al the woods may answer, and their eccho ring.

Behold, whiles she before the altar stands,
Hearing the holy priest that to her speakes,
And blesseth her with his two happy hands,
How the red roses flush up in her cheekes,
And the pure snow with goodly vermill stayne,
Like crimsin dyde in grayne:
That even th' angels, which continually
About the sacred altare doe remaine,
Forget their service and about her fly,
Ofte peeping in her face, that seemes more fayre,
The more they on it stare.
But her sad eyes, still fastened on the ground,
Are governéd with goodly modesty,
That suffers not one looke to glaunce awry,
Which may let in a little thought unsownd.
Why blush ye, love, to give to me your hand,
The pledge of all our band?
Sing, ye sweet angels, Alleluya sing,
That all the woods may answer, and your eccho ring.

Now al is done; bring home the bride againe,
Bring home the triumph of our victory,
Bring home with you the glory of her gaine,
With joyance bring her and with jollity.
Never had man more joyfull day then this,
Whom heaven would heape with blis.
Make feast therefore now all this live-long day;
This day for ever to me holy is;
Poure out the wine without restraint or stay,
Poure not by cups, but by the belly full,
Poure out to all that wull,
And sprinkle all the postes and wals with wine,
That they may sweat, and drunken be withall.
Crowne ye God Bacchus with a coronall.
And Hymen also crowne with wreathes of vine;
And let the Graces daunce unto the rest,
For they can doo it best:
The whiles the maydens doe theyr carroll sing,
The which the woods shal answer, and theyr eccho ring.

Ring ye the bels, ye yong men of the towne,
And leave your wonted labors for this day:
This day is holy; doe ye write it downe,
That ye for ever it remember may.
This day the sunne is in his chiefest hight,
With Barnaby the bright,
From whence declining daily by degrees,
He somewhat loseth of his heat and light,
When once the Crab behind his back he sees.
But for this time it ill ordainéd was,
To chose the longest day in all the yeare,
And shortest night, when longest fitter weare:
Yet never day so long, but late would passe.
Ring ye the bels, to make it weare away,
And bonefiers make all day,
And daunce about them, and about them sing:
That all the woods may answer, and your eccho ring.

Ah! when will this long weary day have end,
And lende me leave to come unto my love?
How slowly do the houres theyr numbers spend!
How slowly does sad Time his feathers move!
Hast thee, O fayrest planet, to thy home
Within the westerne fome:
Thy tyréd steedes long since have need of rest.
Long though it be, at last I see it gloome,
And the bright evening star with golden creast
Appeare out of the east.
Fayre childe of beauty, glorious lampe of love,

That all the host of heaven in rankes doost lead,
And guydest lovers through the nightés dread,
How chearefully thou lookest from above,
And seemst to laugh atweene thy twinkling light,
As joying in the sight
Of these glad many, which for joy doe sing,
That all the woods them answer, and their eccho ring!

Now ceasse, ye damsels, your delights forepast;
Enough is it that all the day was youres:
Now day is doen, and night is nighing fast:
Now bring the bryde into the brydall boures.
The night is come, now soone her disaray,
And in her bed her lay;
Lay her in lillies and in violets,
And silken courteins over her display,
And odourd sheetes, and Arras coverlets.
Behold how goodly my faire love does ly
In proud humility!
Like unto Maia, when as Jove her tooke
In Tempe, lying on the flowry gras,
Twixt sleepe and wake, after she weary was
With bathing in the Acidalian brooke.
Now it is night, ye damsels may be gon,
And leave my love alone,
And leave likewise your former lay to sing:
The woods no more shal answere, nor your eccho ring.

Now welcome, night! thou night so long expected,
That long daies labour doest at last defray,
And all my cares, which cruell Love collected,
Hast sumd in one, and cancelléd for aye:
Spread thy broad wing over my love and me,
That no man may us see,
And in thy sable mantle us enwrap,
From feare of perrill and foule horror free.
Let no false treason seeke us to entrap,
Nor any dread disquiet once annoy
The safety of our joy:
But let the night be calme and quietsome,
Without tempestuous storms or sad afray:
Lyke as when Jove with fayre Alcmena lay,
When he begot the great Tirynthian groome:
Or lyke as when he with thy selfe did lie,
And begot Majesty.
And let the mayds and yong men cease to sing:
Ne let the woods them answer, nor theyr eccho ring.

Let no lamenting cryes, nor dolefull teares,
Be heard all night within, nor yet without:
Ne let false whispers, breeding hidden feares,
Breake gentle sleepe with misconceivéd dout.
Let no deluding dreames, nor dreadful sights,
Make sudden sad affrights;
Ne let house-fyres, nor lightnings helplesse harmes,
Ne let the Pouke, nor other evill sprights,
Ne let mischivous witches with theyr charmes,
Ne let hob goblins, names whose sense we see not,
Fray us with things that be not.
Let not the shriech oule, nor the storke be heard,
Nor the night raven that still deadly yels,
Nor damnéd ghosts cald up with mighty spels,
Nor griesly vultures make us once affeard:
Ne let th' unpleasant quyre of frogs still croking
Make us to wish theyr choking.
Let none of these theyr drery accents sing;
Ne let the woods them answer, nor theyr eccho ring.

But let stil Silence trew night watches keepe,
That sacred Peace may in assurance rayne,
And tymely Sleep, when it is tyme to sleepe,
May poure his limbs forth on your pleasant playne,
The whiles an hundred little wingéd loves,
Like divers fethered doves,
Shall fly and flutter round about our bed,
And in the secret darke that none reproves,
Their prety stealthes shall worke, and snares shal spread
To filch away sweet snatches of delight,
Conceald through covert night.
Ye sonnes of Venus, play your sports at will:
For greedy Pleasure, careless of your toyes,
Thinks more upon her paradise of joyes,
Then what ye do, albe it good or ill.
All night therefore attend your merry play,
For it will soone be day:

Now none doth hinder you, that say or sing,
Ne will the woods now answer, nor your eccho ring.

Who is the same which at my window peepes?
Or whose is that faire face that shines so bright?
Is it not Cinthia, she that never sleepes,
But walkes about high heaven al the night?
O fayrest goddesse, do thou not envy
My love with me to spy:
For thou likewise didst love, though now unthought,
And for a fleece of woll, which privily
The Latmian shephard once unto thee brought,
His pleasures with thee wrought.
Therefore to us be favourable now;
And sith of wemens labours thou hast charge,
And generation goodly dost enlarge,
Encline thy will t' effect our wishfull vow,
And the chast wombe informe with timely seed,
That may our comfort breed:
Till which we cease our hopefull hap to sing,
Ne let the woods us answere, nor our eccho ring.

And thou, great Juno, which with awful might
The lawes of wedlock still dost patronize,
And the religion of the faith first plight
With sacred rites hast taught to solemnize,
And eeke for comfort often callēd art
Of women in their smart,
Eternally bind thou this lovely band,
And all thy blessings unto us impart.
And thou, glad Genius, in whose gentle hand
The bridale bowre and geniall bed remaine,
Without blemish or staine,
And the sweet pleasures of theyr loves delight
With secret ayde doest succour and supply,
Till they bring forth the fruitfull progeny,
Send us the timely fruit of this same night.
And thou, fayre Hebe, and thou, Hymen free,
Grant that it may so be.
Til which we cease your further prayse to sing,
Ne any woods shal answer, nor your eccho ring.

And ye high heavens, the temple of the gods,
In which a thousand torches flaming bright
Doe burne, that to us wretched earthly clods
In dreadful darknesse lend desirēd light,
And all ye powers which in the same remayne,
More than we men can fayne,
Poure out your blessing on us plentiously,
And happy influence upon us raine,
That we may raise a large posterity,
Which from the earth, which they may long possesse
With lasting happinesse,
Up to your haughty pallaces may mount,
And for the guerdon of theyr glorious merit,
May heavenly tabernacles there inherit,
Of blessēd saints for to increase the count.
So let us rest, sweet love, in hope of this,
And cease till then our tymely joyes to sing:
The woods no more us answer, nor our eccho ring.

Song, made in lieu of many ornaments
With which my love should duly have been dect,
Which cutting off through hasty accidents,
Ye would not stay your dew time to expect,
But promist both to recompens,
Be unto her a goodly ornament,
And for short time an endlesse moniment.

MY TRUE-LOVE HATH MY HEART

My true-love hath my heart, and I have his,
By just exchange one for the other given:
I hold his dear, and mine he cannot miss;
There never was a better bargain driven.
His heart in me keeps me and him in one,
My heart in him his thoughts and senses guides;
He loves my heart for once it was his own;
I cherish his because in me it bides.
His heart his wound receivèd from my sight;
My heart was wounded with his wounded heart;
For as from me on him his hurt did light,
So still methought in me his hurt did smart:

Both, equal hurt, in this change sought our bliss,
My true love hath my heart, and I have his.
—*Philip Sidney* (1554-1586)

THE PASSIONATE SHEPHERD TO HIS LOVE

Come live with me and be my Love,
And we will all the pleasures prove
That valleys, groves, hills, and fields,
Woods or steepy mountain yields.

And we will sit upon the rocks,
Seeing the shepherds feed their flocks
By shallow rivers, to whose falls
Melodious birds sing madrigals.

And I will make thee beds of roses
And a thousand fragrant posies;
A cap of flowers, and a kirtle
Embroidered all with leaves of myrtle;

A gown made of the finest wool
Which from our pretty lambs we pull;
Fair linéd slippers for the cold,
With buckles of the purest gold;

A belt of straw and ivy-buds
With coral clasps and amber studs—
And if these pleasures may thee move,
Come live with me and be my Love.

The shepherd swains shall dance and sing
For thy delight each May morning—
If these delights thy mind may move,
Then live with me and be my Love.
—*Christopher Marlowe* (1564-1593)

LOVE'S ETERNITY
Sonnet CXVI

Let me not to the marriage of true minds
Admit impediments. Love is not love
Which alters when it alteration finds,
Or bends with the remover to remove.
Oh, no! it is an ever-fixéd mark
That looks on tempests and is never shaken;
It is the star to every wandering bark,
Whose worth's unknown, although his height be taken.
Love's not Time's fool, though rosy lips and cheeks
Within his bending sickle's compass come;
Love alters not with his brief hours and weeks,
But bears it out even to the edge of doom.
If this be error and upon me proved,
I never writ, nor no man ever loved.
—*William Shakespeare* (1564-1616)

LOVE'S CONCESSION
Sonnet CXXX

My mistress' eyes are nothing like the sun;
Coral is far more red than her lips' red;
If snow be white, why then her breasts are dun;
If hairs be wires, black wires grow on her head.
I have seen roses damasked, red and white,
But no such roses see I in her cheeks;
And in some perfumes is there more delight
Than in the breath that from my mistress reeks.
I love to hear her speak, yet well I know
That music hath a far more pleasing sound;
I grant I never saw a goddess go;
My mistress, when she walks, treads on the ground:
And yet, by heaven, I think my love as rare
As any she belied with false compare.
—*William Shakespeare* (1564-1616)

SONG: TO CELIA

Drink to me only with thine eyes,
And I will pledge with mine;
Or leave a kiss but in the cup
And I'll not ask for wine.
The thirst that from the soul doth rise
Doth ask a drink divine;
But might I of Jove's nectar sup,
I would not change for thine.

I sent thee late a rosy wreath,
Not so much honoring thee
As giving it a hope that there
It could not withered be;
But thou thereon didst only breathe,
And sent'st it back to me:

Since when it grows, and smells, I swear,
  Not of itself but thee!
      —*Ben Jonson* (1573-1637)

LOVE ME NOT FOR COMELY GRACE

Love me not for comely grace,
For my pleasing eye or face,
Nor for any outward part,
No, nor for my constant heart,—
  For those may fail, or turn to ill,
    So thou and I shall sever:
Keep therefore a true woman's eye,
And love me still, but know not why—
  So hast thou the same reason still
    To doat upon me ever!
      —*Anonymous Elizabethan*

SONG

by John Donne (1573-1631)

Go and catch a falling star,
  Get with child a mandrake root,
Tell me where all past years are,
  Or who cleft the devil's foot;
Teach me to hear mermaids singing,
Or to keep off envy's stinging,
    And find
    What wind
Serves to advance an honest mind.

If thou be'st born to strange sights,
  Things invisible to see,
Ride ten thousand days and nights
  Till age snow white hairs on thee;
Thou, when thou return'st, wilt tell me
All strange wonders that befell thee,
    And swear
    No where
Lives a woman true and fair.

If thou find'st one, let me know;
  Such a pilgrimage were sweet.
Yet do not; I would not go,
  Though at next door we might meet.
Though she were true when you met her,
And last till you write your letter,
    Yet she
    Will be
False, ere I come, to two or three.

LOVE'S DEITY

by John Donne (1573-1631)

I long to talk with some old lover's ghost
  Who died before the god of love was born.
I cannot think that he who then loved most
  Sunk so low as to love one which did scorn.
But since this god produced a destiny
And that vice-nature, custom, lets it be,
  I must love her that loves not me.

Sure, they which made him god, meant not so much,
  Nor he in his young godhead practiced it.
But when an even flame two hearts did touch,
  His office was indulgently to fit
Actives to passives. Correspondency
Only his subject was; it cannot be
  Love till I love her who loves me.

But every modern god will now extend
  His vast prerogative as far as Jove;
To rage, to lust, to write to, to commend,
  All is the purlieu of the god of love.
O! were we wakened by this tyranny
To ungod this child again, it could not be
  I should love her who loves not me.

Rebel and atheist too, why murmur I,
  As though I felt the worst that love could do?
Love may make me leave loving, or might try
  A deeper plague, to make her love me too;
Which, since she loves before, I'm loath to see.
Falsehood is worse than hate; and that must be,
  If she whom I love, should love me.

TO ANTHEA, WHO MAY COMMAND HIM ANYTHING

Bid me to live, and I will live
  Thy protestant to be;
Or bid me love, and I will give
  A loving heart to thee.

A heart as soft, a heart as kind,
  A heart as sound and free

As in the whole world thou canst find,
  That heart I'll give to thee.

Bid that heart stay, and it will stay
  To honor thy decree:
Or bid it languish quite away,
  And't shall do so for thee.

Bid me to weep, and I will weep
  While I have eyes to see:
And, having none, yet will I keep
  A heart to weep for thee.

Bid me despair, and I'll despair
  Under that cypress tree:
Or bid me die, and I will dare
  E'en death, to die for thee.

—*Robert Herrick* (1591-1674)

SONG

Ask me no more where Jove bestows,
When June is past, the fading rose;
For in your beauty's orient deep
These flowers, as in their causes, sleep.

Ask me no more whither do stray
The golden atoms of the day;
For in pure love heaven did prepare
Those powders to enrich your hair.

Ask me no more whither doth haste
The nightingale when May is past;
For in your sweet, dividing throat
She winters and keeps warm her note.

Ask me no more where those stars 'light
That downwards fall in dead of night;
For in your eyes they sit, and there
Fixéd become as in their sphere.

Ask me no more if east or west
The phoenix builds her spicy nest;
For unto you at last she flies,
And in your fragrant bosom dies.

—*Thomas Carew* (1598-1639)

HAST THOU SEEN THE DOWN IN THE AIR?

Hast thou seen the down in the air,
When wanton blasts have tossed it?
Or the ship on the sea,
When ruder winds have crossed it?
Hast thou marked the crocodile's weeping,
Or the fox's sleeping?
Or hast thou viewed the peacock in his pride,
Or the dove by his bride? . . .
O so fickle, O so vain, O so false, so false is she!

—*John Suckling* (1609-1642)

TO LUCASTA, GOING TO THE WARS

Tell me not, Sweet, I am unkind,
  That from the nunnery
Of thy chaste breast and quiet mind
  To war and arms I fly.

True, a new mistress now I chase,
  The first foe in the field;
And with a stronger faith embrace
  A sword, a horse, a shield.

Yet this inconstancy is such
  As thou too shalt adore;
I could not love thee, Dear, so much,
  Loved I not honor more.

—*Richard Lovelace* (1618-1658)

TO ALTHEA, FROM PRISON

by Richard Lovelace (1618-1658)

When Love with unconfinéd wings
  Hovers within my gates,
And my divine Althea brings
  To whisper at the grates;
When I lie tangled in her hair
  And fettered to her eye,
The birds that wanton in the air
  Know no such liberty.

When flowing cups run swiftly round
  With no allaying Thames,
Our careless heads with roses bound,
  Our hearts with loyal flames;
When thirsty grief in wine we steep,
  When healths and drafts go free—
Fishes that tipple in the deep
  Know no such liberty.

When, like committed linnets, I
  With shriller throat shall sing

The sweetness, mercy, majesty,
And glories of my King;
When I shall voice aloud how good
He is, how great should be,
Enlargéd winds, that curl the flood,
Know no such liberty.

Stone walls do not a prison make,
Nor iron bars a cage;
Minds innocent and quiet take
That for an hermitage;
If I have freedom in my love
And in my soul am free,
Angels alone, that soar above,
Enjoy such liberty.

PRISONER OF LOVE

How sweet I roamed from field to field,
And tasted all the summer's pride,
Till I the Prince of Love beheld
Who in the sunny beams did glide.

He showed me lilies for my hair,
And blushing roses for my brow:
He led me through his gardens fair
Where all his golden pleasures grow.

With sweet May-dews my wings were wet,
And Phoebus fired my vocal rage;
He caught me in his silken net,
And shut me in his golden cage.

He loves to sit and hear me sing,
Then laughing, sports and plays with me;
Then stretches out my golden wing,
And mocks my loss of liberty.

—*William Blake* (1757-1827)

LOVE'S SECRET

Never seek to tell thy love,
Love that never told can be;
For the gentle wind doth move
Silently, invisibly.

I told my love, I told my love,
I told her all my heart,
Trembling, cold, in ghastly fears,
Ah! she did depart!

Soon after she was gone from me,
A traveller came by,
Silently, invisibly:
He took her with a sigh.

—*William Blake* (1757-1827)

A RED, RED ROSE

O my luve is like a red, red rose,
That's newly sprung in June:
O my luve is like the melodie,
That's sweetly played in tune.

As fair art thou, my bonie lass,
So deep in luve am I;
And I will luve thee still, my dear,
Till a' the seas gang dry.

Till a' the seas gang dry, my dear,
And the rocks melt wi' the sun;
And I will luve thee still, my dear,
While the sands o' life shall run.

And fare-thee-weel, my only luve!
And fare-thee-weel a while!
And I will come again, my luve,
Tho' it were ten thousand mile.

—*Robert Burns* (1759-1796)

SHE WAS A PHANTOM OF DELIGHT

by William Wordsworth (1770-1850)

She was a phantom of delight
When first she gleamed upon my sight;
A lovely apparition, sent
To be a moment's ornament;
Her eyes as stars of twilight fair;
Like twilight's, too, her dusky hair;
But all things else about her drawn
From Maytime and the cheerful dawn;
A dancing shape, an image gay,
To haunt, to startle, and waylay.

I saw her upon nearer view,
A spirit, yet a woman, too!
Her household motions light and free,
And steps of virgin liberty;
A countenance in which did meet
Sweet records, promises as sweet;
A creature not too bright or good
For human nature's daily food;
For transient sorrows, simple wiles,
Praise, blame, love, kisses, tears, and smiles.

And now I see with eyes serene
The very pulse of the machine:
A being breathing thoughtful breath,
A traveler between life and death;
The reason firm, the temperate will,
Endurance, foresight, strength, and skill;
A perfect woman, nobly planned,
To warn, to comfort, and command;
And yet a spirit still, and bright
With something of angelic light.

ROSE AYLMER

Ah, what avails the sceptred race,
  Ah, what the form divine!
What every virtue, every grace!
  Rose Aylmer, all were thine.

Rose Aylmer, whom these wakeful eyes
  May weep, but never see,
A night of memories and of sighs
  I consecrate to thee.

—*Walter Savage Landor* (1775-1864)

THE INDIAN SERENADE

I arise from dreams of thee
  In the first sweet sleep of night,
When the winds are breathing low,
  And the stars are shining bright;
I arise from dreams of thee,
  And a spirit in my feet
Hath led me—who knows how?
  To thy chamber window, sweet!

The wandering airs, they faint
  On the dark, the silent stream;
The champak odors fail
  Like sweet thoughts in a dream;
The nightingale's complaint,
  It dies upon her heart,
As I must die on thine,
  Oh, belovèd as thou art!

Oh, lift me from the grass!
  I die! I faint! I fail!
Let thy love in kisses rain
  On my lips and eyelids pale.
My cheek is cold and white, alas!
  My heart beats loud and fast,
Oh! press it close to thine again,
  Where it will break at last.

—*Percy Bysshe Shelley* (1792-1822)

TO ——

Music, when soft voices die,
Vibrates in the memory—
Odours, when sweet violets sicken,
Live within the sense they quicken.

Rose leaves, when the rose is dead,
Are heaped for the belovèd's bed;
And so thy thoughts, when thou art gone,
Love itself shall slumber on.

—*Percy Bysshe Shelley* (1792-1822)

SHE IS NOT FAIR TO OUTWARD VIEW

She is not fair to outward view,
  As many maidens be;
Her loveliness I never knew
  Until she smiled on me.
O then I saw her eye was bright,
A well of love, a spring of light.

But now her looks are coy and cold,
  To mine they ne'er reply,
And yet I cease not to behold
  The love-light in her eye:
Her very frowns are fairer far
Than smiles of other maidens are.

—*Hartley Coleridge* (1796-1849)

SERENADE

Look out upon the stars, my love,
  And shame them with thine eyes,
On which, than on the lights above,
  There hang more destinies.
Night's beauty is the harmony
  Of blending shades and light;
Then, lady, up,—look out, and be
  A sister to the night!

Sleep not!—thine image wakes for aye
  Within my watching breast:
Sleep not!—from her soft sleep should fly,

Who robs all hearts of rest.
Nay, lady, from thy slumbers break,
And make this darkness gay
With looks, whose brightness well might make
Of darker nights a day.
—*Edward Coote Pinkney* (1802-1828)

COME INTO THE GARDEN MAUD

by Alfred, Lord Tennyson (1809-1892)

I

Come into the garden, Maud,
For the black bat, night, has flown
Come into the garden, Maud,
I am here at the gate alone;
And the woodbine spices are wafted abroad,
And the musk of the rose is blown.

II

For a breeze of morning moves,
And the planet of Love is on high,
Beginning to faint in the light that she loves
On a bed of daffodil sky,
To faint in the light of the sun she loves,
To faint in his light, and to die.

III

All night have the roses heard
The flute, violin, bassoon;
All night has the casement jessamine stirred
To the dancers dancing in tune;
Till a silence fell with the waking bird,
And a hush with the setting moon.

IV

I said to the lily, "There is but one,
With whom she has heart to be gay.
When will the dancers leave her alone?
She is weary of dance and play."
Now half to the setting moon are gone,
And half to the rising day;
Low on the sand and loud on the stone
The last wheel echoes away.

V

I said to the rose, "The brief night goes
In babble and revel and wine.
O young lord-lover, what sighs are those,
For one that will never be thine?
But mine, but mine," so I sware to the rose,
"For ever and ever, mine."

VI

And the soul of the rose went into my blood
As the music clashed in the hall;
And long by the garden lake I stood,
For I heard your rivulet fall
From the lake to the meadow and on to the wood,
Our wood, that is dearer than all;

VII

From the meadow your walks have left so sweet
That whenever a March-wind sighs
He sets the jewel-print of your feet
In violets blue as your eyes,
To the woody hollows in which we meet
And the valleys of Paradise.

VIII

The slender acacia would not shake
One long milk-bloom on the tree;
The white lake-blossom fell into the lake
As the pimpernel dozed on the lea;
But the rose was awake all night for your sake,
Knowing your promise to me;
The lilies and roses were all awake,
They sighed for the dawn and thee.

IX

Queen rose of the rosebud garden of girls,
Come hither, the dances are done,
In gloss of satin and glimmer of pearls,
Queen lily and rose in one;
Shine out, little head, sunning over with curls,
To the flowers, and be their sun.

X

There has fallen a splendid tear
From the passion-flower at the gate.
She is coming, my dove, my dear;
She is coming, my life, my fate.
The red rose cries, "She is near, she is near";
And the white rose weeps, "She is late";

The larkspur listens, "I hear, I hear";
  And the lily whispers, "I wait."

XI

She is coming, my own, my sweet;
  Were it ever so airy a tread,
My heart would hear her and beat,
  Were it earth in an earthy bed;
My dust would hear her and beat,
  Had I lain for a century dead,
Would start and tremble under her feet,
  And blossom in purple and red.

WAYS OF LOVE
(from "Sonnets from the Portuguese")

by Elizabeth Barrett Browning (1806-1861)

If thou must love me, let it be for naught
Except for love's sake only. Do not say
"I love her for her smile—her look—her way
Of speaking gently—for a trick of thought
That falls in well with mine, and certes brought
A sense of pleasant ease on such a day"—
For these things in themselves, Beloved, may
Be changed, or change for thee—and love, so wrought,
May be unwrought so. Neither love me for
Thine own dear pity's wiping my cheeks dry—
A creature might forget to weep, who bore
Thy comfort long, and lose thy love thereby!
But love me for love's sake, that evermore
Thou mayst love on, through love's eternity.

✦

How do I love thee? Let me count the ways.
I love thee to the depth and breadth and height
My soul can reach, when feeling out of sight
For the ends of Being and ideal Grace.
I love thee to the level of every day's
Most quiet need, by sun and candlelight.
I love thee freely, as men strive for Right;
I love thee purely, as they turn from Praise.
I love thee with the passion put to use
In my old griefs, and with my childhood's faith.
I love thee with a love I seemed to lose
With my lost saints—I love thee with the breath,
Smiles, tears, of all my life!—and, if God choose,
I shall but love thee better after death.

MY STAR

All that I know
  Of a certain star
Is, it can throw
  (Like the angled spar)
Now a dart of red,

Now a dart of blue,
Till my friends have said
They would fain see, too,
My star that dartles the red and the blue!
Then it stops like a bird; like a flower, hangs furled.
They must solace themselves with the Saturn above it.
What matter to me if their star is a world?
Mine has opened its soul to me; therefore I love it.
—*Robert Browning* (1812-1889)

SONG

Nay, but you, who do not love her,
Is she not pure gold, my mistress?
Holds earth aught—speak truth—above her?
Aught like this tress, see, and this tress,
And this last fairest tress of all,
So fair, see, ere I let it fall!

Because, you spend your lives in praising;
To praise, you search the wide world over;
So, why not witness, calmly gazing,
If earth holds aught—speak truth—above her?
Above this tress, and this I touch
But cannot praise, I love so much!
—*Robert Browning* (1812-1889)

THE MARRIED LOVER

by Coventry Patmore (1823-1896)

Why, having won her, do I woo?
Because her spirit's vestal grace
Provokes me always to pursue,
But, spirit-like, eludes embrace;
Because her womanhood is such
That, as on court-days subjects kiss
The Queen's hand, yet so near a touch
Affirms no mean familiarness;
Nay, rather marks more fair the height
Which can with safety so neglect
To dread, as lower ladies might,
That grace could meet with disrespect,
Thus she with happy favour feeds
Allegiance from a love so high
That thence no false conceit proceeds
Of difference bridged, or state put by;
Because, although in act and word
As lowly as a wife can be,
Her manners, when they call me lord,
Remind me 'tis by courtesy;
Not with her least consent of will,
Which would my proud affection hurt,
But by the nobler style that still
Imputes an unattained desert;
Because her gay and lofty brows,
When all is won which hope can ask,
Reflect a light of hopeless snows
That bright in virgin ether bask;
Because, though free of the outer court
I am, this Temple keeps its shrine
Sacred to Heaven; because, in short,
She's not and never can be mine.

MODERN LOVE: XVI

In our old shipwrecked days there was an hour
When in the firelight steadily aglow,
Joined slackly, we beheld the red chasm grow
Among the clicking coals. Our library-bower
That eve was left to us; and hushed we sat
As lovers to whom Time is whispering.
From sudden-opened doors we heard them sing;
The nodding elders mixed good wine with chat.
Well knew we that Life's greatest treasure lay
With us, and of it was our talk. "Ah, yes!
Love dies!" I said (I never thought it less).

She yearned to me that sentence to unsay.
Then when the fire domed blackening, I found
Her cheek was salt against my kiss, and swift
Up the sharp scale of sobs her breast did lift:—
Now am I haunted by that taste! that sound!

—*George Meredith* (1828-1909)

LOVE-SWEETNESS

Sweet dimness of her loosened hair's downfall
About thy face; her sweet hands round thy head
In gracious fostering union garlanded;
Her tremulous smiles; her glances' sweet recall
Of love; her murmuring sighs memorial;
Her mouth's culled sweetness by thy kisses shed
On cheeks and neck and eyelids, and so led
Back to her mouth which answers there for all:—
What sweeter than these things, except the thing
In lacking which all these would lose their sweet:—
The confident heart's still fervor; the swift beat
And soft subsidence of the spirit's wing,
Then when it feels, in cloud-girt wayfaring,
The breath of kindred plumes against its feet?

—*Dante Gabriel Rossetti* (1828-1882)

WHEN I AM DEAD, MY DEAREST

When I am dead, my dearest,
Sing no sad songs for me;
Plant thou no roses at my head,
Nor shady cypress tree:
Be the green grass above me
With showers and dewdrops wet:
And if thou wilt, remember,
And if thou wilt, forget.

I shall not see the shadows,
I shall not feel the rain;
I shall not hear the nightingale
Sing on as if in pain:
And dreaming through the twilight
That doth not rise nor set,
Haply I may remember,
And haply may forget.

—*Christina Georgina Rossetti* (1830-1894)

A BIRTHDAY

My heart is like a singing bird
  Whose nest is in a watered shoot;
My heart is like an apple-tree
  Whose bough is bent with thick-set fruit;
My heart is like a rainbow shell
  That paddles in a halcyon sea;
My heart is gladder than all these
  Because my love is come to me.

Raise me a dais of silk and down;
  Hang it with vair and purple dyes;
Carve it in doves, and pomegranates,
  And peacocks with a hundred eyes;
Work it in gold and silver grapes,
  In leaves, and silver fleurs-de-lys;
Because the birthday of my life
  Is come, my love is come to me.

—*Christina Georgina Rossetti* (1830-1894)

ALTER? WHEN THE HILLS DO

Alter? When the hills do.
Falter? When the sun
Question if his glory
Be the perfect one.
Surfeit? When the daffodil

Doth of the dew:
Even as herself, O friend!
I will of you!
—*Emily Dickinson*
(1830-1886)

CHOICE

Of all the souls that stand create
I have elected one,
When sense from spirit files away
And subterfuge is done;

When that which is and that which was
Apart, intrinsic, stand,
And this brief tragedy of flesh
Is shifted like a sand;

When figures show their royal front
And mists are carved away,—
Behold the atom I preferred
To all the lists of clay!
—*Emily Dickinson* (1830-1886)

SONG

Love laid his sleepless head
On a thorny rosy bed;
And his eyes with tears were red,
And pale his lips as the dead.

And fear and sorrow and scorn
Kept watch by his head forlorn,
Till the night was overworn,
And the world was merry with morn.

And joy came up with the day,
And kissed Love's lips as he lay,
And the watchers ghostly and gray
Sped from his pillow away.

And his eyes as the dawn grew bright,
And his lips waxed ruddy as light:
Sorrow may reign for a night,
But day shall bring back delight.
—*Algernon Charles Swinburne*
(1837-1909)

THE BLACKBIRD

The nightingale has a lyre of gold,
The lark's is a clarion call,
And the blackbird plays but a boxwood flute,
But I love him best of all.

For his song is all of the joy of life,
And we in the mad, spring weather,
We two have listened till he sang
Our hearts and lips together.
—*William Ernest Henley* (1849-1903)

WHAT LIPS MY LIPS HAVE KISSED

What lips my lips have kissed, and where, and why,
I have forgotten, and what arms have lain
Under my head till morning; but the rain
Is full of ghosts tonight, that tap and sigh
Upon the glass and listen for reply;
And in my heart there stirs a quiet pain
For unremembered lads that not again
Will turn to me at midnight with a cry.

Thus in the winter stands the lonely tree,
Nor knows what birds have vanished one by one,
Yet knows its boughs more silent than before:
I cannot say what loves have come and gone;
I only know that summer sang in me
A little while, that in me sings no more.
—*Edna St. Vincent Millay* (1892-)

WARNING TO ONE

Death is the strongest of all living things;
And when it happens do not look in the eyes
For a dead fire or a lackluster there,
But listen for the words that fall from lips
Or do not fall. Silence is not death;
It merely means that one conserving breath
Is not concerned with tattle and small quips.

Watch the quick fingers and the way they move
During unguarded moments—words of love
And love's caresses may be cold as ice
And cold the glitter of engagement rings.
Death is the sword that hangs on a single hair,
And that thin tenuous hair is no more than love—
And yours is the silly head it hangs above.
—*Merrill Moore* (1903-)

PATRIOTISM

George Santayana has declared that the emotion of patriotism is "merely a passion for ascendency." Such an opinion would probably also imply that love of country is not one of the nobler emotions fit for the poet to express. Nevertheless, if we consider the poetry of the world, most of the epics, a multitude of didactic poems, and thousands of songs have found their origins in the spirit of nationalism. "I would rather write a nation's songs than make its laws" was no mere passing witticism; it showed knowledge of what makes people act. Frequently patriotic verse is too blatant to convince and too narrowly nationalistic to have universal appeal. The task for some future poet may well be to create a new poetry of internationalism, reaching beyond race or geographical borders.

The poems which follow express the emotions of both the British and their defiant offspring; it is interesting to compare Scott's calm affection with Whitman's challenging chauvinism.

SCOTS, WHA HAE

Scots, wha hae wi' Wallace bled,
Scots, wham Bruce has aften led,
Welcome to your gory bed,
  Or to victory!
Now's the day, and now's the hour;
See the front o' battle lour;
See approach proud Edward's power—
  Chains and slavery!

Wha will be a traitor knave?
Wha can fill a coward's grave?
Wha sae base as be a slave?
  Let him turn and flee!
Wha for Scotland's king and law
Freedom's sword will strongly draw,
Freeman stand, or Freeman fa',
  Let him follow me!

By oppression's woes and pains
By your sons in servile chains!
We will drain our dearest veins,
  But they shall be free!
Lay the proud usurpers low!
Tyrants fall in every foe!
Liberty's in every blow!—
  Let us do or die!

—*Robert Burns* (1759-1796)

NATIVE LAND
(from "The Lay of the Last Minstrel")

Breathes there the man with soul so dead,
Who never to himself hath said,
  "This is my own, my native land!"
Whose heart hath ne'er within him burned
As home his footsteps he hath turned
  From wandering on a foreign strand?
If such there breathe, go, mark him well;
For him no minstrel raptures swell;
High though his titles, proud his name,
Boundless his wealth as wish can claim;
Despite those titles, power, and pelf,
The wretch, concentered all in self,
Living, shall forfeit fair renown,
And, doubly dying, shall go down
To the vile dust from whence he sprung,
Unwept, unhonored, and unsung.

—*Walter Scott* (1771-1832)

CONCORD HYMN
Sung at the Completion of the Battle Monument, July 4, 1837

By the rude bridge that arched the flood,
  Their flag to April's breeze unfurled,
Here once the embattled farmers stood
  And fired the shot heard round the world.

The foe long since in silence slept;
  Alike the conqueror silent sleeps;
And Time the ruined bridge has swept

Down the dark stream which seaward creeps.

On this green bank, by this soft stream,
We set today a votive stone,
That memory may their deed redeem,
When, like our sires, our sons are gone.

Spirit, that made those heroes dare
To die, and leave their children free,
Bid Time and Nature gently spare
The shaft we raise to them and thee.
—*Ralph Waldo Emerson* (1803-1882)

PIONEERS! O PIONEERS!

by Walt Whitman (1819-1892)

Come, my tan-faced children,
Follow well in order, get your weapons ready,
Have you your pistols? have you your sharp-edged axes?
Pioneers! O pioneers!

For we cannot tarry here,
We must march my darlings, we must bear the brunt of danger,
We the youthful sinewy races, all the rest on us depend,
Pioneers! O pioneers!

O you youths, Western youths,
So impatient, full of action, full of manly pride and friendship,
Plain I see you Western youths, see you tramping with the foremost,
Pioneers! O pioneers!

Have the elder races halted?
Do they droop and end their lesson, wearied over there beyond the seas?
We take up the task eternal, and the burden and the lesson,
Pioneers! O pioneers!

All the past we leave behind,
We debouch upon a newer mightier world, varied world,
Fresh and strong the world we seize, world of labor and the march,
Pioneers! O pioneers!

We detachments steady throwing,
Down the edges, through the passes, up the mountains steep,
Conquering, holding, daring, venturing as we go the unknown ways,
Pioneers! O pioneers!

We primeval forests felling,
We the rivers stemming, vexing we and piercing deep the mines within,
We the surface broad surveying, we the virgin soil upheaving,
Pioneers! O pioneers!

Colorado men are we,
From the peaks gigantic, from the great sierras and the high plateaus,
From the mine and from the gully, from the hunting trail we come,
Pioneers! O pioneers!

From Nebraska, from Arkansas,
Central inland race are we, from Missouri, with the continental blood intervein'd,

All the hands of comrades clasping, all the Southern, all the Northern,
Pioneers! O pioneers!

O resistless restless race!
O beloved race in all! O my breast aches with tender love for all!
O I mourn and yet exult, I am rapt with love for all,
Pioneers! O pioneers!

Raise the mighty mother mistress,
Waving high the delicate mistress, over all the starry mistress (bend your heads all),
Raise the fang'd and warlike mistress, stern, impassive, weapon'd mistress,
Pioneers! O pioneers!

See my children, resolute children,
By those swarms upon our rear we must never yield or falter,
Ages back in ghostly millions frowning there behind us urging,
Pioneers! O pioneers!

On and on the compact ranks,
With accessions ever waiting, with the places of the dead quickly fill'd,
Through the battle, through defeat, moving yet and never stopping,
Pioneers! O pioneers!

O to die advancing on!
Are there some of us to droop and die? has the hour come?
Then upon the march we fittest die, soon and sure the gap is fill'd,
Pioneers! O pioneers!

All the pulses of the world,
Falling in they beat for us, with the Western movement beat,
Holding single or together, steady moving to the front, all for us,
Pioneers! O pioneers!

Life's involv'd and varied pageants,
All the forms and shows, all the workmen at their work,
All the seamen and the landsmen, all the masters with their slaves,
Pioneers! O pioneers!

All the hapless silent lovers,
All the prisoners in the prisons, all the righteous and the wicked,
All the joyous, all the sorrowing, all the living, all the dying,
Pioneers! O pioneers!

I too with my soul and body,
We, a curious trio, picking, wandering on our way,
Through these shores amid the shadows, with the apparitions pressing,
Pioneers! O pioneers!

Lo, the darting bowling orb!
Lo, the brother orbs around, all the clustering suns and planets,
All the dazzling days, all the mystic nights with dreams,
Pioneers! O pioneers!

These are of us, they are with us,
All for primal needed work, while the followers there in embryo wait behind,

We today's procession heading, we the route for travel clearing,
Pioneers! O pioneers!

O you daughters of the West!
O you young and elder daughters! O you mothers and you wives!
Never must you be divided, in our ranks you move united,
Pioneers! O pioneers!

Minstrels latent on the prairies!
(Shrouded bards of other lands, you may rest, you have done your work),
Soon I hear you coming warbling, soon you rise and tramp amid us,
Pioneers! O pioneers!

Not for delectations sweet
Not the cushion and the slipper, not the peaceful and the studious,
Not the riches safe and palling, not for us the tame enjoyment,
Pioneers! O pioneers!

Do the feasters gluttonous feast?
Do the corpulent sleepers sleep? Have they lock'd and bolted doors?
Still be ours the diet hard, and the blanket on the ground,
Pioneers! O pioneers!

Has the night descended?
Was the road of late so toilsome? did we stop discouraged nodding on our way?
Yet a passing hour I yield you in your tracks to pause oblivious,
Pioneers! O pioneers!

Till with sound of trumpet,
Far, far off the daybreak call—hark! how loud and clear I hear it wind,
Swift! to the head of the army!—swift! spring to your places,
Pioneers! O pioneers!

THE SOLDIER

If I should die, think only this of me:
That there's some corner of a foreign field
That is forever England. There shall be
In that rich earth a richer dust concealed;
A dust whom England bore, shaped, made aware,
Gave, once, her flowers to love, her ways to roam,
A body of England's, breathing English air,
Washed by the rivers, blessed by suns of home.
And think, this heart, all evil shed away,
A pulse in the eternal mind, no less
Gives somewhere back the thoughts by England given;
Her sights and sounds; dreams happy as her day;
And laughter, learned of friends; and gentleness,
In hearts at peace, under an English heaven.

—*Rupert Brooke* (1887-1915)

HUMANITARIANISM

It sometimes surprises us to discover that features which we have been led to consider "elements of human nature" have had their beginning, rise, and fall along with human institutions. Sympathy with the down-trodden, with the "under-dog," would seem a natural trait in all ages; yet it has had its fluctuations no less than religion. Despite the fact that "the gentle Christ" sowed the seed of the love of man two thousand years ago, human sympathy was buried under a mountain of fear, hate, and superstition during the later Roman Empire, the Dark Ages, and the Renaissance. Yet from the study and imitation of the classics grew a realization of the nobility of man, and from the surge of the Reformation rose a faith in the individual in place of the institution. With Rousseau, Shaftesbury, and the eighteenth-century sentimentalists, this faith in humanity was combined with a belief in the ultimate goodness of life and the universe; the Calvinist concept of an unforgiving God, predestination of infants to eternal damnation, and the ascetic life was supplanted by the Quaker-Methodist-Romanticist doctrine of a deity who scattered blessings, loved the poor and weak, and forgave all who repented. Not content with mere doctrine, these "Humanitarians" sought for practical reform in the shape of democratic governments, organized charities, protection of the rights of orphans and widows, consideration of dumb animals, and fought for their ideals with speech and sword. The war continues; such poets as Walt Whitman, Elizabeth Barrett Browning, in her "Cry of the Children," Margaret Widdemer, in "Factories," and Edwin Markham, in "The Man with the Hoe," belong to the humanitarian armies.

In the poems which follow, Blake is the mystic who loves "all things both great and small," Burns is the ardent democrat and friend of man, and Moody is the social reformer.

FROM "AUGURIES OF INNOCENCE"

by William Blake (1757-1827)

To see a world in a grain of sand
And a heaven in a wild flower;
Hold infinity in the palm of your hand,
And eternity in an hour.

A robin redbreast in a cage
Puts all Heaven in a rage;
A dove-house filled with doves and pigeons
Shudders hell through all its regions.
A dog starved at his master's gate
Predicts the ruin of the state;
A game-cock clipped and armed for fight
Doth the rising sun affright.
A horse misused upon the road
Calls to Heaven for human blood.
Every wolf's and lion's howl
Raises from hell a human soul;
Each outcry of the hunted hare
A fibre from the brain doth tear;
A skylark wounded on the wing
Doth make a cherub cease to sing.

He who shall hurt the little wren
Shall never be beloved by men;
He who the ox to wrath has moved
Shall never be by woman loved.

✦

The wanton boy that kills the fly
Shall feel the spider's enmity;
He who torments the chafer's sprite
Weaves a bower in endless night.
The caterpillar on the leaf
Repeats to thee thy mother's grief.

✦

Every night and every morn
Some to misery are born;
Every morn and every night
Some are born to sweet delight;
Some are born to sweet delight,
Some are born to endless night.
Joy and woe are woven fine,
A clothing for the soul divine.

A MAN'S A MAN FOR A' THAT

by Robert Burns (1759-1796)

Is there, for honest poverty,
  That hings his head, an' a' that;
The coward slave, we pass him by,
  We dare be poor for a' that!
    For a' that, an' a' that,
      Our toils obscure, an' a' that;
    The rank is but the guinea's stamp;
      The man's the gowd[1] for a' that.

What though on hamely fare we dine,
  Wear hodden-gray, an' a' that;
Gie fools their silks, and knaves their wine,
  A man's a man for a' that.
    For a' that, an' a' that,
      Their tinsel show, an' a' that;
    The honest man, though e'er sae poor,
      Is king o' men for a' that.

Ye see yon birkie, ca'd a lord,
  Wha struts, an' stares, an' a' that;
Though hundreds worship at his word,
  He's but a coof[2] for a' that.
    For a' that, an' a' that,
      His riband, star, an' a' that,
    The man o' independent mind,
      He looks and laughs at a' that.

A prince can mak a belted knight,
  A marquis, duke, an' a' that;
But an honest man's aboon his might,
  Guid faith he maunna fa' that!
    For a' that, an' a' that,
      Their dignities, an' a' that,
The pith o' sense, an' pride o' worth,
  Are higher rank than a' that.

Then let us pray that come it may,
  (As come it will for a' that),
That sense and worth, o'er a' the earth,
  Shall bear the gree, an' a' that.
    For a' that, an' a' that,
      It's coming yet, for a' that,
    That man to man, the warld o'er,
      Shall brithers be for a' that.

[1] Gold.
[2] Fool.

GLOUCESTER MOORS

by William Vaughn Moody (1869-1910)

A mile behind is Gloucester town
Where the fishing fleets put in,
A mile ahead the land dips down
And the woods and farms begin.
Here, where the moors stretch free
In the high blue afternoon,
Are the marching sun and talking sea,
And the racing winds that wheel and flee
On the flying heels of June.

Jill-o'er-the-ground is purple blue,
Blue is the quaker-maid,
The wild geranium holds its dew
Long in the boulder's shade.
Wax-red hangs the cup
From the huckleberry boughs,
In barberry bells the gray moths sup
Or where the choke-cherry lifts high up
Sweet bowls for their carouse.

Over the shelf of the sandy cove
Beach-peas blossom late.
By copse and cliff the swallows rove
Each calling to his mate.
Seaward the sea-gulls go,
And the land-birds all are here;
That green-gold flash was a vireo,
And yonder flame where the marsh-flags grow
Was a scarlet tanager.

This earth is not the steadfast place
We landsmen build upon;
From deep to deep she varies pace,
And while she comes is gone.
Beneath my feet I feel
Her smooth bulk heave and dip;
With velvet plunge and soft upreel
She swings and steadies to her keel
Like a gallant, gallant ship.

These summer clouds she sets for sail,
The sun is her masthead light,

She tows the moon like a pinnace frail
Where her phosphor wake churns bright.
Now hid, now looming clear,
On the face of the dangerous blue
The star fleets tack and wheel and veer,
But on, but on does the old earth steer
As if her port she knew.

God, dear God! Does she know her port,
Though she goes so far about?
Or blind astray, does she make her sport
To brazen and chance it out?
I watched when her captains passed:
She were better captainless.
Men in the cabin, before the mast,
But some were reckless and some aghast,
And some sat gorged at mess.

By her battened hatch I leaned and caught
Sounds from the noisome hold,—
Cursing and sighing of souls distraught
And cries too sad to be told.
Then I strove to go down and see;
But they said, "Thou art not of us!"
I turned to those on the deck with me
And cried, "Give help!" But they said, "Let be:
Our ship sails faster thus."

Jill-o'er-the-ground is purple blue,
Blue is the quaker-maid,
The alder-clump where the brook comes through
Breeds cresses in its shade.
To be out of the moiling street
With its swelter and its sin!
Who has given me this sweet,
And given my brother dust to eat?
And when will his wage come in?

Scattering wide or blown in ranks,
Yellow and white and brown,
Boats and boats from the fishing banks
Come home to Gloucester town.
There is cash to purse and spend,
There are wives to be embraced,
Hearts to borrow and hearts to lend,
And hearts to take and keep to the end,—
O little sails, make haste!

But thou, vast outbound ship of souls,
What harbor town for thee?
What shapes, when thy arriving tolls,
Shall crowd the banks to see?
Shall all the happy shipmates then
Stand singing brotherly?
Or shall a haggard ruthless few
Warp her over and bring her to,
While the many broken souls of men
Fester down in the slaver's pen,
And nothing to say or do?

SCORN AND HATE

Rage is said to be fiercest when it is speechless, but it can be bitter enough in words. We may mingle hate with envy when it turns toward one on a higher plane than ourselves—the feeling of the monk speaking in Browning's vindictive "Soliloquy of the Spanish Cloister"—or it may join with scorn if the object of anger is low enough for contempt. Browning's "Lost Leader" and Whittier's "Ichabod" both add a touch of sorrow to this commingling of emotions. Milton's "On the Late Massacre in Piedmont" is hatred of an institution, roused by devotion to a cause and, therefore, adds religious zeal to the mixture of emotions.

SOLILOQUY OF THE SPANISH CLOISTER

by Robert Browning (1812-1889)

Gr-r-r—there go, my heart's abhorrence!
  Water your damned flower-pots, do!
If hate killed men, Brother Lawrence,
  God's blood, would not mine kill you!
What? your myrtle-bush wants trimming?
  Oh, that rose has prior claims—
Needs its leaden vase filled brimming?
  Hell dry you up with its flames!

At the meal we sit together;
  Salve tibi! I must hear

Wise talk of the kind of weather,
  Sort of season, time of year:
Not a plenteous cork-crop: scarcely
  Dare we hope oak-galls, I doubt:
What's the Latin name for "parsley"?
  What's the Greek name for Swine's Snout?

Whew! We'll have our platter burnished,
  Laid with care on our own shelf!
With a fire-new spoon we're furnished,
  And a goblet for ourself,
Rinsed like something sacrificial
  Ere 'tis fit to touch our chaps—
Marked with L. for our initial!
  (He-he! There his lily snaps!)

Saint, forsooth! While brown Dolores
  Squats outside the Convent bank
With Sanchicha, telling stories,
  Steeping tresses in the tank,
Blue-black, lustrous, thick like horsehairs,
  —Can't I see his dead eye glow,
Bright as 'twere a Barbary corsair's?
  (That is, if he'd let it show!)

When he finishes refection,
  Knife and fork he never lays
Cross-wise, to my recollection,
  As do I, in Jesu's praise.
I, the Trinity illustrate,
  Drinking watered orange-pulp—
In three sips the Arian frustrate;
  While he drains his at one gulp!

Oh, those melons! If he's able
  We're to have a feast; so nice!
One goes to the Abbot's table,
  All of us get each a slice.
How go on your flowers? None double?
  Not one fruit-sort can you spy?
Strange!—And I, too, at such trouble,
  Keep them close-nipped on the sly!

There's a great text in Galatians,
  Once you trip on it, entails
Twenty-nine distinct damnations,
  One sure, if another fails;
If I trip him just a-dying,
  Sure of heaven as sure can be,
Spin him round and send him flying
  Off to hell, a Manichee?

Or, my scrofulous French novel
  On grey paper with blunt type!
Simply glance at it, you grovel
  Hand and foot in Belial's gripe;
If I double down its pages
  At the woeful sixteenth print,
When he gathers his greengages,
  Ope a sieve and slip it in't?

Or, there's Satan!—one might venture
  Pledge one's soul to him, yet leave
Such a flaw in the indenture
  As he'd miss, till, past retrieve,
Blasted lay that rose-acacia
  We're so proud of. *Hy, Zy, Hine . . .*
'St! There's Vespers! *Plena gratiâ,*
  Ave, Virgo. Gr-r-r—you swine!

THE LOST LEADER

by Robert Browning (1812-1889)

Just for a handful of silver he left us,
  Just for a riband to stick in his coat—
Found the one gift of which fortune bereft us,
  Lost all the others she lets us devote;
They, with the gold to give, doled him out silver,
  So much was theirs who so little allowed:
How all our copper had gone for his service!
  Rags—were they purple, his heart had been proud!
We that had loved him so, followed him, honored him,
  Lived in his mild and magnificent eye,
Learned his great language, caught his clear accents,
  Made him our pattern to live and to die!
Shakespeare was of us, Milton was for us,

Burns, Shelley, were with us,—they watch from their graves!
He alone breaks from the van and the freemen,
—He alone sinks to the rear and the slaves!

We shall march prospering,—not through his presence;
Songs may inspirit us,—not from his lyre;
Deeds will be done,—while he boasts his quiescence,
Still bidding crouch whom the rest bade aspire:
Blot out his name, then, record one lost soul more,
One task more declined, one more footpath untrod,
One more devils'-triumph and sorrow for angels,
One wrong more to man, one more insult to God!
Life's night begins: let him never come back to us!
There would be doubt, hesitation and pain,
Forced praise on our part—the glimmer of twilight,
Never glad confident morning again!
Best fight on well, for we taught him—strike gallantly,
Menace our heart ere we master his own;
Then let him receive the new knowledge and wait us,
Pardoned in heaven, the first by the throne!

ICHABOD

by John Greenleaf Whittier (1807-1892)

So fallen! so lost! the light withdrawn
Which once he wore!
The glory from his gray hairs gone
Forevermore!

Revile him not, the Tempter hath
A snare for all:
And pitying tears, not scorn and wrath,
Befit his fall!

Oh, dumb be passion's stormy rage,
When he who might
Have lighted up and led his age,
Falls back in night.

Scorn! would the angels laugh, to mark
A bright soul driven,
Fiend-goaded, down the endless dark,
From hope and heaven!

Let not the land once proud of him
Insult him now,
Nor brand with deeper shame his dim,
Dishonored brow.

But let its humbled sons, instead,
From sea to lake,
A long lament, as for the dead,
In sadness make.

Of all we loved and honored, naught
Save power remains;
A fallen angel's pride of thought,
Still strong in chains.

All else is gone; from those great eyes
The soul has fled:
When faith is lost, when honor dies,
The man is dead!

Then, pay the reverence of old days
To his dead fame;
Walk backward, with averted gaze,
And hide the shame!

ON THE LATE MASSACRE IN PIEDMONT

Avenge, O Lord, thy slaughtered saints, whose bones
Lie scattered on the Alpine mountains cold;
Even them who kept thy truth so pure of old,
When all our fathers worshiped stocks and stones,

Forget not: in thy book record their groans
Who were thy sheep, and in their ancient fold
Slain by the bloody Piedmontese, that rolled
Mother with infant down the rocks. Their moans
The vales redoubled to the hills, and they
To heaven. Their martyred blood and ashes sow
O'er all the Italian fields, where still doth sway
The triple tyrant; that from these may grow
A hundredfold, who, having learnt thy way,
Early may fly the Babylonian woe.

—*John Milton* (1608-1674)

PRAISE

We have already seen the emotion of admiration combined with veneration in the poems about Abraham Lincoln. Poems of tribute appear by the thousand when a great leader dies; poets vie with one another to praise their rivals who have been removed from the competition. Ben Jonson's tribute to Shakespeare was indeed a generous gesture, for Shakespeare's plays were still competing with Jonson's upon the stage, and they outshone Jonson's in every respect. (It is interesting to compare this poem with E. A. Robinson's piercing analysis in "Ben Jonson Entertains a Man from Stratford.") Henry Wotton's praise of Elizabeth of Bohemia is one of the loveliest of Elizabethan lyrics—the reference to the stars as "you common people of the skies" being startling in its freshness and "modernity." Difficult though it is for a man to pay tribute to his own father without becoming mawkishly sentimental, yet in "Rugby Chapel" Matthew Arnold avoids this pitfall by attempting to see his father's accomplishments as headmaster of Rugby in the light of history. The poem is more than personal praise; it is a stirring call to duty.

ELIZABETH OF BOHEMIA

You meaner beauties of the night,
  That poorly satisfy our eyes
More by your number than your light,
  You common people of the skies;
  What are you when the moon shall rise?

You curious chanters of the wood,
  That warble forth Dame Nature's lays,
Thinking your passions understood
  By your weak accents; what's your praise
  When Philomel her voice shall raise?

You violets that first appear,
  By your pure purple mantles known
Like the proud virgins of the year,
  As if the spring were all your own;
  What are you when the rose is blown?

So, when my mistress shall be seen
  In form and beauty of her mind,
By virtue first, then choice, a Queen,
  Tell me, if she were not designed
  Th' eclipse and glory of her kind.

—*Henry Wotton* (1568-1639)

TO THE MEMORY OF MY BELOVED MASTER WILLIAM SHAKESPEARE

by Ben Jonson (1573-1637)

To draw no envy, Shakespeare, on thy name,
Am I thus ample to thy book and fame;

While I confess thy writings to be such
As neither man, nor Muse, can praise too much.
'Tis true, and all men's suffrage. But these ways
Were not the paths I meant unto thy praise;
For silliest ignorance on these may light,
Which, when it sounds at best, but echoes right;
Or blind affection, which doth ne'er advance
The truth, but gropes, and urgeth all by chance;
Or crafty malice might pretend this praise,
And think to ruin, where it seemed to raise.
These are, as some infamous bawd or whore
Should praise a matron. What could hurt her more?
But thou art proof against them, and, indeed,
Above the ill fortune of them, or the need.
I therefore will begin. Soul of the age!
The applause, delight, the wonder of our stage!
My Shakespeare, rise! I will not lodge thee by
Chaucer, or Spenser, or bid Beaumont lie
A little further, to make thee a room;
Thou art a monument without a tomb,
And art alive still while thy book doth live
And we have wits to read and praise to give.
That I not mix thee so, my brain excuses,
I mean with great, but disproportioned Muses;
For if I thought my judgment were of years,
I should commit thee surely with thy peers,
And tell how far thou didst our Lyly outshine,
Or sporting Kyd, or Marlowe's mighty line.
And though thou hadst small Latin and less Greek,
From thence to honor thee, I would not seek
For names; but call forth thundering Aeschylus,
Euripides, and Sophocles to us;
Pacuvius, Accius, him of Cordova dead,
To life again, to hear thy buskin tread,
And shake a stage; or, when thy socks were on,
Leave thee alone for the comparison
Of all that insolent Greece or haughty Rome
Sent forth, or since did from their ashes come.
Triumph, my Britain, thou hast one to show
To whom all scenes of Europe homage owe.
He was not of an age, but for all time!
And all the Muses still were in their prime,
When, like Apollo, he came forth to warm
Our ears, or like a Mercury to charm!
Nature herself was proud of his designs
And joyed to wear the dressing of his lines!
Which were so richly spun, and woven so fit,
As, since, she will vouchsafe no other wit.
The merry Greek, tart Aristophanes,
Neat Terence, witty Plautus, now not please,
But antiquated and deserted lie,

As they were not of Nature's family.
Yet must I not give Nature all; thy art,
My gentle Shakespeare, must enjoy a part.
For though the poet's matter nature be,
His art doth give the fashion; and, that he
Who casts to write a living line, must sweat
(Such as thine are) and strike the second heat
Upon the Muses' anvil; turn the same
(And himself with it) that he thinks to frame,
Or, for the laurel, he may gain a scorn;
For a good poet's made, as well as born.
And such wert thou! Look how the father's face
Lives in his issue; even so the race
Of Shakespeare's mind and manners brightly shines
In his well turnéd, and true filéd lines;
In each of which he seems to shake a lance,
As brandished at the eyes of ignorance.
Sweet Swan of Avon! what a sight it were
To see thee in our waters yet appear,
And make those flights upon the banks of Thames,
That so did take Eliza, and our James!
But stay, I see thee in the hemisphere
Advanced, and made a constellation there!
Shine forth, thou Star of poets, and with rage
Or influence, chide or cheer the drooping stage,
Which, since thy flight from hence, hath mourned like night,
And despairs day, but for thy volume's light.

RUGBY CHAPEL

November, 1857

by Matthew Arnold (1822-1888)

Coldly, sadly descends
The autumn evening. The field,
Strewn with its dank yellow drifts
Of withered leaves, and the elms,
Fade into dimness apace,
Silent—hardly a shout
From a few boys late at their play!
The lights come out in the street,
In the school-room windows—but cold,
Solemn, unlighted, austere,
Through the gathering darkness, arise
The chapel-walls, in whose bound
Thou, my father! art laid.

There thou dost lie, in the gloom
Of the autumn evening. But ah,
That word, *gloom,* to my mind
Brings thee back, in the light
Of thy radiant vigor, again;
In the gloom of November we passed
Days not dark at thy side;
Seasons impaired not the ray
Of thy buoyant cheerfulness clear.
Such thou wast! and I stand
In the autumn evening, and think
Of bygone autumns with thee.

Fifteen years have gone round
Since thou arosest to tread,
In the summer-morning, the road
Of death, at a call unforeseen,
Sudden. For fifteen years,
We who till then in thy shade
Rested as under the boughs
Of a mighty oak have endured
Sunshine and rain as we might,
Bare, unshaded, alone,
Lacking the shelter of thee.

O strong soul, by what shore
Tarriest thou now? For that force,

Surely, has not been left vain!
Somewhere, surely, afar,
In the sounding labor-house vast
Of being, is practiced that strength,
Zealous, beneficent, firm!

Yes, in some far-shining sphere,
Conscious or not of the past,
Still thou performest the word
Of the Spirit in whom thou dost live—
Prompt, unwearied, as here!
Still thou upraisest with zeal
The humble good from the ground,
Sternly repressest the bad!
Still, like a trumpet, dost rouse
Those who with half-open eyes
Tread the border-land dim
'Twixt vice and virtue; reviv'st,
Succorest! This was thy work,
This was thy life upon earth.

What is the course of the life
Of mortal men on the earth?
Most men eddy about
Here and there—eat and drink,
Chatter and love and hate,
Gather and squander, are raised
Aloft, are hurled in the dust,
Striving blindly, achieving
Nothing; and then they die—
Perish—and no one asks
Who or what they have been,
More than he asks what waves,
In the moonlit solitudes mild
Of the midmost ocean, have swelled,
Foamed for a moment, and gone.

And there are some, whom a thirst
Ardent, unquenchable, fires,
Not with the crowd to be spent,
Not without aim to go round
In an eddy of purposeless dust,
Effort unmeaning and vain.
Ah, yes! some of us strive
Not without action to die
Fruitless, but something to snatch
From dull oblivion, nor all
Glut the devouring grave!
We, we have chosen our path—
Path to a clear-purposed goal,
Path of advance!—but it leads
A long, steep journey, through sunk
Gorges, o'er mountains in snow.
Cheerful, with friends, we set forth—
Then, on the height, comes the storm.
Thunder crashes from rock
To rock, the cataracts reply,
Lightnings dazzle our eyes.
Roaring torrents have breached
The track, the stream-bed descends
In the place where the wayfarer once
Planted his footstep—the spray
Boils o'er its borders! aloft
The unseen snow-beds dislodge
Their hanging ruin! alas,
Havoc is made in our train!
Friends, who set forth at our side,
Falter, are lost in the storm.
We, we only are left!
With frowning foreheads, with lips
Sternly compressed, we strain on,
On—and at nightfall at last
Come to the end of our way,
To the lonely inn 'mid the rocks;
Where the gaunt and taciturn host
Stands on the threshold, the wind
Shaking his thin white hairs—
Holds his lantern to scan
Our storm-beat figures, and asks:
Whom in our party we bring,
Whom we have left in the snow?

Sadly we answer: We bring
Only ourselves! we lost
Sight of the rest in the storm;
Hardly ourselves we fought through,
Stripped, without friends, as we are.
Friends, companions, and train,
The avalanche swept from our side.

But thou would'st not *alone*
Be saved, my father! *alone*
Conquer and come to thy goal,
Leaving the rest in the wild.
We were weary, and we
Fearful, and we in our march
Fain to drop down and to die.
Still thou turnedst, and still
Beckonedst the trembler, and still
Gavest the weary thy hand.
If, in the paths of the world,
Stones might have wounded thy feet,
Toil or dejection have tried
Thy spirit, of that we saw

Nothing—to us thou wast still
Cheerful, and helpful, and firm!
Therefore to thee it was given
Many to save with thyself;
And, at the end of thy day,
Oh, faithful shepherd! to come,
Bringing thy sheep in thy hand.

And through thee I believe
In the noble and great who are gone;
Pure souls honored and blest
By former ages, who else—
Such, so soulless, so poor,
Is the race of men whom I see—
Seemed but a dream of the heart,
Seemed but a cry of desire.
Yes! I believe that there lived
Others like thee in the past,
Not like the men of the crowd
Who all round me today
Bluster or cringe, and make life
Hideous, and arid, and vile;
But souls tempered with fire,
Fervent, heroic, and good,
Helpers and friends of mankind.

Servants of God!—or sons
Shall I not call you? because
Not as servants ye knew
Your Father's innermost mind,
His, who unwillingly sees
One of his little ones lost—
Yours is the praise, if mankind
Hath not as yet in its march
Fainted, and fallen, and died!

See! In the rocks of the world
Marches the host of mankind,
A feeble, wavering line.
Where are they tending?—A God
Marshaled them, gave them their goal.
Ah, but the way is so long!

Years they have been in the wild!
Sore thirst plagues them, the rocks,
Rising all round, overawe;
Factions divide them, their host
Threatens to break, to dissolve.
—Ah, keep, keep them combined!
Else, of the myriads who fill
That army, not one shall arrive;
Sole they shall stray; on the rocks
Labor forever in vain,
Die one by one in the waste.

Then, in such hour of need
Of your fainting, dispirited race,
Ye, like angels, appear,
Radiant with ardor divine!
Beacons of hope ye appear!
Languor is not in your heart,
Weakness is not in your word,
Weariness not on your brow.
Ye alight in our van! at your voice,
Panic, despair, flee away.
Ye move through the ranks, recall
The stragglers, refresh the outworn,
Praise, reinspire the brave!
Order, courage, return.
Eyes rekindling, and prayers,
Follow your steps as ye go.
Ye fill up the gaps in our files,
Strengthen the wavering line,
Stablish, continue our march,
On, to the bound of the waste,
On, to the City of God.

JOY

Joy unalloyed is a rare emotion in poetry. Pippa dancing by, singing her song of good cheer, seems the embodiment of joy; a paean of triumph from the Psalms combines racial and nationalist pride with exultation; religious ecstasy is a type of joy which we would not confuse with happiness. But joy which is not the joy of the lover or the nature-worshiper or the religious devotee or the triumphing football player is seldom found in life. Emotions rarely come singly, and the more powerful will usually predominate; therefore joy rarely triumphs alone. Richard Hovey and Bliss Carman, in their *Songs from Vagabondia,* tried to express the abandoned happiness of the wanderer. "Three of a Kind" shows this type of joy. Yet even here sheer high spirits merge with a love of wild nature, an irresponsible wanderlust, as an escape from the tragic sense of life.

THREE OF A KIND

by Richard Hovey (1864-1900)

Three of us without a care
In the red September,
Tramping down the roads of Maine,
Making merry with the rain,
With the fellow winds a-fare,
Where the winds remember.

Three of us with shocking hats,
Tattered and unbarbered,
Happy with the splash of mud,
With the highways in our blood,
Bearing down on Deacon Platt's,
Where last year we harbored.

We've come down from Kennebec,
Tramping since last Sunday,
Loping down the coast of Maine,
With the sea for a refrain,
And the maples neck and neck
All the way to Fundy.

Sometimes lodging in an inn,
Cosy as a dormouse—
Sometimes sleeping on a knoll,
With no rooftree but the pole—
Sometimes halely welcomed in
At an old-time farmhouse.

Loafing under ledge and tree,
Leaping over boulders,
Sitting on the pasture bars,
Hail-fellow with storm or stars—
Three of us alive and free,
With unburdened shoulders!

Three of us with hearts like pine
That the lightnings splinter,
Clean of cleave and white of grain—
Three of us afoot again,
With a rapture fresh and fine
As a spring in winter!

All the hills are red and gold;
And the horns of vision
Call across the crackling air
Till we shout back to them there,
Taken captive in the hold
Of their bluff derision.

Spray-salt gusts of ocean blow
From the rocky headlands;
Overhead the wild geese fly,
Honking in the autumn sky;
Black sinister flocks of crow
Settle in the dead lands.

Three of us in love with life,
Roaming like wild cattle,
With the stinging air a-reel
As a warrior might feel
The swift orgasm of the knife
Slay him in mid-battle.

Three of us to march abreast
Down the hills of morrow!
With a clean heart and a few
Friends to clench the spirit to—
Leave the gods to rule the rest,
And good-bye, sorrow!

GRIEF

"Melancholy," said Poe in *The Philosophy of Composition,* "is the most legitimate of all the poetic tones. . . . I asked myself, 'Of all melancholy topics, what, according to the universal understanding of mankind, is the most melancholy?' 'Death' was the obvious reply. 'And when,' I said, 'is this most melancholy of topics most poetical?' . . . The answer, here also, is obvious—'When it most closely allies itself to Beauty: the death, then, of a beautiful woman is, unquestionably, the most poetical topic in the world.' " From this germ came "The Raven," the poem which gripped the fancy of the world within a fortnight. In the same vein, the expression of sorrow, Poe wrote "Ulalume" and "Annabel Lee." In answer to his blank despair, Dante Gabriel Rossetti a few years later wrote "The Blessed Damozel." It gives a hopeful answer to the questions of "The Raven," and makes of sorrow a thing of beauty.

THE BLESSED DAMOZEL

by Dante Gabriel Rossetti (1828-1882)

The blessed damozel leaned out
 From the gold bar of Heaven;
Her eyes were deeper than the depth
 Of waters stilled at even;
She had three lilies in her hand,
 And the stars in her hair were seven.

Her robe, ungirt from clasp to hem,
 No wrought flowers did adorn,
But a white rose of Mary's gift,
 For service meetly worn;
Her hair that lay along her back
 Was yellow like ripe corn.

Herseemed she scarce had been a day
 One of God's choristers;
The wonder was not yet quite gone
 From that still look of hers;
Albeit, to them she left, her day
 Had counted as ten years.

(To *one,* it is ten years of years.
 . . . Yet now, and in this place,
Surely she leaned o'er me—her hair
 Fell all about my face. . . .
Nothing: the autumn fall of leaves.
 The whole year sets apace.)

It was the rampart of God's house
 That she was standing on;
By God built over the sheer depth
 The which is Space begun;
So high, that looking downward thence
 She scarce could see the sun.

It lies in Heaven, across the flood
 Of ether, as a bridge.
Beneath the tides of day and night
 With flame and darkness ridge
The void, as low as where this earth
 Spins like a fretful midge.

Around her, lovers, newly met
 'Mid deathless love's acclaims,
Spoke evermore among themselves
 Their heart-remembered names;
And the souls mounting up to God
 Went by her like thin flames.

And still she bowed herself and stooped
 Out of the circling charm;
Until her bosom must have made
 The bar she leaned on warm,
And the lilies lay as if asleep
 Along her bended arm.

From the fixed place of Heaven she saw
 Time like a pulse shake fierce
Through all the worlds. Her gaze still strove
 Within the gulf to pierce
Its path; and now she spoke as when
 The stars sang in their spheres.

The sun was gone now; the curled moon
 Was like a little feather
Fluttering far down the gulf; and now
 She spoke through the still weather.
Her voice was like the voice the stars
 Had when they sang together.

(Ah sweet! Even now, in that bird's song,
 Strove not her accents there,
Fain to be harkened? When those bells
 Possessed the mid-day air,
Strove not her steps to reach my side
 Down all the echoing stair?)

"I wish that he were come to me,
 For he will come," she said.
"Have I not prayed in Heaven?—on earth,
 Lord, Lord, has he not pray'd?
Are not two prayers a perfect strength?
 And shall I feel afraid?

"When round his head the aureole clings,
 And he is clothed in white,
I'll take his hand and go with him
 To the deep wells of light;
As unto a stream we will step down,
 And bathe there in God's sight.

"We two will stand beside that shrine,
 Occult, withheld, untrod,
Whose lamps are stirred continually

With prayer sent up to God;
And see our old prayers, granted, melt
Each like a little cloud.

"We two will lie i' the shadow of
That living mystic tree
Within whose secret growth the Dove
Is sometimes felt to be,
While every leaf that His plumes touch
Saith His Name audibly.

"And I myself will teach to him,
I myself, lying so,
The songs I sing here; which his voice
Shall pause in, hushed and slow,
And find some knowledge at each pause,
Or some new thing to know."

(Alas! We two, we two, thou say'st!
Yea, one wast thou with me
That once of old. But shall God lift
To endless unity
The soul whose likeness with thy soul
Was but its love for thee?)

"We two," she said, "will seek the groves
Where the lady Mary is,
With her five handmaidens, whose names
Are five sweet symphonies,
Cecily, Gertrude, Magdalen,
Margaret and Rosalys.

"Circlewise sit they, with bound locks
And foreheads garlanded;
Into the fine cloth white like flame
Weaving the golden thread,
To fashion the birth-robes for them
Who are just born, being dead.

"He shall fear, haply, and be dumb:
Then will I lay my cheek
To his, and tell about our love,
Not once abashed or weak:
And the dear Mother will approve
My pride, and let me speak.

"Herself shall bring us, hand in hand,
To Him round whom all souls
Kneel, the clear-ranged unnumbered heads
Bowed with their aureoles:
And angels meeting us shall sing
To their citherns and citoles.

"There will I ask of Christ the Lord
Thus much for him and me:—
Only to live as once on earth
With Love, only to be,
As then awhile, for ever now
Together, I and he."

She gazed and listened and then said,
Less sad of speech than mild:—
"All this is when he comes." She ceased.
The light thrilled toward her, fill'd
With angels in strong level flight.
Her eyes prayed, and she smiled.

(I saw her smile.) But soon their path
Was vague in distant spheres:
And then she cast her arms along
The golden barriers,
And laid her face between her hands,
And wept. (I heard her tears.)

DEATH

The most powerful cause of sorrow is death, but it is not always, in poetry, the death of a beautiful woman. Memories of children cut off in infancy bring tears to Wordsworth, who records them in "Three Years She Grew" and to Ralph Waldo Emerson, who commemorates his sorrow in "Threnody." Arnold finds bitter pain in the song of the nightingale, "Philomela," Whitman elaborates the death-chant of a mocking-bird in "Out of the Cradle Endlessly Rocking." The death of a friend, one who had been closely allied by nature, stung Tennyson to a first cry of anguish in "Break, break, break," which led him on to the greatest of Victorian elegies, "In Memoriam." It was a friend of the spirit rather than a personal acquaintance whose death inspired Walt Whitman to compose what is perhaps the nation's greatest death-poem, certainly the most beautiful tribute to Lincoln, "When Lilacs Last in the Dooryard

Bloomed." Housman sighs for all who are gone before him, without specification, and finds consolation in the fact that he will soon be lying with them.

BREAK, BREAK, BREAK

Break, break, break,
On thy cold gray stones, O Sea!
And I would that my tongue could utter
The thoughts that arise in me.

O well for the fisherman's boy,
That he shouts with his sister at play!
O well for the sailor lad,
That he sings in his boat on the bay!

And the stately ships go on
To their haven under the hill;
But O for the touch of a vanish'd hand,
And the sound of a voice that is still!

Break, break, break,
At the foot of thy crags, O Sea!
But the tender grace of a day that is dead
Will never come back to me.

—*Alfred, Lord Tennyson* (1809-1892)

WHEN LILACS LAST IN THE DOORYARD BLOOMED

by Walt Whitman (1819-1892)

I

When lilacs last in the dooryard bloomed,
And the great star early drooped in the western sky in the night,
I mourned, and yet shall mourn with ever-returning spring.
Ever-returning spring, trinity sure to me you bring,
Lilac blooming perennial and drooping star in the west,
And thought of him I love.

II

O powerful western fallen star!
O shades of night—O moody, tearful night!
O great star disappeared—O the black murk that hides the star!
O cruel hands that hold me powerless—O helpless soul of me!
O harsh surrounding cloud that will not free my soul.

III

In the dooryard fronting an old farmhouse near the whitewashed palings,
Stands the lilac-bush tall-growing with heart-shaped leaves of rich green,
With many a pointed blossom rising delicate, with the perfume strong I love,
With every leaf a miracle—and from this bush in the dooryard,
With delicate-colored blossoms and heart-shaped leaves of rich green,
A sprig with its flower I break.

IV

In the swamp in secluded recesses,
A shy and hidden bird is warbling a song.

Solitary the thrush,
The hermit withdrawn to himself, avoiding the settlements,
Sings by himself a song.

Song of the bleeding throat,
Death's outlet song of life (for well, dear brother, I know,
If thou wast not granted to sing thou would'st surely die).

V

Over the breast of the spring, the land, amid cities,
Amid lanes and through old woods, where lately the violets peeped from the ground, spotting the gray débris,
Amid the grass in the fields each side of the lanes, passing the endless grass,
Passing the yellow-speared wheat, every grain from its shroud in the dark-brown fields uprisen,
Passing the apple-tree blows of white and pink in the orchards,
Carrying a corpse to where it shall rest in the grave,
Night and day journeys a coffin.

VI

Coffin that passes through lanes and streets,
Through day and night with the great cloud darkening the land,
With the pomp of the inlooped flags with the cities draped in black,
With the show of the States themselves as of crape-veiled women standing,
With processions long and winding and the flambeaus of the night,
With the countless torches lit, with the silent sea of faces and the unbared heads,
With the waiting depot, the arriving coffin, and the somber faces,
With dirges through the night, with the thousand voices rising strong and solemn,
With all the mournful voices of the dirges poured around the coffin,
The dim-lit churches and the shuddering organs—where amid these you journey,
With the tolling, tolling bells' perpetual clang,
Here, coffin that slowly passes,
I give you my sprig of lilac.

VII

(Nor for you, for one alone,
Blossoms and branches green to coffins all I bring,
For fresh as the morning, thus would I chant a song for you, O sane and sacred death.

All over bouquets of roses,
O death, I cover you over with roses and early lilies,
But mostly and now the lilac that blooms the first,
Copious I break, I break the sprigs from the bushes,
With loaded arms I come, pouring for you,
For you and the coffins all of you, O death.)

VIII

O western orb sailing the heaven,
Now I know what you must have meant as a month since I walked,
As I walked in silence the transparent shadowy night,
As I saw you had something to tell as you bent to me night after night,
As you drooped from the sky low down as if to my side (while the other stars all looked on),
As we wandered together the solemn night (for something I know not what kept me from sleep),
As the night advanced, and I saw on the rim of the west how full you were of woe,
As I stood on the rising ground in the breeze in the cool, transparent night,
As I watched where you passed, and was lost in the netherward black of the night,

As my soul in its trouble dissatisfied sank, as where you sad orb,
Concluded, dropped in the night, and was gone.

IX

Sing on there in the swamp,
O singer bashful and tender, I hear your notes, I hear your call,
I hear, I come presently, I understand you;
But a moment I linger, for the lustrous star has detained me,
The star my departing comrade holds and detains me.

X

O how shall I warble myself for the dead one there I loved?
And how shall I deck my song for the large sweet soul that has gone?
And what shall my perfume be for the grave of him I love?

Sea-winds blown from east and west,
Blown from the Eastern sea and blown from the Western sea, till there on the prairies meeting,
These and with these and the breath of my chant,
I'll perfume the grave of him I love.

XI

O what shall I hang on the chamber walls?
And what shall the pictures be that I hang on the walls,
To adorn the burial-house of him I love?

Pictures of growing spring and farms and homes,
With the fourth-month eve at sundown, and the gray smoke lucid and bright,
With floods of the yellow gold of the gorgeous, indolent, sinking sun, burning, expanding the air,
With the fresh sweet herbage under foot, and the pale green leaves of the trees prolific,
In the distance the flowing glaze, the breast of the river, with a wind-dapple here and there,
With ranging hills on the banks, with many a line against the sky, and shadows,
And the city at hand with dwellings so dense, and stacks of chimneys,
And all the scenes of life and the workshops, and the workmen homeward returning.

XII

Lo, body and soul—this land,
My own Manhattan with spires, and the sparkling and hurrying tides, and the ships,
The varied and ample land, the South and the North in the light, Ohio's shores and flashing Missouri,
And ever the far-spreading prairies covered with grass and corn.

Lo, the most excellent sun so calm and haughty,
The violet and purple morn with just-felt breezes,
The gentle soft-born measureless light,
The miracle spreading bathing all, the fulfilled noon,
The coming eve delicious, the welcome night and the stars,
Over my cities shining all, enveloping man and land.

XIII

Sing on, sing on you gray-brown bird,
Sing from the swamps, the recesses, pour your chant from the bushes,
Limitless out of the dusk, out of the cedars and pines.
Sing on dearest brother, warble your reedy song,
Loud human song, with voice of uttermost woe.

O liquid and free and tender!
O wild and loose to my soul—O wondrous singer!
You only I hear—yet the star holds me (but will soon depart),
Yet the lilac with mastering odor holds me.

XIV

Now while I sat in the day and looked forth,
In the close of the day with its light and the fields of spring, and the farmers preparing their crops,
In the large unconscious scenery of my land with its lakes and forests,
In the heavenly aërial beauty (after the perturbed winds and the storms),
Under the arching heavens of the afternoon swift passing, and the voices of children and women,
The many-moving sea-tides, and I saw the ships how they sailed,
And the summer approaching with richness, and the fields all busy with labor,
And the infinite separate houses, how they all went on, each with its meals and minutia of daily usages,
And the streets how their throbbings throbbed, and the cities pent—lo, then and there,
Falling upon them all and among them all, enveloping me with the rest,
Appeared the cloud, appeared the long black trail,
And I knew death, its thought, and the sacred knowledge of death.

Then with the knowledge of death as walking one side of me,
And the thought of death close-walking the other side of me,
And I in the middle as with companions, and as holding the hands of companions,
I fled forth to the hiding receiving night that talks not,
Down to the shores of the water, the path by the swamp in the dimness,
To the solemn shadowy cedars and ghostly pines so still.

And the singer so shy to the rest received me,
The gray-brown bird I know received us comrades three,
And he sang the carol of death, and a verse for him I love.

From deep secluded recesses,
From the fragrant cedars and the ghostly pines so still,
Came the carol of the bird.

And the charm of the carol rapt me,
As I held as if by their hands my comrades in the night,
And the voice of my spirit tallied the song of the bird.

Come, lovely and soothing death,
Undulate round the world, serenely arriving, arriving,

In the day, in the night, to all, to each,
Sooner or later delicate death.

Praised be the fathomless universe,
For life and joy, and for objects and knowledge curious,
And for love, sweet love—but praise! praise! praise!
For the sure-enwinding arms of cool-enfolding death.

Dark mother always gliding near with soft feet,
Have none chanted for thee a chant of fullest welcome?
Then I chant it for thee, I glorify thee above all,
I bring thee a song that when thou must indeed come, come unfalteringly.

Approach, strong deliveress,
When it is so, when thou hast taken them, I joyously sing the dead,
Lost in the loving floating ocean of thee,
Laved in the flood of thy bliss, O death.

From me to thee glad serenades,
Dances for thee I propose saluting thee, adornments and feastings for thee,
And the sights of the open landscape and the high-spread sky are fitting,
And life and the fields, and the huge and thoughtful night.

The night in silence under many a star,
The ocean shore and the husky whispering wave whose voice I know,
And the soul turning to thee, O vast and well-veiled death,
And the body gratefully nestling close to thee.

Over the tree-tops I float thee a song,
Over the rising and sinking waves, over the myriad fields and the prairies wide,
Over the dense-packed cities all and the teeming wharves and ways,
I float this carol with joy, with joy to thee, O death.

XV

To the tally of my soul,
Loud and strong kept up the gray-brown bird,
With pure deliberate notes spreading, filling the night.

Loud in the pines and cedars dim,
Clear in the freshness moist and the swamp-perfume,
And I with my comrades there in the night.

While my sight that was bound in my eyes unclosed,
As to long panoramas of visions.

And I saw askant the armies,
I saw as in noiseless dreams hundreds of battle-flags,
Borne through the smoke of the battles and pierced with missiles I saw them,
And carried hither and yon through the smoke, and torn and bloody,
And at last but a few shreds left on the staffs (and all in silence),
And the staffs all splintered and broken.

I saw battle-corpses, myriads of them,
And the white skeletons of young men, I saw them,
I saw the débris and débris of all the slain soldiers of the war,

But I saw they were not as was thought;
They themselves were fully at rest, they suffered not,
The living remained and suffered, the mother suffered,
And the wife and the child and the musing comrade suffered,
And the armies that remained suffered.

XVI

Passing the visions, passing the night,
Passing, unloosing the hold of my comrades' hands,
Passing the song of the hermit bird and the tallying song of my soul,
Victorious song, death's outlet song, yet varying ever-altering song,
As low and wailing, yet clear the notes, rising and falling, flooding the night,
Sadly sinking and fainting, as warning and warning, and yet again bursting with
joy,
Covering the earth and filling the spread of the heaven,
As that powerful psalm in the night I heard from recesses,
Passing, I leave thee, lilac with heart-shaped leaves,
I leave thee there in the dooryard, blooming, returning with spring.

I cease from my song for thee,
From my gaze on thee in the west, fronting the west, communing with thee,
O comrade lustrous with silver face in the night.

Yet each to keep and all, retrievements out of the night,
The song, the wondrous chant of the gray-brown bird,
And the tallying chant, the echo aroused in my soul,
With the lustrous and drooping star with the countenance full of woe,
With the holders holding my hand nearing the call of the bird,
Comrades mine and I in the midst, and their memory ever to keep, for the dead I
loved so well,
For the sweetest, wisest soul of all my days and lands—and this for his dear sake,
Lilac and star and bird twined with the chant of my soul,
There in the fragrant pines and the cedars dusk and dim.

FROM "A SHROPSHIRE LAD"

With rue my heart is laden
For golden friends I had,
For many a rose-lipped maiden
And many a lightfoot lad.

By brooks too broad for leaping
The lightfoot boys are laid;
The rose-lipped girls are sleeping
In fields where roses fade.

—*A. E. Housman*
(1859-)

THE ARTS

Poets are not satisfied with composing literature; they must also praise it. Keats describes his emotion "On First Looking into Chapman's *Homer*," and

Andrew Lang sums up his deep study of the *Odyssey*. Among the most sustained eulogies of one poet by another are Swinburne's apostrophes to the Elizabethan dramatists and Longfellow's sonnet sequence to Dante, "Divina Commedia." James R. Clemens extends the territory to a general "Love of Books."

DIVINA COMMEDIA

by Henry Wadsworth Longfellow (1807-1882)

I

Oft have I seen at some cathedral door
A laborer, pausing in the dust and heat,
Lay down his burden, and with reverent feet
Enter, and cross himself, and on the floor
Kneel to repeat his paternoster o'er;
Far off the noises of the world retreat;
The loud vociferations of the street
Become an undistinguishable roar.
So, as I enter here from day to day,
And leave my burden at this minster gate,
Kneeling in prayer, and not ashamed to pray,
The tumult of the time disconsolate
To inarticulate murmurs dies away,
While the eternal ages watch and wait.

II

How strange the sculptures that adorn these towers!
This crowd of statues, in whose folded sleeves
Birds build their nests; while canopied with leaves
Parvis and portal bloom like trellised bowers,
And the vast minster seems a cross of flowers!
But fiends and dragons on the gargoyled eaves
Watch the dead Christ between the living thieves,
And, underneath, the traitor Judas lowers!
Ah! from what agonies of heart and brain,
What exultations trampling on despair,
What tenderness, what tears, what hate of wrong,
What passionate outcry of a soul in pain,
Uprose this poem of the earth and air,
This medieval miracle of song!

III

I enter, and I see thee in the gloom
Of the long aisles, O poet saturnine!
And strive to make my steps keep pace with thine.
The air is filled with some unknown perfume;
The congregation of the dead make room
For thee to pass; the votive tapers shine;
Like rooks that haunt Ravenna's groves of pine
The hovering echoes fly from tomb to tomb.

From the confessionals I hear arise
Rehearsals of forgotten tragedies,
And lamentations from the crypts below;
And then a voice celestial that begins
With the pathetic words, "Although your sins
As scarlet be," and ends with "as the snow."

IV

With snow-white veil and garments as of flame,
She stands before thee, who so long ago
Filled thy young heart with passion and the woe
From which thy song and all its splendors came;
And while with stern rebuke she speaks thy name,
The ice about thy heart melts as the snow
On mountain heights, and in swift overflow
Comes gushing from thy lips in sobs of shame.
Thou makest full confession; and a gleam,
As of the dawn on some dark forest cast,
Seems on thy lifted forehead to increase;
Lethe and Eunoë—the remembered dream
And the forgotten sorrow—bring at last
That perfect pardon which is perfect peace.

V

I lift mine eyes, and all the windows blaze
With forms of Saints and holy men who died,
Here martyred and hereafter glorified;
And the great Rose upon its leaves displays
Christ's Triumph, and the angelic roundelays,
With splendor upon splendor multiplied;
And Beatrice again at Dante's side
No more rebukes, but smiles her words of praise.
And then the organ sounds, and unseen choirs
Sing the old Latin hymns of peace and love
And benedictions of the Holy Ghost;
And the melodious bells among the spires
O'er all the housetops and through heaven above
Proclaim the elevation of the Host!

VI

O star of morning and of liberty!
O bringer of the light, whose splendor shines
Above the darkness of the Apennines,
Forerunner of the day that is to be!
The voices of the city and the sea,
The voices of the mountains and the pines,
Repeat thy song, till the familiar lines
Are footpaths for the thought of Italy!
Thy flame is blown abroad from all the heights,
Through all the nations, and a sound is heard,

As of a mighty wind, and men devout,
Strangers of Rome, and the new proselytes,
In their own language hear the wondrous word,
And many are amazed and many doubt.

THE LOVE OF BOOKS

Happy he
Who, in his home at night,
Finds in his books delight,
And sweet society;
Whilst he who sees no profit in their use,
Will live a fool and die as great a goose.

At my call
Great Shakespeare and his fellows
Stand ready, like my bellows,
For service menial;
Thus kingly do I sit and at mine ease,
Whilst they, when summoned, do their best to please.

Who pines more
For earthly rank and pelf,
Than good books on his shelf,
Is like a sycamore;
A tree so plagued by density of shade,
That well-intending light shrinks back dismayed.

With a book,
A man is richer far
Than kings and princes are,
Though he no cities took;
For in good books a vein of thought is found,
Which, mined, exhaustless gold yields from the ground.

—*James R. Clemens* (1866-)

Music and the plastic arts receive their share of praise. Keats renders homage to the Elgin marbles as he did to a Grecian urn. Shakespeare's immortal song from "Henry VIII" and Herrick's "To Music to Becalm His Fever" are eloquent in their homage to the healing charm of music. Wordsworth finds an elevation of spirit growing from a song sung by a solitary reaper. John Dryden runs the gamut of effects achieved and the emotions aroused by "the only universal tongue."

ON THE ELGIN MARBLES

My spirit is too weak; mortality
Weighs heavily on me like unwilling sleep,
And each imagined pinnacle and steep
Of godlike hardship tells me I must die
Like a sick eagle looking at the sky.
Yet 'tis a gentle luxury to weep
That I have not the cloudy winds to keep

Fresh for the opening of the morning's eye.
Such dim-conceivèd glories of the brain,
Bring round the heart an indescribable feud;
So do these wonders a most dizzy pain,
That mingles Grecian grandeur with the rude
Wasting of old Time—with a billowy main—
A sun, a shadow of a magnitude.
—*John Keats* (1795-1821)

THE SOLITARY REAPER

by William Wordsworth (1770-1850)

Behold her, single in the field,
Yon solitary highland lass!
Reaping and singing by herself;
Stop here, or gently pass!
Alone she cuts and binds the grain,
And sings a melancholy strain;
O listen! for the vale profound
Is overflowing with the sound.

No nightingale did ever chaunt
More welcome notes to weary bands
Of travellers in some shady haunt,
Among Arabian sands:
A voice so thrilling ne'er was heard
In spring-time from the cuckoo-bird,
Breaking the silence of the seas
Among the farthest Hebrides.

Will no one tell me what she sings?—
Perhaps the plaintive numbers flow
For old, unhappy, far-off things,
And battles long ago:
Or is it some more humble lay,
Familiar matter of today?
Some natural sorrow, loss, or pain,
That has been, and may be again?

Whate'er the theme, the maiden sang
As if her song could have no ending;
I saw her singing at her work,
And o'er the sickle bending;—
I listened, motionless and still;
And, as I mounted up the hill
The music in my heart I bore,
Long after it was heard no more.

ALEXANDER'S FEAST, OR, THE POWER OF MUSIC

by John Dryden (1631-1700)

'Twas at the royal feast for Persia won
By Philip's warlike son—
Aloft in awful state
The godlike hero sate
On his imperial throne;
His valiant peers were placed around,
Their brows with roses and with myrtles bound
(So should desert in arms be crown'd);
The lovely Thais by his side
Sat like a blooming eastern bride
In flower of youth and beauty's pride:—
Happy, happy, happy pair!
None but the brave,
None but the brave,
None but the brave deserves the fair!

Timotheus, placed on high
Amid the tuneful choir,

With flying fingers touch'd the lyre:
The trembling notes ascend the sky
And heavenly joys inspire.
The song began from Jove
Who left his blissful seats above—
Such is the power of mighty love!
A dragon's fiery form belied the god;
Sublime on radiant spires he rode
When he to fair Olympia prest,
And while he sought her snowy breast,
Then round her slender waist he curl'd,
And stamp'd an image of himself, a sovereign of the world.
—The listening crowd admire the lofty sound!
A present deity! they shout around:
A present deity! the vaulted roofs rebound!
With ravish'd ears
The monarch hears,
Assumes the god,
Affects to nod,
And seems to shake the spheres.

The praise of Bacchus then the sweet musician sung,
Of Bacchus ever fair and ever young:
The jolly god in triumph comes!
Sound the trumpets, beat the drums!
Flush'd with a purple grace
He shows his honest face;
Now give the hautboys breath. He comes! he comes!
Bacchus, ever fair and young,
Drinking joys did first ordain;
Bacchus' blessings are a treasure,
Drinking is the soldier's pleasure:
Rich the treasure,
Sweet the pleasure,
Sweet is pleasure after pain.

Soothed with the sound, the king grew vain;
Fought all his battles o'er again,
And thrice he routed all his foes, and thrice he slew the slain!
The master saw the madness rise,
His glowing cheeks, his ardent eyes;
And while he heaven and earth defied
Changed his hand and check'd his pride.
He chose a mournful Muse
Soft pity to infuse:
He sung Darius great and good,
By too severe a fate
Fallen, fallen, fallen, fallen,
Fallen from his high estate,
And weltering in his blood;
Deserted at his utmost need

By those his former bounty fed;
On the bare earth exposed he lies
With not a friend to close his eyes.
—With downcast looks the joyless victor sat,
Revolving in his alter'd soul
The various turns of chance below;
And now and then a sigh he stole,
And tears began to flow.

The mighty master smiled to see
That love was in the next degree;
'Twas but a kindred sound to move,
For pity melts the mind to love.
Softly sweet, in Lydian measures
Soon he soothed his soul to pleasures.
War, he sung, is toil and trouble,
Honour but an empty bubble;
Never ending, still beginning,
Fighting still, and still destroying;
If the world be worth thy winning,
Think, O think, it worth enjoying:
Lovely Thais sits beside thee,
Take the good the gods provide thee!

—The many rend the skies with loud applause;
So Love was crown'd, but Music won the cause.
The prince, unable to conceal his pain,
Gazed on the fair
Who caused his care,
And sigh'd and look'd, sigh'd and look'd again:
Sigh'd and look'd, and sigh'd again:
At length with love and wine at once opprest
The vanquish'd victor sunk upon her breast.

Now strike the golden lyre again:
A louder yet, and yet a louder strain!
Break his bands of sleep asunder
And rouse him like a rattling peal of thunder.
Hark! hark! the horrid sound
Has raiséd up his head:
As awakéd from the dead
And amazed he stares around.
"Revenge, revenge," Timotheus cries,
"See the Furies arise!
See the snakes that they rear!
How they hiss in their hair,
And the sparkles that flash from their eyes!

Behold a ghastly band,
Each a torch in his hand!
Those are Grecian ghosts, that in battle were slain
And unburied remain

Inglorious on the plain:
Give the vengeance due
To the valiant crew!
Behold how they toss their torches on high,
How they point to the Persian abodes
And glittering temples of their hostile gods."
—The princes applaud with a furious joy:
And the King seized a flambeau with zeal to destroy;
Thais led the way
To light him to his prey,
And like another Helen, fired another Troy!

—Thus, long ago,
Ere heaving bellows learn'd to blow,
While organs yet were mute,
Timotheus, to his breathing flute
And sounding lyre
Could swell the soul to rage, or kindle soft desire.
At last divine Cecilia came,
Inventress of the vocal frame;
The sweet enthusiast from her sacred store
Enlarged the former narrow bounds,
And added length to solemn sounds,
With Nature's mother-wit, and arts unknown before.

Let old Timotheus yield the prize
Or both divide the crown;
He raised a mortal to the skies;
She drew an angel down!

TO MUSIC, TO BECALM HIS FEVER

by Robert Herrick (1591-1674)

Charm me asleep, and melt me so
With thy delicious numbers;
That being ravished, hence I go
Away in easy slumbers.
Ease my sick head,
And make my bed,
Thou power that canst sever
From me this ill,
And quickly still,
Though thou not kill
My fever.

Thou sweetly canst convert the same
From a consuming fire
Into a gentle-licking flame,
And make it thus expire.
Then make me weep
My pains asleep,
And give me such reposes
That I, poor I,
May think, thereby,
I live and die
'Mongst roses.

Fall on me like the silent dew,
Or like those maiden showers,
Which, by the peep of day, do strew
A baptism o'er the flowers.
Melt, melt my pains
With thy soft strains;
That having ease me given,
With full delight
I leave this light,
And take my flight
For Heaven.

SWEET MUSIC

Orpheus with his lute made trees,
And the mountain tops that freeze,

Bow themselves, when he did sing:
To his music plants and flowers
Ever sprung; as sun and showers
There had made a lasting spring.

Every thing that heard him play,
Even the billows of the sea,
Hung their heads, and then lay by.
In sweet music is such art,
Killing care and grief of heart
Fall asleep, or hearing, die.

—*William Shakespeare* (1564-1616)

SUGGESTIONS FOR ADDITIONAL READING

LOVE POEMS

Ben Jonson, *The Triumph*
John Lyly, *Cupid and My Campaspe*
John Donne, *The Will*
John Donne, *The Funeral*
George Wither, *Lover's Resolution*
Henry Carey, *Sally in Our Alley*
William Blake, *Song* (*"My silks and fine array"*)
Robert Burns, *Mary Morison*
Robert Burns, *Highland Mary*
Thomas Moore, *Believe Me, If All*
Robert Browning, *Summum Bonum*
Laurence Binyon, *O World, Be Nobler*
Christina Rossetti, *Mirage* (*"The hope I dreamed"*)
William Morris, *Love Is Enough*
F. W. Bourdillon, *The Night Has a Thousand Eyes*
Sara Teasdale, *Love Songs*
Elinor Wylie, *Parting Gift*
Elinor Wylie, *One Person*

PATRIOTIC POEMS

Michael Drayton, *Agincourt*
Edmund Waller, *English Verse*
William Collins, *How Sleep the Brave*
William Cowper, "England," from *The Task*
Robert Burns, *The Whistle*
Walt Whitman, *I Hear America Singing*
James R. Lowell, *Commemoration Ode*

HUMANITARIAN POEMS

Thomas Hood, *The Bridge of Sighs*
Leigh Hunt, *Abou Ben Adhem*
P. B. Shelley, *Song in Time of Revolution*
E. B. Browning, *The Cry of the Children*
Walt Whitman, *Starting from Paumanok*
Margaret Widdemer, *Factories*
John Masefield, *Consecration*
Edwin Markham, *The Man with the Hoe*

POEMS OF ANGER

William Collins, *Ode: The Passions*
P. B. Shelley, *Hate Song*
Robert Browning, *Up at a Villa, Down in the City*
D. G. Rossetti, *On the Refusal of Aid*

POEMS OF PRAISE

William Wordsworth, *At the Grave of Burns*
Lord Byron, *Tom Moore*
E. B. Browning, *Cowper's Grave*
Matthew Arnold, *Heine's Grave*
Austin Dobson, *In Praise of Pope*

POEMS OF SORROW

William Shakespeare, *Dirge from "Cymbeline"*
Thomas Hood, *The Death-Bed*
John Keats, *Ode on Melancholy*
E. A. Poe, *The Raven*
E. A. Poe, *Ulalume*
Matthew Arnold, *Philomela*
R. W. Emerson, *Threnody*
Walt Whitman, *Out of the Cradle Endlessly Rocking*
Conrad Aiken, *Tetelestai*

8

THE EMOTIONS OF POETRY—2: THE FORMS OF NATURE

THE TENDENCY of most people to begin a conversation with a remark about the weather is not merely a confession of inability to think of something to say, but also a recognition of the fact that all human beings are interested in the condition of the physical world which surrounds them. The man whose first act upon rising is to run to the window to observe the condition of the universe outside is not only expressing a healthy desire for physical comfort, but is also revealing the natural pleasure aroused by the prospect of a beautiful day. The world of nature is around us from our cradle to our grave, and colors all our experiences, memories, emotions, and ideas.

The term "nature" is used in so many senses that we must here limit its meaning to "the sum of all appearances of the physical world which reach us through the senses." All that we can know with certainty is the product of sensation. Nature, in one sense, might include both God and man, but in the restricted meaning—the one usually employed when we speak of "nature poetry"—man is the contemplator, and nature the object contemplated.

Man's reactions to the contemplation of nature, particularly when the man also happens to be a poet, take many forms. His approach ranges from the purely objective through the subjective to the symbolic, from extreme materialism to extreme idealism. His views vary in proportion to his cultural background, his physical needs, his mentality, and his emotional apparatus.

The most obvious attitude for man to take toward nature is that of the utilitarian—what is it good for? The engineer who forgets the beauty of a waterfall as he calculates its potential horsepower, the hunter who evaluates his day according to the number of pheasants he has bagged, the farmer who spends his life plowing, planting seed, cultivating weedy ground, and harvesting the crop in stony soil—all these may have difficulty in combining a poetic approach with the practical. Yet Robert Burns composed his most touching poem when his plow drove a fieldmouse from its nest and Robert Frost became New England's unofficial laureate on a mountain-farm in New Hampshire. One reason frequently given for the lack of nature poetry among the early American settlers or the pioneering group in any civilization is that while nature presented obstacles to comfort in the shape of impassable rivers and impenetrable forests, all energy was used in conquering nature rather than celebrating it. Walt Whitman has sung the joys of the broad-axe and the pioneers, but he chanted them in the comparative comfort of a Brooklyn newspaper-office.

The materialistic mind, having put nature to its proper use, next turns to a scientific study of its laws. John Keats is said to have accused Sir Isaac Newton of removing all the poetry from the rainbow by reducing it to a prismatic phenomenon. The knowledge of the workings of nature, acquired through scientific investigation, should be no impediment to the poet, however, for science merely explains, never personalizes. The realms of poetry and science are no more in conflict than those of science and religion; they are complementary, not antagonistic. Poetry humanizes the new realms opened to the mind of man by science. James Thomson found no difficulty in creating poetry from the science of Newton, and Wordsworth in one of his prefaces goes so far as to enunciate the friendship of science and poetry as a fundamental principle.

If the time should ever come when what is now called Science becomes familiarized to men, then the remotest discoveries of the chemist, the botanist, the mineralogist, will be as proper objects of the poet's art as any upon which it can be employed. He will be ready to follow the steps of the man of Science, he will be at his side, carrying sensation into the midst of the objects of Science itself. The poet will lend his divine spirit to aid the transfiguration, and will welcome the being thus produced as a dear and genuine inmate of the household of man.

It is noticeable that Wordsworth does not confuse the functions of the poet and the scientist; he merely harmonizes them. John Ruskin, in *Modern Painters,* distinguished clearly between the methods employed by the two types of minds.

This is the difference between the mere botanist's knowledge of plants and the great poet's or painter's knowledge of them. The one notes their distinctions for the sake of swelling his herbarium; the other that he may render them vehicles of expression and emotion. The one counts the stamens, affixes a name, and is content. The other observes every character of the plant's color and form; considering each of its attributes as an element of expression, he seizes on its lines of grace or energy, rigidity or repose, notes the feebleness or the vigor, the serenity or tremulousness of its hues; observes its local habits, its love or fear of peculiar places, its nourishment or destruction by particular influences; he associates it in his mind with all the features of the situations it inhabits and the ministering agencies necessary to its support. Thenceforward the flower is to him a living creature, with histories written on its leaves and passions breathing in its motion. Its occurrence in his picture is no mere point of color, no meaningless spark of light. It is a voice rising from the earth, a new chord of the mind's music, a necessary note in the harmony of his picture, contributing alike to its tenderness and its dignity, nor less to its loveliness and truth.

Nature can also be looked upon as material for pure objective description, valuable in and of itself, without use, explanation or any human associations. This is the use made of it by the Imagists, H. D., Amy Lowell, and John Gould Fletcher in particular, in scores of poems: "Orchard," "The Garden by Moonlight," "Sand and Spray," and the like. That nature could be a picture beautiful in and of itself was apparently incomprehensible to early artists; eighteenth-century landscapes are filled with human figures in order to endow the painting with "value." James Thomson was one of the first of modern poets to appreciate nature's beauty without drawing a moral from it.

In these instances nature is the center of attention. As soon as man happens upon the scene, however, nature is relegated to secondary importance. In the classical epics, as well as in much of the neo-classical poetry of Pope and his contemporaries, nature is used merely as a picture-frame for the portrait of man in action. Every drama must be given on a stage representing a place, every action must occur "on location," so that there may be some recognition of setting. Classical epic poetry and classical drama, however, compel the scene to be so formalized that it no longer attracts attention and the reader can concentrate upon the persons and plot. In this type of poetry nature fulfills much the same function as was served in the mid-Victorian photographer's studio by the canvas background depicting a sylvan scene or the papier-mâché stump upon which the subject leaned in pensive mood. Rendered meaningless, nature becomes not only artificial but "unnatural."

When Byron, in the person of Childe Harold, sailed up the Rhine to the base of the Alps, he dwelt upon the majesty of the river and its banks for only a moment, and then the flood of historical associations swept over him and the scene was forgotten. For one stanza about the glory of the Alpine peaks he produced ten concerning the battlefields whereon Swiss independence was established; Lake Geneva meant only Rousseau and *La Nouvelle Héloïse* to him. This same attitude toward nature was held by Oliver Goldsmith in *The Deserted Village,* where every spot was dear because of the people whom he had known there. To many people nature is beautiful or interesting only because of its human associations; actually the Rubicon, the Tiber, and the Cam are no more individual as streams than any Goose Creek in America, but their associations have made them memorable. Poets have often given fame to places otherwise undistinguished: the S'wanee River, "sweet Afton," Loch Lomond, Tintern Abbey, Hamelin, Tintagil, Grantchester, Sherwood Forest.

For some poets—especially for the minor poet—nature is merely a source-book of similes, metaphors, and analogies—an extended allegory of human life. This might be part of the artist's utilitarian attitude: to such a poet the flowing stream presents a parallel to the passing of time, the upright oak is an emblem of rectitude, the storm mirrors the hurly-burly of life. Here nature takes a distinctly subordinate rank and we come upon the "pathetic fallacy" or nature falsified.

In all the preceding approaches, nature has been viewed objectively. Lyricism, however, is subjective, and the greatest nature poetry is lyrical. When nature arouses in the poet the simple and spontaneous emotions which are common to children, the product is purely lyric. This is immediately recognizable in the poems of Blake, Burns, Wordsworth, Shelley, Emily Dickinson and that most simple-hearted of contemporary naturalists, W. H. Davies.

The great majority of nature-poems, however, pass beyond this unreflective lyricism to the point where nature becomes a reflector of the moods and emotions of man, calmer of his fears, soother of his sorrows, inspiration for his thoughts, and model for his virtues. Nature thus becomes either an echo of man or his other self. As Coleridge expresses the idea in his "Ode on Dejection":

> We receive but what we give,
> And in our life alone doth Nature live;
> Ours is the wedding garment, ours the shroud.

John Ruskin felt that this attitude toward nature is illogical and inartistic, and tried to bring public condemnation upon it by labelling it "the pathetic fallacy." He pointed out that the waves of the ocean are not inherently cruel nor the summer breezes gentle and kind. The "fallacy" is inherent in that nature is falsely used to express a pathos which only man can feel, not the objects or elements about him. Though the reader of such a poem as Edward Young's *Night Thoughts* may be inclined to agree with Ruskin that the inanimate objects of nature should not be endowed with artificial life, the reading of man's feelings into nature makes half the beauty of Gray, Cowper, Wordsworth and Keats.

The next step beyond interpreting nature as a reflector of man's emotions is that of entering into and interpreting nature itself. Here the poet's imaginative sympathy finds full scope. Walt Whitman and Shelley attempt to become a part of nature instead of making nature a part of humanity. Matthew Arnold, in his essay on Maurice de Guérin, explains this method:

> The grand power of Poetry is its interpretative power . . . the power of so dealing with things as to awaken in us a wonderfully full, new, and intimate sense of them, and of our relations with them. When this sense is awakened in us as to objects without us, we feel ourselves to be in contact with the essential nature of those objects, to be no longer bewildered and oppressed by them, but to have their secret, and to be in harmony with them; and this feeling calms and satisfies us as no other can.

Since what man knows has come to him through his senses, most of his concepts of the world and life beyond this present one have been drawn from his sensory perceptions of the world about him. To Vaughan, Blake and other mystics, nature becomes a symbol of the personal immortality of the spirit. Bryant finds in the birds of the air and the flowers of the field object-lessons of God's care for his creatures. Cardinal Newman finds in the Spring a foreshadowing of the resurrection, and goes on to say:

> The earth that we see does not satisfy us; it is but a beginning; it is but a promise of something beyond it; even when it is gayest, with all its blossoms on, and shows most touchingly what lies hid in it, yet it is not enough. We know much more lies hid in it than we see. . . . What we see is the outward shell of an eternal Kingdom, and on that Kingdom we fix the eyes of our faith.

But to the poet who cannot accept this mystical interpretation, the natural universe may represent an infinity unresponsive to human sorrow and desire, impersonal, the embodiment of unchangeable law. This is the picture of the universe which Meredith has projected in "Lucifer in Starlight." Though both were essentially religious, Meredith and Newman write from an entirely different point of view; one is cosmic, the other primarily terrestrial. Meredith's is the view of nature accepted by Thomas Hardy and other naturalistic pessimists. It carries the wheel full circle, and man is back to much the same attitude as is held by the utilitarian.

These eleven different methods of approaching nature—the utilitarian, the scientific, the imagist, the decorative, the associational, the analogical, the emotional, the "pathetically fallacious," the interpretative, the symbolically mystic, and the fatalistic—are to be found in poetry, though the first two occur rarely. In the history of poetry each of the attitudes has had its day. The primitive man reacted first in the purely emotional manner, making of the sea and the mountains objects of fear and awe. The analogical stage also is clear in the early formative days of the language; many of our most expressive words are merely nature metaphors, "fossil poetry." The myth-making age is the universalization of the "pathetic fallacy," for it gives to natural objects and forces not only the emotions of man, but also his shape and personality. *Beowulf* and other early folk-epics have been interpreted as sun-myths; Olympus was peopled with the offspring of the "earth-mother."

As man began to lose his fear of the forces of nature and turned to the inventing of methods for subjecting them to his control, his mood became utilitarian. Hesiod and others wrote versified directions for the care of the garden; in the eighteenth century the poet Dyer gave all necessary particulars for the raising and utilization of wool. At the time that the formal garden was popular in France and England, the poetry of the day used nature merely for formalized border-decorations. As long as Pope's dictum to the effect that "the proper study of mankind is man" was accepted, the prim verse of the drawing-room superseded the outdoor songs of William Browne. As soon as reaction set in, Burns, Shelley, Keats and Wordsworth sought in nature for an escape from the world of men; the emotional and interpretative stages were begun, and lasted brilliantly for a century; Byron and Browning emphasized the associations. In the poetry of today, though there is more of the fatalistic naturalism than ever before, no one mood seems to be predominant. Even the mysticism of the seventeenth century has its followers in the Meynells, Francis Thompson, Gerard Manley Hopkins, and other moderns.

The aspects of nature which have inspired poetry are quite as varied as the types of reactions. The subject-matter of most of the poetry, however, would seem to fall into three great divisions: (1) Poetry dealing with the material aspects of the universe, the sky, the earth, and the seas. (2) Poetry concerned with life—chiefly the life of the land, though we can occasionally find a lyric to a whale or sea-serpent—the birds, the beasts, the insects, and the plant life. (3) Poetry inspired by the changes occurring in nature—the seasons and the day from dawn to dark. For the purpose of ease in discussion, the nature poems have been grouped according to that plan.

SKY, EARTH, AND SEA

The sky, immense and continuously changing, has puzzled and appealed to all men in all times, from the Chaldean shepherds to the learned astronomers of today. The classicists preferred the sky at noon-day, blue and cloudless; the romanticists wanted the days cloudy and filled with storms or nights filled with stars. "The spacious firmament on high, and all the blue ethereal sky" were for Addison the perfect proof of divinity; to Edna St. Vincent Millay, in "Renascence," perhaps the most powerful sky-poem of our generation, the heaven is big with transforming magic and personal deity. "The Winds" of Cawein approaches the "pathetic fallacy" but the poem is full of movement and struggle. Shelley's "The Cloud" has appealed to a wider audience than any of Shelley's imaginative lyrics. The reason for its popularity has been brilliantly expressed by Francis Thompson in his essay on the poet in this unforgettable paragraph:

> Perhaps none of the poems is more purely and typically Shelleian than "The Cloud," and it is interesting to note how essentially it springs from the faculty of make-believe. The same thing is conspicuous, though less purely conspicuous, throughout his singing; it is the child's faculty of make-believe raised to the *n*th power. He is still at play, save only that his play is such as manhood stops to watch, and his playthings are those which the gods give their children. The universe is his box of toys. He dabbles his fingers in the day-fall. He is gold-dusty with tumbling amidst the stars. He makes bright mischief with the moon. The meteors nuzzle their noses in his hand. He teases into growling the kennelled thunder, and laughs at the shaking of its fiery chain. He dances in and out of the gates of heaven: its floor is littered with his broken fancies. He runs wild over the fields of ether. He chases the rolling world. He gets between the feet of the horses of the sun. He stands in the lap of patient Nature and twines her loosened tresses after a hundred wilful patterns to see how she will look nicest in his song.

THE CLOUD

by Percy Bysshe Shelley (1792-1822)

I bring fresh showers for the thirsting flowers
  From the seas and the streams;
I bear light shade for the leaves when laid
  In their noonday dreams.
From my wings are shaken the dews that waken
  The sweet buds every one,
When rocked to rest on their mother's breast,
  As she dances about the sun.
I wield the flail of the lashing hail,
  And whiten the green plains under,
And then again I dissolve it in rain,
  And laugh as I pass in thunder.

I sift the snow on the mountains below,
  And their great pines groan aghast;
And all the night 'tis my pillow white,
  While I sleep in the arms of the blast.
Sublime on the towers of my skiey bowers
  Lightning, my pilot, sits;
In a cavern under is fettered the thunder,
  It struggles and howls at fits;
Over earth and ocean, with gentle motion,

This pilot is guiding me,
Lured by the love of the genii that move
In the depths of the purple sea;
Over the rills, and the crags, and the hills,
Over the lakes and the plains,
Wherever he dream, under mountain or stream,
The Spirit he loves remains;
And I all the while bask in Heaven's blue smile,
Whilst he is dissolving in rains.

The sanguine Sunrise, with his meteor eyes,
And his burning plumes outspread,
Leaps on the back of my sailing rack,
When the morning star shines dead;
As on the jag of a mountain crag,
Which an earthquake rocks and swings,
An eagle alit one moment may sit
In the light of its golden wings.
And when Sunset may breathe, from the lit sea beneath,
Its ardours of rest and of love,
And the crimson pall of eve may fall
From the depth of Heaven above,
With wings folded I rest, on mine aery nest,
As still as a brooding dove.

That orbèd maiden with white fire laden,
Whom mortals call the Moon,
Glides glimmering o'er my fleece-like floor,
By the midnight breezes strewn;
And wherever the beat of her unseen feet,
Which only the angels hear,
May have broken the woof of my tent's thin roof,
The stars peep behind her and peer;
And I laugh to see them whirl and flee,
Like a swarm of golden bees,
When I widen the rent in my wind-built tent,
Till the calm rivers, lakes, and seas,
Like strips of the sky fallen through me on high,
Are each paved with the moon and these.

I bind the Sun's throne with a burning zone,
And the Moon's with a girdle of pearl;
The volcanoes are dim, and the stars reel and swim
When the whirlwinds my banner unfurl.
From cape to cape, with a bridge-like shape,
Over a torrent sea,
Sunbeam-proof, I hang like a roof,—
The mountains its columns be.
The triumphal arch through which I march
With hurricane, fire, and snow,
When the Powers of the air are chained to my chair,
Is the million-coloured bow;

The sphere-fire above its soft colours wove,
  While the moist Earth was laughing below.

I am the daughter of Earth and Water,
  And the nursling of the Sky;
I pass through the pores of the ocean and shores;
  I change, but I cannot die.
For after the rain when with never a stain
  The pavilion of Heaven is bare,
And the winds and sunbeams with their convex gleams
  Build up the blue dome of air,
I silently laugh at my own cenotaph,
  And out of the caverns of rain,
Like a child from the womb, like a ghost from the tomb,
  I arise and unbuild it again.

THE WINDS

Those hewers of the clouds, the Winds, that lair
At the four compass-points, are out tonight;
I hear their sandals trample on the height,
I hear their voices trumpet through the air:
Builders of storm, God's workmen, now they bear
Up the steep stair of sky, on backs of might,
Huge tempest bulks, while—sweat that blinds their sight—
The rain is shaken from tumultuous hair:
Now, sweepers of the firmament, they broom
Like gathered dust, the rolling mists along
Heaven's floors of sapphire; all the beautiful blue
Of skyey corridor and celestial room—
Preparing, with large laughter and loud song,
For the white moon and stars to wander through.
—*Madison Cawein* (1865-1914)

Of the four primal elements of early science—earth, fire, air and water—man has always clung most affectionately to earth. Since he has seen the plants rise from the ground and gain their sustenance from it, he has pictured himself as an uprooted plant, torn from the bosom of his mother earth, but eventually returning to it. "Dust thou art to dust returnest" was more than a figure of speech to the myth-makers. Mountains have always fascinated man with the pure power of architectural thrust, the symbol of the upward climb and the victorious summit.

Bryant, in "Monument Mountain," combines some of the emotion aroused by the view with a description of the mountain itself. One of the very best of modern mountain-poems is E. A. Robinson's "Monadnock from Wachusett," a sonnet describing the sense of age which a mountain gives. Elinor Wylie's noble "Hymn to Earth" and Wheelock's moving "Earth" offer many a comparison and contrast; the underlying theme is the life-and-death motif which animated Bryant's "Thanatopsis," yet the differences in tone are even greater than the differences in treatment.

MONUMENT MOUNTAIN

by William Cullen Bryant (1794-1878)

Thou who wouldst see the lovely and the wild
Mingled in harmony on Nature's face,
Ascend our rocky mountains. Let thy foot
Fail not with weariness, for on their tops
The beauty and the majesty of earth,
Spread wide beneath, shall make thee to forget
The steep and toilsome way. There, as thou stand'st,
The haunts of men below thee, and around
The mountain-summits, thy expanding heart
Shall feel a kindred with that loftier world
To which thou art translated, and partake
The enlargement of thy vision. Thou shalt look
Upon the green and rolling forest-tops,
And down into the secrets of the glens,
And streams that with their bordering thickets strive
To hide their windings. Thou shalt gaze, at once,
Here on white villages, and tilth, and herds,
And swarming roads, and there on solitudes
That only hear the torrent, and the wind,
And eagle's shriek. There is a precipice
That seems a fragment of some mighty wall,
Built by the hand that fashioned the old world,
To separate its nations, and thrown down
When the flood drowned them. To the north, a path
Conducts you up the narrow battlement.
Steep is the western side, shaggy and wild
With mossy trees, and pinnacles of flint,
And many a hanging crag. But, to the east,
Sheer to the vale go down the bare old cliffs—
Huge pillars, that in middle heaven upbear
Their weather-beaten capitals, here dark
With moss, the growth of centuries, and there
Of chalky whiteness where the thunder-bolt
Has splintered them. It is a fearful thing
To stand upon the beetling verge, and see
Where storm and lightning, from that huge gray wall,
Have tumbled down vast blocks, and at the base
Dashed them in fragments, and to lay thine ear
Over the dizzy depth, and hear the sound
Of winds, that struggle with the woods below,
Come up like ocean murmurs. But the scene
Is lovely round; a beautiful river there
Wanders amid the fresh and fertile meads,
The paradise he made unto himself,
Mining the soil for ages. On each side
The fields swell upward to the hills; beyond,
Above the hills, in the blue distance, rise
The mountain-columns with which earth props heaven.

HYMN TO EARTH

by Elinor Wylie (1887-1928)

Farewell, incomparable element,
Whence man arose, where he shall not return;
And hail, imperfect urn
Of his last ashes, and his firstborn fruit;
Farewell, the long pursuit,
And all the adventures of his discontent;
The voyages which sent
His heart averse from home:
Metal of clay, permit him that he come
To thy slow-burning fire as to a hearth;
Accept him as a particle of earth.

Fire, being divided from the other three,
It lives removed, or secret at the core;
Most subtle of the four,
When air flies not, nor water flows,
It disembodied goes,
Being light, elixir of the first decree,
More volatile than he;
With strength and power to pass
Through space, where never his least atom was:
He has no part in it, save as his eyes
Have drawn its emanation from the skies.

A wingless creature heavier than air,
He is rejected of its quintessence;
Coming and going hence,
In the twin minutes of his birth and death,
He may inhale as breath,
As breath relinquish heaven's atmosphere,
Yet in it have no share,

Nor can survive therein
Where its outer edge is filtered pure and thin:
It doth but lend its crystal to his lungs
For his early crying, and his final songs.

The element of water has denied
Its child; it is no more his element;
It never will relent;
Its silver harvests are more sparsely given
Than the rewards of heaven,
And he shall drink cold comfort at its side:
The water is too wide:
The seamew and the gull
Feather a nest made soft and pitiful
Upon its foam; he has not any part
In the long swell of sorrow at its heart.

Hail and farewell, belovèd element,
Whence he departed, and his parent once;
See where thy spirit runs
Which for so long hath had the moon to wife;
Shall this support his life
Until the arches of the waves be bent
And grow shallow and spent?
Wisely it cast him forth
With his dead weight of burdens nothing worth
Leaving him, for the universal years,
A little seawater to make his tears.

Hail, element of earth, receive thy own,
And cherish, at thy charitable breast,
This man, this mongrel beast:
He plows the sand, and, at his hardest need,
He sows himself for seed;
He plows the furrow, and in this lies down
Before the corn is grown;
Between the apple bloom
And the ripe apple is sufficient room
In time, and matter, to consume his love
And make him parcel of a cypress grove.

Receive him as thy lover for an hour
Who will not weary, by a longer stay,
The kind embrace of clay;
Even within thine arms he is dispersed
To nothing, as at first;
The air flings downward from its four-quartered tower
Him whom the flames devour;
At the full tide, at the flood,
The sea is mingled with his salty blood:
The traveler dust, although the dust be vile,
Sleeps as thy lover for a little while.

EARTH

by John Hall Wheelock (1886-)

Grasshopper, your fairy song
And my poem alike belong
To the dark and silent earth
From which all poetry has birth.
All we say and all we sing
Is but as the murmuring
Of that drowsy heart of hers
When from her deep dream she stirs:
If we sorrow, or rejoice,
You and I are but her voice.

Deftly does the dust express
In mind her hidden loveliness,
And from her cool silence stream
The cricket's cry and Dante's dream;
For the earth that breeds the trees
Breeds cities too, and symphonies.
Equally her beauty flows
Into a savior, or a rose—
Looks down in dream, and from above
Smiles at herself in Jesus' love.
Christ's love and Homer's art
Are but the workings of her heart;
Through Leonardo's hand she seeks
Herself, and through Beethoven speaks
In holy thunderings around
The awful message of the ground.

The serene and humble mold
Does in herself all selves enfold—
Kingdoms, destinies, and creeds,
Great dreams, and dauntless deeds,
Science that metes the firmament,
The high, inflexible intent
Of one for many sacrificed—
Plato's brain, the heart of Christ;
All love, all legend, and all lore
Are in the dust forevermore.

Even as the growing grass,
Up from the soil religions pass,
And the field that bears the rye
Bears parables and prophecy.

Out of the earth the poem grows
Like the lily, or the rose;
And all man is, or yet may be,
Is but herself in agony
Toiling up the steep ascent
Toward the complete accomplishment
When all dust shall be, the whole
Universe, one conscious soul.

Yea, the quiet and cool sod
Bears in her breast the dream of God.
If you would know what earth is, scan
The intricate, proud heart of man,
Which is the earth articulate,
And learn how holy and how great,
How limitless and how profound
Is the nature of the ground—
How without terror or demur
We may entrust ourselves to her
When we are wearied out and lay
Our faces in the common clay.
For she is pity, she is love,
All wisdom, she, all thoughts that move
About her everlasting breast
Till she gathers them to rest:
All tenderness of all the ages,
Seraphic secrets of the sages,
Vision and hope of all the seers,
All prayer, all anguish, and all tears
Are but the dust that from her dream
Awakes, and knows herself supreme—
Are but earth, when she reveals
All that her secret heart conceals
Down in the dark and silent loam,
Which is ourselves, asleep, at home.

Yea, and this, my poem, too,
Is part of her as dust and dew,
Wherein herself she doth declare
Through my lips, and say her prayer.

It is with the sea as with the mountains—love was not at first sight. The sagas of the Norse sea-rovers show that the cold North Sea and the Baltic were feared and respected, but never loved. The voyage from Greece to Troy was more to be dreaded than the Trojans, and the return trip was for Ulysses a ten-year struggle with the forces of the waters. Ships were never quite secure enough to awaken in sailors the poetic mood; none but a romantic landlubber could exult in a storm on the ocean. It must not be supposed that none of the sailors enjoyed plowing the sounding furrows, but early poetry reflects much more fear than affection.

The later poetry—Byron in "Childe Harold," Keats's sonnet, Swinburne in "The Triumph of Time," and the lyrics of Whitman, Hovey, and Joyce—shows that the old respect has not disappeared when the new love has come. John Masefield has drawn powerfully on his own experiences in his great poems of the sea, "Dauber" and "Sea-Fever," and the reader can usually tell at first reading whether the poet is writing from the land or from the deck of a ship.

OCEAN

(from "Childe Harold's Pilgrimage," Canto IV)

by Lord Byron (1788-1824)

Roll on, thou deep and dark blue Ocean—roll!
Ten thousand fleets sweep over thee in vain;
Man marks the earth with ruin; his control
Stops with the shore; upon the watery plain
The wrecks are all thy deed, nor doth remain
A shadow of man's ravage, save his own,
When for a moment, like a drop of rain,

He sinks into thy depths with bubbling groan,
Without a grave, unknell'd, uncoffin'd and unknown.

His steps are not upon thy paths—thy fields
Are not a spoil for him—thou dost arise
And shake him from thee; the vile strength he wields
For earth's destruction thou dost all despise,
Spurning him from thy bosom to the skies,
And send'st him, shivering in thy playful spray,
And howling, to his Gods, where haply lies
His petty hope in some near port or bay,
And dashest him again to earth—there let him lay.

The armaments which thunderstrike the walls
Of rock-built cities, bidding nations quake,
And monarchs tremble in their capitals,
The oak leviathans, whose huge ribs make
Their clay creator the vain title take
Of lord of thee, and arbiter of war;
These are thy toys, and, as the snowy flake,
They melt into thy yeast of waves, which mar
Alike the Armada's pride, or spoils of Trafalgar.

Thy shores are empires, changed in all save thee—
Assyria, Greece, Rome, Carthage, what are they?
Thy waters washed them power while they were free.
And many a tyrant since: their shores obey
The stranger, slave or savage; their decay
Has dried up realms to deserts:—not so thou,
Unchangeable save to thy wild wave's play—
Time writes no wrinkle on thine azure brow—
Such as creation's dawn beheld, thou rollest now.

Thou glorious mirror, where the Almighty's form
Glasses itself in tempests: in all time,
Calm or convulsed—in breeze, or gale, or storm,
Icing the pole, or in the torrid clime
Dark-heaving; boundless, endless, and sublime—
The image of Eternity—the throne
Of the Invisible; even from out thy slime
The monsters of the deep are made; each zone
Obeys thee; thou goest forth, dread, fathomless, alone.

ON THE SEA

It keeps eternal whisperings around
Desolate shores, and with its mighty swell
Gluts twice ten thousand caverns, till the spell
Of Hecate leaves them their old shadowy sound.
Often 'tis in such gentle temper found,
That scarcely will the very smallest shell
Be moved for days from where it sometime fell,

When last the winds of heaven were unbound.
Oh ye! who have your eye-balls vexed and tired,
Feast them upon the wideness of the Sea;
Oh ye! whose ears are dinned with uproar rude,
Or fed too much with cloying melody—
Sit ye near some old cavern's mouth, and brood
Until ye start, as if the sea-nymphs quired!

—*John Keats* (1795-1821)

THE SEA

(from "The Triumph of Time")

by Algernon Charles Swinburne (1837-1909)

I will go back to the great sweet mother,
  Mother and lover of men, the sea.
I will go down to her, I and none other,
  Close with her, kiss her and mix her with me;
Cling to her, strive with her, hold her fast;
O fair white mother, in days long past
Born without sister, born without brother,
  Set free my soul as thy soul is free.

O fair green-girdled mother of mine,
  Sea, that art clothed with the sun and the rain,
Thy sweet hard kisses are strong like wine,
  Thy large embraces are keen like pain.
Save me and hide me with all thy waves,
Find me one grave of thy thousand graves,
Those pure cold populous graves of thine,
  Wrought without hand in a world without stain.

I shall sleep, and move with the moving ships,
  Change as the winds change, veer in the tide;
My lips will feast on the foam of thy lips,
  I shall rise with thy rising, with thee subside;
Sleep, and not know if she be, if she were,
Filled full with life to the eyes and hair,
As a rose is fulfilled to the roseleaf tips
  With splendid summer and perfume and pride.

This woven raiment of nights and days,
  Were it once cast off and unwound from me,
Naked and glad would I walk in thy ways,
  Alive and aware of thy ways and thee;
Clear of the whole world, hidden at home,
Clothed with the green and crowned with the foam,
A pulse of the life of thy straits and bays,
  A vein in the heart of the streams of the sea.

WITH HUSKY-HAUGHTY LIPS, O SEA!

With husky-haughty lips, O sea!
Where day and night I wend thy surf-beat shore,
Imaging to my sense thy varied strange suggestions,
(I see and plainly list thy talk and conference here)
Thy troops of white-maned racers racing to the goal,
Thy ample, smiling face, dash'd with the sparkling dimples of the sun,
Thy brooding scowl and murk—thy unloos'd hurricanes,
Thy unsubduedness, caprices, wilfulness;
Great as thou art above the rest, thy many tears—a lack from all eternity in thy content,
(Naught but the greatest struggles, wrongs, defeats, could make thee greatest—no less could make thee,)
Thy lonely state—something thou ever seek'st and seek'st, yet never gain'st,
Surely some right withheld—some voice, in huge monotonous rage, of freedom-lover pent,
Some vast heart, like a planet's, chain'd and chafing in those breakers,
By lengthen'd swell, and spasm, and panting breath,
And rhythmic rasping of thy sands and waves,
And serpent hiss, and savage peals of laughter,
And undertones of distant lion roar,
(Sounding, appealing to the sky's deaf ear—but now, rapport for once,
A phantom in the night thy confidant for once,)
The first and last confession of the globe,
Outsurging, muttering from thy soul's abysms,
The tale of cosmic elemental passion,
Thou tellest to a kindred soul.

—*Walt Whitman* (1819-1892)

THE SEA GYPSY

I am fevered with the sunset,
I am fretful with the bay,
For the wander-thirst is on me
And my soul is in Cathay.

There's a schooner in the offing,
With her topsails shot with fire;
And my heart has gone aboard her
For the Islands of Desire.

I must forth again tomorrow!
With the sunset I must be
Hull down on the trail of rapture
In the wonder of the sea.

—*Richard Hovey* (1864-1900)

ALL DAY I HEAR

All day I hear the noise of waters
Making moan,
Sad as the sea-bird is when, going
Forth alone,
He hears the winds cry to the waters'
Monotone.

The gray winds, the cold winds are blowing
Where I go.
I hear the noise of many waters
Far below.
All day, all night, I hear them flowing
To and fro.

—*James Joyce* (1882-)

BIRDS, BEASTS, AND FLOWERS

Of all living creatures, birds have most stirred the poets to song. Perhaps there is a kinship between the two natures: the sudden flight, the impulse to sing, the cleaving of space. Certainly the bird songs were the first melodies heard by man, and, according to some musical theorists, have been the basis of all music since.

Though occasionally a raven, a waterfowl, or an eagle may inspire a poem, the heroes are usually the smaller songbirds. In English and continental poetry, the nightingale and the skylark, with occasionally a cuckoo as the harbinger of spring, almost monopolize the poet's attention. In America, since nightingales are absent and our meadow-larks do not soar in song, the first rank in the poet's affection is occupied by the thrush and the mocking-bird, with the robin famous for his personality rather than his voice, and the sea-gull admired for grace in the air. The poet who has never written about a bird is indeed a *rara avis.*

THE ROBIN AND THE WREN[1]

The robin and the wren
Are God Almighty's cock and hen;
The martin and the swallow
Are God Almighty's bow and arrow.
—*Anonymous* (before 1700)

THE RIVALS

The nightingale, the organ of delight,
The nimble lark, the blackbird, and the thrush,
And all the pretty quiristers of flight,
That chant their music-notes on every bush,
Let them no more contend who shall excel—
The cuckoo is the bird that bears the bell.
—*Anonymous* (about 1600)

TO A SKYLARK

Ethereal minstrel! pilgrim of the sky!
Dost thou despise the earth where cares abound?
Or, while the wings aspire, are heart and eye
Both with thy nest upon the dewy ground?
Thy nest which thou canst drop into at will,
Those quivering wings composed, that music still!

Leave to the nightingale her shady wood;
A privacy of glorious light is thine;
Whence thou dost pour upon the world a flood
Of harmony, with instinct more divine;
Type of the wise who soar, but never roam;
True to the kindred points of Heaven and Home!
—*William Wordsworth* (1770-1850)

[1] This quaint verse recalls the legend that a drop of blood fell from the Cross upon a resting robin and, since then, the robin's breast is red.

TO A SKYLARK

by Percy Bysshe Shelley (1792-1822)

Hail to thee, blithe spirit!
Bird thou never wert,
That from heaven, or near it,
Pourest thy full heart
In profuse strains of unpremeditated art.

Higher still and higher
From the earth thou springest
Like a cloud of fire;
The blue deep thou wingest,
And singing still dost soar, and soaring ever singest.

In the golden lightning
Of the sunken sun,
O'er which clouds are bright'ning,
Thou dost float and run;
Like an unbodied joy whose race is just begun.

The pale purple even
Melts around thy flight;
Like a star of heaven
In the broad daylight
Thou art unseen, but yet I hear thy shrill delight,

Keen as are the arrows
Of that silver sphere,

Whose intense lamp narrows
In the white dawn clear,
Until we hardly see, we feel that it is there.

All the earth and air
With thy voice is loud,
As, when night is bare,
From one lonely cloud
The moon rains out her beams, and heaven is overflowed.

What thou art we know not;
What is most like thee?
From rainbow clouds there flow not
Drops so bright to see
As from thy presence showers a rain of melody.

Like a poet hidden
In the light of thought,
Singing hymns unbidden,
Till the world is wrought
To sympathy with hopes and fears it heeded not;

Like a high-born maiden
In a palace tower,
Soothing her love-laden
Soul in secret hour
With music sweet as love, which overflows her bower;

Like a glowworm golden
In a dell of dew,
Scattering unbeholden
Its aërial hue
Among the flowers and grass which screen it from the view;

Like a rose embowered
In its own green leaves,
By warm winds deflowered,
Till the scent it gives
Makes faint with too much sweet those heavy-wingéd thieves.

Sound of vernal showers
On the twinkling grass,
Rain-awakened flowers,
All that ever was
Joyous, and clear, and fresh, thy music doth surpass.

Teach us, sprite or bird,
What sweet thoughts are thine;
I have never heard
Praise of love or wine
That panted forth a flood of rapture so divine:

Chorus Hymeneal,
Or triumphal chaunt,
Matched with thine, would be all
But an empty vaunt,
A thing wherein we feel there is some hidden want.

What objects are the fountains
Of thy happy strain?
What fields, or waves, or mountains?
What shapes of sky or plain?
What love of thine own kind? what ignorance of pain?

With thy clear keen joyance
Languor cannot be—
Shadow of annoyance
Never came near thee:
Thou lovest—but ne'er knew love's sad satiety.

Waking or asleep,
Thou of death must deem
Things more true and deep
Than we mortals dream,
Or how could thy notes flow in such a crystal stream?

We look before and after
And pine for what is not;
Our sincerest laughter
With some pain is fraught;
Our sweetest songs are those that tell of saddest thought.

Yet if we could scorn
Hate, and pride, and fear;
If we were things born
Not to shed a tear,
I know not how thy joy we ever should come near.

Better than all measures
Of delightful sound—
Better than all treasures

That in books are found—
Thy skill to poet were, thou scorner of the ground!

Teach me half the gladness
That thy brain must know,
Such harmonious madness
From my lips would flow,
The world should listen then—as I am listening now.

TO A WATERFOWL

by William Cullen Bryant (1794-1878)

Whither, 'midst falling dew,
While glow the heavens with the last steps of day,
Far, through their rosy depths, dost thou pursue
Thy solitary way!

Vainly the fowler's eye
Might mark thy distant flight to do thee wrong,
As, darkly painted on the crimson sky,
Thy figure floats along.

Seek'st thou the plashy brink
Of weedy lake, or marge of river wide,
Or where the rocking billows rise and sink
On the chafed ocean side?

There is a Power whose care
Teaches thy way along that pathless coast,—
The desert and illimitable air,—
Lone wandering, but not lost.

All day thy wings have fanned,
At that far height, the cold, thin atmosphere,
Yet stoop not, weary, to the welcome land,
Though the dark night is near.

And soon that toil shall end;
Soon shalt thou find a summer home, and rest,
And scream among thy fellows; reeds shall bend,
Soon, o'er thy sheltered nest.

Thou'rt gone, the abyss of heaven
Hath swallowed up thy form; yet, on my heart
Deeply hath sunk the lesson thou hast given,
And shall not soon depart.

He who, from zone to zone,
Guides through the boundless sky thy certain flight,
In the long way that I must tread alone,
Will lead my steps aright.

THE EAGLE

He clasps the crag with crooked hands;
Close to the sun in lonely lands,
Ring'd with the azure world, he stands.

The wrinkled sea beneath him crawls;
He watches from his mountain walls,
And like a thunderbolt he falls.

—*Alfred, Lord Tennyson*
(1809-1892)

VESPERS

O blackbird, what a boy you are!
How you do go it!
Blowing your bugle to that one sweet star—
How you do blow it!
And does she hear you, blackbird boy, so far?
Or is it wasted breath?
"Good Lord! she is so bright
Tonight!"
The blackbird saith.

—*Thomas Edward Brown* (1830-1897)

JENNY WREN

Her sight is short, she comes quite near;
A foot to me's a mile to her;
And she is known as Jenny Wren,
The smallest bird in England. When
I heard that little bird at first,
Methought her frame would surely burst
With earnest song. Oft had I seen
Her running under leaves so green,
Or in the grass when fresh and wet,
As though her wings she would forget.
And, seeing this, I said to her—
"My pretty runner, you prefer
To be a thing to run unheard
Through leaves and grass, and not a bird!"
'Twas then she burst, to prove me wrong,
Into a sudden storm of song;
So very loud and earnest, I
Feared she would break her heart and die.
"Nay, nay," I laughed, "be you no thing
To run unheard, sweet scold, but sing!
O I could hear your voice near me,
Above the din in that oak tree,
When almost all the twigs on top
Had starlings chattering without stop."

—*William H. Davies* (1870-)

A MEMORY

Four ducks on a pond,
A grass-bank beyond,
A blue sky of spring,
White clouds on the wing:
What a little thing
To remember for years—
To remember with tears.

—*William Allingham*
(1824-1889)

Man has always admired the efficiency of beasts of prey, except when that efficiency was turned against himself. Considering that most members of the animal kingdom were heaven-appointed enemies of man, it is not unnatural that it was long before he turned to them with poetic affection. Even the domestic animals were for use rather than amusement and, as long as hunting was a real source of family support, no mercy could be shown to game. With Rousseau's theory that all nature is beneficent, however, came a wave of humanitarianism, and the desire to protect animals from cruelty led to affection, even to affectation. Safe in his cities, man ceased to fear the lion and the wolf; he began to sentimentalize a bit over them. Sometimes, as in Blake's "The Tiger" and Emily Dickinson's "The Snake," his observations were touched with vision and the result is magnificence.

In Frost's "The Runaway" a fine gift of observation is reinforced by an even finer imagination, while G. K. Chesterton's "The Donkey" is a startling revaluation of the grotesque "son of affliction."

THE TIGER

Tiger! Tiger! burning bright
In the forests of the night,
What immortal hand or eye
Could frame thy fearful symmetry?

In what distant deeps or skies
Burnt the fire of thine eyes?
On what wings dare he aspire?
What the hand dare seize the fire?

And what shoulder, and what art,
Could twist the sinews of thy heart?
And when thy heart began to beat,
What dread hand? and what dread feet?

What the hammer? what the chain?
In what furnace was thy brain?
What the anvil? what dread grasp
Dare its deadly terrors clasp?

When the stars threw down their spears
And water'd heaven with their tears,
Did he smile his work to see?
Did he who made the Lamb make thee?

Tiger! Tiger! burning bright
In the forests of the night,
What immortal hand or eye
Dare frame thy fearful symmetry?

—*William Blake* (1757-1827)

THE SNAKE

A narrow fellow in the grass
Occasionally rides;
You may have met him,—did you not?
His notice sudden is.

The grass divides as with a comb,
A spotted shaft is seen;
And then it closes at your feet
And opens further on.

He likes a boggy acre,
A floor too cool for corn.
Yet when a child, and barefoot,
I more than once, at morn,

Have passed, I thought, a whip-lash
Unbraiding in the sun,—
When, stooping to secure it,
It wrinkled, and was gone.

Several of nature's people
I know, and they know me;
I feel for them a transport
Of cordiality;

But never met this fellow,
Attended or alone,
Without a tighter breathing,
And zero at the bone.

—*Emily Dickinson* (1830-1886)

THE RUNAWAY

Once when the snow of the year was beginning to fall,
We stopped by a mountain pasture to say "Whose colt?"
A little Morgan had one forefoot on the wall,
The other curled at his breast. He dipped his head
And snorted at us. And then he had to bolt.
We heard the miniature thunder when he fled,
And we saw him, or thought we saw him, dim and gray,
Like a shadow against the curtain of falling flakes.
"I think the little fellow's afraid of the snow.
He isn't winter-broken. It isn't play
With the little fellow at all. He's running away.
I doubt if even his mother could tell him, 'Sakes,
It's only weather.' He'd think she didn't know!
Where is his mother? He can't be out alone."
And now he comes again with a clatter of stone
And mounts the wall again with whited eyes
And all his tail that isn't hair up straight.

He shudders his coat as if to throw off flies.
"Whoever it is that leaves him out so late,
When other creatures have gone to stall and bin,
Ought to be told to come and take him in."
—*Robert Frost* (1875-)

THE DONKEY

When fishes flew and forests walked
And figs grew upon thorn,
Some moment when the moon was blood,
Then surely I was born;

With monstrous head and sickening cry
And ears like errant wings,
The devil's walking parody
On all four-footed things.

The tattered outlaw of the earth,
Of ancient crooked will;
Starve, scourge, deride me: I am dumb;
I keep my secret still.

Fools! For I also had my hour;
One far, fierce hour and sweet.
There was a shout about my ears,
And palms before my feet!
—*G. K. Chesterton* (1874-)

THE GREY SQUIRREL

Like a small grey
coffee-pot,
sits the squirrel.
He is not

all he should be,
kills by dozens
trees, and eats
his red-brown cousins.

The keeper, on the
other hand
, who shot him, is
a Christian, and

loves his enemies,
which shows
the squirrel was not
one of those.
—*Humbert Wolfe*
(1885-)

THE RABBIT

All day this spring—the first he's known—
He lets himself be sideways blown
When the wind comes; he'll leap and pounce,
And try to rush two ways at once,
On feet that catch the very sound
Cascades make spattering to the ground.
Though men with difficulty sing how soon
They die, how seldom living they can thrive,
He makes a little dancing-tune
By only being alive;
No leaf that April winds blow off the tree
Falls and leaps round again so gay as he.
—*Camilla Doyle* (1898-)

TO FISH

You strange, astonished-looking, angle-faced,
Dreary-mouthed, gaping wretches of the sea,
Gulping salt-water everlastingly,
Cold-blooded, though with red your blood be graced,
And mute, though dwellers in the roaring waste;
And you, all shapes beside, that fishy be,—
Some round, some flat, some long, all devilry,
Legless, unloving, infamously chaste:—

O scaly, slippery, wet, swift, staring wights,
What is't ye do? what life lead? eh, dull goggles?

How do ye vary your vile days and nights?
How pass your Sundays? Are ye still but joggles
In ceaseless wash? Still nought but gapes, and bites,
And drinks, and stares, diversified with boggles?
—*Leigh Hunt* (1784-1859)

That anything so minute as an insect could reveal what appeared to be wisdom and form the complex social organizations of bees and ants has always been a matter of amazement to human beings. Because of this resemblance to man, much of the poetry dealing with insects has stressed the moral lesson involved in their habits; Bernard de Mandeville, eighteenth-century satirist, built up a huge philosophy of life and human society around his "Fable of the Bees" and the twentieth century W. H. Davies draws an example from a resting butterfly.

THE GRASSHOPPER

by Richard Lovelace (1618-1658)

O thou that swing'st upon the waving hair
  Of some well-fillèd oaten beard,
Drunk ev'ry night with a delicious tear
  Dropt thee from heav'n, where now th'art rear'd;

The joys of earth and air are thine entire,
  That with thy feet and wings dost hop and fly;
And when thy poppy works thou dost retire
  To thy carv'd acorn-bed to lie.

Up with the day, the sun thou welcom'st then,
  Sport'st in the gilt plats of his beams,
And all these merry days mak'st merry men,
  Thyself, and melancholy streams.

But ah the sickle! golden ears are cropt;
  Ceres and Bacchus bid good night;
Sharp frosty fingers all your flow'rs have topt,
  And what scythes spar'd, winds shave off quite.

Poor verdant fool, and now green ice! thy joys,
  Large and as lasting as thy perch of grass,
Bid us lay in 'gainst winter rain, and poise
  Their floods with an o'erflowing glass.

Thou best of men and friends! we will create
  A genuine Summer in each other's breast;
And spite of this cold Time and frozen Fate,
  Thaw us a warm seat to our rest.

Our sacred hearths shall burn eternally
  As vestal flames; the North-wind, he
Shall strike his frost-stretch'd wings, dissolve, and fly
  This Etna in epitome.

Dropping December shall come weeping in,
  Bewail th' usurping of his reign;
But when in show'rs of old Greek we begin,
  Shall cry he hath his crown again.

Night as clear Hesper shall our tapers whip
  From the light casements where we play,
And the dark hag from her black mantle strip,
  And stick there everlasting day.

Thus richer than untempted kings are we,
  That asking nothing, nothing need:
Though lord of all what seas embrace, yet he
  That wants himself is poor indeed.

THE HUMBLE-BEE

by Ralph Waldo Emerson (1803-1882)

Burly, dozing humble-bee,
Where thou art is clime for me,
Let them sail for Porto Rique,
Far-off heats through seas to seek;
I will follow thee alone,
Thou animated torrid-zone!
Zigzag steerer, desert cheerer,
Let me chase thy waving lines;
Keep me nearer, me thy hearer,
Singing over shrubs and vines.

Insect lover of the sun,
Joy of thy dominion!
Sailor of the atmosphere;
Swimmer through the waves of air;
Voyager of light and noon;
Epicurean of June;
Wait, I prithee, till I come
Within earshot of thy hum,—
All without is martyrdom.

When the south wind, in May days,
With a net of shining haze
Silvers the horizon wall,
And with softness touching all,
Tints the human countenance
With a color of romance,
And infusing subtle heats,
Turns the sod to violets,
Thou, in sunny solitudes,
Rover of the underwoods,
The green silence dost displace
With thy mellow, breezy bass.

Hot midsummer's petted crone,
Sweet to me thy drowsy tone
Tells of countless sunny hours,
Long days, and solid banks of flowers;
Of gulfs of sweetness without bound
In Indian wildernesses found;
Of Syrian peace, immortal leisure,
Firmest cheer, and bird-like pleasure.

Aught unsavory or unclean
Hath my insect never seen;
But violets and bilberry bells,
Maple-sap and daffodils,
Grass with green flag half-mast high,
Succory to match the sky,
Columbine with horn of honey,
Scented fern and agrimony,
Clover, catchfly, adder's-tongue
And brier-roses, dwelt among;
All beside was unknown waste,
All was picture as he passed.

Wiser far than human seer,
Yellow-breeched philosopher!
Seeing only what is fair,
Sipping only what is sweet,
Thou dost mock at fate and care,
Leave the chaff, and take the wheat.
When the fierce northwestern blast
Cools sea and land so far and fast,
Thou already slumberest deep;
Woe and want thou canst outsleep;
Want and woe, which torture us,
Thy sleep makes ridiculous.

THE EXAMPLE

Here's an example from
  A Butterfly;
That on a rough, hard rock
  Happy can lie;

Friendless and all alone
On this unsweetened stone.

Now let my bed be hard,
No care take I;
I'll make my joy like this
Small Butterfly,
Whose happy heart has power
To make a stone a flower.

—*William H. Davies* (1870-)

In the study of poetry dealing with plant life, it is interesting to note how steadily the development has been from the general to the specific, from "trees and flowers, shrubs and grasses," to "hemlock and tamarack, tulip and rose, barberry and lilac, the tall grass that blows." The cultivated, formal garden appealed to the eighteenth-century Pope at Twickenham, but to rebellious Shelley in the nineteenth century the wild forests on the banks of the Susquehanna seemed a true, untamed Paradise. A legion of associations cluster around flowers and trees, and it is not merely to Wordsworth that "the meanest flower that blows" carries a thought of deep significance.

THOUGHTS IN A GARDEN

by Andrew Marvell (1621-1678)

How vainly men themselves amaze
To win the palm, the oak, or bays;
And their incessant labours see
Crowned from some single herb, or tree,
Whose short and narrow-vergèd shade
Does prudently their toils upbraid;
While all flow'rs and all trees do close
To weave the garlands of repose.

Fair Quiet, have I found thee here,
And Innocence, thy sister dear?
Mistaken long, I sought you then
In busy companies of men.
Your sacred plants, if here below,
Only among the plants will grow;
Society is all but rude
To this delicious solitude.

No white nor red was ever seen
So amorous as this lovely green.
Fond lovers, cruel as their flame,
Cut in these trees their mistress' name:
Little, alas! they know or heed
How far these beauties hers exceed!
Fair trees! wheres'e'er your barks I wound
No name shall but your own be found.

When we have run our passion's heat,
Love hither makes his best retreat.
The Gods, that mortal beauty chase,
Still in a tree did end their race;
Apollo hunted Daphne so,
Only that she might laurel grow;
And Pan did after Syrinx speed,
Not as a nymph, but for a reed.

What wondrous life is this I lead!
Ripe apples drop about my head;
The luscious clusters of the vine
Upon my mouth do crush their wine;
The nectarine, and curious peach,
Into my hands themselves do reach;
Stumbling on melons, as I pass,
Insnared with flowers, I fall on grass.

Meanwhile, the mind, from pleasure less,
Withdraws into its happiness:
The mind, that ocean where each kind
Does straight its own resemblance find;
Yet it creates, transcending these,
Far other worlds, and other seas;
Annihilating all that's made
To a green thought in a green shade.

Here at the fountain's sliding foot,
Or at some fruit-tree's mossy root,
Casting the body's vest aside,
My soul into the boughs does glide:
There like a bird it sits, and sings;
Then whets and claps its silver wings;
And, till prepared for longer flight,
Waves in its plumes the various light.

Such was that happy garden-state,
While man there walked without a mate:
After a place so pure and sweet,
What other help could yet be meet!
But 'twas beyond a mortal's share

To wander solitary there:
Two paradises 'twere in one,
To live in Paradise alone.

How well the skilful gardener drew
Of flowers, and herbs, this dial new;
Where, from above, the milder sun
Does through a fragrant zodiac run;
And, as it works, the industrious bee
Computes its time as well as we.
How could such sweet and wholesome hours
Be reckon'd but with herbs and flowers!

A CONTEMPLATION UPON FLOWERS

Brave flowers—that I could gallant it like you,
  And be as little vain!
You come abroad, and make a harmless show,
  And to your beds of earth again.
You are not proud: you know your birth:
For your embroidered garments are from earth.

You do obey your months and times, but I
  Would have it ever Spring:
My fate would know no Winter, never die,
  Nor think of such a thing.
O that I could my bed of earth but view
And smile, and look as cheerfully as you!

O teach me to see Death and not to fear,
  But rather to take truce!
How often have I seen you at a bier,
  And there look fresh and spruce!
You fragrant flowers. Then teach me, that my breath
Like yours may sweeten and perfume my death.

—*Henry King* (1592-1669)

TO DAFFODILS

Fair daffodils, we weep to see
  You haste away so soon:
As yet the early-rising Sun
  Has not attain'd his noon.
    Stay, stay,
  Until the hasting day
    Has run
  But to the even-song;
And, having pray'd together, we
  Will go with you along.

We have short time to stay, as you,
  We have as short a Spring!
As quick a growth to meet decay
  As you, or any thing.
    We die,
  As your hours do, and dry
    Away
  Like to the Summer's rain;
Or as the pearls of morning's dew
  Ne'er to be found again.

—*Robert Herrick* (1591-1674)

THE DAFFODILS

I wander'd lonely as a cloud
That floats on high o'er vales and hills,
When all at once I saw a crowd,
A host of golden daffodils,
Beside the lake, beneath the trees
Fluttering and dancing in the breeze.

Continuous as the stars that shine
And twinkle on the milky way,
They stretched in never-ending line
Along the margin of a bay:
Ten thousand saw I at a glance
Tossing their heads in sprightly dance.

The waves beside them danced, but they
Out-did the sparkling waves in glee:
A poet could not but be gay
In such a jocund company!
I gazed—and gazed—but little thought
What wealth the show to me had brought.

For oft, when on my couch I lie
In vacant or in pensive mood,
They flash upon that inward eye
Which is the bliss of solitude;
And then my heart with pleasure fills,
And dances with the daffodils.

—*William Wordsworth* (1770-1850)

TO A MOUNTAIN DAISY

On Turning One Down with the Plow

by Robert Burns (1759-1796)

Wee modest crimson-tippéd flow'r,
Thou's met me in an evil hour;
For I maun crush amang the stoure [1]
Thy slender stem:
To spare thee now is past my pow'r,
Thou bonnie gem.

Alas! it's no thy neibor sweet,
The bonnie lark, companion meet,
Bending thee 'mang the dewy weet
Wi' spreckled breast,
When upward springing, blithe, to greet
The purpling east.

Cauld blew the bitter-biting north
Upon thy early humble birth;
Yet cheerfully thou glinted forth
Amid the storm,
Scarce reared above the parent-earth
Thy tender form.

The flaunting flow'rs our gardens yield
High shelt'ring woods and wa's maun shield,
But thou, beneath the random bield [2]
O' clod or stane,
Adorns the histie stibble-field,[3]
Unseen, alane.

There, in thy scanty mantle clad,
Thy snawy bosom sun-ward spread,
Thou lifts thy unassuming head
In humble guise;
But now the share uptears thy bed,
And low thou lies!

Such is the fate of artless maid,
Sweet flow'ret of the rural shade,
By love's simplicity betrayed,
And guileless trust,
Till she like thee, all soiled, is laid
Low i' the dust.

Such is the fate of simple bard,
On life's rough ocean luckless starred:
Unskillful he to note the card
Of prudent lore,
Till billows rage, and gales blow hard,
And whelm him o'er!

Such fate to suffering worth is giv'n,
Who long with wants and woes has striv'n,
By human pride or cunning driv'n
To mis'ry's brink,
Till wrenched of ev'ry stay but Heav'n,
He, ruined, sink!

E'en thou who mourn'st the Daisy's fate,
That fate is thine—no distant date;
Stern Ruin's plowshare drives elate
Full on thy bloom,
Till crushed beneath the furrow's weight
Shall be thy doom!

[1] Dust.

[2] Shelter.

[3] Bare stubble-field.

THE RHODORA

On Being Asked, Whence Is the Flower?

In May, when sea-winds pierced our solitudes,
I found the fresh Rhodora in the woods,
Spreading its leafless blooms in a damp nook,
To please the desert and the sluggish brook.
The purple petals, fallen in the pool,
Made the black water with their beauty gay;

Here might the red-bird come his plumes to cool,
And court the flower that cheapens his array.

Rhodora! if the sages ask thee why
This charm is wasted on the earth and sky,
Tell them, dear, that if eyes were made for seeing,
Then Beauty is its own excuse for being:
Why thou wert there, O rival of the rose!
I never thought to ask, I never knew:
But, in my simple ignorance, suppose
The self-same Power that brought me there brought you.

—*Ralph Waldo Emerson* (1803-1882)

THE DAISY

The daisy lives, and strikes its little root
Into the lap of time: centuries come
And pass away into the silent tomb,
And still the child, hid in the womb of time,
Shall smile and pluck them, when this simple rhyme
Shall be forgotten like a churchyard stone,
Or, lingering, lie unnoticed and unknown. . . .
Aye, still the child, with pleasure in his eye,
Shall cry "The Daisy!" a familiar cry—
And run to pluck it, in the selfsame state
As when Time found it in his infant date;
And, like a child himself, when all was new,
Might smile with wonder, and take notice, too.

—*John Clare* (1793-1864)

THE GRASS
(from "Song of Myself")

by Walt Whitman (1819-1892)

A child said, *What is the grass?* fetching it to me with full hands;
How could I answer the child? I do not know what it is any more than he.

I guess it must be the flag of my disposition, out of hopeful green stuff woven.

Or I guess it is the handkerchief of the Lord,
A scented gift and remembrancer designedly dropt,
Bearing the owner's name someway in the corners, that we may see and remark, and say *Whose?*

Or I guess the grass is itself a child, the produced babe of the vegetation.

Or I guess it is a uniform hieroglyphic,
And it means, Sprouting alike in broad zones and narrow zones,
Growing among black folks as among white,
Kanuck, Tuckahoe, Congressman, Cuff, I give them the same, I receive them the same.

And now it seems to me the beautiful uncut hair of graves.

Tenderly will I use you curling grass,
It may be you transpire from the breasts of young men,
It may be if I had known them I would have loved them,
It may be you are from old people, or from offspring taken soon out of their mothers' laps,
And here you are the mothers' laps.

This grass is very dark to be from the white heads of old mothers,
Darker than the colourless beards of old men,
Dark to come from under the faint red roofs of mouths.
O I perceive after all so many uttering tongues,
And I perceive they do not come from the roofs of mouths for nothing.

I wish I could translate the hints about the dead young men and women,
And the hints about old men and mothers, and the offspring taken soon out of their laps.

What do you think has become of the young and old men?
And what do you think has become of the women and children?

They are alive and well somewhere,
The smallest sprout shows there is really no death,
And if ever there was it led forward life, and does not wait at the end to arrest it,
And ceas'd the moment life appear'd.

All goes onward and outward, nothing collapses,
And to die is different from what anyone supposed, and luckier.

HOURS AND DAYS

No two days are alike in all their parts, yet all are alike in their changes. Night and the disappearance of the sun were the first mystery and tragedy of man's drama; dawn gave it the required happy ending. The classicist loves the clear brilliance of day, the romanticist the kind transformations of the night. From dawn to dawn the shifting pageant is unfolded; the poets are not merely the audience, but also the critics and interpreters. Even dawn may be as variously revealed as in the bright calls of Shakespeare's "Morning Song from 'Cymbeline'" and Davenant's "Awake! Awake!" and the slow introspection of Conrad Aiken's "Morning Song from 'Senlin.'" Evening may suggest gentle fancy, as in Collins's "Ode to Evening," or death, as in Henley's "Margaritae Sorori." No treatments of night could show more differences than Westwood's, Shelley's and Whitman's.

MORNING SONG FROM "CYMBELINE"

Hark! hark! the lark at heaven's gate sings,
And Phoebus 'gins arise,
His steeds to water at those springs
On chaliced flowers that lies;
And winking Mary-buds begin
To ope their golden eyes;
With every thing that pretty is,
My lady sweet, arise;
Arise, arise!

—*William Shakespeare* (1564-1616)

WELCOME TO DAY

Pack, clouds, away, and welcome day,
With night we banish sorrow;

Sweet air, blow soft, mount, larks, aloft
  To give my Love good-morrow!
Wings from the wind to please her mind,
  Notes from the lark I'll borrow;
Bird, prune thy wing, nightingale, sing,
  To give my Love good-morrow;
    To give my Love good-morrow
    Notes from them both I'll borrow.

Wake from thy nest, Robin-red-breast,
  Sing, birds, in every furrow!
And from each hill, let music shrill
  Give my fair Love good-morrow!
Blackbird and thrush in every bush,
  Stare, linnet, and cock-sparrow!
You pretty elves, amongst yourselves
  Sing my fair Love good-morrow;
    To give my Love good-morrow
    Sing, birds, in every furrow!

—*Thomas Heywood* (1573-1650)

AWAKE! AWAKE!

The lark now leaves his watery nest,
  And, climbing, shakes his dewy wings.
He takes this window for the East,
  And to implore your light he sings—
Awake! awake! The morn will never rise
Till she can dress her beauty at your eyes.

The merchant bows unto the seaman's star,
  The ploughman from the sun his season takes;
But still the lover wonders what they are
  Who look for day before his mistress wakes.
Awake! awake! Break thro' your veils of lawn!
Then draw your curtains, and begin the dawn!

—*William Davenant* (1606-1668)

MORNING SONG FROM "SENLIN"

by Conrad Aiken (1889-)

It is morning, Senlin says, and in the morning
When the light drips through the shutters like the dew,
I arise, I face the sunrise,
And do the things my fathers learned to do.
Stars in the purple dusk above the rooftops
Pale in a saffron mist and seem to die,
And I myself on a swiftly tilting planet
Stand before a glass and tie my tie.

Vine-leaves tap my window,
Dew-drops sing to the garden stones,
The robin chirps in the chinaberry tree
Repeating three clear tones.

It is morning. I stand by the mirror
And tie my tie once more.
While waves far off in a pale rose twilight
Crash on a white sand shore.
I stand by a mirror and comb my hair:

How small and white my face!—
The green earth tilts through a sphere of air
And bathes in a flame of space.
There are houses hanging above the stars
And stars hung under a sea . . .
And a sun far off in a shell of silence
Dapples my walls for me . . .

It is morning, Senlin says, and in the morning
Should I not pause in the light to remember God?
Upright and firm I stand on a star unstable,
He is immense and lonely as a cloud.
I will dedicate this moment before my mirror
To him alone, for him I will comb my hair.
Accept these humble offerings, clouds of silence!
I will think of you as I descend the stair.

Vine-leaves tap my window,
The snail-track shines on the stones;
Dew-drops flash from the chinaberry tree
Repeating two clear tones.

It is morning, I awake from a bed of silence,
Shining I rise from the starless waters of sleep.
The walls are about me still as in the evening,
I am the same, and the same name still I keep.
The earth revolves with me, yet makes no motion,
The stars pale silently in a coral sky.
In a whistling void I stand before my mirror,
Unconcerned, and tie my tie.

There are horses neighing on far-off hills
Tossing their long white manes,
And mountains flash in the rose-white dusk,
Their shoulders black with rains. . . .
It is morning, I stand by the mirror
And surprise my soul once more;
The blue air rushes above my ceiling,
There are suns beneath my floor. . . .

. . . It is morning, Senlin says, I ascend from darkness
And depart on the winds of space for I know not where;
My watch is wound, a key is in my pocket,
And the sky is darkened as I descend the stair.
There are shadows across the windows, clouds in heaven,
And a god among the stars; and I will go
Thinking of him as I might think of daybreak
And humming a tune I know. . . .

Vine leaves tap at the window,
Dew-drops sing to the garden stones,
The robin chirps in the chinaberry tree
Repeating three clear tones.

SILENT NOON

Your hands lie open in the long fresh grass,
The finger-points look through like rosy blooms;
Your eyes smile peace. The pasture gleams and glooms
'Neath billowing skies that scatter and amass.
All round our nest, far as the eye can pass,
Are golden kingcup-fields with silver edge
Where the cow-parsley skirts the hawthorn-hedge.
'Tis visible silence, still as the hour-glass.
Deep in the sun-searched growths the dragon-fly
Hangs like a blue thread loosened from the sky—
So this winged hour is dropt to us from above.
Oh! clasp we to our hearts, for deathless dower,
This close-companioned inarticulate hour
When twofold silence was the song of love.

—*Dante Gabriel Rossetti* (1828-1882)

ODE TO EVENING

by William Collins (1721-1759)

If ought of oaten stop or pastoral song
May hope, O pensive Eve, to soothe thine ear,
  Like thy own solemn springs,
  Thy springs, and dying gales,
O nymph reserv'd, while now the bright-hair'd sun
Sits in yon western tent, whose cloudy skirts,
  With brede ethereal wove,
  O'erhang his wavy bed:

Now air is hush'd, save where the weak-eyed bat,
With short shrill shriek, flits by on leathern wing,
  Or where the beetle winds
  His small but sullen horn,
As oft he rises 'midst the twilight path,
Against the pilgrim born in heedless hum:
  Now teach me, maid compos'd,
  To breathe some soften'd strain,
Whose numbers stealing thro' thy darkening vale,
May not unseemly with its stillness suit,
  As, musing slow, I hail
  Thy genial lov'd return!

For when thy folding-star arising shows
His paly circlet, at his warning lamp
  The fragrant hours, and elves
  Who slept in flow'rs the day,
And many a nymph who wreathes her brows with sedge,
And sheds the fresh'ning dew, and lovelier still,
  The pensive pleasures sweet
  Prepare thy shadowy car.

Then lead, calm votaress, where some sheety lake
Cheers the lone heath, or some time-hallowed pile,
  Or upland fallows grey
  Reflect its last cool gleam.
Or if chill blust'ring winds, or driving rain,
Prevent my willing feet, be mine the hut,
  That from the mountain's side,
  Views wilds, and swelling floods,
And hamlets brown, and dim-discover'd spires,
And hears their simple bell, and marks o'er all
  Thy dewy fingers draw
  The gradual dusky veil.

While Spring shall pour his showers, as oft he wont,
And bathe thy breathing tresses, meekest Eve!
  While Summer loves to sport
  Beneath thy lingering light;
While sallow autumn fills thy lap with leaves;
Or winter, yelling through the troublous air,
  Affrights thy shrinking train
  And rudely rends thy robes;
So long, sure-found beneath the sylvan shed,
Shall fancy, friendship, science, rose-lipped health,
  Thy gentlest influence own,
  And love thy favourite name!

MARGARITAE SORORI

A late lark twitters from the quiet skies;
And from the west,
Where the sun, his day's work ended,
Lingers as in content,
There falls on the old, gray city
An influence luminous and serene,
A shining peace.

The smoke ascends
In a rosy-and-golden haze. The spires
Shine, and are changed. In the valley
Shadows rise. The lark sings on. The sun,
Closing his benediction,
Sinks, and the darkening air
Thrills with the sense of the triumphing night—
Night with her train of stars
And her great gift of sleep.

So be my passing!
My task accomplished and the long day done,
My wages taken, and in my heart
Some late lark singing,
Let me be gathered to the quiet west,
The sundown splendid and serene,
Death.

—*William Ernest Henley* (1849-1903)

TO NIGHT

by Percy Bysshe Shelley (1792-1822)

Swiftly walk o'er the western wave,
  Spirit of Night!
Out of the misty eastern cave,
Where, all the long and lone day-light,
Thou wovest dreams of joy and fear,
Which make thee terrible and dear—
  Swift be thy flight!

Wrap thy form in a mantle gray,
  Star-inwrought!
Blind with thine hair the eyes of day;
Kiss her until she be wearied out,
Then wander o'er city, and sea, and land
Touching all with thine opiate wand—
  Come, long-sought!

When I arose and saw the dawn,
  I sighed for thee;

When light rode high, and the dew was gone,
And noon lay heavy on flower and tree,
And the weary day turned to his rest,
Lingering like an unloved guest,
I sighed for thee.

Thy brother Death came, and cried,
Wouldst thou me?
Thy sweet child Sleep, the filmy-eyed,
Murmured like a noontide bee,
Shall I nestle near thy side?
Wouldst thou me?—And I replied,
No, not thee!

Death will come when thou art dead,
Soon, too soon—
Sleep will come when thou art fled;
Of neither would I ask the boon
I ask of thee, belovèd Night—
Swift be thine approaching flight,
Come soon, soon!

THE MOON

I

Art thou pale for weariness
Of climbing heaven, and gazing on the earth,
Wandering companionless
Among the stars that have a different birth,—
And ever-changing, like a joyless eye
That finds no object worth its constancy?

II

And like a dying lady, lean and pale,
Who totters forth, wrapped in a gauzy veil,
Out of her chamber, led by the insane
And feeble wanderings of her fading brain,
The moon arose up in the murky East,
A white and shapeless mass—

—*Percy Bysshe Shelley* (1792-1822)

NIGHT OF SPRING

Slow, horses, slow,
As through the wood we go—
We would count the stars in heaven,
Hear the grasses grow:

Watch the cloudlets few
Dappling the deep blue,
In our open palms outspread
Catch the blessèd dew.

Slow, horses, slow,
As through the wood we go—
We would see fair Dian rise
With her huntress bow:

We would hear the breeze
Ruffling the dim trees,
Hear its sweet love-ditty set
To endless harmonies.

Slow, horses, slow,
As through the wood we go—
All the beauty of the night
We would learn and know!

—*Thomas Westwood* (1814-1888)

EARTH AT NIGHT
(from "Song of Myself")

Press close, bare-bosom'd night—press close magnetic nourishing night!
Night of south winds—night of the large few stars—
Still nodding night—mad naked summer night.

Smile, O voluptuous cool-breath'd earth!
Earth of the slumbering and liquid trees!
Earth of departed sunset—earth of the mountains misty-top!
Earth of the vitreous pour of the full moon just tinged with blue!
Earth of shine and dark mottling the tide of the river!
Earth of the limpid grey of clouds brighter and clearer for my sake!
Far-swooping elbow'd earth—rich apple-blossom'd earth!
Smile, for your lover comes.

—*Walt Whitman* (1819-1892)

THE SEASONS

The years roll their circle as well as the days, each unique. From the dawn of spring to the close of the winter night, the poet is almost too aware of the beauty and significance of the panorama, too sensitive to its mutations. The joy of English and all northern poets at the coming of the spring is scarcely shared by the Mediterranean singers, whose seasons have no dramatic changes; yet Browning cried out from his Florentine villa with deep nostalgia, "O to be in England, now that April's there!" The festive harvest-songs and the winter wassail-songs are as distinctly national as the languages. Spenser's "Shepherd's Calendar" carries the reader from January to December, and a hundred other poets have been as assiduous as he in recording the seasons.

HOME-THOUGHTS, FROM ABROAD

Oh, to be in England
Now that April's there,
And whoever wakes in England
Sees, some morning, unaware,
That the lowest boughs and the brush-wood sheaf
Round the elm-tree bole are in tiny leaf,
While the chaffinch sings on the orchard bough
In England—now!

And after April, when May follows,
And the whitethroat builds, and all the swallows—
Hark! where my blossomed pear-tree in the hedge
Leans to the field and scatters on the clover
Blossoms and dewdrops—at the bent-spray's edge—
That's the wise thrush; he sings each song twice over,
Lest you should think he never could recapture
The first fine careless rapture!
And though the fields look rough with hoary dew,
All will be gay when noontide wakes anew
The buttercups, the little children's dower,
—Far brighter than this gaudy melon-flower!

—*Robert Browning* (1812-1889)

WHEN THE HOUNDS OF SPRING
(from "Atalanta in Calydon")

by Algernon Charles Swinburne (1837-1909)

When the hounds of spring are on winter's traces,
  The mother of months in meadow or plain
Fills the shadows and windy places
  With lisp of leaves and ripple of rain;
And the brown bright nightingale amorous
Is half assuaged for Itylus,
For the Thracian ships and the foreign faces,
  The tongueless vigil, and all the pain.

Come with bows bent and with emptying of quivers,
  Maiden most perfect, lady of light,
With a noise of winds and many rivers,
  With a clamor of waters, and with might;
Bind on thy sandals, O thou most fleet,
Over the splendor and speed of thy feet;
For the faint east quickens, the wan west shivers,
  Round the feet of the day and the feet of the night.

Where shall we find her, how shall we sing to her,
  Fold our hands round her knees, and cling?
O that man's heart were as fire and could spring to her,
  Fire, or the strength of the streams that spring!
For the stars and the winds are unto her
As raiment, as songs of the harp-player;
For the risen stars and the fallen cling to her,
  And the southwest-wind and the west-wind sing.

For winter's rains and ruins are over,
  And all the season of snows and sins;
The days dividing lover and lover,
  The light that loses, the night that wins;
And time remembered is grief forgotten,
And frosts are slain and flowers begotten,
And in green underwood and cover
  Blossom by blossom the spring begins.

The full streams feed on flower of rushes,
  Ripe grasses trammel a traveling foot,
The faint fresh flame of the young year flushes
  From leaf to flower and flower to fruit,
And fruit and leaf are as gold and fire,
And the oat is heard above the lyre,
And the hoofèd heel of a satyr crushes
  The chestnut-husk at the chestnut-root.

And Pan by noon and Bacchus by night,
  Fleeter of foot than the fleet-foot kid,
Follows with dancing and fills with delight
  The Maenad and the Bassarid;
And soft as lips that laugh and hide
The laughing leaves of the trees divide,
And screen from seeing and leave in sight
  The god pursuing, the maiden hid.

The ivy falls with the Bacchanal's hair
  Over her eyebrows hiding her eyes;
The wild vine slipping down leaves bare
  Her bright breast shortening into sighs;
The wild vine slips with the weight of its leaves,
But the berried ivy catches and cleaves
To the limbs that glitter, the feet that scare
  The wolf that follows, the fawn that flies.

SONG ON MAY MORNING

Now the bright morning-star, Day's harbinger,
Comes dancing from the East, and leads with her
The flowery May, who from her green lap throws
The yellow cowslip and the pale primrose.
Hail, bounteous May, that dost inspire
Mirth, and youth, and warm desire!
Woods and groves are of thy dressing;
Hill and dale doth boast thy blessing.
Thus we salute thee with our early song,
And welcome thee, and wish thee long.
—*John Milton* (1608-1674)

JUNE

Broom out the floor now, lay the fender by,
And plant this bee-sucked bough of woodbine there,
And let the window down. The butterfly
Floats in upon the sunbeam, and the fair
Tanned face of June, the nomad gypsy, laughs
Above her widespread wares, the while she tells
The farmers' fortunes in the fields, and quaffs
The water from the spider-peopled wells.

The hedges all are drowned in green grass seas,
And bobbing poppies flare like Elmo's light,
While siren-like the pollen-stainèd bees
Drone in the clover depths. And up the height
The cuckoo's voice is hoarse and broke with joy.
And on the lowland crops the crows make raid,
Nor fear the clappers of the farmer's boy
Who sleeps, like drunken Noah, in the shade.
And loop this red rose in that hazel ring
That snares your little ear, for June is short
And we must joy in it and dance and sing,
And from her bounty draw her rosy worth.
Aye, soon the swallows will be flying south,
The wind wheel north to gather in the snow,
Even the roses spilt on youth's red mouth
Will soon blow down the road all roses go.
—*Francis Ledwidge* (1891-1917)

AUGUST

Why should this Negro insolently stride
Down the red noonday on such noiseless feet?
Piled in his barrow, tawnier than wheat,
Lie heaps of smoldering daisies, somber-eyed,
Their copper petals shriveled up with pride,
Hot with a superfluity of heat,

Like a great brazier borne along the street
By captive leopards, black and burning-pied.

Are there no water-lilies, smooth as cream,
With long stems dripping crystal? Are there none
Like those white lilies, luminous and cool,
Plucked from some hemlock-darkened northern stream
By fair-haired swimmers, diving where the sun
Scarce warms the surface of the deepest pool?
—*Elinor Wylie* (1887-1928)

ODE TO AUTUMN

by John Keats (1795-1821)

Season of mists and mellow fruitfulness!
Close bosom-friend of the maturing sun;
Conspiring with him how to load and bless
With fruit the vines that round the thatch-eaves run;
To bend with apples the moss'd cottage-trees,
And fill all fruit with ripeness to the core;
To swell the gourd, and plump the hazel shells
With a sweet kernel; to set budding more,
And still more, later flowers for the bees,
Until they think warm days will never cease,
For Summer has o'er-brimm'd their clammy cells.

Who hath not seen thee oft amid thy store?
Sometimes whoever seeks abroad may find
Thee sitting careless on a granary floor,
Thy hair soft-lifted by the winnowing wind;
Or on a half-reap'd furrow sound asleep,
Drowsed with the fume of poppies, while thy hook
Spares the next swath and all its twinèd flowers;
And sometimes like a gleaner thou dost keep
Steady thy laden head across a brook;
Or by a cider-press, with patient look,
Thou watchest the last oozings, hours by hours.

Where are the songs of Spring? Ay, where are they?
Think not of them, thou hast thy music too,
While barrèd clouds bloom the soft-dying day,
And touch the stubble-plains with rosy hue;
Then in a wailful choir, the small gnats mourn
Among the river sallows, borne aloft
Or sinking as the light wind lives or dies;
And full-grown lambs loud bleat from hilly bourn;
Hedge-crickets sing; and now with treble soft
The redbreast whistles from a garden-croft,
And gathering swallows twitter in the skies.

WINTER
(from "Love's Labor's Lost")

When icicles hang by the wall,
And Dick the shepherd blows his nail,
And Tom bears logs into the hall,
And milk comes frozen home in pail,
When blood is nipped and ways be foul,
Then nightly sings the staring owl,
"Tu-whit, tu-who!" a merry note,
While greasy Joan doth keel the pot.

When all aloud the wind doth blow,
And coughing drowns the parson's saw,
And birds sit brooding in the snow,
And Marian's nose looks red and raw,
When roasted crabs hiss in the bowl,
Then nightly sings the staring owl,
"Tu-whit, tu-who!" a merry note,
While greasy Joan doth keel the pot.

—*William Shakespeare* (1564-1616)

WINTER

A widow bird sat mourning for her love
Upon a wintry bough;
The frozen wind crept on above,
The freezing stream below.

There was no leaf upon the forest bare,
No flower upon the ground,
And little motion in the air
Except the mill-wheel's sound.

—*Percy Bysshe Shelley* (1792-1822)

THIS MEASURE

This measure was a measure to my mind,
Still musical through the unlikely hush.
The cold goes wide as doors, and in will come
Those notes of May set ringing through the brush,
Where every voice by natural law is dumb.

How many seasons I have watched the boughs,
That first are happy-tongued and happy-leaved,
Then bleed, as though an autumn were the last,
While that great life was with them undeceived,
Which all a wintering world seals home more fast.

Now visibly indeed I am assailed,
Yet I seem come clap on my very thing;
And now I learn I only asked as much:
It was in blooming weeks I lacked a spring
Rooted and blowing beyond sense or touch.

—*Léonie Adams* (1899-)

TO A SNOWFLAKE

What heart could have thought you?—
Past our devisal
(O filigree petal!)
Fashioned so purely,
Fragilely, surely,
From what Paradisal
Imagineless metal,
Too costly for cost?
Who hammered you, wrought you,
From argentine vapor?—

"God was my shaper.
Passing surmisal,
He hammered, He wrought me,
From curled silver vapor,
To lust of his mind:—
Thou couldst not have thought me!
So purely, so palely,
Tinily, surely,
Mightily, frailly,
Insculped and embossed,
With His hammer of wind,
And His graver of frost."

—*Francis Thompson* (1859-1907)

THE SNOWSTORM

by Ralph Waldo Emerson (1803-1882)

Announced by all the trumpets of the sky,
Arrives the snow, and, driving o'er the fields,
Seems nowhere to alight: the whited air
Hides hills and woods, the river, and the heaven,
And veils the farmhouse at the garden's end.
The sled and traveler stopped, the courier's feet

Delayed, all friends shut out, the housemates sit
Around the radiant fireplace, enclosed
In a tumultuous privacy of storm.

Come, see the north wind's masonry.
Out of an unseen quarry evermore
Furnished with tile, the fierce artificer
Curves his white bastions with projected roof
Round every windward stake or tree or door.
Speeding, the myriad-handed, his wild work
So fanciful, so savage, naught cares he
For number or proportion. Mockingly
On coop or kennel he hangs Parian wreaths;
A swan-like form invests the hidden thorn;
Fills up the farmer's lane from wall to wall,
Maugre the farmer's sighs; and at the gate
A tapering turret overtops the work.
And when his hours are numbered, and the world
Is all his own, retiring, as he were not,
Leaves, when the sun appears, astonished Art
To mimic in slow structures, stone by stone,
Built in an age, the mad wind's night-work,
The frolic architecture of the snow.

WINTER
(from "The Seasons")

by James Thomson (1700-1748)

See, Winter comes to rule the varied year,
Sullen and sad, with all his rising train—
Vapors, and clouds, and storms. Be these my theme;
These, that exalt the soul to solemn thought
And heavenly musing. Welcome, kindred glooms!
Cogenial horrors, hail! With frequent foot,
Pleased have I, in my cheerful morn of life,
When nursed by careless solitude I lived
And sung of Nature with unceasing joy,
Pleased have I wandered through your rough domain;
Trod the pure virgin-snows, myself as pure;
Heard the winds roar, and the big torrent burst;
Or seen the deep-fermenting tempest brewed
In the grim evening-sky. Thus passed the time,
Till through the lucid chambers of the south
Looked out the joyous Spring—looked out and smiled.

✦

Now, when the cheerless empire of the sky
To Capricorn the Centaur-Archer yields,
And fierce Aquarius stains the inverted year—
Hung o'er the farthest verge of heaven, the sun
Scarce spreads o'er ether the dejected day.
Faint are his gleams, and ineffectual shoot
His struggling rays in horizontal lines
Through the thick air; as clothed in cloudy storm,
Weak, wan, and broad, he skirts the southern sky;
And, soon descending, to the long dark night,
Wide-shading all, the prostrate world resigns.
Nor is the night unwished; while vital heat,
Light, life, and joy the dubious day forsake.
Meantime, in sable cincture, shadows vast,
Deep-tinged and damp, and congregated clouds,
And all the vapory turbulence of heaven
Involve the face of things. Thus Winter falls,
A heavy gloom oppressive o'er the world,
Through Nature shedding influence malign,
And rouses up the seeds of dark disease.
The soul of man dies in him, loathing life,
And black with more than melancholy views.

✦

The keener tempests come: and, fuming dun
From all the livid east or piercing north,
Thick clouds ascend, in whose capacious womb
A vapory deluge lies, to snow congealed.
Heavy they roll their fleecy world along,
And the sky saddens with the gathered storm.
Through the hushed air the whitening shower descends,
At first thin-wavering; till at last the flakes
Fall broad and wide and fast, dimming the day
With a continual flow. The cherished fields
Put on their winter-robe of purest white.
'Tis brightness all; save where the new snow melts

Along the mazy current. Low the woods
Bow their hoar head; and, ere the languid sun
Faint from the west emits his evening ray,
Earth's universal face, deep-hid and chill,
Is one wild dazzling waste, that buries wide
The works of man. Drooping, the laborer-ox
Stands covered o'er with snow, and then demands
The fruit of all his toil. The fowls of heaven,
Tamed by the cruel season, crowd around
The winnowing store, and claim the little boon
Which Providence assigns them. One alone,
The redbreast, sacred to the household gods,
Wisely regardful of the embroiling sky,
In joyless fields and thorny thickets leaves
His shivering mates, and pays to trusted man
His annual visit. Half afraid, he first
Against the window beats; then brisk alights
On the warm hearth; then, hopping o'er the floor,
Eyes all the smiling family askance,
And pecks, and starts, and wonders where he is—
Till, more familiar grown, the table-crumbs
Attract his slender feet. The foodless wilds
Pour forth their brown inhabitants. The hare,
Though timorous of heart, and hard beset
By death in various forms, dark snares, and dogs,
And more unpitying men, the garden seeks,
Urged on by fearless want. The bleating kine
Eye the bleak heaven, and next the glistening earth,
With looks of dumb despair; then, sad-dispersed,
Dig for the withered herb through heaps of snow.

✦

By wintry famine roused, from all the tract
Of horrid mountains which the shining Alps,
And wavy Apennines, and Pyrenees
Branch out stupendous into distant lands,
Cruel as death, and hungry as the grave!
Burning for blood, bony, and gaunt, and grim!
Assembling wolves in raging troops descend;
And, pouring o'er the country, bear along,
Keen as the north-wind sweeps the glossy snow.
All is their prize. They fasten on the steed,
Press him to earth, and pierce his mighty heart.
Nor can the bull his awful front defend,
Or shake the murdering savages away.
Rapacious, at the mother's throat they fly,
And tear the screaming infant from her breast.
The godlike face of man avails him naught.
Even Beauty, force divine! at whose bright glance
The generous lion stands in softened gaze,
Here bleeds, a hapless undistinguished prey.
But if, apprised of the severe attack,
The country be shut up, lured by the scent,
On churchyards drear (inhuman to relate!)
The disappointed prowlers fall, and dig
The shrouded body from the grave; o'er which,
Mixed with foul shades and frighted ghosts, they howl.
Among those hilly regions, where, embraced
In peaceful vales, the happy Grisons dwell,
Oft, rushing sudden from the loaded cliffs,
Mountains of snow their gathering terrors roll.
From steep to steep, loud thundering, down they come,
A wintry waste in dire commotion all;
And herds, and flocks, and travelers, and swains,
And sometimes whole brigades of marching troops,
Or hamlets sleeping in the dead of night,
Are deep beneath the smothering ruin whelmed.

✦

Meantime the village rouses up the fire;
While, well attested, and as well believed,
Heard solemn, goes the goblin-story round,
Till superstitious horror creeps o'er all.
Or frequent in the sounding hall they wake
The rural gambol. Rustic mirth goes round—
The simple joke that takes the shepherd's heart,
Easily pleased; the long loud laugh sincere;
The kiss, snatched hasty from the sidelong maid

On purpose guardless, or pretending sleep;
The leap, the slap, the haul; and, shook to
notes
Of native music, the respondent dance.
Thus jocund fleets with them the winter-
night.

FROM "SNOW-BOUND: A WINTER IDYL"

by John Greenleaf Whittier (1807-1892)

The sun that brief December day
Rose cheerless over hills of gray,
And, darkly circled, gave at noon
A sadder light than waning moon.
Slow tracing down the thickening sky
Its mute and ominous prophecy,
A portent seeming less than threat,
It sank from sight before it set.
A chill no coat, however stout,
Of homespun stuff could quite shut out,
A hard, dull bitterness of cold,
That checked, mid-vein, the circling race
Of life-blood in the sharpened face,
The coming of the snow-storm told.
The wind blew east: we heard the roar
Of Ocean on his wintry shore,
And felt the strong pulse throbbing there
Beat with low rhythm our inland air.
Meanwhile we did our nightly chores,—
Brought in the wood from out of doors,
Littered the stalls, and from the mows
Raked down the herd's-grass for the cows;
Heard the horse whinnying for his corn;
And, sharply clashing horn on horn,
Impatient down the stanchion rows
The cattle shake their walnut bows;
While, peering from his early perch
Upon the scaffold's pole of birch,
The cock his crested helmet bent
And down his querulous challenge sent.
Unwarmed by any sunset light
The gray day darkened into night,
A night made hoary with the swarm
And whirl-dance of the blinding storm,
As zigzag wavering to and fro
Crossed and recrossed the wingèd snow:
And ere the early bedtime came
The white drift piled the window-frame,
And through the glass the clothes-line posts
Looked in like tall and sheeted ghosts.

So all night long the storm roared on:
The morning broke without a sun;
In tiny spherule traced with lines
Of Nature's geometric signs,
In starry flake and pellicle,
All day the hoary meteor fell;
And, when the second morning shone,
We looked upon a world unknown,
On nothing we could call our own.
Around the glistening wonder bent
The blue walls of the firmament,
No cloud above, no earth below,—
A universe of sky and snow!
The old familiar sights of ours
Took marvelous shapes; strange domes and
towers
Rose up where sty or corn-crib stood,
Or garden-wall or belt of wood;
A smooth white mound the brush-pile
showed,
A fenceless drift what once was road;
The bridle-post an old man sat
With loose-flung coat and high cocked hat;
The well-curb had a Chinese roof;
And even the long sweep, high aloof,
In its slant splendor, seemed to tell
Of Pisa's leaning miracle.

A prompt, decisive man, no breath
Our father wasted: "Boys, a path!"
Well pleased, (for when did farmer boy
Count such a summons less than joy?)
Our buskins on our feet we drew;
With mittened hands, and caps drawn low,
To guard our necks and ears from snow,
We cut the solid whiteness through.
And, where the drift was deepest, made
A tunnel walled and overlaid
With dazzling crystal: we had read
Of rare Aladdin's wondrous cave,
And to our own his name we gave,
With many a wish the luck were ours
To test his lamp's supernal powers.
We reached the barn with merry din,
And roused the prisoned brutes within.
The old horse thrust his long head out,
And grave with wonder gazed about;
The cock his lusty greeting said,
And forth his speckled harem led;

The oxen lashed their tails, and hooked,
And mild reproach of hunger looked;
The hornèd patriarch of the sheep,
Like Egypt's Amun roused from sleep,
Shook his sage head with gesture mute,
And emphasized with stamp of foot.

All day the gusty north-wind bore
The loosening drift its breath before;
Low circling round its southern zone,
The sun through dazzling snow-mist shone.
No church-bell lent its Christian tone
To the savage air, no social smoke
Curled over woods of snow-hung oak.
A solitude made more intense
By dreary-voicèd elements,
The shrieking of the mindless wind,
The moaning tree-boughs swaying blind,
And on the glass the unmeaning beat
Of ghostly finger-tips of sleet.
Beyond the circle of our hearth
No welcome sound of toil or mirth
Unbound the spell, and testified
Of human life and thought outside.
We minded that the sharpest ear
The buried brooklet could not hear,
The music of whose liquid lip
Had been to us companionship
And, in our lonely life, had grown
To have an almost human tone.

As night drew on, and, from the crest
Of wooded knolls that ridged the west,
The sun, a snow-blown traveler, sank
From sight beneath the smothering bank,
We piled with care our nightly stack
Of wood against the chimney-back,—
The oaken log, green, huge, and thick,
And on its top the stout back-stick;
The knotty foresticks laid apart,
And filled between with curious art
The ragged brush; then, hovering near,
We watched the first red blaze appear,
Heard the sharp crackle, caught the gleam
On whitewashed wall and sagging beam,
Until the old, rude-furnished room
Burst, flower-like, into rosy bloom;
While radiant with a mimic flame
Outside the sparkling drift became,
And through the bare-boughed lilac-tree
Our own warm hearth seemed blazing free.
The crane and pendent trammels showed,
The Turks' heads on the andirons glowed;
While childish fancy, prompt to tell
The meaning of the miracle,
Whispered the old rime: *Under the tree*
When fire outdoors burns merrily,
There the witches are making tea.

The moon above the eastern wood
Shone at its full; the hill-range stood
Transfigured in the silver flood,
Its blown snows flashing cold and keen,
Dead white, save where some sharp ravine
Took shadow, or the somber green
Of hemlocks turned to pitchy black
Against the whiteness at their back.
For such a world and such a night
Most fitting that unwarming light,
Which only seemed where'er it fell
To make the coldness visible.

Shut in from all the world without,
We sat the clean-winged hearth about,
Content to let the north-wind roar
In baffled rage at pane and door,
While the red logs before us beat
The frost-line back with tropic heat;
And ever, when a louder blast
Shook beam and rafter as it passed,
The merrier up its roaring draught
The great throat of the chimney laughed,
The house-dog on his paws outspread
Laid to the fire his drowsy head,
The cat's dark silhouette on the wall
A couchant tiger's seemed to fall;
And, for the winter fireside meet,
Between the andirons' straddling feet,
The mug of cider simmered slow,
The apples sputtered in a row,
And, close at hand, the basket stood
With nuts from brown October's wood.

At last the great logs, crumbling low,
Sent out a dull and duller glow,
The bull's-eye watch that hung in view,
Ticking its weary circuit through,
Pointed with mutely-warning sign
Its black hand to the hour of nine.
That sign the pleasant circle broke:
My uncle ceased his pipe to smoke,

Knocked from its bowl the refuse gray
And laid it tenderly away,
Then roused himself to safely cover
The dull red brand with ashes over.
And while, with care, our mother laid
The work aside, her steps she stayed
One moment, seeking to express
Her grateful sense of happiness
For food and shelter, warmth and health,
And love's contentment more than wealth,
With simple wishes (not the weak,
Vain prayers which no fulfilment seek,
But such as warm the generous heart,
O'er-prompt to do with Heaven its part)
That none might lack, that bitter night,
For bread and clothing, warmth and light.

Within our beds awhile we heard
The wind that round the gables roared,
With now and then a ruder shock,
Which made our very bedsteads rock.
We heard the loosened clapboards tost,
The board-nails snapping in the frost;
And on us, through the unplastered wall,
Felt the light-sifted snow-flakes fall;
But sleep stole on, as sleep will do
When hearts are light and life is new;
Faint and more faint the murmurs grew,
Till in the summer-land of dreams
They softened to the sound of streams,
Low stir of leaves, and dip of oars,
And lapsing waves on quiet shores.

Next morn we wakened with the shout
Of merry voices high and clear;
And saw the teamsters drawing near
To break the drifted highways out.
Down the long hillside treading slow
We saw the half-buried oxen go,
Shaking the snow from heads uptost,
Their straining nostrils white with frost.
Before our door the straggling train
Drew up, an added team to gain.
The elders threshed their hands a-cold,
Passed, with the cider-mug, their jokes
From lip to lip; the younger folks
Down the loose snow-banks, wrestling, rolled,
Then toiled again the cavalcade
O'er windy hill, through clogged ravine,
And woodland paths that wound between
Low drooping pine-boughs winter-weighed.
From every barn a team afoot,
At every house a new recruit,
Where, drawn by Nature's subtlest law,
Haply the watchful young men saw
Sweet doorway pictures of the curls
And curious eyes of merry girls,
Lifting their hands in mock defense
Against the snow-balls' compliments,
And reading in each missive tost
The charm which Eden never lost.

PHILOSOPHY OF THE PHYSICAL WORLD

For the philosophic mind, however, the great effect comes not from a single tree or the song of a bird, but from the totality of the physical world. Wordsworth has shown clearly in his "Lines Composed a Few Miles Above Tintern Abbey" how the meaning and influence of nature passed in his life through at least three distinct stages. The poem is in a way a summary of this whole chapter. Walt Whitman's few lines voice an acceptance which is an all-inclusive exultation.

LINES

Composed a Few Miles Above Tintern Abbey, on Revisiting the Banks of the Wye During a Tour. July 13, 1798

by William Wordsworth (1770-1850)

Five years have passed; five summers, with
the length
Of five long winters! and again I hear
These waters, rolling from their mountain-
springs
With a soft inland murmur.—Once again
Do I behold these steep and lofty cliffs,
That on a wild secluded scene impress
Thoughts of more deep seclusion; and con-
nect
The landscape with the quiet of the sky.
The day is come when I again repose

Here, under this dark sycamore, and view
These plots of cottage-ground, these orchard-tufts,
Which at this season, with their unripe fruits,
Are clad in one green hue, and lose themselves
'Mid groves and copses. Once again I see
These hedge-rows, hardly hedge-rows, little lines
Of sportive wood run wild: these pastoral farms,
Green to the very door; and wreaths of smoke
Sent up, in silence, from among the trees!
With some uncertain notice, as might seem
Of vagrant dwellers in the houseless woods
Or of some Hermit's cave, where by his fire
The Hermit sits alone.
These beauteous forms,
Through a long absence, have not been to me
As is a landscape to a blind man's eye:
But oft, in lonely rooms, and 'mid the din
Of towns and cities, I have owed to them
In hours of weariness, sensations sweet,
Felt in the blood, and felt along the heart;
And passing even into my purer mind,
With tranquil restoration:—feelings too
Of unremembered pleasure: such, perhaps,
As have no slight or trivial influence
On that best portion of a good man's life,
His little, nameless, unremembered acts
Of kindness and of love. Nor less, I trust,
To them I may have owed another gift,
Of aspect more sublime; that blessed mood,
In which the burthen of the mystery,
In which the heavy and the weary weight
Of all this unintelligible world,
Is lightened:—that serene and blessed mood,
In which the affections gently lead us on,—
Until, the breath of this corporeal frame
And even the motion of our human blood
Almost suspended, we are laid asleep
In body, and become a living soul:
While with an eye made quiet by the power
Of harmony, and the deep power of joy,
We see into the life of things.
If this
Be but a vain belief, yet, oh! how oft—
In darkness and amid the many shapes
Of joyless daylight; when the fretful stir
Unprofitable, and the fever of the world,
Have hung upon the beatings of my heart—
How oft, in spirit, have I turned to thee,
O sylvan Wye! thou wanderer through the woods,
How often has my spirit turned to thee!
And now, with gleams of half-extinguished thought,
With many recognitions dim and faint,
And somewhat of a sad perplexity,
The picture of the mind revives again:
While here I stand, not only with the sense
Of present pleasure, but with pleasing thoughts
That in this moment there is life and food
For future years. And so I dare to hope,
Though changed, no doubt, from what I was when first
I came among these hills; when like a roe
I bounded o'er the mountains, by the sides
Of the deep rivers, and the lonely streams,
Wherever nature led: more like a man
Flying from something that he dreads, than one
Who sought the thing he loved. For nature then
(The coarser pleasures of my boyish days,
And their glad animal movements all gone by)
To me was all in all.—I cannot paint
What then I was. The sounding cataract
Haunted me like a passion; the tall rock,
The mountain, and the deep and gloomy wood,
Their colors and their forms, were then to me
An appetite; a feeling and a love,
That had no need of a remoter charm,
By thought supplied, nor any interest
Unborrowed from the eye.—That time is past,
And all its aching joys are now no more,
And all its dizzy raptures. Not for this
Faint I, nor mourn nor murmur; other gifts
Have followed; for such loss, I would believe,
Abundant recompense. For I have learned
To look on nature, not as in the hour
Of thoughtless youth; but hearing oftentimes
The still, sad music of humanity,
Nor harsh nor grating, though of ample power
To chasten and subdue. And I have felt
A presence that disturbs me with the joy
Of elevated thoughts; a sense sublime

Of something far more deeply interfused,
Whose dwelling is the light of setting suns,
And the round ocean and the living air,
And the blue sky, and in the mind of man;
A motion and a spirit, that impels
All thinking things, all objects of all thought,
And rolls through all things. Therefore am I still
A lover of the meadows and the woods,
And mountains; and of all that we behold
From this green earth; of all the mighty world
Of eye, and ear,—both what they half create,
And what perceive; well pleased to recognize
In nature and the language of the sense,
The anchor of my purest thoughts, the nurse,
The guide, the guardian of my heart, and soul
Of all my moral being.
Nor perchance,
If I were not thus taught, should I the more
Suffer my genial spirits to decay:
For thou art with me here upon the banks
Of this fair river; thou my dearest Friend,
My dear, dear Friend; and in thy voice I catch
The language of my former heart, and read
My former pleasures in the shooting lights
Of thy wild eyes. Oh! yet a little while
May I behold in thee what I was once,
My dear, dear Sister! and this prayer I make,
Knowing that Nature never did betray
The heart that loved her; 'tis her privilege,
Through all the years of this our life, to lead
From joy to joy: for she can so inform
The mind that is within us, so impress
With quietness and beauty, and so feed
With lofty thoughts, that neither evil tongues,
Rash judgments, nor the sneers of selfish men,
Nor greetings where no kindness is, nor all
The dreary intercourse of daily life,
Shall e'er prevail against us, or disturb
Our cheerful faith, that all which we behold
Is full of blessings. Therefore let the moon
Shine on thee in thy solitary walk;
And let the misty mountain-winds be free
To blow against thee: and, in after years,
When these wild ecstasies shall be matured
Into a sober pleasure; when thy mind
Shall be a mansion for all lovely forms,
Thy memory be as a dwelling-place
For all sweet sounds and harmonies; oh! then,
If solitude, or fear, or pain, or grief,
Should be thy portion, with what healing thoughts
Of tender joy wilt thou remember me,
And these my exhortations! Nor, perchance—
If I should be where I no more can hear
Thy voice, nor catch from thy wild eyes these gleams
Of past existence—wilt thou then forget
That on the banks of this delightful stream
We stood together; and that I, so long
A worshiper of Nature, hither came
Unwearied in that service: rather say
With warmer love—oh! with far deeper zeal
Of holier love. Nor wilt thou then forget,
That after many wanderings, many years
Of absence, these steeps woods and lofty cliffs,
And this green pastoral landscape, were to me
More dear, both for themselves and for thy sake!

FROM "GIVE ME THE SPLENDID SILENT SUN"

Give me the splendid silent sun with all his beams full-dazzling,
Give me juicy autumnal fruit ripe and red from the orchard,
Give me a field where the unmow'd grass grows,
Give me an arbour, give me the trellis'd grape,
Give me fresh corn and wheat, give me serene-moving animals teaching content,
Give me nights perfectly quiet as on high plateaus west of the Mississippi, and I looking up at the stars,
Give me odorous at sunrise a garden of beautiful flowers where I can walk undisturb'd,
Give me for marriage a sweet-breath'd woman of whom I should never tire,

Give me a perfect child, give me a way aside from the noise of the world, a rural
domestic life,
Give me to warble spontaneous songs recluse by myself, for my own ears only,
Give me solitude, give me Nature, give me again, O Nature, your primal sanities!

—*Walt Whitman* (1819-1892)

THE CITY

It must not be thought, however, that the poet establishes close contact with nature only when he "murmurs near the running brooks a music sweeter than their own" or "babbles of green fields." The city has its flora and fauna, too, its "moral aspects" and, in the case of the worshippers of the machine, its "pathetic fallacies." The poet is the first to realize the truth of the proverb *magna civitas, magna solitudo*—a great city, a great solitude—and he knows that nature expresses herself not only through prairie silences but through stone and steel. Three hundred years ago Milton knew that "meadows trim with daisies pied" were not enough; after a dinner of herbs and dancing in the checkered shade, we turn to the town.

Towered cities please us then,
And the busy hum of men.

The late laureate of England, Robert Bridges, saw the city transformed and men's minds diverted by the common miracle of snow. Carl Sandburg, "the laureate of industrial America," sees glamor as well as vitality in this urban civilization. Robert Frost, E. E. Cummings and others have made it imaginatively clear that city streets are not outside of nature. A new imagery has sprung up with the new architecture. Riveters seem to be "the woodpeckers of the town," electric street-lamps have become "iron lilies," skyscrapers are "waterfalls of stone." There is no bar to the alert and image-making impulse; the metaphorical sense is never fettered or defeated. "Stone walls do not a prison make nor iron bars a cage" might have been written with the girder-built metropolis in mind.

The following poems represent only a few of the innumerable illustrations of the growing importance of the city from the eighteenth century to the present day. Eda Lou Walton has compiled an entire anthology, *The City Day,* especially for those students in metropolitan centers to whom the countryside is remote. Her preface suggests that historically city poetry can be traced from the development of the cities as trade centers and she gives reasons for new ideas of beauty in urban poetry, reasons which spring from environmental and psychological sources. Moreover, she shows that language and imagery, being from a much older background than the city, must use older associational words in a new way to convey new impressions and sensations.

VENICE

Venice, thou Siren of sea-cities, wrought
By mirage, built on water, stair o'er stair,
Of sunbeams and cloud-shadows, phantom-fair,
With naught of earth to mar thy sea-born thought!

Thou floating film upon the wonder-fraught
Ocean of dreams! Thou hast no dream so rare
As are thy sons and daughters, they who wear
Foam-flakes of charm from thine enchantment caught!
O dark brown eyes! O tangles of dark hair!
O heaven-blue eyes, blonde tresses where the breeze
Plays over sun-burned cheeks in sea-blown air!
Firm limbs of moulded bronze! frank debonair
Smiles of deep-bosomed women! Loves that seize
Man's soul, and waft her on storm-melodies!

—*John Addington Symonds* (1840-1893)

LONDON VOLUNTARY

by William Ernest Henley (1849-1903)

Forth from the dust and din,
The crush, the heat, the many-spotted glare,
The odour and sense of life and lust aflare,
The wrangle and jangle of unrests,
Let us take horse, Dear Heart, take horse and win—
As from swart August to the green lap of May—
To quietness and the fresh and fragrant breasts
Of the still, delicious night, not yet aware
In any of her innumerable nests
Of that first sudden plash of dawn,
Clear, sapphirine, luminous, large,
Which tells that soon the flowing springs of day
In deep and ever deeper eddies drawn
Forward and up, in wider and wider way,
Shall float the sands, and brim the shores,
On this our lith of the World, as round it roars
And spins into the outlook of the Sun
(The Lord's first gift, the Lord's especial charge),
With light, with living light, from marge to marge
Until the course He set and staked be run.

Through street and square, through square and street,
Each with his home-grown quality of dark
And violated silence, loud and fleet,
Waylaid by a merry ghost at every lamp,
The hansom wheels and plunges. Hark, O, hark,
Sweet, how the old mare's bit and chain
Ring back a rough refrain
Upon the marked and cheerful tramp
Of her four shoes! Here is the Park,
And O, the languid midsummer wafts adust,
The tired midsummer blooms!
O, the mysterious distances, the glooms
Romantic, the august
And solemn shapes! At night this City of Trees

Turns to a tryst of vague and strange
And monstrous Majesties,
Let loose from some dim underworld to range
These terrene vistas till their twilight sets:
When, dispossessed of wonderfulness, they stand
Beggared and common, plain to all the land
For stooks of leaves! And lo! the Wizard Hour,
His silent, shining sorcery winged with power!
Still, still the streets, between their carcanets
Of linking gold, are avenues of sleep.
But see how gable ends and parapets
In gradual beauty and significance
Emerge! And did you hear
That little twitter-and-cheep,
Breaking inordinately loud and clear
On this still, spectral, exquisite atmosphere?
'Tis a first nest at matins! And behold
A rakehell cat—how furtive and acold!
A spent witch homing from some infamous dance—
Obscene, quick-trotting, see her tip and fade
Through shadowy railings into a pit of shade!
And now! a little wind and shy,
The smell of ships (that earnest of romance),
A sense of space and water, and thereby
A lamplit bridge touching the troubled sky,
And look, O, look! a tangle of silver gleams
And dusky lights, our River and all his dreams,
His dreams that never save in our deaths can die.

What miracle is happening in the air,
Charging the very texture of the gray
With something luminous and rare?
The night goes out like an ill-parcelled fire,
And, as one lights a candle, it is day.
The extinguisher, that perks it like a spire
On the little formal church, is not yet green
Across the water: but the house-tops nigher,
The corner-lines, the chimneys—look how clean,
How new, how naked! See the batch of boats,
Here at the stairs, washed in the fresh-sprung beam!
And those are barges that were goblin floats,
Black, hag-steered, fraught with devilry and dream!
And in the piles the water frolics clear,
The ripples into loose rings wander and flee,
And we—we can behold that could but hear
The ancient River singing as he goes,
New-mailed in morning, to the ancient Sea.
The gas burns lank and jaded in its glass:
The old Ruffian soon shall yawn himself awake,
And light his pipe, and shoulder his tools, and take
His hobnailed way to work!

Let us too pass—

Pass ere the sun leaps and your shadow shows—
Through these long, blindfold rows
Of casements staring blind to right and left,
Each with his gaze turned inward on some piece
Of life in death's own likeness—Life bereft
Of living looks as by the Great Release—
Pass to an exquisite night's more exquisite close!

Reach upon reach of burial—so they feel,
These colonies of dreams! And as we steal
Homeward together, but for the buxom breeze,
Fitfully frolicking to heel
With news of dawn-drenched woods and tumbling seas,
We might—thus awed, thus lonely that we are—
Be wandering some dispeopled star,
Some world of memories and unbroken graves,
So broods the abounding Silence near and far:
Till even your footfall craves
Forgiveness of the majesty it braves.

LONDON SNOW

by Robert Bridges (1844-1930)

When men were all asleep the snow came flying,
In large white flakes falling on the city brown,
Stealthily and perpetually settling and loosely lying,
  Hushing the latest traffic of the drowsy town;
Deadening, muffling, stifling its murmurs failing;
Lazily and incessantly floating down and down:
  Silently sifting and veiling road, roof and railing;
Hiding difference, making unevenness even,
Into angles and crevices softly drifting and sailing.
  All night it fell, and when full inches seven
It lay in the depth of its uncompacted lightness,
The clouds blew off from a high and frosty heaven;
  And all woke earlier for the unaccustomed brightness
Of the winter dawning, the strange unheavenly glare:
The eye marveled—marveled at the dazzling whiteness;
  The ear hearkened to the stillness of the solemn air;
No sound of wheel rumbling nor of foot falling,
And the busy morning cries came thin and spare.
  Then boys I heard, as they went to school, calling,
They gathered up the crystal manna to freeze
Their tongues with tasting, their hands with snowballing;
  Or rioted in a drift, plunging up to the knees;
Or peering up from under the white-mossed wonder,
"O look at the trees!" they cried, "O look at the trees!"
  With lessened load a few carts creak and blunder,
Following along the white deserted way,
A country company long dispersed asunder:

When now already the sun, in pale display
Standing by Paul's high dome, spread forth below
His sparkling beams, and awoke the stir of the day.
For now doors open, and war is waged with the snow;
And trains of somber men, past tale of number,
Tread long brown paths, as toward their toil they go:
But even for them awhile no cares encumber
Their minds diverted; the daily word is unspoken,
The daily thoughts of labor and sorrow slumber
At the sight of the beauty that greets them, for the charm they have broken.

A BROOK IN THE CITY

The farm house lingers, though averse to square
With the new city street it has to wear
A number in. But what about the brook
That held the house as in an elbow-crook?
I ask as one who knew the brook, its strength
And impulse, having dipped a finger length
And made it leap my knuckle, having tossed
A flower to try its currents where they crossed.
The meadow grass could be cemented down
From growing under pavements of a town;
The apple trees be sent to hearth-stone flame.
Is water wood to serve a brook the same?
How else dispose of an immortal force
No longer needed? Staunch it at its source
With cinder loads dumped down? The brook was thrown
Deep in a sewer dungeon under stone
In fetid darkness still to live and run—
And all for nothing it had ever done
Except forget to go in fear perhaps.
No one would know except for ancient maps
That such a brook ran water. But I wonder
If from its being kept forever under,
These thoughts may not have risen that so keep
This new-built city from both work and sleep.

—*Robert Frost* (1875-)

FROM "THE WINDY CITY"

by Carl Sandburg (1878-)

Night gathers itself into a ball of dark yarn.
Night loosens the ball and it spreads.
The lookouts from the shores of Lake Michigan
find night follows day, and ping! ping! across
sheet gray the boat lights put their signals.
Night lets the dark yarn unravel, Night speaks and
the yarns change to fog and blue strands.

The lookouts turn to the city.

The canyons swarm with red sand lights of the sunset.
The atoms drop and sift, blues cross over, yellows plunge.
Mixed light-shafts stack their bayonets, pledge with crossed handles.
So, when the canyons swarm, it is then the lookouts speak
Of the high spots over a street . . . mountain language
Of skyscrapers in dusk, the Railway Exchange,
The People's Gas, the Monadnock, the Transportation,
Gone to the gloaming.

The river turns in a half circle.
The Goose Island bridges curve
    over the river curve.
    Then the river panorama
    performs for the bridge,
    dots . . . lights . . . dots . . . lights,
    sixes and sevens of dots and lights,
    a lingo of lanterns and searchlights,
    circling sprays of gray and yellow.

✦

A man came as a witness saying:
"I listened to the Great Lakes
And I listened to the Grand Prairie,
And they had little to say to each other,
A whisper or so in a thousand years.
'Some of the cities are big,' said one.
'And some not so big,' said another.
'And sometimes the cities are all gone,'
Said a black knob bluff to a light green sea."

Winds of the Windy City, come out of the prairie,
    all the way from Medicine Hat.
Come out of the inland sea blue water, come where
    they nickname a city for you.

Corn wind in the fall, come off the black lands,
    come off the whisper of the silk hangers,
    the lap of the flat spear leaves.

Blue water wind in summer, come off the blue miles
    of lake, carry your inland sea-blue fingers,
    carry us cool, carry your blue to our homes.

White spring winds, come off the bag wool clouds,
    come off the running melted snow, come white
    as the arms of snow-born children.

Gray fighting winter winds, come along on the tearing
    blizzard tails, the snouts of the hungry
    hunting storms, come fighting gray in winter.

Winds of the Windy City,
Winds of corn and sea blue,

Spring wind white and fighting winter gray,
Come home here—they nickname a city for you.

The wind of the lake shore waits and wanders.
The heave of the shore wind hunches the sand piles.
The winkers of the morning stars count out cities
And forget the numbers.

BLUE ISLAND INTERSECTION

Six street ends come together here.
They feed people and wagons into the center.
In and out all day horses with thoughts of nose-bags,
Men with shovels, women with baskets and baby buggies.
Six ends of streets and no sleep for them all day.
The people and wagons come and go, out and in.
Triangles of banks and drug stores watch.
The policemen whistle, the trolley cars bump:
Wheels, wheels, feet, feet, all day.

In the false dawn when the chickens blink
And the east shakes a lazy baby toe at tomorrow,
And the east fixes a pink half-eye this way,
In the time when only one milk wagon crosses
These three streets, these six street ends,
It is the sleep time and they rest.
The triangle banks and drug stores rest.
The policeman is gone, his star and gun sleep.
The owl car blutters along in a sleep-walk.

—*Carl Sandburg* (1878-   )

BEFORE DAWN

What is this that I have heard?
Scurrying rat or stirring bird?
Scratching in the wall of sleep?
Twitching on the eaves of sleep?
I can hear it working close
Through a space along the house,
Through a space obscure and thin.
Night is swiftly running out,
Dawn has yet to ripple in,
Dawn has yet to clear the doubt,—
Rat within or bird without.

—*Melville Cane* (1879-   )

IMPRESSION: IV

by E. E. Cummings (1896-   )

the hours rise up putting off stars and it is
dawn
into the street of the sky light walks scattering poems

on earth a candle is
extinguished   the city
wakes
with a song upon her
mouth having death in her eyes

and it is dawn
the world
goes forth to murder dreams. . . .

i see in the street where strong
men are digging bread
and i see the brutal faces of
people contented hideous hopeless cruel happy

and it is day

in the mirror
i see a frail
man
dreaming
dreams
dreams in the mirror
and it
is dusk   on earth

a candle is lighted
and it is dark
the people are in their houses
the frail man is in his bed
the city

sleeps with death upon her mouth having a song in her eyes
the hours descend
putting on stars. . . .

in the street of the sky night walks scattering poems

WATERFALLS OF STONE

Buildings are waterfalls of stone
That, spurting up with marble crest,
Are frozen and enchained in air,
Poised in perpetual rest.

But water seeks its level out.
So, when these fountains are unbound,
The cataracts of melting stone
Will sink into the ground.

—*Louis Ginsberg* (1896-   )

SUGGESTIONS FOR ADDITIONAL READING

POEMS OF INANIMATE NATURE

Lord Byron, *Childe Harold's Pilgrimage*
William Cullen Bryant, *Evening Wind*
William Wordsworth, *The Excursion*
P. B. Shelley, *Ode to the West Wind*
Alfred Tennyson, *The Brook*
Sidney Lanier, *Song of the Chattahoochee*
Walt Whitman, *Song of the Open Road*
Richard W. Gilder, *In the White Mountains*
William Butler Yeats, *The Lake Isle of Innisfree*
Madison Cawein, *The First Quarter*
E. A. Robinson, *Monadnock Through the Trees*
John Masefield, *Sea-Fever*
John Masefield, *The West Wind*
Edna St. Vincent Millay, *Renascence*
Edna St. Vincent Millay, *God's World*

Frank Ernest Hill, *Earth and Air*
Léonie Adams, *Country Summer*

POEMS OF ANIMATE NATURE

William Cowper, *Epitaph on a Hare*
William Wordsworth, *To the Cuckoo*
William Blake, *The Fly*
P. B. Shelley, *The Sensitive Plant*
Philip Freneau, *The Caty-did*
Philip Freneau, *The Honey-bee*
Philip Freneau, *To the Wild Honey-suckle*
William Cullen Bryant, *Robert O'Lincoln*
William Cullen Bryant, *To the Fringed Gentian*
Robert Browning, *Muléykeh*
R. W. Emerson, *Woodnotes*
Alfred Tennyson, *The Daisy*
Sidney Lanier, *Tampa Robins*
Paul H. Hayne, *The Mocking-Bird*
Bret Harte, *Chiquita*
Austin Dobson, *A Flower Song of Angiola*
Joyce Kilmer, *Trees*
John Masefield, *Tewkesbury Road*
Carl Sandburg, *Grass*
George Meredith, *The Lark Ascending*
Humbert Wolfe, *Lilac*
Humbert Wolfe, *Rose*
Humbert Wolfe, *Two Sparrows*
W. H. Davies, *The Kingfisher*
W. H. Davies, *Sheep*

POEMS OF CHANGES IN NATURE

Robert Herrick, *Corinna's Gone A-Maying*
Thomas Gray, *Ode to Spring*
James Thomson, *The Seasons*
William Cullen Bryant, *June*
Thomas Hood, *November*
William Ernest Henley, *Pastorale*
H. W. Longfellow, *Hymn to the Night*
Sidney Lanier, *Sunrise*
Francis Thompson, *Ode to the Setting Sun*
Emily Dickinson, *Autumn*
Emily Dickinson, *Indian Summer*
Carl Sandburg, *Slabs of the Sunburnt West*
Carl Sandburg, *Chicago*
Robert Frost, *To Earthward*
Robert Frost, *Nothing Gold Can Stay*
Edwin Arlington Robinson, *The Sheaves*
Sara Teasdale, *August Moonrise*

9

THE THOUGHTS OF POETRY: THE POEM AS IDEA

"YE SHALL know the truth, and the truth shall make you free," Jesus said to his disciples and to all mankind. Together with all great philosophers, and quite in opposition to some evangelical preachers, he realized that man will never be completely happy until he has security, some assurance of the meaning of life. He also knew that man himself can never reach absolute certainty, and that for most minds the law must be interpreted through institutions, creeds, and social customs. Man's hope of discovering some of "the eternal verities," however, has made him desire to establish systems which might explain the universe.

Descartes upset the whole self-satisfied authoritarian system of mediaeval philosophy by asking: Is any truth undeniable? His own method of systematic doubt led to his theory that there is only one absolute, undeniable truth —one's own existence. From the central idea of *Cogito, ergo sum* he rebuilt a universe in orderly fashion. The method which he provided gripped the minds of others, and systematic philosophers became as numerous as the mediaeval casuists had been before. It became obvious to the thoughtful that though appearances might satisfy the requirements of daily life, *reality* was an entirely different matter. To Bishop Berkeley and the "Idealists" it was obvious that a stone had many different appearances, according to the point of view from which it was seen, the different eyes which saw it, and the other variations in sensory perceptions; but there was, after all, only one stone, which possessed a reality entirely apart from appearance. Apparently one could have a full and excellent knowledge of *things* without the slightest conception of *truth*. When his belief and all the facts were perfectly coherent in every respect, then and then only could man feel reasonably sure that he had found the truth.

This was the path followed by philosophy, one of the five great paths which man has trod in his search for reality. Philosophy at one time embraced the whole of human knowledge, a condition reflected today in the fact that a graduate student in Chemistry or Sanskrit still works for a degree of "Doctor of Philosophy." As this body of information became organized, branches grew great on the parent tree, until some branches, such as Science and Religion, were felt to be self-supported, separate trees, if not the only tree in the world. The new science of psychology is perhaps philosophy's latest rebellious product. Today people have come to think of the philosopher as "man reasoning," whereas the artist is "man expressing," the scientist is "man experimenting," the preacher is "man spiritualizing," and most of us are merely "man experiencing."

These have been the five roads of destiny which direct man toward that truth which will explain life and the universe. Experience has always been called the most tedious and rocky of the roads, yet all the others have been forced to conform to the contours of experience if they were to be accepted as true highways. Every reader of poetry can recognize the truth of a figure or a statement when it agrees with his own experience. Distance covered on the road of experience does not usually have to be retraced. It is in this respect that the biography of poets is valuable. Have they arrived at an idea through their own experience? Is Poe a pessimist because of the life he led? Housman? Hardy? Jeffers? Does Milton admire a stoic because his own blindness made him one? Is Swinburne expressing his over-sensuous self, or dramatizing himself, or challenging opinion from an entirely different point of view?

The pathway of art is the most pleasant of all. Through the contemplation of beauty the emotions are calmed and the mind perceives the harmony of the universe. After gazing upon the lines and figures on a Grecian urn, Keats decided that "Beauty is truth, truth beauty." By creating a thing of beauty, such as a poem, the artist becomes momentarily the agent of universal truth, the conduit through which run the waters from the springs of reality.

Science views the universe as a place of law and order, and tries to discover what the laws and order may be. It can work without emotions, unconscious of beauty and unconcerned with the ultimate purpose of it all. It conforms to experience, and applies many of the methods of philosophy, but desires nothing more than is necessary to explain the physical workings of the parts. When man goes beyond this into the realm of purpose, he leaves science for religion.

For religion is the attempt on the part of man to find his own place in the scheme. It is more concerned than philosophy with the rules of human conduct, more insistent upon conformity with the "ethical laws" of the universe. Philosophy discovers their existence; religion glorifies and spiritualizes them. Like philosophy, it is farther from experience than either art or science, and therefore is more open to argument; like art, it is more dependent upon emotion than either science or philosophy; like experience, we must acknowledge it whether we wish to or not—no sensitive man can be without some religion, though his eyes may be closed to beauty and his mind to logic.

The problems treated by poets appear to fall into three main categories: problems concerning the conduct of life, problems of the purpose of life, and problems of the nature of the universe and man's relation to it. The order in which they are listed here is probably the order in which they have arisen in man's consciousness—surely the first difficulty faced by man was learning how to interpret and govern his own conduct.

The greatest ethical poetry of the world is Oriental rather than Occidental; it is Buddhist or Sufi or Hebrew rather than Christian. The eastern mind seems more concerned with things of the spirit than the western mind; it is less concerned with time and more with eternity. As a result, the western mind has attained a greater speed, a sharper viewpoint on immediate details, a shrewder sense of material values and other practical advantages. The book which works against the materialistic outlook and which continues to color the western mind is a product of the Orient: the Bible. It is interesting to note that the poetry of the Anglo-Saxon race is filled with more ethical implications than that of any other European people.

The Christian attitude toward the conduct of life is so bound up with the ideas of the purpose of life and our place in the universe that its intent is direct and inescapable. George Herbert's long "Church Porch" in *The Temple* serves excellently as an example of poetry on Christian conduct. Three other attitudes which man assumes in his conduct and his method of existence are represented by Stoicism, Pragmatism, and Hedonism.

STOICISM

Stoicism, taught by Zeno in the third century before Christ, made virtue the highest good, inculcated control of the passions and complete indifference to both pleasure and pain. Its modern expression might be summarized thus: "Though life is hard and unyielding, let us bear it bravely to the end, enduring calmly, even grimly, whatever it brings." This is the message of Milton's famous sonnet "On His Blindness," quoted on page 365, of Emily Brontë's "The Old Stoic," and of Wordsworth's ode, though the "Ode to Duty" and the "Ode on the Intimations of Immortality" seem to emanate from two quite different poets.

As fighting stoics Arnold, Henley, and Browning are more definite, even defiant. They call upon us to face a harsh and inimical world with courage, even though defeat seems certain. Browning's "Prospice," like so many of his other poems, might well be placed in the group under Optimism; yet its courageous disposal of death makes it a stoical expression as well.

ODE TO DUTY

by William Wordsworth (1770-1850)

Stern Daughter of the Voice of God!
O Duty! if that name thou love,
Who art a light to guide, a rod
To check the erring, and reprove;
Thou, who art victory and law
When empty terrors overawe;
From vain temptations dost set free;
And calm'st the weary strife of frail humanity!

There are who ask not if thine eye
Be on them; who, in love and truth,
Where no misgiving is, rely
Upon the genial sense of youth:
Glad Hearts! without reproach or blot;
Who do thy work, and know it not:
O if through confidence misplaced
They fail, thy saving arms, dread Power, around them cast.

Serene will be our days and bright,
And happy will our nature be,
When love is an unerring light,
And joy its own security.
And they a blissful course may hold
Even now, who, not unwisely bold,
Live in the spirit of this creed;
Yet seek thy firm support, according to their need.

I, loving freedom, and untried;
No sport of every random gust,
Yet being to myself a guide,
Too blindly have reposed my trust:

And oft, when in my heart was heard
Thy timely mandate, I deferred
The task, in smoother walks to stray;
But thee I now would serve more strictly, if I may.

Through no disturbance of my soul,
Or strong compunction in me wrought,
I supplicate for thy control;
But in the quietness of thought:
Me this unchartered freedom tires;
I feel the weight of chance-desires:
My hopes no more must change their name,
I long for a repose that ever is the same.

Stern Lawgiver! yet thou dost wear
The Godhead's most benignant grace;
Nor know we anything so fair
As is the smile upon thy face:
Flowers laugh before thee on their beds
And fragrance in thy footing treads;
Thou dost preserve the stars from wrong;
And the most ancient heavens, through Thee, are fresh and strong.

To humbler functions, awful Power!
I call thee: I myself commend
Unto thy guidance from this hour;
Oh, let my weakness have an end!
Give unto me, made lowly wise,
The spirit of self-sacrifice;
The confidence of reason give;
And in the light of truth thy Bondman let me live!

THE OLD STOIC

Riches I hold in light esteem,
And love I laugh to scorn;
And lust of fame was but a dream,
That vanished with the morn:

And if I pray, the only prayer
That moves my lips for me
Is, "Leave the heart that now I bear,
And give me liberty!"

Yes, as my swift days near their goal,
'Tis all that I implore;
In life and death a chainless soul,
With courage to endure.

—*Emily Brontë* (1818-1848)

THE LAST WORD

Creep into thy narrow bed,
Creep, and let no more be said!
Vain thy onset! all stands fast.
Thou thyself must break at last.

Let the long contention cease!
Geese are swans, and swans are geese.
Let them have it how they will!
Thou art tired; best be still.

They out-talked thee, hissed thee, tore thee?
Better men fared thus before thee;
Fired their ringing shot and passed,
Hotly charged—and sank at last.

Charge once more, then, and be dumb!
Let the victors, when they come,
When the forts of folly fall,
Find thy body by the wall!

—*Matthew Arnold* (1822-1888)

INVICTUS

Out of the night that covers me,
Black as the Pit from pole to pole,
I thank whatever gods may be
For my unconquerable soul.

In the fell clutch of circumstance
I have not winced nor cried aloud.
Under the bludgeonings of chance
My head is bloody, but unbowed.

Beyond this place of wrath and tears
Looms but the Horror of the shade,
And yet the menace of the years
Finds, and shall find me, unafraid.

It matters not how strait the gate,
How charged with punishments the scroll,
I am the master of my fate:
I am the captain of my soul.

—*William Ernest Henley* (1849-1903)

THE CELESTIAL SURGEON

If I have faltered more or less
In my great task of happiness;
If I have moved among my race
And shown no glorious morning face;

If beams from happy human eyes
Have moved me not; if morning skies,
Books, and my food, and summer rain
Knocked on my sullen heart in vain:—
Lord, thy most pointed pleasure take
And stab my spirit broad awake;
Or, Lord, if too obdurate I,
Choose thou, before that spirit die,
A piercing pain, a killing sin,
And to my dead heart run them in!

—*Robert Louis Stevenson* (1850-1894)

PROSPICE

by Robert Browning (1812-1889)

Fear death? to feel the fog in my throat,
The mist in my face,
When the snows begin, and the blasts denote
I am nearing the place,
The power of the night, the press of the storm,
The post of the foe;
Where he stands, the Arch Fear in a visible form,
Yet the strong man must go:
For the journey is done and the summit attained,
And the barriers fall,
Though a battle's to fight ere the guerdon be gained,
The reward of it all.
I was ever a fighter, so—one fight more,
The best and the last!
I would hate that death bandaged my eyes, and forbore,
And bade me creep past.
No! let me taste the whole of it, fare like my peers
The heroes of old,
Bear the brunt, in a minute pay glad life's arrears
Of pain, darkness and cold.
For sudden the worst turns the best to the brave,
The black minute's at end,
And the elements' rage, the fiend-voices that rave,
Shall dwindle, shall blend,
Shall change, shall become first a peace out of pain,
Then a light, then thy breast,
O thou soul of my soul! I shall clasp thee again,
And with God be the rest!

PRAGMATISM

The pragmatist feels that he goes a step further than the stoic when he declares, "I can endure my lot as well as the others, but I prefer to make it better if I can, by work in the line of progress." Pragmatism and the theory of progress are both products of the industrial revolution, and are deeply influenced by the ideals of science. Rossetti has given three excellent contrasting pictures of attitudes toward the conduct of life in "The Choice"; the reader, however, cannot avoid feeling that the poet is preaching the acceptance of the last program. Tennyson is speaking to Victorian England through Ulysses both in "The Lotos-Eaters" and "Ulysses," urging the Carlylian doctrine of the sanctity of work, the necessity of going on. Matthew Arnold's "Empedocles' Song" seems to be more than a dramatic monologue. It is the embodiment of all Arnold's deepest convictions on the necessity for self-reliance in this world; there is certainly no conflict in idea between this poem and "The Last Word" or "Dover Beach."

THE CHOICE

by Dante Gabriel Rossetti (1828-1882)

I

Eat thou and drink; tomorrow thou shalt die.
Surely the earth, that's wise (being very old),
Needs not our help. Then loose me, love, and hold
Thy sultry hair up from my face; that I
May pour for thee this golden wine, brim-high,
Till round the glass thy fingers glow like gold.
We'll drown all hours; thy song, while hours are tolled,
Shall leap, as fountains veil the changing sky.
Now kiss, and think that there are really those,
My own high-bosomed beauty, who increase
Vain gold, vain lore, and yet might choose our way!
Through many years they toil; then on a day
They die not,—for their life was death,—but cease;
And round their narrow lips the mold falls close.

II

Watch thou and fear; tomorrow thou shalt die.
Or art thou sure thou shalt have time for death?
Is not the day which God's word promiseth
To come man knows not when? In yonder sky,
Now while we speak, the sun speeds forth; can I
Or thou assure him of his goal? God's breath
Even at this moment haply quickeneth
The air to a flame; till spirits, always nigh
Though screened and hid, shall walk the daylight here.
And dost thou prate of all that man shall do?
Canst thou, who hast but plagues, presume to be
Glad in his gladness that comes after thee?
Will *his* strength slay *thy* worm in hell? Go to:
Cover thy countenance, and watch, and fear.

III

Think thou and act; tomorrow thou shalt die.
Outstretched in the sun's warmth upon the shore,
Thou say'st: "Man's measured path is all gone o'er;
Up all his years, steeply, with strain and sigh,
Man clomb until he touched the truth; and I,
Even I, am he whom it was destined for."
How should this be? Art thou then so much more
Than they who sowed, that thou shouldst reap thereby?

Nay, come up hither. From this wave-washed mound
Unto the furthest flood-brim look with me;
Then reach on with thy thought till it be drowned.
Miles and miles distant though the gray line be,
And though thy soul sail leagues and leagues beyond,—
Still, leagues beyond those leagues, there is more sea.

ULYSSES

by Alfred, Lord Tennyson (1809-1892)

It little profits that an idle king,
By this still hearth, among these barren crags,
Matched with an agèd wife, I mete and dole
Unequal laws unto a savage race,
That hoard, and sleep, and feed, and know not me.
I cannot rest from travel; I will drink
Life to the lees. All time I have enjoyed
Greatly, have suffered greatly, both with those
That loved me, and alone; on shore, and when
Through scudding drifts the rainy Hyades
Vext the dim sea. I am become a name;
For always roaming with a hungry heart
Much have I seen and known,—cities of men
And manners, climates, councils, governments,
Myself not least, but honored of them all,—
And drunk delight of battle with my peers,
Far on the ringing plains of windy Troy.
I am a part of all that I have met;
Yet all experience is an arch wherethrough
Gleams that untravelled world whose margin fades
Forever and forever when I move.
How dull it is to pause, to make an end,
To rust unburnished, not to shine in use!
As though to breathe were life! Life piled on life
Were all too little, and of one to me
Little remains; but every hour is saved
From that eternal silence, something more,
A bringer of new things; and vile it were
For some three suns to store and hoard myself,
And this gray spirit yearning in desire
To follow knowledge like a sinking star,
Beyond the utmost bound of human thought.

This is my son, mine own Telemachus,
To whom I leave the sceptre and the isle—
Well-loved of me, discerning to fulfil
This labor, by slow prudence to make mild
A rugged people, and through soft degrees
Subdue them to the useful and the good.
Most blameless is he, centred in the sphere
Of common duties, decent not to fail
In offices of tenderness, and pay
Meet adoration to my household gods,
When I am gone. He works his work, I mine.

There lies the port; the vessel puffs her sail;
There gloom the dark, broad seas. My mariners,
Souls that have toiled, and wrought, and thought with me,—
That ever with a frolic welcome took
The thunder and the sunshine, and opposed
Free hearts, free foreheads,—you and I are old;
Old age hath yet his honor and his toil.
Death closes all; but something ere the end,
Some work of noble note, may yet be done,
Not unbecoming men that strove with Gods.
The lights begin to twinkle from the rocks;
The long day wanes; the slow moon climbs; the deep
Moans round with many voices. Come, my friends,
'Tis not too late to seek a newer world.
Push off, and sitting well in order smite
The sounding furrows; for my purpose holds
To sail beyond the sunset, and the baths
Of all the western stars, until I die.
It may be that the gulfs will wash us down;
It may be we shall touch the Happy Isles,
And see the great Achilles, whom we knew.
Though much is taken, much abides; and though
We are not now that strength which in old days

Moved earth and heaven; that which we are, we are;
One equal temper of heroic hearts,
Made weak by time and fate, but strong in will
To strive, to seek, to find, and not to yield.

EMPEDOCLES' SONG
(from "Empedocles on Etna")

by Matthew Arnold (1822-1888)

The out-spread world to span
A cord the Gods first slung,
And then the soul of man
There, like a mirror, hung,
And bade the winds through space impel the gusty toy.

Hither and thither spins
The wind-borne, mirroring soul,
A thousand glimpses wins,
And never sees a whole;
Looks once, and drives elsewhere, and leaves its last employ.

The Gods laugh in their sleeve
To watch man doubt and fear,
Who knows not what to believe
Since he sees nothing clear,
And dares stamp nothing false where he finds nothing sure.

Is this, Pausanias, so?
And can our souls not strive,
But with the winds must go,
And hurry where they drive?
Is fate indeed so strong, man's strength indeed so poor?

I will not judge. That man,
Howbeit, I judge as lost,
Whose mind allows a plan,
Which would degrade it most;
And he treats doubt the best who tries to see least ill.

Be not, then, fear's blind slave!
Thou art my friend; to thee,
All knowledge that I have,
All skill I wield, are free.
Ask not the latest news of the last miracle,

Ask not what days and nights
In trance Pantheia lay,
But ask how thou such sights
May'st see without dismay;
Ask what most helps when known, thou son of Anchitus!

What! hate, and awe, and shame
Fill thee to see our time;
Thou feelest thy soul's frame
Shaken and out of chime?
What! life and chance go hard with thee too, as with us;

Thy citizens, 'tis said,
Envy thee and oppress,
Thy goodness no men aid,
All strive to make it less;
Tyranny, pride, and lust, fill Sicily's abodes;

Heaven is with earth at strife,
Signs make thy soul afraid,
The dead return to life,
Rivers are dried, winds stayed;
Scarce can one think in calm, so threatening are the Gods;

And we feel, day and night,
The burden of ourselves—
Well, then, the wiser wight
In his own bosom delves,
And asks what ails him so, and gets what cure he can.

The sophist sneers: 'Fool, take
Thy pleasure, right or wrong.'
The pious wail: 'Forsake
A world these sophists throng.'
Be neither saint nor sophist-led, but be a man!

These hundred doctors try
To preach thee to their school.
'We have the truth!' they cry;
And yet their oracle,
Trumpet it as they will, is but the same as thine.

Once read thy own breast right,
And thou hast done with fears;
Man gets no other light,
Search he a thousand years.
Sink in thyself! there ask what ails thee, at that shrine!

What makes thee struggle and rave?
Why are men ill at ease?—
'Tis that the lot they have
Fails their own will to please,
For man would make no murmuring, were his will obeyed.

And why is it, that still
Man with his lot thus fights?—
'Tis that he makes this *will*
The measure of his *rights,*
And believes Nature outraged if his will's gainsaid.

Couldst thou, Pausanias, learn
How deep a fault is this;
Couldst thou but once discern
Thou hast no *right* to bliss,
No title from the Gods to welfare and repose;

Then thou wouldst look less mazed
Whene'er of bliss debarred,
Nor think the Gods were crazed
When thy own lot went hard.
But we are all the same—the fools of our own woes!

For, from the first faint morn
Of life, the thirst for bliss
Deep in man's heart is born;
And, skeptic as he is,
He fails not to judge clear if this be quenched or no.

Nor is the thirst to blame.
Man errs not that he deems
His welfare his true aim,
He errs because he dreams
The world does but exist that welfare to bestow.

We mortals are no kings
For each of whom to sway
A new-made world up-springs,
Meant merely for his play;
No, we are strangers here; the world is from of old.

In vain our pent wills fret,
And would the world subdue.
Limits we did not set
Condition all we do;
Born into life we are, and life must be our mold.

Born into life!—man grows
Forth from his parents' stem,
And blends their bloods, as those
Of theirs are blent in them;
So each new man strikes root into a far foretime.

Born into life!—we bring
A bias with us here,
And, when here, each new thing
Affects us we come near;
To tunes we did not call our being must keep chime.

Born into life!—in vain,
Opinions, those or these,
Unaltered to retain
The obstinate mind decrees;
Experience, like a sea, soaks all-effacing in.

Born into life!—who lists
May what is false hold dear,
And for himself make mists
Through which to see less clear;
The world is what it is, for all our dust and din.

Born into life!—'tis we,
And not the world, are new;
Our cry for bliss, our plea,
Others have urged it too—
Our wants have all been felt, our errors made before.

No eye could be too sound
To observe a world so vast,
No patience too profound
To sort what's here amassed;
How man may here best live no care too great to explore.

But we—as some rude guest
Would change, where'er he roam,
The manners there professed
To those he brings from home—
We mark not the world's course, but would have *it* take *ours.*

The world's course proves the terms
On which man wins content;

Reason the proof confirms—
We spurn it, and invent
A false course for the world, and for our-
selves, false powers.

Riches we wish to get,
Yet remain spendthrifts still;
We would have health, and yet
Still use our bodies ill;
Bafflers of our own prayers, from youth to
life's last scenes.

We would have inward peace,
Yet will not look within;
We would have misery cease,
Yet will not cease from sin;
We want all pleasant ends, but will use no
harsh means;

We do not what we ought,
What we ought not, we do,
And lean upon the thought
That chance will bring us through;
But our own acts, for good or ill, are might-
ier powers.

Yet, even when man forsakes
All sin,—is just, is pure,
Abandons all which makes
His welfare insecure,—
Other existences there are, that clash with
ours.

Like us, the lightning-fires
Love to have scope and play;
The stream, like us, desires
An unimpeded way;
Like us, the Libyan wind delights to roam
at large.

Streams will not curb their pride
The just man not to entomb,
Nor lightnings go aside
To give his virtues room;
Nor is that wind less rough which blows a
good man's barge.

Nature, with equal mind,
Sees all her sons at play;
Sees man control the wind,
The wind sweep man away;
Allows the proudly riding and the founder-
ing bark.

And, lastly, though of ours
No weakness spoil our lot,
Though the non-human powers
Of Nature harm us not,
The ill deeds of other men make often *our*
life dark.

✦

Yet still, in spite of truth,
In spite of hopes entombed,
That longing of our youth
Burns ever unconsumed,
Still hungrier for delight as delights grow
more rare.

We pause; we hush our heart,
And thus address the Gods:
'The world hath failed to impart
The joy our youth forbodes,
Failed to fill up the void which in our breasts
we bear.

'Changeful till now, we still
Looked on to something new;
Let us, with changeless will,
Henceforth look on to you,
To find with you the joy we in vain here
require!'

Fools! That so often here
Happiness mocked our prayer,
I think, might make us fear
A like event elsewhere;
Make us, not fly to dreams, but moderate
desire.

And yet, for those who know
Themselves, who wisely take
Their way through life, and bow
To what they cannot break,
Why should I say that life need yield but
moderate bliss?

Shall we, with temper spoiled,
Health sapped by living ill,
And judgment all embroiled
By sadness and self-will,
Shall *we* judge what for man is not true bliss
or is?

Is it so small a thing
To have enjoyed the sun,

To have lived light in the spring,
To have loved, to have thought, to have done;
To have advanced true friends, and beat down baffling foes—

That we must feign a bliss
Of doubtful future date,
And, while we dream on this,
Lose all our present state,
And relegate to worlds yet distant our repose?

Not much, I know, you prize
What pleasures may be had,
Who look on life with eyes
Estranged, like mine, and sad;
And yet the village-churl feels the truth more than you,
Who's loath to leave this life
Which to him little yields—
His hard-tasked sunburnt wife,
His often-labored fields,
The boors with whom he talked, the country-spots he knew.

But thou, because thou hear'st
Men scoff at Heaven and Fate,
Because the Gods thou fear'st
Fail to make blest thy state,
Tremblest, and wilt not dare to trust the joys there are!

I say: Fear not! Life still
Leaves human effort scope.
But, since life teems with ill,
Nurse no extravagant hope;
Because thou must not dream, thou need'st not then despair!

HEDONISM

We have already met the doctrine of hedonism in Rossetti's first sonnet of "The Choice," but it has not yet been given its full expression. There have always been cults which believed in "pure sensation," even among the Hebrews. The Greek Epicureans, though they were in theory quite simple in their pursuit of pleasure, belonged to the group of hedonists; so did the sybarites of Cyrene and the courtiers of the Stuarts and the Bourbons, who held that pleasure was the final object of life.

Robert Herrick has perfectly expressed the Cavalier attitude in his winning "To the Virgins." But the greatest of all epicurean poems is the "Rubáiyát of Omar Khayyám," that rallying-point of those who cry, "Life is a cheat, a conjurer's trick, so be merry while you can." (The word "rubáiyát" means "quatrains.") The poem is not only a complete expression of a love of mental nonchalance and physical sensuousness which is much more than Persian; in the epigrammatic translation of Edward Fitzgerald, it has become the textbook of revolt against the Victorian tradition. Its brilliantly colored and fine-pointed verses continue to be quoted by lovers, rebels, and light-hearted readers of all ages.

TO THE VIRGINS TO MAKE MUCH OF TIME

Gather ye rosebuds while ye may,
Old Time is still a-flying;
And this same flower that smiles today,
Tomorrow will be dying.

The glorious lamp of heaven, the sun,
The higher he's a-getting,
The sooner will his race be run,
The nearer he's to setting.

That age is best which is the first,
When youth and blood are warmer;
But being spent, the worse and worst
Times still succeed the former.

Then be not coy, but use your time,
And while ye may, go marry;

For, having lost but once your prime,
You may forever tarry.
—*Robert Herrick* (1591-1674)

RUBÁIYÁT OF OMAR KHAYYÁM
(Condensed)

translated by Edward Fitzgerald (1809-1883)

Wake! For the Sun, who scattered into flight
The Stars before him from the field of Night,
Drives Night along with them from heav'n, and strikes
The Sultán's turret with a shaft of light.

Before the phantom of False Morning died,
Methought a Voice within the Tavern cried:
"When all the temple is prepared within,
Why nods the drowsy Worshiper outside?"

And, as the cock crew, those who stood before
The Tavern shouted: "Open, then, the door!
You know how little while we have to stay,
And, once departed, may return no more."

Now the New Year reviving old desires,
The thoughtful soul to solitude retires,
Where the WHITE HAND OF MOSES on the bough
Puts out, and Jesus from the ground suspires.

Iram indeed is gone with all his Rose,
And Jamshyd's Sev'n-ringed Cup where no one knows:
But still a ruby kindles in the vine,
And many a garden by the water blows.

And David's lips are locked; but in divine
High-piping Pehleví, with "Wine! Wine! Wine!
Red Wine!"—the Nightingale cries to the Rose
That sallow cheek of hers to incarnadine.

Come, fill the cup, and in the fire of Spring
Your winter-garment of repentance fling:
The Bird of Time has but a little way
To flutter—and the Bird is on the wing.

Whether at Naishápúr or Babylon,
Whether the Cup with sweet or bitter run,
The Wine of Life keeps oozing drop by drop,
The Leaves of Life keep falling one by one.

✦

A book of verses underneath the bough,
A jug of wine, a loaf of bread—and Thou
Beside me singing in the wilderness—
Oh, wilderness were Paradise enow!

Some for the glories of this world; and some
Sigh for the Prophet's Paradise to come;
Ah, take the cash, and let the credit go,
Nor heed the rumble of a distant drum!

Look to the blowing Rose about us—"Lo,
Laughing," she says, "into the world I blow,
At once the silken tassel of my purse
Tear, and its treasure on the garden throw."

And those who husbanded the golden grain,
And those who flung it to the winds like rain,
Alike to no such aureate earth are turned
As, buried once, men want dug up again.

The worldly hope men set their hearts upon
Turns ashes—or it prospers; and anon,
Like snow upon the desert's dusty face,
Lighting a little hour or two—is gone.

Think, in this battered Caravanserai
Whose portals are alternate Night and Day,
How Sultán after Sultán with his pomp
Abode his destined hour, and went his way.

They say the lion and the lizard keep
The Courts where Jamshyd gloried and drank deep:
And Bahrám, that great Hunter—the wild ass
Stamps o'er his head, but cannot break his sleep.

I sometimes think that never blows so red
The rose as where some buried Caesar bled;
That every hyacinth the garden wears
Dropped in her lap from some once lovely head.

And this reviving herb whose tender green
Fledges the river-lip on which we lean—

Ah, lean upon it lightly! for who knows
From what once lovely lip it springs unseen!

Ah, my Belovéd, fill the cup that clears
Today of past regrets and future fears:
Tomorrow!—Why, tomorrow I may be
Myself with yesterday's Sev'n Thousand Years.

For some we loved, the loveliest and the best
That from his vintage rolling Time hath pressed,
Have drunk their Cup a round or two before,
And one by one crept silently to rest.

And we that now make merry in the room
They left, and Summer dresses in new bloom,
Ourselves, must we beneath the couch of earth
Descend—ourselves to make a couch—for whom?

Ah, make the most of what we yet may spend,
Before we too into the dust descend:
Dust into dust, and under dust to lie,
Sans wine, sans song, sans singer, and—sans end!

Alike for those who for Today prepare,
And those that after some Tomorrow stare,
A Muezzín from the Tower of Darkness cries,
"Fools! your reward is neither here nor there."

Why, all the Saints and Sages who discussed
Of the Two Worlds so wisely—they are thrust
Like foolish prophets forth: their words to scorn
Are scattered, and their mouths are stopped with dust.

Myself when young did eagerly frequent
Doctor and saint, and heard great argument
About it and about: but evermore
Came out by the same door where in I went.

With them the seed of Wisdom did I sow,
And with mine own hand wrought to make it grow;
And this was all the harvest that I reaped:
"I came like water, and like wind I go."

Into this Universe, and *Why* not knowing
Nor *Whence,* like water willy-nilly flowing;
And out of it, as wind along the waste,
I know not *Whither,* willy-nilly blowing.

What, without asking, hither hurried *Whence?*
And, without asking, *Whither* hurried hence?
Oh, many a cup of this forbidden wine
Must drown the memory of that insolence!

Up from Earth's center through the Seventh Gate
I rose, and on the throne of Saturn sate,
And many a knot unraveled by the road,
But not the Master-knot of Human Fate.

There was the door to which I found no key;
There was the veil through which I might not see:
Some little talk awhile of Me and Thee
There was—and then no more of Thee and Me.

Earth could not answer; nor the seas that mourn
In flowing purple, of their Lord forlorn;
Nor rolling Heaven, with all his Signs revealed
And hidden by the sleeve of Night and Morn.

Then of the Thee in Me who works behind
The Veil, I lifted up my hands to find
A lamp amid the Darkness; and I heard,
As from Without: "The Me within Thee blind!"

Then to the lip of this poor earthen urn
I leaned, the Secret of my Life to learn:
And lip to lip it murmured: "While you live,
Drink!—for, once dead, you never shall return."

I think the vessel, that with fugitive
Articulation answered, once did live,
And drink; and ah! the passive lip I kissed,
How many kisses might it take—and give!

For I remember stopping by the way
To watch a Potter thumping his wet Clay:
And with its all-obliterated tongue
It murmured: "Gently, Brother, gently, pray!"

And has not such a story from of old
Down Man's successive generations rolled
Of such a clod of saturated earth
Cast by the Maker into human mold?

And not a drop that from our cups we throw
For Earth to drink of, but may steal below
To quench the fire of anguish in some eye
There hidden—far beneath, and long ago.

As then the Tulip, for her morning sup
Of heav'nly vintage, from the soil looks up,
Do you devoutly do the like, till Heav'n
To Earth invert you—like an empty Cup.

✦

So when that Angel of the Darker Drink
At last shall find you by the river-brink,
And, offering his cup, invite your Soul
Forth to your lips to quaff—you shall not shrink.

Why, if the Soul can fling the dust aside,
And naked on the air of Heaven ride,
Were't not a shame—were't not a shame for him
In this clay carcase crippled to abide?

'Tis but a tent where takes his one day's rest
A Sultán to the realm of Death addressed:
The Sultán rises, and the dark Ferrásh
Strikes and prepares it for another Guest.

And fear not lest Existence closing your
Account, and mine, should know the like no more:
The Eternal Sákí from that bowl has poured
Millions of bubbles like us, and will pour.

✦

You know, my Friends, with what a brave carouse
I made a second marriage in my house;
Divorced old barren Reason from my bed,
And took the Daughter of the Vine to spouse.

✦

And lately, by the Tavern Door agape,
Came shining through the dusk an Angel Shape
Bearing a vessel on his shoulder; and
He bid me taste of it; and 'twas—the Grape!

The Grape that can with Logic absolute
The two-and-seventy jarring sects confute,
The sovereign Alchemist that in a trice
Life's leaden metal into gold transmute;

✦

Why, be this Juice the growth of God, who dare
Blaspheme the twisted tendril as a snare?
A blessing, we should use it, should we not?
And if a curse—why, then, Who set it there?

✦

Oh, threats of Hell and hopes of Paradise!
One thing at least is certain,—*This* Life flies;
One thing is certain and the rest is lies;
The flower that once has blown forever dies.

Strange, is it not? that of the myriads who
Before us passed the door of Darkness through,
Not one returns to tell us of the Road,
Which to discover we must travel too.

The revelations of Devout and Learn'd
Who rose before us, and as prophets burned,
Are all but stories which, awoke from sleep,
They told their comrades, and to sleep returned.

I sent my Soul through the Invisible,
Some letter of that After-life to spell:
And by and by my Soul returned to me,
And answered, "I myself am Heav'n and Hell"—

Heav'n but the vision of fulfilled desire,
And Hell the shadow from a soul on fire,
Cast on the Darkness into which Ourselves,
So late emerged from, shall so soon expire.

We are no other than a moving row
Of magic shadow-shapes that come and go

Round with the Sun-illumined Lantern held
In midnight by the Master of the Show;

But helpless Pieces of the game He plays
Upon this checker-board of nights and days;
Hither and thither moves, and checks, and slays,
And one by one back in the closet lays.

The ball no question makes of Ayes and Noes,
But here or there, as strikes the player, goes;
And He that tossed you down into the field,
He knows about it all—HE knows—HE knows!

The Moving Finger writes; and, having writ,
Moves on: nor all your piety nor wit
Shall lure it back to cancel half a line;
Nor all your tears wash out a word of it.

And that inverted bowl they call the Sky,
Whereunder crawling cooped we live and die,
Lift not your hands to *It* for help—for It
As impotently moves as you or I.

With Earth's first clay they did the last man knead,
And there of the last harvest sowed the seed;
And the first morning of Creation wrote
What the last dawn of reckoning shall read.

Yesterday *This* Day's Madness did prepare,
Tomorrow's silence, triumph, or despair:
Drink! for you know not whence you came, nor why;
Drink! for you know not why you go, nor where.

✦

As under cover of departing day
Slunk hunger-stricken Ramazán away,
Once more within the Potter's house alone
I stood, surrounded by the shapes of clay:

Shapes of all sorts and sizes, great and small,
That stood along the floor and by the wall;
And some loquacious vessels were; and some
Listened perhaps, but never talked at all.

Said one among them: "Surely not in vain
My substance of the common earth was ta'en
And to this figure molded, to be broke,
Or trampled back to shapeless earth again."

Then said a second: "Ne'er a peevish boy
Would break the bowl from which he drank in joy;
And He that with his hand the vessel made
Will surely not in after wrath destroy."

After a momentary silence spake
Some vessel of a more ungainly make:
"They sneer at me for leaning all awry—
What! did the hand, then, of the Potter shake?"

Whereat some one of the loquacious lot—
I think a Súfi pipkin—waxing hot:
"All this of Pot and Potter—Tell me, then,
Who is the Potter, pray, and who the Pot?"

"Why," said another, "some there are who tell
Of one who threatens he will toss to Hell
The luckless Pots he marred in making—Pish!
He's a Good Fellow, and 'twill all be well."

"Well," murmured one, "let whoso make or buy,
My clay with long oblivion is gone dry:
But fill me with the old familiar Juice,
Methinks I might recover by and by."

So while the vessels one by one were speaking,
The little Moon looked in that all were seeking;
And then they jogged each other: "Brother! Brother!
Now for the Porter's shoulder-knot a-creaking!"

✦

Ah, with the Grape my fading life provide;
And wash the body whence the life has died,
And lay me, shrouded in the living Leaf,
By some not unfrequented garden-side—

That ev'n my buried ashes such a snare
Of vintage shall fling up into the air
As not a True-believer passing by
But shall be overtaken unaware.

Indeed, the Idols I have loved so long
Have done my credit in this World much wrong:
Have drowned my glory in a shallow cup,
And sold my reputation for a song.

Indeed, indeed, repentance oft before
I swore—but was I sober when I swore?
And then, and then came Spring, and rose-in-hand
My threadbare penitence apieces tore.

And much as Wine has played the Infidel,
And robbed me of my robe of Honor—Well,
I wonder often what the vintners buy
One half so precious as the stuff they sell.

Yet ah, that Spring should vanish with the rose!
That Youth's sweet-scented manuscript should close!
The nightingale that in the branches sang,
Ah whence, and whither flown again, who knows!

✦

Ah Love! could you and I with Him conspire
To grasp this sorry Scheme of Things entire,
Would not we shatter it to bits—and then
Remold it nearer to the Heart's desire!

Yon rising Moon that looks for us again—
How oft hereafter will she wax and wane;
How oft hereafter rising look for us
Through this same garden—and for *one* in vain!

And when like her, O Sákí, you shall pass
Among the guests star-scattered on the grass,
And in your joyous errand reach the spot
Where I made one—turn down an empty glass!

OPTIMISM

All men must live in society; rules of conduct thus become necessary for the good of all. All men are not, however, concerned with the purpose of life. The hedonist regards life with a shrug; "as long as we sleep, eat, and enjoy ourselves, what does the purpose of life—if any—matter?" The poet, nevertheless, cannot be satisfied with so complacent an acceptance of the world. If life is without reason, why live at all? If it has purpose, then let us find that purpose and work in harmony with it. Just as in the conduct of life, Christianity and Pragmatism follow much the same paths, so when the problem is one of purpose, the teachings of Christianity are much the same as those of Optimism. It must not be thought that Optimism is a system of philosophy; it is frequently quite irrational, almost as irrational, or unreasonable, as many of the principles by which we live. The Optimist and the Christian may differ in this respect: the former feels that life is, somehow, good—this being for him "the best of all possible worlds"—whereas the latter may feel that another life is necessary to make up for the injustices of this one. Of all the poems dealing with the volatile optimism of youth, perhaps Tennyson's "Locksley Hall" has attained the widest fame. Of all optimists among the great poets, Browning appears the most determined, even dogged; the thoughts of "Rabbi Ben Ezra" may not have been uttered by the rabbi, but they are characteristic of the poet. Tennyson's poem, though no part of his own biography, is autobiographical in feeling, Browning's in effect.

LOCKSLEY HALL

by Alfred, Lord Tennyson (1809-1892)

Comrades, leave me here a little, while as yet 'tis early morn;
Leave me here, and when you want me, sound upon the bugle-horn.

'Tis the place, and all around it, as of old, the curlews call,
Dreary gleams about the moorland flying over Locksley Hall;

Locksley Hall, that in the distance overlooks the sandy tracts,
And the hollow ocean-ridges roaring into cataracts.

Many a night from yonder ivied casement, ere I went to rest,
Did I look on great Orion sloping slowly to the West.

Many a night I saw the Pleiads, rising through the mellow shade
Glitter like a swarm of fire-flies tangled in a silver braid.

Here about the beach I wandered, nourishing a youth sublime
With the fairy tales of science, and the long result of Time;

When the centuries behind me like a fruitful land reposed;
When I clung to all the present for the promise that it closed;

When I dipped into the future far as human eye could see,
Saw the vision of the world, and all the wonder that would be.—

In the Spring a fuller crimson comes upon the robin's breast;
In the Spring the wanton lapwing gets himself another crest;

In the Spring a livelier iris changes on the burnished dove;
In the Spring a young man's fancy lightly turns to thoughts of love.

Then her cheek was pale and thinner than should be for one so young,
And her eyes on all my motions with a mute observance hung.

And I said, "My cousin Amy, speak, and speak the truth to me,
Trust me, cousin, all the current of my being sets to thee."

On her pallid cheek and forehead came a color and a light,
As I have seen the rosy red flushing in the northern night.

And she turned—her bosom shaken with a sudden storm of sighs—
All the spirit deeply dawning in the dark of hazel eyes—

Saying, "I have hid my feelings, fearing they should do me wrong;"
Saying, "Dost thou love me, cousin?" weeping, "I have loved thee long."

Love took up the glass of Time, and turned it in his glowing hands;
Every moment, lightly shaken, ran itself in golden sands.

Love took up the harp of Life, and smote on all the chords with might;
Smote the chord of Self, that, trembling, passed in music out of sight.

Many a morning on the moorland did we hear the copses ring,
And her whisper thronged my pulses with the fulness of the Spring.

Many an evening by the waters did we watch the stately ships,
And our spirits rushed together at the touching of the lips.

O my cousin, shallow-hearted! O my Amy, mine no more!
O the dreary, dreary moorland! O the barren, barren shore!

Falser than all fancy fathoms, falser than all songs have sung,
Puppet to a father's threat, and servile to a shrewish tongue!

Is it well to wish thee happy?—having known me—to decline
On a range of lower feelings and a narrower heart than mine!

Yet it shall be; thou shalt lower to his level day by day,
What is fine within thee growing coarse to sympathize with clay.

As the husband is, the wife is: thou art mated with a clown,
And the grossness of his nature will have weight to drag thee down.

He will hold thee, when his passion shall have spent its novel force,
Something better than his dog, a little dearer than his horse.

What is this? his eyes are heavy; think not they are glazed with wine.
Go to him, it is thy duty; kiss him, take his hand in thine.

It may be my lord is weary, that his brain is overwrought;
Soothe him with thy finer fancies, touch him with thy lighter thought.

He will answer to the purpose, easy things to understand—
Better thou wert dead before me, though I slew thee with my hand!

Better thou and I were lying, hidden from the heart's disgrace,
Rolled in one another's arms, and silent in a last embrace.

Cursèd be the social wants that sin against the strength of youth!
Cursèd be the social lies that warp us from the living truth!

Cursèd be the sickly forms that err from honest Nature's rule!
Cursèd be the gold that gilds the straitened forehead of the fool!

Well—'tis well that I should bluster!—Hadst thou less unworthy proved
Would to God—for I had loved thee more than ever wife was loved.

Am I mad, that I should cherish that which bears but bitter fruit?
I will pluck it from my bosom, though my heart be at the root.

Never, though my mortal summers to such length of years should come
As the many-wintered crow that leads the clanging rookery home.

Where is comfort? in division of the records of the mind?
Can I part her from herself, and love her, as I knew her, kind?

I remember one that perished; sweetly did she speak and move;
Such a one do I remember, whom to look at was to love.

Can I think of her as dead, and love her for the love she bore?
No—she never loved me truly; love is love for evermore.

Comfort! comfort scorned of devils! this is truth the poet sings,
That a sorrow's crown of sorrow is remembering happier things.

Drug thy memories, lest thou learn it, lest thy heart be put to proof,
In the dead unhappy night, and when the rain is on the roof.

Like a dog, he hunts in dreams, and thou art staring at the wall,
Where the dying night-lamp flickers, and the shadows rise and fall.

Then a hand shall pass before thee, pointing to his drunken sleep,
To thy widowed marriage-pillows, to the tears that thou wilt weep.

Thou shalt hear the "Never, never," whispered by the phantom years,
And a song from out the distance in the ringing of thine ears;

And an eye shall vex thee, looking ancient kindness on thy pain.
Turn thee, turn thee on thy pillow; get thee to thy rest again.

Nay, but Nature brings thee solace; for a tender voice will cry
'Tis a purer life than thine, a lip to drain thy trouble dry.

Baby lips will laugh me down; my latest rival brings thee rest.
Baby fingers, waxen touches, press me from the mother's breast.

O, the child too clothes the father with a dearness not his due.
Half is thine and half is his; it will be worthy of the two.

O, I see thee old and formal, fitted to thy petty part,
With a little hoard of maxims preaching down a daughter's heart.

"They were dangerous guides, the feelings—she herself was not exempt—
Truly, she herself had suffered"—Perish in thy self-contempt!

Overlive it—lower yet—be happy! wherefore should I care?
I myself must mix with action, lest I wither by despair.

What is that which I should turn to, lighting upon days like these?
Every door is barred with gold, and opens but to golden keys.

Every gate is thronged with suitors, all the markets overflow.
I have but an angry fancy; what is that which I should do?

I had been content to perish, falling on the foeman's ground,
When the ranks are rolled in vapor, and the winds are laid with sound.

But the jingling of the guinea helps the hurt that Honor feels,
And the nations do but murmur, snarling at each other's heels.

Can I but relive in sadness? I will turn that earlier page.
Hide me from my deep emotion, O thou wondrous Mother-Age!

Make me feel the wild pulsation that I felt before the strife,
When I heard my days before me, and the tumult of my life;

Yearning for the large excitement that the coming years would yield,
Eager-hearted as a boy when first he leaves his father's field,

And at night along the dusky highway near and nearer drawn,
Sees in heaven the light of London flaring like a dreary dawn;

And his spirit leaps within him to be gone before him then,
Underneath the light he looks at, in among the throngs of men:

Men, my brothers, men the workers, ever reaping something new;
That which they have done but earnest of the things that they shall do.

For I dipped into the future, far as human eye could see,
Saw the Vision of the world, and all the wonder that would be;

Saw the heavens filled with commerce, argosies of magic sails,
Pilots of the purple twilight, dropping down with costly bales;

Heard the heavens fill with shouting, and there rained a ghastly dew
From the nations' airy navies grappling in the central blue;

Far along the world-wide whisper of the south-wind rushing warm,
With the standards of the peoples plunging through the thunder-storm;

Till the war-drum throbbed no longer, and the battle-flags were furled
In the Parliament of man, the Federation of the world.

There the common sense of most shall hold a fretful realm in awe,
And the kindly earth shall slumber, lapped in universal law.

So I triumphed ere my passion sweeping through me left me dry,
Left me with the palsied heart, and left me with the jaundiced eye;

Eye, to which all order festers, all things here are out of joint.
Science moves, but slowly, slowly, creeping on from point to point;

Slowly comes a hungry people, as a lion, creeping nigher,
Glares at one that nods and winks behind a slowly-dying fire.

Yet I doubt not through the ages one increasing purpose runs,
And the thoughts of men are widened with the process of the suns.

What is that to him that reaps not harvest of his youthful joys,
Though the deep heart of existence beat for ever like a boy's?

Knowledge comes, but wisdom lingers, and I linger on the shore,
And the individual withers, and the world is more and more.

Knowledge comes, but wisdom lingers, and he bears a laden breast,
Full of sad experience, moving toward the stillness of his rest.

Hark, my merry comrades call me, sounding on the bugle-horn,
They to whom my foolish passion were a target for their scorn:

Shall it not be scorn to me to harp on such a mouldered string?
I am shamed through all my nature to have loved so slight a thing.

Weakness to be wroth with weakness! woman's pleasure, woman's pain—
Nature made them blinder motions bounded in a shallower brain.

Woman is the lesser man, and all thy passions, matched with mine,
Are as moonlight unto sunlight, and as water unto wine—

Here at least, where nature sickens, nothing. Ah, for some retreat
Deep in yonder shining Orient, where my life began to beat,

Where in wild Mahratta-battle fell my father evil-starred;—
I was left a trampled orphan, and a selfish uncle's ward.

Or to burst all links of habit—there to wander far away,
On from island unto island at the gateways of the day.

Larger constellations burning, mellow moons and happy skies,
Breadths of tropic shade and palms in cluster, knots of Paradise.

Never comes the trader, never floats an European flag,
Slides the bird o'er lustrous woodland, swings the trailer from the crag;

Droops the heavy-blossomed bower, hangs the heavy-fruited tree—
Summer isles of Eden lying in dark-purple spheres of sea.

There methinks would be enjoyment more than in this march of mind,
In the steamship, in the railway, in the thoughts that shake mankind.

There the passions cramped no longer shall have scope and breathing space;
I will take some savage woman, she shall rear my dusky race.

Iron-jointed, supple-sinewed, they shall dive, and they shall run,
Catch the wild goat by the hair, and hurl their lances in the sun;

Whistle back the parrot's call, and leap the rainbows of the brooks,
Not with blinded eyesight poring over miserable books—

Fool, again the dream, the fancy! but I *know* my words are wild,
But I count the gray barbarian lower than the Christian child.

I, to herd with narrow foreheads, vacant of our glorious gains,
Like a beast with lower pleasures, like a beast with lower pains!

Mated with a squalid savage—what to me were sun or clime?
I the heir of all the ages, in the foremost files of time—

I that rather held it better men should perish one by one,
Than that earth should stand at gaze like Joshua's moon in Ajalon!

Not in vain the distance beacons. Forward, forward let us range,
Let the great world spin forever down the ringing grooves of change.

Through the shadow of the globe we sweep into the younger day;
Better fifty years of Europe than a cycle of Cathay.

Mother-Age (for mine I knew not) help me as when life begun;
Rift the hills, and roll the waters, flash the lightnings, weigh the sun.

O, I see the crescent promise of my spirit hath not set.
Ancient founts of inspiration well through all my fancy yet.

Howsoever these things be, a long farewell to Locksley Hall!
Now for me the woods may wither, now for me the roof-tree fall.

Comes a vapor from the margin, blackening over heath and holt,
Cramming all the blast before it, in its breast a thunderbolt.

Let it fall on Locksley Hall, with rain or hail, or fire or snow;
For the mighty wind arises, roaring seaward, and I go.

RABBI BEN EZRA

by Robert Browning (1812-1889)

Grow old along with me!
The best is yet to be,
The last of life, for which the first was made:
Our times are in His hand
Who saith, "A whole I planned,
Youth shows but half; trust God: see all, nor be afraid!"

Not that, amassing flowers,
Youth sighed, "Which rose make ours,
Which lily leave and then as best recall?"
Not that, admiring stars,
It yearned, "Nor Jove, nor Mars;
Mine be some figured flame which blends, transcends them all!"

Not for such hopes and fears
Annulling youth's brief years,
Do I remonstrate: folly wide the mark!
Rather I prize the doubt
Low kinds exist without,
Finished and finite clods, untroubled by a spark.

Poor vaunt of life indeed,
Were man but formed to feed
On joy, to solely seek and find and feast;
Such feasting ended, then
As sure an end to men;
Irks care the crop-full bird? Frets doubt the maw-crammed beast?

Rejoice we are allied
To that which doth provide
And not partake, effect and not receive!
A spark disturbs our clod;
Nearer we hold of God
Who gives, than of his tribes that take, I must believe.

Then, welcome each rebuff
That turns earth's smoothness rough,
Each sting that bids nor sit nor stand but go!
Be our joys three-parts pain!
Strive, and hold cheap the strain;
Learn, nor account the pang; dare, never grudge the throe!

For thence,—a paradox
Which comforts while it mocks,—
Shall life succeed in that it seems to fail:
What I aspired to be,
And was not, comforts me:
A brute I might have been, but would not sink i' the scale.

What is he but a brute
Whose flesh has soul to suit,
Whose spirit works lest arms and legs want play?
To man, propose this test—
Thy body at its best,
How far can that project thy soul on its lone way?

Yet gifts should prove their use:
I own the Past profuse
Of power each side, perfection every turn:
Eyes, ears took in their dole,
Brain treasured up the whole;
Should not the heart beat once "How good to live and learn"?

Not once beat "Praise be thine!
I see the whole design,
I, who saw power, see now Love perfect too:
Perfect I call thy plan:

Thanks that I was a man!
Maker, remake, complete,—I trust what thou shalt do!"

For pleasant is this flesh;
Our soul, in its rose-mesh
Pulled ever to the earth, still yearns for rest:
Would we some prize might hold
To match those manifold
Possessions of the brute,—gain most, as we did best!

Let us not always say,
"Spite of this flesh today
I strove, made head, gained ground upon the whole!"
As the bird wings and sings,
Let us cry, "All good things
Are ours, nor soul helps flesh more, now, than flesh helps soul!"

Therefore I summon age
To grant youth's heritage,
Life's struggle having so far reached its term:
Thence shall I pass, approved
A man, for aye removed
From the developed brute; a God though in the germ.

And I shall thereupon
Take rest, ere I be gone
Once more on my adventure brave and new:
Fearless and unperplexed,
When I wage battle next,
What weapons to select, what armor to indue.

Youth ended, I shall try
My gain or loss thereby;
Leave the fire ashes, what survives is gold:
And I shall weigh the same,
Give life its praise or blame:
Young, all lay in dispute; I shall know, being old.

For note, when evening shuts,
A certain moment cuts
A deed off, calls the glory from the gray:
A whisper from the west
Shoots—"Add this to the rest,
Take it and try its worth: here dies another day."

So, still within this life,
Though lifted o'er its strife,
Let me discern, compare, pronounce at last,
"This rage was right i' the main,
That acquiescence vain:
The Future I may face now I have proved the Past."

For more is not reserved
To man, with soul just nerved
To act tomorrow what he learns today:
Here, work enough to watch
The Master work, and catch
Hints of the proper craft, tricks of the tool's true play.

As it were better, youth
Should strive, through acts uncouth,
Toward making, than repose on aught found made:
So, better, age, exempt
From strife, should know, than tempt
Further. Thou waitedst age: wait death nor be afraid!

Enough now, if the Right
And Good and Infinite
Be named here, as thou callest thy hand thine own,
With knowledge absolute,
Subject to no dispute
From fools that crowded youth, nor let thee feel alone.

Be there, for once and all,
Severed great minds from small,
Announced to each his station in the Past!
Was I, the world arraigned,
Were they, my soul disdained,
Right? Let age speak the truth and give us peace at last!

Now, who shall arbitrate?
Ten men love what I hate,
Shun what I follow, slight what I receive;
Ten, who in ears and eyes
Match me: we all surmise,
They this thing, and I that: whom shall my soul believe?

Not on the vulgar mass
Called "work," must sentence pass,

Things done, that took the eye and had the price;
O'er which, from level stand,
The low world laid its hand,
Found straightway to its mind, could value in a trice:

But all, the world's coarse thumb
And finger failed to plumb,
So passed in making up the main account;
All instincts immature,
All purposes unsure,
That weighed not as his work, yet swelled the man's amount:

Thoughts hardly to be packed
Into a narrow act,
Fancies that broke through language and escaped;
All I could never be,
All, men ignored in me,
This, I was worth to God, whose wheel the pitcher shaped.

Ay, note that Potter's wheel,
That metaphor! and feel
Why time spins fast, why passive lies our clay,—
Thou, to whom fools propound,
When the wine makes its round,
"Since life fleets, all is change; the Past gone, seize today!"

Fool! All that is, at all,
Lasts ever, past recall;
Earth changes, but thy soul and God stand sure:
What entered into thee,
That was, is, and shall be:
Time's wheel runs back or stops: Potter and clay endure.

He fixed thee mid this dance
Of plastic circumstance,
This Present, thou, forsooth, wouldst fain arrest:
Machinery just meant
To give thy soul its bent,
Try thee and turn thee forth, sufficiently impressed.

What though the earlier grooves
Which ran the laughing loves
Around thy base, no longer pause and press?
What though about thy rim,
Skull-things in order grim
Grow out, in graver mood, obey the sterner stress?

Look not thou down but up!
To uses of a cup,
The festal board, lamp's flash and trumpet's peal,
The new wine's foaming flow,
The Master's lips a-glow!
Thou, heaven's consummate cup, what need'st thou with earth's wheel?

But I need, now as then,
Thee, God, who moldest men;
And since, not even while the whirl was worst,
Did I—to the wheel of life
With shapes and colors rife,
Bound dizzily,—mistake my end, to slake thy thirst:

So, take and use thy work:
Amend what flaws may lurk,
What strain o' the stuff, what warpings past the aim!
My times be in thy hand!
Perfect the cup as planned!
Let age approve of youth, and death complete the same!

FATALISM

Thomas Gray's "Elegy Written in a Country Churchyard" is probably the best loved of the longer poems in the English language. The reason for this is not far to seek: it is most soothing for those who have failed. The attitude taken is that, no matter what may be the outcome of life, it is not the fault of the individual but of circumstance. Fatalism has been defined as the doctrine that all things are subject to a whim of fate or the unpredictable decree of some arbiter of destiny. This theory is closely allied to stoicism, and is found in the *Rubáiyát;* here it assumes a provincial rather than an Oriental character.

The concluding epitaph of the "Elegy" is not, as some have maintained, a superfluous addition, but an integral part of the poem.

ELEGY

Written in a Country Churchyard

by Thomas Gray (1716-1771)

The curfew tolls the knell of parting day,
The lowing herd wind slowly o'er the lea,
The ploughman homeward plods his weary way,
And leaves the world to darkness and to me.

Now fades the glimmering landscape on the sight,
And all the air a solemn stillness holds,
Save where the beetle wheels his droning flight,
And drowsy tinklings lull the distant folds:

Save that from yonder ivy-mantled tower
The moping owl does to the moon complain
Of such as, wandering near her secret bower,
Molest her ancient solitary reign.

Beneath those rugged elms, that yew-tree's shade
Where heaves the turf in many a mouldering heap,
Each in his narrow cell for ever laid,
The rude forefathers of the hamlet sleep.

The breezy call of incense-breathing morn,
The swallow twittering from the straw-built shed,
The cock's shrill clarion, or the echoing horn,
No more shall rouse them from their lowly bed.

For them no more the blazing hearth shall burn
Or busy housewife ply her evening care:
No children run to lisp their sire's return,
Or climb his knees the envied kiss to share.

Oft did the harvest to their sickle yield,
Their furrow oft the stubborn glebe has broke;
How jocund did they drive their team afield!
How bow'd the woods beneath their sturdy stroke!

Let not Ambition mock their useful toil,
Their homely joys, and destiny obscure;
Nor Grandeur hear with a disdainful smile
The short and simple annals of the poor.

The boast of heraldry, the pomp of power,
And all that beauty, all that wealth e'er gave
Awaits alike th' inevitable hour:—
The paths of glory lead but to the grave.

Nor you, ye proud, impute to these the fault
If memory o'er their tomb no trophies raise,
Where through the long-drawn aisle and fretted vault
The pealing anthem swells the note of praise.

Can storied urn or animated bust
Back to its mansion call the fleeting breath?
Can Honour's voice provoke the silent dust,
Or Flattery soothe the dull, cold ear of death?

Perhaps in this neglected spot is laid
Some heart once pregnant with celestial fire;
Hands, that the rod of empire might have sway'd,
Or waked to ecstasy the living lyre:

But Knowledge to their eyes her ample page,
Rich with the spoils of time, did ne'er unroll;
Chill Penury repress'd their noble rage,
And froze the genial current of the soul.

Full many a gem of purest ray serene
The dark unfathom'd caves of ocean bear:
Full many a flower is born to blush unseen,
And waste its sweetness on the desert air.

Some village-Hampden, that with dauntless breast
The little tyrant of his fields withstood,
Some mute inglorious Milton here may rest,
Some Cromwell, guiltless of his country's blood.

Th' applause of listening senates to command,
The threats of pain and ruin to despise,
To scatter plenty o'er a smiling land,
And read their history in a nation's eyes,

Their lot forbade: nor circumscribed alone
Their growing virtues, but their crimes confined;
Forbade to wade through slaughter to a throne,
And shut the gates of mercy on mankind;

The struggling pangs of conscious truth to hide,
To quench the blushes of ingenuous shame,
Or heap the shrine of luxury and pride
With incense kindled at the Muse's flame.

Far from the madding crowd's ignoble strife
Their sober wishes never learn'd to stray;
Along the cool sequester'd vale of life
They kept the noiseless tenor of their way.

Yet e'en these bones from insult to protect
Some frail memorial still erected nigh,
With uncouth rhymes and shapeless sculpture deck'd
Implores the passing tribute of a sigh.

Their name, their years, spelt by th' unletter'd Muse,
The place of fame and elegy supply:
And many a holy text around she strews,
That teach the rustic moralist to die.

For who, to dumb forgetfulness a prey,
This pleasing anxious being e'er resign'd,
Left the warm precincts of the cheerful day,
Nor cast one longing lingering look behind?

On some fond breast the parting soul relies,
Some pious drops the closing eye requires;
E'en from the tomb the voice of Nature cries,
E'en in our ashes live their wonted fires.

For thee, who, mindful of th' unhonour'd dead,
Dost in these lines their artless tale relate;
If chance, by lonely contemplation led,
Some kindred spirit shall enquire thy fate,—

Haply some hoary-headed swain may say,
"Oft have we seen him at the peep of dawn
Brushing with hasty steps the dews away,
To meet the sun upon the upland lawn;

"There at the foot of yonder nodding beech
That wreathes its old fantastic roots so high,
His listless length at noon-tide would he stretch,
And pore upon the brook that babbles by.

"Hard by yon wood, now smiling as in scorn,
Muttering his wayward fancies he would rove;
Now drooping, woeful-wan, like one forlorn,
Or crazed with care, or cross'd in hopeless love.

"One morn I miss'd him on the 'custom'd hill,
Along the heath, and near his favourite tree;
Another came; nor yet beside the rill,
Nor up the lawn, nor at the wood was he;

"The next with dirges due in sad array
Slow through the church-way path we saw him borne,—
Approach and read (for thou canst read) the lay
Graved on the stone beneath yon agèd thorn."

The Epitaph

Here rests his head upon the lap of earth,
A youth to fortune and to fame unknown.
Fair Science frowned not on his humble birth,
And Melancholy marked him for her own.

Large was his bounty, and his soul sincere,
Heaven did a recompense as largely send.
He gave to misery, all he had, a tear,
He gained from Heaven ('twas all he wished) a friend.

No farther seek his merits to disclose,
Or draw his frailties from their dread abode,
(There they alike in trembling hope repose),
The bosom of his Father and his God.

PESSIMISM

Pessimism has become increasingly popular as a code of living ever since Schopenhauer erected it into a philosophic system. His theme, that pain is the only reality and that the universe, if it has any purpose at all, is inimical to man, has been reëchoed by hundreds of modern poets. James Thomson finds life a nightmare, a "City of Dreadful Night"; T. S. Eliot suggests that the modern world is a "Waste Land" of disintegrated memories and futile craving for an idyllic past, which probably never existed. Poe uncovers enough tragedy in his own life to justify that bitter picture, "The Conqueror Worm," and Arnold expresses in "Dover Beach" the fears of the old orthodox religion at the coming of the new science. The poetry of Housman, Santayana, and Jeffers is steeped in philosophic pessimism, though often—especially in the blithe quatrains of Housman and the dark, long-rolling lines of Jeffers—it has a brave and even heroic ring.

PESSIMIST AND OPTIMIST

This one sits shivering in Fortune's smile,
  Taking his joy with hated, doubtful breath.
This other, gnawed by hunger, all the while
  Laughs in the teeth of death.

—*Thomas Bailey Aldrich* (1836-1907)

THE CONQUEROR WORM

by Edgar Allan Poe (1809-1849)

Lo! 'tis a gala night
  Within the lonesome latter years!
An angel throng, bewinged, bedight
  In veils, and drowned in tears,
Sit in a theater, to see
  A play of hopes and fears,
While the orchestra breathes fitfully
  The music of the spheres.

Mimes, in the form of God on high,
  Mutter and mumble low,
And hither and thither fly—
  Mere puppets they, who come and go
At bidding of vast formless things
  That shift the scenery to and fro,
Flapping from out their Condor wings
  Invisible Woe!

That motley drama—oh, be sure
  It shall not be forgot!
With its Phantom chased for evermore,
  By a crowd that seize it not,
Through a circle that ever returneth in
  To the selfsame spot,
And much of madness, and more of sin,
  And horror the soul of the plot.

But see, amid the mimic rout,
  A crawling shape intrude!
A blood-red thing that writhes from out
  The scenic solitude!
It writhes!—it writhes!—with mortal pangs
  The mimes become its food,
And seraphs sob at vermin fangs
  In human gore imbued.

Out—out are the lights—out all!
  And, over each quivering form,
The curtain, a funeral pall,
  Comes down with the rush of a storm,
While the angels, all pallid and wan,
  Uprising, unveiling, affirm
That the play is the tragedy, "Man,"
  And its hero the Conqueror Worm.

DOVER BEACH

by Matthew Arnold (1822-1888)

The sea is calm tonight,
The tide is full, the moon lies fair
Upon the straits;—on the French coast the light
Gleams and is gone; the cliffs of England stand,
Glimmering and vast, out in the tranquil bay.
Come to the window, sweet is the night-air!
Only, from the long line of spray
Where the sea meets the moon-blanched land,
Listen! you hear the grating roar
Of pebbles which the waves draw back, and fling,
At their return, up the high strand,
Begin, and cease, and then again begin,
With tremulous cadence slow, and bring
The eternal note of sadness in.

Sophocles long ago
Heard it on the Aegean, and it brought

Into his mind the turbid ebb and flow
Of human misery; we
Find also in the sound a thought,
Hearing it by this distant northern sea.

The sea of faith
Was once, too, at the full, and round earth's shore
Lay like the folds of a bright girdle furled.
But now I only hear
Its melancholy, long, withdrawing roar,
Retreating, to the breath
Of the night-wind, down the vast edges drear
And naked shingles of the world.

Ah, love, let us be true
To one another! for the world, which seems
To lie before us like a land of dreams,
So various, so beautiful, so new,
Hath really neither joy, nor love, nor light,
Nor certitude, nor peace, nor help for pain;
And we are here as on a darkling plain
Swept with confused alarms of struggle and flight,
Where ignorant armies clash by night.

BE STILL, MY SOUL

Be still, my soul, be still; the arms you bear are brittle,
  Earth and high heaven are fixt of old and founded strong.
Think rather,—call to thought, if now you grieve a little,
  The days when we had rest, O soul, for they were long.

Men loved unkindness then, but lightless in the quarry
  I slept and saw not; tears fell down, I did not mourn;
Sweat ran and blood sprang out and I was never sorry;
  Then it was well with me, in days ere I was born.

Now, and I muse for why and never find the reason,
  I pace the earth, and drink the air, and feel the sun.
Be still, be still, my soul; it is but for a season:
  Let us endure an hour and see injustice done.

Ay, look: high heaven and earth ail from the prime foundation;
  All thoughts to rive the heart are here, and all are vain:
Horror and scorn and hate and fear and indignation—
  Oh, why did I awake? When shall I sleep again?

—*A. E. Housman* (1859-   )

FROM "THE BROKEN BALANCE"

by Robinson Jeffers (1887-   )

IV

Rain, hail and brutal sun, the plow in the roots,
The pitiless pruning-iron in the branches,
Strengthen the vines, they are all feeding friends
Or powerless foes until the grapes purple.
But when you have ripened your berries, it is time to begin to perish.

The world sickens with change, rain becomes poison,
The earth is a pit, it is time to perish.
The vines are fey, the very kindness of nature
Corrupts what her cruelty before strengthened.
When you stand on the peak of time it is time to begin to perish.

Reach down the long morbid roots that forget the plow,
Discover the depths; let the long pale tendrils
Spend all to discover the sky, now nothing is good
But only the steel mirrors of discovery . . .
And the beautiful enormous dawns of time, after we perish.

V

Mourning the broken balance, the hopeless prostration of the earth
Under men's hands and their minds,
The beautiful places killed like rabbits to make a city,
The spreading fungus, the slime-threads
And spores; my own coast's obscene future: I remember the farther
Future, and the last man dying
Without succession under the confident eyes of the stars.
It was only a moment's accident,
The race that plagued us; the world resumes the old lonely immortal
Splendor; from here I can even
Perceive that that snuffed candle had something . . . a fantastic virtue,
A faint and unshapely pathos . . .
So death will flatter them at last: what, even the bald ape's by-shot
Was moderately admirable?

VI

All summer neither rain nor wave washes the cormorants'
Perch, and their droppings have painted it shining white.
If the excrement of fish-eaters make the brown rock a snow-mountain
At noon, a rose in the morning, a beacon at moonrise
On the black water: it is barely possible that even men's present
Lives are something; their arts and sciences (by moonlight)
Not wholly ridiculous, nor their cities merely an offense.

VII

Under my windows, between the road and the sea-cliff, bitter wild grass
Stands narrowed between the people and the storm.
The ocean winter after winter gnaws at its earth, the wheels and the feet
Summer after summer encroach and destroy.
Stubborn green life, for the cliff-eater I cannot comfort you, ignorant which color,
Gray-blue or pale-green, will please the late stars;
But laugh at the other, your seed shall enjoy wonderful vengeances and suck
The arteries and walk in triumph on the faces.

AGNOSTICISM

Just as the number of people with well-formulated ideas on human conduct is greater than the number convinced about the purpose of life, so is the latter number greater than the number of those intelligently acquainted with the relation of man to the universe. Man is very slow in gaining concepts of universals; anything beyond his own birth or death seems relatively unimportant. Poets, however, have not neglected this field of philosophic thought. Here we enter definitely into the realm of religion. English religious poetry ranges all the way from doubt and complete denial of God through agnosticism, pantheism, and rationalism to mysticism and orthodox Christianity.

Swinburne, in "The Garden of Proserpine," approaches complete denial as nearly as any of the great poets.

THE GARDEN OF PROSERPINE

by Algernon Charles Swinburne (1837-1909)

Here, where the world is quiet,
  Here, where all trouble seems
Dead winds' and spent waves' riot
  In doubtful dreams of dreams;
I watch the green field growing
For reaping folk and sowing,
For harvest-time and mowing,
  A sleepy world of streams.

I am tired of tears and laughter,
  And men that laugh and weep;
Of what may come hereafter
  For men that sow to reap:
I am weary of days and hours,
Blown buds of barren flowers,
Desires and dreams and powers,
  And everything but sleep.

Here life has death for neighbor,
  And far from eye or ear
Wan waves and wet winds labor,
  Weak ships and spirits steer;
They drive adrift, and whither
They wot not who make thither;
But no such winds blow hither,
  And no such things grow here.

No growth of moor or coppice,
  No heather-flower or vine,
But bloomless buds of poppies,
  Green grapes of Proserpine,
Pale beds of blowing rushes,
Where no leaf blooms or blushes
Save this whereout she crushes
  For dead men deadly wine.

Pale, without name or number,
  In fruitless fields of corn,
They bow themselves and slumber
  All night till light is born;
And like a soul belated,
In hell and heaven unmated,
By cloud and mist abated
  Comes out of darkness morn.

Though one were strong as seven,
  He too with death shall dwell,
Nor wake with wings in heaven,
  Nor weep for pains in hell;
Though one were fair as roses,
His beauty clouds and closes;
And well though love reposes,
  In the end it is not well.

Pale, beyond porch and portal,
  Crowned with calm leaves, she stands
Who gathers all things mortal
  With cold immortal hands;
Her languid lips are sweeter
Than love's who fears to greet her
To men that mix and meet her
  From many times and lands.

She waits for each and other,
  She waits for all men born;
Forgets the earth her mother,
  The life of fruits and corn;
And spring and seed and swallow
Take wing for her and follow
Where summer song rings hollow
  And flowers are put to scorn.

There go the loves that wither,
  The old loves with wearier wings;
And all dead years draw thither,
  And all disastrous things;
Dead dreams of days forsaken,
Blind buds that snows have shaken,
Wild leaves that winds have taken,
  Red strays of ruined springs.

We are not sure of sorrow,
  And joy was never sure;
Today will die tomorrow;
  Time stoops to no man's lure;
And love, grown faint and fretful,
With lips but half regretful
Sighs, and with eyes forgetful
  Weeps that no loves endure.

From too much love of living,
  From hope and fear set free,
We thank with brief thanksgiving

Whatever gods may be
That no life lives for ever;
That dead men rise up never;
That even the weariest river
Winds somewhere safe to sea.

Then star nor sun shall waken,
Nor any change of light:
Nor sound of waters shaken,
Nor any sound or sight:
Nor wintry leaves nor vernal,
Nor days nor things diurnal:
Only the sleep eternal
In an eternal night.

PANTHEISM

The greatest pantheistic poetry is that of the Hindus, but even the most orthodox Christians have used the arguments of the pantheists to prove that God dwells in every living thing. Here we come close to nature-poetry, pantheism being a worship of the elements, and particularly of earth. There is a philosophic justification for it in the system of Hegel, which assumes that the Universe is a Whole, and therefore that any one part is just as much a fragment of the "soul of the universe" as any other part. Hegel deduces the nature of the "Over-Soul" from a study of its minute manifestations in the world of nature, just as the anthropologist can deduce the story of prehistoric man from a bone found in a gravel-pit.

Swinburne was the most pantheistic as well as the most agnostic of poets; his "Hertha" is a rhapsody in praise of the spirit of Nature which includes All. The basic idea is unfolded in the opening stanzas:

FROM "HERTHA"

I am that which began;
Out of me the years roll;
Out of me God and man;
I am equal and whole;
God changes, and man, and the form of them bodily; I am the soul.

Before ever land was,
Before ever the sea,
Or soft hair of the grass,
Or fair limbs of the tree,
Or the flesh-colour'd fruit of my branches, I was, and thy soul was in me.

First life on my sources
First drifted and swam;
Out of me are the forces
That save it or damn;
Out of me man and woman, and wild-beast and bird: before God was, I am. . . .

—*Algernon Charles Swinburne* (1837-1909)

Coleridge's pantheism was of a stricter sort; it demanded something beyond earth, beyond nature, to give an integral meaning to life.

HYMN BEFORE SUNRISE, IN THE VALE OF CHAMOUNI

by Samuel Taylor Coleridge (1772-1834)

Hast thou a charm to stay the morning-star
In his steep course? So long he seems to pause
On thy bald awful head, O sovran Blanc!
The Arve and Arveiron at thy base
Rave ceaselessly; but thou, most awful Form!
Risest from forth thy silent sea of pines,
How silently! Around thee and above
Deep is the air and dark, substantial, black,
An ebon mass: methinks thou piercest it,
As with a wedge! But when I look again,
It is thine own calm home, thy crystal shrine,
Thy habitation from eternity!
O dread and silent Mount! I gazed upon thee,
Till thou, still present to the bodily sense,
Didst vanish from my thought: entranced in prayer
I worshiped the Invisible alone.

Yet, like some sweet beguiling melody,
So sweet, we know not we are listening to it,
Thou, the meanwhile, wast blending with my Thought,
Yea, with my Life and Life's own secret joy:
Till the dilating Soul, enrapt, transfused,
Into the mighty vision passing—there
As in her natural form, swelled vast to Heaven!

Awake, my soul! not only passive praise
Thou owest! not alone these swelling tears,
Mute thanks and secret ecstasy! Awake,
Voice of sweet song! Awake, my heart, awake!
Green vales and icy cliffs, all join my hymn.

Thou first and chief, sole sovereign of the Vale!
O struggling with the darkness all the night,
And visited all night by troops of stars,
Or when they climb the sky or when they sink:
Companion of the morning-star at dawn,
Thyself Earth's rosy star, and of the dawn
Co-herald: wake, O wake, and utter praise!
Who sank thy sunless pillars deep in Earth?
Who filled thy countenance with rosy light?
Who made thee parent of perpetual streams?

And you, ye five wild torrents fiercely glad!
Who called you forth from night and utter death,
From dark and icy caverns called you forth,
Down those precipitous, black, jaggéd rocks,
For ever shattered and the same for ever?
Who gave you your invulnerable life,
Your strength, your speed, your fury, and your joy,
Unceasing thunder and eternal foam?
And who commanded (and the silence came),
Here let the billows stiffen, and have rest?

Ye Ice-falls! ye that from the mountain's brow
Adown enormous ravines slope amain—
Torrents, methinks, that heard a mighty voice,
And stopped at once amid their maddest plunge!
Motionless torrents! silent cataracts!
Who made you glorious as the Gates of Heaven
Beneath the keen full moon? Who bade the sun
Clothe you with rainbows? Who, with living flowers
Of loveliest blue, spread garlands at your feet?—
God! let the torrents, like a shout of nations,
Answer! and let the ice-plains echo, God!
God! sing ye meadow-streams with gladsome voice!
Ye pine-groves, with your soft and soul-like sounds!
And they too have a voice, yon piles of snow,
And in their perilous fall shall thunder, God!

Ye living flowers that skirt the eternal frost!
Ye wild goats sporting round the eagle's nest!
Ye eagles, play-mates of the mountain-storm!
Ye lightnings, the dread arrows of the clouds!

Ye signs and wonders of the element!
Utter forth God, and fill the hills with praise!

Thou too, hoar Mount! with thy sky-pointing peaks,
Oft from whose feet the avalanche, unheard,
Shoots downward, glittering through the pure serene
Into the depth of clouds, that veil thy breast—
Thou too again, stupendous Mountain! thou
That as I raise my head, awhile bowed low
In adoration, upward from thy base
Slow traveling with dim eyes suffused with tears,
Solemnly seemest, like a vapory cloud,
To rise before me—Rise, O ever rise,
Rise like a cloud of incense from the Earth!
Thou kingly Spirit throned among the hills,
Thou dread ambassador from Earth to Heaven,
Great Hierarch! tell thou the silent sky,
And tell the stars, and tell yon rising sun
Earth, with her thousand voices, praises God.

RATIONALISM

The rationalist desires to reduce everything to order and then apply the principles of mathematics and logic to arrive at a demonstrable conclusion. It is natural, therefore, that most examples of rationalistic religious verse should come from the eighteenth century, the "age of reason." Addison finds proof of God in the mathematical perfection of the movements of the heavenly bodies; Pope, placing man at the head of a carefully arranged series of creations, rejoices in the orderliness of the universe. Tennyson's "In Memoriam," that high note of Victorian religious poetry, is rationalism lifted to a pitch of vision.

HYMN

The spacious firmament on high,
With all the blue ethereal sky,
And spangled heavens, a shining frame,
Their great Original proclaim.
Th' unwearied sun from day to day
Does his Creator's power display;
And publishes to every land
The work of an Almighty hand.

Soon as the evening shades prevail,
The Moon takes up the wondrous tale;
And nightly to the listening earth
Repeats the story of her birth;
Whilst all the stars that round her burn,
And all the planets in their turn,
Confirm the tidings as they roll,
And spread the truth from pole to pole.

What though in solemn silence all
Move round the dark terrestrial ball;
What though no real voice nor sound
Amidst their radiant orbs be found?
In Reason's ear they all rejoice,
And utter forth a glorious voice;
Forever singing as they shine,
"The Hand that made us is divine."

—*Joseph Addison* (1672-1719)

FROM "AN ESSAY ON MAN"

by Alexander Pope (1688-1744)

Epistle I

Awake, my St. John! leave all meaner things
To low ambition, and the pride of Kings.
Let us (since Life can little more supply
Than just to look about us and to die)
Expatiate free o'er all this scene of Man;
A mighty maze! but not without a plan;
A Wild, where weeds and flow'rs promiscuous shoot;
Or Garden, tempting with forbidden fruit.
Together let us beat this ample field,
Try what the open, what the covert yield;
The latent tracts, the giddy heights, explore
Of all who blindly creep, or sightless soar;
Eye Nature's walks, shoot Folly as it flies,
And catch the Manners living as they rise;
Laugh where we must, be candid where we can;
But vindicate the ways of God to Man.

Say first, of God above, or Man below,
What can we reason, but from what we know?
Of Man, what see we but his station here,

From which to reason, or to which refer?
Through worlds unnumbered though the God be known,
'Tis ours to trace him only in our own,
He, who through vast immensity can pierce,
See worlds on worlds compose one universe,
Observe how system into system runs,
What other planets circle other suns,
What varied Being peoples ev'ry star,
May tell why Heav'n has made us as we are.
But of this frame the bearings, and the ties,
The strong connections, nice dependencies,
Gradations just, has thy pervading soul
Looked through? or can a part contain the whole?
  Is the great chain, that draws all to agree,
And drawn supports, upheld by God, or thee?

Presumptuous Man! the reason wouldst thou find,
Why formed so weak, so little, and so blind?
First, if thou canst, the harder reason guess,
Why formed no weaker, blinder, and no less?
Ask of thy mother earth, why oaks are made
Taller or stronger than the weeds they shade?
Or ask of yonder argent fields above,
Why Jove's satellites are less than Jove?
  Of Systems possible, if 'tis confessed
That Wisdom infinite must form the best,
Where all must full or not coherent be,
And all that rises, rise in due degree;
Then, in the scale of reas'ning life, 'tis plain,
There must be, somewhere, such a rank as Man:
And all the question (wrangle e'er so long)
Is only this, if God has placed him wrong?
  Respecting Man, whatever wrong we call,
May, must be right, as relative to all.
In human works, though labored on with pain,
A thousand movements scarce one purpose gain;
In God's, one single can its end produce;
Yet serves to second too some other use.
So Man, who here seems principal alone,
Perhaps acts second to some sphere unknown,
Touches some wheel, or verges to some goal:
'Tis but a part we see, and not a whole.
  When the proud steed shall know why Man restrains
His fiery course, or drives him o'er the plains:
When the dull Ox, why now he breaks the clod,
Is now a victim, and now Egypt's God:
Then shall Man's pride and dullness comprehend
His actions', passions', being's, use and end;
Why doing, suff'ring, checked, impelled; and why
This hour a slave, the next a deity.
  Then say not Man's imperfect, Heav'n in fault;
Say rather, Man's as perfect as he ought:
His knowledge measured to his state and place;
His time a moment, and a point his space.
If to be perfect in a certain sphere,
What matter, soon or late, or here or there?
The bless'd today is as completely so,
As who began a thousand years ago.

Heav'n from all creatures hides the book of Fate,
All but the page prescribed, their present state:
From brutes what men, from men what spirits know:
Or who could suffer Being here below?
The lamb thy riot dooms to bleed today,
Had he thy Reason, would he skip and play?
Pleased to the last, he crops the flow'ry food,
And licks the hand just raised to shed his blood.
O blindness to the future! kindly giv'n,
That each may fill the circle marked by Heav'n:
Who sees with equal eye, as God of all,
A hero perish, or a sparrow fall,
Atoms or systems into ruin hurled,
And now a bubble burst, and now a world.
  Hope humbly then; with trembling pinions soar;
Wait the great teacher Death: and God adore.
What future bliss, he gives not thee to know,
But gives that Hope to be thy blessing now.
Hope springs eternal in the human breast:
Man never Is, but always To be bless'd:
The soul, uneasy and confined from home,

Rests and expatiates in a life to come.
  Lo, the poor Indian! whose untutored mind
Sees God in clouds, or hears him in the wind:
His soul proud Science never taught to stray
Far as the solar walk, or milky way;
Yet simple Nature to his hope has giv'n,
Behind the cloud-topped hill, an humbler heav'n;
Some safer world in depth of woods embraced,
Some happier island in the wat'ry waste,
Where slaves once more their native land behold,
No fiends torment, no Christians thirst for gold.
To Be, contents his natural desire,
He asks no Angel's wing, no Seraph's fire;
But thinks, admitted to that equal sky,
His faithful dog shall bear him company.

Go, wiser thou! and, in thy scale of sense,
Weigh thy Opinion against Providence;
Call imperfection what thou fanci'st such,
Say, here he gives too little, there too much:
Destroy all Creatures for thy sport or gust,
Yet cry, If Man's unhappy, God's unjust;
If Man alone engross not Heav'n's high care,
Alone made perfect here, immortal there:
Snatch from his hand the balance and the rod,
Re-judge his justice, be the God of God.
In Pride, in reas'ning Pride, our error lies;
All quit their sphere, and rush into the skies.
Pride still is aiming at the bless'd abodes,
Men would be Angels, Angels would be Gods
Aspiring to be Gods, if Angels fell,
Aspiring to be Angels, Men rebel:
And who but wishes to invert the laws
Of Order, sins against th' Eternal Cause.

Ask for what end the heav'nly bodies shine,
Earth for whose use? Pride answers, " 'Tis for mine:
For me kind Nature wakes her genial Pow'r,
Suckles each herb, and spreads out ev'ry flow'r;
Annual for me, the grape, the rose renew
The juice nectareous, and the balmy dew;
For me, the mine a thousand treasures brings;
For me, health gushes from a thousand springs;
Seas roll to waft me, suns to light me rise;
My foot-stool earth, my canopy the skies."
  But errs not Nature from his gracious end,
From burning suns when livid deaths descend,
When earthquakes swallow, or when tempests sweep
Towns to one grave, whole nations to the deep?
"No," ('tis replied) "the first Almighty Cause
Acts not by partial, but by gen'ral laws;
Th' exceptions few; some change since all began:
And what created perfect?"—Why then Man?
If the great end be human Happiness,
Then Nature deviates; and can Man do less?
As much that end a constant course requires
Of show'rs and sun-shine, as of Man's desires;
As much eternal springs and cloudless skies,
As Men for ever temp'rate, calm, and wise.
If plagues or earthquakes break not Heav'n's design,
Why then a Borgia, or a Catiline?
Who knows but he, whose hand the lightning forms,
Who heaves old Ocean, and who wings the storms;
Pours fierce Ambition in a Caesar's mind,
Or turns young Ammon loose to scourge mankind?
From pride, from pride, our very reas'ning springs;
Account for moral as for nat'ral things:
Why charge we Heav'n in those, in these acquit?
In both, to reason right is to submit.
  Better for Us, perhaps, it might appear,
Were there all harmony, all virtue here;
That never air or ocean felt the wind;
That never passion discomposed the mind.
But all subsists by elemental strife;
And Passions are the elements of Life.
The gen'ral Order, since the whole began
Is kept in Nature, and is kept in Man.

What would this Man? Now upward will he soar,
And, little less than Angel, would be more;
Now looking downwards, just as grieved appears
To want the strength of bulls, the fur of bears.
Made for his use all creatures if he call,
Say what their use, had he the pow'rs of all?
Nature to these, without profusion, kind,
The proper organs, proper pow'rs assign'd;
Each seeming want compensated of course,
Here with degrees of swiftness, there of force;
All in exact proportion to the state;
Nothing to add, and nothing to abate.
Each beast, each insect, happy in its own:
Is Heav'n unkind to Man, and Man alone?
Shall he alone, whom rational we call,
Be pleased with nothing, if not bless'd with all?
  The bliss of Man (could Pride that blessing find)
Is not to act or think beyond mankind;
No pow'rs of body or of soul to share,
But what his nature and his state can bear.
Why has not Man a microscopic eye?
For this plain reason, Man is not a Fly.
Say what the use, were finer optics giv'n,
T' inspect a mite, not comprehend the heav'n?
Or touch, if tremblingly alive all o'er,
To smart and agonize at every pore?
Or quick effluvia darting through the brain,
Die of a rose in aromatic pain?
If Nature thundered in his op'ning ears,
And stunned him with the music of the spheres,
How would he wish that Heav'n had left him still
The whisp'ring Zephyr, and the purling rill?
Who finds not Providence all good and wise,
Alike in what it gives, and what denies?

Far as Creation's ample range extends,
The scale of sensual, mental pow'rs ascends:
Mark how it mounts, to Man's imperial race,
From the green myriads in the peopled grass:
What modes of sight betwixt each wide extreme,
The mole's dim curtain, and the lynx's beam:
Of smell, the headlong lioness between,
And hound sagacious on the tainted green:
Of hearing, from the life that fills the Flood,
To that which warbles through the vernal wood:
The spider's touch, how exquisitely fine!
Feels at each thread, and lives along the line:
In the nice bee, what sense so subtly true
From pois'nous herbs extracts the healing dew?
How Instinct varies in the grov'ling swine,
Compared, half-reas'ning elephant, with thine!
'Twixt that, and Reason, what a nice barrier,
For ever sep'rate, yet for ever near!
Remembrance and Reflection how allied;
What thin partitions Sense from Thought divide:
And Middle natures, how they long to join,
Yet never pass th' insuperable line!
Without this just gradation, could they be
Subjected, these to those, or all to thee?
The pow'rs of all subdued by thee alone,
Is not thy Reason all these pow'rs in one?

See, through this air, this ocean, and this earth,
All matter quick, and bursting into birth.
Above, how high progressive life may go!
Around, how wide! how deep extend below!
Vast chain of Being! which from God began,
Natures ethereal, human, angel, man,
Beast, bird, fish, insect, what no eye can see,
No glass can reach; from Infinite to thee,
From thee to Nothing.—On superior pow'rs
Were we to press, inferior might on ours:
Or in the full creation leave a void,
Where, one step broken, the great scale's destroyed:
From Nature's chain whatever link you strike,
Tenth or ten-thousandth, breaks the chain alike.
  And, if each system in gradation roll
Alike essential to th' amazing Whole,
The least confusion but in one, not all
That system only, but the Whole must fall.
Let Earth unbalanced from her orbit fly,
Planets and Suns run lawless through the sky;
Let ruling Angels from their spheres be hurled,

Being on Being wrecked, and world on world;
Heav'n's whole foundations to their center nod,
And Nature tremble to the throne of God.
All this dread Order break—for whom? for thee?
Vile worm!—O Madness! Pride! Impiety!

What if the foot, ordained the dust to tread,
Or hand, to toil, aspired to be the head?
What if the head, the eye, or ear repined
To serve mere engines to the ruling Mind?
Just as absurd for any part to claim
To be another, in this gen'ral frame:
Just as absurd, to mourn the tasks or pains,
The great directing Mind of all ordains.
All are but parts of one stupendous whole,
Whose body Nature is, and God the soul;
That, changed through all, and yet in all the same;
Great in the earth, as in th' ethereal frame;
Warms in the sun, refreshes in the breeze,
Glows in the stars, and blossoms in the trees,
Lives through all life, extends through all extent,
Spreads undivided, operates unspent;
Breathes in our soul, informs our mortal part,
As full, as perfect, in a hair as heart:
As full, as perfect, in vile Man that mourns,
As the rapt Seraph that adores and burns:
To him no high, no low, no great, no small;
He fills, he bounds, connects, and equals all.

Cease then, nor Order Imperfection name:
Our proper bliss depends on what we blame.
Know thy own point: This kind, this due degree
Of blindness, weakness, Heav'n bestows on thee.
Submit.—In this, or any other sphere,
Secure to be as bless'd as thou canst bear:
Safe in the hand of one disposing Pow'r,
Or in the natal, or the mortal hour.
All Nature is but Art, unknown to thee;
All Chance, Direction, which thou canst not see;
All Discord, Harmony not understood;
All partial Evil, universal Good:
And, spite of Pride, in erring Reason's spite,
One truth is clear, *Whatever is, is right.*

FROM "IN MEMORIAM"

by Alfred, Lord Tennyson (1809-1892)

Proem

Strong Son of God, immortal Love,
Whom we, that have not seen thy face,
By faith, and faith alone, embrace,
Believing where we cannot prove;

Thine are these orbs of light and shade;
Thou madest life in man and brute;
Thou madest death; and lo, thy foot
Is on the skull which thou hast made.

Thou wilt not leave us in the dust:
Thou madest man, he knows not why,
He thinks he was not made to die;
And thou hast made him: thou art just.

Thou seemest human and divine,
The highest, holiest manhood, thou.
Our wills are ours, we know not how;
Our wills are ours, to make them thine.

Our little systems have their day;
They have their day and cease to be;
They are but broken lights of thee,
And thou, O Lord, art more than they.

We have but faith; we cannot know,
For knowledge is of things we see;
And yet we trust it comes from thee,
A beam in darkness: let it grow.

Let knowledge grow from more to more,
But more of reverence in us dwell;
That mind and soul, according well,
May make one music as before,

But vaster. We are fools and slight;
We mock thee when we do not fear.
But help thy foolish ones to bear;
Help thy vain worlds to bear thy light.

Forgive what seemed my sin in me,
What seemed my worth since I began;
For merit lives from man to man,
And not from man, O Lord, to thee.

Forgive my grief for one removed,
Thy creature, whom I found so fair.
I trust he lives in thee, and there
I find him worthier to be loved.

Forgive these wild and wandering cries,
  Confusions of a wasted youth;
  Forgive them where they fail in truth,
And in thy wisdom make me wise.

XXVII

I envy not in any moods
  The captive void of noble rage,
  The linnet born within the cage,
That never knew the summer woods;

I envy not the beast that takes
  His license in the field of time,
  Unfettered by the sense of crime,
To whom a conscience never wakes;

Nor, what may count itself as blest,
  The heart that never plighted troth
  But stagnates in the weeds of sloth;
Nor any want-begotten rest.

I hold it true, whate'er befall;
  I feel it, when I sorrow most;
  'Tis better to have loved and lost
Than never to have loved at all.

XLVII

That each, who seems a separate whole,
  Should move his rounds, and fusing all
  The skirts of self again, should fall
Remerging in the general Soul,

Is faith as vague as all unsweet.
  Eternal form shall still divide
  The eternal soul from all beside;
And I shall know him when we meet:

And we shall sit at endless feast,
  Enjoying each the other's good.
  What vaster dream can hit the mood
Of Love on earth? He seeks at least

Upon the last and sharpest height,
  Before the spirits fade away,
  Some landing-place, to clasp and say,
"Farewell! We lose ourselves in light."

LI

Do we indeed desire the dead
  Should still be near us at our side?
  Is there no baseness we would hide?
No inner vileness that we dread?

Shall he for whose applause I strove,
  I had such reverence for his blame,
  See with clear eye some hidden shame
And I be lessened in his love?

I wrong the grave with fears untrue:
  Shall love be blamed for want of faith?
  There must be wisdom with great Death;
The dead shall look me through and through.

Be near us when we climb or fall.
  Ye watch, like God, the rolling hours
  With larger other eyes than ours,
To make allowance for us all.

LV

The wish, that of the living whole
  No life may fail beyond the grave,
  Derives it not from what we have
The likest God within the soul?

Are God and Nature then at strife,
  That Nature lends such evil dreams?
  So careful of the type she seems,
So careless of the single life,

That I, considering everywhere
  Her secret meaning in her deeds,
  And finding that of fifty seeds
She often brings but one to bear,

I falter where I firmly trod,
  And falling with my weight of cares
  Upon the great world's altar-stairs
That slope through darkness up to God,

I stretch lame hands of faith, and grope,
  And gather dust and chaff, and call
  To what I feel is Lord of all,
And faintly trust the larger hope.

LVI

"So careful of the type?" but no.
  From scarpéd cliff and quarried stone
  She cries, "A thousand types are gone.
I care for nothing, all shall go.

"Thou makest thine appeal to me;
  I bring to life, I bring to death;
  The spirit does but mean the breath.
I know no more." And he, shall he,

Man, her last work, who seemed so fair,
  Such splendid purpose in his eyes,

Who rolled the psalm to wintry skies,
Who built him fanes of fruitless prayer,

Who trusted God was love indeed
And love Creation's final law—
Though Nature, red in tooth and claw
With ravine, shrieked against his creed—

Who loved, who suffered countless ills,
Who battled for the True, the Just,
Be blown about the desert dust,
Or sealed within the iron hills?

No more? A monster then, a dream,
A discord. Dragons of the prime,
That tear each other in their slime,
Were mellow music matched with him.

O life as futile, then, as frail!
O for thy voice to soothe and bless!
What hope of answer, or redress?
Behind the veil, behind the veil.

XCVI

You say, but with no touch of scorn,
Sweet-hearted, you, whose light-blue eyes
Are tender over drowning flies,
You tell me, doubt is Devil-born.

I know not: one indeed I knew
In many a subtle question versed,
Who touched a jarring lyre at first,
But ever strove to make it true;

Perplexed in faith, but pure in deeds,
At last he beat his music out.
There lives more faith in honest doubt,
Believe me, than in half the creeds.

He fought his doubts and gathered strength,
He would not make his judgment blind,
He faced the specters of the mind
And laid them; thus he came at length

To find a stronger faith his own,
And Power was with him in the night,
Which makes the darkness and the light,
And dwells not in the light alone,

But in the darkness and the cloud,
As over Sinaï's peaks of old,
While Israel made their gods of gold,
Although the trumpet blew so loud.

CXVIII

Contemplate all this work of Time,
The giant laboring in his youth;
Nor dream of human love and truth,
As dying Nature's earth and lime;

But trust that those we call the dead
Are breathers of an ampler day
For ever nobler ends. They say,
The solid earth whereon we tread

In tracts of fluent heat began,
And grew to seeming-random forms,
The seeming prey of cyclic storms,
Till at the last arose the man;

Who throve and branched from clime to clime,
The herald of a higher race,
And of himself in higher place,
If so he type this work of time

Within himself, from more to more;
Or, crowned with attributes of woe
Like glories, move his course, and show
That life is not as idle ore,

But iron dug from central gloom,
And heated hot with burning fears,
And dipped in baths of hissing tears,
And battered with the shocks of doom

To shape and use. Arise and fly
The reeling Faun, the sensual feast;
Move upward, working out the beast,
And let the ape and tiger die.

CXXX

Thy voice is on the rolling air;
I hear thee where the waters run;
Thou standest in the rising sun,
And in the setting thou art fair.

What art thou then? I cannot guess;
But though I seem in star and flower
To feel thee some diffusive power,
I do not therefore love thee less.

My love involves the love before;
My love is vaster passion now;
Though mix'd with God and Nature thou,
I seem to love thee more and more.

Far off thou art, but ever nigh;
I have thee still, and I rejoice;
I prosper, circled with thy voice;
I shall not lose thee though I die.

CXXXI

O living will that shalt endure
When all that seems shall suffer shock,
Rise in the spiritual rock,
Flow through our deeds and make them pure,

That we may lift from out of dust
A voice as unto him that hears,
A cry above the conquered years
To one that with us works, and trust,

With faith that comes of self-control,
The truths that never can be proved
Until we close with all we loved,
And all we flow from, soul in soul.

MYSTICISM

Religion, however, is more emotional than intellectual, and the greatest religious poems are the products of mystics, poets of deep emotional power, rather than of the rational Popes and the agnostic Swinburnes. Blake, that God-intoxicated visionary, has left us a library of prophetic poetry which often requires a new dictionary of angels to interpret, but its fervor and nobility must persuade the most skeptical. Francis Thompson, perhaps the greatest of modern Catholic poets, has created in "The Hound of Heaven" a daring symbol which at first shocks our imagination, but later lifts us with its power of phrase and magnificence of effect.

Tennyson's "In Memoriam" deserves to be placed among the great orthodox religious poems; Queen Victoria is said to have kept it by her bedside with her Bible. "In Memoriam," quoted as part of the preceding group, is a curious blend of radiance and rationalism. It combines fervor with ethical purpose and is a definite attempt to hold religious values through a Victorian stability.

Mysticism is the doctrine that the ultimate nature of reality or divine essence may be known in an immediate apprehension. It is intuition or insight as opposed to observation and logic. It is the sense of absorption in and union with an ultimate spirit far beyond earthly experience. This was Blake's power and, in a lesser degree, Francis Thompson's: a pure revelation that has little concern with plodding reason. Even in this era of frayed nerves its sense of rapture illuminates the unaffected lines of the contemporary Léonie Adams.

Browning, that most varied of poets, sounded the religious mystical note again and again. Space does not permit the inclusion of his "Saul" in its entirety; but the final sections of "Saul," here given, contain the climactic conclusion of the poem, the pith of its message.

A NEW JERUSALEM
(from "Milton")

And did those feet in ancient time
Walk upon England's mountains green?
And was the Holy Lamb of God
On England's pleasant pastures seen?

And did the countenance divine
Shine forth upon our clouded hills?
And was Jerusalem builded here
Among these dark satanic mills?

Bring me my bow of burning gold!
Bring me my arrows of desire!

Bring me my spear! O clouds, unfold!
Bring me my chariot of fire!

I will not cease from mental fight,
Nor shall my sword sleep in my hand,
Till we have built Jerusalem
In England's green and pleasant land.

—*William Blake* (1757-1827)

FROM "SAUL"

by Robert Browning (1812-1889)

Then the truth came upon me. No harp more—no song more! outbroke—
"I have gone the whole round of creation: I saw and I spoke:
I, a work of God's hand for that purpose, received in my brain
And pronounced on the rest of his handwork—returned him again
His creation's approval or censure: I spoke as I saw:
I report, as a man may of God's work—all's love, yet all's law.
Now I lay down the judgeship he lent me. Each faculty tasked
To perceive him, has gained an abyss, where a dewdrop was asked.
Have I knowledge? confounded it shrivels at Wisdom laid bare.
Have I forethought? how purblind, how blank, to the Infinite Care!
Do I task any faculty highest, to image success?
I but open my eyes,—and perfection, no more and no less,
In the kind I imagined, full-fronts me, and God is seen God
In the star, in the stone, in the flesh, in the soul and the clod.
And thus looking within and around me, I ever renew
(With that stoop of the soul which in bending upraises it too)
The submission of man's nothing-perfect to God's all-complete,
As by each new obeisance in spirit, I climb to his feet.
Yet with all this abounding experience, this deity known,
I shall dare to discover some province, some gift of my own.
There's a faculty pleasant to exercise, hard to hoodwink,
I am fain to keep still in abeyance (I laugh as I think)
Lest, insisting to claim and parade in it, wot ye, I worst
E'en the Giver in one gift.—Behold, I could love if I durst!
But I sink the pretension as fearing a man may o'ertake
God's own speed in the one way of love: I abstain for love's sake.
—What, my soul? see thus far and no farther? when doors great and small,
Nine-and-ninety flew ope at our touch, should the hundredth appall?
In the least things have faith, yet distrust in the greatest of all?
Do I find love so full in my nature, God's ultimate gift,
That I doubt his own love can compete with it? Here, the parts shift?
Here, the creature surpass the Creator,—the end, what Began?
Would I fain in my impotent yearning do all for this man,
And dare doubt he alone shall not help him, who yet alone can?
Would it ever have entered my mind, the bare will, much less power,
To bestow on this Saul what I sang of, the marvelous dower
Of the life he was gifted and filled with? to make such a soul,
Such a body, and then such an earth for insphering the whole?
And doth it not enter my mind (as my warm tears attest)
These good things being given, to go on, and give one more, the best?
Aye, to save and redeem and restore him, maintain at the height

This perfection,—succeed with life's day-spring, death's minute of night?
Interpose at the difficult minute, snatch Saul the mistake,
Saul the failure, the ruin he seems now,—and bid him awake
From the dream, the probation, the prelude, to find himself set
Clear and safe in new light and new life,—a new harmony yet
To be run, and continued, and ended—who knows?—or endure!
The man taught enough, by life's dream, of the rest to make sure;
By the pain-throb, triumphantly winning intensified bliss,
And the next world's reward and repose, by the struggles in this.

"I believe it! 'Tis thou, God, that givest, 'tis I who receive:
In the first is the last, in thy will is my power to believe.
All's one gift: thou canst grant it moreover, as prompt to my prayer
As I breathe out this breath, as I open these arms to the air.
From thy will, stream the worlds, life and nature, thy dread Sabaoth:
I will?—the mere atoms despise me! Why am I not loath
To look that, even that in the face too? Why is it I dare
Think but lightly of such impuissance? What stops my despair?
This;—'tis not what man Does which exalts him, but what man Would do!
See the King—I would help him but cannot, the wishes fall through.
Could I wrestle to raise him from sorrow, grow poor to enrich,
To fill up his life, starve my own out, I would—knowing which,
I know that my service is perfect. Oh, speak through me now!
Would I suffer for him that I love? So wouldst thou—so wilt thou!
So shall crown thee the topmost, ineffablest, uttermost crown—
And thy love fill infinitude wholly, nor leave up nor down
One spot for the creature to stand in! It is by no breath,
Turn of eye, wave of hand, that salvation joins issue with death!
As thy Love is discovered almighty, almighty be proved
Thy power, that exists with and for it, of being Beloved!
He who did most, shall bear most; the strongest shall stand the most weak.
'Tis the weakness in strength, that I cry for! my flesh, that I seek
In the Godhead! I seek and I find it. O Saul, it shall be
A Face like my face that receives thee; a Man like to me,
Thou shalt love and be loved by, forever: a Hand like this hand
Shall throw open the gates of new life to thee! See the Christ stand!"

I know not too well how I found my way home in the night.
There were witnesses, cohorts about me, to left and to right,
Angels, powers, the unuttered, unseen, the alive, the aware:
I repressed, I got through them as hardly, as strugglingly there,
As a runner beset by the populace famished for news—
Life or death. The whole earth was awakened, hell loosed with her crews;
And the stars of night beat with emotion, and tingled and shot
Out in fire the strong pain of pent knowledge: but I fainted not,
For the Hand still impelled me at once and supported, suppressed
All the tumult, and quenched it with quiet, and holy behest,
Till the rapture was shut in itself, and the earth sank to rest.
Anon at the dawn, all that trouble had withered from earth—
Not so much, but I saw it die out in the day's tender birth;
In the gathered intensity brought to the gray of the hills;

In the shuddering forests' held breath; in the sudden wind-thrills;
In the startled wild beasts that bore off, each with eye sidling still
Tho' averted with wonder and dread; in the birds stiff and chill
That rose heavily, as I approached them, made stupid with awe:
E'en the serpent that slid away silent,—he felt the new law.
The same stared in the white humid faces upturned by the flowers;
The same worked in the heart of the cedar and moved the vine-bowers:
And the little brooks witnessing murmured, persistent and low,
With their obstinate, all but hushed voices—"E'en so, it is so!"

THE HOUND OF HEAVEN

by Francis Thompson (1859-1907)

I fled Him, down the nights and down the days;
  I fled Him, down the arches of the years;
I fled Him, down the labyrinthine ways
  Of my own mind; and in the mist of tears
I hid from Him, and under running laughter.
      Up vistaed hopes I sped;
      And shot, precipitated,
Adown Titanic glooms of chasmed fears,
  From those strong Feet that followed, followed after.
      But with unhurrying chase,
      And unperturbèd pace,
    Deliberate speed, majestic instancy,
      They beat—and a Voice beat
      More instant than the Feet—
    "All things betray thee, who betrayest Me."

      I pleaded, outlaw-wise,
By many a hearted casement, curtained red,
  Trellised with intertwining charities
(For, though I knew His love Who followèd,
      Yet was I sore adread
Lest, having Him, I must have naught beside);
But, if one little casement parted wide,
  The gust of His approach would clash it to:
  Fear wist not to evade, as Love wist to pursue.
Across the margent of the world I fled,
  And troubled the gold gateways of the stars,
  Smiting for shelter on their clangèd bars;
      Fretted to dulcet jars
And silvern chatter the pale ports o' the moon.
I said to Dawn: Be sudden—to Eve: Be soon;
  With thy young skiey blossoms heap me over
      From this tremendous Lover—
Float thy vague veil about me, lest He see!
  I tempted all His servitors, but to find
My own betrayal in their constancy,
In faith to Him their fickleness to me,

Their traitorous trueness, and their loyal deceit.
To all swift things for swiftness did I sue;
Clung to the whistling mane of every wind.
But whether they swept, smoothly fleet,
The long savannahs of the blue;
Or whether, Thunder-driven,
They clanged his chariot 'thwart a heaven,
Plashy with flying lightnings round the spurn o' their feet:—
Fear wist not to evade as Love wist to pursue.
Still with unhurrying chase,
And unperturbèd pace,
Deliberate speed, majestic instancy,
Came on the following Feet,
And a Voice above their beat—
"Naught shelters thee, who wilt not shelter Me."

I sought no more that after which I strayed
In face of man or maid;
But still within the little children's eyes
Seems something, something that replies,
They at least are for me, surely for me!
I turned me to them very wistfully;
But just as their young eyes grew sudden fair
With dawning answers there,
Their angel plucked them from me by the hair.
"Come then, ye other children, Nature's—share
With me" (said I) "your delicate fellowship;
Let me greet you lip to lip,
Let me twine with you caresses,
Wantoning
With our Lady-Mother's vagrant tresses,
Banqueting
With her in her wind-walled palace,
Underneath her azured daïs,
Quaffing, as your taintless way is,
From a chalice
Lucent-weeping out of the dayspring."
So it was done:
I in their delicate fellowship was one—
Drew the bolt of Nature's secrecies.
I knew all the swift importings
On the willful face of skies;
I knew how the clouds arise
Spumèd of the wild sea-snortings;
All that's born or dies
Rose and drooped with; made them shapers
Of mine own moods, or wailful or divine;
With them joyed and was bereaven.
I was heavy with the even,
When she lit her glimmering tapers
Round the day's dead sanctities.

I laughed in the morning's eyes.
I triumphed and I saddened with all weather,
Heaven and I wept together,
And its sweet tears were salt with mortal mine.

Against the red throb of its sunset-heart
I laid my own to beat,
And share commingling heat;
But not by that, by that, was eased my human smart.
In vain my tears were wet on Heaven's gray cheek.
For ah! we know not what each other says,
These things and I; in sound *I* speak—
Their sound is but their stir, they speak by silences.
Nature, poor stepdame, cannot slake my drouth;
Let her, if she would owe me,
Drop yon blue bosom-veil of sky, and show me
The breasts o' her tenderness:
Never did any milk of hers once bless
My thirsting mouth.
Nigh and nigh draws the chase,
With unperturbèd pace,
Deliberate speed, majestic instancy;
And past those noisèd Feet
A Voice comes yet more fleet—
"Lo! naught contents thee, who content'st not Me."

Naked I wait Thy love's uplifted stroke!
My harness piece by piece Thou hast hewn from me,
And smitten me to my knee;
I am defenseless utterly.
I slept, methinks, and woke,
And, slowly gazing, find me stripped in sleep.
In the rash lustihead of my young powers,
I shook the pillaring hours
And pulled my life upon me; grimed with smears,
I stand amid the dust o' the mounded years—
My mangled youth lies dead beneath the heap.
My days have crackled and gone up in smoke,
Have puffed and burst as sun-starts on a stream.
Yea, faileth now even dream
The dreamer, and the lute the lutanist;
Even the linked fantasies, in whose blossomy twist
I swung the earth a trinket at my wrist,
Are yielding; cords of all too weak account
For earth with heavy griefs so overplused.
Ah! is Thy love indeed
A weed, albeit an amaranthine weed,
Suffering no flowers except its own to mount?
Ah! must—
Designer infinite!—
Ah! must Thou char the wood ere Thou canst limn with it?

My freshness spent its wavering shower i' the dust;
And now my heart is as a broken fount,
Wherein tear-drippings stagnate, spilt down ever
From the dank thoughts that shiver
Upon the sighful branches of my mind.
Such is; what is to be?
The pulp so bitter, how shall taste the rind?
I dimly guess what Time in mists confounds;
Yet ever and anon a trumpet sounds
From the hid battlements of Eternity;
Those shaken mists a space unsettle, then
Round the half-glimpsèd turrets slowly wash again.
But not ere him who summoneth
I first have seen, enwound
With glooming robes purpureal, cypress-crowned;
His name I know, and what his trumpet saith.
Whether man's heart or life it be which yields
Thee harvest, must Thy harvest-fields
Be dunged with rotten death?

Now of that long pursuit
Comes on at hand the bruit;
That Voice is round me like a bursting sea:
"And is thy earth so marred,
Shattered in shard on shard?
Lo, all things fly thee, for thou fliest Me!
Strange, piteous, futile thing!
Wherefore should any set thee love apart?
Seeing none but I makes much of naught" (He said),
"And human love needs human meriting:
How hast thou merited—
Of all man's clotted clay the dingiest clot?
Alack, thou knowest not
How little worthy of any love thou art!
Whom wilt thou find to love ignoble thee
Save Me, save only me?
All which I took from thee I did but take,
Not for thy harms,
But just that thou might'st seek it in My arms.
All which thy child's mistake
Fancies as lost, I have stored for thee at home:
Rise, clasp My hand, and come!"

Halts by me that footfall:
Is my gloom, after all,
Shade of His hand, outstretched caressingly?
"Ah, fondest, blindest, weakest,
I am He Whom thou seekest!
Thou dravest love from thee, who dravest Me."

SUGGESTIONS FOR ADDITIONAL READING

POEMS ON THE CONDUCT OF LIFE

George Herbert, *The Church Porch*
Alfred, Lord Tennyson, *The Lotos-Eaters*
H. W. Longfellow, *The Psalm of Life*
O. W. Holmes, *The Chambered Nautilus*
Edwin Markham, *The Man with the Hoe*

POEMS ON THE PURPOSE OF LIFE

William Blake, *The Everlasting Gospel*
William Blake, *Night*
Gerard Manley Hopkins, *The Habit of Perfection*
John Keats, *Ode to a Nightingale*
Stephen Crane, *The Wayfarer*
Stephen Crane, *A Man Said to the Universe*
R. W. Emerson, *Terminus*
A. E. Housman, *Epilog to "A Shropshire Lad"*

POEMS ON MAN AND THE UNIVERSE

George Herbert, *The Collar*
Henry Vaughan, *The Retreat*
Henry Vaughan, *The World*
Thomas Traherne, *Wonder*
Thomas Traherne, *The Anticipation*
William Blake, *The Divine Image*
William Wordsworth, *Ode on Intimations of Immortality*
W. C. Bryant, *Thanatopsis*
A. C. Swinburne, *Hertha*
R. W. Emerson, *The Problem*
Sidney Lanier, *The Marshes of Glynn*
Robert Bridges, *The Testament of Beauty*

10

SATIRE IN POETRY: THE POEM AS WEAPON

MODERN psychiatrists have found the well-spring of most satirical writing in disease—disease of the mind if not of the body. The theory appears very convincing at first, until one realizes that the satirists have seen more coolly and thought more sanely than most of their contemporaries. A satirist has been defined as "a well-born soul out of luck," which is an admission of marked mental superiority of the satirical spirit. When a man or woman with a sense of humor or proportion is chafed by some aspect of life until a strong antipathy is roused, the result—if it finds expression in the written or spoken word—is usually satire.

Byron's club-foot may have made him extremely self-conscious and easily irritated, but the objects of his scorn would have irritated him just as much if he had been perfect. Pope was a hunchback, and hated Mary Wortley Montagu with the bitterness of rejected love when she poked fun at his figure; "The Dunciad" may have been written that the world might see how a powerful mind could overcome the handicap of a deformed body, but it upheld standards in literature which had little to do with personal antipathies. The master-satirist, Jonathan Swift, may have succumbed in the end to madness, but *Gulliver's Travels* and *The Tale of a Tub* show him as only too candid, too bitterly sane. The case for the personal grudge theory of satire might be built up by other examples, but "the spot that has been rubbed raw" will not always be found. The spirit of evangelism may cause a writer to set up a program to change the world—Voltaire with a plan for clear thinking which hastened the French Revolution, Juvenal with a moral indignation which almost converted Rome. Others may engage in it merely for the pleasure of pointing out life's incongruities—satire is closely linked with comedy, though all comedy need not be satiric. For Meredith the functions of the two are essentially the same: to throw light into the dark corners, much as the scientist discovers diseases and their antidotes.

Satire may frequently have a greater effect than positive preaching—the cartoonists of the past and the caricaturists of today have discovered that. Its greatest effectiveness, however, lies in the destruction of affectations. Acid satire which burns and cuts too brutally is always less popular and, in the end, less effective than the playful taunts of Horace or the witty exposure by an Aristophanes or a Molière.

The popular subjects for satire have changed with society itself—the mediaeval *fabliaus* attacking priests and noblemen from the point of view of the common yeoman, the works of Rabelais being typical of this *genre;* the Renaissance religious and political diatribes of Erasmus and his friends and enemies; eighteenth-century literary quips of Pope and the salon-leaders; nineteenth-century attacks upon the social maladjustments rising from the industrial revolution. Today religion and literature no longer occupy the center of the satirical stage; politics, sex, and money are the favorite themes. The best examples of literary satire, however, deal with religion, politics and literature.

Satire is not necessarily prosaic, though one would not expect to find lyrical outbursts in the middle of "MacFlecknoe." The modern novel, especially since Samuel Butler's *Erewhon,* is strongly flavored with satire, as is the drama of Shaw and others. In the kingdom of poetry satire will always occupy a prosperous if not noble province.

RELIGIOUS SATIRE

In English poetry, perhaps religion holds the honored place as the most venerable subject of satire. *Piers Plowman* and Chaucer both belabored the sinful priests and monks; after the Reformation, Samuel Butler, in *Hudibras,* ridiculed the Puritan in burlesque fashion; Jonathan Swift, a dean of St. Patrick's cathedral in Dublin, defended his faith by attacking its counterfeits; Robert Burns, thrown out of a Scotch Presbyterian church, turned upon his persecutors in wrath; the discoveries of Victorian science set the arrows of satire flying in all directions. Beneath the destructive irony of the following poems the reader should be able to find the implication of a constructive philosophy.

THE BEASTS' CONFESSION

by Jonathan Swift (1667-1745)

When beasts could speak (the learned say
They still can do so every day),
It seems they had religion then,
As much as now we find in men.
It happened, when a plague broke out,
(Which therefore made them more devout)
The king of brutes (to make it plain,
Of quadrupeds I only mean)
By proclamation gave command
That every subject in the land
Should to the priest confess their sins;
And thus the pious Wolf begins:—
"Good father, I must own with shame,
That often I have been to blame:
I must confess, on Friday last,
Wretch that I was! I broke my fast:
But I defy the basest tongue
To prove I did my neighbor wrong;
Or ever went to seek my food,
By rapine, theft, or thirst of blood."
The Ass approaching next, confessed
That in his heart he loved a jest:
A wag he was, he needs must own,
And could not let a dunce alone:
Sometimes his friend he would not spare,
And might perhaps be too severe:
But yet the worst that could be said,
He was a wit both born and bred;
And, if it be a sin and shame,
Nature alone must bear the blame:
One fault he has, is sorry for't,
His ears are half a foot too short;
Which could he to the standard bring,
He'd show his face before the king:
Then for his voice, there's none disputes
That he's the nightingale of brutes.
The Swine with contrite heart allowed
His shape and beauty made him proud:
In diet was perhaps too nice,
But gluttony was ne'er his vice:
In every turn of life content,

And meekly took what fortune sent:
Inquire through all the parish round,
A better neighbor ne'er was found;
His vigilance might some displease;
'Tis true, he hated sloth-like peace.
  The mimic Ape began his chatter,
How evil tongues his life bespatter;
Much of the censuring world complained,
Who said, his gravity was feigned:
Indeed, the strictness of his morals
Engaged him in a hundred quarrels:
He saw, and he was grieved to see't,
His zeal was sometimes indiscreet:
He found his virtues too severe
For our corrupted times to bear;
Yet such a lewd licentious age
Might well excuse a stoic's rage.
  The Goat advanced with decent pace,
And first excused his youthful face;
Forgiveness begged that he appeared
('Twas Nature's fault) without a beard.
'Tis true, he was not much inclined
To fondness for the female kind:
Not, as his enemies object,
From chance, or natural defect;
Not by his frigid constitution;
But through a pious resolution:
For he had made a holy vow
Of Chastity, as monks do now:
Which he resolved to keep for ever hence
And strictly too, as doth his reverence.
  Apply the tale, and you shall find
How just it suits with human kind.
Some faults we own; but can you guess?
—Why, virtues carried to excess,
Wherewith our vanity endows us,
Though neither foe nor friend allows us.
  The Lawyer swears (you may rely on't)
He never squeezed a needy client;
And this he makes his constant rule,
For which his brethren call him fool;
His conscience always was so nice,
He freely gave the poor advice;
By which he lost, he may affirm,
A hundred fees last Easter term;
While others of the learnèd robe,
Would break the patience of a Job.
No pleader at the bar could match
His diligence and quick dispatch;
Ne'er kept a cause, he well may boast,
Above a term or two at most.
  The cringing Knave, who seeks a place
Without success, thus tells his case:
Why should he longer mince the matter?
He failed, because he could not flatter;
He had not learned to turn his coat,
Nor for a party give his vote:
His crime he quickly understood;
Too zealous for the nation's good;
He found the ministers resent it,
Yet could not for his heart repent it.
  The Chaplain vows, he cannot fawn,
Though it would raise him to the lawn:
He passed his hours among his books;
You find it in his meagre looks:
He might, if he were worldly wise,
Preferment get, and spare his eyes;
But owns he had a stubborn spirit,
That made him trust alone to merit;
Would rise by merit to promotion;
Alas! a mere chimeric notion.
  The Doctor, if you will believe him,
Confessed a sin; (and God forgive him!)
Called up at midnight, ran to save
A blind old beggar from the grave:
But see how Satan spreads his snares;
He quite forgot to say his prayers.
He cannot help it, for his heart,
Sometimes to act the parson's part:
Quotes from the Bible many a sentence,
That moves his patients to repentance;
And, when his medicines do no good,
Supports their minds with heavenly food:
At which, however well intended;
He hears the clergy are offended;
And grown so bold behind his back,
To call him hypocrite and quack.
In his own church he keeps a seat;
Says grace before and after meat;
And calls, without affecting airs,
His household twice a day to prayers.
He shuns apothecaries' shops,
And hates to cram the sick with slops;
He scorns to make his art a trade;
Nor bribes my lady's favorite maid.
Old nurse-keepers would never hire,
To recommend him to the squire;
Which others, whom he will not name,
Have often practised to their shame.
  The Statesman tells you, with a sneer,
His fault is to be too sincere;
And having no sinister ends,

Is apt to disoblige his friends.
The nation's good, his master's glory,
Without regard to Whig or Tory,
Were all the schemes he had in view,
Yet he was seconded by few:
Though some had spread a thousand lies,
'Twas he defeated the excise.
'Twas known, though he had borne aspersion,
That standing troops were his aversion:
His practice was, in every station,
To serve the king, and please the nation.
Though hard to find in every case
The fittest man to fill a place:
His promises he ne'er forgot,
But took memorials on the spot;
His enemies, for want of charity,
Said he affected popularity:
'Tis true, the people understood,
That all he did was for their good;
Their kind affections he has tried;
No love is lost on either side.
He came to court with fortune clear,
Which now he runs out every year;
Must, at the rate that he goes on,
Inevitably be undone:
O! if his majesty would please
To give him but a writ of ease,
Would grant him license to retire,
As it has long been his desire,
By fair accounts it would be found,
He's poorer by ten thousand pound.
He owns, and hopes it is no sin,
He ne'er was partial to his kin;
He thought it base for men in stations,
To crowd the court with their relations:
His country was his dearest mother,
And every virtuous man his brother;
Through modesty or awkward shame,
(For which he owns himself to blame,)
He found the wisest man he could,
Without respect to friends or blood;
Nor ever acts on private views,
When he has liberty to choose.
The Sharper swore he hated play,
Except to pass an hour away:
And well he might; for, to his cost,
By want of skill, he always lost;
He heard there was a club of cheats,
Who had contrived a thousand feats;
Could change the stock, or cog a die,
And thus deceive the sharpest eye:
Nor wonder how his fortune sunk,
His brothers fleece him when he's drunk.
I own the moral not exact,
Besides, the tale is false, in fact;
And so absurd, that could I raise up,
From fields Elysian, fabling Aesop,
I would accuse him to his face,
For libeling the four-foot race.
Creatures of every kind but ours
Well comprehend their natural powers,
While we, whom reason ought to sway,
Mistake our talents every day.
The Ass was never known so stupid
To act the part of Tray or Cupid;
Nor leaps upon his master's lap,
There to be stroked, and fed with pap,
As Aesop would the world persuade;
He better understands his trade:
Nor comes whene'er his lady whistles,
But carries loads, and feeds on thistles.
Our author's meaning, I presume, is
A creature *bipes et implumis;*
Wherein the moralist designed
A compliment on human kind;
For here he owns, that now and then
Beasts may degenerate into men.

HOLY WILLIE'S PRAYER

by Robert Burns (1759-1796)

O Thou, wha in the heavens dost dwell,
Wha, as it pleases best Thysel',
Sends ane to heaven an' ten to hell,
A' for Thy glory,
And no for ony guid or ill
They've done afore Thee!

I bless and praise Thy matchless might,
Whan thousands Thou hast left in night,
That I am here before Thy sight,
For gifts an' grace
A burning an' a shining light,
To a' this place.

What was I, or my generation,
That I should get sic exaltation?
I, wha deserv'd most just damnation,
For broken laws,
Sax thousand years ere my creation,
Through Adam's cause.

Vhen from my mither's womb I fell,
'hou might hae plungéd me in hell,
'o gnash my gums, and weep and wail,
In burning lakes,
Vhere damnéd devils roar and yell,
Chained to their stakes;

et I am here, a chosen sample,
'o show Thy grace is great and ample;
m here a pillar o' Thy temple,
Strong as a rock,
. guide, a buckler, and example
To a' thy flock.

'ut yet, O Lord! confess I must
.t times I'm fashed wi' fleshly lust;
.n' sometimes too, in warldly trust,
Vile self gets in;
.ut Thou remembers we are dust,
Defiled wi' sin.

1ay be Thou lets this fleshly thorn
Beset Thy servant e'en and morn
.est he owre proud and high should turn,
That he's sae gifted;
f sae, Thy hand maun e'en be borne,
Until Thou lift it.

.ord, bless Thy chosen in this place,
'or here Thou hast a chosen race;
But God confound their stubborn face,
An' blast their name,
Vha bring Thy elders to disgrace
An' open shame!

.ord, mind Gaw'n Hamilton's deserts,
Ie drinks, an' swears, an' plays at cartes,
'et has sae mony takin' arts
Wi' grit an' sma',
'rae God's ain Priest the people's hearts
He steals awa.

An' when we chastened him therefor,
Thou kens how he bred sic a splore
As set the warld in a roar
O' laughin' at us;
Curse Thou his basket and his store,
Kail and potatoes!

.ord, hear my earnest cry an' prayer,
Against that Presbyt'ry o' Ayr!
Thy strong right hand, Lord, make it bear
Upo' their heads!
Lord, visit them, and dinna spare,
For their misdeeds.

O Lord my God, that glib-tongued Aiken,
My vera heart and soul are quakin',
To think how we stood sweatin', shakin',
An' filled wi' dread,
While he, wi' hingin' lips and snakin',
Held up his head.

Lord, in Thy day of vengeance try him!
Lord, visit him wha did employ him,
And pass not in Thy mercy by them,
Nor hear their prayer;
But, for Thy people's sake, destroy them,
And dinna spare.

But, Lord, remember me and mine
Wi' mercies temp'ral and divine,
That I for grace and gear may shine
Excelled by nane,
And a' the glory shall be Thine,
Amen, Amen!

THE LATEST DECALOGUE

Thou shalt have one God only; who
Would be at the expense of two?
No graven images may be
Worshiped, except the currency:
Swear not at all; for, for thy curse
Thine enemy is none the worse:
At church on Sunday to attend
Will serve to keep the world thy friend:
Honor thy parents: that is, all
From whom advancement may befall;
Thou shalt not kill; but need'st not strive
Officiously to keep alive:
Do not adultery commit;
Advantage rarely comes of it:
Thou shalt not steal; an empty feat,
When it's so lucrative to cheat:
Bear not false witness; let the lie
Have time on its own wings to fly:
Thou shalt not covet, but tradition
Approves all forms of competition.

—*Arthur Hugh Clough* (1819-1861)

POLITICAL SATIRE

A limerick or a popular song directed against a political candidate today will wreak havoc in his fortunes; the ballads hawked about the streets of London in the sixteenth and seventeenth centuries produced much the same effect then. Poetry as a political weapon reached its highest state of development, perhaps, in John Dryden's "Absalom and Achitophel," which almost quelled a rebellion. Spenser's "Mother Hubberd's Tale" had been much more general in its satire, but Byron's "Vision of Judgment" left very little of the reputation of George III behind it.

Goldsmith's "The Deserted Village" is familiar to all as a classic bucolic poem; beneath its idyllic surface it is a satire, directed against the policy of driving the farmers and villagers into the cities and overseas during the eighteenth century. Southey's "After Blenheim" aimed at the institution of war in the Napoleonic period, and Lowell's two series of *Biglow Papers,* one written at the time of the Mexican War and the other during the Civil War, are even more outspoken.

AFTER BLENHEIM

by Robert Southey (1774-1843)

It was a summer evening,
  Old Kaspar's work was done,
And he before his cottage door
  Was sitting in the sun;
And by him sported on the green
His little grandchild Wilhelmine.

She saw her brother Peterkin
  Roll something large and round
Which he beside the rivulet
  In playing there had found;
He came to ask what he had found
That was so large and smooth and round.

Old Kaspar took it from the boy
  Who stood expectant by;
And then the old man shook his head,
  And with a natural sigh,
" 'Tis some poor fellow's skull," said he,
"Who fell in the great victory.

"I find them in the garden,
  For there's many here about;
And often when I go to plough
  The ploughshare turns them out.
For many thousand men," said he,
"Were slain in that great victory."

"Now tell us what 'twas all about,"
  Young Peterkin he cries;
And little Wilhelmine looks up
  With wonder-waiting eyes;
"Now tell us all about the war,
And what they fought each other for."

"It was the English," Kaspar cried,
  "Who put the French to rout;
But what they fought each other for
  I could not well make out.
But every body said," quoth he,
"That 'twas a famous victory.

"My father lived at Blenheim then,
  Yon little stream hard by;
They burnt his dwelling to the ground,
  And he was forced to fly:
So with his wife and child he fled,
Nor had he where to rest his head.

"With fire and sword the country round
  Was wasted far and wide,
And many a childing mother then
  And newborn baby died:
But things like that, you know, must be
At every famous victory.

"Great praise the Duke of Marlb'ro' won
  And our good Prince Eugene."
"Why, 'twas a very wicked thing!"
  Said little Wilhelmine;

"Nay . . . nay . . . my little girl," quoth he,
"It was a famous victory.

"And every body praised the Duke
Who this great fight did win."
"But what good came of it at last?"
Quoth little Peterkin:—
"Why, that I cannot tell," said he,
"But 'twas a famous victory."

THE PIOUS EDITOR'S CREED
(from "The Biglow Papers")

by James Russell Lowell (1819-1891)

I du believe in Freedom's cause,
Ez fur away ez Payris is;
I love to see her stick her claws
In them infarnal Phayrisees;
It's wal enough agin a king
To dror resolves an' triggers,—
But libbaty's a kind o' thing
Thet don't agree with niggers.

I du believe the people want
A tax on teas an' coffees,
Thet nothin' ain't extravygunt,—
Purvidin' I'm in office;
Fer I hev loved my country sence
My eye-teeth filled their sockets,
An' Uncle Sam I reverence,
Partic'larly his pockets.

I du believe in any plan
O' levyin' the taxes,
Ez long ez, like a lumberman,
I git jest wut I axes;
I go free-trade thru thick an' thin,
Because it kind o' rouses
The folks to vote,—an' keeps us in
Our quiet custom-houses.

I du believe it's wise an' good
To sen' out furrin missions,
Thet is, on sartin understood
An' orthydox conditions;—
I mean nine thousan' dolls. per ann.,
Nine thousan' more fer outfit,
An' me to recommend a man
The place 'ould jest about fit.

I du believe in special ways
O' prayin' an' convartin';
The bread comes back in many days,
An' buttered, tu, fer sartin;
I mean in preyin' till one busts
On wut the party chooses,
An' in convartin' public trusts
To very privit uses.

I du believe hard coin the stuff
Fer 'lectioneers to spout on;
The people's ollers soft enough
To make hard money out on;
Dear Uncle Sam pervides fer his,
An' gives a good-sized junk to all,—
I don't care how hard money is,
Ez long ez mine's paid punctooal.

I du believe with all my soul
In the gret Press's freedom,
To pint the people to the goal
An' in the traces lead 'em;
Palsied the arm thet forges yokes
At my fat contracts squintin',
An' withered be the nose thet pokes
Inter the gov'ment printin'!

I du believe thet I should give
Wut's his'n unto Caesar,
Fer it's by him I move an' live,
Frum him my bread an' cheese air;
I du believe thet all o' me
Doth bear his superscription,—
Will, conscience, honor, honesty,
An' things o' thet description.

I du believe in prayer an' praise
To him thet hez the grantin'
O' jobs,—in every thin' thet pays,
But most of all in cantin';
This doth my cup with marcies fill,
This lays all thought o' sin to rest,—
I don't believe in princerple,
But oh, I du in interest.

I du believe in bein' this
Or thet, ez it may happen
One way or t'other hendiest is
To ketch the people nappin';
It ain't by princerples nor men
My preudunt course is steadied,—
I scent wich pays the best, an' then
Go into it baldheaded.

I du believe thet holdin' slaves
  Comes nat'ral to a Presidunt,
Let 'lone the rowdedow it saves
  To hev a wal-broke precedunt;
Fer any office, small or gret,
  I couldn't ax with no face,
'uthout I'd ben, thru dry an' wet,
  Th' unrizzest kind o' doughface.

I du believe wutever trash
  'll keep the people in blindness,—
Thet we the Mexicuns can thrash
  Right inter brotherly kindness,
Thet bombshells, grape, an' powder 'n' ba
  Air good-will's strongest magnets,
Thet peace, to make it stick at all,
  Must be druv in with bagnets.

In short, I firmly du believe
  In Humbug generally,
Fer it's a thing thet I perceive
  To hev a solid vally;
This heth my faithful shepherd ben,
  In pasturs sweet heth led me,
An' this'll keep the people green
  To feed ez they hev fed me.

LITERARY SATIRE

In "Sir Thopas" Chaucer burlesqued the mediaeval chivalric romance; satire on literary men and their practices has been popular ever since. Dryden's "MacFlecknoe," Pope's "Dunciad," and Byron's "English Bards and Scotch Reviewers" are perhaps historically more famous literary satires than the one example reproduced here, but Pope's "Essay on Criticism" contains some of the most famous lines on literary faults and virtues that can be found.

Pope's "Essay on Criticism" is the most distinguished of this *genre.* In it he exposes the foibles of poets—or, rather, of versifiers—and points his epigrams with devastating wit. The version that follows is a condensation of Pope's more than seven hundred lines.

FROM "AN ESSAY ON CRITICISM"

by Alexander Pope (1688-1744)

'Tis hard to say, if greater want of skill
Appear in writing or in judging ill;
But, of the two, less dang'rous is th' offense
To tire our patience, than mislead our sense.
Some few in that, but numbers err in this,
Ten censure wrong for one who writes amiss;
A fool might once himself alone expose,
Now one in verse makes many more in prose.
  'T is with our judgments as our watches, none
Go just alike, yet each believes his own.
In Poets as true genius is but rare,
True Taste as seldom is the Critic's share;
Both must alike from Heav'n derive their light,
These born to judge, as well as those to write.
Let such teach others who themselves excel,
And censure freely who have written well.
Authors are partial to their wit. 't is true,
But are not Critics to their judgment too?
  Yet if we look more closely, we shall fin
Most have the seeds of judgment in thei mind:
Nature affords at least a glimm'ring light;
The lines, though touched but faintly, ar drawn right.
But as the slightest sketch, if justly traced,
Is by ill-coloring but the more disgraced,
So by false learning is good sense defaced:
Some are bewildered in the maze of schools
And some made coxcombs Nature meant bu fools.
In search of wit these lose their commor sense,
And then turn Critics in their own defense:
Each burns alike, who can, or cannot write,
Or with a Rival's, or an Eunuch's spite.
All fools have still an itching to deride,
And fain would be upon the laughing side.
If Maevius scribble in Apollo's spite,
There are who judge still worse than he can write.

Some have at first for Wits, then Poets passed,
Turned Critics next, and proved plain fools at last.
Some neither can for Wits nor Critics pass,
As heavy mules are neither horse nor ass.
Those half-learn'd witlings, num'rous in our isle,
As half-formed insects on the banks of Nile;
Unfinished things, one knows not what to call,
Their generation's so equivocal:
To tell 'em, would a hundred tongues require,
Or one vain wit's, that might a hundred tire.
  But you who seek to give and merit fame,
And justly bear a Critic's noble name,
Be sure yourself and your own reach to know,
How far your genius, taste, and learning go;
Launch not beyond your depth, but be discreet,
And mark that point where sense and dullness meet.
  Nature to all things fixed the limits fit,
And wisely curbed proud man's pretending wit.
As on the land while here the ocean gains,
In other parts it leaves wide sandy plains;
Thus in the soul while memory prevails,
The solid pow'r of understanding fails;
Where beams of warm imagination play,
The memory's soft figures melt away.
One science only will one genius fit;
So vast is art, so narrow human wit:
Not only bounded to peculiar arts,
But oft in those confined to single parts.
Like kings we lose the conquests gained before,
By vain ambition still to make them more;
Each might his sev'ral province well command,
Would all but stoop to what they understand.
  First follow Nature, and your judgment frame
By her just standard, which is still the same:
Unerring Nature, still divinely bright,
One clear, unchanged, and universal light,
Life, force, and beauty, must to all impart,
At once the source, and end, and test of Art.
Art from that fund each just supply provides,
Works without show, and without pomp presides:
In some fair body thus th' informing soul
With spirits feeds, with vigor fills the whole,
Each motion guides, and ev'ry nerve sustains;
Itself unseen, but in th' effects, remains.
Some, to whom Heav'n in wit has been profuse,
Want as much more, to turn it to its use;
For wit and judgment often are at strife,
Though meant each other's aid, like man and wife.
'T is more to guide, than spur the Muse's steed;
Restrain his fury, than provoke his speed;
The wingéd courser, like a gen'rous horse,
Shows most true mettle when you check his course.
  Those Rules of old discovered, not devised,
Are Nature still, but Nature methodized;
Nature, like liberty, is but restrained
By the same laws which first herself ordained.

✦

  Of all the Causes which conspire to blind
Man's erring judgment, and misguide the mind,
What the weak head with strongest bias rules,
Is Pride, the never-failing voice of fools.
Whatever Nature has in worth denied,
She gives in large recruits of needful pride;
For as in bodies, thus in souls, we find
What wants in blood and spirits, swelled with wind:
Pride, where wit fails, steps in to our defense,
And fills up all the mighty Void of sense.
If once right reason drives that cloud away,
Truth breaks upon us with resistless day.
Trust not yourself; but your defects to know,
Make use of ev'ry friend—and ev'ry foe.
  A little learning is a dang'rous thing;
Drink deep, or taste not the Pierian spring.
There shallow draughts intoxicate the brain,
And drinking largely sobers us again.
Fired at first sight with what the Muse imparts,

In fearless youth we tempt the heights of Arts,
While from the bounded level of our mind
Short views we take, nor see the lengths behind;
But more advanced, behold with strange surprise
New distant scenes of endless science rise!
So pleased at first the tow'ring Alps we try,
Mount o'er the vales, and seem to tread the sky,
Th' eternal snows appear already past,
And the first clouds and mountains seem the last;
But, those attained, we tremble to survey
The growing labors of the lengthened way,
Th' increasing prospect tires our wand'ring eyes,
Hills peep o'er hills, and Alps on Alps arise!
A perfect Judge will read each work of Wit
With the same spirit that its author writ:
Survey the Whole, nor seek slight faults to find
Where Nature moves, and rapture warms the mind;
Nor lose, for that malignant dull delight,
The gen'rous pleasure to be charmed with Wit.
But in such lays as neither ebb, nor flow,
Correctly cold, and regularly low,
That, shunning faults, one quiet tenor keep,
We cannot blame indeed—but we may sleep.
In wit, as Nature, what affects our hearts
Is not th' exactness of peculiar parts;
'T is not a lip, or eye, we beauty call,
But the joint force and full result of all.

✦

Some to Conceit alone their taste confine,
And glitt'ring thoughts struck out at ev'ry line;
Pleased with a work where nothing 's just or fit;
One glaring Chaos and wild heap of wit.
Poets like painters, thus, unskilled to trace
The naked nature and the living grace,
With gold and jewels cover ev'ry part,
And hide with ornaments their want of art.
True Wit is Nature to advantage dressed,
What oft was thought, but ne'er so well expressed;
Something, whose truth convinced at sight we find,
That gives us back the image of our mind.
As shades more sweetly recommend the light,
So modest plainness sets off sprightly wit.
For works may have more wit than does 'em good,
As bodies perish through excess of blood.
Others for Language all their care express,
And value books, as women men, for Dress:
Their praise is still—the Style is excellent:
The Sense, they humbly take upon content.
Words are like leaves; and where they most abound,
Much fruit of sense beneath is rarely found,
False Eloquence, like the prismatic glass,
Its gaudy colors spreads on ev'ry place;
The face of Nature we no more survey,
All glares alike, without distinction gay:
But true expression, like th' unchanging Sun,
Clears and improves whate'er it shines upon,
It gilds all objects, but it alters none.

✦

But most by Numbers judge a Poet's song;
And smooth or rough, with them is right or wrong:
In the bright Muse though thousand charms conspire,
Her voice is all these tuneful fools admire;
Who haunt Parnassus but to please their ear,
Not mend their minds; as some to Church repair,
Not for the doctrine, but the music there.
These equal syllables alone require,
Though oft the ear the open vowels tire;
While expletives their feeble aid do join;
And ten low words oft creep in one dull line:
While they ring round the same unvaried chimes,
With sure returns of still expected rhymes;
Where'er you find "the cooling western breeze,"
In the next line, it "whispers through the trees"; [1]

[1] It is interesting to observe that while Pope ridiculed the prevalence of this rhyme, out of the five times in which he used "breeze" as a rhyme-word "trees" followed dutifully no less than four times!

If crystal streams "with pleasing murmurs creep,"
The reader's threatened (not in vain) with "sleep";
Then, at the last and only couplet fraught
With some unmeaning thing they call a thought,
A needless Alexandrine ends the song
That, like a wounded snake, drags its slow length along.
Leave such to tune their own dull rhymes, and know
What 's roundly smooth or languishingly slow;
And praise the easy vigor of a line,
Where Denham's strength, and Waller's sweetness join.
True ease in writing comes from art, not chance,
As those move easiest who have learned to dance.

SUGGESTIONS FOR ADDITIONAL READING

POEMS OF RELIGIOUS SATIRE

John Skelton, *Colin Clout*
Geoffrey Chaucer, *The Frere's Tale*
Samuel Butler, *Hudibras*
Robert Burns, *Address to the Unco Guid*
O. W. Holmes, *The Deacon's Masterpiece*
A. C. Swinburne, *The Higher Pantheism*
Rupert Brooke, *Heaven*

POEMS OF POLITICAL SATIRE

Edmund Spenser, *Mother Hubberd's Tale*
John Dryden, *Absalom and Achitophel*
Lord Byron, *A Vision of Judgment*
Oliver Goldsmith, *The Deserted Village*
Edwin Arlington Robinson, *Dionysus in Doubt*
Edgar Lee Masters, *Godbey*

POEMS OF LITERARY SATIRE

John Dryden, *MacFlecknoe*
Alexander Pope, *The Dunciad*
Alexander Pope, *Epistle to Dr. Arbuthnot*
Jonathan Swift, *On the Death of Dr. Swift*
Oliver Goldsmith, *Retaliation*
Lord Byron, *English Bards and Scotch Reviewers*
James Russell Lowell, *A Fable for Critics*
Amy Lowell, *A Critical Fable*
Arthur Guiterman, *Afternoon Tea*
Leonard Bacon, *The Furioso*

11

PLAY IN POETRY: THE POEM AS EXERCISE OR AMUSEMENT

If poetry is to reflect life, it must mirror not only its serious aspects—"Life is real, life is earnest"—but its sense of play. And if the sense of play is to be appreciated, it must be given a wider application than is usually accorded the term. For one thing, play is not the opposite of passion, but another, a lighter and, often, subtler form of it. There is, in life, the play of courtship, athletic play, play with a purpose and sportiveness for its own sake—the game whose strict rules make it the more fascinating—and the mere impulse of fun-making which is an escape from insistence upon the grim struggle of life.

So in poetry. The range of the play-instinct is almost as varied as life itself. There is the obvious gayety of sheer nonsense in the verse of Edward Lear and Lewis Carroll, but there is an intricate, even unhappy, play in the elaborate conceits of John Donne, in which metaphor often attains a monstrous exaggeration. There are the "light fantastic" bucolics of Robert Herrick—a reaction from the profound to the playful—and there are the native pastorals of Robert Frost, with their casual philosophic banter. The most metaphysical of poets have not disdained the desire to play. Gerard Hopkins delighted in verbal riotousness with a kind of wild and passionate whimsicality. Emerson indulged in grave raillery, Emily Dickinson in a divine impudence.

No poet better illustrates the tendency to mingle passion and playfulness than "holy George Herbert." In Herbert's ardent poetry, there is a devout fancifulness, a devotion no less intense for being dexterous. Herbert's fondness for typographical tricks—antedating, by more than three hundred years, E. E. Cummings' linear eccentricities—his rhymed oddities and curious religious conceits reveal the poet and minister at play, enjoying the difficult pastime of treating the most solemn themes in the most unexpected manner. Herbert reveled in metaphysical puns—one of his sacred poems has its climax in "Jesu" and "I ease you"—in anagrams and acrostics, in echo-verses ("Heaven"), poems where the lines are shaped to simulate the subject ("Easter Wings" and "The Altar") and teasing ingenuities, as in "Paradise," where a poem is constructed thus: "charm—harm—arm," "start—tart—art," etc., each new rhyme being furnished by dropping a single letter at a time. His couplet to the Virgin, playing on the anagram "Mary-Army," is typical:

ANA { MARY / ARMY } GRAM

How well her name an "Army" doth present,
In whom the Lord of Hosts did pitch His tent!
—*George Herbert* (1593-1632)

Browning's playful side is shown not only by his tricks of characterization, but by his delight in intricate and unexpected rhyme. None of Browning's intellectual calisthenics are more brilliant than the amazing rhyming effects in "Youth and Art," "A Likeness" and "The Glove." In the first two he revels in rhymes as nimbly turned as *fortunes—short tunes, piano—can know, jasmine —alas! mine, mark ace—cigar-case, examine it—Lamb in it, Vichy—is she, crony owes—Antonios, portfolio—imbroglio, keepsake—leaps ache.* In "The Glove" Browning achieves one of his greatest pieces of virtuosity; not only does he play with his technique, but he romps away with his subject. The subject was an old one in literature. In the *Essais Historiques sur Paris,* Saint Croix (or Sainfoix) told the story thus: "One day while Francis I was watching a fight between two of his lions, a lady, having dropped her glove into the arena, said to De Lorge, 'If you love me as much as you protest you do, fetch me my glove.' De Lorge went down, recovered the glove, and threw it in the lady's face." Schiller used the anecdote as early as 1797 in "Der Handschuh," adding nothing to the story. Leigh Hunt elaborated it somewhat in "The Glove and the Lions," adding King Francis' approval of the lover's scornful gesture. ("No love, quoth he, but vanity sets love a task like that!") Browning is not content to leave the tale where others had left it. With a light hand and an ironic turn, he retells the narrative through the medium of Ronsard, the Court-poet—which makes the flexible rhyming quite appropriate—gives us a view of the customs of the sixteenth-century court, wholly changes the characters of the chief actors, differs with Hunt and Schiller by defending the lady, and adds an entirely new—and logical—conclusion.

THE GLOVE
(Peter Ronsard *loquitur*)

by Robert Browning (1812-1889)

"Heigho," yawned one day King Francis,
"Distance all value enhances!
When a man's busy, why, leisure
Strikes him as wonderful pleasure,—
'Faith, and at leisure once is he?
Straightway he wants to be busy.
Here we've got peace; and aghast I'm
Caught thinking war the true pastime!
Is there a reason in metre?
Give us your speech, master Peter!"
I who, if mortal dare say so,
Ne'er am at loss with my Naso,
"Sire," I replied, "joys prove cloudlets:
Men are the merest Ixions"—
Here the King whistled aloud, "Let's
. . . Heigho . . . go look at our lions!"
Such are the sorrowful chances
If you talk fine to King Francis.

And so, to the courtyard proceeding,
Our company, Francis was leading,
Increased by new followers tenfold
Before he arrived at the penfold;
Lords, ladies, like clouds which bedizen
At sunset the western horizon.
And Sir De Lorge pressed 'mid the foremost
With the dame he professed to adore most—

Oh, what a face! One by fits eyed
Her, and the horrible pitside;
For the penfold surrounded a hollow
Which led where the eye scarce dared follow,
And shelved to the chamber secluded
Where Bluebeard, the great lion, brooded.
The king hailed his keeper, an Arab
As glossy and black as a scarab,
And bade him make sport and at once stir
Up and out of his den the old monster.
They opened a hole in the wirework
Across it, and dropped there a firework,
And fled; one's heart's beating redoubled;
A pause, while the pit's mouth was troubled,
The blackness and silence so utter,
By the firework's slow sparkling and sputter;
Then earth in a sudden contortion
Gave out to our gaze her abortion!
Such a brute! Were I friend Clement Marot
(Whose experience of nature's but narrow,
And whose faculties move in no small mist
When he versifies David the Psalmist)
I should study that brute to describe you
Illum Juda Leonem de Tribu! [1]

One's whole blood grew curdling and creepy
To see the black mane, vast and heapy,
The tail in the air stiff and straining,
The wide eyes, nor waxing nor waning,
As over the barrier which bounded
His platform, and us who surrounded
The barrier, they reached and they rested
On the space that might stand him in best stead:
For who knew, he thought, what the amazement,
The eruption of clatter and blaze meant,
And if, in this minute of wonder,
No outlet, 'mid lightning and thunder,
Lay broad, and, his shackles all shivered,
The lion at last was delivered?
Ay, that was the open sky o'erhead!
And you saw by the flash on his forehead,
By the hope in those eyes wide and steady,
He was leagues in the desert already,
Driving the flocks up the mountain,
Or catlike couched hard by the fountain
To waylay the date-gathering negress:
So guarded he entrance or egress.

[1] That lion of the tribe of Judah!

"How he stands!" quoth the King: "we may well swear,
(No novice, we've won our spurs elsewhere,
And so can afford the confession),
We exercise wholesome discretion
In keeping aloof from his threshold;
Once hold you, those jaws want no fresh hold,
Their first would too pleasantly purloin
The visitor's brisket or sirloin;
But who's he would prove so fool-hardy?
Not the best man of Marignan, pardie?"

The sentence no sooner was uttered,
Than over the rails a glove fluttered,
Fell close to the lion, and rested:
The dame 'twas, who flung it and jested
With life so, De Lorge had been wooing
For months past; he sate there pursuing
His suit, weighing out with nonchalance
Fine speeches like gold from a balance.

Sound the trumpet, no true knight's a tarrier!
De Lorge made one leap at the barrier,
Walked straight to the glove,—while the lion
Ne'er moved, kept his far-reaching eye on
The palm-tree-edged desert-spring's sapphire,
And the musky oiled skin of the Kaffir,—
Picked it up, and as calmly retreated,
Leaped back where the lady was seated,
And full in the face of its owner
Flung the glove—

"Your heart's queen, you dethrone her?
So should I"—cried the King—" 'twas mere vanity,
"Not love, set that task to humanity!"
Lords and ladies alike turned with loathing
From such a proved wolf in sheep's clothing.

Not so, I; for I caught an expression
In her brow's undisturbed self-possession
Amid the Court's scoffing and merriment,—
As if from no pleasing experiment
She rose, yet of pain not much heedful
So long as the process was needful—
As if she had tried in a crucible,
To what "speeches like gold" were reducible,
And, finding the finest prove copper,
Felt the smoke in her face was but proper;
To know what she had *not* to trust to,

Was worth all the ashes, and dust too.
She went out 'mid hooting and laughter;
Clement Marot stayed; I followed after,
And asked, as a grace, what it all meant—
If she wished not the rash deed's recallment?
"For I"—so I spoke—"am a Poet:
Human nature,—behoves that I know it!"

She told me, "Too long had I heard
Of the deed proved alone by the word:
For my love,—what De Lorge would not dare!
With my scorn—what De Lorge could compare!
And the endless descriptions of death
He would brave when my lip formed a breath,
I must reckon as braved, or, of course,
Doubt his word—and moreover, perforce,
For such gifts as no lady could spurn,
Must offer my love in return.
When I looked on your lion, it brought
All the dangers at once to my thought,
Encountered by all sorts of men,
Before he was lodged in his den,—
From the poor slave whose club or bare hands
Dug the trap, set the snare on the sands,
With no King and no Court to applaud,
By no shame, should he shrink, overawed,
Yet to capture the creature made shift,
That his rude boys might laugh at the gift,
To the page who last leaped o'er the fence
Of the pit, on no greater pretence
Than to get back the bonnet he dropped,
Lest his pay for a week should be stopped—
So, wiser I judged it to make
One trial what 'death for my sake'
Really meant, while the power was yet mine,
Than to wait until time should define
Such a phrase not so simply as I,
Who took it to mean just 'to die.'
The blow a glove gives is but weak—
Does the mark yet discolour my cheek?
But when the heart suffers a blow,
Will the pain pass so soon, do you know?"

I looked, as away she was sweeping,
And saw a youth eagerly keeping
As close as he dared to the doorway:
No doubt that a noble should more weigh
His life than befits a plebeian;
And yet, had our brute been Nemean—
(I judge by a certain calm fervor
The youth stepped with, forward to serve her)
—He'd have scarce thought you did him the worst turn
If you whispered, "Friend, what you'd get, first earn!"
And when, shortly after, she carried
Her shame from the Court, and they married,
To that marriage some happiness, maugre
The voice of the Court, I dared augur.

For De Lorge, he made women with men vie,
Those in wonder and praise, these in envy;
And in short stood so plain a head taller
That he wooed and won . . . How do you call her?
The beauty, that rose in the sequel
To the King's love, who loved her a week well;
And 'twas noticed he never would honour
De Lorge (who looked daggers upon her)
With the easy commission of stretching
His legs in the service, and fetching
His wife, from her chamber, those straying
Sad gloves she was always mislaying,
While the King took the closet to chat in,—
But of course this adventure came pat in;
And never the King told the story,
How bringing a glove brought such glory,
But the wife smiled—"His nerves are grown firmer—
Mine he brings now and utters no murmur!"

Venienti occurrite morbo! [2]
With which moral I drop my theorbo.[3]

[2] "Meet the coming disease!" A proverb indicating that it is wiser to forestall misfortune, as the lady did, than suffer unhappiness.

[3] Theorbo: a musical instrument, similar to the lute, used by Court poets and pages.

From this it is only a step to light verse. This is the division of poetry which Cowper called "familiar verse" to designate the lyric which combined sentiment and playfulness, the type which is more commonly called *vers de société*. The poetry of this kind is, as Brander Matthews wrote in *American Familiar Verse,* "less emotional, or at least less expansive than the regular lyric; and it seeks to veil the depth of its feeling behind a debonair assumption of gaiety." But true light verse does not *attempt* depth of feeling; its debonair attitude is not assumed, but natural. The colloquial, and usually gentle, flow of *vers de société* has been explained and its limitations have been defined by various commentators, by none more notably than by Frederick Locker-Lampson. Himself a skilled artisan in the medium, Locker-Lampson, in his Preface to the collection he called *Lyra Elegantiarum,* maintained it was the manner rather than the matter which determined light verse, and that such verse need not be confined to topics of everyday life. The verse itself, however, should be "graceful, refined and fanciful, not seldom distinguished by chastened sentiment, and playful. The tone should not be pitched too high; it should be terse and idiomatic and rather in the conversational key; the rhythm should be crisp and sparkling and the rhyme frequent and never forced, while the entire poem should be marked by tasteful moderation, high finish and completeness . . . for, however trivial the subject-matter may be, subordination to the rules of composition and perfection of execution are of the utmost importance."

Among the poets who have excelled in compositions of this sort first rank must be accorded Robert Herrick (1591-1674), Matthew Prior (1664-1721), W. M. Praed (1802-1839), Walter Savage Landor (1775-1864), Thomas Moore (1782-1852), Thomas Hood (1798-1845), C. S. Calverley (1831-1894), and Austin Dobson (1840-1921). Yet no writer of these brief and buoyant pieces obeyed Locker-Lampson's strictures more faithfully than Locker-Lampson himself. His "My Mistress's Boots" is characterized by the qualities he advocated—crisp rhythm, unforced rhyme, conversational tone, tasteful moderation and, "however trivial the subject-matter may be," perfection of execution.

MY MISTRESS'S BOOTS

by Frederick Locker-Lampson (1821-1895)

They nearly strike me dumb,—
I tremble when they come
Pit-a-pat:
This palpitation means
These Boots are Geraldine's—
Think of that!

O, where did hunter win
So delicate a skin
For her feet?
You lucky little kid,
You perish'd, so you did,
For my Sweet.

The faëry stitching gleams
On the sides, and in the seams,
And reveals
That the Pixies were the wags
Who tipt these funny tags,
And these heels.

What soles to charm an elf!
Had Crusoe, sick of self,
Chanced to view
One printed near the tide,
O, how hard he would have tried
For the two!

For Gerry's debonair,
And innocent and fair
As a rose;
She's an Angel in a frock,—
She's an Angel with a clock
To her hose!

The simpletons who squeeze
Their pretty toes to please
Mandarins,

Would positively flinch
From venturing to pinch
Geraldine's!

Cinderella's *left* and *rights*
To Geraldine's were frights:
And I trow
The Damsel, deftly shod,
Has dutifully trod
Until now.

Come, Gerry, since it suits
Such a pretty Puss (in Boots)
These to don,
Set your dainty hand awhile
On my shoulder, Dear, and I'll
Put them on.

Such verse has, as Locker-Lampson maintained *vers d'occasion* should have, "the same relation to the poetry of lofty imagination and deep feeling that the Dresden China shepherds and shepherdesses bear to the sculptures of Donatello and Michelangelo." No less smoothly written, preserving the same decorum, "where sentiment never surges into passion and where humor never overflows into boisterous sentiment," are Thackeray's "Peg of Limavaddy" and his "The Cane-Bottom'd Chair," Thomas Hood's "I'm Not a Single Man" and his "The Broken Dish," Thomas Moore's "The time I've lost in wooing" and his "Dear Fanny," C. S. Calverley's "Flight" and his "Ode to Tobacco," Austin Dobson's "A Song of the Four Seasons" and his "The Old Sedan Chair." Hood's tiny "To Minerva" is somewhat more jovial in spirit and the concluding pun almost violates Locker-Lampson's strictures about boisterousness.

TO MINERVA

My temples throb, my pulses boil,
I'm sick of Song and Ode and Ballad;
So, Thyrsis, take the midnight oil
And pour it on a lobster salad.

My brain is dull, my sight is foul,
I cannot write a verse, or read—
Then, Pallas, take away thine Owl,
And let us have a Lark instead.

—*Thomas Hood* (1799-1845)

Thus far no mention has been made of the American contribution to light verse; yet there has been no lack of it. The Colonial versifiers reveled in occasional verse, and the contemporaries have surpassed their English cousins in verve and variety. Eugene Field, Paul Laurence Dunbar, and James Whitcomb Riley used dialect and "straight" speech to excellent effect. Even the proverbially staid New Englanders relished the rounding and polishing of social verse. James Russell Lowell, Bayard Taylor, John Godfrey Saxe, and especially Oliver Wendell Holmes were skilled in constructing stanzas centering about the moods or manners of well-bred people. Justifying the French designation, *vers de société,* the matter was usually limited to the more cultured aspect of society, the tone was delicate, the touch was dexterous, the note was flippant or graceful or gay. When pathos was sounded, as in Holmes's exquisite "The Last Leaf," it remained decorously sad, carefully avoiding the tragic. Locker-Lampson admired this poem to the extent of copying the stanza form in his "My Mistress's Boots," quoted on page 308.

THE LAST LEAF

by Oliver Wendell Holmes (1809-1894)

I saw him once before,
As he passed by the door,
And again
The pavement stones resound,
As he totters o'er the ground
With his cane.

They say that in his prime,
Ere the pruning-knife of Time
Cut him down,
Not a better man was found
By the Crier on his round
Through the town.

But now he walks the streets,
And he looks at all he meets
Sad and wan,
And he shakes his feeble head,
That it seems as if he said,
"They are gone."

The mossy marbles rest
On the lips that he has prest
In their bloom,
And the names he loved to hear
Have been carved for many a year
On the tomb.

My grandmamma has said—
Poor old lady, she is dead
Long ago—
That he had a Roman nose,
And his cheek was like a rose
In the snow.

But now his nose is thin,
And it rests upon his chin
Like a staff,
And a crook is in his back,
And a melancholy crack
In his laugh.

I know it is a sin
For me to sit and grin
At him here;
But the old three-cornered hat,
And the breeches, and all that,
Are so queer!

And if I should live to be
The last leaf upon the tree
In the spring,
Let them smile, as I do now,
At the old forsaken bough
Where I cling.

Guy Wetmore Carryl did more than any one individual in recent times to broaden the confines of *vers de société*. His work was, as Edmund Clarence Stedman insisted light verse should be, "marked by humor, by spontaneity, joined with extreme elegance of finish, above all, by lightness of touch," but he discarded the artificiality which, too often, gave light verse the falsely patrician air of an affected *salon*. His very choice of subjects is revealing. Instead of writing about porcelain ladies and elegantly erudite gentlemen, he used, as spring-boards for his wit, Aesop, Mother Goose, and the tales of the brothers Grimm. No more brilliant verse has been published in America than Carryl's perversions of the Greek parables in *Fables for the Frivolous,* his inflation and parodying of the nursery rhymes in *Mother Goose for Grown-ups* and his wild re-writing of the familiar fairy tales in *Grimm Tales Made Gay*—all of them being crammed with surprising yet appropriate puns and all of them ending with a wholly inappropriate Moral. It is impossible to gauge how far Carryl's gifts would have taken him if he had lived to apply his extraordinary technique through maturity. He died at the age of thirty-one.

THE HARMONIOUS HEEDLESSNESS OF LITTLE BOY BLUE

by Guy Wetmore Carryl (1873-1904)

Composing scales beside the rails
That flanked a field of corn,
A farmer's boy with vicious joy
Performed upon a horn:
The vagrant airs, the fragrant airs
Around that field that strayed,
Took flight before the flagrant airs
That noisome urchin played.

He played with care "The Maiden's Prayer;"
He played "God Save the Queen,"
"Die Wacht am Rhein," and "Auld Lang Syne,"
And "Wearing of the Green:"
With futile toots, and brutal toots,
And shrill chromatic scales,
And utterly inutile toots,
And agonizing wails.

The while he played, around him strayed,
And calmly chewed the cud,
Some thirty-nine assorted kine,
All ankle-deep in mud:
They stamped about and tramped about
That mud, till all the troupe
Made noises, as they ramped about,
Like school-boys eating soup.

Till, growing bored, with one accord
They broke the fence forlorn:
The field was doomed. The cows consumed
Two-thirds of all the corn,
And viciously, maliciously,
Went prancing o'er the loam.
That landscape expeditiously
Resembled harvest-home.

"Most idle ass of all your class,"
The farmer said with scorn:
"Just see, my son, what you have done!
The cows are in the corn!"
"Oh drat," he said, "the brat!" he said.
The cowherd seemed to rouse.
"My friend, it's worse than that," he said.
"The corn is in the cows."

THE MORAL lies before your eyes.
When tending kine and corn,
Don't spend your noons in tooting tunes
Upon a blatant horn:
Or scaling, and assailing, and
With energy immense,
Your cows will take a railing, and
The farmer take offense.

Since Carryl, light verse has grown more broadly humorous and more biting. Without sacrificing its despatch and neatness of execution, it has changed from polite persiflage to ironic commentary. It may be more accurate to describe the process as a return rather than a change, for the satires of Horace, the edged lyrics of Catullus, and many of the barbed flippancies of Heine are a kind of incisive, even savage, light verse. At all events, the decorous *vers de société* of Praed and Prior, Bunner and Bret Harte, Calverley and Dobson has little except technical dexterity in common with the modern light verse of such Americans as Franklin P. Adams, Bert Leston Taylor, Arthur Guiterman, Don Marquis, Burges Johnson, Keith Preston, Alice Duer Miller, R. R. Kirk, Newman Levy, Dorothy Parker, Samuel Hoffenstein, Ogden Nash, Paul James, Selma Robinson, Marie Luhrs, and Morrie Ryskind, who, with George S. Kaufman, received the Pulitzer Prize in 1932 for the musical satire, *Of Thee I Sing*. Thus light verse, in common with every other form of poetry, has reflected the temper of the times. Here, too, the spirit is not merely one of mockery; it has turned from social badinage to social criticism.

HAPPY THOUGHT FOR SOME STRUGGLING NATION

Though the privates may never return
To the hearths and the homes that are theirs,

Since the dukes and the viscounts are safe
Need we burden the Lord with our prayers?
—*Morrie Ryskind* (1895-)

No less satiric, but quieter in tone, is Marie Luhrs' semi-historical triptych. In a flexible idiom and a half-quizzical, half-conversational key, the foreign scene, the background of intrigue, the casual amours, the very eccentricities of the characters are cannily projected.

ARIA IN AUSTRIA

by Marie Luhrs (1909-)

The Meeting

The Archduke's wife, a German princess with a jaw,
Spoke Greek with a French accent, dreamt about cube roots,
And was a high authority on Roman law;
She bore two half-wit children as their marriage fruits.

It was not strange that the Archduke loved at first sight
Ernestine pinning a tall, be-ribboned red wig
On his wife, Elsa, Princess Schwarzdorf-Neckenheit
Who was quite bald and, when her stays were off, quite big.

Ernestine was a barber's daughter, young and blonde;
The Archduke took her dancing one night—the next day
He made her a Baroness; told her he was fond
Of her—wanted to take her to the Alps to stay.

Ernestine loved the boy who drove the Archduke's carriage;
Her father explained that it was better to be
Dishonored by an Archduke than to make a marriage
Of honor with a coachman—yet how handsome he!

The barber told his daughter that the same technique
Which fascinates a coachman, fascinates a prince;
With these parting words and a kiss upon her cheek
He gave his child to royalty and did not wince.

The coachman drove her to the Tyrolean Alps;
The house was small, the garden large, its flowers scented;
She loved the Archduke instead of shampooing scalps
Or wigs for his wife who was brilliant and demented.

First the affair was a scandal; then a commonplace.
The old Emperor played chess with Elsa, let her win
To keep her and her lands and treaties in good grace
While his son went hunting in the Alps with his sin.

The Italian Dancing Master

Now and again the Archduke visited his wife
Or went to war, and his mistress was left alone

To meditate over her beads on death and life
And to walk in the garden where trees made their moan.

She listened to the waters of the fountains weep
For a day. For a day she listened to the crying
Of leaves. She opened her French book and fell asleep;
She longed for gay Paris but the French verbs were trying.

Then she sent her maid into blue Italian skies
To fetch the man who trained the Roman opera girls.
She planned to give the Archduke a pleasant surprise
By learning the new dances in costume and curls.

Before the Archduke's lady the master would caper,
His slender, turning body was cased in black satin;
Under cream lace she noted the delicate taper
Of his wrist, and his hand that hung so long and Latin.

The dancing master had a dwarf who played the clavier;
Outdoors the fountains harmonized their silver sprinkle;
Indoors beneath a plaque of the merciful Savior
The lady learned a new dance to the clavier's tinkle.

Once when the master explained a step their hands brushed . . .
The Archduke was pleased with the dance on his return,
But as time passed and a dark son was born she blushed:—
The Archduke raged and boxed her ears and made them burn.

The Parting

Perhaps the roast pork gave the Archduke indigestion,
Perhaps the heat made it too unpleasant to dine;
At any rate his mistress did not ask a question
When he flung down his napkin and left his white wine,

And strode down the garden walk and mounted his horse;
His mistress sighed, shook her head, wiped the children's noses,
While the Archduke galloped a dusty summer course
Through air that was sweet with haying and leaves and roses.

The brilliant peasant girls in the fields swung their forks
At him. Still he galloped on the road to Vienna.
Life, lately, instead of waltzes and popping corks,
Had been a hymn—and his mistress was using henna.

Thus he mused as the horse's mouth started to foam:
"We might as well be married—with three squawking brats
And one of them not mine; I'll never turn back home;
I meant to leave her like this: without any spats,

Without her tears, without a hysterical scene—
Just ride off some dreaming day and never come back;"
The evening was coming down sweet and cool and green.
The horse went slower and the reins were hanging slack.

The horse went slower, but the Archduke dangled his whip.
"I might just as well be married to her," he said,
And yet two of the children had his Hapsburg lip;
By this time all of the children would be in bed.

Before him lay Vienna and court etiquette;
Behind him a garden changing blossom with season
And three small children—he would not leave them just yet.
Later, with the ballet in town, he would have reason.

She said to him crossly, patting the horse's flanks,
"I thought you were never coming back—how I worried!"
And he said to her: "Foolish child! Is that my thanks
For bringing you a bracelet? The horse knows I hurried."

Another contemporary American, Newman Levy, has sharpened light verse with a keen critical edge. Just as Carryl burlesqued the story-element in nursery rhymes and fairy tales, so Levy reduces the "plots" of well-known operas and dramas to gay ridicule. Like Carryl, also, he luxuriates in a variety of odd verse-forms, his rhyming is adroit, the sense of play in his *Opera Guyed* and *Theatre Guyed* is alternately delicate and broad. No recent writer has been so happy in his use of "split" or "run-over" rhyme; "Thais" alone is rich in such skilful pairings as *courtesan—report is an, holy men—solely men*(tion), *wonder where—underwear, stupor sent—two per cent, solitude—folly to d*(evote), *exposure he—hosiery.* Anatole France, himself, would have relished the impudence of the burlesque. Another variation of a familiar theme—Shakespeare's *Othello*—is equally ingenious and surprising with its piling up of internal rhymes.

OTHELLO

by Newman Levy (1888-)

There lived a bold and valiant dinge who made the heathen Paynim cringe,
A gallant chap in any scrap, a brave and warlike fellow.
In Venice, by the broad canals, the lustrous-eyed Venetian gals
Exclaimed with joy, "He's quite a boy, this warrior Othello."

The rapturous adoring frails would listen to his warlike tales,
"This gallant smoke's a fearless bloke, this offspring of Bellona."
Of all the janes who listened to his thrilling deeds of derring-do
The hardest hit, I must admit, was lovely Desdemona.

She'd gaze upon his swarthy pan and coyly murmur, "What a man!"
Her aged dad felt rather sad to see this romance brewing.
"Although," he said, "I like this shine, I have to draw the color line.
I can't consent to let this gent continue with his wooing."

And so one night when all was clear they hailed a passing gondolier
And soon were tied as man and bride in lawful matrimony.
Her ancient dad was thunderstruck; said he, "My child is badly stuck.
Alas, alack, the outlook's black." Othello said, "Boloney!"

Iago was Othello's aide, a crafty double-crossing blade,
A crooked knave who viewed his brave superior with loathing.
Said he, "I think I have a plan to trick this Ethiopian.
I'll gyp the coon, and pretty soon I'll wear Othello's clothing."

Now came the bugle-call to war, and off to battle sailed the Moor,
And by his side his blushing bride looked on with fond devotion.
The enemy they quickly met and ere the evening sun had set
The Turkish fleet in grim defeat was scattered o'er the ocean.

Then brave Othello and his host sailed proudly to the Cyprus coast.
The natives cheered as he appeared, "He licked the heathen proper!"
Othello, turning to his wife, exclaimed, "I'm through with war for life.
I've done my bit and now I quit; so, baby, come to popper!"

Iago whispered, "Listen, boss, we threw them pagans for a loss.
The heathen Turks they got the works the way I knew it would be.
But now that war is left behind there's something else that's on my mind,
The Mrs., here, I greatly fear is not all that she should be."

Othello cried, "Look here, you louse, how dare you thus defame my spouse!
Like Caesar's wife, I'll stake my life, that kid's above suspicion."
Iago muttered with a cough, "I simply thought I'd tip you off.
If you don't care, that's your affair. I've stated my position.

"For I've been watching her of late with Cassio, your trusted mate,
And he's the bird, I'll give my word, that Desdemona goes with.
That handkerchief you gave your bride the night your nuptial knot was tied,
I've heard him brag that very rag's the one he blows his nose with."

"He little thinks," he said aside, "I swiped the kerchief from his bride.
I know he'd rave to find I gave his wedding gift to Cassio.
But now I think the warlike dinge begins to feel a jealous twinge;
My dusky chief with rage and grief is green as a pistachio."

Othello swore a fearful oath, "If that's the case I'll kill them both.
I'm grieved and hurt to think that skirt would willingly deceive me."
Iago sneered, "Look, here they come; observe the kerchief on that bum.
Conclusive proof, you trusting goof. Perhaps now you'll believe me."

That night the Moor with angry tread approached in rage the bridal bed,
And there the maid reclined arrayed in picturesque kimona.
She said, "My darling, why this grouch? Our interrupted bridal couch
Awaits you here, Othello dear, so come to Desdemona."

"Shut up, you jade!" Othello cried. "At last my eyes are open wide.
I've stood enough of that there stuff, you double-crossing trollop!"
He seized a pillow from the bed and crushed it down upon her head,
A smashing blow that laid her low, a cruel vicious wallop.

Attracted by Othello's shout in rushed the neighbors from without.
"You done her wrong!" exclaimed the throng that gathered there in terror.
"The handkerchief you saw was lost. Your faithful bride was double-crossed.
Iago framed your lovely dame." Othello said, "My error."

"Alas!" he cried in great distress, "what matters now a Moor or less.
My time has come. I knew that bum Iago was a Jonah!"
With that a gleaming knife he drew; into his breast the blade plunged true,
And there he died beside his bride, unhappy Desdemona.

Modern American light verse is far more varied than the *vers de société* of the past. It ranges from the whimsical suavity of Oliver Herford to the half-sentimental, half-ludicrous dialect of T. A. Daly, from the gracious courtliness of Clinton Scollard to the swift buffooneries of Ogden Nash, whose *Free Wheeling* was almost called *The King's English Murder Case* and *The Golden Trashery of Ogden Nashery*. The following seven examples by contemporary Americans are evidence of that variety. Charlotte Perkins Stetson Gilman's "A Conservative" is mocking satire; Bert Leston Taylor's "Canopus" is quiet irony; Franklin P. Adams' "On the Day After Christmas" is brilliant fooling pointed with equally brilliant rhymes; Dr. Richard Hoffmann's "Post-Mortem" is in the traditional manner of Prior with an epigrammatic twist; Richard Kirk's "Bees" is a delightful bit of malice with a touch of parody; Selma Robinson's "City Childhood" is an altogether charming flash of reminiscence, in which tenderness and irony are neatly blended; and David McCord's "A Stropshire Lad" justifies its pun by catching Housman's keen inflection.

A CONSERVATIVE

by Charlotte Perkins Stetson Gilman
(1860-)

The garden beds I wandered by
  One bright and cheerful morn,
When I found a new-fledged butterfly,
  A-sitting on a thorn,
A black and crimson butterfly
  All doleful and forlorn.

I thought that life could have no sting
  To infant butterflies,
So I gazed on this unhappy thing
  With wonder and surprise.
While sadly with his waving wing
  He wiped his weeping eyes.

Said I, "What can the matter be?
  Why weepest thou so sore?
With garden fair and sunlight free
  And flowers in goodly store,"—
But he only turned away from me
  And burst into a roar.

Cried he, "My legs are thin and few
  Where once I had a swarm!
Soft fuzzy fur—a joy to view—
  Once kept my body warm,
Before these flapping wing-things grew,
  To hamper and deform!"

At that outrageous bug I shot
  The fury of mine eye;
Said I, in scorn all burning hot,
  In rage and anger high,
"You ignominious idiot!
  Those wings are made to fly!"

"I do not want to fly," said he,
  "I only want to squirm!"
And he drooped his wings dejectedly,
  But still his voice was firm:
"I do not want to be a fly!
  I want to be a worm!"

O yesterday of unknown lack
  Today of unknown bliss!
I left my fool in red and black;
  The last I saw was this,—
The creature madly climbing back
  Into his chrysalis.

CANOPUS

When quacks with pills political would dope
  us,
When politics absorbs the livelong day,

I like to think about that star Canopus,
So far, so far away.

Greatest of visioned suns, they say who list 'em;
To weigh it science almost must despair.
Its shell would hold our whole dinged solar system,
Nor even know 'twas there.

When temporary chairmen utter speeches,
And frenzied henchmen howl their battle hymns,
My thoughts float out across the cosmic reaches
To where Canopus swims.

When men are calling names and making faces,
And all the world's ajangle and ajar,
I meditate on interstellar spaces
And smoke a mild seegar.

For after one has had about a week of
The argument of friends as well as foes,
A star that has no parallax to speak of
Conduces to repose.

—*Bert Leston Taylor* (1866-1921)

ON THE DAY AFTER CHRISTMAS

by Franklin P. Adams (1881-)

Oh, yesterday was the merry Yuletide,
But I am by a column-rule tied
To ceaseless labor. This the pay-off:
I never, never get a day off.

For if I had no daily fetters
To bind me to The Beautiful Letters,
What games there are, and how I'd play 'em
From 1 p. m. to 7 *a.* m!

Oh, what a wild and wasteful winter
I'd have were it not for the printer
And his demand for copious copy!
Verse? In the bucket but a droppie.

With ne'er a shackle I'd be able
To dally at the gaming table
Without that sorrow's crown of sorrow:
"I've got to quit, or I'm sunk tomorrow."

No one would say, when I read at night time,
"Papa, it's putting-out-the-light time.
It's twenty minutes to eleven;
Remember, you must rise at seven."

And when I'm out with this or that one,
I wouldn't leave at 12 or *at* 1;
And would I give the baby bow-boy
A target? Oh boy! *oh* boy! *OH* boy!

Gyveless, I'd seek the barracuda
In Florida or in Bermuda.
(Untrue; but that rhyme was a strangler.
I am the Incompleatest Angler).

And I could have a primrose time at
Some softly semi-tropic climate,
Where, with some elderly palooka,
I'd play six sets on green en-tout-cas.[1]

"Tut! tut!" I hear you say, explicit,
"You love your work, and how you'd miss it!"
My mental music and my mind's tone
May be the whirring of the grindstone.

(The trouble with these feathery-hearted
Poetics is, that once they're started,
Though interest—mine and yours—diminish,
They're somewhat difficult to finish.)

Although sincere and analytic
The verses seem, they're hypocritic;
For though I shout my shackles gall so,
I do those things I like to, also.

POST-MORTEM

When I shall answer Charon's call
They'll find I have no heart at all;
At my post-mortem they will say,
"He must have given it away."

When you are freed from worldly woes
What will your autopsy disclose?
Pathologists amazed shall be—
Two hearts instead of one they'll see.

And wonder shall on wonder fall;
This miracle will not be all—

[1] En-tout-cas: "at all events"—so called because of a recently invented composition used on tennis-courts which makes the court easier and faster in spite of the changes in weather.

For of the two hearts in your breast
There'll be but one shall be at rest.
—*Richard Hoffmann* (1887-)

BEES

My enemy, by a wild bee gored
(Lord, I thank Thee! I thank Thee, Lord!)

Indifferently my lampoon read,
Unhurt by anything I said—

My words, like arrow-heads of tin,
Blunting on that ass's skin!

Poets are witty men like me,
But only God can make a bee!
—*Richard R. Kirk* (1877-)

A STROPSHIRE LAD

by David McCord (1897-)

"Experience has taught me, when I am shaving of a morning, to keep watch over my thoughts, because, if a line of poetry strays into my memory, my skin bristles so that the razor ceases to act."—A. E. Housman in "The Name and Nature of Poetry."

When I was one and twenty,
With down upon the chin,
A little soap was plenty
As daily I'd begin.

Then reading Blake and William
From dark to dewy morn,
I sprang up like a trillium
Amid the Ludlow corn;

And like the starry gazer,
Myself would wrap in thought
And let the ragged razor
Attend me as it ought.

With foamy lips, and mouthy
Of Latin verbs and Greek,
I'd say a little Southey
And shave the other cheek.

But now that I am bristled,
Needs I must quote with care:
For one as over-thistled
There's little skin to spare.

By silly prose and blather
I'll not be troubled much,
But lads are hell for lather
Who think of poems and such.

So Collins, Smart, and Cowper
And him of lovely bars
I swear at like a trooper,
And furrow fresh the scars.

CITY CHILDHOOD

by Selma Robinson (1905-)

When I was a child
There was nothing I'd rather
Do than visit
My Roumanian grandfather;

He had a blonde beard
And rosy cheeks
And he lived on a street
Full of Russians and Greeks.

I was not allowed to speak
To the Greeks or Lithuanians,
For they were foreigners
And we were Roumanians.

In the afternoons
I was taken to call
In an old wine-cellar
With sausage on the wall.

I can't recollect
The wine-merchant's name,
But he gave me walnuts
Whenever I came.

Walnuts and filberts
In a trough made of wood
And told me to eat
As many as I could.

And then Grandpa would say,
"Give her water and wine
So that I may see
If she's grandchild of mine."

And I'd reach for the wine,
But not for the water,
To show that I really
Was his granddaughter.

And they fed me a sausage
  And a caraway roll
And bright red beet-soup
  In a pottery bowl. . . .

If I have a daughter
  Or if I have a son
They'll probably have little
  Of my kind of fun.

A healthier stomach
  And a better bladder
May make them stronger
  But not much gladder,

With nothing to remember
  But vegetable stews
And cod-liver doses
  And orthopedic shoes.

Closely allied to light verse, and even more obviously a result of play in poetry, is nonsense verse. Sometimes, as in Lewis Carroll's "You are old, Father William," and "How doth the little Crocodile," the nonsense is made to parody eminent poets; sometimes, as in Heinrich Hoffmann's "Struwelpeter" series, the purpose is moralizing; but, generally, nonsense verse is the expression of sheer high spirits. Here melody takes the place of meaning and ordinary words convey wild and absurd ideas. Frequently the poet is unable to reach the height of the ridiculous because of the limitations of the dictionary, so words are coined to serve his purpose. "Meloobious," "borascible," "himmeltaneous," "flumpetty," and "runcible," among others, were invented by Edward Lear, while "whiffling," "burbled," "frumious," "galumphing" and "chortled" —all from Carroll's "Jabberwocky"—have become part of literature if not of our language.

The best nonsense verse may be recognized by two features: a lovely if illogical series of sounds and a headlong, ludicrous departure from reality—all accompanied by an air of extreme seriousness. Most of the classic refrains— "With a hey, and a ho, and a hey nonino!", "Tillyvally, lady, tillyvally!" "Down-a-derry, down-a-derry"—combine these two features, features which establish a relation between the simple nonsense of Lear and much of the elaborate pretentiousness of Swinburne, which Swinburne himself realized and burlesqued. One of the chief charms of nonsense verse is the way in which the madcap music takes on a meaning of its own, a meaning seemingly profound though it makes no demands upon the intelligence. The motto of all creators of nonsense might well be, "Take care of the sounds and the sense will take care of itself."

THE POBBLE WHO HAS NO TOES

by Edward Lear (1812-1888)

The Pobble who has no toes
  Had once as many as we;
When they said, "Some day you may lose
    them all,"
  He replied, "Fish fiddle de-dee!"
And his Aunt Jobiska made him drink
Lavender water tinged with pink;
For she said, "The World in general knows
There's nothing so good for a Pobble's toes!"

The Pobble who has no toes
  Swam across the Bristol Channel;
But before he set out he wrapped his nose
  In a piece of scarlet flannel.
For his Aunt Jobiska said, "No harm
Can come to his toes if his nose is warm;
And it's perfectly known that a Pobble's toes
Are safe—provided he minds his nose."

The Pobble swam fast and well,
  And when boats or ships came near him,
He tinkledy-binkledy-winkled a bell
  So that all the world could hear him.

And all the Sailors and Admirals cried,
When they saw him nearing the farther side,
"He has gone to fish for his Aunt Jobiska's
Runcible Cat with crimson whiskers!"

But before he touched the shore—
The shore of the Bristol Channel—
A sea-green Porpoise carried away
His wrapper of scarlet flannel.
And when he came to observe his feet,
Formerly garnished with toes so neat,
His face at once became forlorn
On perceiving that all his toes were gone!

And nobody ever knew,
From that dark day to the present,
Whoso had taken the Pobble's toes,
In a manner so far from pleasant.
Whether the shrimps or crawfish gray,
Or crafty mermaids stole them away,
Nobody knew; and nobody knows
How the Pobble was robbed of his twice five toes!

The Pobble who has no toes
Was placed in a friendly Bark,
And they rowed him back and carried him up
To his Aunt Jobiska's Park.
And she made him a feast at his earnest wish,
Of eggs and buttercups fried with fish;
And she said, "It's a fact the whole world knows,
That Pobbles are happier without their toes."

An air of mock solemnity is maintained throughout *Alice in Wonderland* and *Through the Looking-Glass*. In the poems punctuating these volumes Carroll takes care of the sounds and lets the sense take care of itself; "The Lobster Quadrille," "The Walrus and the Carpenter," and "Jabberwocky" combine magic of sound and madness of meaning with such genius that their appeal is not confined to children or nonsense lovers but to all who delight in the wild interplay of serious tones and surprising syllables.

JABBERWOCKY

by Lewis Carroll (1832-1898)

'Twas brillig, and the slithy toves
Did gyre and gimble in the wabe:
All mimsy were the borogoves,
And the mome raths outgrabe.

"Beware the Jabberwock, my son!
The jaws that bite, the claws that catch!
Beware the Jubjub bird, and shun
The frumious Bandersnatch!"

He took his vorpal sword in hand;
Long time the manxome foe he sought—
So rested he by the Tumtum tree,
And stood awhile in thought.

And, as in uffish thought he stood,
The Jabberwock, with eyes of flame,
Came whiffling through the tulgey wood,
And burbled as it came!

One, two! One, two! And through and through
The vorpal blade went snicker-snack!
He left it dead, and with its head
He went galumphing back.

"And hast thou slain the Jabberwock?
Come to my arms, my beamish boy!
O frabjous day! Callooh, Callay!"
He chortled in his joy.

'Twas brillig, and the slithy toves
Did gyre and gimble in the wabe:
All mimsy were the borogoves,
And the mome raths outgrabe.

Most limericks belong in the category of nonsense verses; so do most of the jingles of Mother Goose—a circumstance which gave rise to the vogue of D'Arcy Thompson and William Brighty Rands, whose *Lilliput Levee* is still a favorite. Rands accomplished a delightful medley of nursery rhymes in "Topsy-Turvey World," the chorus of which runs:

CHORUS

Ba-ba, black wool,
Have you any sheep?
Yes, sir, a pack-full,
Creep, mouse, creep!
Four-and-twenty little maids
Hanging out the pie,
Out jumped the honey-pot,
Guy-Fawkes, Guy!
Cross-latch, cross-latch,
Sit and spin the fire,
When the pie was opened,
The bird was on the brier!

William Brighty Rands
(1823-1882)

Among the more recent writers of nonsense verse the three most original are C. S. Calverley, W. S. Gilbert and Gelett Burgess. Calverley's gift was the most literary, and his "The Cock and the Bull," though pure nonsense, is a cruel parody of Browning, while "The Auld Wife" is a broad burlesque of the ballad with a cryptic refrain.

THE AULD WIFE

by C. S. Calverley (1831-1884)

The auld wife sat at her ivied door,
(*Butter and eggs and a pound of cheese*)
A thing she had frequently done before;
And her spectacles lay on her aproned knees.

The piper he piped on the hill-top high,
(*Butter and eggs and a pound of cheese*)
Till the cow said "I die" and the goose asked "Why;"
And the dog said nothing, but searched for fleas.

The farmer he strode through the square farmyard;
(*Butter and eggs and a pound of cheese*)
His last brew of ale was a trifle hard,
The connection of which with the plot one sees.

The farmer's daughter hath frank blue eyes,
(*Butter and eggs and a pound of cheese*)
She hears the rooks caw in the windy skies,
As she sits at her lattice and shells her peas.

The farmer's daughter hath ripe red lips;
(*Butter and eggs and a pound of cheese*)
If you try to approach her, away she skips
Over tables and chairs with apparent ease.

The farmer's daughter hath soft brown hair;
(*Butter and eggs and a pound of cheese*)
And I met with a ballad, I can't say where,
Which wholly consisted of lines like these.

She sat with her hands 'neath her dimpled cheeks,
(*Butter and eggs and a pound of cheese*)
And spake not a word. While a lady speaks
There is hope, but she didn't even sneeze.

She sat with her hands 'neath her crimson cheeks;
(*Butter and eggs and a pound of cheese*)
She gave up mending her father's breeks,
And let the cat roll in her best chemise.

She sat with her hands 'neath her burning cheeks
(*Butter and eggs and a pound of cheese*),
And gazed at the piper for thirteen weeks;
Then she followed him out o'er the misty leas.

Her sheep followed her as their tails did them
(*Butter and eggs and a pound of cheese*),
And this song is considered a perfect gem,
And as to the meaning, it's what you please.

W. S. Gilbert is known throughout the world for the "book and lyrics" of *The Pirates of Penzance, Patience, H. M. S. Pinafore, The Mikado* and other comic operas for which Arthur Sullivan supplied the inimitable music. The raw metal for many of his plots may be found in *The Bab Ballads,* that priceless treasury, by which Gilbert won enduring fame as craftsman, satirist and fashioner of nonsense verse *summa cum laude*. Unlike Lear or Carroll, Gilbert did not invent curious words; his ingenuity consisted in inventing absurd situations and then treating them with the greatest gravity. His technical facility emphasized the humor of his effects, his most ridiculous plots being set to precise and unusually difficult metres.

GENTLE ALICE BROWN

by W. S. Gilbert (1836-1911)

It was a robber's daughter, and her name was Alice Brown.
Her father was the terror of a small Italian town;
Her mother was a foolish, weak, but amiable old thing;
But it isn't of her parents that I'm going for to sing.

As Alice was a-sitting at her window-sill one day,
A beautiful young gentleman he chanced to pass that way;
She cast her eyes upon him, and he looked so good and true,
That she thought, "I could be happy with a gentleman like you!"

And every morning passed her house that cream of gentlemen,
She knew she might expect him at a quarter unto ten,
A sorter in the Custom-house, it was his daily road
(The Custom-house was fifteen minutes' walk from her abode).

But Alice was a pious girl, who knew it wasn't wise
To look at strange young sorters with expressive purple eyes;
So she sought the village priest to whom her family confessed,
The priest by whom their little sins were carefully assessed.

"Oh, holy father," Alice said, " 'twould grieve you, would it not?
To discover that I was a most disreputable lot!

Of all unhappy sinners I'm the most unhappy one!"
The padre said, "Whatever have you been and gone and done?"

"I have helped mamma to steal a little kiddy from its dad,
I've assisted dear papa in cutting up a little lad.
I've planned a little burglary and forged a little check,
And slain a little baby for the coral on its neck!"

The worthy pastor heaved a sigh, and dropped a silent tear—
And said, "You mustn't judge yourself too heavily, my dear—
It's wrong to murder babies, little corals for to fleece;
But sins like these one expiates at half-a-crown apiece.

"Girls will be girls—you're very young, and flighty in your mind;
Old heads upon young shoulders we must not expect to find:
We mustn't be too hard upon these little girlish tricks—
Let's see—five crimes at half-a-crown—exactly twelve-and-six."

"Oh, father," little Alice cried, "your kindness makes me weep,
You do these little things for me so singularly cheap—
Your thoughtful liberality I never can forget;
But O there is another crime I haven't mentioned yet!

"A pleasant-looking gentleman, with pretty purple eyes,
I've noticed at my window, as I've sat a-catching flies;
He passes by it every day as certain as can be—
I blush to say I've winked at him and he has winked at me!"

"For shame," said Father Paul, "my erring daughter! On my word
This is the most distressing news that I have ever heard.
Why, naughty girl, your excellent papa has pledged your hand
To a promising young robber, the lieutenant of his band!

"This dreadful piece of news will pain your worthy parents so!
They are the most remunerative customers I know;
For many, many years they've kept starvation from my doors,
I never knew so criminal a family as yours!

"The common country folk in this insipid neighborhood
Have nothing to confess, they're so ridiculously good;
And if you marry anyone respectable at all,
Why, you'll reform, and what will then become of Father Paul?"

The worthy priest, he up and drew his cowl upon his crown,
And started off in haste to tell the news to Robber Brown;
To tell him how his daughter, who now was for marriage fit,
Had winked upon a sorter, who reciprocated it.

Good Robber Brown, he muffled up his anger pretty well,
He said, "I have a notion, and that notion I will tell;
I will nab this gay young sorter, terrify him into fits,
And get my gentle wife to chop him into little bits.

"I've studied human nature, and I know a thing or two,
Though a girl may fondly love a living gent, as many do—
A feeling of disgust upon her senses there will fall
When she looks upon his body chopped particularly small."

He traced that gallant sorter to a still suburban square;
He watched his opportunity and seized him unaware;
He took a life-preserver and he hit him on the head,
And Mrs. Brown dissected him before she went to bed.

And pretty little Alice grew more settled in her mind,
She nevermore was guilty of a weakness of the kind,
Until at length good Robber Brown bestowed her pretty hand
On the promising young robber, the lieutenant of his band.

Nonsense verse is not as prevalent today as it was; the delight of "nonsense, pure and absolute" has given way to erudite irony and satire with a purpose. Yet Hilaire Belloc, Anthony C. Deane, A. T. Quiller-Couch, and Col. D. Streamer (Harry Graham) are among the most accomplished contemporary writers of nonsense verse in England while, in this country, Gelett Burgess, Oliver Herford, Laura E. Richards, Nancy Byrd Turner, and Carolyn Wells have kept the madcap art alive. Of the latter group none has offered so rich a contribution as Gelett Burgess, inventor of the Huldy Ann Epics and the featureless Goops, who put upon his title-page "Nonsense is the Fourth Dimension of Literature," a jest which has been turned into earnest by Eugene Jolas and other exponents of "the vertigral age," "verbirrupta," "hypnologs," "mantic poetry," and a general revolution of language. The following are four of Burgess's best "antidotes to modern neurasthenia":

THE MUSE OF NONSENSE

This is the Muse of Nonsense: See!
Preposterously strained is she;
Her Figures have nor Rule nor Joint,
And so it's hard to See the Point.

✦

THE SUNSET

Picturing the Glow It Casts upon a Dish of Dough

The Sun is Low, to Say the Least,
Although it is Well-Red;
Yet, Since it Rises in the Yeast,
It Should be Better Bred!

✦

THE WINDOW PAIN

A Theme Symbolic, Pertaining to the Melon Colic

The Window has Four Little Panes;
But One have I—
The Window Pains are in its Sash;
I Wonder Why!

✦

THE PURPLE COW

I never saw a Purple Cow,
I never hope to see one;
But I can tell you, anyhow,
I'd rather see than be one!

—*Gelett Burgess*
(1866-)

SUGGESTIONS FOR ADDITIONAL READING

VERS DE SOCIÉTÉ, LIGHT OR OCCASIONAL VERSE

Robert Herrick, *Upon Julia's Clothes*
Robert Herrick, *Delight in Disorder*
Robert Herrick, *The Night Piece*
Robert Herrick, *The Bracelet*
John Suckling, *A Wedding*
John Suckling, *To My Love*
Edmund Waller, *On a Girdle*
John Milton, *On the Oxford Carrier*
Abraham Cowley, *A Lover's Chronicle*
Abraham Cowley, *The Wish*
William Cowper, *The Poplar Field*
William Cowper, *The Diverting History of John Gilpin*
Oliver Goldsmith, *An Elegy on the Death of a Mad Dog*
Matthew Prior, *Cupid Mistaken*
Matthew Prior, *An Ode*
W. M. Praed, *A Letter of Advice*
W. M. Praed, *The Belle of the Ball-Room*
W. S. Landor, *Her Lips*
W. S. Landor, *Sixteen*
W. S. Landor, *Defiance*
Thomas Moore, *The Time I've Lost in Wooing*
Thomas Moore, *Reason, Folly and Beauty*
Thomas Hood, *The Time of Roses*
Thomas Hood, *"Please to Ring the Belle"*
W. M. Thackeray, *The Ballad of Bouillabaise*
W. M. Thackeray, *The Mahogany Tree*
W. M. Thackeray, *The Cane-Bottom'd Chair*
Robert Browning, *Youth and Art*
Robert Browning, *Garden Fancies*
Robert Browning, *The Pied Piper of Hamelin*
A. C. Swinburne, *A Match*
A. C. Swinburne, *An Interlude*
C. S. Calverley, *Companions*
C. S. Calverley, *Love*
C. S. Calverley, *On the Brink*
C. S. Calverley, *Changed*
Frederick Locker-Lampson, *Geraldine*
Frederick Locker-Lampson, *A Terrible Infant*
Austin Dobson, *A Garden Idyl*
Austin Dobson, *Avice*
Austin Dobson, *The Old Sedan Chair*
Austin Dobson, *A Dialogue from Plato*
Austin Dobson, *The Ballad of Beau Brocade*
Austin Dobson, *Proverbs in Porcelain*
John Godfrey Saxe, *My Familiar*
John Godfrey Saxe, *The Coquette*
Oliver Wendell Holmes, *To an Insect*
Oliver Wendell Holmes, *Dorothy Q*
Oliver Wendell Holmes, *My Aunt*
Oliver Wendell Holmes, *Contentment*
Oliver Wendell Holmes, *The Deacon's Masterpiece*
James Russell Lowell, *Scherzo*
James Russell Lowell, *Auf Wiedersehen*
James Russell Lowell, *Without and Within*
James Russell Lowell, *Aladdin*
Bret Harte, *Her Letter*
Bret Harte, *Dolly Varden*
H. C. Bunner, *Da Capo*
H. C. Bunner, *The Maid of Murray Hill*
H. C. Bunner, *Forfeits*
Eugene Field, *To Mistress Pyrrha*
Eugene Field, *Lydia Dick*
Eugene Field, *Apple Pie and Cheese*
Guy Wetmore Carryl, *Fables for the Frivolous*
Guy Wetmore Carryl, *Mother Goose for Grown-ups*
Paul Laurence Dunbar, *Lyrics of Love and Laughter*
Oliver Herford, *The Bashful Earthquake*
Bert Leston Taylor, *Motley Measures*
Carolyn Wells, *Idle Idylls*

CONTEMPORARY LIGHT VERSE

Arthur Guiterman, *Ballads of Old New York*
Arthur Guiterman, *The Laughing Muse*
T. A. Daly, *Canzoni*
T. A. Daly, *McAroni Ballads*

Franklin P. Adams, *Tobogganing on Parnassus*
Franklin P. Adams, *Something Else Again*
R. R. Kirk, *First Editions*
Newman Levy, *Opera Guyed*
Newman Levy, *Theatre Guyed*
Morrie Ryskind, *Unaccustomed As I Am*
Dorothy Parker, *Enough Rope*
Dorothy Parker, *Sunset Gun*
Samuel Hoffenstein, *Poems in Praise of Practically Nothing*
T. S. Eliot, *Conversation Galante*
Ogden Nash, *Hard Lines*
Ogden Nash, *Free Wheeling*
Ira Gershwin, *Of Thee I Sing*
Paul James, *Shoes and Ships and Sealing Wax*
Selma Robinson, *City Child*

NONSENSE VERSE AND BURLESQUE

Edward Lear, *Nonsense Books*
Lewis Carroll, *The Hunting of the Snark*
Lewis Carroll, *Sylvie and Bruno*
Lewis Carroll, *Rhyme? and Reason?*
William Brighty Rands, *Lilliput Levee*
C. S. Calverley, *The Cock and the Bull*
C. S. Calverley, *Lovers and a Reflection*
W. S. Gilbert, *The Bab Ballads*
Col. D. Streamer, *Ruthless Rhymes for Heartless Homes*
Col. D. Streamer, *Baby's Baedecker*
A. T. Quiller-Couch, *The Famous Ballad of the Jubilee Cup*
Hilaire Belloc, *The Bad Child's Book of Beasts*
Hilaire Belloc, *More Beasts for Worse Children*
Anthony C. Deane, *New Rhymes for Old*
Gelett Burgess, *The Burgess Nonsense Book*
Laura E. Richards, *Tirra Lirra*
Nancy Byrd Turner, *Contrary Mary*
Ilo Orleans, *Father Gander*

BOOK TWO

STRUCTURE AND TECHNIQUE

CONTENTS FOR BOOK TWO

12

THE RHYTHMS OF POETRY: THE POEM AS MUSICAL MOVEMENT

Rhythm: Movement in time, characterized by equality of measures and by alternation of tension (stress) and relaxation.

—*The Century Dictionary.*

RHYTHM

POETRY, and for that matter, every form of art, is founded on rhythm, the subtle "movement in time." But rhythm and the laws of versification are scarcely the same thing. Rhythm is organic, prehistoric, embedded in the blood; versification is one of man's pleasant ingenuities, a comparatively recent invention, a by-product of his brain. Man moved to rhythm before he was conscious of it. For countless thousands of years he watched the rhythmical rotation of light and dark, felt the pulse of cold January and hot June, heard the almost metrical beat of tide-heaving seas. Long before he understood their cycles he responded to them. Later he tried to echo these rhythms, to imitate them, to summon them while fanning a fire or furling sail or composing a poem. Then he began to analyze them.

Thus man, the distance-annihilating, time-binding animal, triumphed over his environment not so much because of his physical energy or his creative activities as through his power of interpretation. He charted space, even infinity, by defining it; he exorcised the nameless ghosts by giving them a name. Poetry escaped him; it resisted definition. Interpreters succeeded only in revealing fragments of the process; the poets themselves, instruments only half aware of what twitched or caressed their strings, unriddled their art only a little more clearly than a violin attempting to explain the genius of music.

The problem of rhythm, in whose complexities is written the history of art, is a study more puzzling and profound than the most intricate of its manifestations. Were the first savage chants, outbursts of terror and triumph, shaped by the drumming of insistent feet? And were those rhythmic patterns, fundamentally urgent and regular, prompted from without by such manifestations as the pounding of tides or swung within the blood by the definite beat of the pulse? Whatever the origins, the potency of rhythm lies close to the heart of poetry's secret. Lacking intimate knowledge of the Cro-Magnons, one need not relinquish the search for its beginnings; one can trace its wavering development through the child, an emotional as well as an aesthetic primitive. The infant delights not so much in sheer clamor as in *ordered* sound: he craves a regularity in the clapping of hands, the accents of a savagely simple tune, the reiteration of alliterative syllables. He is rocked with an even motion, sung to and soothed in rhythmic measures. "The child," says Robert Lynd, "is a poet from the age at which he learns to beat a spoon on the table. He likes to make not only a noise, but a noise with something of an echo. Later on, he himself trots gloriously in reins with bells that jingle in rhythm as he runs. His pleasure in swings, in sitting behind a horse, in travelling in a train, with its puff-puff as regular as an uncle's watch and its wheels thudding out endless hexameters, arise from the same delight in rhythm. . . . Cynics may pretend that it is nurses and foolish parents who invent the language of babyhood. It is the child, however, who feels that a sound does not mean enough till it has rhymed itself double, and who of its own accord will gravely murmur 'cawr-cawr' to a scratching hen, 'wow-wow' to a dog," and, as Lynd might have added, "moo-moo" to the casual cow or "quack-quack" to describe a duck with onomatopoeic precision.

From this earliest delight in elementary rhythm, childhood may be said to sing its way to youth through poetry. Children learn the intricacies of language through verse rather than prose; their first accounts of a bewildering world do not come from a prosy father but through the chiming cadences of a melodic Mother Goose. They ring changes on the bells of rhyme before they sound the duller gamut of colloquial speech. It is in the flush of awakening life that this rhythmic impulse finds its highest gratification; mornings are saturated with sentiments that sing themselves into tune; strophes fall in prodigal showers through the burning air. Almost every boy is not only a potential but a practising poet, every girl a half-sister to Sappho. Lyrics, flowering with a punctuality of pattern, outnumber the daffodils. So through adolescence the young life turns to poetry for its clearest and most intense expression.

Suddenly we are aware of a complete change. Maturity proclaims itself by contradicting the poetic attitude of youth; "shades of the prison-house begin to close." Fancy has no place in a world of facts; the "practical" person ceases to be concerned not only with the writing of poetry but the reading of it. Even the thinker whose search for finalities is the pursuit of a vision, treats the imaginative mind with the same smiling depreciation that he bestows upon the immature one. The nature of maturity seems to fasten upon this defensive revulsion, a sweeping disavowal of all that man cherished during his formative years. The child in the grown man must be denied, a process generally accomplished by simultaneously scorning and eradicating (as far as consciousness can perform the task) all the creative images and associations of childhood. And poetry, being the earliest, most closely intertwined, suffers the heaviest repudiation.

The fluctuations of the poetic attitude, still less than half-explained, will not be clarified until the depths themselves are analyzed. And beneath the undercurrent of self-hypnotic states, emotional conflicts, poetry's occasional employment of the dream-mechanism and the still deeper mystery of language, there lies the wellspring of rhythm. It is, first of all, physical—we feel it in the breath, the pulse; we measure it in our walking stride; we quicken to it in the sway of the dance. It is psychological—we listen, with dread or delight, to the ticking of a clock; we are lulled by the swing of a cradle-song, excited by a drum or the roaring beat of an airplane motor. It is emotional—we release our passions through simulating larger rhythms; we shape our dreams and desires, hates and hungers through the creation of sonnets and symphonies, canvases and cathedrals, only through the understanding of the laws of rhythm. Cazamian speaks even of a "national rhythm" or the "rhythm of a century" in thought.

Thus rhythm is the nucleus, the germinal power of life, flowing through all natural forces, the carrier of every form of energy. There is nothing in nature from the swing of the solar system to the climb of a blade of grass that does not persist in recurrent movements. Day and night, the march of seasons, the pattern of a leaf, the wave-lengths of light, and the periodic functions of human life have a rhythm that is as regular as it is insistent. Applied to the arts, and in particular to the art of writing, it becomes obvious that rhythm is not, as many interpreters have defined it, a pleasant accompaniment, a colorful accessory of poetry, but the quality by virtue of which literature exists, the power which poetry has exploited and made articulate.

FOOT AND METER

How fully can these rhythms communicate themselves without analysis? How much will they permit dissection without losing their life-blood? Only the sensitive surgeon can determine the degree, only the dexterous student can tell when to probe and when to hold his hand.

It is a question whether rhythm can actually be "taught," whether much should be done beyond "exposing" the pupil to the poem. It seems certain, however, that the pedantic application of rules and technical terms is an obstacle to the appreciation of poetry. Nothing can so quickly quench the young reader's delight in verse as the suspicion that he is not meant to share an enjoyment which the poet felt in the act of creation, but that the poem is merely an excuse for studies in scansion and problems in involved metrics—problems of which the poet was, usually, unaware. Robert Frost once heard a teacher say to his class, "We will read this poem three times—first for syntax, second for meaning, third for beauty." If any "beauty" survived, it was not because of the process; after a poem has been so taken apart it resembles nothing so much as a dismembered jig-saw puzzle—the pieces are there, many of them curiously shaped and quaintly colored, but the picture, the poem itself, has vanished.

Poetry is not founded on the laws of versification. One might go further and say that these laws have been imposed upon poetry—and that most poets are ignorant of them, or have violated them or, pointing to the constant exceptions, have disputed the rules. The poets' rhythms, they will tell you, are alive and fluctuant, dependent not upon a metrical yardstick, but upon the breath, the temperament and the emotional response of the reader; the accents may well vary with various interpreters—just as the notes of a Beethoven symphony may be variously stressed by different conductors.

Nevertheless, before the rules can be interpreted they must be known. For convenience as well as criticism, the technical terms and traditional forms are given in this chapter without, however, attempting such classifications (dubious and controversial) as "ascending" and "falling" meters. Nor will there be any account of such exotic divisions as the *pyrrhic* foot, or the *amphimacer,* or the *amphibrach*—Latin units which have no real equivalents in English.

The very nature of accent has given rise to controversy, some scholars maintaining it is due to a change in pitch of the voice, others to an increase of volume of tone. It is, however, generally accepted as *stress* and it is this stress or accent which determines the rhythms in English verse. The meaning of spoken English and even the differentiation of words depend upon accentuation. This is not true of French, where there is very little if any differentiation in syllabic accent. The result is that French poetry is written in units of the line, with rigid insistence upon the *number* of syllables. For example: "J'aime de tes concerts la sauvage harmonie" (Lamartine). The measures of Greek and Latin poetry were not governed by accent, but based upon quantity—the time consumed in pronouncing a syllable, a long syllable being considered equal to two short syllables—the laws governing quantity being far stricter than the rules determining English verse. Classical prosody lists about thirty different "feet," but the fundamental ones in English are four—a fifth (the *spondee*) being occasionally employed.

FEET

A "foot" is the rhythmical unit of a line of poetry. The dissyllabic (two syllable) feet are *iambic* and *trochaic* and form "duple" (or double) meters; the trisyllabic (three syllable) feet are *dactylic* and *anapestic* and form "triple" meters.

THE IAMBIC FOOT

The iambic foot consists of an unaccented syllable followed by an accented one, such as the child experiences in "skipping"—the light touch of the toe followed by the firm planting of the foot. We might, therefore, Anglicize the name to "skipping foot." It may be expressed thus: ˘ ´ . Such words as *again, oppose, delight, began,* are, in themselves, iambic feet. It is the commonest of rhythmical stresses, seen in its musical form in "The Farmer in the Dell" and other simple melodies. English verse is founded on the iambic beat; it is claimed that our ordinary speech tends to fall into iambics partly because of the great prevalence of monosyllabic and disyllabic words, partly because our minds enjoy the finality of end-stress. Two examples of varying length:

> The grave's a fine and private place,
> But none, I think, do there embrace.
>
> —*Marvell*

> Or where the beetle winds
> His small but sullen horn.
>
> —*Collins*

THE TROCHAIC FOOT

The trochaic foot consists of an accented syllable followed by an unaccented one. It is the rhythm of the military march—the "1, 2, 3, 4, hep,—hep,—" of the sergeant calling step. It might be called the "marching foot." It may be expressed thus: ´ ˘. Such words as *heartless, answer, tender, softly, going* are, in themselves, trochaic feet. Four examples:

> I a light canoe will build me . . .
> Like a yellow leaf in Autumn.
> —*Longfellow*

> Double, double, toil and trouble;
> Fire burn and cauldron bubble.
> —*Shakespeare*

> Once upon a midnight dreary,
> While I pondered, weak and weary—
> —*Poe*

> Meadows trim with daisies pied,
> Shallow brooks and rivers wide.
> —*Milton*

It should be noted that the fourth example of trochaic feet lacks the last unaccented syllable at the end of the line. This deficiency (the scholarly term being *catalectic*) is more common than a completed trochaic line (*acatalectic*) and complete trochaic meters of the "Hiawatha" type are comparatively rare.

THE DACTYLIC FOOT

The dactylic foot consists of three syllables: an accented syllable followed by two unaccented ones. This is the "waltz rhythm," the "three-quarters" time of "The Beautiful Blue Danube." It often has a lulling affect. It may be expressed thus: ´ ˘ ˘. Such words as *violet, rhapsody, fugitive, tenderness, silently,* are, in themselves, dactylic feet. Two illustrative examples of different line lengths:

> Perishing gloomily,
> Spurred by contumely,
> Cold inhumanity,
> Burning insanity.
> —*Hood*

> This is the forest primeval. The murmuring pines and the hemlocks,
> Bearded with moss and in garments green, indistinct in the twilight . . .
> —*Longfellow*

In the second example, it will be observed that the second line skips a beat and that the last foot is not completed, lacking one syllable *(catalectic)*, a common feature of dactylic poems of any length.

THE ANAPESTIC FOOT

The anapestic foot consists of three syllables: two unaccented syllables followed by an accented syllable. This, too, is waltz rhythm, starting on the "off beat," as in a gallop. We hear it in the notes of the bugle-call, "To the Colors." It may be expressed thus: ˘ ˘ ´ . Such words as *cavalier, supersede, disappear, intervene, rataplan* are, in themselves, anapestic feet. It is usually (not always, as Swinburne's "Forsaken Garden" will show) a speedy and propulsive rhythm, difficult to maintain. An example:

The Assyrian came down like a wolf on the fold,
And his cohorts were gleaming in purple and gold.
—*Byron*

THE SPONDEE

The spondee consists of two strong, equally accented syllables, such as *barnyard, wine-glass, homesick, farewell.* Few lines can be composed exclusively of spondees, the foot being used chiefly for occasional emphasis.

Samuel Taylor Coleridge has written an amusing rhymed diagram in his "Lesson for a Boy," which begins:

Trochee trips from long to short.
From long to long in solemn sort
Slow Spondee stalks: strong foot! yet ill able
Ever to come up with Dactyl trisyllable.
Iambics march from short to long—
With a leap and a bound the swift Anapests throng . . .

Poetry, like music, can secure variations in its rhythmical effects by rests, substitutions of one type of foot for another, elisions, and changes of tempo. Thus:

Break, break, break,
On thy cold grey stones, O sea.

METERS

THE METER

The meter (or measure) of a verse is determined by the number of feet in the line. The terms explain themselves: *monometer:* one foot; *dimeter:* two feet; *trimeter:* three feet; *tetrameter:* four feet; *pentameter:* five feet; *hex-*

ameter: six feet; *heptameter:* seven feet; *octameter:* eight feet. The combination of accent and meter give the verse its classic characterization. Thus:

Ĭngrát | ĭtúde, | thŏu már | blĕ-heárt | ĕd fiénd.

The alternating unaccented and accented beat shows this to be an iambic line; the division shows the line to consist of five feet. Therefore, the verse is an example of *iambic pentameter.*

A poem in *monometer,* the shortest of all measures, is a rarity, but one of the loveliest comes from the seventeenth century:

UPON HIS DEPARTURE HENCE

Thus I
Pass by
And die:

As one
Unknown
And gone

I'm made
A shade
And laid

I' th' grave:
There have
My cave,

Where tell
I dwell.
Farewell.

—*Robert Herrick*
(1591-1674)

The poem, it will be seen, is in *iambic monometer* and, since it is divided into stanzas of three lines, is built of *tercets.*

It will be interesting to compare the set of tercets just quoted with those that follow. Both poems are composed of three-line stanzas; the preceding poem is in the shortest of meters (*monometer*), the following is in the longest *(octameter);* the movement of the first is *iambic,* that of the second is *trochaic.*

A TOCCATA OF GALUPPI'S

by Robert Browning (1812-1889)

O Galuppi, Baldassare, this is very sad to find!
I can hardly misconceive you; it would prove me deaf and blind;
But although I take your meaning, 'tis with such a heavy mind!

Here you come with your old music, and here's all the good it brings.
What, they lived once thus at Venice where the merchants were the kings,
Where St. Mark's is, where the Doges used to wed the sea with rings?

Ay, because the sea's the street there; and 'tis arched by . . . what you call
. . . Shylock's bridge with houses on it, where they kept the carnival:
I was never out of England—it's as if I saw it all.

Did young people take their pleasure when the sea was warm in May?
Balls and masks begun at midnight, burning ever to mid-day,
When they made up fresh adventures for the morrow, do you say?

Was a lady such a lady, cheeks so round and lips so red,—
On her neck the small face buoyant, like a bell-flower on its bed,
O'er the breast's superb abundance where a man might base his head?

Well, and it was graceful of them—they'd break talk off and afford
—She, to bite her mask's black velvet—he, to finger on his sword,
While you sat and played Toccatas, stately at the clavichord?

What? Those lesser thirds so plaintive, sixths diminished, sigh on sigh,
Told them something? Those suspensions, those solutions—"Must we die?"
Those commiserating sevenths—"Life might last! we can but try!"

"Were you happy?"—"Yes."—"And are you still as happy?"—"Yes. And you?"
—"Then, more kisses!"—"Did *I* stop them, when a million seemed so few?"
Hark, the dominant's persistence till it must be answered to!

So, an octave struck the answer. Oh, they praised you, I dare say!
"Brave Galuppi! that was music! good alike at grave and gay!
I can always leave off talking when I hear a master play!"

Then they left you for their pleasure: till in due time, one by one,
Some with lives that came to nothing, some with deeds as well undone,
Death stepped tacitly and took them where they never see the sun.

But when I sit down to reason, think to take my stand nor swerve,
While I triumph o'er a secret wrung from nature's close reserve,
In you come with your cold music till I creep through every nerve.

Yes, you, like a ghostly cricket, creaking where a house was burned:
"Dust and ashes, dead and done with, Venice spent what Venice earned.
The soul, doubtless, is immortal—where a soul can be discerned.

"Yours for instance: you know physics, something of geology,
Mathematics are your pastime; souls shall rise in their degree;
Butterflies may dread extinction,—you'll not die, it cannot be!

"As for Venice and her people, merely born to bloom and drop,
Here on earth they bore their fruitage, mirth and folly were the crop:
What of soul was left, I wonder, when the kissing had to stop?

"Dust and ashes!" So you creak it, and I want the heart to scold.
Dear dead women, with such hair, too—what's become of all the gold
Used to hang and brush their bosoms? I feel chilly and grown old.

The remarks on rhythm and the analyses of metrical feet are applicable in retrospect to all poems previously read as well as to all others which may be encountered. They have a particular bearing upon the study of stanza-structure in the following chapter. Meanwhile a warning should be issued against accepting too literally the old categories of "falling" and "rising" rhythms. These "ascending" or "descending" classifications are scarcely fundamental; they are actually misleading, for much depends upon the interpreter, on the very ascent or decline of the reader's voice. Nor is it true that the duple meters (*iambic* and *trochaic*) are more adapted to slower-paced themes while the triple meters (*dactylic* and *anapestic*) are the more rapidly running. The dactylic measure may well gather speed in Browning's "Cavalier Tune," but nothing can be graver than the same rhythm in Longfellow's "Evangeline."

FROM "EVANGELINE"

This is the forest primeval. The murmuring pines and the hemlocks,
Bearded with moss, and in garments green, indistinct in the twilight,
Stand like Druids of eld, with voices sad and prophetic,
Stand like harpers hoar, with beards that rest on their bosoms.
Loud from its rocky caverns, the deep-voiced neighboring ocean
Speaks, and in accents disconsolate answers the wail of the forest.

This is the forest primeval; but where are the hearts that beneath it
Leaped like the roe, when he hears in the woodland the voice of the huntsman?
Where is the thatch-roofed village, the home of Acadian farmers,—
Men whose lives glided on like rivers that water the woodlands,
Darkened by shadows of earth, but reflecting an image of heaven?
Waste are those pleasant farms, and the farmers forever departed!
Scattered like dust and leaves, when the mighty blasts of October
Seize them, and whirl them aloft, and sprinkle them far o'er the ocean.
Naught but tradition remains of the beautiful village of Grand-Pré.

—*Henry Wadsworth Longfellow* (1807-1882)

CAVALIER TUNE

Boot, saddle, to horse, and away!
Rescue my castle before the hot day
Brightens to blue from its silvery gray.
Chorus—Boot, saddle, to horse, and away!

Ride past the suburbs, asleep as you'd say;
Many's the friend there, will listen and pray
"God's luck to gallants that strike up the lay—
Chorus—Boot, saddle, to horse, and away!"

Forty miles off, like a roebuck at bay,
Flouts Castle Brancepeth the Roundheads' array:
Who laughs, "Good fellows ere this, by my fay,
Chorus—Boot, saddle, to horse, and away!"

Who? My wife Gertrude; that, honest and gay,
Laughs when you talk of surrendering, "Nay!
I've better counsellors; what counsel they?
Chorus—Boot, saddle, to horse, and away!"

—*Robert Browning* (1812-1889)

Contrast the use of iambics in the two poems that follow, two poems which illustrate variety of speeds as well as serenity of contemplation contrasted with swift action—both being achieved by the same accent.

THE WAR SONG OF DINAS VAWR

by Thomas Love Peacock (1785-1866)

The mountain sheep are sweeter,
But the valley sheep are fatter;
We therefore deemed it meeter
To carry off the latter.
We made an expedition;
We met a host and quelled it;
We forced a strong position,
And killed the men who held it.

On Dyfed's richest valley,
Where herds of kine were browsing,
We made a mighty sally,
To furnish our carousing.
Fierce warriors rushed to meet us;
We met them, and o'erthrew them:
They struggled hard to beat us;
But we conquered them, and slew them.

As we drove our prize at leisure,
The king marched forth to catch us:
His rage surpassed all measure,
But his people could not match us.
He fled to his hall-pillars;
And, ere our force we led off,
Some sacked his house and cellars,
While others cut his head off.

We there, in strike bewildering,
Spilt blood enough to swim in:
We orphaned many children,
And widowed many women.
The eagles and the ravens
We glutted with our foemen;
The heroes and the cravens,
The spearmen and the bowmen.

We brought away from battle,
And much their land bemoaned them,
Two thousand head of cattle,
And the head of him who owned them:
Ednyfed, King of Dyfed,
His head was borne before us;
His wine and beasts supplied our feasts,
And his overthrow, our chorus.

VIRTUE

Sweet day, so cool, so calm, so bright!
The bridal of the earth and sky—
The dew shall weep thy fall tonight;
    For thou must die.

Sweet rose, whose hue angry and brave
Bids the rash gazer wipe his eye,
Thy root is ever in its grave,
    And thou must die.

Sweet spring, full of sweet days and roses,
A box where sweets compacted lie,
My music shows ye have your closes,
    And all must die.

Only a sweet and virtuous soul,
Like seasoned timber, never gives;
But though the whole world turn to coal
    Then chiefly lives.

—*George Herbert* (1593-1632)

13

THE PATTERNS OF POETRY—1: THE POEM AS ARCHITECTURE

Architecture has been characterized as "frozen music." Poetry might well be termed a "verbal architecture." The rules governing the composition of a ballade are as fixed as the laws determining the construction of a bridge; the structure of a sonnet is as precise as that of a skyscraper. The poet enjoys working with a resisting medium; inspired though he may be, he knows inspiration alone will not do the work for him. He becomes a craftsman, realizing with Gautier:

> Fair things grow fairer still
> When polished clean as bone
> With skill—
> The stanza or the stone.

The sculpture or architecture of poetry is an intricate one, but its elements are simple. Feet—as analyzed in the preceding chapter—are combined into the structure of a line; lines are combined into the pattern of a poem. Each pattern, or stanza-form, has distinct characteristics and is immediately recognizable, whether it is as unpretentious as the couplet or as elaborate as *ottava rima* and the Spenserian stanza. Before analyzing these structures, it may be well to examine two common but "looser" forms: free verse and blank verse.

FREE VERSE

Free Verse or, as it is sometimes called by its French equivalent, *vers libre,* is based upon a broad (and often irregular) movement rather than on a fixed pattern; it might be said to be founded on a *general* rhythm rather than on any precise meter. The late Amy Lowell, a pioneer as well as one of the chief modern exponents of this form, declared that "since verse is verse just *because* it has more pattern than prose, free verse is a misnomer; verse can never be free. The best name for this form in English would be 'cadenced verse' for it is based upon cadence rather than upon actual meter. Metrical verse seeks its effects chiefly through definite lilt of meter and the magic and satisfaction of chime. 'Cadenced verse' gets its effects through subtle shades of changing rhythms and through a delicate sense of balance."

The unit of free verse is the *strophe,* not the line nor the foot as in regular meter. The strophe, in Greek drama, was the full circle made by the chorus while walking about the altar, chanting the ode. The length of time varied, but it was always one completed movement. Therefore, the strophe applied to modern verse means one completed round (a cadence), or a series of such units. In short free-verse poems the strophe may be the entire poem; in longer ones there is usually a succession of strophes. However, though free verse dispenses with any decided meter, it employs all the other assets of poetry: assonance, alliteration, balance—even, though not always, rhyme.

Derided as "shredded prose" free verse has often degenerated into mere uncontrolled garrulity. But so, its defenders may retort, has much formal verse. Its uncertain outlines make it a dangerous model, but at its best it is capable of undeniable eloquence and flexibility.

In America, Whitman blazed the path for all followers of the form as early as 1855 with the publication of the elemental *Leaves of Grass*. Half a century earlier Heinrich Heine had employed the form to express the hoarse music of the tides in his two cycles entitled *The North Sea*. Anticipating the modern poets by more than two thousand years, the Hebrew seers and psalmists evoked their God and their greatest effects in this medium. The Bible is built up of "cadenced verse." Ancient Hebrew poetry is founded on balance and repetition: instead of rhyme it makes use of alliteration and assonance; instead of fixed meter, it is composed in a "strophic" measure. The King James version recaptures the flow and fervor of the Hebraic music. The Psalms, the Song of Songs, the Lamentations of Jeremiah, the tremendous images in Job are couched in a free verse which delights the ear and which the mind will not relinquish.

My belovèd spake, and said unto me,
"Rise up, my love, my fair one, and come away.
For lo! the winter is past, the rain is over and gone;
The flowers appear upon earth; the time of the singing birds is come;
And the voice of the turtle is heard in our land.
The fig-tree putteth forth her green figs,
And the vines with the tender grape give a good smell.
Arise, my love, my fair one, and come away . . ."
My belovèd is mine, and I am his—
He feedeth among the lilies.
Until the day break and the shadows flee away,
Turn, my belovèd, and be thou like a roe
Or a young hart upon the mountains of Bether.

—*The Song of Songs*

Hast thou given the horse strength?
Hast thou clothed his neck with thunder?
Canst thou make him afraid as a grasshopper?
The glory of his nostrils is terrible.
He paweth in the valley, and rejoiceth in his strength;
He goeth on to meet the armed men.
He mocketh at fear, and is not affrighted,
Neither turneth he back from the sword.
The quiver rattleth against him,
The glittering spear and the shield,

He swalloweth the ground with fierceness and rage;
Neither believeth he that it is the sound of the trumpet.
He saith among the trumpets, Ha, ha!
And he smelleth the battle afar off.

✦

Where wast thou when I laid the foundations of the earth?
Declare, if thou hast understanding.
Who hath laid the measures thereof, if thou knowest,
Or who hath stretched the line upon it?
Whereupon are the foundations thereof fastened?
Or who laid the cornerstone thereof,
When the morning stars sang together,
And all the sons of God shouted for joy?
Or who shut up the sea with doors
When it brake forth, as if it had issued out of the womb?
When I made the cloud the garment thereof
And thick darkness a swaddling band for it,
And brake up for it my decreed place,
And set bars and doors,
And said, Hitherto shalt thou come, but no further:
And here shall thy proud waves be stayed? . . .
Hath the rain a father? Or who hath begotten the drops of dew?
Out of whose womb came the ice?
And the hoar-frost of Heaven, who hath 'gendered it?
The waters are hid as with a stone,
And the face of the deep is frozen.
Canst thou bind the sweet influences of Pleiades?
Or loose the bands of Orion?
Canst thou bring forth Mazzaroth in his season?
Or canst thou guide Arcturus with his sons?

—*The Book of Job*

Other examples of free verse quoted in this volume are "Lilacs" by Amy Lowell (page 31), "The Gale" by John Gould Fletcher (page 32), "Images" by Richard Aldington (page 32), "From 'Crossing Brooklyn Ferry' " by Walt Whitman (page 42), "Smoke and Steel" by Carl Sandburg (page 54), "When Lilacs Last in the Dooryard Bloomed" by Walt Whitman (page 179), "With Husky-Haughty Lips" by Walt Whitman (page 206), "The Grass" by Walt Whitman (page 218), "Margaritae Sorori" by W. E. Henley (page 223), "Give Me the Splendid Silent Sun" by Walt Whitman (page 236), "From 'The Windy City' " by Carl Sandburg (page 241), "Blue Island Intersection" by Carl Sandburg (page 243), "Impression: IV" by E. E. Cummings (page 243), "From 'The Broken Balance' " by Robinson Jeffers (page 273), and "Dirge for Two Veterans" by Walt Whitman (page 438).

BLANK VERSE

The term "blank verse" commonly refers to the unrhymed five-foot iambic line, that most majestic and sonorous instrument of English verse. It is the medium of the dramas of Marlowe and Shakespeare, the epics of Milton, the panoramas of Browning. Although the term *iambic pentameter* immediately suggests the Elizabethan plays, unrhymed "fives" were originally introduced into English verse from the Italian by Henry Howard, Earl of Surrey (1517-1547). But the iambic pentameter which Howard used to translate Virgil's *Aeneid* was a far less flexible form than the fiery blank verse fashioned by Marlowe. Of all Marlowe's "purple patches" none is more brilliant and breath-catching than the address of Faustus to Helen of Troy, whom the magician has called forth from the grave.

FROM "DOCTOR FAUSTUS"

Was this the face that launch'd a thousand ships,
And burnt the topless towers of Ilium?—
Sweet Helen, make me immortal with a kiss.—
Her lips suck forth my soul: see, where it flies!—
Come, Helen, come, give me my soul again.
Here will I dwell, for heaven is in these lips,
And all is dross that is not Helena.
I will be Paris, and for love of thee,
Instead of Troy, shall Wittenberg be sack'd;
And I will combat with weak Menelaus,
And wear thy colours on my plumèd crest;
Yea, I will wound Achilles in the heel,
And then return to Helen for a kiss.
O, thou art fairer than the evening air
Clad in the beauty of a thousand stars;
Brighter art thou than flaming Jupiter
When he appear'd to hapless Semele;
More lovely than the monarch of the sky
In wanton Arethusa's azur'd arms;
And none but thou shalt be my paramour!

—*Christopher Marlowe* (1564-1593)

In the hands of Shakespeare blank verse gradually attained an incredible richness and flexibility. In Shakespeare's dramas it ranges from the most direct colloquial speech to the highest reach of rhetoric. It can be as quietly carved as this passage from "Twelfth Night":

. . . She never told her love,
But let concealment, like a worm i' the bud,
Feed on her damask cheek: she pin'd in thought,
And with a green and yellow melancholy,
She sat like Patience on a monument,
Smiling at grief.

It can cry out its passion with the agony of the tortured Othello:

. . . O, now, forever
Farewell the tranquil mind; farewell content!
Farewell the plumèd troop and the big wars
That make ambition virtue! O, farewell!

Farewell the neighing steed, and the shrill trump,
The spirit-stirring drum, the ear-piercing fife,
The royal banner, and all quality,
Pride, pomp, and circumstance of glorious war!
And, O you mortal engines, whose rude throats
The immortal Jove's dread clamours counterfeit,
Farewell! Othello's occupation's gone!

Or it can move as confidently and proudly as the famous speech from "King Richard the Second," perhaps the noblest patriotic apostrophe ever composed:

This royal throne of kings, this scepter'd isle,
This earth of majesty, this seat of Mars,
This other Eden, demi-paradise,
This fortress built by Nature for herself
Against infection and the hand of war,
This happy breed of men, this little world,
This precious stone set in the silver sea,
Which serves it in the office of a wall,
Or as a moat defensive to a house,
Against the envy of less happier lands,
This blessèd plot, this earth, this realm, this England.
—*William Shakespeare* (1564-1616)

The "Puritan" blank verse of John Milton is of an entirely different texture. Less luxuriant than the Elizabethans', it moves with an almost divine dignity; it is less ecstatic than Shakespeare's but more exalted. The blank verse of Milton's "Paradise Lost," "Paradise Regained," and "Samson Agonistes" sacrifices sensuousness for sonority—and the effect is sublimity. An illustrative fragment is the speech of Satan in Book Four of "Paradise Lost":

SATAN SPEAKS

O Thou, that with surpassing glory crowned,
Look'st from thy sole dominion like the god
Of this new world; at whose sight all the stars
Hide their diminished heads; to thee I call,
But with no friendly voice, and add thy name,
O sun! to tell thee how I hate thy beams,
That bring to my remembrance from what state
I fell, how glorious once above thy sphere,
Till pride and worse ambition threw me down
Warring in heaven against heaven's matchless king. . . .

Me miserable! which way shall I fly
Infinite wrath and infinite despair?
Which way I fly is hell; myself am hell;
And, in the lowest deep, a lower deep
Still threatening to devour me opens wide,
To which the hell I suffer seems a heaven.
—*John Milton* (1608-1674)

The blank verse of William Wordsworth is more pedestrian; his "The Prelude" affects us because of its autobiographical sincerity, not because of its music. Far more resonant is the blank verse of Keats—at its purest in "Hyperion"—and that of Tennyson, notably in his "Ulysses." The form itself has grown so flexible that it can deviate from strict metrical regularity without injuring the onrolling line—in fact the departures, the endless kaleidoscope of effects, reveal its inexhaustible power. As in a clog or tap dance, the pattern is established, and then varied upon. Possibly its greatest asset is this adaptability; such sharply differentiated poets as Robert Browning and Robert Frost have implanted their own idioms upon the measure without distorting it.

But, though the term "blank verse" is commonly associated with the five-foot iambic line, it is not confined to it. Strictly speaking, it can mean any unrhymed regularly patterned verse, no matter how short the line or how long the poem may be. Longfellow's "Evangeline" is no less blank verse for being in dactylic hexameter instead of iambic pentameter. The four-footed trochaic line of "Hiawatha" is equally an example of blank verse. Collins' "Ode to Evening," Lamb's "The Old Familiar Faces," Tennyson's "Tears, Idle Tears" show that blank verse may be employed in lyrics of varying meters as well as in sustained passages of a prescribed measure.

THE OLD FAMILIAR FACES

I have had playmates, I have had companions,
In my days of childhood, in my joyful school-days,
All, all are gone, the old familiar faces.

I have been laughing, I have been carousing,
Drinking late, sitting late, with my bosom cronies,
All, all are gone, the old familiar faces.

I loved a love once, fairest among women;
Closed are her doors on me, I must not see her—
All, all are gone, the old familiar faces.

I have a friend, a kinder friend has no man;
Like an ingrate, I left my friend abruptly;
Left him, to muse on the old familiar faces.

Ghost-like I paced round the haunts of my childhood.
Earth seemed a desert I was bound to traverse,
Seeking to find the old familiar faces.

Friend of my bosom, thou more than a brother,
Why wert not thou born in my father's dwelling?
So might we talk of the old familiar faces—

How some they have died, and some they have left me,
And some are taken from me; all are departed;
All, all are gone, the old familiar faces.

—*Charles Lamb* (1775-1834)

Blank verse and free verse do not conform to any particular stanza pattern. The stanza is a verse or set of verses of predetermined number of lines, the smallest unit being the couplet.

THE COUPLET

The couplet (formerly called a "distich") is, as the name implies, a pair of rhymes. It consists of two lines of matched verse in immediate succession. Rhyme is imperative although the line-lengths may differ. The most popular forms are the octosyllabic (four-foot) and the "heroic" (five-foot) couplet—the latter being a rhymed form of iambic pentameter. The latter form has been a favorite since Chaucer's use of it in "The Canterbury Tales" and Dryden brought it to a kind of perfection which Pope tightened into a "thought couplet," each couplet being a unit in itself. (See pages 278 and 300.) Thus Pope, in "An Essay on Criticism":

A little learning is a dangerous thing;
Drink deep, or taste not the Pierian Spring. . . .

True ease in writing comes from art, not chance,
As those move easiest who have learned to dance.

Among the couplets of irregular length is Browning's "Love Among the Ruins," which begins:

Where the quiet-colored end of evening smiles
    Miles on miles.

Although so brief that it rarely stands alone, a couplet may constitute a complete poem. Many of the sharpest epigrams point themselves into perfect couplets. Seven examples among many are quoted:

CHLOE

Bright as the day, and like the morning fair,
Such Chloe is—and common as the air.
—*Lord Lansdowne* (1667-1735)

ENGRAVED ON THE COLLAR OF HIS HIGHNESS' DOG

I am his Highness' dog at Kew.
Pray tell me, sir, whose dog are you?
—*Alexander Pope* (1688-1744)

LOVE

Love is a circle that doth restless move
In the same sweet eternity of Love.
—*Robert Herrick* (1591-1674)

ON THE DEATH OF SIR ALBERTUS AND LADY MORTON

He first deceased. She, for a little, tried
To live without him; liked it not, and died.
—*Henry Wotton* (1568-1639)

TO WILLIAM HAYLEY

Thy friendship oft has made my heart to ache:
Do be my enemy, for friendship's sake!
—*William Blake* (1757-1827)

ON A DEAD HOSTESS

Of this bad world the loveliest and best
Has smiled and said "Good Night," and gone to rest.
—*Hilaire Belloc* (1870-   )

ON SEEING WEATHER-BEATEN TREES

Is it so plainly in our living shown,
By slant and twist, which way the wind hath blown?
—*Adelaide Crapsey* (1878-1914)

Until recently the shortest poem in English was thought to be Strickland Gillilan's couplet:

ON THE ANTIQUITY OF MICROBES

Adam
Had 'em.

But a contemporary versifier challenged the length of Gillilan's effort; four syllables, said he, were two too many. In proof of his claim that a poem could be still briefer, he produced this couplet:

LINES (2) ON THE QUESTIONABLE IMPORTANCE OF THE INDIVIDUAL

I . . .
Why?

It might be well to compare the couplets of Chaucer, Marvell, Pope, Cowper, and Keats to see the variety which the paired line can accomplish, for, as a rule, the couplet is used in poems of some length. Examples of the running couplet appear everywhere, a particularly delightful instance being one of the most recently published poems.

CRYSTAL MOMENT

by Robert P. T. Coffin (1892-)

Once or twice this side of death
Things can make one hold his breath.

From my boyhood I remember
A crystal moment of September.

A wooded island rang with sounds
Of church bells in the throats of hounds.

A buck leaped out and took the tide
With jewels flowing past each side.

With his high head like a tree,
He swam within a yard of me.

I saw the golden drop of light
In his eyes turned dark with fright.

I saw the forest's holiness
On him like a fierce caress.

Fear made him lonely past belief,
My heart was trembling like a leaf.

He leaned towards the land and life
With need above him like a knife.

In his wake the hot hounds churned,
They stretched their muzzles out and yearned.

They cried no more, but swam and throbbed,
Hunger drove them till they sobbed.

Pursued, pursuers reached the shore
And vanished. I saw nothing more.

So they passed, a pageant such
As only gods could witness much.

Life and death upon one tether
And running beautiful together.

THE TERCET

The tercet (sometimes called "triplet") is a stanza of three lines rhyming together. Three poems in tercets (Herrick's "Upon His Departure Hence," Browning's "A Toccata of Galuppi's" and his "Cavalier Tune") have been quoted in the preceding chapter on pages 335, 335, 337. Here are three other triplets in varying lengths and different meters:

Beauty, truth and rarity,
Grace in all simplicity,
Here enclosed in cinders lie.
—"The Eagle and the Phoenix," *William Shakespeare*

Whoe'er she be—
That not impossible she
That shall command my heart and me.
—"Wishes for the Supposed Mistress," *Richard Crashaw*

But John P.
Robinson, he
Sez he wunt vote for Guverner B.
—"The Biglow Papers," *James Russell Lowell*

One of the shortest poems in this form—a poem made of only two tercets—is Herrick's charming:

WHENAS IN SILKS MY JULIA GOES

Whenas in silks my Julia goes,
Then, then, me thinks, how sweetly flows
That liquefaction of her clothes.

Next, when I cast mine eyes and see
That brave vibration each way free,
O how that glittering taketh me!
—*Robert Herrick* (1591-1674)

TERZA RIMA

Terza Rima ("third rhyme") is a form of tercet in which the first and third lines rhyme together, while the second line introduces a new rhyme to be carried on by the first and third lines of the next tercet. The effect gained is of remarkable continuity and the interlocking arrangement of rhymes may be expressed thus: *a-b-a, b-c-b, c-d-c, d-e-d,* and so on until the end of the poem. The problem of closing the uncompleted rhyme of the second line is solved either by ending the poem with an extra line, making the last stanza one of four lines, or by closing with a couplet. Dante's *Divina Commedia* is written entirely in *terza rima.* Examples in English are comparatively rare, but among them are Shelley's "Ode to the West Wind" (page 43), Browning's "The Statue and the Bust" (page 96), Mrs. Browning's "Casa Guidi Windows" and William Morris' "The Defense of Guenevere."

THE QUATRAIN

The quatrain (or "quatorzain") is any four-line stanza. The lines may be of any length, the rhymes (when rhymes occur) may be arranged in any order. The possible variations of this stanza form are so numerous that only the more important patterns can be shown here. Perhaps the most familiar arrangement is the "ballad stanza" in which the rhyme is either *a-b-a-b* or *a-b-x-b* —*x* representing the unrhymed third line. It is employed in "The Douglas Tragedy" (page 385), "Sir Patrick Spence" (page 387), "Jesse James" (page 394), "Proud Maisie" (page 395), "La Belle Dame sans Merci" (page 396), "The Image" (page 398), "Ballad of the Huntsman" (page 399), "The Enchanted Shirt" (page 113) and other poems in this volume. The rhyme-scheme is usually:

She set her foot upon the ship, a
No mariners could she behold, b
But the sails were o' the taffeta x
And the masts o' the beaten gold. b

When the third line is rhymed, the pattern becomes more musical—*a-b-a-b*— as in Emerson's:

By the rude bridge that arched the flood, a
Their flag to April's breezes furled, b
Here once the embattled farmers stood a
And fired the shot heard round the world. b

This form of the quatrain has infinite possibilities, particularly in its manipulation of meter, accent, and length of line. One of the most musical effects is achieved by alternating single ("masculine") rhymes with double ("feminine") ones, an effect which has been strikingly yet delicately achieved by a modern poet who deserves to be better known.

MERCIFUL MEDUSA

Sleep is a merciful Medusa, bending, a
  Under her sluggish and outrageous hair, b
A steady gaze of bronze, superbly blending a
  All creatures in her one impersonal stare. b

Bird, beast and man, worn out with lovely moving
  Seek her at night, forlornly and alone,
Cry to her to be pitilessly loving,
  Look on her face and turn to grateful stone.

—*Winifred Welles* (1893-)

An uncommon and ingenious use of the popular *a-b-a-b* quatrain, in which originality is achieved by contrasted line-lengths, may be observed in the following noble poem:

DISCIPLINE

by George Herbert (1593-1632)

Throw away Thy rod, a
Throw away Thy wrath; b
  O my God, a
Take the gentle path! b

For my heart's desire
Unto Thine is bent:
  I aspire
To a full consent.

Not a word or look
I affect to own,
  But by book,
And Thy Book alone.

Though I fail, I weep;
Though I halt in pace,
  Yet I creep
To the throne of grace.

Then let wrath remove;
Love will do the deed;
  For with love
Stony hearts will bleed.

Love is swift of foot;
Love's a man of war,
  And can shoot,
And can hit from far.

Who can 'scape his bow?
That which wrought on Thee,
  Brought Thee low,
Needs must work on me.

Throw away Thy rod;
Though man frailties hath,
  Thou art God:
Throw away Thy wrath.

A less common but interesting variant is the quatrain rhymed *a-a-b-b,* a unit formed of two couplets. Sometimes the coupled lines are identical in length; sometimes they are sharply contrasted. Three examples follow:

The boys are up in the woods with day a
To fetch the daffodils away, a
And home at noonday from the hills b
They bring no dearth of daffodils. b

—*A. E. Housman*

As sap foretastes the spring, a
As Earth ere blossoming a

Thrills b
With far daffodills. b
—*Francis Thompson*

It will last till men weary of pleasure a
In measure; a
It will last till men weary of laughter . . . b
And after! b
—*Austin Dobson*

Another interesting variation of the quatrain is the form used in Tennyson's "In Memoriam." Here one pair of rhymes encloses another—*a-b-b-a*—as:

FROM "IN MEMORIAM"

O yet we trust that somehow good a
Will be the final goal of ill, b
To pangs of nature, sins of will, b
Defects of doubt, and taints of blood; a

That nothing walks with aimless feet;
That not one life shall be destroy'd,
Or cast as rubbish to the void,
When God hath made the pile complete;

That not a worm is cloven in vain;
That not a moth with vain desire
Is shrivell'd in a fruitless fire,
Or but subserves another's gain.

Behold, we know not anything;
I can but trust that good shall fall
At last—far off—at last, to all,
And every winter change to spring.

So runs my dream: but what am I?
An infant crying in the night:
An infant crying for the light:
And with no language but a cry.
—*Alfred, Lord Tennyson* (1809-1892)

The quatrain known to us chiefly through Fitzgerald's adaptation of Omar Khayyám's "Rubáiyát" is one which rhymes the first, second, and fourth line, leaving the third unrhymed—*a-a-x-a*—as on pages 257 to 261. Swinburne also employed the blank third line of the "Omar stanza" in his resounding "Laus Veneris." Swinburne, however, used the third unrhymed line of each verse to rhyme with the same line in the verse immediately following it, a striking and unexpected device. The illustration which follows is the concluding four stanzas of the poem.

Ah, love, there is no better life than this; a
To have known love, how bitter a thing it is, a
And afterward be cast out of God's *sight;* x
Yea, these that know not, shall they have such bliss a

High up in barren heaven before his face
As we twain in the heavy-hearted place,
Remembering love and all the dead *delight,*
And all that time was sweet with for a space?

For till the thunder in the trumpet be,
Soul may divide from body, but not we
One from another; I told thee with my *hand,*
I let mine eyes have all their will of thee,

I seal myself upon thee with my might,
Abiding alway out of all men's sight
  Until God loosen over sea and *land*
The thunder of the trumpets of the night.
    —*Algernon Charles Swinburne* (1837-1909)

Sometimes a single quatrain forms a complete poem. Such a poem is usually of an epigrammatic nature—*vide* the poems on pages 426 to 433 in Chapter 17. The following illustrations, epigrammatic in character, show two different rhyme-schemes.

IANTHE

From you, Ianthe, little troubles pass — a
  Like little ripples down a sunny river; — b
Your pleasures spring like daisies in the grass, — a
  Cut down, and up again as blithe as ever. — b
    —*Walter Savage Landor* (1775-1864)

ON HIS SEVENTY-FIFTH BIRTHDAY

I strove with none; for none was worth my strife, — a
Nature I loved and, next to Nature, Art; — b
I warmed both hands before the fire of life. — a
It sinks, and I am ready to depart. — b
    —*Walter Savage Landor* (1775-1864)

WOMAN

Not she with traitorous kiss her Saviour stung, — a
Not she denied him with unholy tongue; — a
She, while apostles shrank, could dangers brave, — b
Last at the cross and earliest at the grave. — b
    —*Eaton Stannard Barrett* (1786-1820)

Other examples occur frequently throughout these chapters, the quatrain being the most commonly employed of all the stanza forms.

THE QUINTET

The quintet is a five-line stanza variously rhymed. The favorite formula seems to be *a-b-a-b-b*. Shelley's "To a Skylark" (page 207) makes use of this pattern as does Swinburne's "Hertha" with its long-rolling last line:

I the grain and the furrow, — a
    The plough-cloven clod — b
And the ploughshare drawn thorough, — a
    The germ and the sod, — b
The deed and the doer, the seed and the sower, the dust which is God. — b
    —*Algernon Charles Swinburne* (1837-1909)

Christina Rossetti's "The Bourne," one of the loveliest of her elegiac poems, employs a rather uncommon form of the quintet in which the rhyme scheme is *a-b-b-b-a*.

THE BOURNE

Underneath the growing grass, a
Underneath the living flowers, b
Deeper than the sound of showers: b
There we shall not count the hours b
By the shadows as they pass. a

Youth and health will be but vain,
Beauty reckoned of no worth:
There a very little girth
Can hold round what once the earth
Seemed too narrow to contain.
—*Christina Georgina Rossetti* (1830-1894)

Another form of the quintet is employed with exquisite grace in Waller's seventeenth-century love song which blends light passion and a fashionable philosophy.

SONG

Go, lovely Rose! a
Tell her, that wastes her time and me, b
That now she knows, a
When I resemble her to thee, b
How sweet, and fair, she seems to be. b

Tell her that's young,
And shuns to have her graces spy'd,
That had'st thou sprung
In deserts where no men abide,
Thou must have uncommended dy'd.

Small is the worth
Of beauty from the light retir'd;
Bid her come forth,
Suffer herself to be desir'd,
And not blush so to be admir'd.

Then die! that she
The common fate of all things rare
May read in thee;
How small a part of time they share
That are so wondrous sweet and fair!
—*Edmund Waller* (1606-1687)

Another variation of the quintet is the form perfected by Adelaide Crapsey. Her "cinquains," as she termed them, lack rhyme, but the line-pattern is strict in structure—the five lines having, respectively, two, four, six, eight, and two syllables each, bearing a close relation to the Japanese *hokku.* Two of these delicate designs are quoted.

NOVEMBER NIGHT

Listen . . .
With faint dry sound,
Like steps of passing ghosts,
The leaves, frost-crisp'd, break from the trees
And fall.

THE WARNING

Just now,
Out of the strange
Still dusk . . . as strange, as still . . .
A white moth flew. Why am I grown
So cold?
—*Adelaide Crapsey* (1878-1914)

THE SESTET

In its particular application the "sestet" is the six-line unit of the sonnet as contrasted with the "octave," the preceding eight lines. In a general sense, the sestet is a six-line stanza in which the possibilities of line and rhyme arrangement are almost endless. It may be composed of interlacing couplets as in Holmes' "The Last Leaf" (page 310) and Shakespeare's "Orpheus with His Lute" (page 191); it may be constructed with a mingling of rhymed and unrhymed lines as in Rossetti's "The Blessed Damozel" (page 177), formed of a quatrain and a supplementary couplet as in Clemens' "The Love of Books" (page 187), or built on the interesting pattern devised as early as the sixteenth century by some unknown contributor to Robert Jones' *Second Book of Airs.*

Love winged my Hopes and taught me how to fly a
Far from base earth, but not to mount too high: a
For true pleasure b
Lives in measure, b
Which if men forsake, c
Blinded they into folly run and grief for pleasure take. c
—*Anonymous* (about 1590)

A particularly musical sestet achieves an echo-like reverberation through its alternation of two single contrasting rhymes—*a-b-a-b-a-b*—as in Andrew Lang's "Romance":

And through the silver Northern night a
The sunset slowly died away, b
And herds of strange deer, lily-white, a
Stole forth among the branches gray; b
About the coming of the light, a
They fled like ghosts before the day. b
—*Andrew Lang* (1844-1912)

Perhaps the best-known form of the sestet is the "tail rhyme" six-line stanza perfected if not invented by Burns. His frequent and skilful use of the form is so closely associated with him that it is often referred to as the "Burns stanza." The form is as in these lines from "The Hermit":

In this lone cave, in garments lowly, a
Alike a foe to noisy folly, a
And brow-bent gloomy melancholy, a
  I wear away b
My life, and in my office holy, a
  Consume the day. b
  —*Robert Burns* (1759-1796)

More famous examples of the six-line "Burns stanza" are "To a Mountain Daisy" (page 217) and "Holy Willie's Prayer" (page 296).

THE SEPTET

The septet is any seven-line stanza. It is an uncommon but extremely flexible form, its possibilities of combination being countless. The following example is built on only two rhymes—*a-b-a-b-b-a-a*—and is one of the more unusual variations:

MISCONCEPTIONS

This is a spray the Bird clung to, a
  Making it blossom with pleasure, b
Ere the high tree-top she sprung to, a
  Fit for her nest and her treasure. b
  Oh, what a hope beyond measure b
Was the poor spray's, which the flying feet hung to,— a
So to be singled out, built in, and sung to! a

This is a heart the Queen leant on,
  Thrilled in a minute erratic,
Ere the true bosom she bent on,
  Meet for love's regal dalmatic.
  Oh, what a fancy ecstatic
Was the poor heart's, ere the wanderer went on—
Love to be saved for it, proffered to, spent on!
  —*Robert Browning* (1812-1889)

One particular form of the septet has been much esteemed. It is *rime royal* —so called because it was supposedly first employed by a royal poet, King James I of Scotland. Chaucer used it in his "Tale of the Man of Lawe," "Troilus and Criseyde" and "The Parlement of Foules"; Shakespeare's "The Rape of Lucrece" is written in *rime royal,* and so modern a poet as John Masefield has given it new life in "Dauber" and "The Widow in the Bye Street." The rhyme-scheme is *a-b-a-b-b-c-c,* and the two concluding couplets give the stanza particular force. A fragment from "The Rape of Lucrece" shows the pattern:

Without the bed her other fair hand was a
On the green coverlet, whose perfect white b
Show'd like an April daisy on the grass a
With pearly sweat, resembling dew of night. b
Her eyes, like marigolds, had sheathed their light, b
And, canopied in darkness, sweetly lay c
Till they might open to adorn the day. c
—*William Shakespeare*

THE OCTAVE

In its particular application the "octave" is the eight-line unit of the sonnet as contrasted with the six-line sestet which follows it. In a general sense the octave is any eight-line stanza, whether it is composed of a pair of quatrains, or two tercets with a pair of rhyming lines after each (*a-a-a-b-c-c-c-b*), as in Drayton's "Agincourt," or in the form (*a-b-a-b-c-c-c-b*) which Swinburne used so eloquently in "The Garden of Proserpine" and the Chorus from "Atalanta in Calydon" which begins "When the hounds of spring are on winter's traces." A stanza of each of the first and last types:

Upon Saint Crispin's Day a
Fought was this noble fray, a
Which fame did not delay a
To England to carry. b
O when shall English men c
With such acts fill a pen? c
Or England breed again c
Such a King Harry? b
—*Michael Drayton*

Here, where the world is quiet, a
Here, where all trouble seems b
Dead winds' and spent waves' riot a
In doubtful dreams of dreams, b
I watch the green field growing c
For reaping folk and sowing, c
For harvest-time and mowing, c
A sleepy world of streams. b
—*Algernon Charles Swinburne*

A particular form of the eight-line stanza is known as *ottava rima* (rhymed octave), so called because it is taken from the Italian. The rhyme-pattern is *a-b-a-b-a-b-c-c*. Boccaccio first fashioned it and, in the hands of Tasso and Ariosto, it became the regular Italian heroic meter. In English it has been largely employed for satiric purposes, but it is capable of sweeping and even sustained effects. Byron's *ottava rima* is well known through his "Don Juan" and "The Vision of Judgment," a stanza from the latter being quoted below. Keats's "Isabella," however, shows a dramatic use of *ottava rima,* this paraphrase of a story from Boccaccio making an appropriate link with the Italian verse-form.

The angels were all singing out of tune, a
And hoarse with having little else to do, b
Excepting to wind up the sun and moon, a
Or curb a runaway young star or two, b
Or wild colt of a comet, which too soon a
Broke out of bounds o'er the ethereal blue, b
Splitting some planet with its playful tail, c
As boats are sometimes by a wanton whale. c
—*Lord Byron*

THE SPENSERIAN STANZA

The Spenserian stanza is a majestic nine-line stanza invented by Spenser in "The Faerie Queene." The rhyme scheme is intricately knit—*a-b-a-b-b-c-b-c-c*—and the ninth line, called the Alexandrine, is one foot longer than the preceding eight, rounding out the stanza with sonorous finality. An illustrative and picturesque segment is the opening of Spenser's classic:

FROM "THE FAERIE QUEENE"

by Edmund Spenser (1552-1599)

A gentle knight was pricking on the plaine, a
Ycladd in mightie armes and silver shielde, b
Wherein old dints of deepe woundes did remaine, a
The cruell markes of many a bloody fielde; b
Yet armes till that time did he never wield: b
His angry steed did chide his foming bitt, c
As much disdayning to the curbe to yield: b
Full jolly knight he seemd, and faire did sitt, c
As one for knightly giusts and fierce encounters fitt. c

But on his brest a bloodie crosse he bore,
The deare remembrance of his dying Lord,
For whose sweete sake that glorious badge he wore,
And dead as living ever him adored:
Upon his shield the like was also scored,
For soveraine hope, which in his helpe he had:
Right faithfull true he was in deede and word,
But of his cheere [1] did seeme too solemne sad;
Yet nothing did he dread, but ever was ydrad.

Upon a great adventure he was bond,
That greatest Gloriana [2] to him gave,
That greatest glorious queene of Faery Lond,
To winne him worshippe, and her grace to have,
Which of all earthly thinges he most did crave;
And ever as he rode his hart did earne
To prove his puissance in battell brave
Upon his foe, and his new force to learne;
Upon his foe, a dragon horrible and stearne.

[1] Countenance.
[2] Queen Elizabeth.

A lovely ladie rode him faire beside,
Upon a lowly asse more white than snow,
Yet she much whiter, but the same did hide
Under a vele, that wimpled was full low,
And over all a blacke stole shee did throw:
As one that inly mournd, so was she sad,
And heavie sate upon her palfrey slow:
Seemèd in heart some hidden care she had;
And by her in a line a milkewhite lambe she lad.

So pure and innocent, as that same lambe,
She was in life and every vertuous lore,
And by descent from royall lynage came
Of ancient kinges and queenes, that had of yore
Their scepters stretched from east to westerne shore,
And all the world in their subjection held,
Till that infernall feend with foule uprore
Forwasted all their land, and them expeld:
Whom to avenge, she had this knight from far compeld.

Among the memorable poems in the Spenserian stanza are Thomson's "The Castle of Indolence," Burns' "The Cotter's Saturday Night," Byron's "Childe Harold," Tennyson's "The Lotos-Eaters," Keats's "The Eve of St. Agnes" (page 68), Shelley's "The Revolt of Islam" and "Adonais." The opening and concluding stanzas of the last poem, that passionate elegy on the death of Keats, are quoted.

FROM "ADONAIS"

by Percy Bysshe Shelley (1792-1822)

I weep for Adonais—he is dead! a
Oh, weep for Adonais! though our tears b
Thaw not the frost which binds so dear a head! a
And thou, sad Hour, selected from all years b
To mourn our loss, rouse thy obscure compeers, b
And teach them thine own sorrow! Say: "With me c
Died Adonais; till the Future dares b
Forget the Past, his fate and fame shall be c
An echo and a light unto eternity!" c

Where wert thou, mighty Mother, when he lay,
When thy Son lay, pierced by the shaft which flies
In darkness? where was lorn Urania
When Adonais died? With veilèd eyes,
'Mid listening Echoes, in her Paradise
She sate, while one, with soft enamoured breath
Rekindled all the fading melodies,
With which, like flowers that mock the corse beneath,
He had adorned and hid the coming bulk of Death.

Oh, weep for Adonais—he is dead!
Wake, melancholy Mother, wake and weep!

Yet wherefore? Quench within their burning bed
Thy fiery tears, and let thy loud heart keep
Like his, a mute and uncomplaining sleep;
For he is gone, where all things wise and fair
Descend;—oh, dream not that the amorous Deep
Will yet restore him to the vital air;
Death feeds on his mute voice, and laughs at our despair.

Most musical of mourners, weep again!
Lament anew, Urania!—He died,
Who was the Sire of an immortal strain,
Blind, old, and lonely, when his country's pride,
The priest, the slave, and the liberticide,
Trampled and mocked with many a loathèd rite
Of lust and blood. He went, unterrified,
Into the gulf of death; but his clear Sprite
Yet reigns o'er earth; the third among the sons of light.

✦

The One remains, the many change and pass;
Heaven's light forever shines, Earth's shadows fly;
Life, like a dome of many-coloured glass,
Stains the white radiance of Eternity,
Until Death tramples it to fragments.—Die,
If thou wouldst be with that which thou dost seek!
Follow where all is fled!—Rome's azure sky,
Flowers, ruins, statues, music, words, are weak
The glory they transfuse with fitting truth to speak.

Why linger, why turn back, why shrink, my Heart?
Thy hopes are gone before: from all things here
They have departed; thou shouldst now depart!
A light is passed from the revolving year,
And man, and woman; and what still is dear
Attracts to crush, repels to make thee wither.
The soft sky smiles,—the low wind whispers near:
'Tis Adonais calls! oh, hasten thither,
No more let Life divide what Death can join together.

That Light whose smile kindles the Universe,
That Beauty in which all things work and move,
That Benediction which the eclipsing Curse
Of birth can quench not, that sustaining Love
Which through the web of being blindly wove
By man and beast and earth and air and sea,
Burns bright or dim, as each are mirrors of
The fire for which all thirst, now beams on me,
Consuming the last clouds of cold mortality.

The breath whose might I have invoked in song
Descends on me; my spirit's bark is driven,

Far from the shore, far from the trembling throng
Whose sails were never to the tempest given;
The massy earth and spherèd skies are riven!
I am borne darkly, fearfully, afar;
Whilst, burning through the inmost veil of Heaven,
The soul of Adonais, like a star,
Beacons from the abode where the Eternal are.

SUGGESTIONS FOR ADDITIONAL READING ILLUSTRATING VARIOUS STANZA FORMS

POEMS IN DUPLE METER (IAMBIC AND TROCHAIC)

Henry Wadsworth Longfellow, *Hiawatha*
A. E. Housman, *Bredon Hill, On Wenlock Edge,* and, for that matter, most of *A Shropshire Lad*
Robert Burns, *Bonny Lesley*
Robert Burns, *The Vowels: A Tale*
William Blake, *The Lamb*
William Blake, *To Winter*
John Keats, *Lamia*
John Keats, *Isabella, or the Pot of Basil*
P. B. Shelley, *Queen Mab*
Alfred, Lord Tennyson, *Ring Out, Wild Bells*
Edna St. Vincent Millay, *Renascence*
Sara Teasdale, *"I shall not care"*
Edwin Arlington Robinson, *The Man Against the Sky*
Amy Lowell, *Evelyn Ray*

POEMS IN TRIPLE METER (DACTYLIC AND ANAPESTIC)

P. B. Shelley, *The Cloud*
P. B. Shelley, *Arethusa*
William Blake, *The Shepherd*
William Blake, *Nurse's Song*
Austin Dobson, *The Ballad of "Beau Brocade"*
Henry Wadsworth Longfellow, *Evangeline*
Sidney Lanier, *Marsh Song at Sunset*
Sidney Lanier, *The Song of the Chattahoochee*
Robert Browning, *The Lost Leader*
Robert Browning, *The Year's at the Spring*
Robert Frost, *Blueberries*
Edwin Arlington Robinson, *John Evereldown*
Vachel Lindsay, *The Kallyope Yell*
Elinor Wylie, *Sea Lullaby*

14

THE PATTERNS OF POETRY—2: THE SONNET

"We say that just as the inherent spirit of poetry at its highest and noblest forces itself into the mould of blank verse or the decasyllabic stanza, so it is, on occasion prescribed by itself, forced into the mould of the sonnet, which is just as glorious, just as gracious, and just as free, powerful and effective."

—*T. W. H. Crosland* in "The English Sonnet"

None of the stanza forms has been more exploited and exalted than the sonnet, and none has achieved so wide a variety of effects. Though there are differences among the types—mainly differences in the arrangement of rhymes—all sonnets have fourteen lines, the lines themselves being composed (with few exceptions) of ten syllables: iambic pentameter. These fourteen lines are usually divided into the opening eight (the octave) and the concluding six (the sestet). This stanza-form creates a complete poem, possibly the finest medium for the communication of a single idea. The shape of the sonnet sharpens its outlines, the limitation of length condenses its content, the rhyme-scheme adds a subtly interwoven music, while the iambic pentameter line gives it the surge and resonance of blank verse.

In Italian, the language of its origin (one theory of its origin is that it is the result of the impact of Arabian mathematical genius upon Italian poets at the court of Frederick II in Sicily), the sonnet was employed chiefly for grace and gallantry, for compliments and courtly gestures. Dante, relinquishing the terza rima of the *Divina Commedia,* used the form to woo his Beatrice; Petrarch employed it to immortalize his Laura; Tasso, turning from his epic, composed a thousand sonnets; Michelangelo left sculpture long enough to carve words in this more durable medium; Cavalcanti's ballads, popular though they were, never surpassed his "perfect" sonnets.

In English, however, the structure has been employed more gravely. Although Spenser's "Amoretti" and Sidney's "Astrophel and Stella" abound in pretty conceits and the light artifice of the early Elizabethans, the sonnet has reached its full expression as the embodiment of high seriousness. No other stanza form is capable of holding such intense meditation or pouring out so concentrated a measure of thought. Poets have always vied with each other to pay homage to the form; none of the tributes being more memorable than Wordsworth's famous "Sonnet on the Sonnet":

SONNET ON THE SONNET

Scorn not the Sonnet. Critic, you have frowned,
Mindless of its just honours; with this key

Shakespeare unlocked his heart; the melody
Of this small lute gave ease to Petrarch's wound;
A thousand times this pipe did Tasso sound;
With it Camoëns soothed an exile's grief;
The Sonnet glittered a gay myrtle leaf
Amid the cypress with which Dante crowned
His visionary brow: a glow-worm lamp,
It cheered mild Spenser, called from Faery-land
To struggle through dark ways; and, when a damp
Fell round the path of Milton, in his hand
The thing became a trumpet; whence he blew
Soul-animating strains—alas, too few!
—*William Wordsworth* (1770-1850)

Scholars have been uncertain in their division of the various types of sonnets, but it may be said that the three chief types are (1) the Petrarchan, or Italian, (2) The Shakespearian, (3) the Miltonic. Added classifications would include (4) the Spenserian and (5) the Composite, or "Irregular" sonnet.

THE PETRARCHAN, OR ITALIAN, SONNET

The Petrarchan is the strictest type of sonnet. It permits of no more than two rhymes in the octave—always arranged *a-b-b-a-a-b-b-a*. The sestet allows somewhat more liberty with three rhymes—arranged *c-d-e-c-d-e* or *c-d-e-e-d-c* or *c-d-e-d-c-e*—although many of the Italian sestets are built on only two rhymes *c-d-c-d-c-d*. Before citing any traditional English sonnet of the pure Petrarchan type, it might be well to show an example of the strict Italian form as rendered by an English poet of the nineteenth century. This is Rossetti's version of Dante's famous sonnet on the conflict of beauty and duty.

BEAUTY AND DUTY

Two ladies to the summit of my mind a
Have clomb, to hold an argument of love. b
The one has wisdom with her from above, b
For every noblest virtue well designed: a
The other, beauty's tempting power refined a
And the high charm of perfect grace approve: b
And I, as my sweet Master's will doth move, b
At feet of both their favors am reclined. a

Beauty and Duty in my soul keep strife, c
At question if the heart such course can take d
And 'twixt the ladies hold its love complete. e
The fount of gentle speech yields answer meet: e
That Beauty may be loved for gladness' sake, d
And Duty in the lofty ends of life. c
—*Dante Alighieri* (1265-1321), *translated by*
Dante Gabriel Rossetti (1828-1882)

Two things besides the rhyme-scheme will be observed in the poem quoted, two features which characterize the Italian sonnet: (1) the definite division into two parts, (2) the ascent of the octave and the "dying fall" of the sestet. This gives the Petrarchan sonnet its wave-like effect, the eighth line representing the crest of the wave and the rest of the sonnet being an ebbing away. To change the metaphor, the octave and sestet contrast a statement with its consequence or philosophy; the octave presents the thought, the sestet offers a fulfilment or conclusion of the idea, a circumstance which has given rise to the theory—a rather far-fetched one—that the sonnet is a condensed form of the Greek ode. Many of the sestets make this premise-and-conclusion formula explicit by beginning the octave with *As* or *When* and the sestet with *So* or *Then.* An excellent instance of this formation is Longfellow's "Nature," a Petrarchan sonnet in every sense:

NATURE

As a fond mother, when the day is o'er — a
Leads by the hand her little child to bed, — b
Half willing, half reluctant to be led — b
And leave his broken playthings on the floor, — a
Still gazing at them through the open door, — a
Nor wholly reassured and comforted — b
By promises of others in their stead, — b
Which, though more splendid, may not please him more; — a

So Nature deals with us, and takes away — c
Our playthings one by one, and by the hand — d
Leads us to rest so gently that we go — e
Scarce knowing if we wish to go or stay, — c
Being too full of sleep to understand — d
How far the unknown transcends the what we know. — e

—*Henry Wadsworth Longfellow* (1807-1882)

The wave-like quality of the Italian sonnet has been recognized by countless poets, but it remained for Watts-Dunton to express it in pure Petrarchan:

THE SONNET'S VOICE

Yon silvery billows breaking on the beach — a
Fall back in foam beneath the star-shine clear, — b
The while my rhymes are murmuring in your ear — b
A restless lore like that the billows teach; — a
For on those sonnet-waves my soul would reach — a
From its own depths and rest within you, dear, — b
As, through the billowy voices yearning here, — b
Great Nature strives to find a human speech. — a

A sonnet is a wave of melody: — c
From heaving waters of the impassioned soul — d
A billow of tidal music one and whole — d
Flows in the "octave;" then, returning free, — c
Its ebbing surges in the "sestet" roll — d
Back to the deeps of Life's tumultuous sea. — c

—*Theodore Watts-Dunton* (1836-1914)

Another example of Petrarchan sonnet is the beautiful brief elegy "Rest" by Christina Rossetti, sister of Dante Gabriel Rossetti, and author of some of the clearest sonnets and lyrics in the language:

REST

O Earth, lie heavily upon her eyes; a
Seal her sweet eyes weary of watching, Earth; b
Lie close around her: leave no room for mirth b
With its harsh laughter, nor for sound of sighs. a
She hath no questions, she hath no replies, a
Hushed in and curtained with a blessèd dearth b
Of all that irked her from the hour of birth; b
With stillness that is almost Paradise. a

Darkness more clear than noonday holdeth her, c
Silence more musical than any song; d
Even her very heart has ceased to stir: c
Until the morning of Eternity e
Her rest shall not begin nor end, but be; e
And when she wakes she will not think it long. d

—*Christina Georgina Rossetti* (1830-1894)

A superb example of the Petrarchan model, a poet's tribute to a translator, is, at the same time, one of the most famous poems in English literature. Its sensitive use of association, its central symbolism, above all its colorful suggestiveness lift the words into that atmosphere of wonder, into the very "realms of gold," which Keats and only a few other poets inhabited.

ON FIRST LOOKING INTO CHAPMAN'S HOMER

Much have I travell'd in the realms of gold, a
  And many goodly states and kingdoms seen; b
  Round many western islands have I been b
Which bards in fealty to Apollo hold. a
Oft of one wide expanse had I been told a
  That deep-brow'd Homer ruled as his demesne; b
  Yet did I never breathe its pure serene b
Till I heard Chapman speak out loud and bold: a

Then felt I like some watcher of the skies c
  When a new planet swims into his ken; d
Or like stout Cortez, when with eagle eyes c
  He stared at the Pacific—and all his men d
Look'd at each other with a wild surmise— c
  Silent, upon a peak in Darien. d

—*John Keats* (1795-1821)

THE SHAKESPEARIAN SONNET

The Shakespearian sonnet was not invented by Shakespeare, but by his predecessors, chiefly by Henry Howard, Earl of Surrey. Shakespeare took the model which had been used tentatively, enriched it with his powerful line, and perfected it. The Shakespearian sonnet reveals an abrupt departure from the Petrarchan model. The pause between octave and sestet is still observed, but it is less pronounced; the structure consisting less of the two independent parts than of three quatrains, each with independent rhymes, and a concluding couplet. The rhyme-pattern is thus: *a-b-a-b c-d-c-d e-f-e-f g-g*—a total of seven rhymes as contrasted with the Petrarchan four or five. The radical re-arrangement, and especially the concluding couplet, seemed such a violation of the original form that several purists have refused to consider the Shakespearian sonnets *as* sonnets and have called them "fourteeners." On the other hand, only a pedant would deny the vitality which Shakespeare brought to the form not only by his magnificent rhetoric, but by the very freedom of the new pattern. Comparing the two forms, William Sharp wrote with rare discrimination, "The Petrarchan sonnet is like a wind, gathering in volume and dying away again immediately upon attaining culminating force; the Shakespearian sonnet is like a red-hot bar being moulded upon a forge till—in the closing couplet—it receives a final clinching blow from the hammer." It is the couplet which, as Sharp implied, "clinches" the Shakespearian sonnet; it is not only the crux but the test of this type of sonnet: it reveals the master and betrays the tyro.

Three Shakespearian sonnets follow with their annotated rhyme-schemes. The first is one of the one hundred and fifty-four unparalleled sonnets by Shakespeare himself; the second is the fierce outcry from Shakespeare's contemporary, Michael Drayton; the third is a passionate declaration by that modern Elizabethan, Edna St. Vincent Millay.

SONNET XXXIII

Full many a glorious morning have I seen a
Flatter the mountain tops with sovereign eye, b
Kissing with golden face the meadows green, a
Gilding pale streams with heavenly alchemy; b
Anon permit the basest clouds to ride c
With ugly rack on his celestial face, d
And from the forlorn world his visage hide, c
Stealing unseen to west with this disgrace: d

Even so my sun one early morn did shine e
With all-triumphant splendour on my brow; f
But out, alack! he was but one hour mine; e
The region[1] cloud hath masked him from me now. f
Yet him for this my love no whit disdaineth; g
Suns of the world may stain, when heaven's sun staineth. g

—*William Shakespeare* (1564-1616)

THE PARTING

Since there's no help, come, let us kiss and part,— a
Nay I have done, you get no more of me; b

[1] Airy.

And I am glad, yea, glad with all my heart, a
That thus so cleanly I myself can free; b
Shake hands for ever, cancel all our vows, c
And when we meet at any time again, d
Be it not seen in either of our brows c
That we one jot of former love retain. d

Now at the last gasp of Love's latest breath, e
When, his pulse failing, Passion speechless lies, f
When Faith is kneeling by his bed of death, e
And Innocence is closing up his eyes,— f
Now if thou would'st, when all have given him over, g
From death to life thou might'st him yet recover! g
—*Michael Drayton* (1563-1631)

PITY ME NOT

Pity me not because the light of day a
At close of day no longer walks the sky; b
Pity me not for beauties passed away a
From field and thicket as the year goes by; b
Pity me not the waning of the moon, c
Nor that the ebbing tide goes out to sea, d
Nor that a man's desire is hushed so soon, c
And you no longer look with love on me. d

This have I known always: love is no more e
Than the wide blossom which the wind assails; f
Than the great tide that treads the shifting shore, e
Strewing fresh wreckage gathered in the gales. f
Pity me that the heart is slow to learn g
What the swift mind beholds at every turn. g
—*Edna St. Vincent Millay* (1892-)

THE MILTONIC SONNET

The Miltonic sonnet returns to the rhyme-scheme of the Petrarchan sonnet with its strict emphasis on four or five rhymes. It differs strikingly from its model in one essential: In the Petrarchan the octave usually projected a general idea while the sestet pointed it and made it particular; in the Miltonic sonnet there is no pause, the octave and sestet being moulded into one firm unit. Milton unrolled his thought without interruption, the "run on" eighth line carrying the crest of the poem to the end of the sonnet, instead of the peak being (as in the Petrarchan) at the end of the octave. The rhyme scheme is *a-b-b-a-a-b-b-a-c-d-e-c-d-e* as in the following moving and immortal poem:

ON HIS BLINDNESS

When I consider how my light is spent, a
Ere half my days, in this dark world and wide, b
And that one talent which is death to hide, b

Lodged with me useless, though my soul more bent a
To serve therewith my Maker, and present a
My true account, lest He returning chide, b
"Doth God exact day-labour, light denied?" b
I fondly ask; but Patience, to prevent a
That murmur, soon replies, "God doth not need c
Either man's work or His own gifts: who best d
Bear his mild yoke, they serve Him best. His state e
Is kingly: Thousands at His bidding speed c
And post o'er land and ocean without rest; d
They also serve who only stand and wait." e

—*John Milton* (1608-1674)

Wordsworth employed the sonnet in a variety of ways from the pure Petrarchan model to the composite form. In none did he attain higher quality than in his Miltonic sonnets, particularly in those where the ardent revolutionary spoke—that eager spirit whose later abandonment of liberalism was mourned by Browning in "The Lost Leader." One of Wordsworth's fiery sonnets, compact with dissatisfaction of smug materialistic civilization. is the following:

THE WORLD

The world is too much with us; late and soon, a
Getting and spending, we lay waste our powers: b
Little we see in Nature that is ours; b
We have given our hearts away, a sordid boon! a
The Sea that bares her bosom to the moon; a
The winds that will be howling at all hours, b
And are up-gathered now like sleeping flowers; b
For this, for everything, we are out of tune; a
It moves us not.—Great God! I'd rather be c
A Pagan suckled in a creed outworn; d
So might I, standing on this pleasant lea, c
Have glimpses that would make me less forlorn; d
Have sight of Proteus rising from the sea; c
Or hear old Triton blow his wreathèd horn. d

—*William Wordsworth* (1770-1850)

THE SPENSERIAN SONNET

The Spenserian sonnet is a curious combination of the Petrarchan and the Shakespearian sonnet with an entirely new feature. It has exactly five rhymes as against the seven found in the Shakespearian form, but it resembles the Shakespearian in its use of the concluding couplet. Its innovation is an "interlocking" rhyme-scheme: *a-b-a-b-b-c-b-c-c-d-c-d-e-e*. This continuous linking of paired sounds is a happy and ingenious device, a silver chain of rhyme, neither too loose nor too constricted.

FAIR IS MY LOVE

Fair is my Love, when her fair golden hairs a
With the loose wind ye waving chance to mark; b

Fair, when the rose in her red cheeks appears; a
Or in her eyes the fire of love does spark. b
Fair, when her breast, like a rich laden bark, b
With precious merchandise she forth doth lay; c
Fair, when that cloud of pride, which oft doth dark b
Her goodly light, with smiles she drives away. c
But fairest she, when so she doth display c
The gate with pearls and rubies richly dight; d
Through which her words so wise do make their way c
To bear the message of her gentle spright. d
The rest be works of Nature's wonderment; e
But this the work of heart's astonishment. e

—*Edmund Spenser* (1552-1599)

Such music lingers in the ear after the graceful content has left the mind. One remembers the chiming syllables even though the elaborate conceits and artificially fervid compliments are out of date.

THE COMPOSITE SONNET

The Composite or "Irregular" sonnet is, as the name implies, a combination of other sonnet-types. Some of the most notable of English sonnets fall into this category, the possibilities of variation being unlimited. Philip Sidney's cycle of sonnets, "Astrophel and Stella," would be in this class. The octaves of Sidney's sonnets are irreproachably Petrarchan while the sestets, employing the final couplet forbidden in the Petrarchan, are Shakespearian—Sidney's rhyme-scheme being *a-b-b-a-a-b-b-a c-d-c-d-e-e*.

TO THE MOON

With how sad steps, O Moon, thou climb'st the skies! a
How silently, and with how wan a face! b
What! may it be that even in heavenly place b
That busy archer his sharp arrows tries? a
Sure, if that long-with-love-acquainted eyes a
Can judge of love, thou feel'st a lover's case; b
I read it in thy looks. Thy languished grace b
To me, that feel the like, thy state descries. a

Then, even of fellowship, O Moon, tell me, c
Is constant love deemed there but want of wit? d
Are beauties there as proud as here they be? c
Do they above love to be loved, and yet d
Those lovers scorn whom that love doth possess? e
Do they call virtue there ungratefulness? e

—*Philip Sidney* (1554-1586)

Somewhat different is Wordsworth's "Sonnet on the Sonnet" quoted on page 360. This, too, is in the composite or "irregular" form, but its origins are less obvious than the Sidney sonnets. Its octave—*a-b-b-a-a-c-c-a*—is a compromise between the Petrarchan and Spenserian type, but the sestet—*d-e-d-e-f-f*—

is quite Shakespearian. Yet the uninterrupted thought, the "run on" eighth line, the lack of pause between the octave and sestet are definitely Miltonic!

Similarly hybrid is Swinburne's tribute to Shakespeare, which, inconsistently, is not written in the Shakespearian form, but in a cross between the Petrarchan and an altered form of the Miltonic. The octave is the orthodox *a-b-b-a-a-b-b-a* while the sestet violates the tradition and begins with a couplet, presenting this curious arrangement: *c-c-d-e-e-d*.

WILLIAM SHAKESPEARE

Not if men's tongues and angels' all in one a
Spake, might the word be said that might speak Thee. b
Streams, winds, woods, flowers, fields, mountains, yea, the sea, b
What power is in them all to praise the sun? a
His praise is this,—he can be praised of none. a
Man, woman, child, praise God for him; but he b
Exults not to be worshipped, but to be. b
He is; and, being, beholds his work well done. a
All joy, all glory, all sorrow, all strength, all mirth, c
Are his: without him, day were night on earth. c
Time knows not his from time's own period. d
All lutes, all harps, all viols, all flutes, all lyres, e
Fall dumb before him ere one string suspires. e
All stars are angels; but the sun is God. d

—*Algernon Charles Swinburne* (1837-1909)

An equally impressive tribute to the great poet-dramatist is the sonnet written by Matthew Arnold. This, also, is written in a composite form rather than in the Shakespearian pattern, although the sestet has the rhymes—and the ring —of Shakespeare's own.

SHAKESPEARE

Others abide our question. Thou art free. a
We ask and ask. Thou smilest, and art still, b
Out-topping knowledge. For the loftiest hill, b
Who to the stars uncrowns his majesty, a
Planting his steadfast footsteps in the sea, a
Making the heaven of heavens his dwelling-place, c
Spares but the cloudy border of his base c
To the foiled searching of mortality; a
And thou, who didst the stars and sunbeams know, d
Self-schooled, self-scanned, self-honoured, self-secure, e
Didst tread on earth unguessed at.—Better so! d
All pains the immortal spirit must endure, e
All weakness which impairs, all griefs which bow, f
Find their sole speech in that victorious brow. f

—*Matthew Arnold* (1822-1888)

It is almost impossible to assign a particular form to one of the greatest sonnets ever written. As a poem Shelley's "Ozymandias" is tremendous in pictorial power, superb in irony; as a pattern it is so "irregular" as to be nondescript. Were it not that its ten-syllable iambics confine themselves to fourteen lines, its standing as a sonnet would be doubtful. The rhyme-scheme is haphazard, catch-as-catch-can—*a-b-a-b-a-c-d-c-e-d-e-f-e-f*—yet the spell of the poem is such that we are unconscious of the shortcomings in its design.

OZYMANDIAS

I met a traveller from an antique land a
Who said: Two vast and trunkless legs of stone b
Stand in the desert . . . Near them, on the sand, a
Half sunk, a shattered visage lies, whose frown, b
And wrinkled lip, and sneer of cold command, a
Tell that its sculptor well those passions read c
Which yet survive, stamped on these lifeless things, d
The hand that mocked them, and the heart that fed: c
And on the pedestal these words appear: e
"My name is Ozymandias, king of kings: d
Look on my works, ye Mighty, and despair!" e
Nothing beside remains. Round the decay f
Of that colossal wreck, boundless and bare e
The lone and level sands stretch far away. f

—*Percy Bysshe Shelley* (1792-1822)

The sonnets which follow include all the varieties previously analyzed. Apart from the importance of their content, an added pleasure may be derived from recognizing and classifying the type, there being a number of composite or "irregular" sonnets as well as Petrarchan, Shakespearian, Miltonic, and Spenserian forms. The arrangement is chronological.

VOW TO LOVE FAITHFULLY

Set me whereas the sun doth parch the green,
Or where his beams do not dissolve the ice,
In temperate heat where he is felt and seen;
In presence 'prest of people, mad or wise;
Set me in high or yet in low degree,
In longest night or in the shortest day,
In clearest sky or where clouds thickest be,
In lusty youth or when my hairs are gray.
Set me in heaven, in earth, or else in hell;
In hill, or dale, or in the foaming flood;
Thrall or at large, alive, whereso I dwell,
Sick or in health, in evil fame or good;
Hers will I be, and only with this thought
Content myself although my chance be nought.

—*Henry Howard, Earl of Surrey* (1517-1547)

LIKE AS A SHIP

Like as a ship, that through the ocean wide,
By conduct of some star doth make her way,
Whenas a storm hath dimmed her trusty guide,
Out of her course doth wander far astray;
So I, whose star, that wont with her bright ray
Me to direct, with clouds is overcast,
Do wander now, in darkness and dismay,
Through hidden perils round about me placed;
Yet hope I well that, when this storm is past,
My Helicè, the lodestar of my life,
Will shine again, and look on me at last,
With lovely light to clear my cloudy grief:
Till then I wander care-full, comfortless,
In secret sorrow, and sad pensiveness.

—*Edmund Spenser* (1552-1599)

SLEEP

Come, Sleep! O Sleep, the certain knot of peace,
The baiting-place of wit, the balm of woe,
The poor man's wealth, the prisoner's release,
The indifferent judge between the high and low!
With shield of proof, shield me from out the prease [1]
Of those fierce darts Despair at me doth throw:
O make in me those civil wars to cease!
I will good tribute pay if thou do so.

Take thou of me, smooth pillows, sweetest bed,
A chamber deaf to noise and blind to light,
A rosy garland, and a weary head:
And if these things, as being thine by right,
Move not thy heavy grace, thou shalt in me,
Livelier than elsewhere, Stella's image see.

—*Philip Sidney* (1554-1586)

DESIRE

Thou blind man's mark, thou fool's self-chosen snare,
Fond fancy's scum, and dregs of scattered thought,
Band of all evils; cradle of causeless care;
Thou web of ill, whose end is never wrought:
Desire! Desire! I have too dearly bought
With price of mangled mind, thy worthless ware;
Too long, too long, asleep thou hast me brought,
Who should my mind to higher things prepare.

But yet in vain thou hast my ruin sought;
In vain thou mad'st me to vain things aspire;
In vain thou kindlest all thy smoky fire;
For Virtue hath this better lesson taught—
Within myself to seek my only hire,
Desiring nought but how to kill Desire.

—*Philip Sidney* (1554-1586)

TO DELIA

When men shall find thy flower, thy glory pass,

[1] Prease: press.

And thou, with careful brow, sitting alone,
Receivèd hast this message from thy glass,
That tells the truth, and says that all is gone;
Fresh shalt thou see in me the wounds thou madest,
Though spent thy flame, in me the heat remaining:
I that have loved thee thus before thou fadest,
My faith shall wax, when thou art in thy waning!

The world shall find this miracle in me,
That fire can burn when all the matter's spent:
Then what my faith hath been, thyself shall see,
And that thou wast unkind, thou may'st repent!
Thou may'st repent that thou hast scorned my tears,
When Winter snows upon thy sable hairs.

—*Samuel Daniel* (1562-1619)

THE PARADOX

When first I ended, then I first began;
Then more I travelled further from my rest.
Where most I lost, there most of all I won;
Pinèd with hunger, rising from a feast.
Methinks I fly, yet want I legs to go;
Wise in conceit, in act a very sot;
Ravished with joy amidst a hell of woe;
What most I seem that surest I am not.

I build my hopes a world above the sky,
Yet with the mole I creep into the earth;
In plenty, I am starved with penury,
And yet I surfeit in the greatest dearth.
I have, I want; despair, and yet desire;
Burned in a sea of ice, and drowned amidst a fire.

—*Michael Drayton* (1563-1631)

SONNETS

by William Shakespeare (1564-1616)

XVIII

Shall I compare thee to a summer's day?
Thou art more lovely and more temperate:
Rough winds do shake the darling buds of May,

And summer's lease hath all too short a date:
Sometime too hot the eye of heaven shines,
And often is his gold complexion dimm'd;
And every fair from fair sometime declines,
By chance, or nature's changing course un-
  trimm'd.

But thy eternal summer shall not fade,
Nor lose possession of that fair thou ow'st,
Nor shall death brag thou wander'st in his
  shade,
When in eternal lines to time thou grow'st;
So long as men can breathe, or eyes can see,
So long lives this, and this gives life to thee.

XXX

When to the sessions of sweet silent thought
I summon up remembrance of things past,
I sigh the lack of many a thing I sought,
And with old woes new wail my dear time's
  waste:
Then can I drown an eye, unus'd to flow,
For precious friends hid in death's dateless
  night,
And weep afresh love's long since cancell'd
  woe,
And moan the expense of many a vanish'd
  sight.

Then can I grieve at grievances forgone,
And heavily from woe to woe tell o'er
The sad account of fore-bemoanèd moan,
Which I new pay as if not paid before.
But if the while I think on thee, dear friend,
All losses are restor'd and sorrows end.

LXV

Since brass, nor stone, nor earth, nor bound-
  less sea,
But sad mortality o'ersways their power,
How with this rage shall beauty hold a plea,
Whose action is no stronger than a flower?
O! how shall summer's honey breath hold out
Against the wrackful siege of battering days,
When rocks impregnable are not so stout,
Nor gates of steel so strong, but Time decays?

O fearful meditation! where, alack,
Shall Time's best jewel from Time's chest lie
  hid?
Or what strong hand can hold his swift foot
  back?
Or who his spoil of beauty can forbid?
O! none, unless this miracle have might,
That in black ink my love may still shine
  bright.

LXVI

Tired with all these, for restful death I cry—
As, to behold desert a beggar born,
And needy nothing trimm'd in jollity,
And purest faith unhappily forsworn,
And gilded honour shamefully misplaced,
And maiden virtue rudely strumpeted,
And right perfection wrongfully disgraced,
And strength by limping sway disablèd,
And art made tongue-tied by authority,
And folly, doctor-like, controlling skill,
And simple truth miscall'd simplicity,
And captive good attending captain ill:—
—Tired with all these, from these would I
  be gone,
Save that, to die, I leave my love alone.

LXXI

No longer mourn for me when I am dead
Than you shall hear the surly sullen bell
Give warning to the world that I am fled
From this vile world with vilest worms to
  dwell;
Nay, if you read this line, remember not
The hand that writ it, for I love you so
That I in your sweet thoughts would be for-
  got
If thinking on me then should make you
  woe.

O if, I say, you look upon this verse
When I perhaps compounded am with clay,
Do not so much as my poor name rehearse,
But let your love even with my life decay,
Lest the wise world should look into your
  moan
And mock you with me after I am gone.

LXXXVII

Farewell! thou art too dear for my possessing,
And like enough thou know'st thy estimate:
The charter of thy worth gives thee releasing;
My bonds in thee are all determinate.
For how do I hold thee but by thy granting?
And for that riches where is my deserving?
The cause of this fair gift in me is wanting,
And so my patent back again is swerving.

Thyself thou gav'st, thy own worth then not knowing,
Or me, to whom thou gav'st it, else mistaking;
So thy great gift, upon misprision growing,
Comes home again, on better judgment making.
Thus have I had thee, as a dream doth flatter,
In sleep a king, but, waking, no such matter.

XCVII

How like a winter hath my absence been
From thee, the pleasure of the fleeting year!
What freezings have I felt, what dark days seen!
What old December's bareness everywhere!
And yet this time remov'd was summer's time;
The teeming autumn, big with rich increase,
Bearing the wanton burden of the prime,
Like widow'd wombs after their lords' decease.

Yet this abundant issue seem'd to me
But hope of orphans and unfather'd fruit;
For summer and his pleasures wait on thee,
And, thou away, the very birds are mute:
Or, if they sing, 'tis with so dull a cheer,
That leaves look pale, dreading the winter's near.

XCIX

The forward violet thus did I chide:
"Sweet thief, whence didst thou steal thy sweet that smells,
If not from my love's breath? The purple pride,
Which on thy soft cheek for complexion dwells,
In my love's veins thou hast too grossly dyed."
The lily I condemnèd for thy hand
And buds of marjoram had stolen thy hair;
The roses fearfully on thorns did stand,
One blushing shame, another white despair;
A third, nor red nor white, had stolen of both,
And to his robbery had annexed thy breath;
But for his theft, in pride of all his growth,
A vengeful canker eat him up to death.
More flowers I noted, yet none could I see
But sweet or color it had stolen from thee.

CVI

When in the chronicle of wasted time
I see descriptions of the fairest wights,
And beauty making beautiful old rhyme
In praise of ladies dead and lovely knights,
Then, in the blazon of sweet beauty's best,
Of hand, of foot, of lip, of eye, of brow,
I see their antique pen would have express'd
Even such a beauty as you master now.

So all their praises are but prophecies
Of this our time, all you prefiguring;
And, for they look'd but with divining eyes,
They had not skill enough your worth to sing:
For we, which now behold these present days,
Have eyes to wonder, but lack tongues to praise.

CXLVI

Poor soul, the center of my sinful earth,
Fool'd by those rebel powers that thee array,
Why dost thou pine within and suffer dearth,
Painting thy outward walls so costly gay?
Why so large cost, having so short a lease,
Dost thou upon thy fading mansion spend?
Shall worms, inheritors of this excess
Eat up thy charge? Is this thy body's end?

Then soul, live thou upon thy servant's loss
And let that pine to aggravate thy store;
Buy terms divine in selling hours of dross;
Within be fed, without be rich no more;
So shall thou feed on death, that feeds on men,
And death once dead, there's no more dying then.

DEATH, BE NOT PROUD

Death, be not proud, though some have callèd thee
Mighty and dreadful, for thou art not so:
For those whom thou think'st thou dost overthrow
Die not, poor Death; nor yet canst thou kill me.
From Rest and Sleep, which but thy picture be,
Much pleasure, then from thee much more must flow;
And soonest our best men with thee do go—

Rest of their bones and souls' delivery!
Thou'rt slave to Fate, chance, kings, and desperate men,
And dost with poison, war, and sickness dwell;
And poppy or charms can make us sleep as well
And better than thy stroke. Why swell'st thou then?
One short sleep past, we wake eternally,
And Death shall be no more: Death, thou shalt die!

—*John Donne* (1573-1631)

JOHN THE BAPTIST

The last and greatest herald of heaven's King,
Girt with rough skins, hies to the deserts wild,
Among that savage brood the woods forth bring,
Which he more harmless found than man and mild:
His food was locusts, and what there doth spring,
With honey that from virgin hives distilled;
Parched body, hollow eyes, some uncouth thing
Made him appear, long since from earth exiled.
There burst he forth: "All ye, whose hopes rely
On God, with me amidst these deserts mourn;
Repent, repent, and from old errors turn."
Who listened to his voice, obeyed his cry?
Only the echoes, which he made relent,
Rung from their marble caves, "Repent, repent."

—*William Drummond of Hawthornden* (1585-1649)

ON HIS HAVING ARRIVED AT THE AGE OF TWENTY-THREE

How soon hath Time, the subtle thief of youth,
Stolen on his wing my three-and-twentieth year!
My hasting days fly on with full career,
But my late spring no bud or blossom shew'th.
Perhaps my semblance might deceive the truth
That I to manhood am arrived so near;
And inward ripeness doth much less appear,
That some more timely-happy spirits endu'th.
Yet, be it less or more, or soon or slow,
It shall be still in strictest measure even
To that same lot, however mean or high,
Toward which Time leads me, and the will of Heaven.
All is, if I have grace to use it so,
As ever in my great Task-Master's eye.

—*John Milton* (1608-1674)

SLEEP

A flock of sheep that leisurely pass by,
One after one; the sound of rain, and bees
Murmuring; the fall of rivers, winds and seas,
Smooth fields, white sheets of water, and pure sky;
I have thought of all by turns, and yet do lie
Sleepless! and soon the small birds' melodies
Must hear, first uttered from my orchard trees;
And the first cuckoo's melancholy cry.
Even thus last night, and two nights more, I lay,
And could not win thee, Sleep! by any stealth:
So do not let me wear tonight away:
Without Thee what is all the morning's wealth?
Come, blessèd barrier between day and day,
Dear mother of fresh thoughts and joyous health!

—*William Wordsworth* (1770-1850)

AFTER-THOUGHT

To the River Duddon

I thought of Thee, my partner and my guide,
As being past away.—Vain sympathies!
For, backward, Duddon, as I cast my eyes,
I see what was, and is, and will abide;
Still glides the Stream, and shall for ever glide;
The Form remains, the Function never dies;
While we, the brave, the mighty, and the wise,
We Men. who in our morn of youth defied

The elements, must vanish;—be it so!
Enough, if something from our hands have power
To live, and act, and serve the future hour;
And if, as toward the silent tomb we go,
Through love, through hope, and faith's transcendent dower,
We feel that we are greater than we know.

—*William Wordsworth* (1770-1850)

IT IS A BEAUTEOUS EVENING

It is a beauteous evening, calm and free,
The holy time is quiet as a Nun
Breathless with adoration; the broad sun
Is sinking down in its tranquillity;
The gentleness of heaven broods o'er the Sea;
Listen! the mighty Being is awake,
And doth with his eternal motion make
A sound like thunder—everlastingly.
Dear child! dear girl! that walkest with me here,
If thou appear untouched by solemn thought,
Thy nature is not therefore less divine:
Thou liest in Abraham's bosom all the year;
And worship'st at the Temple's inner shrine,
God being with thee when we know it not.

—*William Wordsworth* (1770-1850)

WHEN I HAVE FEARS

When I have fears that I may cease to be
  Before my pen has glean'd my teeming brain,
Before high-pilèd books, in charactery,
  Hold like rich garners the full-ripen'd grain;
When I behold, upon the night's starr'd face,
  Huge cloudy symbols of a high romance,
And think that I may never live to trace
  Their shadows, with the magic hand of chance;
And when I feel, fair creature of an hour,
  That I shall never look upon thee more,
Never have relish in the faery power
  Of unreflecting love;—then on the shore
Of the wide world I stand alone, and think
Till love and fame to nothingness do sink.

—*John Keats* (1795-1821)

ON THE GRASSHOPPER AND CRICKET

The poetry of earth is never dead:
  When all the birds are faint with the hot sun,
  And hide in cooling trees, a voice will run
From hedge to hedge about the new-mown mead.
That is the grasshopper's—he takes the lead
  In summer luxury,—he has never done
  With his delights, for when tired out with fun,
He rests at ease beneath some pleasant weed.
The poetry of earth is ceasing never:
  On a lone winter evening, when the frost
Has wrought a silence, from the stove there shrills
The cricket's song, in warmth increasing ever,

And seems to one, in drowsiness half-lost,
The grasshopper's among some grassy hills.
—*John Keats* (1795-1821)

LAST SONNET

Bright star, would I were stedfast as thou art—
Not in lone splendour hung aloft the night
And watching, with eternal lids apart,
Like nature's patient, sleepless Eremite,
The moving waters at their priestlike task
Of pure ablution round earth's human shores,
Or gazing on the new soft-fallen mask
Of snow upon the mountains and the moors—
No—yet still stedfast, still unchangeable,
Pillow'd upon my fair love's ripening breast,
To feel for ever its soft fall and swell,
Awake for ever in a sweet unrest,
Still, still to hear her tender-taken breath,
And so live ever—or else swoon to death.
—*John Keats* (1795-1821)

THREE SONNETS "FROM THE PORTUGUESE"

by Elizabeth Barrett Browning (1806-1861)

III

Unlike are we, unlike, O princely Heart!
Unlike our uses and our destinies.
Our ministering two angels look surprise
On one another, as they strike athwart
Their wings in passing. Thou, bethink thee, art
A guest for queens to social pageantries,
With gages from a hundred brighter eyes
Than tears even can make mine, to play thy part
Of chief musician. What hast *thou* to do
With looking from the lattice-lights at me—
A poor, tired, wandering singer, singing through
The dark, and leaning up a cypress tree?
The chrism is on thine head—on mine the dew—
And Death must dig the level where these agree.

VI

Go from me. Yet I feel that I shall stand
Henceforward in thy shadow. Nevermore
Alone upon the threshold of my door
Of individual life I shall command
The uses of my soul, nor lift my hand
Serenely in the sunshine as before,
Without the sense of that which I forbore—
Thy touch upon the palm. The widest land
Doom takes to part us, leaves thy heart in mine
With pulses that beat double. What I do
And what I dream include thee, as the wine
Must taste of its own grapes. And when I sue
God for myself, He hears that name of thine,
And sees within my eyes the tears of two.

XXII

When our two souls stand up erect and strong,
Face to face, silent, drawing nigh and nigher,
Until the lengthening wings break into fire
At either curvèd point,—what bitter wrong
Can the earth do us, that we should not long
Be here contented? Think! In mounting higher,
The angels would press on us, and aspire
To drop some golden orb of perfect song
Into our deep, dear silence. Let us stay
Rather on earth, Belovèd—where the unfit
Contrarious moods of men recoil away

And isolate pure spirits, and permit
A place to stand and love in for a day,
With darkness and the death-hour rounding it.

LUCIFER IN STARLIGHT

On a starred night Prince Lucifer uprose.
Tired of his dark dominion swung the fiend
Above the rolling ball in cloud part screened,
Where sinners hugged their spectre of repose.
Poor prey to his hot fit of pride were those.
And now upon his western wing he leaned,
Now his huge bulk o'er Afric's sands careened,
Now the black planet shadowed Arctic snows.
Soaring through wider zones that pricked his scars
With memory of the old revolt from Awe,
He reached a middle height, and at the stars,
Which are the brain of heaven, he looked, and sank.
Around the ancient track marched, rank on rank,
The army of unalterable law.

—*George Meredith* (1828-1909)

FROM "THE HOUSE OF LIFE"

by Dante Gabriel Rossetti (1828-1882)

Love Enthroned

I marked all kindred Powers the heart finds fair:—
Truth, with awed lips; and Hope, with eyes upcast;
And Fame, whose loud wings fan the ashen Past
To signal-fires, Oblivion's flight to scare;
And Youth, with still some single golden hair
Unto his shoulder clinging, since the last
Embrace wherein two sweet arms held him fast;
And Life, still wreathing flowers for Death to wear.

Love's throne was not with these; but far above
All passionate wind of welcome and farewell
He sat in breathless bowers they dream not of;
Though Truth foreknow Love's heart, and Hope foretell,
And Fame be for Love's sake desirable,
And Youth be dear, and Life be sweet to Love.

Lovesight

When do I see thee most, belovèd one?
When in the light the spirits of mine eyes
Before thy face, their altar, solemnise
The worship of that Love through thee made known?
Or when in the dusk hours, (we two alone,)
Close-kissed and eloquent of still replies
Thy twilight-hidden glimmering visage lies,
And my soul only sees thy soul its own?

O love, my love! if I no more should see
Thyself, nor on the earth the shadow of thee,
Nor image of thine eyes in any spring,—
How then should sound upon Life's darkening slope
The ground-whirl of the perished leaves of Hope,
The wind of Death's imperishable wing?

Lost Days

The lost days of my life until today,
What were they, could I see them on the street
Lie as they fell? Would they be ears of wheat
Sown once for food but trodden into clay?
Or golden coins squandered and still to pay?
Or drops of blood dabbling the guilty feet?
Or such spilt water as in dreams must cheat
The undying throats of Hell, athirst alway?
I do not see them here; but after death
God knows I know the faces I shall see,
Each one a murdered self, with low last breath.
"I am thyself,—what hast thou done to me?"
"And I—and I—thyself," (lo! each one saith,)
"And thou thyself to all eternity!"

REMEMBER

Remember me when I am gone away,
Gone far away into the silent land;
When you can no more hold me by the hand,
Nor I half turn to go yet turning stay.
Remember me when no more day by day
You tell me of our future that you planned:
Only remember me; you understand
It will be late to counsel then or pray.
Yet if you should forget me for a while
And afterwards remember, do not grieve:
For if the darkness and corruption leave
A vestige of the thoughts that once I had,
Better by far you should forget and smile
Than that you should remember and be sad.
—*Christina Georgina Rossetti* (1830-1894)

GOD'S GRANDEUR

The world is charged with the grandeur of God.
It will flame out, like shining from shook foil;
It gathers to a greatness, like the ooze of oil
Crushed. Why do men then now not reck his rod?
Generations have trod, have trod, have trod;
And all is seared with trade; bleared, smeared with toil;
And wears man's smudge and shares man's smell; the soil
Is bare now, nor can foot feel, being shod.

And for all this, nature is never spent;
There lives the dearest freshness deep down things;
And though the last lights off the black West went
Oh, mornings, at the brown brink eastward, springs—
Because the Holy Ghost over the bent
World broods with warm breast and with ah! bright wings.
—*Gerard Manley Hopkins* (1844-1898)

IN HOSPITAL

by William Ernest Henley (1846-1903)

Before

Behold me waiting—waiting for the knife.
A little while, and at a leap I storm
The thick, sweet mystery of chloroform,
The drunken dark, the little death-in-life.
The gods are good to me: I have no wife,
No innocent child, to think of as I near
The fateful minute; nothing all-too dear
Unmans me for my bout of passive strife.
Yet I am tremulous and a trifle sick,
And, face to face with chance, I shrink a little:
My hopes are strong, my will is something weak.
Here comes the basket? Thank you. I am ready.
But, gentlemen my porters, life is brittle:
You carry Caesar and his fortunes.—Steady!

After

Like as a flamelet blanketed in smoke,
So through the anaesthetic shows my life;
So flashes and so fades my thought, at strife
With the strong stupor that I heave and choke
And sicken at, it is so foully sweet.
Faces look strange from space—and disappear.
Far voices, sudden loud, offend my ear—
And hush as sudden. Then my senses fleet
All were a blank, save for this dull, new pain
That grinds my leg and foot; and brokenly
Time and the place glimpse on to me again;
And, unsurprised, out of uncertainty,
I wake—relapsing—somewhat faint and fain,
To an immense, complacent dreamery.

RENOUNCEMENT

I must not think of thee; and, tired yet strong,
I shun the thought that lurks in all delight—
The thought of thee—and in the blue Heaven's height,
And in the sweetest passage of a song.
O just beyond the fairest thoughts that throng
This breast, the thought of thee waits hidden yet bright;
But it must never, never come in sight;
I must stop short of thee the whole day long.

But when sleep comes to close each difficult day,
When night gives pause to the long watch I keep,
And all my bonds I needs must loose apart,
Must doff my will as raiment laid away,
With the first dream that comes with the first sleep
I run, I run, I am gathered to thy heart.

—*Alice Meynell* (1850-1923)

THE HEART

O nothing, in this corporal earth of man,
That to the imminent heaven of his high soul
Responds with colour and with shadow, can
Lack correlated greatness. If the scroll
Where thoughts lie fast in spell of hieroglyph
Be mighty through its mighty habitants;
If God be in His Name; grave potence if
The sounds unbind of hieratic chants;
All's vast that vastness means. Nay, I affirm

Nature is whole in her least things exprest,
Nor know we with what scope God builds the worm.
Our towns are copied fragments from our breast;
And all man's Babylons strive but to impart
The grandeurs of his Babylonian heart.
—*Francis Thompson* (1859-1907)

FROM "WEEK-END"

The train! The twelve o'clock for paradise,
Hurry, or it will try to creep away.
Out in the country everyone is wise!
We can be only wise on Saturday.
There you are waiting, little friendly house:
Those are your chimney-stacks with you between,
Surrounded by old trees and strolling cows,
Staring through all your windows at the green.
Your homely floor is creaking for our tread;
The smiling tea-pot with contented spout
Thinks of the boiling water, and the bread
Longs for the butter. All their hands are out
To greet us, and the gentle blankets seem
Purring and crooning: "Lie in us, and dream."
—*Harold Monro* (1879-1931)

RETURN AT NIGHT

Nothing but darkness enters in this room,
Nothing but darkness and the winter night,
Yet on this bed once years ago a light
Silvered the sheets with an unearthly bloom;
It was the planet Venus in the west
Casting a square of brightness on this bed,
And in that light your dark and lovely head
Lay for a while and seemed to be at rest.

But that the light is gone and that no more
Even if it were here, would you be here—
That is one line in a long tragic play
That has been acted many times before,
And acted best when not a single tear
Falls—when the mind and not the heart holds sway.
—*Sara Teasdale* (1884-1933)

THE DEAD

These hearts were woven of human joys and cares,
Washed marvellously with sorrow, swift to mirth.
The years had given them kindness. Dawn was theirs,
And sunset, and the colours of the earth.
These had seen movement, and heard music; known

Slumber and waking; loved; gone proudly friended;
Felt the quick stir of wonder; sat alone;
Touched flowers and furs and cheeks. All this is ended.
There are waters blown by changing winds to laughter
And lit by the rich skies, all day. And after,
Frost, with a gesture, stays the waves that dance
And wandering loveliness. He leaves a white
Unbroken glory, a gathered radiance,
A width, a shining peace, under the night.
—*Rupert Brooke* (1887-1915)

FROM "WILD PEACHES"

Down to the Puritan marrow of my bones
There's something in this richness that I hate.
I love the look, austere, immaculate,
Of landscapes drawn in pearly monotones.
There's something in my very blood that owns
Bare hills, cold silver on a sky of slate,
A thread of water, churned to milky spate
Streaming through slanted pastures fenced with stones.

I love those skies, thin blue or snowy gray,
Those fields sparse-planted, rendering meager sheaves;
That spring, briefer than apple-blossom's breath,
Summer, so much too beautiful to stay,
Swift autumn, like a bonfire of leaves,
And sleepy winter, like the sleep of death.
—*Elinor Wylie* (1887-1928)

OH, SLEEP FOREVER IN THE LATMIAN CAVE

Oh, sleep forever in the Latmian cave,
Mortal Endymion, darling of the Moon!
Her silver garments by the senseless wave
Shouldered and dropped and on the shingle strewn,
Her fluttering hand against her forehead pressed,
Her scattered looks that trouble all the sky,
Her rapid footsteps running down the west—
Of all her altered state, oblivious lie!
Whom earthen you, by deathless lips adored,
Wild-eyed and stammering to the grasses thrust,
And deep into her crystal body poured
The hot and sorrowful sweetness of the dust:
Whereof she wanders mad, being all unfit
For mortal love, that might not die of it.
—*Edna St. Vincent Millay* (1892-)

THOUGHT'S END

I watched the hills drink the last color of light,
All shapes grow bright and wane on the pale air.
Till down the traitorous east there came the night,
And swept the circle of my seeing bare.
Its intimate beauty like a wanton's veil
Tore from the void as from an empty face.
I felt at being's rim all being fail,
And my one body pitted against space.
O heart more frightened than a wild bird's wings,
Beating at green, now is no fiery mark
Left on the quiet nothingness of things.
Be self no more against the flooding dark:
There thousandwise sown in that cloudy blot
Stars that are worlds look out and see you not.

—*Léonie Adams* (1899-)

HOW SHE RESOLVED TO ACT

"I shall be careful to say nothing at all
About myself or what I know of him
Or the vaguest thought I have—no matter how dim,
Tonight if it so happen that he call."

And not ten minutes later the door-bell rang,
And into the hall he stepped as he always did
With a face and a bearing that quite poorly hid
His brain that burned and his heart that fairly sang
And his tongue that wanted to be rid of the truth.

As well as she could, for she was very loath
To signify how she felt, she kept very still;
But soon her heart cracked loud as a coffee-mill
And her brain swung like a comet in the dark
And her tongue raced like a squirrel in the park.

—*Merrill Moore* (1903-)

No reference to the sonnet, however brief, could pretend to authority without some mention of the sonnet *sequences* which have enriched literature. These groups of interrelated sonnets sometimes form a narrative, sometimes an exposition of character; more often, however, they are purely a set of associated poems in which the "plot" is less important than the range of emotion. Critics have differed in their choice of these, although most of them unite in awarding first place to Shakespeare's group of one hundred and fifty-four. After Shakespeare's immortal series, readers have been divided in their affections, but there can be little doubt that a great majority would select Philip Sidney's "Astrophel and Stella" and Edmund Spenser's "Amoretti" as the leading sonnet cycles prior to Shakespeare, although Drayton's forceful "Idea" should not be forgotten. Students of sonnet sequences should not fail to examine those of Wordsworth, particularly his "Political Sonnets" and the eloquent series addressed to "The River Duddon." The two greatest examples of the "sonnet necklaces" of the Victorian era are Mrs. Elizabeth Barrett Browning's "Sonnets from the Portuguese" and Dante Gabriel Rossetti's "House of Life." In the present period Masefield has used the sonnet sequence "Animula" to unfold a tale of passion.

In America long groups of sonnets have been less popular, but two remarkable sequences have appeared: Arthur Davison Ficke's "Sonnets of a Portrait Painter," and William Ellery Leonard's autobiographical "Two Lives." It might be added that three American sonneteers, Edna St. Vincent Millay, Elinor Wylie, and Edwin Arlington Robinson, have produced some of the most accomplished sonnets of the last half-century, Miss Millay's "Fatal Interview" and Mrs. Wylie's shorter "One Person" being two sonnet-sequences that seem destined to outlive their epoch. Merrill Moore has written several series of related sonnets colloquially pitched and distinctly American in tone.

Sonnets quoted in other chapters of this book are:

15

THE PATTERNS OF POETRY—3: THE BALLAD

POETRY began as a public function and developed, or degenerated, into a private performance. Instead of appealing only to the individual, poetry originally called forth the broadest responses of the entire community. To discover the origins of this appeal one must make an excursion into anthropology.

In Chapter 12 it was maintained that man's deep impulse to make strongly rhythmical sounds was the basis of poetry and, probably, of speech itself. Though there are many conflicting theories concerning primitive language, it is generally agreed that it was "sung" rather than "spoken" and that, in matters of communal concern, it fell into recognizable patterns: short phrases to the drum-beat of a war-dance; a marching chant after victory; a slow, rocking lamentation over a grave.

As the rites increased, the accompanying songs must have grown in range and volume. After tribal ceremonials to the sun and invocations for rain, primitive people turned to more personal jubilations: they began to celebrate the exploits of the clan and the heroism of individual leaders. Song was not yet a pastime; it was a form of magic, and a potent one, a talisman of the tribe. Groups fought, plundered, took prisoners, kept the strongest of the children and the best of the women, and—disdaining nothing they could use—incorporated into their own songs whatever seemed the most powerful parts of the enemy's chants. The more imaginative members of the clan—priests or skalds or bards or gleemen, "Smoothers and Polishers of Speech"—varied the words to suit the occasion, shifted the locality, added adventures that may have happened—or should have happened—and thus a literature came into being. The stuff of poetry must have been used for hundreds, possibly thousands, of years before it was shaped into epics, sagas, and separate metrical tales.

The English ballad developed along the line of primitive poetry. Its roots were widespread in Teutonic and Scandinavian soil; but, as the ballad-singers adapted it to local conditions, it began to assume a distinct shape, an authentic accent of its own. Soon the ballad-singer was employing the medium for current events; his tales became the news of the day. As the stories were repeated, or imitated, or passed from one to another, variations inevitably crept in; every ballad-singer was something of a ballad-maker. Refrains were introduced and these choruses were not only sung by the listeners but often danced to. No one recorded these rhymed stories; they were learned "by ear," carried from group to group, handed down from generation to generation. If, as Professor

Louise Pound insists in *Poetic Origins and the Ballad,* any ballad was the work of a particular individual, his name was forgotten and the changes made in his composition were so many that the ballad became the expression and the property of no one poet but of the people. This was the more reasonable since it was so manifestly a part of their experiences: a truly democratic poetry, being not only of the people and for the people, but—to a great extent—by the people.

Controversy has continued as to whether the early story-poems were improvised spontaneously by groups of people or were, in the manner of later poetry, constructed by an individual and sponsored by the community. It is likely that ballads were both spontaneously born *and* made. Sailors before the mast, soldiers in the trenches, boys at school have always improvised songs and varied them with topical references, and such songs persisted, like the sea chanteys, long after the occupation or occasion which prompted them was forgotten. Ballads are still being made by such a process. Elisabeth Greenleaf and Grace Y. Mansfield relate how one of the contributions to their *Ballads and Sea Songs of Newfoundland* (1933) was composed. "They [the sealer's crew] all started to make up the song at the beginning of the voyage, and someone added a line or two, or even a verse, whenever anything happened, so that the song is a sort of log of the cruise." However, the important thing about a folk-song is not whether it is created by single inspiration or spontaneous group accord, but that it is used, adapted, and colored by the community—it is never a private amusement but a public necessity, the response to a social need.

It was in the Cheviot hills along the Scottish border that the English ballad attained its greatest power; the harpers were, almost always, "of the north country." Aiming at little more than a vivid presentation of dramatic events, the ballads spread to ever wider circles. Some of them were finally written down, but they were haphazardly recorded and few scholars thought them worth studying. It was not until the middle of the eighteenth century that Bishop Thomas Percy discovered and began to decipher some of the old manuscripts. His task was difficult. There were, of course, no "originals" to act as standards of comparison. This, in a way, was just as well; for, as Allingham pointed out, a century after Percy, "the ballads owe no little of their merit to the countless riddlings, shiftings, siftings, omissions and additions of innumerable reciters." Yet Percy had trouble enough deciphering the parchments without judging the final quality of this oral literature. In the preface to his *Reliques of Ancient Poetry* (1765), he defended his versions and complained that the transcriptions were "sometimes extremely incorrect and faulty, being in such instances made from defective copies or the imperfect recitation of illiterate singers, so that a considerable portion of the song or narrative is sometimes omitted, and miserable trash or nonsense not infrequently introduced into pieces of considerable merit."

We must, therefore, accept the ballad with all its defects, its curious transitions, its sometimes annoying gaps, its swift pictures and occasionally startling phrases, its sudden descents from high poetry to banality, for the sake of its sharp characteristic quality. And what are its characteristics? An examination of a typical "border ballad" will reveal what is true of most.

THE DOUGLAS TRAGEDY

"Rise up! rise up, Lord Douglas!" she says,
"And put on your armor sae bright!
Let it never be said that a daughter o' thine
Was married to a lord under night!"

"Rise up! rise up, my seven bold sons!
And put on your armor sae bright;
And take better care o' your younger sister,
For your elder's awa' the last night."

Lady Margaret was on a milk-white steed,
Lord William was on a gray;
With a bugelet horn hung down by his side;
And lightly they rode away.

Lord William look'd owre his left shoulder,
To see what he could see,
And there he spied her seven brethren bold
Come riding over the lea.

"Light down! light down, Lady Margaret!" he said,
"And hold my steed in your hand,
Until that against your seven brethren bold
And your father I make a stand."

She held his steed in her milk-white hand,
And never shed one tear
Until that she saw her seven brethren fa'
And her father who loved her sae dear.

"Oh hold your hand! Lord William!" she said,—
"For your strokes they are wondrous sair; [1]
True lovers I can get many an ane,
But a father I can never get mair." [2]

O she's ta'en out her handkerchief,
It was o' the holland sae fine;
And aye she dighted [3] her father's bloody wounds,
That were redder than the wine.

"O choose! O choose, Lady Margaret!" he said,—
"O whether will ye gang or bide!"
"I'll gang, I'll gang, Lord William!" she said,—
"For ye hae left me nae other guide."

He's lifted her on a milk-white steed,
And himself on a dapple gray,
With a bugelet horn hung down by his side:
And slowly they rade away.

[1] Sore. [2] More. [3] Dressed.

O they rade on and on they rade,
  And a' by the light of the moon
Until they came to yon wan water,
  And there they lighted down.

They lighted down to take a drink
  Of the spring that ran sae clear;
And down the stream ran his gude heart's blood,
  And sair she began to fear.

"Hold up! hold up, Lord William!" she says,—
  "For I fear that you are slain."
" 'Tis naething but the shadow of my scarlet cloak,
  That shines in the water so plain."

O they rade on and on they rade,
  And a' by the light of the moon,
Until they came to his mother's door,
  And there they lighted down.

"Get up! get up, lady mother!" he says,—
  "Get up and let me in!
Get up! get up, lady mother!" he says,—
  "For this night my fair lady I've win.

"O make my bed, lady mother!" he says,—
  "O make it braid and deep!
And lay Lady Margaret close at my back!
  And the sounder I will sleep."

Lord William was dead lang ere midnight,
  Lady Margaret lang ere day:
And a' true lovers that go thegither,
  May they have mair luck than they!

Lord William was buried in St. Mary's kirk,
  Lady Margaret in Mary's choir;
Out o' her grave grew a bonny red rose,
  And out o' the knight's a briar.

What are the salient characteristics of such a poem? First of all, it moves swiftly. The ballad is primarily a story—a story in which action and movement are so speeded up that there is little if any time for anything else. There are no preliminaries, no digressions, no after-thoughts. The ballad starts in *medias res;* the persons involved are thrust upon the reader without introduction; we meet them loving and fighting and riding rapidly to their doom. The outraged mother rousing her husband and sons, the reckless Lord William defying every convention by the elopement, the desperate Lady Margaret, torn between loyalty to her father and passion for her lover—their motives, their very gestures, are stamped suddenly upon us. All is definite, decisive, direct.

A second feature of the ballad is its manipulation of the spoken, rather than the written, word. The language matches the action; it is equally direct, vivid, and spare. Metaphors are seldom encountered; the balladist was too intent upon his tale to stop for fine or ornate figures of speech.

Another characteristic of the ballad is its undeviating realism; it does not mince or evade or attempt subterfuge. If the tale is bloody—and it usually is—the ballad-singer makes no effort to soften the shock or placate the squeamish reader. The verse is keenly, uncompromisingly realistic; but as Herbert Read remarks,[1] "What, inheriting the jargon of our fathers, we call realism is no more than definiteness." This definiteness intensifies the details of the ballads and points the particularities with rude exactness. Lady Margaret's brothers were not "many," they were "Seven bold brothers;" in "Thomas the Rhymer" the Queen of Elfland's horse was not adorned with "dozens" of silver bells, but hung with "fifty silver bells and nine." Certain symbolic numbers—three, seven, and forty—seem to have been favored by the balladists.

Another, though less general, feature of the ballad is the employment of repetition. Sometimes the repetition consists only of a phrase; sometimes it is a line repeated in almost identical form; sometimes the device is extended and becomes a refrain. (The refrain may originally have been used as a dance measure or as the "chorus" in which the listeners joined—the narrative part of the ballad being sung or recited by the soloist.) Though it no longer serves such a purpose, so effective is this antique device that modern poets have adopted it—Rossetti in "Sister Helen," Kipling in "Mandalay," William Morris in "The Gilliflower of Gold," to name only three instances.

The last, and possibly the most remarkable, feature of the ballad is its impersonal tone. The objective attitude is maintained throughout; the narrator tells what there is to tell without adding any emotion of his own. He is not horrified by murder, shocked by illicit love, outraged by betrayal. The balladist knew that most communities were composed of hard-worked, commonplace people who relished gossip and a downright bloody deed, whose sympathies were with the outlaw, and who were far more interested in the frank event than in his feeling about it. Accordingly, the ballad-poet effaced himself as commentator or interpreter.

An excellent example of this detached attitude, unmoved in the face of catastrophe, is "Sir Patrick Spence." No criticism is made of the treachery, the bad judgment, or the rival faction which influenced the King to send the Scots nobles to sea at the most perilous time of year. The facts are given, the picture is swiftly painted, the betrayal and the inevitable tragedy are related as grim matters of course. The version quoted is somewhat more concentrated than most.

[1] In *Phases of English Poetry*. Harcourt, Brace and Company. 1929.

SIR PATRICK SPENCE

The king sits in Dumferline town,
  Drinking the blude-red wine.
"O, where will I get me a skeely[1] skipper
  To sail this ship of mine?"

O, up and spak an eldern knicht,
  Sat at the king's right knee:
"Sir Patrick Spence is the best sailòr,
  That sails upon the sea."

[1] Skilful.

The king has written a braid letter,[2]
  And signed it wi' his hand;
And sent it to Sir Patrick Spence,
  Was walking on the sand.

The first line that Sir Patrick read,
  A loud laugh laughèd he:
The next line that Sir Patrick read,
  The tear blinded his e'e.

"O wha is this hae done this deed,
  This ill deed done to me;
To send me out this time o' the year,
  To sail upon the sea?

"Mak haste, mak haste, my merry men all,
  Our good ship sails the morn."
"O say na sae, my master dear,
  For I fear a deadlie storm.

Late, late yestreen I saw the new moon
  Wi' the auld moon in her arme;
And I fear, I fear my dear mastèr,
  That we will come to harme."

They hadna sailed a league, a league,
  A league but barely three,

[2] "A braid letter," i.e. open, or patent; in opposition to close rolls.

When the lift grew dark, the wind blew loud
  And gurly [3] grew the sea.

The anchors brak, the topmast split,
  'Twas sic a deadlie storm;
The waves cam owre the broken ship
  Till a' her sides were torn.

O loth, loth were our gude Scots lords
  To wet their cork-heeled shoon;
But lang or a' the play were played
  Their hats they swam aboon.[4]

O lang, lang, may their ladies sit
  Wi' their fans into their hand,
Or e'er they see Sir Patrick Spence
  Come sailing to the land.

O lang, lang, may the maidens stand
  Wi' their gold kems [5] in their hair,
Waiting for their ain dear loves,
  For they'll see them na mair.

Half owre, half owre to Aberdour,[6]
  'Tis fifty fathom deep:
And there lies gude Sir Patrick Spence,
  Wi' the Scots lords at his feet.

[3] Angry.
[4] Above (them).
[5] Combs.
[6] Aberdour, a fishing town on the Firth.

Thus, as Professor Francis B. Gummere summarizes it in *The Beginnings of Poetry,* "the subjective, the reflective, the sentimental, are characteristics impossible in throng-made verse. . . . The diction of a traditional ballad is spontaneous, simple, objective as speech itself, and close to actual life."

The metrical structure of the ballad is equally "simple and spontaneous." The form is variable, but the preference is for quatrains with a straightforward, deliberate beat. The meter is usually iambic tetrameter with alternating lines of iambic trimeter. "Sir Patrick Spence" is a model of this structure, as is "The Daemon Lover," from which a stanza is diagrammed.

He stráck | the tóp- | mast wí' | his hánd,
  The fóre- | mast wí' | his knée;
He brák | that gál | lant shíp | in twáin,
  And sánk | her ín | the séa.

This example not only illustrates the traditional "ballad stanza" (see page 348), but the usual rhyme-scheme, which is *a-b-x-b*. Sometimes, the first and third as well as the second and fourth lines are rhymed, but this is rare. A commoner device is that which adds an internal rhyme in the third line to compensate for the lack of end-rhyme. Thus:

Yestreen the Queen had four Maries,
The night she'll hae but three;
There was Marie Seaton, and Marie Beaton,
And Marie Carmichael, and me.

Assonance (see page 464) is freely employed in the ballads, either to take the place of or to supplement "true" rhyme. Thus in "Sir Patrick Spence," there are such characteristic assonances as "deep-feet," "morn-storm," and a whole quatrain in assonance:

The anchors brak, the topmast *split,*
'Twas sic a deadlie *storm;*
The waves cam owre the broken *ship*
Till a' her sides were *torn.*

Occasionally the quatrain form is discarded and the couplet is employed. Rhymes following close upon each other give an effect of terseness as well as tension, as in "The Two Sisters of Binnorie," "Hynd Horn," "The Cruel Brother," and "Cospatrick." Another ballad composed in couplets, although arranged in four-line stanzas, is the quietly blood-curdling song known variously as "Lord Randal," and "Lord Donald."

LORD RANDAL

"O where ha'e ye been, Lord Randal, my son?
O where ha'e ye been, my handsome young man?"—
"I ha'e been to the wild wood; mother, make my bed soon,
For I'm weary with hunting, and fain would lie down."

"Who gave ye your dinner, Lord Randal, my son?
Who gave ye your dinner, my handsome young man?"—
"I dined with my true-love; mother, make my bed soon,
For I'm weary with hunting, and fain would lie down."

"What had ye for dinner, Lord Randal, my son?
What had ye for dinner, my handsome young man?"—
"I had eels boiled in broo';[1] mother, make my bed soon,
For I'm weary with hunting, and fain would lie down."

"And where are your bloodhounds, Lord Randal, my son?
And where are your bloodhounds, my handsome young man?"—
"O they swelled and they died; mother, make my bed soon,
For I'm weary with hunting, and fain would lie down."

"O I fear ye are poisoned, Lord Randal, my son!
O I fear ye are poisoned, my handsome young man!"—
"O yes! I am poisoned; mother, make my bed soon,
For I'm sick at the heart, and I fain would lie down."

Most of the characteristics of the ballad are in the five foregoing stanzas. The narrative is remarkably condensed; the statements are concise to the point

[1] Broth.

of being stripped; the language is sharp and decisive; the pitch is tensely dramatic. Suggestion also plays a great part here. The mother's anxiety is contrasted with the son's sick weariness, her questions heighten the suspense and gradually reveal the truth, summoning the enigmatic figure of the boy's sweetheart, and leaving the air heavy with horror. None of the characters is described, yet each is completely revealed: the distraught mother, the trusting son, and the malevolent creature who, offering love and food, did him to death.

Another powerful and even more terrible drama is suggested in "Edward, Edward," one of the oldest of the ballads.

EDWARD, EDWARD

"Why does your brand sae drip wi' blude,
Edward, Edward?
Why does your brand sae drip wi' blude,
And why sae sad gang ye, O?"
"O I ha'e killed my hawk sae good,
Mither, mither,
O I ha'e killed my hawk sae good
And I had no more but he, O."

"Your hawk's blude was never sae red,
Edward, Edward,
Your hawk's blude was never sae red,
My dear son, I tell thee, O."
"O I ha'e killed my red-roan steed,
Mither, mither,
O I ha'e killed my red-roan steed,
That erst was sae fair and free, O."

"Your steed was old and ye ha'e gat mair,
Edward, Edward,
Your steed was old and ye ha'e gat mair,
Some other dule ye dree, O." [1]
"O, I ha'e killed my father dear,
Mither, mither,
O, I ha'e killed my father dear,
Alas, and woe is me, O."

"What penance will ye dree for that,
Edward, Edward?
What penance will ye dree for that,
My dear son, now tell me, O?"
"I'll set my feet in yonder boat,
Mither, mither,
I'll set my feet in yonder boat,
And I'll fare across the sea, O."

"What will ye do wi' your towers and hall,
Edward, Edward?
What will ye do wi' your towers and hall,
That were sae fair to see, O?"
"I'll let them stand till down they fall,
Mither, mither,
I'll let them stand till down they fall,
For here never mair may I be, O."

"What will ye leave to your bairns and wife,
Edward, Edward?
What will ye leave to your bairns and wife,
When ye gang owre the sea, O?"
"The world's room: let them beg through life,
Mither, mither,
The world's room: let them beg through life,
For them never mair will I see, O."

"And what will ye leave to your ain mither dear,
Edward, Edward?
And what will ye leave to your ain mither dear,
My dear son, now tell me, O?"
"The curse o' hell frae me shall ye bear,
Mither, mither,
The curse o' hell frae me shall ye bear,
Sic counsels ye gave to me, O."

[1] "Dule ye dree": grief you suffer.

Here, again, the core of the tragedy is concealed until the sudden, incredible climax. It is only with the last line that we realize the diabolic extent of the crime and the revulsion of the weak-willed son who has murdered his father at the instigation of his mother.

It is interesting to observe the growth and variation of folk-songs, and such an opportunity is afforded in America. When the Scotch and English settlers came to the States they brought many of the ballads with them. Local conditions, popular names, indigenous items soon crept into the imported narratives; the departures began to color the tale; the tune changed. Finally the ballad as sung in the mountains of Kentucky would scarcely have been recognized by those who heard the original in the Cheviot hills. Until recently "backwoods ballads" connoted, in the minds of most readers, a few primitive fragments discovered in the Appalachians. But, as the interest in folk-lore increased, it became evident that there was a wealth of song—adapted, transformed, and original—in every corner of the country. In *Folk-Songs of the South,* John Harrington Cox cites no less than fourteen variants of "Sir Hugh or the Jew's Daughter," while Arthur Kyle Davis, Jr., pursuing other folk material, records still greater changes. In his *Traditional Ballads of Virginia* Davis, as researcher, calls attention to the rich variety that the same ballad may attain within one state. Professor Davis collected no less than ninety-two Virginia versions and fragments of "Bonny Barbara Allen," many of them presenting "healthy and different texts," of which he presented an annotated thirty-six set to an even dozen melodies! Barbara Allen's "ninety-two progeny are something of a record achievement," writes Professor Davis, "certainly for a lady who, according to the ballad, scorned her lover. One is thankful that she did not encourage him!"

Some of the difficulties of the folk-lorist are revealed in Professor Davis's preface to his monumental volume. He began his work of editing fifty Virginia ballads nonchalantly enough. "Only fifty? What were fifty ballads to him, fresh from the rigors of a dissertation! He did not foresee the magnitude of the task: the long period of preparation for work in a highly specialized field; the fifty ballads expanding into six hundred and fifty versions, variants and fragments with one hundred and forty-eight melodies; the tediousness of recapturing the data of collection for each of these six hundred and fifty items; the often illegible and unsatisfactory state of the material . . . the bulky files of correspondence extending over a dozen years from hundreds of correspondents . . . the tedious and microscopic process of comparing all the versions and variants of a single ballad with each other and with all the other printed texts of the same ballad. . . ." These represent only a portion of the labors of the folk-song researcher, quite apart from his field-work.

The local variations tend to combine parts of the older ballads, a tendency illustrated by "Johnny Randolph" (also known in other versions as "John Ramsey," "Johnny Reeler" and "Johnny Randall"), which is a composite of the two ballads reprinted on pages 389 and 390, "Lord Randal" and "Edward, Edward." (A particularly vigorous and racily American version of "Edward, Edward" is the piece called "Blood on the P'int o' Your Knife," quoted by Vance Randolph in his *Ozark Mountain Folks.*) The version which follows is one heard in Tennessee, but, in a slightly different form, is common to Kentucky, West Virginia, and the more remote parts of the Appalachians.

JOHNNY RANDALL

"Now where have you been, Johnny Randall, my son?
Now where have you been, my rambling young man?"

"I've been courting pretty Polly; mother, make my bed soon,
I've a pain in my heart and I need to lie down."

"What was your supper, Johnny Randall, my son?
What was your supper, my rambling young man?"
"Fried eels and fresh butter; mother, make my bed soon,
I've a pain in my heart and I need to lie down."

"What do you will to your father, Johnny Randall, my son?
What do you will to your father, my rambling young man?"
"A dead son to bury; mother, make my bed soon,
I've a pain in my heart and I need to lie down."

"What do you leave to your brothers, Johnny Randall, my son?
What do you leave to your brothers, my rambling young man?"
"My horse and my buggy; mother, make my bed soon,
I've a pain in my heart and I need to lie down."

"What do you will to your sweetheart, Johnny Randall, my son?
What do you will to your sweetheart, my rambling young man?"
"Hell's fire and brimstone to scorch her so brown!
She caused this pain in my heart and I need to lie down."

Another example of "transplanting" is furnished by the two following ballads. The first is ancient and is found, slightly varied, in many compilations. Its chief characteristic is the idyllic refrain. This striking device not only adds an unexpected music to the gruesome verses, but, with its burden of fine flowers and green leaves, intensifies the tragedy.

FINE FLOWERS IN THE VALLEY

She lean'd her back upon a thorn;
Fine flowers in the valley,
And there she has her sweet babe born,
And the green leaves they grow rarely.

She's ta'en the ribbon frae her hair
And bound its body fast and sair.

"Smile na sae sweet, my bonny babe,
An ye smile sae sweet, ye'll smile me dead."

She's ta'en out her little pen-knife
And twinn'd[1] the sweet babe o' its life.

She's howket[2] a grave sae deep and wide
And there she's buried her babe inside.

She's covered it wi' a marble stane
Thinking she would gang maiden hame

As she was going to the church
She saw a sweet babe in the porch.

"O sweet babe, if thou wert mine
I wad cleed[3] thee in silk and sabelline."[4]

"O mother mine, when I was thine,
You did na prove to me sae kind."

"But now I'm in the heavens hie,
Fine flowers in the valley,
And ye have the pains o' hell to dree—"
And the green leaves they grow rarely.

[1] Robbed.
[2] Dug.
[3] Clothe.
[4] Sable.

It is interesting to contrast this original from the Cheviot hills with an American adaptation found in the Appalachian mountains. Cecil J. Sharp, the folk-lorist, recorded almost a thousand songs from the lips of unlettered musicians in Kentucky, Tennessee, Virginia and the Carolinas, songs which sometimes betray and sometimes conceal their English origin. The following variant of "Fine Flowers in the Valley," still current in the Southern hills, shows how the local idiom has altered the language of the original.

THE CRUEL MOTHER

There was a lady from the town
Low, so low, so lonely—
She walked her up, she walked her down
Down by the greenwood sidey.

First she leaned against an oak;
First it bent and then it broke.

Next she leaned against a thorn,
Two sweet little babes to her were born.

She got a rope so long and neat;
She tied them down both hands and feet.

She got a knife so keen and sharp
And pierced it through each young thing's heart.

She walked the road one moonlit night—
There stood her two babes, dressed in white.

"O babes, O babes, if you were mine
I'd dress you up in silks so fine."

"O mother, O mother, when we were thine
You neither dressed us coarse nor fine.

"In seven years you'll hear a bell;
Low, so low, so lonely—
In seven years you'll land in hell."
Down by the greenwood sidey.

But the impulse to make new ballads is even greater than the wish to adapt old ones. In America, the machine has not prevented anonymous singers from putting into rhyme such catastrophes as the Johnstown flood or the exploits of the engineer Casey Jones or the sinking of the *Vestris* (Brunswick record 277). The spread of the phonograph and the radio may temporarily discourage folk-singing, but the pleasure of personal recitation and improvisation cannot be satisfied by vicarious mediums. The very diversity of industries has produced a great variety of American ballads, naïve and sophisticated, ballads of the cowboys in cattle-camps, lumberjacks in Maine and Michigan, hoboes riding the rails, negroes in the cotton-fields. There is even *(vide* "Frankie and Johnny") an American balladry of city streets. No résumé of folk-literature in this country would be complete without a recognition of the racy authentic quality in "Jesse James," "The Boll Weevil Song," "John Henry," "Deep River," "The Lone Prairie," "The Big Rock Candy Mountains," "The Shanty Boy," "Casey Jones" and "Frankie and Johnny."

Of these "Jesse James" is typical. A popular outlaw, the Robin Hood of the Middle West, Jesse James was the leader of a gang who befriended the needy and "fought square." Like his model, Jesse James robbed only the rich, was beloved by the poor, and was treacherously done to death. His betrayer, one of his own gang, was Robert Ford, who surrendered to the authorities and collected the ten thousand dollars offered by the governor of Missouri as the price on the outlaw's head. The seeming confusion of names in the ballad is due to the fact that when Jesse James—unarmed at the time—was shot down he was living under the name of "Howard." The version given here is practically identical with the one in Carl Sandburg's excellent and comprehensive *The American Songbag.*

JESSE JAMES

It was on a Wednesday night, the moon was shining bright,
They robbed the Danville train.
And the people they did say, for many miles away,
'Twas the outlaws Frank and Jesse James.

Jesse had a wife to mourn him all her life,
The children they are brave.
'Twas a dirty little coward shot Mister Howard,
And laid Jesse James in his grave.

Jesse was a man was a friend to the poor,
He never left a friend in pain.
And with his brother Frank he robbed the Chicago bank
And then held up the Glendale train.

It was Robert Ford, the dirty little coward,
I wonder how he does feel,
For he ate of Jesse's bread and he slept in Jesse's bed,
Then he laid Jesse James in his grave.

It was his brother Frank that robbed the Gallatin bank,
And carried the money from the town.
It was in this very place that they had a little race,
For they shot Captain Sheets to the ground.

They went to the crossing not very far from there,
And there they did the same;
And the agent on his knees he delivered up the keys
To the outlaws Frank and Jesse James.

It was on a Saturday night, Jesse was at home
Talking to his family brave,
When the thief and the coward, little Robert Ford,
Laid Jesse James in his grave.

How people held their breath when they heard of Jesse's death,
And wondered how he ever came to die.
'Twas one of the gang, dirty Robert Ford,
That shot Jesse James on the sly.

Jesse went to rest with his hand on his breast;
He died with a smile on his face.
He was born one day in the county of Clay,
And came from a solitary race.

Of the many original cowboy ballads none is more popular than "Home on the Range," which has been sung since the time of the early buffalo-hunters and is heard nightly on the air through the radio, to a hundred harmonies, none of which are more skilfully arranged than the setting by David Guion of Dallas, Texas. The anonymous author has voiced the hunger of all homesick cowboys for the "free country" beyond the reach of the cities, a region fast dwindling and, therefore, all the more dear.

HOME ON THE RANGE

Oh, give me a home where the buffalo roam,
  Where the deer and the antelope play;
Where never is heard a discouraging word
  And the skies are not cloudy all day.

How often at night when the heavens are bright
  With a light from the glittering stars,
Have I stood here amazed and asked as I gazed
  If their glory was greater than ours.

So give me the land where the bright diamond sand
  Flows leisurely down to the stream;
Oh, give me the rocks and the faraway flocks
  That graze on the mountains so green.

Then I would not exchange my home on the range
  Where the deer and the antelope play;
Where never is heard a discouraging word
  And the skies are not cloudy all day.

It has been the fashion to divide ballad literature into (a) the "popular" or ancient ballads and (b) the "literary" or modern ballads. Actually no such division exists. Many of the so-called "art" or "literary" ballads are as direct and simple as their forerunners, and the best of them are even more spirited. The chief difference is one of time. The Romantic Movement revived interest in the medieval and marked a reaction from the complex to the naïve. Wordsworth and Coleridge sounded the note with their *Lyrical Ballads* in 1798. They swung clear of the literary conventions of their day and carried the simplest themes to an unexpected emotional pitch. "The Rime of the Ancient Mariner" (see page 76) is an extended and glorified ballad, perhaps the richest ever written. Sir Walter Scott's "Jock of Hazeldean," "Proud Maisie," and "Lochinvar" (see page 67) owe more to the ancient models, for Scott was an inveterate collector of popular ballads—the bride-stealing theme in "Lochinvar" being found in the old "Katharine Jaffray." "Proud Maisie" has much of the grim concision characteristic of the terse Border ballads.

PROUD MAISIE

Proud Maisie is in the wood,
  Walking so early;
Sweet Robin sits on the bush,
  Singing so rarely.

"Tell me, thou bonny bird,
  When shall I marry me?"
"When six braw gentlemen
  Kirkward shall carry ye."

"Who makes the bridal bed,
  Birdie, say truly?"
"The grey-headed sexton
  That delves the grave duly."

"The glow-worm o'er grave and stone
  Shall light thee steady.
The owl from the steeple sing
  'Welcome, proud lady.' "

—*Walter Scott* (1771-1832)

Even more indebted to the medieval love of legend and superstition are Keats's "La Belle Dame sans Merci," Rossetti's "Sister Helen" (see page 91) and Masefield's "Cap on Head." The influence of "Sir Patrick Spence" may be traced in Longfellow's "The Wreck of the Hesperus" and Whittier's "Skipper Ireson's Ride" (see page 99) both of which (like "Sir Patrick Spence") were founded on actual events. Perhaps no poet ever combined the tone of the old ballads with the sheer magic of pure poetry as did Keats in "La Belle Dame sans Merci."

LA BELLE DAME SANS MERCI

by John Keats (1795-1821)

Ah, what can ail thee, wretched wight,
  Alone and palely loitering?
The sedge is wither'd from the lake,
  And no birds sing.

Ah, what can ail thee, wretched wight,
  So haggard and so woe-begone?
The squirrel's granary is full,
  And the harvest's done.

I see a lily on thy brow,
  With anguish moist and fever dew;
And on thy cheek a fading rose
  Fast withereth too.

I met a lady in the meads
  Full beautiful, a faery's child;
Her hair was long, her foot was light,
  And her eyes were wild.

I set her on my pacing steed,
  And nothing else saw all day long;
For sideways would she lean, and sing
  A faery's song.

I made a garland for her head,
  And bracelets too, and fragrant zone;
She look'd at me as she did love,
  And made sweet moan.

She found me roots of relish sweet,
  And honey wild, and manna dew,
And sure in language strange she said,
  "I love thee true."

She took me to her elfin grot
  And there she wept and sigh'd full sore,
And there I shut her wild, wild eyes
  With kisses four.

And there we slumber'd on the moss
  And there I dream'd—ah! woe betide!
The latest dream I ever dream'd
  On the cold hill side.

I saw pale kings, and princes too,
  Pale warriors, death-pale were they all;
Who cry'd—"La belle Dame sans merci
  Hath thee in thrall!"

I saw their starv'd lips in the gloam
  With horrid warning gapèd wide,
And I awoke, and found me here
  On the cold hill side.

And this is why I sojourn here
  Alone and palely loitering,
Though the sedge is wither'd from the lake,
  And no birds sing.

No list of modern ballads could be compiled without including Poe's "Annabel Lee"—a true ballad in spite of its departures in form—Lanier's "The Revenge of Hamish," Morris's "The Gilliflower of Gold," John Davidson's "A Ballad of a Nun," on which the play "The Miracle" was founded, and his "A Ballad of Hell," and John Hay's native "Pike County Ballads," including the famous "Jim Bludso." Nor has contemporary poetry neglected the ballad. Poems saturated with legend and folk-flavor have been composed by Stephen Vincent Benét and his brother William Rose Benét, Marjorie Allen Seiffert, Hervey Allen, Alfred Noyes, John Masefield, William Butler Yeats, and Sylvia Townsend Warner. But of all modern examples of the form the most popular in appeal and the most authentic in tone are Rudyard Kipling's *Barrack Room Ballads*. Compared to those of his immediate predecessors—Swinburne, Rossetti and Morris—Kipling's are far more vivid, free and spontaneous, unaffected by literature. They recapture and retain the old straightforwardness, the direct and vigorous communication of what Gummere calls "throng-poetry." "Danny Deever," "Mandalay," "The Ballad of East and West," "Fuzzy Wuzzy" and "Gunga Din" have been imitated, parodied and, like their ancient prototypes, have been varied by anonymous adapters. They bid fair to be handed down to generations remote from ours; popular pieces today, they are likely to become the folk-songs of tomorrow. It is interesting to note that, in most of these ballads—"Mandalay" being particularly effective—Kipling employs the old refrain-device, the burden being used for emphasis as well as music.

MANDALAY

by Rudyard Kipling (1865-)

By the old Moulmein Pagoda, lookin' eastward to the sea,
There's a Burma girl a-settin', an' I know she thinks o' me;
For the wind is in the palm-trees, an' the temple-bells they say:
"Come you back, you British soldier; come you back to Mandalay!"
Come you back to Mandalay,
Where the old Flotilla lay:
Can't you 'ear their paddles chunkin' from Rangoon to Mandalay?
On the road to Mandalay,
Where the flyin'-fishes play,
An' the dawn comes up like thunder outer China 'crost the Bay!

'Er petticut was yaller an' 'er little cap was green,
An' 'er name was Supi-yaw-lat—jes' the same as Theebaw's Queen,
An' I seed her fust a-smokin' of a whackin' white cheroot,
An' a-wastin' Christian kisses on an 'eathen idol's foot:
Bloomin' idol made o' mud—
What they called the Great Gawd Budd—
Plucky lot she cared for idols when I kissed 'er where she stud!
On the road to Mandalay—

When the mist was on the rice-fields an' the sun was droppin' slow,
She'd git 'er little banjo an' she'd sing *"Kulla-lo-lo!"*
With 'er arm upon my shoulder an' her cheek agin my cheek
We useter watch the steamers an' the *hathis* pilin' teak.
Elephints a-pilin' teak
In the sludgy, squdgy creek,
Where the silence 'ung that 'eavy you was 'arf afraid to speak!
On the road to Mandalay—

But that's all shove be'ind me—long ago an' fur away,
An' there ain't no 'busses runnin' from the Bank to Mandalay;

An' I'm learnin' 'ere in London what the ten-year sodger tells:
"If you've 'eard the East a-callin', why, you won't 'eed nothin' else."
No! you won't 'eed nothin' else
But them spicy garlic smells
An' the sunshine an' the palm-trees an' the tinkly temple bells!
On the road to Mandalay—

I am sick o' wastin' leather on these gritty pavin'-stones,
An' the blasted Henglish drizzle wakes the fever in my bones;
Tho' I walks with fifty 'ousemaids outer Chelsea to the Strand,
An' they talks a lot o' lovin', but wot do they understand?
Beefy face an' grubby 'and—
Law! wot *do* they understand?
I've a neater, sweeter maiden in a cleaner, greener land!
On the road to Mandalay—

Ship me somewheres east of Suez where the best is like the worst,
Where there aren't no Ten Commandments, an' a man can raise a thirst;
For the temple-bells are callin', an' it's there that I would be—
By the old Moulmein Pagoda, lookin' lazy at the sea—
On the road to Mandalay,
Where the old Flotilla lay,
With our sick beneath the awnings when we went to Mandalay!
Oh, the road to Mandalay,
Where the flyin'-fishes play,
An' the dawn comes up like thunder outer China 'crost the Bay!

Sylvia Townsend Warner is known chiefly for her remarkable prose. But her volumes of poetry (chiefly *The Espalier* and *Time Importuned*) are as characteristic of this distinguished creator as her exquisite *Mr. Fortune's Maggot* and its poignant sequel *The Salutation*. Her ballad "The Image" combines the old ballad spirit with an idiom which is Miss Warner's own. The reference in the first stanza ("as it says in the song") is to the ballad "Lord Randal," quoted on page 389. Miss Warner's handling of the theme—the malevolent sweetheart being a practitioner in black magic instead of a poisoner—is a triumph of re-creation.

THE IMAGE

by Sylvia Townsend Warner (1893-)

"Why do you look so pale, my son William?
Where have you been so long?"
"I've been to my sweetheart, Mother,
As it says in the song."

"Though you be pledged and cried to the parish
'Tis not fitting or right
To visit a young maiden
At this hour of night."

"I went not for her sweet company,
I meant not any sin,
But only to walk round her house
And think she was within.

"Unbeknown I looked in at the window;
And there I saw my bride

Sitting lonesome in the chimney-nook,
With the cat alongside.

"Slowly she drew out from under her apron
An image made of wax,
Shaped like a man, and all stuck over
With pins and with tacks.

"Hair it had, hanging down to its shoulders,
Straight as any tow—
Just such a lock she begged of me
But three days ago.

"She set it down to stand in the embers—
The wax began to run,
Mother! Mother! That waxen image,
I think it was your son!"

" 'Twas but a piece of maiden's foolishness,
Never think more of it.
I warrant that when she's a wife
She'll have a better wit."

"Maybe, maybe, Mother.
I pray you, mend the fire.
For I am cold to the knees
With walking through the mire.

"The snow is melting under the rain,
The ways are full of mud;
The cold has crept into my bones,
And glides along my blood.

"Take out, take out my winding sheet
From the press where it lies,
And borrow two pennies from my money-box
To put upon my eyes;

"For now the cold creeps up to my heart,
My ears go Ding, go Dong:
I shall be dead long before day,
For winter nights are long."

"Cursèd, cursèd be that Devil's vixen
To rob you of your life!
And cursèd be the day you left me
To go after a wife!"

"Why do you speak so loud, Mother?
I was almost asleep.
I thought the churchbells were ringing
And the snow lay deep.

"Over the white fields we trod to our wedding,
She leant upon my arm—
What have I done to her that she
Should do me this harm?"

The impulse to make ballads persists in spite of changing fashions in everything else. Another skilful employment of an old theme—in this instance the tale of Apollo and Daphne—is Phelps Putnam's "Ballad of a Strange Thing," in which the mythological figures are transported to the American scene, the setting being Pollard Mill at harvest time. One of the most recent examples, and one in the best traditional manner, is by one of the younger American poets whose short stories are even more striking than the lyrics in her *City Child.*

BALLAD OF THE HUNTSMAN

by Selma Robinson (1905-)

And "No" she answered to his plea;
"We never can be wed
Though you ask me a hundred times," said she.
"Or a thousand times," she said.

"Oh, then, farewell my golden dear,
Farewell my stony-hearted.
I shall go away, far, far from here."
Said she: "It's time you started."

"I shall go away with my bag and my gun
To hunt and forget," said he.
"I shall put my woven jacket on
And my boots that lace to the knee."

"It's time you left and I wish you luck.
If you bag a grouse or a pheasant
Or a spotted quail," she said, "or a duck,
Bring one to me for a present."

"Each time I aim into the blue
Of the sky or the brown of the marsh,
I shall think I point my gun at you,"
Said he, and his voice was harsh.

A day and a week and a month went by
And again he stood at her door
Pale and worn, with his cap awry,
And stained were the clothes he wore;

Stained was his coat of woven wool
And stained his boots of calf.
"But I've brought you a gift, my beautiful,"
And he began to laugh.

"That's neither grouse nor spotted quail
That you hide from me," she said.
"And why is your face so pale, so pale
And why are your hands so red?"

"Nor grouse nor quail nor duck I give,"
He said, and spread apart
His hands, and there like a crimson sieve
He offered his riddled heart.

SUGGESTIONS FOR ADDITIONAL READING

BALLADS OF THE SUPERNATURAL

Anonymous, *Thomas the Rhymer*
Anonymous, *The Boy and the Mantle*
Anonymous, *Clerk Saunders*
Anonymous, *The Wife of Usher's Well*
Anonymous, *Binnorie*
Anonymous, *Sir Cauline*
John Davidson, *A Ballad of a Nun*
A. E. Housman, *The True Lover*
William Butler Yeats, *Father Gilligan*
John Masefield, *Cap on Head*
Elizabeth Madox Roberts, *Orpheus*
Phelps Putnam, *Ballad of a Strange Thing*

HISTORICAL BALLADS

Anonymous, *The Queen's Marie*
Anonymous, *Hugh of Lincoln*
Anonymous, *Bonny George Campbell*
Anonymous, *King John and the Abbot of Canterbury*
Anonymous, *Chevy Chase*
Anonymous, *Sir Andrew Barton*
Anonymous, *Edom o' Gordon*

BALLADS OF LOVE AND ROMANCE

Anonymous, *Childe Maurice*
Anonymous, *The Twa Sisters*
Anonymous, *Young Beichan*
Anonymous, *The Twa Corbies*
Anonymous, *Lord Thomas and Fair Annet*
Anonymous, *Fair Margaret and Sweet William*
Anonymous, *Sir Aldingar*
Anonymous, *May Colvin*
Anonymous, *The Baffled Knight*
Anonymous, *Barbara Allen's Cruelty*
Thomas Campbell, *Lord Ullin's Daughter*
John Davidson, *A Ballad of Hell*
Alfred Noyes, *The Highwayman*
Marjorie Allen Seiffert, *Ballads of the Singing Bowl*
Elinor Wylie, *The Puritan's Ballad*

BALLADS OF ADVENTURE

Anonymous, *Robin Hood and Sir Guy*
Anonymous, *Robin Hood and the Monk*
Anonymous, *The Death of Robin Hood*
Anonymous, *Lord Bateman*
Rudyard Kipling, *Gunga Din*
Rudyard Kipling, *The Ballad of East and West*
John Hay, *Pike County Ballads*
Alfred Noyes, *Forty Singing Seamen*
Stephen Vincent Benét, *The Ballad of William Sycamore*
William Rose Benét, *The Horse Thief*
William Rose Benét, *Merchants from Cathay*
Robert P. T. Coffin, *Ballads of Square-Toed Americans*

BALLADS OF HUMOR AND HIGH NONSENSE

Anonymous, *Get Up and Bar the Door*
Anonymous, *The Old Cloak*

Anonymous, *Widdicombe Fair*
Edward Lear, *The Yonghy-Bonghy-Bo*
Edward Lear, *The Owl and the Pussy-Cat*
Lewis Carroll, *Jabberwocky*
Lewis Carroll, *The Hunting of the Snark*
W. S. Gilbert, *The Bab Ballads*
T. A. Daly, *McAroni Ballads*

NATIVE AMERICAN BALLADS

Anonymous, *Casey Jones*
Anonymous, *Frankie and Johnny*
Anonymous, *The Boll-Weevil Song*
Anonymous, *The Shanty Boy*
Anonymous, *Noah's Ark*
Anonymous, *The Lone Prairie*
Anonymous, *The Big Rock Candy Mountains*
Badger Clark, *Sun and Saddle-Leather*

16

THE PATTERNS OF POETRY—4: THE STRICTER FORMS

THE PATTERNS analyzed in the preceding chapters are definite in outline but variable in detail. Stanza-forms vary in meter, rhyme-scheme and length of line; ballads are extremely flexible and may be of any length; even the sonnet permits, within the fourteen prescribed lines, different arrangements in rhyme. The patterns to be discussed in this chapter are far stricter. The shapes are rigid, the rules regarding the rhymes are iron-clad. Each of these "fixed forms" has its own laws, but all of them agree on one rule in regard to the rhymes: *No word or syllable once used as a rhyme can be used again throughout the entire poem, not even if it is spelled differently.* The rhyming syllable, in each case, must be a new one in *sound*. Thus if the word "right" is used in the first stanza of any of the French forms, it cannot be used in any of the other stanzas, nor can the word "write" or "rite" (which are not rhymes, but actually the same sound) be used in any part of the poem. It is this very limitation of rhyme which makes the French forms so difficult—and so delightful.

The term "French forms" has prevailed because these constructions originated in the country of the troubadours. They are found as early as the fourteenth century and attained instant popularity. Originally religious in character, the ballades and their kind became highly popular at court and castle, and even the gutters of Paris echoed with their technical ingenuities when Villon wrote his immortal refrain, *"Mais où sont les neiges d'antan?"* ("But where are the snows of yester-year?")

The French forms have been adapted and much employed by English poets, but they remain exotics. No English craftsman has ever put a very considerable fraction of the force and passion which Villon burned into his ballades. Villon's compositions, strict in pattern, are bitter and bawdy and brilliantly spontaneous; the English counterparts are light in tone, graceful rather than grave, and, with few exceptions, conscious of their artificiality. In a "Note on Some Foreign Forms of Verse," written in 1878, Austin Dobson defined the limitations for his compatriots: "Most of the French forms are not yet suited for, nor are they intended to rival, the more approved natural rhythms in the treatment of grave and elevated themes. What is modestly advanced for them is that they may add a new charm of buoyancy, a lyric freshness, to amatory and light verse."

Chaucer wrote several ballades and rondels which are assumed to be the earliest English examples of these verse-forms. Although several other English poets of the early fifteenth century experimented in the difficult constructions, it was not until the end of the nineteenth century that the French forms were fully established in England. It was Austin Dobson, following the French poet Banville, who reintroduced the old "refrain poetry." Dobson and his followers—notably W. E. Henley, Andrew Lang, Edmund Gosse, and Richard Le Gallienne—made the French forms a vogue, and the "naughty nineties" luxuriated in the far from naughty sentiments enshrined in proper and intricate stanzas. Swinburne, for whom no form was too difficult, accepted the challenge and surpassed his fellows in the number and variety of his exercises.

The most important of the French forms are the ballade (with its amplifications in the double ballade, the ballade with two refrains, and the chant royal), the rondeau, the rondel, the rondeau redoublé, the triolet, the villanelle, and the sestina. The one strict form which is wholly English is the limerick.

THE BALLADE GROUP

THE BALLADE

The ballade, not to be confused with the ballad, is not only the oldest of the French forms but easily the most favored. In France, its greatest vogue occurred in the fourteenth and fifteenth centuries. Little interest was displayed in its possibilities for more than two hundred years until Théodore de Banville (1802-1891) brought back the intricate rhyme-scheme, since when it has not been forgotten. A modern French dramatist, Edmond Rostand, has employed the form as a medium for heroic comedy. In the first act of *Cyrano de Bergerac,* the duel between the hero and the viscount is fought to metrical strokes as Cyrano improvises a ballade and "touches" at the very end of the envoy. In England, as has been said, the ballade, although used as early as the time of Chaucer, never was popular until Austin Dobson introduced the involved foreign forms and displayed their liveliness as well as their limitations.

The structure of the ballade is extremely strict. It consists of three stanzas of eight (a few examples have ten) lines and another stanza (or half-stanza) of four lines called the *envoy* which, following the old custom, is generally addressed to some prince or imaginary power. The rhymes of the first stanza are arranged *a-b-a-b-b-c-b-c,* and the rhyme-sounds as well as the arrangement are repeated in all the others—the envoy (or half-stanza) being *b-c-b-c.* No rhyme-word or rhyming sound may be used again throughout the entire ballade. Thus if the word "sight" occurs in the first stanza, it cannot be repeated (nor can the words "cite" or "excite" or "insight" be used) in any other stanza.

The outstanding feature of the ballade is its *refrain.* The refrain is the line which ends all the stanzas and the envoy. It is thus repeated *in its entirety* and gives balance and unity to the poem.

In Henley's hands the ballade attained an outdoor gaiety of its own, as may be seen in the following example with its annotated rhyme-scheme, the capital *C* denoting the refrain.

BALLADE OF SPRING

by William Ernest Henley (1849-1903)

There's a noise of coming, going, a
Budding, waking, vast and still. b
Hark, the echoes are yeo-hoing a
Loud and sweet from vale and hill! b
Do you hear it? With a will, b
In a grandiose lilt and swing, c
Nature's voices shout and trill. . . . b
'Tis the symphony of Spring! C

Rains are singing, clouds are flowing, a
Ocean thunders, croons the rill, b
And the West his clarion's blowing, a
And the sparrow tunes his quill, b
And the thrush is fluting shrill, b
And the skylark's on the wing, c
And the merles their hautboys fill— b
'Tis the symphony of Spring! C

Lambs are bleating, steers are lowing, a
Brisk and rhythmic clacks the mill. b
Kapellmeister April, glowing a
And superb with glee and skill, b
Comes, his orchestra to drill b
In a music that will ring c
Till the grey world yearn and thrill. b
'Tis the symphony of Spring! C

Envoy

Princes, though your blood be chill, b
Here's shall make you leap and fling, c
Fling and leap like Jack and Jill! b
'Tis the symphony of Spring. C

Another excellent use of the ballade—this time for pictorial purpose—is Richard Le Gallienne's "A Ballade Catalogue of Lovely Things" on page 53.

A favorite device of the writers of ballades is the use of a refrain which asks a question. One of the most famous is the *ubi sunt* theme. Villon popularized this in his *"Mais où sont les neiges d'antan?"* Andrew Lang imitated it in the refrain "Nay, but where is the last year's snow?" Other poets asked: "Where are the gods of Yesterday?" "Where are the ships of Tyre?" "Where are the cities of old time?" "Where are the singers of golden deeds?" "Where are the galleons of Spain?" "What has become of last year's love?" etcetera. One of the best of these is Andrew Lang's skilful adaptation from Villon, although Lang's use of "away" and "way" in the first and second stanza is a violation of the rule about not repeating the same sound.

BALLADE OF DEAD LADIES

by Andrew Lang (1844-1912)

Nay, tell me now in what strange air
The Roman Flora dwells today.
Where Archippiada hides, and where
Beautiful Thais has passed away?
Whence answers Echo, afield, astray,
By mere or stream,—around, below?
Lovelier she than a woman of clay;
Nay, but where is the last year's snow?

Where is wise Héloïse, that care
Brought on Abeilard, and dismay?
All for her love he found a snare,
A maimed poor monk in orders grey;
And where's the Queen who willed to slay
Buridan, that in a sack must go
Afloat down Seine,—a perilous way—
Nay, but where is the last year's snow?

Where's that White Queen, a lily rare,
With her sweet song, the Siren's lay?
Where's Bertha Broad-foot, Beatrice fair?
Alys and Ermengarde, where are they?
Good Joan, whom English did betray
In Rouen town, and burned her? No,
Maiden and Queen, no man may say;
Nay, but where is the last year's snow?

Envoy

Prince, all this week thou need'st not pray,
Nor yet this year the thing to know.
One burden answers, ever and aye,
"Nay, but where is the last year's snow?"

Helen Louise Cohen's *Lyric Forms from France* goes far beyond Gleeson White's pioneering *Ballades and Rondeaux* and quotes almost one hundred and fifty examples of the ballade group, from G. K. Chesterton's satirical "A Ballade of Suicide" (with its refrain, "I think I will not hang myself today") to Swinburne's incredibly long—and incredibly dull—"A Ballade at Parting," with its ten-line stanzas, its five-line envoy and its ponderous refrain, "Here the limitless north-eastern, there the strait south-western sea." Recently there has been a tendency to use the ballade for broadly humorous effects, even to turn it upon itself in burlesque. This impulse is illustrated by most of the contributions to *One Hundred and One Ballades,* published in 1931, some of the more notable contributors being G. K. Chesterton, Maurice Baring, E. C. Bentley, Theodore Maynard, C. K. Scott-Moncrieff, and J. C. Squire. Chesterton printed no less than twelve high-spirited, whimsical and satirical ballades, of which the following is one of the most Chestertonian:

A BALLADE OF THE GROTESQUE

by G. K. Chesterton (1874-)

I was always the Elephant's Friend,
  I never have caused him to grieve;
Though monstrous and mighty to rend
  He was fed from the fingers of Eve,
  He is wise, but he will not deceive,
He is kind in his wildest career;
  But still I will say, with his leave,
The shape is decidedly queer.

I was light as a penny to spend,
  I was thin as an arrow to cleave,
I could stand on a fishing-rod's end,
  With composure, though on the *qui vive,*
  But from Time, all a-flying to thieve
The suns and the moons of the year,
  A different shape I receive;
The shape is decidedly queer.

I am proud of the world as I wend,
  What hills could Omnipotence heave,
I consider the heaven's blue bend
  A remarkable feat to achieve;
  —But think of the Cosmos—conceive
The universe—system and sphere,
  I must say with my heart on my sleeve,
The shape is decidedly queer.

Envoy

  Prince, Prince, what is this I perceive
On the top of your collar appear?
  You say it's your face, you believe,
. . . The shape is decidedly queer.

In spite of the lightness and dexterity of Chesterton's verses, it must be pointed out that the author of the foregoing ballade violated the rule concerning the rhyme-scheme. No rhyme-word or rhyming sound is allowed to be used more than once in the ballade, and Chesterton uses "deceive," "conceive," "receive" and "perceive," although all four words are actually the same rhyme sound: *'ceive.* Similarly, having used the word "leave" in the first stanza, to be technically correct, he should not have chosen the rhyme "believe" in the last stanza, since this is really not a new rhyme, but the identical sound.

J. C. Squire's fourteen contributions to the same volume may be more special in their application, but they are equally gay and somewhat more exact in technique. All of them reveal the poet who is also one of the most brilliant of living parodists. The following, one of the most amusing, has not yet been quoted in any other collection:

A BALLADE OF ANY FATHER TO ANY SON

by J. C. Squire (1883-)

To be read in the Cockney, Lancashire, Scotch, American or other marked accent

I 'ad no education, and my pile
  Began with pennies from the boots I blacked;
I said, "I'll raise my son in first-rate style,
  He shall start life with everything I lacked."
  You learnt some Greek and Latin, you were whacked,
While I coughed up at least 5,000 cool,
  Then you forgot it all, and then you slacked:
What was the use of sending you to school?

You cannot spell, your handwriting is vile,
  Your notions of geography are cracked,
You said the Danube flowed into the Nile,
  And then that Etna was a cataract,
  And the Sahara quite a fertile tract:
And now you say that you've been playing Boule
  And lost on every number that you backed:
What was the use of sending you to school?

Your car eats juice a gallon to the mile—
  If I'd been my old man I'd had you smacked!—
Don't stand there grinning like a crocodile!
  I'm damn well sick of you, and that's a fact:
  My study with your bills is simply stacked,
And now yer Ma and me, it's something crool,
  We've had to have the under 'ousemaid sacked:
What was the use of sending you to school?

Envoy

  Prince, it is not my way to fail in tact,
But you are such an utter bloody fool,
  HEY? You have never *heard* of Kellogg's Pact?
—What *was* the use of sending you to school?

In America the ballade has found favor with the best of contemporary versifiers. Among those who have excelled in the form are Franklin P. Adams, Don Marquis, Arthur Guiterman, Bert Leston Taylor, Christopher Morley, Gelett Burgess, Clinton Scollard, T. A. Daly, Edwin Arlington Robinson, and James Branch Cabell. One of the most recent by the Pepysian "conductor" of "The Conning Tower" is reprinted, with its appropriate reference to Samuel Pepys himself:

A BALLADE OF 1933

by Franklin P. Adams (1881-)

I am a puny opinion-moulder;
I am a chap of cheap chit-chatter;
I am a bird's-eye-view beholder;
Motley my wear, and worn to a tatter,
Madder am I than the famous hatter;
Keen for a kiss as was Samuel P.;
Maybe his record I'll try to shatter
For Nineteen Hundred and Thirty-three.

Darling, I know I am growing older;
Time is a wall that I cannot batter.
Enemies say I'm a cynic scolder;
Say that my intellect's growing fatter;
Say that my jests are getting flatter;
Say that my singing is off the key.
What of the seeds that I hope to scatter
For Nineteen Hundred and Thirty-three?

Timider I, or shall I be bolder?
Noisier I, or cease my clatter?
Warmer my love, or even colder?
Shall I write poems, or metric patter?
Will money over me shower and spatter,
Or Love surge over me like the sea?
Vote for one? I'd elect the latter
For Nineteen Hundred and Thirty-three.

Envoy

Pure as the purest of reading matter,
Here is my heart, and the rest of me—
Here on a beautiful silver platter
For Nineteen Hundred and Thirty-three.

In spite of the occasional parodies and perversions of the form, the ballade remains an instrument for evoking straightforward sentiment. That it is still employed to express unashamed tenderness may be proved by the following contemporary ballade by one whose work in the French forms has hitherto appeared above the pseudonym of "George Jester."

BALLADE OF REMEMBERED ROSES

(After a sketch by Turgenieff)

by George Macy (1900-)

Here on my lap an open volume lies,
Outside a winter wind is wildly blowing;
Here by the fire my dear one sits and sighs,
Outside the day is dead and it is snowing.
I read: a sylvan tale, of roosters crowing,
Of roses . . . oh! what memories they stir,
These words I read, so plain yet freely flowing:
"How beautiful, how fresh those roses were!"

For now I see, what time I close my eyes,
A rolling farm, the farmers at their hoeing;
A house all sunny under summer skies;
A little lake with boats too small for rowing;
An old red barn, the cattle gently lowing;
A fragrance everywhere of mint and myrrh;
And in the garden roses, roses growing—
How beautiful, how fresh those roses were!

The room is cold, the fire slowly dies;
I look across to where my wife is sewing
But hear her warm young voice, her eager cries
And feel the petals of the rose she's throwing.
I see the colors of the rose she's showing:
Its bud so like the cherry lips of her,
Its petal like her cheek, so pink, so glowing . . .
How beautiful, how fresh those roses were!

Sweet wife! I know how white my hair is going,
How fleet the years, and how the senses blur;
Yet I have known eternal youth in knowing
How beautiful, how fresh those roses were.

THE DOUBLE BALLADE

The double ballade is not to be confused with the Ballade à Double Refrain; it is merely a more extended ballade, with double the number of stanzas—six instead of three. The verses themselves usually consist of eight lines, though there are several examples with ten, and one splendid poem (Henley's "Double Ballade of the Nothingness of Things") employs eleven lines, but in every case there are six stanzas. The envoy is optional, and, though Swinburne and Henley, both of whom were fond of this overlengthy and tiring form, added it to their half-dozen stanzas, most writers discard the envoy. Henley's "Double

Ballade on the Nothingness of Things," seventy-two lines long, is one of the most astonishing of these "endurance contests," but Alfred Noyes has gone it one better with his "A Triple Ballade of Old Japan," which runs to eighty lines.

Owing to the double difficulty of this variation, there are comparatively few contemporary authors who attempt to wrestle with its complexities, and the double ballade has gone almost entirely out of favor. However, Swinburne's "Double Ballade of August" and Henley's "Double Ballade of Life and Fate" are occasionally quoted.

THE BALLADE À DOUBLE REFRAIN

The ballade à double refrain is, as the name indicates, a ballade with two "burdens" or refrains. One of these refrains occurs in the middle of each stanza, being repeated in its entirety as the fourth line of every verse, the other at the end of each stanza. Both refrains occur in the envoy, and the charm of this type of ballade is its skilful use of the repetition without letting it become tiresome. In order to avoid monotony, the two refrains are usually opposite in character—forming either an actual contradiction or a sharp contrast in mood and sentiment. The ballade à double refrain has always been a more appealing form than the double ballade and it continues to be favored by the skilled practitioner as well as the apprentice. One of the best known of this type of ballade is the following:

THE BALLADE OF PROSE AND RHYME

by Austin Dobson (1840-1921)

When the roads are heavy with mire and rut, a
  In November fogs, in December snows, b
When the North Wind howls, and the doors are shut, a
  There is place and enough for the pains of prose; B
  But whenever a scent from the whitethorn blows, b
And the jasmine-stars at the casement climb, c
  And a Rosalind-face at the lattice shows, b
Then hey!—for the ripple of laughing rhyme! C

When the brain gets dry as an empty nut, a
  When the reason stands on its squarest toes, b
When the mind (like a beard) has a "formal cut," a
  There is place and enough for the pains of prose; B
  But whenever the May-blood stirs and glows b
And the young year draws to the "golden prime,"— c
  And Sir Romeo sticks in his ear a rose, b
Then hey!—for the ripple of laughing rhyme! C

In a theme where the thoughts have a pedant-strut a
  In a changing quarrel of "Ayes" and "Noes," b
In a starched procession of "If" and "But," a
  There is place and enough for the pains of prose; B

But whenever a soft glance softer glows, b
And the light hours dance to the trysting-time, c
And the secret is told "that no one knows," b
Then hey!—for the ripple of laughing rhyme! C

Envoy

In the workaday world, for its needs and woes, b
There is place and enough for the pains of prose; B
But wherever the May-bells clash and chime, c
Then hey!—for the ripple of laughing rhyme! C

THE CHANT ROYAL

The chant royal is one of the most difficult of the ballade group; it is, in fact, one of the most uncommon of the French forms. It owes its imposing title to the legend that it was a form selecced for composition before the king, and poets who succeeded in the making of chants royal were considered worthy of regal honors. It is actually a larger form of the ballade, consisting of five verses of eleven lines and an envoy of five. In common with all other types of the ballade, the order of rhymes is the same in every stanza and each verse ends with the same refrain. Twelve examples of the chant royal may be found in Helen Louise Cohen's *Lyric Forms from France* including the excellent burlesque by H. C. Bunner entitled "Behold the Deeds!"

The rhyme order of the chant royal varies somewhat with the different practitioners of this form. Usually, however, it is as follows: *a-b-a-b-c-c-d-d-e-d-e*. The rhymes of the envoy follow in the same order as those in the last five lines, namely *d-d-e-d-e*. There are, in all, sixty lines to be strictly rhymed. In spite of its difficulty, this form has found more favor than the double ballade to which it is related; even such contemporaries as Richard Le Gallienne, Clinton Scollard, and Don Marquis have written in this form. With most of the poets, however, the chant royal begins as an example of dexterity and remains little more than a *tour de force*. Occasionally a poet carries the form beyond an exhibition of skill and achieves a poem instead of a technical performance. Such a chant royal is Dobson's sonorous "The Dance of Death" and Don Marquis' "Chant of the Changing Hours." The following, which has not yet been anthologized, is another worthy example, a variation of the *ubi sunt* theme with modern overtones:

CHANT ROYAL OF LOVE

by Michael Lewis (1885-)

All gods were deathless once. All mortals knew a
That death would beckon and brook no delay b
Beyond a little turning of the screw. a
But gods held death a plaything; such as they b
Had everlastingness for daily bread c
And could not die. . . . And now the gods are dead. c
Their effigies in marble, bronze or bone d
Are buried shards or a thin powder blown d

Beyond the furthest cranny of the skies, e
And but one god still comes into his own: d
Love is the only lord that never dies. E

Where now are Thor and Odin and their crew a
Of girls like goddesses, who sought the fray; b
Thunder-shod, stormy ranks of Valkyrs, who a
Swooped down to bear the chosen ones away? b
Where is Osiris, with unlimited c
Rule of the underworld, and Ra the dread? c
Where has the power of high Olympus gone? d
Where's Bacchus and his magic vine and cone? d
Though Mercury was shrewd, Minerva wise, e
And Zeus learned all men's frailties to condone, d
Love is the only lord that never dies. E

Where are those Eastern deities that drew a
Syria and Babylon and brought dismay b
Upon the proud Egyptian and the Jew? a
Where's fire-limbed Moloch and his human prey? b
Astarte, with the moon upon her head? c
Tammuz, for whom all streams in Spring ran red? c
Bel-Marduk, and his hide of evil roan, d
More bull than god? Fish-Dagon, monstrous grown? d
No longer will these terrors victimize— e
One god remains, eternally alone: d
Love is the only lord that never dies. E

And all the fond beliefs on which we grew a
In simple trust. . . . What happened? Who can say b
Where clear-eyed Kindness went? What overthrew a
Virtue with sneers and Honor with a bray? b
Comforting, life-renewing Faith has fled; c
Peace has been spat upon and stoned and bled; c
Mercy expired with unavailing moan; d
Terror has reaped where Tolerance had sown . . . d
And still—more radiant with each disguise, e
More resonant with each triumphant tone— d
Love is. The only lord that never dies! E

Countless his forms and fancies. Seldom true a
To any pattern that men would obey. b
Motley is oft his wear, madness his hue, a
Turning all topsyturvy in his play. b
Putting a torn world mercifully to bed, c
Careless if those who love are ever wed, c
Twitching aside the virgin's bashful zone, d
Inflaming with a gust some poor old crone, d
He spins the world; his element is surprise. e
And, since his rules and reasons are unknown, d
Love is the only lord that never dies. E

Envoy

Prince, there is dust upon an empty throne; d
The very monuments of kings are prone, d
And every pretty lord and lady lies e
Beneath an ancient custody of stone . . . d
Love is the only lord. That never dies! E

THE RONDEAU GROUP

THE RONDEAU

The rondeau is, next to the ballade, the most popular of the French forms. Its characteristic note is badinage and sprightliness, although it must be recalled that Dobson's often-quoted "In After Days" and Charlotte Gilman's "A Man Must Live" are essentially serious, and one of the most famous poems of the World War, John McCrae's "In Flanders Fields," is—although most readers were unaware of it—a strict rondeau.

There are two types of rondeau, one consisting of thirteen lines, the other of ten, both written throughout on two rhymes, the lines being usually of eight syllables. The first is the more frequent and is the one considered here. The refrain of the rondeau differs from that of the ballade by occurring at the very *beginning* of the poem as well as at the conclusion of the next and also the last stanzas. It is always the first part of the first line—in some cases the first word only is used as the refrain. Allowing *R* to represent the refrain, the rhyme-scheme of the rondeau would be *Ra-a-b-b-a a-a-b-R a-a-b-b-a-R*.

The following rondeau is quoted not only as an excellent example of the form, but as one of the best of the serious employments of this model.

"A MAN MUST LIVE"

A man must live! We justify Ra
Low shift and trick to treason high, a
  A little vote for a little gold, b
  To a whole senate bought and sold b
With this self-evident reply. a

But is it so? Pray tell me why a
Life at such cost you have to buy? a
  In what religion were you told b
    "A man must live"? R

There are times when a man must die. a
Imagine for a battle-cry a
  From soldier with a sword to hold— b
  From soldiers with the flag unrolled— b
This coward's whine, this liar's lie, a
    "A man must live"! R

—*Charlotte Perkins Stetson Gilman*
(1860-)

It is at once evident that the refrain (or repetition of the opening phrase) not only forms an inseparable part of each stanza but is also the climax of the rondeau. Many poets have given this refrain a humorous twist by punning or playing on the sound and meaning of the refrain with each repetition. However, in such an instance, though the spelling may be changed or the actual words altered, the *sound* of the refrain must reappear *exactly* in each case. Thus a strict rondeau may be built on a refrain which appears the first time as "Immortal Eyes," the second time as "immortal lies," and the third time as "immortalize." A certain paraphrase of Horace begins by quoting the first phrase of one of the odes in Latin and the refrain of the rondeau appears in this order: *"Cum tu, Lydia,"* "Come to Lydia," and "Come to! Lydia!" A well-known writer of light verse begins a rondeau " 'Tis Labor Day" and, after rambling through the thirteen lines, ends his poem apologetically with " 'Tis labored. Eh?"

An extremely neat instance of the rondeau with a punning refrain is the following by T. A. Daly. It will be noted that this rondeau maintains its serious sentiment throughout; even the play of meaning in the refrain adds to the delicacy of the tribute and does not—as commonly occurs with such devices—break into a grimace.

A SONG TO ONE

If few are won to read my lays Ra
And offer me a word of praise, a
If there are only one or two b
To take my rhymes and read them through, b
I may not claim the poet's bays. a

I care not, when my Fancy plays a
Its one sweet note, if it should raise a
A host of listeners or few— b
If you are one. R

The homage that my full heart pays a
To Womanhood in divers ways, a
Begins and ends, my love, in you. b
My lines may halt, but strong and true b
My soul shall sing through all its days, a
If you are won. R

—*T. A. Daly* (1871-)

A broader example of the playful, punning rondeau is one which begins as a distinctly amorous tribute and ends in derisive burlesque. Its point, as well as its humor, lies in the way the refrain is treated and turned:

A REGRETFUL RONDEAU

My lady's eyes are fire and jet,
A dark allure, a laughing threat;
Her coiled hair is a living mass
Of copper strands and burnished brass,
Holding men's hearts in that bright net.

Her mouth is Beauty's epithet
Phrased in a double rhyme. And yet
I do not love her—so, alas,
My lady sighs.

How can I? Much to my regret
I have beheld her silhouette
Blot out a haystack, cows, a class
Of little girls who tried to pass. . . .
Love her? I would—could I forget
My lady's size!

—*Michael Lewis* (1885-)

In the following rondeau the refrain is also twisted in meaning and emphasis, though not—obeying the strict rule—in sound. But here the rondeau combines sentiment and sententiousness, with just a suspicion of mockery at the end.

TO A NEGLECTFUL LOVER

Do write, my love, for but the sight
Of your so-cherished hand brings light
Into each dull, disheartening day
That darkens when you are away
And burns a beacon through the night.

Oh, do not pause for wit or bright
Appraisals of the hour. Be trite,

Be trivial. But, whate'er you say,
Do write, "My love . . ."

My heart becomes a tugging kite
Straining toward some too perilous height
Where your heart plays serene and gay.
Play, then, awhile, but do not stay
Too long or leave me in this plight.
Do right, my love!

—*Nancy Birckhead* (1908-)

THE ROUNDEL

The roundel, a charming variant of the rondeau, may claim to be an English form for it was shaped by an English poet, who, shortening the original model, called his version "roundel," or a little "round," the literal translation of "rondeau." One or two old French poems bear a resemblance to this form, but Swinburne must be given credit not only for its introduction but for the remarkable use he made of it. Swinburne wrote one hundred of these experiments (*A Century of Roundels*), many of them unreservedly sentimental, but none without a delicate craftsmanship. The roundel has always eleven lines—two of the eleven lines being the refrain. The rhymes, with *R* as the refrain, are arranged: *Ra-b-a-R b-a-b a-b-a-R*. In almost every case, the refrain (*R*) rhymes with the *b*-lines. An excellent example, as well as a description of the form itself, is the following:

THE ROUNDEL

A roundel is wrought as a ring or a star-bright sphere, Ra
With craft of delight and with cunning of sound unsought, b
That the heart of the hearer may smile if to pleasure his ear a
A roundel is wrought. R

Its jewel of music is carven of all or of aught— b
Love, laughter or mourning—remembrance of rapture or fear— a
That fancy may fashion to hang in the ear of thought. b

As a bird's quick song runs round, and the hearts in us hear a
Pause answer to pause, and again the same strain caught, b
So moves the device whence, round as a pearl or a tear, a
A roundel is wrought. R

—*Algernon Charles Swinburne* (1837-1909)

THE RONDEL

The rondel is the early form of the rondeau and was employed lavishly in the fourteenth century. It is a cross between the rondeau and the triolet for, like the latter, it repeats two of the lines in their entirety. The rondel is composed of thirteen lines arranged in three stanzas; the rhymes are limited to two and may be expressed thus: *A-B-b-a a-b-A-B a-b-b-a-A*—the capital letters representing the lines which are repeated in their entirety. Though many have delighted in the wit and brevity of the form, no poet has made better use of it than Henley, Gosse, and Dobson. Henley was particularly apt in this variant, as may be proved by his paraphrase of Ronsard's *"Ainsi qu'aux fleurs la vieillesse."*

AND LIGHTLY LIKE THE FLOWERS

And lightly, like the flowers, A
  Your beauties Age will dim, B
  Who makes the song a hymn, b
And turns the sweets to sours. a

Alas, the chubby Hours a
  Grow lank and gray and grim, b
And lightly, like the flowers, A
  Your beauties Age will dim. B

Still rosy are the bowers, a
  The walks yet green and trim. b
  Among them let your whim b
Pass sweetly, like the showers, a
And lightly, like the flowers. A

—*William Ernest Henley* (1849-1903)

THE TRIOLET

The triolet, so called because of the triple recurrence of the first line, is one of the neatest and, by all odds, the nimblest of the French forms. Like the rondeau, it is built on only two rhymes; like the rondel it repeats two of its lines as echoing refrains. The triolet differs from its related forms by being a single stanza of eight lines—the first line (A) being repeated as the fourth, the first and second (A B) being repeated as the seventh and eighth lines of the triolet. If the lower case letters represent the rhymes and the capitals indicate the repeated lines, the formula for the triolet would be: *A-B-a-A-a-b-A-B*. An example which characterizes the form:

THE TRIOLET

A gesture in space A
  And lo! there's the triolet. B
Less grandeur than grace— a
A gesture in space— A
Words made of old lace a
  With a fragrance like violet . . . b
A gesture in space— A
  And lo! there's the triolet. B

—*Michael Lewis* (1885-)

Austin Dobson's accomplishments in this *genre* are flawless. No one has given the triolet so airy and spontaneous a turn as his translation of Horace's "Persicos Odi" and the little sequence entitled "Rose Leaves," one of which is quoted:

FROM "ROSE LEAVES"

I intended an Ode,
  And it turned to a Sonnet.
It began *à la mode,*
I intended an Ode;
But Rose crossed the road
  In her latest new bonnet!
I intended an Ode;
  And it turned to a Sonnet.

—*Austin Dobson* (1840-1921)

It may be supposed that the triolet is not adapted for serious emotion, its spirit being heel-and-toe pertness, a musical vivacity and an artful artlessness. The best triolets are not only ingenious, but as one poet has put it, "playful, sly, this tiny trill of melody turning on its own axis." Nevertheless, a few triolets have succeeded in stepping out of their own limitations and appealing to the reader as straightforward, dramatic, and even bitter poems. Such exceptions are H. C. Bunner's "A Pitcher of Mignonette," Robert Bridges' "All women born are so perverse" and Ernest Radford's cycle of six, notably this condensed "psychograph" of George Hall, released from Birmingham prison after serving a twenty years' sentence.

OUT

I killed her? Ah, why do they cheer?
  Are those twenty years gone today?
Why, she was my wife, sir,—so dear.
I killed her? Ah, why do they cheer?
  . . . Ah, hound! He was shaking with fear,
And I rushed—with a knife, they say. . . .
I killed her? Ah, why do they cheer?
  Are those twenty years gone today?

—*Ernest Radford*

Thus the quick turn of grace-notes which comprise the triolet may be used for sombre purposes. Another instance of this power is to be found in the few lines by one of the younger American poets and novelists.

TRIOLET

The night is full of the crying
Of dreams that will not die,—
Deathless and time-defying,—
The night is full of the crying
Of restless phantoms flying
Mysteriously by.
The night is full of the crying
Of dreams that will not die.

—*Alexander K. Laing*
(1903-)

THE RONDEAU REDOUBLÉ

The rondeau redoublé is not, as the name suggests, a double rondeau, but so wide a departure from the parent model as scarcely to resemble the rondeau at all. Like the rondeau it is written on two rhymes, and the first part of the first line is used as a refrain at the end of the poem, but here the resemblance ceases. The rondeau redoublé is composed of six quatrains and a final refrain. The rhyme-scheme for the first, third and fifth stanzas is *a-b-a-b,* for the second, fourth and sixth *b-a-b-a*. But the distinguishing feature is this: *Each line of the first quatrain* is employed *in its entirety* as the *last* line of each succeeding verse—that is, the first line of the poem acts as the last line of the second stanza, the second line of the poem as the final line of the third stanza, the third line becomes the last line of the fourth stanza, the fourth line ends the fifth stanza. The last line of the sixth quatrain is a new line, but it is *followed* by the first phrase of the first line. The opening quatrain, therefore, is a kind of text on which the rondeau redoublé is built. These intricate directions will seem somewhat simpler when an example is read and analyzed. The structure itself is anything but elaborate, as may be learned by examining Graham R. Tomson's "I will go hence" or John Payne's "My Day and Night" which is reprinted here. (R, as usual, represents the refrain.)

MY DAY AND NIGHT

My day and night are in my lady's hand; RA1
I have no other sunrise than her sight; B2
For me her favour glorifies the land; A3
Her anger darkens all the cheerful light. B4

Her face is fairer than the hawthorn white, b
When all a-flower in May the hedgerows stand; a
While she is kind, I know of no affright; b
My day and night are in my lady's hand. A1

All heaven in her glorious eyes is spanned; a
Her smile is softer than the summer's night, b
Gladder than daybreak on the Faery strand; a
I have no other sunrise than her sight. B2

Her silver speech is like the singing flight b
Of runnels rippling o'er the jewelled sand; a
Her kiss a dream of delicate delight; b
For me her favour glorifies the land. A3

What if the Winter chase the Summer bland! a
The gold sun in her hair burns ever bright. b
If she be sad, straightway all joy is banned; a
Her anger darkens all the cheerful light. B4

Come weal or woe, I am my lady's knight b
And in her service every ill withstand; a
Love is my Lord in all the world's despite b
And holdeth in the hollow of his hand a
My day and night. R

—*John Payne* (1835-1900)

THE VILLANELLE

The villanelle was originally used for purely pastoral subjects, but it rapidly became stylized and now bears the same relation to its origins as Marie Antoinette's beribboned dairy resembled the cowsheds of the peasantry. It has become a piece of rhymed Dresden china, a pastoral in porcelain.

Nevertheless, the villanelle remains one of the most musical of the French forms; the triplet stanzas embody the plan of *terza rima* with a teasing suspense and the repetition of the two lines—like an extended triolet—contributes a bell-like echo. It is composed of five three-line stanzas, each stanza ending with an alternating line of the first stanza, followed by a concluding four-line stanza. The first line of the first stanza is repeated as the last line of the even-numbered stanzas, the third line of the first stanza is repeated as the last line of the odd-numbered stanzas. In the last stanza both of these lines appear together as a concluding couplet. Only two rhymes are permitted throughout the verses. Using capitals for the repeated lines, the formula for the villanelle may be expressed thus: *A1-b-A2 a-b-A1 a-b-A2 a-b-A1 a-b-A2 a-b-A1-A2.* An example:

THEOCRITUS

O Singer of Persephone! A1
In the dim meadows desolate, b
Dost thou remember Sicily? A2

Still through the ivy flits the bee a
Where Amaryllis lies in state; b
O Singer of Persephone! A1

Simaetha calls on Hecate, a
And hears the wild dogs at the gate; b
Dost thou remember Sicily? A2

Still by the light and laughing sea a
Poor Polypheme bemoans his fate; b
O Singer of Persephone! A1

And still in boyish rivalry a
Young Daphnis challenges his mate; b
Dost thou remember Sicily? A2

Slim Lacon keeps a goat for thee; a
For thee the jocund shepherds wait; b
O Singer of Persephone! A1
Dost thou remember Sicily? A2

—*Oscar Wilde* (1856-1900)

Another and more graphic picture is presented in the following villanelle. Here the plucking of the daisy petals is skilfully simulated by the measured fall of the repeated lines.

VILLANELLE OF MARGUERITES

"A little, passionately, not at all." A1
She casts the snowy petals on the air; b
And what care we how many petals fall? A2

Nay, wherefore seek the seasons to forestall? a
It is but playing, and she will not care, b
A little, passionately, not at all! A1

She would not answer us if we should call a
Across the years; her visions are too fair; b
And what care we how many petals fall! A2

She knows us not, nor recks if she enthrall a
With voice and eyes and fashion of her hair, b
A little, passionately, not at all! A1

Knee-deep she goes in meadow-grasses tall, a
Kissed by the daisies that her fingers tear; b
And what care we how many petals fall! A2

We pass and go; but she shall not recall a
What men we were, nor all she made us bear; b
"A little, passionately, not at all!" A1
And what care we how many petals fall! A2

—*Ernest Dowson* (1876-1900)

Edwin Arlington Robinson's "The House on the Hill" (see page 33) uses the repetition to sound a note of mournful loneliness: "They are all gone away; There is nothing more to say," while Franklin P. Adams, in "Villanelle, with Stevenson's Assistance," makes his light-hearted catalogue revolve about the familiar couplet, "The world is so full of a number of things, I'm sure we should all be as happy as kings." A more modern poem returns, curiously enough, to the original bucolic note with a mixture of mockery and tenderness.

ARCTIC AGRARIAN

Scene: The Adirondacks

Here in these hills the Spring comes slow
  To those who learn her backwood way,
Who plough in ice and reap in snow.

First, there's a tremor; then, a throe;
  Then splintering of bells that play
"Hear!" In these hills the Spring comes slow.

We are not tricked for long. We know
  The paradox of frost in May,
Who plough in ice and reap in snow.

A mole sniffs the new earth; a crow
  Measures our field, decides to stay.
(Here in these hills the Spring comes slow.)

These are our vernal auguries. We go,
  Stopping at times to curse or pray,
Who plough in ice and reap in snow.

Suddenly white is green, although
  When it occurred we cannot say,
Who plough in ice and reap in snow,
Here in these hills . . .
                    The Spring comes slow.

—*Louis Untermeyer* (1885-   )

THE SESTINA

The sestina is, by all odds, the most complicated—and it might be added, the least gratifying—of the French forms. It is lengthy, its arrangement is not only arbitrary but awkward, and its conclusion seldom wins from the reader anything more than a sigh of relief. Suffice it to say that the sestina is composed of six stanzas of six lines each, the lines of the six verses ending with *the same six words,* and the arrangement of these six terminal words following a definite and extremely intricate order. To make the matter still more difficult, there is a final stanza, or "tornada," of three lines in which *all* of the six words must be used, three at the ends and three in the middle of the lines. As may be imagined, the form is so forbidding that most of the poems in this form are nothing more than tiresome technical exercises. However, Rudyard

Kipling's "Sestina of the Tramp-Royal" is not only a particularly successful example, but a splendid poem in its own right, and Swinburne, for whom no form was complex enough, actually wrote a double sestina of twelve verses of twelve lines each—revolving through all its one hundred and fifty lines (there is an added "tcrnada" of six lines) around a fragment from the Decameron!

The pattern of the sestina permits of rhyme although it does not demand it. It is the order in which the words are used that is imperative. It was once thought that there was a mystic significance in the rigid placing of the end-words, but no one has ever explained the symbolism—if there was one. The arrangement of final words in each of the stanzas may be learned from this table:

1-2-3-4-5-6	in	first	stanza
6-1-5-2-4-3	"	second	"
3-6-4-1-2-5	"	third	"
5-3-2-6-1-4	"	fourth	"
4-5-1-3-6-2	"	fifth	"
2-4-6-5-3-1	"	sixth	"

In the envoy, or "tornada," there is some slight variation; usually, however, 1 comes in the middle and 2 comes at the end of the first line; 3 comes in the middle and 4 comes at the end of the second line; 5 comes in the middle and 6 at the end of the third and last line. By this arrangement each stanza has at the end of its first line the last word of the preceding stanza and, therefore, no word occurs more than once in the same place.

Although, as has been said, the most famous sestinas have been written by Swinburne, Edmund Gosse and Kipling have excelled in the form (there is also the stirring "Sestina: Altaforte" by Ezra Pound), and James Branch Cabell, known to contemporary readers as the author of a series of brilliantly colored novels, has composed a volume of verse (*From the Hidden Way*) rich in the French Forms, among which his sestina "The Conqueror Passes" is notable. Gelett Burgess' "Sestina of Youth and Age" is probably the most vital as well as the most flexible of all.

SESTINA OF YOUTH AND AGE

by Gelett Burgess (1866-)

My father died when I was all too young, 1
And he too old, too crowded with his care, 2
For me to know he knew my hot fierce hopes; 3
Youth sees wide chasms between itself and Age— 4
How could I think he, too, had lived my life? 5
My dreams were all of war, and his of rest. 6

And so he sleeps (please God), at last at rest, 6
And, it may be, with soul refreshed, more young 1
Than when he left me, for that other life— 5
Free, for a while, at least, from that old Care, 2

The hard, relentless torturer of his age, 4
That cooled his youth, and bridled all his hopes. 3

For now I know he had the longing hopes, 3
The wild desires of youth, and all the rest 6
Of my ambitions ere he came to age; 4
He, too, was bold, when he was free and young— 1
Had I but known that he could feel, and care! 2
How could I know the secret of his life? 5

In my own youth I see his early life 5
So reckless, and so full of flaming hopes— 3
I see him jubilant, without a care, 2
The days too short, and grudging time for rest; 6
He knew the wild delight of being young— 1
Shall I, too, know the calmer joys of age? 4

His words come back, to mind me of that age 4
When, lovingly, he watched my broadening life— 5
And, dreaming of the days when he was young, 1
Smiled at my joys, and shared my fears and hopes. 3
His words still live, for in my heart they rest, 6
Too few not to be kept with jealous care! 2

Ah, little did I know how he could care! 2
That, in my youth, lay joys to comfort age! 4
Not in this world, for him, was granted rest, 6
But as he lived, in me, a happier life, 5
He prayed more earnestly to win my hopes 3
Than ever for his own, when he was young! 1

Envoy

He once was young; I too must fight with Care; 1-2
He knew my hopes, and I must share his age; 3-4
God grant my life be worthy, too, of rest! 5-6

THE LIMERICK

Though pedants may sneer, the "disreputable" limerick deserves a place in any consideration of strict forms if only because it is the one purely English pattern. Frowned on by puritans and purists, denied a mention in most collections, it is, nevertheless, a continuously popular form of verse. Its name is supposed to have been derived from an Irish song, each verse of which dealt with the adventures of different inhabitants of various villages, the chorus being, "Won't you come up to Limerick?" Although several examples of the pattern existed prior to 1830, Edward Lear's immortal moonshine verses, composed between 1832 and 1836, published in his *Book of Nonsense* in 1846, were the first to draw attention to these ingenious and slightly mad brevities.

Ever since the days of Lear, the limerick has flourished, even among those who are wholly ignorant of poetry. Innumerable newspaper competitions have been held in England and America, hundreds of thousands of "missing last lines" have been supplied by contestants and, it has been estimated, at least one million limericks, good, mediocre, and indecent, are in existence today.

The simplicity of the form may account for its wide-spread favor. It is a five-line stanza built on two rhymes (the rhymes being expressed by the symbol *a-a-b-b-a*) with the third and fourth lines one foot shorter than the other three. The measure is almost invariably anapestic trimeter. Edward Lear's limericks depend on their wildness and fantastic "plots" for their effects. Technically they are not as interesting as the modern limericks; from a rhyming point of view they offer no surprise, for in most cases, the rhyme-word of the last line is a mere repetition of a preceding one. The contemporary limerick uses the surprise of a new or curious rhyme as its final twist, often making its point by a freak of spelling or some trick in typographical arrangement. To illustrate the difference, examples of both periods are given. The first two are by Edward Lear.

TWO LIMERICKS

There was an Old Man who said, "How — a
Shall I flee from this horrible Cow? — a
    I will sit on this stile, — b
    And continue to smile, — b
Which may soften the heart of that Cow." — a

✦

There was an Old Man who said, "Hush!
I perceive a young bird in that bush!"
    When they said, "Is it small?"
    He replied, "Not at all.
It is four times as big as the bush!"

—*Edward Lear* (1812-1888)

The modern limerick, as has been implied, disdains to repeat a rhyme-word for its final effect. Even the amateur relishes the sport of giving the last line an extra twist with an absurd idea or unsuspected rhyme. Witness the following anonymous limericks:

There was an old party of Lyme,
Who married three wives at a time.
    When asked, "Why the third?"
    He replied, "One's absurd,
And bigamy, sir, is a crime!"

✦

There was a faith-healer of Deal
Who said, "Although pain isn't real,
    If I sit on a pin
    And I puncture my skin
I dislike what I *fancy* I feel!"

W. S. Gilbert employed the form for one of his most delightful lyrics in "The Sorcerer," two verses of which run:

THE SORCERER

Oh! My name is John Wellington Wells,
I'm a dealer in magic and spells,
    In blessings and curses
    And ever-filled purses,
In prophecies, witches, and knells.

If you want a proud foe to "make tracks"—
If you'd melt a rich uncle in wax—
    You've but to look in
    On our resident Djinn,
Number seventy, Simmery Axe!

—*W. S. Gilbert* (1836-1911)

The variety of limericks is as incalculable as their number. The chapter may well end with a few of the tongue-twisting variety and those which depend on the trick of spelling and pronunciation for their humor. The first one has been credited to Carolyn Wells; the fourth was written, in his teens, by Franklin P. Adams.

FOUR LIMERICKS

There was a young fellow named Tate
Who dined with his girl at 8.8,
    But I'd hate to relate
    What that person named Tate
And his tête-à-tête ate at 8.8.

✦

There was a young lady of Warwick,
Who lived in a castle histarwick,
    On the damp castle mould
    She contracted a could,
And the doctor prescribed paregarwick.

✦

Said a bad little youngster named Beauchamp:
"Those jelly-tarts, how shall I reauchamp?
    To my parents I'd go,
    But they always say 'No,'
No matter how much I beseauchamp."

✦

Said a lady whose surname was Beaulieu,
"Orthography's very unreaulieu;
    The spelling of Belvoir
    Is quite a decelvior"—
Said her husband, "What's wrong with Yours Treaulieu?"

And here, in conclusion, is a limerick by one who might not be suspected of its authorship:

WEAR AND TEAR

There was an old man of the Cape,
Who made himself garments of crêpe.
When asked, "Do they tear?"
He replied, "Here and there,
But they're perfectly splendid for shape!"
—*Robert Louis Stevenson*
(1850-1894)

SUGGESTIONS FOR ADDITIONAL READING

All of the following poems are to be found in Helen Louise Cohen's *Lyric Forms from France,* published by Harcourt, Brace and Company.

BALLADES

Franklin P. Adams, *Ballade of Schopenhauer's Philosophy*
Richard Aldington, *Villon's Epitaph in Ballade Form*
Gelett Burgess, *Ballade of Fog in the Cañon*
James Branch Cabell, *Story of the Flowery Kingdom*
G. K. Chesterton, *A Ballade of Suicide*
T. A. Daly, *Ballade of the Tempting Book*
Austin Dobson, *The Ballade of Imitation*
W. E. Henley, *Ballade of Truisms*
Joyce Kilmer, *Ballade of My Lady's Beauty*
Andrew Lang, *Ballade to Theocritus in Winter*
Richard Le Gallienne, *Ballade of Old Laughter*
Christopher Morley, *Ballade of the Lost Refrain*
Edwin Arlington Robinson, *Ballade by the Fire*
Nate Salsbury and Newman Levy, *Ballade of the Ancient Wheeze*
Clinton Scollard, *A Ballade of Midsummer*
A. C. Swinburne, *A Ballade of Dreamland*
A. C. Swinburne, *Villon's Ballad of the Women of Paris*
Bert Leston Taylor, *Ballade of Spring's Unrest*
Louis Untermeyer, *Ballade from "The Heaven Above Storysende"*
Carolyn Wells, *Ballade of Indignation*

DOUBLE BALLADES

W. E. Henley, *Double Ballade of Life and Fate*
John Payne, *Double Ballade of the Singers of the Time*
A. C. Swinburne, *Villon's Double Ballade of Good Counsel*

BALLADES A DOUBLE REFRAIN

W. E. Henley, *Ballade of Midsummer Days and Nights*
Bert Leston Taylor, *Ballade of Death and Time*
Carolyn Wells, *Ballade of Wisdom and Folly*

CHANTS ROYAL

H. C. Bunner, *Behold the Deeds!*
Gelett Burgess, *Chant Royal of the True Romance*
Austin Dobson, *The Dance of Death*
Edmund Gosse, *The Praise of Dionysus*
Brian Hooker, *Ballade of Farewell*
Don Marquis, *Chant of the Changing Hours*

RONDEAUX

H. C. Bunner, *An April Fool*
James Branch Cabell, *Grave Gallantry*
Austin Dobson, *"Farewell Renown!"*

Austin Dobson, *In After Days*
W. E. Henley, *If I Were King*
Rose Macaulay, *The New Year*
Don Marquis, *The Rondeau*
John McCrae, *In Flanders Fields*
Christopher Morley, *All Lovely Things*
D. G. Rossetti, *Villon's Rondeau to Death*
Louis Untermeyer, *A Father Speaks*
Carolyn Wells, *Her Spinning-Wheel*

RONDELS

H. C. Bunner, *O Honey of Hymettus Hill*
Austin Dobson, *The Wanderer*
John Drinkwater, *Rondels of the Year*
W. E. Henley, *Rondels, from the French*
John Payne, *Rondel ("Kiss Me, Sweetheart")*
Frank Dempster Sherman, *"Awake! Awake!"*
Robert Louis Stevenson, *Since I Am Sworn to Live My Life*

ROUNDELS

James Branch Cabell, *Arcadians Confer in Exile*
Amy Levy, *Between the Showers*
A. C. Swinburne, *Etude Réaliste*
A. C. Swinburne, *Babyhood*
A. C. Swinburne, *Flower-Pieces*
A. C. Swinburne, *Two Preludes*
A. C. Swinburne, *Three Faces*

RONDEAUX REDOUBLES

Cosmo Monkhouse, *Rondeau Redoublé*
Graham R. Tomson, *Rondeau Redoublé*
Louis Untermeyer, *The Passionate Aesthete to His Love*

TRIOLETS

H. C. Bunner, *A Pitcher of Mignonette*
Adelaide Crapsey, *Song*
T. A. Daly, *Mistletoe and Holly*
Austin Dobson, *Rose-Leaves*
Arthur Guiterman, *Apology*
George MacDonald, *Song*
Ernest Radford, *Six Triolets*
Louis Untermeyer, *Triolet from "The Heaven Above Storysende"*

VILLANELLES

Franklin P. Adams, *Villanelle, with Stevenson's Assistance*
Zoe Akins, *Villanelle of City and Country*
Austin Dobson, *"When I saw you last, Rose"*
Ernest Dowson, *Villanelle of the Poet's Road*
Ernest Dowson, *Villanelle of Sunset*
W. E. Henley, *Villanelle*
R. L. Megroz, *Villanelle of Love*
John Payne, *Villanelle ("The air is white")*
Clinton Scollard, *Villanelle to the Daffodil*
Graham R. Tomson, *To Hesperus*

SESTINAS

James Branch Cabell, *The Conqueror Passes*
Edmund Gosse, *Sestina*
Rudyard Kipling, *Sestina of the Tramp-Royal*
A. Mary F. Robinson, *Pulvis et Umbra*
A. C. Swinburne, *Sestina*

DOUBLE SESTINA

A. C. Swinburne, *The Complaint of Lisa*

17

THE PATTERNS OF POETRY—
5: EPIGRAM, EPITAPH, ELEGY, EPIC, AND ODE

This chapter is devoted to the patterns of those forms established by subject-matter rather than by an arrangement of stanzas or scheme of rhymes. It is primarily content, not a fixed design, which governs the Epigram, the Epitaph, the Elegy, the Epic, and the Ode. These divisions are identified more by feeling than by form; they are recognized by the sharp, considered thrust or the impassioned outcry, the impersonal summary of an epoch or a flight of headlong ecstasy. Distantly related, they should be examined separately.

THE EPIGRAM

In Greek literature the epigram originally was an epitaph, a poetical inscription placed upon a monument, a temple, or a tomb—*epi:* upon, *graphein:* to write. The word has come to characterize any short poem confined to one subject which, usually, ends with an ingenious turn of thought. The chief feature of the epigram is not so much its terseness as the sharpness of its condensation. The epigram may be a proverb happily pointed by rhyme, or a political squib, or a large generality compressed into an inch of wit; it is the concision which gives the verse its unmistakable tone. Perhaps the greatest collection of its kind, "The Greek Anthology," is memorable because of the trenchant quality of the epigrams, whether they are amatory, declamatory, or satirical.

There is no rule as to the length or the meter. The greatest number of epigrams, however, seem to be quatrains, although many of the most memorable have been framed in couplets. Coleridge's definition—in itself an excellent epigram—is one of the latter:

AN EPIGRAM

What is an Epigram? A dwarfish whole;
Its body brevity, and wit its soul.

—*Samuel Taylor Coleridge* (1772-1834)

The eighteenth century, with its fondness for neat malice and barbed elegance, was particularly conducive to the fashioning of epigrams. Scarcely a poet of the period failed to take advantage of these brief and brilliant thrusts. Pope's couplets in his "Essay on Criticism" (page 300) and his "Essay on Man" (page 278) could, by themselves, form a small but impressive anthology of epigrams. The following four excerpts are taken from the Second Epistle of the "Essay on Man":

Know then thyself, presume not God to scan;
The proper study of mankind is man.

✦

Extremes in nature equal ends produce;
In man they join to some mysterious use.

✦

Whate'er the passion—knowledge, fame, or pelf,
Not one will change his neighbor with himself.

✦

Vice is a monster of so frightful mien,
As, to be hated, needs but to be seen;
Yet seen too oft, familiar with her face,
We first endure, then pity, then embrace.
—*Alexander Pope* (1688-1744)

Prior was another who relished the precise twist which gave character to the epigram. He preferred the quatrain for his effects, which were light in tone and swift in touch. Three of his most dexterous verses follow, the first being an adaptation from Ausonius.

THE LADY WHO OFFERS HER LOOKING-GLASS TO VENUS

Venus, take my votive glass;
Since I am not what I was,
What from this day I shall be,
Venus, let me never see.

A REPLY

Sir, I admit your general rule,
That every poet is a fool:
But you yourself may serve to show it,
That every fool is not a poet.

A REASONABLE AFFLICTION

On his death-bed poor Lubin lies:
His spouse is in despair:
With frequent sobs, and mutual cries,
They both express their care.

"A different cause," says parson Sly,
"The same effect may give:
Poor Lubin fears that he shall die;
His wife, that he may live."
—*Matthew Prior* (1664-1721)

Far more savage is the epigram of the earlier John Wilmot, an epigram which is also a mock-epitaph and which packs a complete analysis of character into four lines. The daring of these lines cannot be appreciated until it is realized that Wilmot was Earl of Rochester and prominent at the court of Charles II.

ON CHARLES II

Here lies our Sovereign Lord the King,
Whose word no man relies on,

Who never said a foolish thing,
Nor ever did a wise one.
—*John Wilmot, Earl of Rochester* (1647-1680)

Entirely different in character are the epigrams of another eighteenth-century poet, William Blake, whose mystical vision illuminated the least of his lines. His "Auguries of Innocence" (see page 166) are epigrammatic intensities of the highest order. But, though the epigram was brought to full flower in the eighteenth century, no period has been without it. Some of the choicest blossoms of the form, classic and modern, are quoted below, the arrangement being chronological. The first six are from "The Greek Anthology," the translations being by Humbert Wolfe.

FROM "THE GREEK ANTHOLOGY"

Beware lest, Love, too often with your stings
Goaded, my soul takes flight. She too has wings.

✦

You need no torch to light your lamp. The love
That burns my soul up will be fire enough.

✦

Love and Timarion matched their wings and eyes;
And that is why the god no longer flies.

✦

This House was built for Zeus, where he will find
In Athens the heaven he has left behind.

✦

I saw no doctor, but, feeling queer inside,
Just thought of one—and naturally died.

✦

Marcus, when running in the armored race,
Went on till midnight, when they closed the place;
And I don't blame the stewards, for they must
Have thought the fellow was another bust.
But, when they went again next year, the ghost
Of Marcus was still running—at the post.
—*Translated by Humbert Wolfe* (1885-)

DISINHERITED

Thy father all from thee, by his last will,
Gave to the poor; thou hast good title still.
—*John Donne* (1573-1631)

OF COMMON DEVOTION

Our God and soldiers we alike adore
Ev'n at the brink of danger; not before:
After deliverance, both alike requited,
Our God's forgotten, and our soldiers slighted.
—*Francis Quarles* (1592-1644)

INTENDED TO ALLAY THE VIOLENCE OF PARTY SPIRIT

God bless the King! I mean the Faith's Defender;
God bless—no harm in blessing—the Pretender!
But who Pretender is, or who is King,
God bless us all!—that's quite another thing.
—*John Byrom* (1692-1763)

THE MAIDEN'S CHOICE

A fool and knave with different views,
For Julia's hand apply:
The knave, to mend his fortune, sues,
The fool, to please his eye.

Ask you, how Julia will behave?
Depend on't for a rule,
If she's a fool, she'll wed the knave—
If she's a knave, the fool.
—*Samuel Bishop* (1731-1795)

CROMEK SPEAKS

I always take my judgment from a fool
Because his judgment is so very cool;
Not prejudiced by feelings great or small.
Amiable state! He cannot feel at all.
—*William Blake* (1757-1827)

ON THE LATIN GERUNDS

When Dido found Aeneas would not come,
She mourn'd in silence, and was Di-do-dum.
—*Richard Porson* (1759-1808)

THE CRIMEAN HEROES

Hail, ye indomitable heroes, hail!
Despite of all your generals ye prevail.
—*Walter Savage Landor* (1775-1864)

DEATH

Death stands above me, whispering low
I know not what into my ear;
Of his strange language all I know
Is, there is not a word of fear.
—*Walter Savage Landor* (1775-1864)

ON A BROKEN PIPE

Neglected now it lies, a cold clay form,
So late with living inspirations warm;
Type of all other creatures formed of clay—
What more than it for Epitaph have they?
—*James Thomson* (*B. V.*) (1834-1882)

OUTWITTED

He drew a circle that shut me out—
Heretic, rebel, a thing to flout.
But Love and I had the wit to win:
We drew a circle that took him in!
—*Edwin Markham* (1852-)

SCULPTURE AND SONG

The statue—Buonarroti said—doth wait,
Thrall'd in the block, for me to liberate.
The poem—saith the poet—wanders free
Till I betray it to captivity.
—*William Watson* (1858-)

THE SAME COMPLAINT

"What's your most vexing parasite,"
Bawled Earth to Mars, "since Life began?"
Mars roared an answer through the night,
In emphasis of thunder, "Man!"
—*Norman Gale* (1862-)

ON A POLITICIAN

Here richly, with ridiculous display,
The Politician's corpse was laid away.
While all of his acquaintance sneered and slanged,
I wept: for I had longed to see him hanged.
—*Hilaire Belloc* (1870-)

GOD'S LITTLE EPIGRAMS

God's little epigrams, the bees,
Are pointed and impartial.
Could Martial rival one of these?
No, not even Martial.
—*Richard Kirk* (1877-)

SELF-ESTEEM

Love with a liquid ecstasy
Did wholly fill me up,
And since his drink is sweet to me
Can I despise the cup?
—*Anna Wickham* (1884-)

CLOCKS

On what a brave and curious whim
Man gathers clocks to see
And listen to their taunting him
On his mortality.

How sharp a jest it is that man
His own impermanence mocks
To memorize how short his span
Upon a thousand clocks!
—*Louis Ginsberg* (1896-)

ON SOME SOUTH AFRICAN NOVELISTS

You praise the firm restraint with which they write—
I'm with you there, of course.
They use the snaffle and the curb all right;
But where's the bloody horse?

—*Roy Campbell* (1902-)

THE DEAD

Only the living are concerned with living;
"So sharp! so sweet! so swift! so short!" despair
The restless living . . . but the dead do not care.

—*Selma Robinson* (1905-)

The following six epigrams are paraphrases of German proverbs and aphorisms which date from the eighteenth century. Though the idiom is local, the application is universal.

REMINDER

Though pain and care are everywhere,
Give freely, lass, live fully, lover;
For death's a rather long affair,
And when you die, you die all over.

FOOL

The man who shuns Wine, Woman, and Song
Remains a fool his whole life long.

ANCIENT ADAGE

Away with recipes in books!
Hunger is the best of cooks.

DISGRUNTLED GUEST

The meat is high,
The bread is dry,
The wine is bitter
And so am I.

DOCTORS

The good Lord saves us from disease.
Along come the doctors and take their fees.

EMBARRASSMENT OF EYES

When Love suddenly grows jealous
It develops (so they tell us)
Twice two hundred eyes, or nearly—
And not one of them sees clearly.

—*From the German*

Other examples of the epigram may be found under the consideration of the couplet and quatrain in Chapter 13 on pages 345 and 351.

THE EPITAPH

The epitaph, generally speaking, is an inscription in memory of the dead. *Siste, Viator* ("Pause, Traveler") ran the first phrase cut into the tombstones above the Roman graves. It was followed by a summary or tribute or even a denunciation, many of the lines resembling those of the later Elizabethans who gave the epitaph a definite literary form. The last line of Fletcher's "Aspatia's Song" is anticipated by the Latin, "Light lie the earth upon thee."

In verse, the epitaph is a poem, usually brief, composed in honor (or scorn) of the deceased. It differs from the elegy (see page 433) by being particular rather than general; it is addressed to an individual instead of being a universal and, usually, lengthy expression of grief inspired by an individual. The elegy is loose and rounded, whereas the epitaph is compact and pointed, resembling the epigram. Many of the finest epitaphs are distinctly epigrammatic, like the famous summary of Pope's upon the death of Isaac Newton, a mingling of gravity and levity:

EPITAPH ON NEWTON

Nature and Nature's laws lay hid in night:
God said, "Let Newton be!" and all was light.
—*Alexander Pope* (1688-1744)

Newton lies in Westminster Abbey; the lines which Pope wrote for an unnamed poet are engraved upon his own monument in Twickenham church.

FOR ONE WHO WOULD NOT BE BURIED IN WESTMINSTER ABBEY

Heroes, and kings! your distance keep:
In peace let one poor poet sleep,
Who never flattered folks like you:
Let Horace blush, and Virgil too.
—*Alexander Pope* (1688-1744)

John Gay's epitaph upon himself is a satirical, even disillusioned, epigram; yet it is so natural in effect, so perfect in form that no collection is complete without it.

MY OWN EPITAPH

Life is a jest, and all things show it.
I thought so once; but now I know it.
—*John Gay* (1685-1732)

Dryden's much-quoted couplet is still more cynical, but its wit has preserved it.

EPITAPH ON HIS WIFE

Here lies my wife: here let her lie!
Now she's at rest—and so am I.
—*John Dryden* (1631-1700)

The epitaphs of the Elizabethans are graver in character. Those of Raleigh, Fletcher, Carew, Herrick, and Jonson rank among the finest short poems in the language.

HIS OWN EPITAPH

Even such is time, which takes in trust
Our youth, our joys, our all we have,
And pays us but with age and dust;
Who, in the dark and silent grave,
When we have wandered all our ways,
Shuts up the story of our days;
But from this earth, this grave, this dust,
My God shall raise me up, I trust.
—*Walter Raleigh* (1552-1618)

ASPATIA'S SONG

Lay a garland on my hearse
Of the dismal yew:
Maidens, willow branches bear;
Say, I dièd true.

My love was false, but I was firm
From my hour of birth.
Upon my buried body lie
Lightly, gentle earth!
—*John Fletcher* (1579-1625)

EPITAPH ON A YOUNG GIRL

This little vault, this narrow room,
Of love and beauty is the tomb;
The dawning beam, that 'gan to clear
Our clouded sky lies darken'd here,
For ever set to us: by Death
Sent to enflame the world beneath.
'Twas but a bud, yet did contain
More sweetness than shall spring again;
A budding star, that might have grown
Into a sun when it had blown.
This hopeful beauty did create
New life in love's declining state;
But now his empire ends, and we
From fire and wounding darts are free.
His brand, his bow, let no man fear:
The flames, the arrows, all lie here.
—*Thomas Carew* (1596-1638)

AN EPITAPH ON SALATHIEL PAVY, A CHILD OF QUEEN ELIZABETH'S CHAPEL

Weep with me, all you that read
This little story:
And know, for whom a tear you shed
Death's self is sorry.
'Twas a child that so did thrive
In grace and feature,
As Heaven and Nature seem'd to strive
Which own'd the creature.
Years he number'd scarce thirteen
When Fates turn'd cruel,
Yet three fill'd zodiacs had he been
The stage's jewel;
And did act, what now we moan,
Old men so duly,
As, sooth, the Parcae thought him one,
He play'd so truly.
So, by error, to his fate
They all consented;
But viewing him since, alas, too late!
They have repented;
And have sought, to give new birth,
In baths to steep him;
But being so much too good for Earth,
Heaven vows to keep him.
—*Ben Jonson* (1573-1637)

UPON A CHILD

Here a pretty baby lies
Sung asleep with lullabies;
Pray be silent, and not stir
Th' easy earth that covers her.
—*Robert Herrick*
(1591-1674)

FOR SIR JOHN VANBRUGH, ARCHITECT

Lie heavy on him, earth! for he
Laid many a heavy load on thee.
—*Abel Evans* (18th century)

Modern poetry, while not so hospitable to elegiac verse, has produced many notable epitaphs. The following unforgettable quatrain, sometimes credited to George MacDonald, is probably of an earlier period.

HIC JACET

Here lie I, Martin Eldinbrodde,
Ha' mercy on my soul, Lord God,
As I would do, were I Lord God,
An' Thou wert Martin Eldinbrodde.
—*From Norfolk's Epitaphs*
(1861)

No less famous is Stevenson's "Requiem." Stevenson's death in distant Samoa, after the sick author had traversed two continents, added a personal poignance to the lines.

REQUIEM

Under the wide and starry sky
Dig the grave and let me lie.
Glad did I live and gladly die,
  And I laid me down with a will.

This be the verse you grave for me:
Here he lies where he longed to be;
Home is the sailor, home from sea,
  And the hunter home from the hill.
—*Robert Louis Stevenson*
(1850-1894)

A nineteenth-century adaptation from Callimachus is among the shortest of elegies, but powerful and moving in its brief poignance. Its adapter was one of the lesser Victorian poets.

HERACLITUS

They told me, Heraclitus, they told me you were dead,
They brought me bitter news to hear and bitter tears to shed.
I wept as I remembered how often you and I
Had tired the sun with talking and sent him down the sky.

And now that thou art lying, my dear old Carian guest,
A handful of grey ashes, long, long ago at rest,
Still are thy pleasant voices, thy nightingales, awake;
For Death, he taketh all away, but them he cannot take.
—*William (Johnson) Cory* (1823-1892)

Epitaphs in sonnet form are comparatively rare, yet Luella Boynton's "Epitaph for a Young Athlete" successfully employs both patterns and reveals, at the same time, a graphic use of symbolism.

EPITAPH FOR A YOUNG ATHLETE

As spears go down with beauty, so you went,
Shaping the perfect arc in air. O bright
And splendid javelin with power spent,
Ceasing its brief, its unretarded flight.
Not if I could, with pity or with awe,
Would I hold back one moment of your days
From that half-circle drawn without a flaw
And ended here. There are unkinder ways
For men to travel than your airy track
Across the morning. Now the spear is thrust
Deep into earth, but in that sudden, black
Descending was no whimpering of dust.
Safe in the warm, brown sheath forever hide
Your polished beauty and your silver side.
—*Luella Boynton* (1906-   )

Among contemporary examples of the form none has surpassed the more than two hundred free-verse epitaphs in Edgar Lee Masters' *Spoon River Anthology,* in which the dead in a Middle Western town reveal the truth about themselves. Equally pointed are the epitaphs in rhyme by that gifted Englishwoman, Sylvia Townsend Warner, whose "The True Heart" and "Mr. Fortune's Maggot," though in prose, are compact with poetry.

TWO EPITAPHS

John Bird, a labourer, lies here,
Who served the earth for sixty year
With spade and mattock, drill and plow;
But never found it kind till now.

✦

Her grieving parents cradled here
Ann Monk, a gracious child and dear.
Lord, let this epitaph suffice:
Early to Bed and Early to Rise.

—*Sylvia Townsend Warner* (1893-)

THE ELEGY

The elegy is, literally, what the Greek word indicates—*elegos:* a lament, a song of mourning. Unlike the epitaph, it is rarely concise and never caustic, but an extended song of sorrow, an upwelling of grief and regret. In the earlier elegies, and as late as "Lycidas," there was a distinct formula—a pastoral setting, a statement of the cause of mourning, an invocation (either to the Muses or to shepherds), a recalling of happy memories followed by grief over the loss of the person bewailed, a questioning of the Justice that permits such things to occur, and a final consolation in the thought that the ideals of the dead live on forever.

The elegy is no longer a fixed form; it is not cast in any particular mould. It is recognized by its subject and tone. Its outstanding characteristic may be said to be a paradox of emotion and expression: though impassioned in feeling, the tone is calm. The personal outcry is lifted to an impersonal plane; the note turns from the individual to the universal.

Nothing could better illustrate this than Milton's "Lycidas." Here, beginning as an expression of personal loss, roughly following the elegy "formula," the poem proceeds to compensating generalities and ends in large acceptance. In this poem the mythological allusions and Christian theology, the remote references and the immediate music are mingled, as the late Robert Bridges wrote, "in a dreamy passionate flux . . . heightened and inspired."

LYCIDAS

A Lament for a Friend Drowned in His Passage from Chester on the Irish Seas, 1637

by John Milton (1608-1674)

Yet once more, O ye Laurels, and once more,
Ye Myrtles brown, with Ivy never sere,
I come to pluck your berries harsh and crude,
And with forced fingers rude
Shatter your leaves before the mellowing year.
Bitter constraint and sad occasion dear
Compels me to disturb your season due:
For Lycidas is dead, dead ere his prime,
Young Lycidas, and hath not left his peer:
Who would not sing for Lycidas? he knew
Himself to sing, and build the lofty rhyme.
He must not float upon his watery bier

Unwept, and welter to the parching wind,
Without the meed of some melodious tear.
  Begin then, Sisters of the sacred well
That from beneath the seat of Jove doth spring;
Begin, and somewhat loudly sweep the string.
Hence with denial vain, and coy excuse:
So may some gentle Muse
With lucky words favor *my* destined Urn,
And, as he passes, turn
And bid fair peace be to my sable shroud.
For we were nursed upon the self-same hill,
Fed the same flock, by fountain, shade, and rill;
Together both, ere the high Lawns appeared
Under the opening eyelids of the Morn,
We drove a-field, and both together heard
What time the grey-fly winds her sultry horn,
Battening our flocks with the fresh dews of night,
Oft till the Star that rose, at Evening, bright
Toward Heaven's descent had sloped his westering wheel.
Meanwhile the Rural ditties were not mute;
Tempered to the Oaten Flute,
Rough Satyrs danced, and Fauns with cloven heel,
From the glad sound would not be absent long,
And old Damoetas loved to hear our song.
  But O the heavy change, now thou art gone,
Now thou art gone and never must return!
Thee, Shepherd, thee the Woods, and desert Caves,
With wild Thyme and the gadding Vine o'ergrown,
And all their echoes, mourn.
The Willows, and the Hazel Copses green,
Shall now no more be seen,
Fanning their joyous Leaves to thy soft lays.
As killing as the Canker to the Rose,
Or Taint-worm to the weanling Herds that graze,
Or Frost to Flowers, that their gay wardrobe wear,
When first the White-thorn blows;
Such, Lycidas, thy loss to Shepherd's ear.
  Where were ye, Nymphs, when the remorseless deep
Closed o'er the head of your loved Lycidas?
For neither were ye playing on the steep,
Where your old Bards, the famous Druids, lie,
Nor on the shaggy top of Mona high,
Nor yet where Deva spreads her wizard stream:
Ay me! I fondly dream
"Had ye been there"—for what could that have done?
What could the Muse herself that Orpheus bore,
The Muse herself, for her enchanting son
Whom Universal nature did lament,
When, by the rout that made the hideous roar,
His gory visage down the stream was sent,

Down the swift Hebrus to the Lesbian shore?
  Alas! What boots it with uncessant care
To tend the homely slighted Shepherd's trade,
And strictly meditate the thankless Muse?
Were it not better done, as others use,
To sport with Amaryllis in the shade,
Or with the tangles of Neaera's hair?
Fame is the spur that the clear spirit doth raise
(That last infirmity of noble mind)
To scorn delights, and live laborious days;
But the fair Guerdon when we hope to find,
And think to burst out into sudden blaze,
Comes the blind Fury with the abhorrèd shears,
And slits the thin-spun life. "But not the praise,"
Phoebus replied, and touched my trembling ears:
"Fame is no plant that grows on mortal soil,
Nor in the glistening foil
Set off to the world, nor in broad rumor lies,
But lives and spreads aloft by those pure eyes,
And perfect witness of all-judging Jove;
As he pronounces lastly on each deed,
Of so much fame in Heaven expect thy meed."
  O fountain Arethuse, and thou honored flood,
Smooth-sliding Mincius, crowned with vocal reeds,
That strain I heard was of a higher mood:
But now my Oat proceeds,
And listens to the Herald of the Sea
That came in Neptune's plea.
He asked the Waves, and asked the felon winds,
What hard mishap hath doomed this gentle swain?
And questioned every gust of rugged wings
That blows from off each beakèd Promontory.
They knew not of his story,
And sage Hippotades their answer brings,
That not a blast was from his dungeon strayed,
The Air was calm, and on the level brine
Sleek Panope with all her sisters played.
It was that fatal and perfidious Bark
Built in the eclipse, and rigged with curses dark,
That sunk so low that sacred head of thine.
  Next Camus, reverend Sire, went footing slow,
His Mantle hairy, and his Bonnet sedge,
Inwrought with figures dim, and on the edge
Like to that sanguine flower inscribed with woe.
"Ah, who hath reft," (quoth he) "my dearest pledge?"
Last came, and last did go,
The Pilot of the Galilean Lake.
Two massy Keys he bore of metals twain,
(The Golden opes, the Iron shuts amain).
He shook his Mitred locks, and stern bespake,
"How well could I have spared for thee, young swain,

Enow of such as, for their bellies' sake,
Creep and intrude, and climb into the fold!
Of other care they little reckoning make,
Than how to scramble at the shearers' feast,
And shove away the worthy bidden guest.
Blind mouths! that scarce themselves know how to hold
A Sheep-hook, or have learned aught else the least
That to the faithful Herdman's art belongs!
What recks it them? What need they? They are sped;
And when they list, their lean and flashy songs
Grate on their scrannel Pipes of wretched straw;
The hungry Sheep look up, and are not fed,
But swoln with wind, and the rank mist they draw,
Rot inwardly, and foul contagion spread:
Besides what the grim Wolf with privy paw
Daily devours apace, and nothing said.
But that two-handed engine at the door
Stands ready to smite once, and smite no more."
  Return, Alpheus, the dread voice is past,
That shrunk thy streams; return Sicilian Muse,
And call the Vales, and bid them hither cast
Their Bells, and Flowerets of a thousand hues.
Ye valleys low, where the mild whispers use,
Of shades and wanton winds, and gushing brooks,
On whose fresh lap the swart Star sparely looks,
Throw hither all your quaint enamelled eyes,
That on the green turf suck the honey'd showers,
And purple all the ground with vernal flowers.
Bring the rathe Primrose that forsaken dies,
The tufted Crow-toe, and pale Jessamine,
The white Pink, and the Pansy freaked with jet,
The glowing Violet,
The Musk-rose, and the well-attired Woodbine,
With Cowslips wan that hang the pensive head,
And every flower that sad embroidery wears:
Bid Amaranthus all his beauty shed,
And Daffadillies fill their cups with tears,
To strew the Laureate Hearse where Lycid lies.
For so, to interpose a little ease,
Let our frail thoughts dally with false surmise.
Ay me! Whilst thee the shores and sounding Seas
Wash far away, where'er thy bones are hurled;
Whether beyond the stormy Hebrides,
Where thou perhaps under the whelming tide
Visit'st the bottom of the monstrous world;
Or whether thou, to our moist vows denied,
Sleep'st by the fable of Bellerus old,
Where the great vision of the guarded Mount
Looks toward Namancos and Bayona's hold;
Look homeward, Angel, now, and melt with ruth:
And, O ye Dolphins, waft the hapless youth.

Weep no more, woful Shepherds, weep no more,
For Lycidas, your sorrow, is not dead,
Sunk though he be beneath the watery floor.
So sinks the day-star in the Ocean bed,
And yet anon repairs his drooping head,
And tricks his beams, and with new-spangled Ore,
Flames in the forehead of the morning sky:
So Lycidas sunk low, but mounted high,
Through the dear might of Him that walked the waves,
Where, other groves and other streams along,
With Nectar pure his oozy Locks he laves,
And hears the unexpressive nuptial Song,
In the blest Kingdoms meek of joy and love.
There entertain him all the Saints above,
In solemn troops, and sweet Societies,
That sing, and singing in their glory move,
And wipe the tears for ever from his eyes.
Now, Lycidas, the Shepherds weep no more;
Henceforth thou art the Genius of the shore,
In thy large recompense, and shalt be good
To all that wander in that perilous flood.
Thus sang the uncouth Swain to the oaks and rills,
While the still Morn went out with Sandals grey,
He touched the tender stops of various Quills,
With eager thought warbling his Doric lay:
And now the Sun had stretched out all the hills,
And now was dropt into the Western bay;
At last he rose, and twitched his Mantle blue:
Tomorrow to fresh Woods, and Pastures new.

Attention may be called to the fact that the last eight lines of "Lycidas" compose a perfect example of *ottava rima,* for a definition of which see page 355.

Attention has been called to the fact that though the deaths of women have occasioned many moving poems, the greatest elegies have been written upon the deaths of men: Milton's "Lycidas" is a monody in which "the author bewails a learned friend [Edward King, one of Milton's schoolmates] unfortunately drowned in his passage from Chester on the Irish seas in 1637"; Shelley's "Adonais" (see page 357) mourns the death of his fellow-poet Keats; "Thyrsis" commemorates Arnold's friend, the poet Arthur Hugh Clough, who died at Florence in 1861; Tennyson's "In Memoriam" (see pages 281 and 350) was occasioned by the loss of Arthur Henry Hallam; Swinburne's "Ave Atque Vale" is a tribute to the poet Baudelaire; Whitman's "Captain, My Captain" and his "When Lilacs Last in the Dooryard Bloom'd" (see page 179) and E. A. Robinson's "The Master" (see page 140) were inspired by the passing of Lincoln.

All elegies have not been prompted by particular individuals. Whitman's moving "Dirge for Two Veterans" is a poem inspired by the sight of a double grave for two anonymous soldiers; yet the intensity of feeling—the personal mingled with the universal—is as great as though the poet were intimately acquainted with the men he mourns.

DIRGE FOR TWO VETERANS

by Walt Whitman (1819-1892)

The last sunbeam
Lightly falls from the finish'd Sabbath,
On the pavement here, and there beyond it is looking,
Down a new-made double grave,

Lo, the moon ascending,
Up from the east the silvery round moon,
Beautiful over the house-tops ghastly, phantom moon,
Immense and silent moon.

I see a sad procession,
And I hear the sound of coming full-key'd bugles,
All the channels of the city streets they're flooding,
As with voices and with tears.

I hear the great drums pounding,
And the small drums steady whirring,
And every blow of the great convulsive drums,
Strikes me through and through.

For the son is brought with the father,
(In the foremost ranks of the fierce assault they fell,
Two veterans son and father dropt together,
And the double grave awaits them.)

Now nearer blow the bugles,
And the drums strike more convulsive,
And the daylight o'er the pavement quite has faded,
And the strong dead-march enwraps me.

In the eastern sky up-buoying,
The sorrowful vast phantom moves illumin'd,
('Tis some mother's large transparent face,
In heaven brighter growing.)

O strong dead-march you please me!
O moon immense with your silvery face you soothe me!
O my soldiers twain! O my veterans passing to burial!
What I have I also give you.

The moon gives you light,
And the bugles and the drums give you music,
And my heart, O my soldiers, my veterans,
My heart gives you love.

More general in its application and lighter in its music is the song from Scott's "The Lady of the Lake," with its soothing repetitions and lullaby-like overtones. Although it lacks the intimacy of the great elegies, the tone of the poem as well as the key in which it is cast entitles it to a place in this category.

SOLDIER, REST!
(from "The Lady of the Lake")

by Walter Scott (1771-1832)

Soldier, rest! thy warfare o'er,
  Sleep the sleep that knows not breaking;
Dream of battled fields no more,
  Days of danger, nights of waking.
In our isle's enchanted hall,
  Hands unseen thy couch are strewing,
Fairy strains of music fall,
  Every sense in slumber dewing.
Soldier, rest! thy warfare o'er,
Dream of fighting fields no more;
Sleep the sleep that knows not breaking,
Morn of toil, nor night of waking.

No rude sound shall reach thine ear,
  Armour's clang, or war-steed champing,
Trump nor pibroch summon here
  Mustering clan or squadron tramping.
Yet the lark's shrill fife may come
  At the daybreak from the fallow,
And the bittern sound his drum,
  Booming from the sedgy shallow.
Ruder sounds shall none be near,
Guards nor warders challenge here,
Here's no war-steed's neigh and champing,
Shouting clans or squadrons stamping.

Huntsman, rest! thy chase is done;
  While our slumbrous spells assail ye,
Dream not, with the rising sun,
  Bugles here shall sound reveille.
Sleep! the deer is in his den;
  Sleep! thy hounds are by thee lying:
Sleep! nor dream in yonder glen
  How thy gallant steed lay dying.
Huntsman, rest! thy chase is done;
Think not of the rising sun,
For at dawning to assail ye
Here no bugles sound reveille.

Though poems inspired by the death of women cannot be ranked with those that mourn the death of men, a few shorter elegies to women are memorable. These elegies, chiefly modern, are lyric in character and include Oscar Wilde's artfully artless "Requiescat," Matthew Arnold's "Strew on her roses, roses," and Edna St. Vincent Millay's "Memorial to D. C.," five poems to a schoolmate who died at Vassar College in 1918, a set of verses which includes the touching "Elegy" and its accompanying "Dirge." The lines by Wilde are typical of the shorter modern elegy:

REQUIESCAT

Tread lightly, she is near
  Under the snow,
Speak gently, she can hear
  The daisies grow.

All her bright golden hair
  Tarnished with rust,
She that was young and fair
  Fallen to dust.

Lily-like, white as snow,
  She hardly knew
She was a woman, so
  Sweetly she grew.

Coffin-board, heavy stone,
  Lie on her breast;
I vex my heart alone,
  She is at rest.

Peace, Peace, she cannot hear
  Lyre or sonnet,
All my life's buried here,
  Heap earth upon it.

—*Oscar Wilde*
(1856-1900)

Among modern elegies none is more powerful than Archibald MacLeish's "Memorial Rain," an extraordinary poem in which the pompous tone of the ambassador dedicating a graveyard to the dead soldiers is in dramatic contrast with the quiet soliloquy of the poet remembering his friend who lies there. Sara Teasdale's tribute to another poet, Vachel Lindsay, is the more poignant when it is known that he was one of her few close friends. The poem of his which she admired particularly was Lindsay's tribute to the reformer John P. Altgeld ("The Eagle That Is Forgotten"), an elegy that ends with the line "To live in mankind is far more than to live in a name."

IN MEMORY OF VACHEL LINDSAY

"Deep in the ages," you said, "Deep in the ages,"
And "To live in mankind is far more than to live in a name"—
You are deep in the ages now, deep in the ages,
You whom the world could not break, nor the years tame.

Fly out, fly on, eagle that is not forgotten,
Fly straight to the innermost light, you who loved sun in your eyes—
Free of the fret, free of the weight of living,
Bravest among the brave and gayest among the wise.

—*Sara Teasdale* (1884-1933)

THE EPIC

The outstanding characteristic of the epic is the scope and amplitude of its theme. A true epic sums up an epoch. Characters enter it, adventurers emerge, personalities are flashed forth—but they are merely parts of a design which is noble and yet impersonal. Thus the epic not only summarizes an age, it transcends it.

Grandeur and strength maintain the epic throughout its length, for the epic-writer must have unusual power of endurance. A short epic is as much a contradiction in terms as a lengthy sonnet. Morris's *Atalanta's Race* and Arnold's *Sohrab and Rustum* have been called "miniature epics," and, in *The Rape of the Lock,* Pope perfected a "mock epic," but one measures the real epic by its sweep and sublimity. If one accepts Aristotle's dictum in the *Poetics,* that "the longer the story, consistently with its being comprehensible as a whole, the finer it is by reason of its magnitude," then the epic is the highest form of narrative poetry. It is unfortunate that the length of this poetic form precludes the inclusion of a complete example, but a few observations can be made to guide further reading.

Although the genuine racial or "popular" epics have no fixed form, and wander on through endless adventures, frequently without plot connection—as in *Beowulf,* the *Nibelungenlied,* and the *Kalevala*—practically every epic written in western Europe has followed the model established by Homer's *Iliad* and *Odyssey.* Here, as in the epics which followed, the central action embodied either a physical conflict—Greek *vs.* Trojan, Beowulf *vs.* Grendel, Roland *vs.* the Saracens, God *vs.* Satan—or a wearisome search and struggle —Ulysses seeking Ithaca, Aeneas seeking a site for a new empire, Dante seeking Paradise, Columbus seeking a new way to India, in Joel Barlow's ponderous *Columbiad.* Naturally, there were many digressions—Ulysses and Circe,

Raphael's story of the creation of the world in Milton. But the major purpose was to present an idealized hero of a group—Ulysses, the wise Greek; Beowulf, the great Scandinavian warrior; Satan, the undefeatable antagonist—in a situation which would bring glory to the group. *Genesis* and *Exodus* might well be called the epics of the Hebrews; *Paradise Lost* might, in a sense, be considered the Old Testament of the English and the *Iliad* the Bible of the Greeks.

Limitations of space prevent the quotation of an entire epic here, and an adequate analysis of it is, therefore, impossible. However, the formula of the classical epic is clear. It begins with a statement of the subject:

> Achilles' wrath, to Greece the direful spring
> Of woes unnumbered, Heavenly Goddess, sing!
> —*Iliad,* Pope's version

> Arms and the man I sing . . .
> —*Aeneid*

> Of man's first disobedience, and the fruit
> Of that forbidden tree, whose mortal taste
> Brought death into the world, and all our woe . . .
> —Milton, *Paradise Lost*

This same formula has been followed by all epic-poets, even down to Stephen Vincent Benét in his panoramic *John Brown's Body*. Pope burlesqued it delicately:

> What dire offense from amorous causes springs,
> What mighty contests rise from trivial things,
> I sing—
> —*The Rape of the Lock*

Next in the order of the epic "formula" was the invocation of the Muse:

> Sing, Heavenly Muse, that, on the secret top
> Of Oreb, or of Sinai, didst inspire
> That shepherd who first taught the chosen seed
> In the beginnings how the heavens and earth
> Rose out of Chaos.
> —*Paradise Lost*

Thereupon the epic should, according to classical theory, begin the action *in medias res,* in the middle of the story—Aeneas' landing near Carthage, Satan and his army writhing in the fiery sea of Hell. Following the invocation a conflict is visible, a battle inevitable. Before the fighting can begin, however, there must be a careful catalogue of forces: all the leaders of the Greeks and Trojans, all the devils and angels:

> First Moloch, horrid king, besmeared with blood . . .
> Next Chemos, the obscene dread of Moab's sons . . .
> Belial came last; than whom a spirit more lewd
> Fell not from Heaven . . .
> —*Paradise Lost*

After the roll-call of forces come the challenges, the "boastings" of Beowulf about what he will do to Grendel when he catches him, of Achilles foretelling his revenge upon Hector.

The preliminaries now being concluded, the battle begins; the poet, unable to tell it all, confines himself to individual exploits: a day's work by Diomed, the prowess of Gabriel:

> Meanwhile, in other parts, like deeds deserved
> Memorial, where the might of Gabriel fought,
> And with fierce ensigns pierced the deep array
> Of Moloch, furious king, who him defied . . .
> —*Paradise Lost*

Pope has reproduced the same effect satirically in burlesque:

> While through the press enraged Thalestris flies,
> And scatters death around from both her eyes,
> A Beau and Witling perished in the throng,
> One died in metaphor, and one in song.
> —*The Rape of the Lock*

The gods, however, cannot remain outside the story; they must interfere, and before they can act, they must hold a council. It was at a council of the gods that the fates of Hector and Ulysses were decided; Christ and God confer upon the fate of Satan and man. In *The Rape of the Lock*, the guardian sylphs take the place of the gods in guiding the action. After the poem has proceeded through its ten or twelve books, or cantos, the end comes with the death or victory of the hero. Death is perhaps the more effective conclusion in *Beowulf* and the *Song of Roland,* but the suggestion of a new story just beginning gives unusual power and beauty to the concluding lines of *Paradise Lost:*

> The world was all before them, where to choose
> Their place of rest, and Providence their guide.
> They, hand in hand, with wandering steps and slow,
> Through Eden took their solitary way.

America is still awaiting its great epic; there are those who assert that it is an impossibility. It seems certain that a great body of legend, a maturity of tradition, must be assimilated before epics are produced. The closest approach, perhaps, is Stephen Vincent Benét's *John Brown's Body,* although Phelps Putnam's mythical "Bill Williams" is an attempt to create a saga in segments and Archibald MacLeish's *Conquistador* is an epical account of the Spanish conquest of Mexico, a sinewy narrative which is a triumph of heroic poetry. The legends of Johnny Appleseed and the fabulous exploits of Paul Bunyan, the Herculean hero of the lumber-camps, are material from which a rich and highly indigenous epic may some day be fashioned.

THE ODE

In Greek poetry the ode grew out of the choric song and became "a form of stately and elaborate verse." Originally chanted, the ode was built on a set of themes and responses and sung by divided choirs, half the singers intoning the strophe (turn), the other half replying with the antistrophe (counter-turn) and both uniting with the epode (after-song). Pindar's odes attained the greatest fame because of their ingenuity, and his served as models for the first English expressions of that form. Ben Jonson had called some of his irregular rhymed stanzas "odes" and Milton had approximated the form in his "Hymn on the Morning of Christ's Nativity," but Abraham Cowley was the first to pattern his odes after what he believed to be the style of Pindar, Cowley failing to comprehend that Pindar varied the verse-arrangement of his odes but that each was consistently and strictly patterned. "He supposed," said Edmund Gosse, "the Greek poet to be carried away on a storm of heroic emotion in which all the discipline of prosody was disregarded. . . . His idea of an ode, which he impressed with such success upon the British nation that it has never been entirely removed, was a lofty and tempestuous piece of indefinite poetry, conducted 'without sail or oar' in whatever direction the enthusiasm of the poet chose to take it."

Cowley's critical errors were corrected by Congreve and others, and a hundred years later, Gray published his "The Bard" and "The Progress of Poesy" which restored the true form. Gray's "Pindaric" odes are divided into units of threes—three sections, each of which contains three stanzas: the strophe, the antistrophe, and the epode. In a footnote to "The Progress of Poesy," Gray himself wrote, "The subject and simile, as usual with Pindar, are united. The various sources of poetry, which gives life and lustre to all it touches, are here described; its quiet, majestic progress enriching every subject (otherwise dry and barren) with a pomp of diction and luxuriant harmony of numbers; and its more rapid and irresistible course when swollen and hurried away by the conflict of tumultuous passions." The subjects of the three sections are (I) the power of poetry in general, (II) poetry in other countries, and (III) poetry in England.

THE PROGRESS OF POESY

A Pindaric Ode

by Thomas Gray (1716-1771)

I

The Strophe

Awake, Aeolian lyre, awake,
And give to rapture all thy trembling strings.
From Helicon's harmonious springs
A thousand rills their mazy progress take:
The laughing flowers, that round them blow,
Drink life and fragrance as they flow.
Now the rich stream of music winds along
Deep, majestic, smooth and strong,
Through verdant vales, and Ceres' golden reign:
Now rolling down the steep amain,
Headlong, impetuous, see it pour;
The rocks and nodding groves re-bellow to the roar.

The Antistrophe

O Sovereign of the willing soul,
Parent of sweet and solemn-breathing airs,
Enchanting shell! the sullen Cares
And frantic Passions hear thy soft control.
On Thracia's hills the Lord of War
Has curbed the fury of his car,
And dropped his thirsty lance at thy command.
Perching on the sceptred hand
Of Jove, thy magic lulls the feathered king
With ruffled plumes and flagging wing:
Quenched in dark clouds of slumber lie
The terror of his beak, and lightnings of his eye.

The Epode

Thee the voice, the dance, obey,
Tempered to thy warbled lay.
O'er Idalia's velvet-green
The rosy-crownèd Loves are seen
On Cytherea's day,
With antic Sports, and blue-eyed Pleasures,
Frisking light in frolic measures;
Now pursuing, now retreating,
Now in circling troops they meet:
To brisk notes in cadence beating,
Glance their many-twinkling feet.
Slow melting strains their Queen's approach declare:
Where'er she turns, the Graces homage pay.
With arms sublime, that float upon the air,
In gliding state she wins her easy way:
O'er her warm cheek and rising bosom move
The bloom of young Desire and purple light of Love.

II

The Strophe

Man's feeble race what ills await!
Labour, and Penury, the racks of Pain,
Disease, and Sorrow's weeping train,
And Death, sad refuge from the storms of fate!
The fond complaint, my song, disprove,
And justify the laws of Jove.
Say, has he given in vain the heavenly Muse?
Night, and all her sickly dews,
Her spectres wan, and birds of boding cry,
He gives to range the dreary sky:
Till down the eastern cliffs afar
Hyperion's march they spy, and glittering shafts of war.

The Antistrophe

In climes beyond the solar road,
Where shaggy forms o'er ice-built mountains roam,
The Muse has broke the twilight gloom
  To cheer the shivering native's dull abode.
And oft, beneath the odorous shade
Of Chili's boundless forests laid,
She deigns to hear the savage youth repeat
In loose numbers wildly sweet
Their feather-cinctured chiefs, and dusky loves.
Her track, where'er the Goddess roves,
Glory pursue and generous Shame,
The unconquerable Mind, and Freedom's holy flame.

The Epode

Woods, that wave o'er Delphi's steep,[1]
Isles, that crown the Aegean deep,
  Fields, that cool Ilissus laves,
  Or where Maeander's amber waves
In lingering labyrinths creep,
  How do your tuneful echoes languish,
  Mute, but to the voice of anguish?
Where each old poetic mountain
  Inspiration breathed around:
Every shade and hallowed fountain
  Murmured deep a solemn sound:
Till the sad Nine, in Greece's evil hour,
  Left their Parnassus for the Latian plains.
Alike they scorn the pomp of tyrant Power,
  And coward Vice, that revels in her chains.
When Latium had her lofty spirit lost,
They sought, O Albion! next thy sea-encircled coast.

III

The Strophe

  Far from the sun and summer gale,
In thy green lap was Nature's darling laid,[2]
What time, where lucid Avon strayed,
  To him the mighty mother did unveil
Her awful face: the dauntless child
Stretched forth his little arms, and smiled.
This pencil take (she said), whose colours clear
Richly paint the vernal year:
Thine too these golden keys, immortal boy!
This can unlock the gates of joy;

[1] In this epode, Gray symbolizes the progress of poetry from Greece to Italy, and from Italy to England.
[2] Shakespeare.

Of horror that, and thrilling fears,
Or ope the sacred source of sympathetic tears.

The Antistrophe

Nor second he,[3] that rode sublime,
Upon the seraph-wings of Ecstasy,
The secrets of the abyss to spy:
He passed the flaming bounds of place and time:
The living Throne, the sapphire-blaze,
Where Angels tremble while they gaze,
He saw; but, blasted with excess of light,
Closed his eyes in endless night.
Behold, where Dryden's less presumptuous car,
Wide o'er the fields of glory bear
Two coursers of ethereal race,
With necks in thunder clothed, and long-resounding pace.

The Epode

Hark, his hands the lyre explore!
Bright-eyed Fancy, hovering o'er,
Scatters from her pictured urn
Thoughts that breathe, and words that burn.
But ah, 'tis heard no more!—
O Lyre divine! what daring Spirit
Wakes thee now? Though he inherit
Nor the pride, nor ample pinion,
That the Theban Eagle bear,[4]
Sailing with supreme dominion
Through the azure deep of air:
Yet oft before his infant eyes would run
Such forms as glitter in the Muse's ray,
With orient hues, unborrowed of the Sun:
Yet shall he mount, and keep his distant way
Beyond the limits of a vulgar fate,
Beneath the Good how far—but far above the Great.

Collins' odes are less complex in architecture. In his exquisite "Ode to Evening" (see page 222) the simplicity of thought and scene is reflected in the austere pattern of unrhymed stanzas; in his "Ode to Fear" Collins maintains the three-part division into strophe, antistrophe, and epode, although he does not preserve the order or the intricacy.

ODE TO FEAR

by William Collins (1721-1759)

Strophe

Thou, to whom the world unknown
With all its shadowy shapes, is shown;

[3] Here Gray refers to Milton.
[4] Pindar.

Who seest, appalled, the unreal scene,
While fancy lifts the veil between:
  Ah Fear! ah frantic Fear!
  I see, I see thee near.
I know thy hurried step, thy haggard eye!
Like thee I start; like thee disordered fly.
For, lo, what monsters in thy train appear!
Danger, whose limbs of giant mould
What mortal eye can fixed behold?
Who stalks his round, an hideous form,
Howling amidst the midnight storm;
Or throws him on the ridgy steep
Of some loose hanging rock to sleep:
And with him thousand phantoms joined,
Who prompt to deeds accursed the mind:
And those, the fiends, who, near allied,
O'er Nature's wounds and wrecks, preside;
Whilst Vengeance, in the lurid air,
Lifts her red arm, exposed and bare:
On whom that ravening brood of Fate,
Who lap the blood of Sorrow, wait:
Who, Fear, this ghastly train can see,
And look not madly wild, like thee?

Epode

In earliest Greece, to thee, with partial choice,
  The grief-full Muse addrest her infant tongue;
The maids and matrons, on her awful voice,
  Silent and pale, in wild amazement hung.

Yet he, the bard [1] who first invoked thy name,
  Disdained in Marathon its power to feel:
For not alone he nursed the poet's flame,
  But reached from Virtue's hand the patriot's steel.

But who is he whom later garlands grace,
  Who left awhile o'er Hybla's dews to rove,
With trembling eyes thy dreary steps to trace,
  Where thou and furies shared the baleful grove?

Wrapt in thy cloudy veil, the incestuous queen [2]
  Sighed the sad call her son and husband heard,
When once alone it broke the silent scene,
  And he, the wretch of Thebes, no more appeared.

O Fear! I know thee by my throbbing heart:
  Thy withering power inspired each mournful line:
Though gentle Pity claim her mingled part,
  Yet all the thunders of the scene are thine!

[1] Aeschylus. [2] Jocasta.

Antistrophe

Thou who such weary lengths hast past,
Where wilt thou rest, mad nymph, at last?
Say, wilt thou shroud in haunted cell,
Where gloomy Rape and Murder dwell?
  Or, in some hollowed seat,
  'Gainst which the big waves beat,
Hear drowning seamen's cries, in tempests brought?
Dark Power! with shuddering, meek, submitted thought,
Be mine to read the visions old
Which thy awakening bards have told:

And, lest thou meet my blasted view,
Hold each strange tale devoutly true;
Ne'er be I found, by thee o'erawed,
In that thrice hallowed eve, abroad,
When ghosts, as cottage maids believe,
Their pebbled beds permitted leave;
And goblins haunt, from fire, or fen,
Or mine, or flood, the walks of men!

  O thou, whose spirit most possest
The sacred seat of Shakespeare's breast!
By all that from thy prophet broke,
In thy divine emotions spoke;
Hither again thy fury deal,
Teach me but once like him to feel:
His cypress wreath my meed decree,
And I, O Fear, will dwell with thee!

The "irregular" ode, introduced by Cowley, has become a recognized form in English poetry. Differing sharply from the classical pattern, it discards strophe, antistrophe and epode; it is not bound by limitations of shape or size, rhyme-scheme or metre. The odes of Coleridge, Wordsworth, Tennyson, and O'Shaughnessy are so free as to have the character of improvisations; the more shapely odes of Keats and Shelley are actually extended and magnificently sustained lyrics. Keats's odes, though precise in metrical structure, are irregular in form; yet each dictates its own pattern. The "Ode to a Nightingale" is the most exact and altogether regular ode, except for the longer line at the end of the second stanza. These measured odes have appropriately been termed "stanzaic," Shelley's "Ode to the West Wind" (see page 43) and Whitman's "Pioneers! O Pioneers!" (see page 163) being varied examples. The exalted odes of Keats, however, present the "stanzaic" ode at its highest; probably the most eloquent of his raptures being the "Ode to a Nightingale."

ODE TO A NIGHTINGALE

by John Keats (1795-1821)

My heart aches, and a drowsy numbness pains
  My sense, as though of hemlock I had drunk,

Or emptied some dull opiate to the drains
  One minute past, and Lethe-wards had sunk:
'Tis not through envy of thy happy lot,
  But being too happy in thine happiness,—
    That thou, light-wingèd Dryad of the trees,
        In some melodious plot
  Of beechen green, and shadows numberless,
    Singest of summer in full-throated ease.

O for a draught of vintage, that hath been
  Cool'd a long age in the deep-delvèd earth,
Tasting of Flora and the country green,
  Dance, and Provençal song, and sun-burnt mirth!
O for a beaker full of the warm South,
  Full of the true, the blushful Hippocrene,
    With beaded bubbles winking at the brim,
        And purple-stainèd mouth;
That I might drink, and leave the world unseen,
  And with thee fade away into the forest dim:

Fade far away, dissolve, and quite forget
  What thou among the leaves hast never known,
The weariness, the fever, and the fret
  Here, where men sit and hear each other groan;
Where palsy shakes a few, sad, last gray hairs,
  Where youth grows pale, and spectre-thin, and dies;
    Where but to think is to be full of sorrow
        And leaden-eyed despairs;
Where Beauty cannot keep her lustrous eyes,
  Or new Love pine at them beyond tomorrow.

Away! away! for I will fly to thee,
  Not charioted by Bacchus and his pards,
But on the viewless wings of Poesy,
  Though the dull brain perplexes and retards:
Already with thee! tender is the night,
  And haply the Queen-Moon is on her throne,
    Cluster'd around by all her starry Fays;
        But here there is no light,
  Save what from heaven is with the breezes blown
    Through verdurous glooms and winging mossy ways.

I cannot see what flowers are at my feet,
  Nor what soft incense hangs upon the boughs,
But, in embalmèd darkness, guess each sweet
  Wherewith the seasonable month endows
The grass, the thicket, and the fruit-tree wild;
  White hawthorn, and the pastoral eglantine;
    Fast-fading violets cover'd up in leaves;
        And mid-May's eldest child,
  The coming musk-rose, full of dewy wine,
    The murmurous haunt of flies on summer eves.

Darkling I listen; and for many a time
I have been half in love with easeful Death,
Call'd him soft names in many a musèd rhyme,
To take into the air my quiet breath;
Now more than ever seems it rich to die,
To cease upon the midnight with no pain,
While thou art pouring forth thy soul abroad
In such an ecstasy!
Still wouldst thou sing, and I have ears in vain—
To thy high requiem become a sod.

Thou wast not born for death, immortal Bird!
No hungry generations tread thee down;
The voice I hear this passing night was heard
In ancient days by emperor and clown:
Perhaps the self-same song that found a path
Through the sad heart of Ruth, when, sick for home,
She stood in tears amid the alien corn;
The same that oft-times hath
Charm'd magic casements, opening on the foam
Of perilous seas, in faëry lands forlorn.

Forlorn! the very word is like a bell
To toll me back from thee to my sole self.
Adieu! the fancy cannot cheat so well
As she is famed to do, deceiving elf.
Adieu! adieu! thy plaintive anthem fades
Past the near meadows, over the still stream,
Up the hill-side; and now 'tis buried deep
In the next valley-glades:
Was it a vision, or a waking dream?
Fled is that music:—do I wake or sleep?

Mention might be made of the so-called "Horatian ode," an ode built of four-line and six-line stanzas—actually not a formal ode at all. Possibly the best of this type is Andrew Marvell's "An Horatian Ode upon Cromwell's Return from Ireland," although Gray's "On a Distant Prospect of Eton College" is better known.

Today the ode can scarcely be recognized by its form. It may be quite "Horatian," loosely stanzaic, or wholly irregular. It is identified by its tone: an intense, richly elaborated and, usually, profound apostrophe. Of the "irregular" odes none is so impressive as Wordsworth's "Intimations of Immortality," possibly the greatest philosophical ode ever written in English.

ODE

Intimations of Immortality from Recollections of Early Childhood

by William Wordsworth (1770-1850)

There was a time when meadow, grove, and stream,
The earth, and every common sight,
To me did seem

Apparelled in celestial light,
The glory and the freshness of a dream.
It is not now as it hath been of yore;—
Turn wheresoe'er I may,
By night or day,
The things which I have seen I now can see no more.

The Rainbow comes and goes,
And lovely is the Rose;
The Moon doth with delight
Look round her when the heavens are bare;
Waters on a starry night
Are beautiful and fair;
The Sunshine is a glorious birth;
But yet I know, where'er I go,
That there hath passed away a glory from the earth.

Now, while the birds thus sing a joyous song,
And while the young lambs bound
As to the tabor's sound,
To me alone there came a thought of grief;
A timely utterance gave that thought relief,
And I again am strong.
The cataracts blow their trumpets from the steep;
No more shall grief of mine the season wrong;
I hear the Echoes through the mountains throng;
The Winds come to me from the fields of sleep,
And all the earth is gay;
Land and sea
Give themselves up to jollity,
And with the heart of May
Doth every Beast keep holiday—
Thou Child of Joy,
Shout round me, let me hear thy shouts, thou happy Shepherd-boy.

Ye blessèd Creatures, I have heard the call
Ye to each other make; I see
The heavens laugh with you in your jubilee;
My heart is at your festival,
My head hath its coronal,
The fulness of your bliss, I feel—I feel it all.
Oh evil day! if I were sullen
While Earth herself is adorning,
This sweet May-morning,
And the Children are culling
On every side,
In a thousand valleys far and wide,
Fresh flowers; while the sun shines warm,
And the Babe leaps up on his Mother's arm:—
I hear, I hear, with joy I hear!
—But there's a Tree, of many, one,
A single Field which I have looked upon,

Both of them speak of something that is gone:
    The Pansy at my feet
    Doth the same tale repeat:
Whither is fled the visionary gleam?
Where is it now, the glory and the dream?

Our birth is but a sleep and a forgetting:
The Soul that rises with us, our life's Star,
    Hath had elsewhere its setting,
        And cometh from afar:
    Not in entire forgetfulness,
    And not in utter nakedness,
But trailing clouds of glory do we come
    From God, who is our home:
Heaven lies about us in our infancy!
Shades of the prison-house begin to close
    Upon the growing Boy,
But He beholds the light, and whence it flows,
    He sees it in his joy;
The Youth, who daily farther from the east
    Must travel, still is Nature's Priest,
        And by the vision splendid
        Is on his way attended;
At length the Man perceives it die away,
And fade into the light of common day.

Earth fills her lap with pleasures of her own;
Yearnings she hath in her own natural kind,
And, even with something of a Mother's mind,
    And no unworthy aim,
    The homely Nurse doth all she can
To make her Foster-child, her Inmate, Man,
    Forget the glories he hath known,
And that imperial palace whence he came.

Behold the Child among his new-born blisses,
A six years' Darling of a pigmy size!
See, where 'mid work of his own hand he lies,
Fretted by sallies of his mother's kisses,
With light upon him from his father's eyes!
See, at his feet, some little plan or chart,
Some fragment from his dream of human life,
Shaped by himself with newly-learnèd art;
    A wedding or a festival,
    A mourning or a funeral;
        And this hath now his heart,
    And unto this he frames his song:
        Then will he fit his tongue
To dialogues of business, love, or strife;
    But it will not be long
    Ere this be thrown aside,
    And with new joy and pride

The little Actor cons another part;
Filling from time to time his "humorous stage"
With all the Persons, down to palsied Age,
That Life brings with her in her equipage;
    As if his whole vocation
    Were endless imitation.

Thou, whose exterior semblance doth belie
    Thy Soul's immensity;
Thou best Philosopher, who yet dost keep
Thy heritage, thou Eye among the blind,
That, deaf and silent, read'st the eternal deep,
Haunted for ever by the eternal Mind,—
    Mighty Prophet! Seer blest!
    On whom those truths do rest,
Which we are toiling all our lives to find,
In darkness lost, the darkness of the grave;
Thou, over whom thy Immortality
Broods like the Day, a Master o'er a Slave,
A Presence which is not to be put by;
Thou little Child, yet glorious in the might
Of heaven-born freedom on thy being's height,
Why with such earnest pains dost thou provoke
The years to bring the inevitable yoke,
Thus blindly with thy blessedness at strife?
Full soon thy Soul shall have her earthly freight,
And custom lie upon thee with a weight,
Heavy as frost, and deep almost as life!

    O joy! that in our embers
    Is something that doth live,
    That nature yet remembers
    What was so fugitive!
The thought of our past years in me doth breed
Perpetual benediction: not indeed
For that which is most worthy to be blest—
Delight and liberty, the simple creed
Of Childhood, whether busy or at rest,
With new-fledged hope still fluttering in his breast:—
    Not for these I raise
    The song of thanks and praise;
  But for those obstinate questionings
  Of sense and outward things,
  Fallings from us, vanishings;
  Blank misgivings of a Creature
Moving about in worlds not realised,
High instincts before which our mortal Nature
Did tremble like a guilty Thing surprised:
    But for those first affections,
    Those shadowy recollections,
  Which, be they what they may,
Are yet the fountain light of all our day,

Are yet a master light of all our seeing;
  Uphold us, cherish, and have power to make
Our noisy years seem moments in the being
Of the eternal Silence: truths that wake,
    To perish never;
Which neither listlessness, nor mad endeavour,
    Nor Man nor Boy,
Nor all that is at enmity with joy,
Can utterly abolish or destroy!
    Hence in a season of calm weather
        Though inland far we be,
Our Souls have sight of that immortal sea
    Which brought us hither,
    Can in a moment travel thither,
And see the Children sport upon the shore,
And hear the mighty waters rolling evermore.

Then sing, ye Birds, sing, sing a joyous song!
    And let the young Lambs bound
    As to the tabor's sound!
We in thought will join your throng,
    Ye that pipe and ye that play,
    Ye that through your hearts today
    Feel the gladness of the May!
What though the radiance which was once so bright
Be now for ever taken from my sight,
    Though nothing can bring back the hour
Of splendour in the grass, of glory in the flower;
    We will grieve not, rather find
    Strength in what remains behind;
    In the primal sympathy
    Which having been must ever be;
    In the soothing thoughts that spring
    Out of human suffering;
    In the faith that looks through death,
In years that bring the philosophic mind.

And O, ye Fountains, Meadows, Hills, and Groves,
Forbode not any severing of our loves!
Yet in my heart of hearts I feel your might;
I only have relinquished one delight
To live beneath your more habitual sway.
I love the Brooks which down their channels fret,
Even more than when I tripped lightly as they;
The innocent brightness of a new-born Day
        Is lovely yet;
The Clouds that gather round the setting sun
Do take a sober colouring from an eye
That hath kept watch o'er man's mortality;
Another race hath been, and other palms are won.
Thanks to the human heart by which we live,

Thanks to its tenderness, its joys, and fears,
To me the meanest flower that blows can give
Thoughts that do often lie too deep for tears.

SUGGESTIONS FOR ADDITIONAL READING

EPIGRAMS AND EPITAPHS

Ben Jonson, *Epitaph on Elizabeth*
William Browne, *On the Countess Dowager of Pembroke*
John Milton, *On the University Carrier*
Robert Burns, *A Bard's Epitaph*
Walter Savage Landor, *Shorter Poems*
William Blake, *Epigrams*
Edgar Lee Masters, *Spoon River Anthology*
Thomas Hardy, *Rain on a Grave*
Edna St. Vincent Millay, *Epitaph*

ELEGIES

Geoffrey Chaucer, *The Book of the Duchess*
John Dryden, *Eleanora*
John Dryden, *On the Death of a Very Young Gentleman*
Henry King, *Exequy on His Wife*
P. B. Shelley, *Adonais*
Thomas Gray, *Elegy Written in a Country Churchyard*
Alfred, Lord Tennyson, *In Memoriam*
Matthew Arnold, *Thyrsis*
Walt Whitman, *When Lilacs Last in the Dooryard Bloom'd*
Walt Whitman, *Captain, My Captain*
William Watson, *Lachrymae Musarum*
Vachel Lindsay, *The Eagle That Is Forgotten*
Edna St. Vincent Millay, *Elegy*
Archibald MacLeish, *Memorial Rain*

EPICS

Anonymous, *Beowulf*
John Milton, *Paradise Lost*
Abraham Cowley, *The Davideis*
William Morris, *The Story of Sigurd*
Alexander Pope, *The Rape of the Lock (A Mock Epic)*
Stephen Vincent Benét, *John Brown's Body*
Archibald MacLeish, *Conquistador*

ODES

Andrew Marvell, *An Horatian Ode upon Cromwell's Return from Ireland*
Abraham Cowley, *Pindarique Odes*
Abraham Cowley, *Ode of Wit*
John Dryden, *Alexander's Feast*
John Dryden, *A Song for St. Cecilia's Day*
Thomas Gray, *Ode on the Spring*
Thomas Gray, *The Bard: A Pindaric Ode*
Thomas Gray, *Ode on a Distant Prospect of Eton College*
William Collins, *Ode to Evening*
William Wordsworth, *Ode to Duty*
William Wordsworth, *Ode to Lycoris*
John Keats, *Ode on a Grecian Urn*
John Keats, *Ode to Autumn*
John Keats, *Ode to Melancholy*
John Keats, *Ode to Psyche*
John Keats, *Ode to Apollo*
John Keats, *Ode* (*"Bards of Passion and of Mirth"*)
P. B. Shelley, *Ode to the West Wind*
P. B. Shelley, *Ode to Heaven*
P. B. Shelley, *Ode to Liberty*
P. B. Shelley, *Ode to Naples*
Alfred, Lord Tennyson, *Ode on the Death of the Duke of Wellington*
Alfred, Lord Tennyson, *Ode to Memory*
Henry Timrod, *Ode* (*"Sleep sweetly in your humble graves"*)
Arthur O'Shaughnessy, *Ode* (*"We are the music-makers"*)
James Russell Lowell, *Ode Recited at the Harvard Commemoration*
Walt Whitman, *Pioneers! O Pioneers!*
William Vaughn Moody, *An Ode in Time of Hesitation*
William Watson, *Ode in May*
Elinor Wylie, *Hymn to Earth*
Elinor Wylie, *This Corruptible*
Edna St. Vincent Millay, *Ode to Silence*

18

THE WORDS OF POETRY: DEVICES OF SOUND AND SENSE

THE RHYTHMICAL patterns, the types and stanza-forms are the exterior manifestation, the finished architecture of poetry; but it is with words that the poet builds.

Lytton Strachey repeats the story attributed to Mallarmé of Degas, who had turned to sonnet-writing between paintings, complaining of his lack of success. "I cannot understand it," Degas cried, "my poems won't come, and yet I'm full of excellent ideas." "But, my dear Degas," replied Mallarmé, "poetry is not written with ideas; it is written with words."

Poetry is essentially more than ideas or pattern-making. Nor can mechanics alone produce that happy combination of music and meaning which is the essence of poetry. The paradox of poetry is this: although, since the introduction of printing, poetry is taken through the eye, it is seized and held by the ear. We are not conscious of the fortunate joining of vowels and consonants until the ear appreciates them. The visual structure is not enough; when vowels and consonants are unhappily combined even the greatest of poets cannot lift the line into poetry. Possibly the most awkward line of blank verse is Shakespeare's:

> Now minutely revolts upbraid his faith-breach—

a line from the fifth act of *Macbeth* which might serve as a model of cacophony.

The English poet is under a much greater handicap than his French or Italian colleague, for English is essentially a monosyllabic tongue, while the Latin languages are musically polysyllabic. It has been said that a list of Italian towns, or a mere catalogue of Sicilian food, is not spoken but sung. In English, however, even the most complex and erudite vocabulary—Milton's, for example—contains less than ten per cent of words over two syllables in length. Adelaide Crapsey's valuable, though unfortunately incomplete, *A Study in English Metrics* shows that such learned poets as Pope and Tennyson used a vocabulary that was about five per cent polysyllabic and surprises us with the discovery that in Swinburne the amount of words of more than two syllables is scarcely two per cent. This decided leaning toward the short and weighted word sacrifices something of the limpid music of the Italian language and the fluency of the French, but it gains in strength, emphasis, and "masculinity."

For sensuous effects, however, poets have leaned toward words of more than one syllable. A symposium was recently conducted to discover which ten

English words a group of poets might consider the loveliest in sound, not because of meaning. The ten words chosen as sheer music were *violet, lullaby, golden, murmuring, wearily, lovely, tranquilly, fluting, hush, melody.*

Although this list is a controversial one, several things are here disclosed on which there would be common agreement. First, the prevalence of two- and three-syllable words—there being only one monosyllabic word among the ten. Second, the predominance of soft and liquid consonants—l's, m's, n's, w's, v's—and the absence of the awkward th and the sibilant s, with only one harsh guttural g, lightened in this instance (in *golden*) by the open o. The preponderance of words dominated by l recalls the line which Tennyson considered his most musical one:

> The mellow ouzel fluting in the elm,

while the repetition of l, v and related w brings to mind Poe's:

> The viol, the violet and the vine . . .
>
> The melancholy waters lie—

and Lanier's:

> The wilful waterweeds held me thrall,
> The laving laurel turned my tide—

Lastly, there is the blending of "light" and "dark" vowels—the hard bright i and e set off by the rich and solemn o and the soft u. A short drum-beat is effected by the percussive b and t, but the explosive k and p are not here.

But the poet uses words in two ways, and he succeeds or fails in the double use of language—as music and as meaning. To do this he must take advantage of every contrivance, trick, or stratagem. Thus the poet has recourse to various devices which might be grouped under two main heads: the sensual, or devices of sound, and the intellectual, or devices of sense.

The principal devices of sound are *rhyme, assonance, alliteration, repetition,* and *onomatopoeia.*

The principal devices of sense are *metaphor, simile, metonymy, synecdoche, apostrophe,* and *epithet.*

DEVICES OF SOUND

RHYME AND ITS RELATIONS

Rhyme has been variously defined and limited. Its uses are many—as a method of emphasis; as a musical punctuation; as a half-sensual, half-psychological shock of pleasure. This pleasure is accomplished by the reader's expectancy. In a poem built with rhyme, the reader hearing a word instinctively waits for the word which will match it in sound. "Bred" says the poet, ringing the bell at the end of the line:

> Tell me where is fancy bred—

and, unconsciously, the reader faces the possibilities of the corresponding sound. He knows it will be something ending in "-ed." Will it be "said," "dead," "fed," "red," "wed," "bled," "bed," "led," "thread," "dread," "spread" . . . ? Then the poet rings another harmonizing bell:

Or in the heart or in the head—

and the reader is both pleased and surprised. It is this mixture of anticipation, recognition, and surprise which constitutes the pleasure in rhyme. If Shakespeare had followed "bred" with "bread" the reader would have been disappointed, for the words, although spelled differently, make identically the same sound. Had the second line been "Or in the heart or in the brain" the reader would have been equally disappointed, for there would have been *no* correspondence in sound. There must be enough similarity and enough difference—making a kind of game between the poet and his audience. To rouse the reader, suggest a solution and keep him, for a moment, in suspense, is the very purpose of rhyme.

Every poet tries to heighten the rhyme-response not only by the placing of his rhymes, but by their very kind. Recently various experiments have been made in an effort to enlarge the resources of rhyme, some of which may have permanent value. Some of these innovations have been given a name; others are as yet uncharted. Scholars are still uncertain whether or not rhyme can be divided as drastically as the divisions which follow, but since the poets have employed them they might well be examined.

Perfect Rhyme. Until recently this was the only form recognized by the purists. "Perfect" rhyme was the only kind considered worthy of the name; "imperfect" rhyme was held to be a contradiction in terms. One might say that, until the first decade of the twentieth century, there were only two classifications: words that "legitimately" rhymed and those that did not. "Sight rhymes" (such as "move" and "love"), used by all the poets, were frowned on by the pedants. Writing in 1882, Tom Hood, son of the poet, and author of *The Rhymester,* said: "The theory of 'allowable' rhymes is a rank heresy. The linking together in a couplet of *ever* and *river,* of *shadow* and *meadow,* of *heaven* and *driven* is without excuse." Yet the very examples which Hood held up to scorn are those employed by the best poets of the past, while the modern poets have not only dared to use such "heresies," but have employed "imperfect" rhyme—of which more later—assonance, dissonance, and have invented several departures of their own.

Though there will always be differences of taste regarding the "allowability" of certain rhymes, there is a consensus of opinion as to what constitutes a perfect rhyme. A perfect rhyme must commence on a strong or accented syllable. From the accented vowel of that syllable to the end the words intended to rhyme must be identical in sound, but the letter (or letters) *preceding* the accented vowel must be *un*like in sound. Thus *night, light, bright, sprite, quite, height, fight, write, indite, delight* are perfect single (or "masculine") rhymes, having the common sound *ite,* preceded by different, or unlike, consonants. Spelling is never the governing principle. It is the sound—and the sound alone—which determines the rhyme. Thus *prays, gaze, raise, maize,* though spelled differently, are perfect rhymes, obeying the rule of identically sounding vowel and final consonant (where there is a consonant), preceded by a *dis*similar consonant-sound. But *prays* cannot be considered as a rhyme for *praise,* for there is no difference in the consonant preceding the vowel-sound; nor can *night, unite* and *knight* be said to rhyme, for they are the same sound, there being no unlikeness whatsoever in the sound immediately preceding the vowel. Neither can *night* and *ride* be said to rhyme, for though the sound preceding the vowel is different, the sound following the vowel is also different, not identical as it should be to constitute a true rhyme. *Night* and *ride* is an example of imperfect rhyme, which will be considered later.

Adding a suffix gives us double or triple rhymes—these rhymes being commonly called "feminine"—such doubles as *lightly, brightly, sprightly* or, in triple rhyme, *rightfully, spitefully, delightfully.* Besides the addition of suffixes, double and triple—and even quadruple—rhymes are frequently formed by the pairing of words of one or two syllables to complete the rhyme, such as *foeman, Roman, no man,* or *javelins* and *travel-inns,* or *pitiful* and *city-full,* or *basement, casement* and *grace meant,* or to (widen the range) *intellectual* and *affect you all.* An excellent modern example of double rhyming is Elinor Wylie's brilliant "Peregrine," which throughout its more than one hundred lines is composed, with two exceptions, entirely of "feminine" rhymes. A characteristic fragment:

FROM "PEREGRINE"

A stick he carried,
Slept in a lean-to;
He'd never married
And didn't mean to.
He'd tried religion
And found it pleasant;
He relished a pigeon
Stewed with a pheasant. . . .
His sins were serried,
His virtues garish;
His corpse was buried
In the country parish.
—*Elinor Wylie* (1887-1928)

It is sometimes contended that rhymes of more than one syllable should be employed only in verse of a light nature, while rhymes of three or four syllables are downright comic. But one only has to remember such poems as Hood's "The Bridge of Sighs" to find proof to the contrary.

A particularly brilliant alternation of single ("masculine") and double ("feminine") rhymes is Browning's "A Grammarian's Funeral," which begins:

Let us begin and carry up this corpse,
Singing together.
Leave we the common crofts, the vulgar thorpes
Each in its tether
Sleeping safe on the bosom of the plain,
Cared-for till cock-crow:
Look out if yonder be not day again

Rimming the rock-row!
That's the appropriate country; there, man's thought,
Rarer, intenser,
Self-gathered for an outbreak, as it ought,
Chafes in the censer.
Leave we the unlettered plain its herd and crop;
Seek we sepulture
On a tall mountain, citied to the top,
Crowded with culture!

It is unnecessary to give further examples of perfect rhyme. At least ninety per cent of the rhymed poems quoted are composed of perfect rhyme. It can always be recognized by its full round certainty—the chord on the tonic with none of its intervals augmented or diminished—having always the ripe air of musical finality.

Imperfect Rhyme. Less common than perfect rhyme, imperfect rhyme has an ancient if not honorable lineage. Popular ballads are full of imperfect rhyming; the folk-songs of the fifteenth to eighteenth centuries as well as those of today simply reek with them. Perfect rhyme is the matching of identical vowel sounds preceded by unlike consonants and followed by identical consonants (e.g., *time* and *rime, late* and *fate, done* and *won*) whereas imperfect rhyme is the matching of identical vowel sounds preceded *and* followed by unlike consonants (e.g., *time* and *mine, late* and *fade, done* and *long*). Here is an example from the ancient "Childe Maurice":

I got him in my mother's bower
Wi' mickle sin and *shame;*
I brought him up in the good greenwood
Under the dew and *rain.*

And here are two native stanzas from our own brief epic of the Negro steel-driver:

John Henry said to his captain,
"A man ain't nothin' but a *man.*
Before I'd be beaten by an old steam-drill,
I'd die with the hammer in my *hand.*"

John Henry started at the right-hand side,
The steam-drill started at the *left.*
"Before I'd let that steam-drill beat me down,
Lord, I'd hammer my fool self to *death.*"

Suspended Rhyme. This variation has been resented as a suspiciously modern departure, although the Elizabethans indulged in it, and even the New Englanders were not above using such pairs as *earth* and *forth* (Bryant), *poll* and *full* (Longfellow), *coffees* and *office* (Lowell). It is closely related to perfect rhyme inasmuch as it follows the rule of unlike preceding consonant (if any) and identical final consonant sound. But—and in this departure from perfect rhyme lies its charm—*the vowel sound is different.* (E.g., *famine-*

women, ample-temple, ready-study, clergy-orgy). This device, one of the most valuable in extending the gamut of tonal effects, has also been called "slant rhyme," "tangential rhyme," or even "false rhyme." But it seems that the musical analogy is the aptest, since the vowel sound approaching the perfect cadence hangs above it like the chord of the seventh, that suspension which hesitates before it resolves and reaches the tonic. Apart from music, the effect is that of a slight but unmistakable tension, a psychological suspense. Shakespeare employed it in one of the songs in *A Midsummer Night's Dream:*

Now the hungry lion roars,
  And the wolf behowls the *moon;*
Whilst the heavy ploughman snores,
  All with weary task for*done.*

Hero and Leander reveals how Marlowe liked to vary his set of perfect rhymes with occasional suspensions:

For know that underneath this radiant *floor*
Was Danaë's statue in a brazen *tower*. . . .
Of crystal shining fair the pavement *was;*
The town of Sestos called it Venus' *glass*. . . .
The richest corn dies if it be not *reaped;*
Beauty alone is lost, too warily *kept*. . . .
And as she wept, her tears to pearl he *turned*
And wound them on his arm and for her *mourned.*

Until 1915 the use of suspended rhyme was occasional and uncertain; today its manipulators are many and skilled in practice. Among those who have varied the perfect with suspended rhyme are Humbert Wolfe, John Crowe Ransom, Archibald MacLeish, Conrad Aiken, Mark Van Doren, Stephen Spender, Merrill Moore, and Elinor Wylie. John Crowe Ransom's work is rich in suspensions; the following verse from "Husband Betrayed" is an illustration:

But there was heavy *dudgeon*
When he that should have married him a *woman*
To sit and drudge and serve him as was *common*
Discovered he had wived a *pigeon.*

Humbert Wolfe has shown more knowledge of the potentialities of suspension than any of his contemporaries; his "Iliad" is a skilful manipulation of suspended sounds and, incidentally, one of the best poems on poetry since O'Shaughnessy's ode.

ILIAD

by Humbert Wolfe (1885-   )

False dreams, all *false,*
mad heart, were yours.
The word, and nought *else,*
in time endures.
Not you long *after,*
perished and mute,
will last, but the *defter*
viol and lute.
Sweetly they'll *trouble*
the listen*ers*
with the cold dropped *pebble*
of painless *verse.*
Not you will be *offered,*

but the poet's false pain.
You have loved and *suffered,*
mad heart, in vain.
What love doth *Helen*
or Paris *have*
where they lie *still in*
a nameless *grave?*
Her beauty's a *wraith,*
and the boy *Paris*
muffles in *death*
his mouth's cold *cherries.*
Yes! these are *less,*
that were love's *summer,*
than one gold *phrase*
of old blind *Homer.*
Not Helen's *wonder*
nor Paris stirs,
but the bright, un*tender*
hexameters.
And thus, all *passion*
is nothing *made,*
but a star to *flash in*
an Ili*ad.*
Mad heart, you were *wrong!*
No love of yours,
but only what's *sung,*
when love's over, endures.

This division should also include the accords known as "visual" rhyme. Such sight rhymes as *gone-stone, war-far, love-move,* etc., belong in the category of suspended rather than imperfect rhymes.

Dissonance-Consonance. This is the strictest and most difficult of sound-devices. It is an exact pairing of consonants—*all* the consonants—instead of matching the vowels. The vowel-sound is purposely made *not* to match, as in suspended rhyme. But where, in suspended rhyme, the preceding consonant differs (following the rule of orthodox rhyme) in dissonance—often referred to as "consonance"—both succeeding *and* preceding consonant are identical in sound. *Read-rude, blood-blade, grove-grave, grain-green, light-late, fiery-fury* are examples of dissonance. (The term "consonance" is frequently employed because of the identity of consonants; since rhyme generally refers to vowel-and-consonant coupling (see page 458), and since here the vowels are totally unlike, "dissonance" seems the more exact term.) The departure which a contemporary English poet, Frank Kendon, caused to be known as "analyzed rhyme" is an employment of dissonantal effects. The opening stanza of Kendon's "I Spend My Days Vainly" is illustrative:

I spend my days vainly,
  Not in delight;
  Though the world is elate
And tastes her joys finely.

A brief poem by one of the editors of this volume attempts to show the musical possibilities of dissonance. Here the consonants are paired in orthodox couplets (a-b, c-d) while the vowels rhyme a-d, b-c.

DARK FLOWER

Intangibly the intricate vein — a
Perfects its traceries of vine. — b
The hand is taught, the heart is tried — c
Whenever the body can be betrayed. — d

Obedient to an ancient rune — a
It flowers without sun or rain. — b

No branch has borne a richer freight c
But let none sever the sanguine fruit. d
—*Louis Untermeyer* (1885-)

Archibald MacLeish, Conrad Aiken, W. H. Auden and Wilfred Owen are particularly expert in their handling of dissonance. In Auden's "Paid on Both Sides" one of the most arresting of the younger English poets achieves a hard-bitten, hard-biting eloquence, substituting dissonance for rhyme.

CHORUS
(from "Paid on Both Sides")

by W. H. Auden (1906-)

To throw away the key and walk *away*
Not abrupt exile, the neighbours asking *why,*
But following a line with left and *right*
An altered gradient at another *rate*
Learns more than maps upon the whitewashed *wall*
The hand put up to ask; and makes us *well*
Without confession of the ill. All *pasts*
Are single old past now, although some *posts*
Are forwarded, held looking on a new *view;*
The future shall fulfil a surer *vow*
Not smiling at queen over the glass *rim*
Nor making gunpowder in the top *room,*
Not swooping at the surface still like *gulls*
But with prolonged drowning shall develop *gills.*

But there are still to tempt; areas not *seen*
Because of blizzards or an erring *sign*
Whose guessed at wonders would be worth al*leging,*
And lies about the cost of a night's *lodging.*
Travellers may sleep at inns but not at*tach,*
They sleep one night together, not asked to *touch;*
Receive no normal welcome, not the pressed *lip,*
Children to lift, not the assuaging *lap.*
Crossing the pass descend the growing *stream*
Too tired to hear except the pulses' *strum,*
Reach villages to ask for a be*d in*
Rock shutting out the sky, the old life *done.*

Archibald MacLeish is no less certain in his free play of dissonance and consonance. His "American Letter" is a triumph of concealed rhyme and the graphic "Weather" is a model of rhymed consonants and unrhyming vowels. It begins:

The northeast wind was the wind off the *lake*
Blowing the oak-leaves pale side out *like*
Aspen blowing the sound of the surf *far*
Inland over the fences blowing *for*
Miles over smell of earth the ali*en*
Lake smell

The southwest wind was thunder *on*
Afternoon: you saw the wind first in the *vine*
Over the side-porch and the weather *vane*
Whirled and the doors slammed all to*gether.*
After the rain in the grass we used to *gather*
Wind-fallen cold white apples. . . .

The war poetry of Wilfred Owen, killed at twenty-five, is more poïgnant because of this device; Owen carried dissonance to a pitch of psychological as well as technical intensity. In the recently recovered "From My Diary," he wrote a poem whose alternate lines begin with: *Leaves-lives, birds-bards, bees-boys, flashes-fleshes, mead-maid, heat-heart, braiding-brooding, stirs-stars.* "Strange Meeting," which Edmund Blunden has called "the most remote and intimate, tranquil and dynamic of Owen's imaginative statements of war experience," is a dream in which Owen furthers the uncanny phantasma by the prolonged and painful dissonances. Only the beginning and ending are quoted:

FROM "STRANGE MEETING"

It seemed that out of battle I *escaped*
Down some profound dull tunnel, long since *scooped*
Through granites which titanic wars had *groined.*
Yet also there encumbered sleepers *groaned,*
Too fast in thought of death to be be*stirred.*
Then, as I probed them, one sprang up, and *stared*
With piteous recognition in fixed *eyes,*
Lifting distressful hands as if to bl*ess.* . . .
"Strange friend," I said, "here is no cause to mourn."
"None," said the other, "save the undone years. . . .
I am the enemy you killed, my *friend.*
I knew you in this dark; for so you *frowned*
Yesterday through me as you jabbed and *killed.*
I parried; but my hands were loath and *cold.*
Let us sleep now. . . ."

—*Wilfred Owen* (1893-1918)

Assonance. Assonance is the furthest departure from perfect rhyme; it is so far removed that it usually figures in a category of its own. It is a resemblance, rather than a matching; an approximation of sounds. Sometimes the same vowel is used, sometimes a merely similar one, and there is no particular concurrence of consonants, as is found in regular rhyme. *Blazing-flaming, futile-paddle* are examples of assonance. A line from an Irish broad-sheet ballad runs:

I speak in *candour,* one night in *slumber*—

and here are two more from another:

I heard great *lamentation* the small birds they were *making,*
Saying, "We'll have no more *engagements* with the boys of Mullabaun."

Alliteration. Alliteration is a repetition of sounds either at the beginning of two or more words or concealed within the words. To achieve its effect—"apt alliteration's artful aid"—the words must immediately succeed each other or occur at short intervals. It is, next to pure rhyme, the commonest device of sound. We know it in its most familiar form as an aid to memory, a mnemonic trick; many popular phrases and proverbs owe their pithiness to its power: "Sink or swim," "do or die," "fast and furious," "waste not, want not."

It is not only the commonest of sound devices, it is the oldest. The Hebrews delighted in it, and the Anglo-Saxons built an intricate poetic scheme upon it. The lines of *Beowulf* do not rhyme, but each of them has four heavily stressed syllables, the first three of which have to be alliterative. Thus:

Wæs se *g*rimma *g*æst *G*rendel haten
*M*ære *m*earcstapa, se the *m*oras heold.

Shakespeare knew its value and its danger better than any poet who ever lived. The pomp and pageantry of Egypt is sounded in such lines as:

The *b*arge she sat i*n*, like a *b*ur*n*ished th*r*o*n*e,
*B*ur*n*ed on the water. The *p*oo*p* was *b*eate*n* gold;
*P*ur*p*le the *s*ail*s*, and *s*o *p*erfumèd that
The wi*n*ds were love-*s*ick with them.

Shakespeare, also, could use alliteration to burlesque itself. As a parody of the "grand rhetorical manner," nothing is more ludicrous than Peter Quince's:

Whereat with *bl*ade, with *bl*oody *bl*ameful *bl*ade,
He *br*avely *br*oached his *b*oiling *bl*oody *br*east.

The art of alliteration is half to conceal, half to reveal, it; it should not be too prominent a challenge to the eye. Tennyson, one of the greatest of technicians, was skilful in its use:

E*l*aine the fair, E*l*aine the *l*oveab*l*e,
E*l*aine the *l*i*l*y maid of Asto*l*at,

We relish the l's—unconscious that there are eight of them—for they are cunningly hidden. Similarly the drowsy buzzing of bees and the peace of a quiet afternoon are held in Tennyson's famous alliterative lines:

The moan of doves in immemorial elms
And murmur of innumerable bees.

We resent alliteration only when it flaunts itself and dominates the line or sacrifices meaning for an overweight of music. Lanier's poetry suffers from his excessive fondness of its effect, as in

To *w*heel from the *w*ood to the *w*indow *w*here . . .

Swinburne was the worst offender. In Swinburne's poetry we are too often held up by a superfluity of sound; we are not aided but irritated by the very things he hoped alliteration would effect: ease of speech, fluency of narration, musical speed—all of which are frequently lost as we stop to count the obvious sign-posts. For example:

*Shr*ill *shr*ieks in faces the *blind bland* air that was *m*ute as a *m*aiden.
*S*tung in*to s*torm *by* the *s*peed of our *pass*age an*d d*eaf when we *passed*.

And again in "The Garden of Cymodoce":

From the *l*ips ever*l*iving of *l*aughter and *l*ove ever*l*asting that *l*eave
In the *c*left of his heart who shall *k*iss them a sna*k*e to *c*orrode it and *c*leave
So *gl*immers the flower into *gl*ory, the *gl*ory re*c*oils into *gl*oom.

It is only a step from this abuse of alliteration to Swinburne's conscious burlesque of it in "Nephelidia," that delightful self-parody in which Swinburne showed he could be more absurd than any of his imitators:

*M*ild is the *m*irk and *m*onstrous *m*usic of *m*emory, *m*elodiously *m*ute as it *m*ay be,
W*h*ile the *h*ope in the *h*eart of a *h*ero is *b*ruised *b*y the *b*reach of men's *r*apiers, *r*esigned to the *r*od;
*M*ade *m*eek as a *m*other whose *b*osom-*b*eats *b*ound with the *b*liss-*b*ringing *b*ulk of a *b*alm-*b*reathing *b*a*b*y,
As they *gr*ope through the *gr*ave-yards of *c*reeds, under s*k*ies *gr*owing *gr*een at a *gr*oan for the *gr*imness of *G*od.

INTERNAL RHYME

Rhyme, the most pronounced and potent device in emphasizing rhythm, is commonly placed at the end of the line. But, though such an arrangement is usual, it is not inevitable. Often the poet half-hides, half-reveals his rhymed words within the lines, such a device being called internal (or interior) rhyme. Kipling, following certain ballad patterns (see page 388), frequently employs the hidden rhyme. It is especially effective in his "Tomlinson," which ends:

That the sin they *do* by two and *two* they must pay for one by one—
And the God that you *took* from a printed *book* be with you, Tomlinson!

Lanier was especially fond of varying the position of his rhyming words, shifting the pattern from line to line. For example:

O *rain me* down from your darks that *contain me*. . . .
Vanishing, *swerving,* evermore *curving* again into sight. . . .
While the riotous *noon-day* sun of the *June-day* long did shine. . . .

Writers of light verse use internal rhyme freely for comic effect. An example of three internal rhymes within a single line is Wallace Irwin's "Song for a Cracked Voice," which begins:

When I was young and *slender,* a *spender,* a *lender,*
What gentleman adventurer was prankier than I,
Who lustier at *passes* with *glasses*—and *lasses,*
How pleasant was the look of 'em as I came jaunting by!

Sometimes the interior rhyme is found at the beginning instead of at the end of a line. An illustration of this is Thomas Hood's "The Double Knock," in which the rhymes are double. It opens:

"Rat-tat" it went upon the lion's chain;
"That hat, I know it!" cried the joyful girl;
"Summer's it is, I know him by his knock;
Comers like him are welcome as the day!

Lizzy! go down and open the street-door;
Busy I am to anyone but him.
Know him you must—he has been often here;
Show him upstairs, and tell him I'm alone."

Poe's "The Raven" is an example of interior rhyme in which the device is used for emphasis and sustains the reiterative beat. It must, however, be apparent that the demands of the rhyme-scheme turn several of the stanzas from the sombre repetition which was Poe's intention into amiable and even tinkling light verse, which was scarcely what Poe planned to achieve. For example:

Much I marvelled this *ungainly* fowl to hear discourse so *plainly,*
Though its answer little meaning—little relevancy bore;
For we cannot help *agreeing* that no living human *being*
Ever yet was blessed with *seeing* bird above his chamber door,
Bird or beast upon the sculptured bust above his chamber door,
With such name as "Nevermore."

But internal rhymes for humorous effects are the exception rather than the rule. Internal rhyme, mingled with assonance, plays a great part in folk-songs. Irish poetry is rich with interior as well as terminal correspondence of sounds; the English adapters followed the Gaelic pattern when they composed such verses as:

I speak in *candour,* one night in *slumber*
My mind did *wander* near to Athlone,
The centre *station* of the Irish *nation,*
Where a *congregation* unto me was shown.

Modern uses of this mingling of assonance and hidden rhyme are increasingly easy to find. Archibald MacLeish, who has done more to extend the devices of poetry than any living poet, shows how subtly the thing can be done in "Before March." In this poem the *ought* sound is woven through the lines—*water, thought* (of her), *aut*(umn), *thought*(s), *brought* (her) varied with the related sound of *salt, galled, all, alt*(ered).

BEFORE MARCH

The gull's image and the gull
Meet upon the water

All day I have thought of her
There is nothing left of that year

(There is sere grass
Salt colored)

We have annulled it with
Salt

We have galled it clean to the clay with that one autumn
The hedge rows keep the rubbish and the leaves

There is nothing left of that year in our lives but the leaves of it
As though it had not been at all

As though the love the love and the life altered
Even ourselves are as strangers in these thoughts

Why should I weep for this
What have I brought her
Of sorrow of sorrow of sorrow her heart full

The gull
Meets with his image on the winter water
—*Archibald MacLeish* (1892-)

In the following impressionistic poem irregular internal rhyme is employed to intensify the conflict as well as the color; it is used—and overused—so lavishly that almost every other word is a rhyming syllable. Here, too, assonance has been added to rhyme and, though no precise pattern is discernible, the musical effects have been definitely planned. Sometimes the rhymes and assonances are placed in immediate succession, sometimes they are widely separated.

MUNITIONS PLANT

by Louis Untermeyer (1885-)

The *core* of him is *hate.*
Deep in his *stones* he *wait*s and *growls* for *war.*
His *iron bones strain* to destroy; his *bowels*
Are grinding *steel* that *crush* the maggots he *contains.*
His *fire*s are *rush*ing anger.
Every *churn*ing *wheel,*
Fed and well-*greased* with blood,
*Turn*s with a *red*der purpose—
Released through *pass*ion to *create*
Rash agonies of *hate.*

*Thrust*ing his *back* against the *night,*
He *crack*s the *white* moon into *splinter*ed *glass*
And *crust*s of *winter*-bitten *ponds.*
*Tim*idly *clust*ered houses *sleep*
Deep in their *bonds* of silence.
He *howls* to see small hours *pass*
And *roar*s *dark blas*phemies into their *ears*
*Pouring grim spark*s upon the *bleeding* dawn
That *rears* its *head unheeding.*

Scorning the light of *peace,* now that the *stars* are *dead,*
His chimneys *shake* their *bars halt*ing the *east.*
*Morning break*s down their desperate *assault;*
Daylight *plows through* them.
*Rouse*d by the *clamor,*
*Nak*ed, *new,*
The sun,
Answering *hate* with *heat,*
*Beat*s its *great hammer* on the smoking *back.*

Morning. Fresh fires. *Attack.*
Up go *black arms tearing* apart the *sky!*
Down swarms a heaven of *flaring light*
*Bright*ening into *laught*er!
Up go the *shafts* of *fear* and hatred!
Down *fly* the *spears* of love!
The battle never *clears.*
The rhythm never *dies.*
The rhythm has no *ending.*
*Ris*ing. *Rending.*
Death at life's *core.*
War! War!

REPETITION

Repetition is another favorite method of adding emphasis and music to a poem. It may consist of a phrase repeated in various stanzas or a single word at definite intervals, but usually it is a line added to or inserted in a verse. When it appears regularly it is known as a refrain—hence the use of the term in the French forms—and thus it acts as a chorus. It may be a line of happy nonsense syllables, as in so many of the ancient ballads and songs, like Shakespeare's "With a hey, and a ho, and a hey nonino," and Nashe's "Cuckoo, jug-jug, pu-we, to-witta-woo," or it may be as grave and meaningful as the concluding line of each stanza in Lamb's "The Old Familiar Faces," on page 344. Campion's "Cherry Ripe" shows a light-hearted use of the refrain.

CHERRY-RIPE

There is a garden in her face
  Where roses and white lilies blow;
A heavenly paradise is that place,
  Wherein all pleasant fruits do flow.
    There cherries grow which none may buy
    Till "Cherry-ripe" themselves do cry.

Those cherries fairly do inclose
  Of orient pearl a double row,
Which when her lovely laughter shows,
  They look like rosebuds filled with snow;
    Yet them nor peer nor prince can buy
    Till "Cherry-ripe" themselves do cry.

Her eyes like angels watch them still;
  Her brows like bended bows do stand,
Threat'ning with piercing frowns to kill
  All that attempt with eye or hand
    Those sacred cherries to come nigh,
    Till "Cherry-ripe" themselves do cry.

—*Thomas Campion* (1540-1619)

A few of the countless poems making effective use of repetition, chiefly as refrains, are Spenser's exquisite "Prothalamion" and his "Epithalamion," quoted on page 146, Whittier's "Skipper Ireson's Ride" (see page 99), Poe's "The Raven" and his "The Bells," Alfred Noyes's 'The Barrel-Organ" and most of the songs from his *Tales of the Mermaid Tavern,* Vachel Lindsay's "The Congo" and William Rose Benét's "Merchants from Cathay." Tennyson's "The Lady of Shalott" (see page 64) uses the device most effectively by regularly repeating the title-phrase, "The Lady of Shalott." Every slumber-song is built upon a repetition of lulling syllables such as Richard Rowlands' "Upon my lap my sovereign sits," with its oft-repeated

> Sing lullaby, my little boy,
> Sing lullaby, my only joy!

Nashe's magnificent "In Time of Pestilence," a poem written during one of the sixteenth-century epidemics of the black death, has two refrains, a mounting reiteration.

IN TIME OF PESTILENCE

by Thomas Nashe (1567-1601)

Adieu, farewell earth's bliss!
This world uncertain is.
Fond are life's lustful joys;
Death proves them all but toys.
None from his darts can fly;
I am sick, I must die—
Lord, have mercy on us!

Rich men, trust not in wealth;
Gold cannot buy you health;
Physic himself must fade;
All things to end are made;
The plague full swift goes by;
I am sick, I must die—
Lord, have mercy on us!

Beauty is but a flower
Which wrinkles will devour;
Brightness falls from the air;
Queens have died young and fair;
Dust hath closed Helen's eye;
I am sick, I must die—
Lord, have mercy on us!

Strength stoops unto the grave;
Worms feed on Hector brave;
Swords may not fight with fate;
Earth still holds ope her gate;
Come, come! the bells do cry;
I am sick, I must die—
Lord, have mercy on us!

Wit with his wantonness
Tasteth death's bitterness;
Hell's executioner
Hath no ears for to hear
What vain art can reply;
I am sick, I must die—
Lord, have mercy on us!

Haste therefore each degree
To welcome destiny;
Heaven is our heritage,
Earth but a player's stage.
Mount we unto the sky;
I am sick, I must die—
Lord, have mercy on us!

Another poem with two refrains is Christina Rossetti's musical "Wife to Husband."

ONOMATOPOEIA

That awkward and forbidding-looking technical word onomatopoeia merely means "to make a name." The making or forming of a word by imitating its sound is the simplest and probably the oldest of devices; some philologists maintain that all language had its origin in this principle: such verbs as *buzz, hum, twitter, jangle* and such nouns as *pewit, whip-poor-will, yawn, murmur* are produced by onomatopoeia. Infants learn to recognize things by associating them with the sound they produce: they employ onomatopoeia naturally by naming the sound—*bow-wow* is a dog, *ding-dong* is a bell, *buzz-buzz* is a fly, *choo-choo* is a locomotive, *moo-moo* is a cow. The poet utilizes this vivid simplicity: he values the *crack* of thunder, the *tinkle* or *tolling* of bells, the *clatter* of hooves, the *rustling* of dry leaves. Even a reader with little or no knowledge of Latin can hear the gallop of a horse in the sound of the words:

Quadrupedante putrem sonitu quatit ungula campum.
—*VIII Aeneid,* 596

As with alliteration, it is easy to overdo the imitation of physical sound effects, for sounds help sense more than is realized. Many of our most familiar phrases are sharpened because of the graphic power in "the *rattle* of dishes," "the *bubbling* of water," "the *clang* of metal," "the *wash* and *swish* of water," "the *snap* of a branch," "the *thud* of a dull blow," "the *cooing* of doves," "the *slushy* mud," "the *crunch* of bones." "Think," says L. A. G. Strong, "of the shades of meaning with which we differentiate between *scream, squeal, squeak, screech, shout, bellow, bawl*—all onomatopoetic words."

Among modern American poets, Vachel Lindsay was particularly happy in the use of these sound-words. His "Kallyope Yell" is an attempt to put the whole spirit of howling democracy into the tone of the street calliope.

Music of the mob am I,
Circus day's tremendous cry:—
I am the Kallyope, Kallyope, Kallyope!
Tooting hope, tooting hope, tooting hope;
Hoot toot, hoot toot, hoot toot, hoot toot,
Willy willy willy wah Hoo!
Sizz, fizz. . . . .

DEVICES OF SENSE

SIMILE AND METAPHOR

Simile and metaphor are poetry's most constant properties. The power of each lies in the relation of things wholly unlike each other, a comparison between two objects that are alike only in the point of comparison. "Poetry begins in trivial metaphors," said Robert Frost in an address on *Education by Poetry,* "'pretty' metaphors, and goes on to the profoundest thinking that we have. Poetry provides the one permissible way of saying one thing and meaning another."

This "saying one thing and meaning another" is most strikingly achieved by simile and metaphor. "The Lord is my shepherd" sings the psalmist, and the simple metaphor suggests all the protection, the security and the loving-kindness we ask of a universal God by comparing him to the keeper of a casual flock.

When the comparison is direct and introduced by *like* or *as,* it is a simile. When the comparison is indirect or implied, without the use of *like* or *as,* it is a metaphor. "My heart is *like* a singing bird . . . my heart is *like* an apple-tree" sings Christina Rossetti, fashioning the set of similes which begin "A Birthday" on page 160. "O my luve is *like* a red, red rose . . . O my luve is *like* the melody," declares Robert Burns in the immortal song quoted on page 155. (Longfellow's "Nature," the sonnet quoted in Chapter 14, is a continuous simile, a simile extended through fourteen lines.) This definite comparison of the object with a bird, a melody, a flower—a comparison achieved by the imagination only, for, actually, a woman is not the least like a rose nor a heart like an apple-tree—is a device of which the poets never tire.

The suggestion in the metaphor is still more potent. "There is a garden in her face," sings Campion and the comparison is sudden and vivid. "O my luve is *like* a red, red rose," is, as statement, less arresting than "You *are* a tulip." The method is ageless; it is common to the seventeenth-century Robert Herrick and the twentieth-century E. E. Cummings. Herrick's "A Meditation for His Mistress" is a veritable wreath of floral conceits woven about a chain of metaphors.

A MEDITATION FOR HIS MISTRESS

You are a tulip seen today,
But, dearest, of so short a stay
That where you grew scarce man can say.

You are a lovely July-flower,
Yet one rude wind or ruffling shower
Will force you hence, and in an hour.

You are a sparkling rose i' th' bud,
Yet lost ere that chaste flesh and blood
Can show where you or grew or stood.

You are a full-spread, fair-set vine,
And can with tendrils love entwine,
Yet dried ere you distil your wine.

You are like balm enclosèd well
In amber or some crystal shell,
Yet lost ere you transfuse your smell.

You are a dainty violet,
Yet wither'd ere you can be set
Within the virgin's coronet.

You are the queen all flowers among;
But die you must, fair maid, ere long,
As he, the maker of this song.

—*Robert Herrick* (1591-1674)

The power of the metaphor is not because of its "literary" appeal; on the contrary, its popularity is due to its daily use and universal acceptance. The best of language, of conversation itself, rests on metaphor. It is not only the poet who discovers or imagines or forces a comparison between two unrelated things; peasants use naturally poetic and highly suggestive idioms the world over. Our own farmers and folk of the backwoods employ the vivid power of simile and metaphor when they say that "Rumor spreads like wildfire" or that something desirable is "scarce as hen's teeth," or that a colt moves "fast as greased lightning" (the adjective *greased* not only heightening the speed but adding a characteristically American touch of humor!), or that woman has "a heart of gold," or that a hired man is "slow as molasses in winter"—another graphic and humorous figure when one recalls how slow molasses moves even in summer! Recall the dazzling metaphor which named the commonest of wayside blossoms. It must have been some anonymous poet who went into the fields early in June and saw that this most widespread of ordinary flowers seemed to mirror the sun—the white petals like the rays and the glowing golden centre like the sun itself. So, knowing that the sun was the "eye of day," he called its replica "the Day's Eye" or, as we know it today, the Daisy! The word "daybreak" is another metaphor. It represented to the original coiner of the word not a mere division of time, but a dramatic event: a sudden breaking forth of light, as though each morning the day actually broke through its shell of darkness.

With flowers it is much the same. The botanist, with forbidding Latinity, thrusts *Arisaema triphyllum* on an innocent spring blossom, but the countryman rescues the flower for us by calling it a Jack-in-the-Pulpit. It is the metaphorical and poetry-making sense which has given our wild flowers such familiar but imaginative names as Black-Eyed-Susan, Lady's Slipper, Forget-Me-Not, Pearly Everlasting, Heart's Ease, Dutchman's Breeches, Love-in-a-Mist, Bleeding Hearts, Dew-on-the-Mountains, Queen Anne's Lace, Hens-and-Chickens.

We no longer hear the beauty and the daring which went into the making of such metaphors unless we listen with more attentive ears. We need what the poet has: observation plus imagination.

Poetry might be said to be founded on the vigor and range of the metaphorical mind. Its element is surprise. To relate the hitherto unrelated, to make "the strange seem familiar and the familiar seem strange" is the aim of metaphor. Through this heightened awareness, poetry, though variously defined, is invariably pronounced and unmistakably perceived.

KENNING

An interesting though almost forgotten form of metaphor is that which the older poets called *kenning*. Kenning is a device in which the object itself is not named but referred to by another word or phrase describing its use or characteristics. As G. E. Hodgson puts it, "It has the peculiar quality of arriving at the essence of a matter, and so of drawing not just any picture but the only apt one—and this by means of highly picturesque and suggestive words." The force and color of Anglo-Saxon poetry is emphasized by speaking of arrows as "battle-adders," of the harp as "gleewood," of the sea as "the whale's road" or "merstreets," of the king as "the ring-giver," of a ship as "the wave-floater," "the ocean steed," "the foam-girdled" or "the sea-wood."

METONYMY AND SYNECDOCHE

Metonymy and synecdoche are related to metaphor and simile, being forms of comparison. Metonymy (literally "name-change") is the substitution of one thing to represent another. It must be a suggestive substitution, an attribute of the thing meant. Thus Byron, describing the night before Waterloo, says:

> And Belgium's capital had gathered there
> Her beauty and chivalry—

"beauty" and "chivalry" standing for beautiful women and chivalrous men. We say "She sets a good table" when we mean "her table is set with the good things she prepares."

Synecdoche (literally "receiving together") is the figure of speech in which a part represents the whole—"A sail! A sail!" when a ship is meant—or, vice versa, the whole for a part—as "America won the Davis Cup," when the team from the United States is meant.

Both metonymy and synecdoche might be called "figures of association" and though they are recognizable, they are not always easily distinguishable. Thus in Shirley's:

> Sceptre and Crown
> Must tumble down,
> And in the dust be equal made
> With the poor crooked scythe and spade.

"Sceptre and Crown" and "scythe and spade" are used to symbolize the kings and peasants which the phrases suggest. When Kipling in "Recessional" speaks of England holding dominion over "palm and pine" he suggests, by selecting typically northern and tropic trees, the extent of the British Empire.

APOSTROPHE AND ANTITHESIS

Other figures of speech are *allegory* (an extended metaphor in which abstract ideas are personified, as in *The Faerie Queene*), *antithesis* (an opposition or contrast of words and ideas) *hyperbole* (an intentional exaggeration for the sake of surprise, as in Marlowe's "Was this the face that launched a thousand ships, And burnt the topless towers of Ilium!"), *litotes* (the opposite of hyperbole, being the art of understatement) and *apostrophe.*

Of these, apostrophe is the most frequently employed. It is the addressing of some absent person as though he were present or the personification of some object which is directly addressed. Byron makes excellent use of apostrophe in:

> Roll on, thou deep and dark blue ocean, roll.

Various examples of the personification of a bird, flower, insect and tree are Bryant's apostrophes "To a Waterfowl" and "To the Fringed Gentian" ("Thou blossom bright with autumn dew"), Emerson's direct address "The Humble-Bee" ("Burley, dozing humble-bee, where thou art is clime for me") and Robert Frost's:

> Tree at my window, window tree,
> My sash is lowered when night comes on;
> But let there never be curtain drawn
> Between you and me.

Keats's "Ode on a Grecian Urn" is a magnificent example of the address to an inanimate object—"Thou still unravish'd bride of quietness"—while Walt Whitman's apostrophe to Lincoln—"O Captain! My Captain!"—is an addressing of a dead hero as though he were present to hear and appreciate the tribute.

The old trick of antithesis has been given a new turn in the last half-century. The deliberate contrast of beauty and brutality, of classical allusions and harsh commonplaces, is one of the devices by which such poets as T. S. Eliot and Ezra Pound, borrowing the method from Laforgue, reveal their attitude to the difficulties and contradictions of the modern world.

EPITHET

An epithet is a word—usually an adjective—which describes its object with particular exactness. At its best an epithet can be a revelation, disclosing the salient and hitherto unsuspected quality of familiar things: "The *slow, majestic* tide," "the *patient* stars," "the *lazy, leaden-stepping* hours," "*brittle* beauty," "lovely and *soothing* death," "Press close, *bare-bosomed* night—press close, *magnetic nourishing* night . . . *mad, naked* summer night," "the *honeyed* middle of the night," "the *lavish motherliness* of milk," "Tiger, tiger *burning bright* . . . What immortal hand or eye Dare frame thy *fearful* symmetry," "*smooth-sliding* Mincius," "the pansy *freak'd* with jet," "Mount to paradise by the *stairway* of surprise," "a *tumultuous privacy* of storm," "this *quick* misery," "the *accent* of a coming foot," "death's large *democratic* fingers."

To "stab the spirit broad awake" is the poet's privilege, his very duty. And in no way can he rouse the wandering mind of the reader more powerfully than with the arresting word. Sometimes the epithets evoke wonder because of their strangeness, sometimes because of emotional associations or association with other poems. But usually it is the simplest words that move us most, and the poet becomes distinctive not so much by the choice of rare or striking words as by the uses to which he puts the ordinary terms of speech and the order which he imposes on them. Thus Robert Frost says:

The footpath down to the well is *healed.*

And Emily Dickinson, speaking of a railway train, says:

I like to see it *lap* the miles
And *lick* the valleys up—

which is not far from the ordinary—and vivid—advertisement of the modern motorcar which "*eats* up the road!"

This power of epithet—the intensification of the adjective and the quickening of the verb, the active principle in language—is to be found in colloquial speech, even in slang. The choice of the exact word, the surprising but, somehow, inevitable epithet may be found on the streets as living as in the libraries. Most of slang is ephemeral, careless and lazy, but the best of it is highly dramatic, actually charged with that keen condensation which is one of the hallmarks of poetry. What is more exact than the verb "pussyfoot"? One immediately sees the activity of the insidious "pussyfooter" in the sly, cat-like term. Such phrases as to "*crash* a party," to "*muscle* in" (a daring use of a noun as a verb, a phrase which Shakespeare would have appreciated) to "*hit* the high spots" show not only a quality of imagination but a feeling for swift-moving action and terse epithet. "To crash a party," "to muscle in," "to hit the high spots" are actually more powerful—and poetic—than "to come uninvited," "to interfere," "to visit (or dwell on) only the important aspects."

Thus the poets have not merely chosen "the best words in the best order," but the most exact ones. Whether romantic or classical, traditional or experimental, each poet relies upon the peculiar richness of a phrase or new appropriateness in a word—a shade of exactness no other poet has discovered. Thus

Rupert Brooke in "The Great Lover" (page 51) appreciates "the *strong* crust of *friendly* bread," "blue, *bitter* smoke of wood," "the cool *kindliness* of sheets," "the *rough male kiss* of blankets," "the keen *unpassioned* beauty of a great machine," "the *benison* of hot water." And in "The Waste Land" T. S. Eliot sees how "the river *sweats* oil and tar," "the jungle *crouched, humped* in silence," hears the "dry grass *singing*" and how

> A woman drew her long black hair out tight
> And *fiddled whisper music* on those strings.

The youngest of contemporary American poets are no less gifted with a feeling for the exact epithet. Merrill Moore's informal sonnets are keen with shades of observation and expression. He sees small black birds *"peppering* the sky," speaks of allowing *"fish-like* thoughts to escape in thin streams trickling through the mind" and notes how an ardent young dreamer is *"fevering* into Paradise." Christy MacKaye's "Earth Melody," written while she was still an undergraduate, is another poem to confound those who speak of a current "dearth of simplicity and high seriousness." With its skilful and almost uncanny use of epithet, music, and metaphor it may well conclude the chapter.

EARTH MELODY

by Christy MacKaye (1909-)

One day I heard a clear untremorous reed
Played by a boy in wheat fields all alone:
Each note upon the air a scarlet bead,
No joy or sorrow, only birds of tone
Pricking the cords of thought until they bleed,
And in the heart's deep earth red seed are sown.

And in the quiet after, I heard more
Than skies or meadows ever told before:
Cool consolation and a flock of pities
For hearts that drink the nourishment of pain
In music from the trees' small tongues, and cities
Of busy crickets, and from the tread of rain.

Often I listen to music of man's lore
But seldom pause, as then, on the brink of day
To speak with trees and flowers along the way,
To listen to the sigh of fields, the rune
Of inlets where the waves go plodding through,
The untired birds' small penetrating tune
That winds write on a spider-web with dew,
And the slow footfall of silence through the hours
To make articulate and fitly frame
So clear a springing as the will of flowers
Poured out upon the air to build a name.

The pace of the Bible's great grey language came
From contours of the wind, the sound of flame,

The loneliness we pity the old hills for,
Moulding the mind as oceans carve a shore;
But that and these were moulded by much more
Awfully moving among giant powers,
Yet speaking with most purity in flowers
As in that clear, untremorous music blown
From a far reed in wheat fields all alone.

19

GOOD AND BAD POETRY

It is a matter for some jubilation that not quite all men are able to create poetry. However, everyone who expresses any opinion about poetry thereby becomes a critic. "Criticism," says Henry Hazlitt, "is the one art that all humanity practises." The function of criticism, according to Matthew Arnold, is not necessarily lower than the creative function in life; it is merely another art, in no way subservient. The aim of this book is not merely to increase one's understanding and appreciation of poetry, but also to sharpen the critical sense.

There are several points on which good critics differ from poor or pretentious ones. One is knowledge, knowledge of what has been done before, insuring some evaluation of the work criticized by comparison with what has been said and written by others. Here, certainly, Pope's axiom applies—"a little knowledge is a dangerous thing"—but there is the opposite danger, seen at times among the learned, of knowing so much of what has been done before that there is nothing new to be learned; to the past-worshipping scholar, the only good poets, like the proverbial good Indians, are the dead ones. It is impossible to apply the historical method of criticism, to place an author and his work in the proper movement or current of ideas, to see what is of his age and what is of himself, without a background of wide and careful reading, modern or experimental as well as classical. A balance must be maintained.

Another quality, which Aristotle possessed in its most fully developed form, is the ability to analyze a work of art, to reduce it to its components until the parts that are faulty and those that are flawless can be distinguished. The reader who can read a poem without the knowledge that it is meant to be a sonnet and render judgment upon it without considering whether or not it has violated the rules of sonnet structure, could scarcely be considered a competent critic.

The most important quality of all, however, is good taste. Historical knowledge and analytical power may aid taste, but they cannot take its place. It has been argued that good taste is inborn, not acquired; but experience has shown that taste can be immensely improved by use. Everyone has picked up a book which seemed something of a masterpiece some years ago, only to discover that his mind has outgrown his enthusiasm and that the book now seems over-written, sentimental and vapid. This is a simple evidence of change of taste. Good taste is made up of open-mindedness, mental balance, and common sense, but it is more than these. It is not awed by names or dates; it judges a work on what it is, not what others say of it. Anatole France feels that "criticism is the adventure of a soul among masterpieces" and that its function is to record the effects a masterpiece may have upon the adventurer, thus carrying the appreciation over to another. The chief difficulty with this type of criticism is its variability; the subjective unanalyzed pleasure which B enjoys in a poem may be imperceptible to A, and no arguments on B's part will sound convincing if A's taste rejects them.

The faults in poetry which should be readily perceptible are those of content and those of expression or form. Prosaic content makes bad poetry:

> I've measured it from side to side;
> 'Tis four feet long and two feet wide.

This is bad poetry, even if it does occur in Wordsworth. Its author wrote much poetry of the highest quality and much that is worse than mediocre; yet there is always the danger of name-worship when we read a poem by Wordsworth, just as there is danger of carelessness or indifference when we read work by an unknown poet. Some of the catalogues of Whitman are not only prosaic, but particularly unlovely prose.

> The area the eighty-third year of These States—the three and a half millions of square miles;
> The eighteen thousand miles of sea-coast and bay-coast on the main—the thirty thousand miles of river navigation,
> The seven millions of distinct families, and the same number of dwellings—Always these, and more, branching forth into numberless branches . . .

Closely allied to prosiness as a fault is lack of imagination, a lack of ability to see what will arouse the desired response. Oliver Wendell Holmes, in *The Autocrat of the Breakfast Table,* says that he once wrote a poem for a festive, convivial occasion, in which one of the stanzas was:

> The purple globed clusters their life-dews have bled;
> How sweet is the breath of the fragrance they shed!
> For summer's last roses lie hid in the wines
> That were garnered by maidens who laughed through the vines.

Whatever value this may have as poetry, it must be admitted that Holmes knew what he was doing when he "reconstructed" the poem for a social meeting as a "teetotaler" would have it:

> The half-ripened apples their life-dews have bled;
> How sweet is the taste of the sugar of lead!
> For summer's rank poisons lie hid in the wines
> That were garnered by stable-boys smoking long-nines!

Hypocrisy in religion and love has been condemned again and again by society; insincerity in poetry, however, has often escaped punishment, because here hypocrisy is very hard to detect. It is no sin for a dramatic poet to pretend emotions which he himself does not feel, but when a poet writes in his own person, we demand sincerity. Examine the following sonnet:

> Sweet child of woe! who pour'st thy love-lorn lays
> On the dull ear of pensive night,

Who with thy sighs protract'st the pitying gale,
Which seeks with gos'mer wing the infant light.
Daughter of sighs, whose plumy pinions wave
In one dank circle of despair,
Who in the surge of misery lov'st to lave,
And draw'st rich solace from the realms of care.

Offspring of grief! child of extatic woes!
Now night sheds soft her curtained sleep,
And greedy wealth, and vulgar bliss repose,
And only sorrow joys to wake and weep.
Come, child of woe, and let Eliza join
In all your sorrows, for your joys are mine.

—*Royall Tyler* (1757-1826)

The strained sentimentalism and confused imagery of these lines were in vogue during the eighteenth and mid-nineteenth centuries; a new type of sentimentality which indulges in hackneyed rhymes about mother, home, and country is at present so popular a type of verse that it is syndicated daily in hundreds of newspapers. This sententiousness was one of the qualities of Longfellow which made him "the fireside poet," but brought him condemnation from the critics; Longfellow's "Psalm of Life" has been called the most popular American poem, because every line in it contains a platitude.

Not enjoyment, and not sorrow,
Is our destined end or way;
But to act, that each tomorrow
Find us farther than today.

The trouble with such verse is not the sentiment, which is commendable, but the tone, which is commonplace. Longfellow himself knew the difference between the ring of real poetry and the repetition of flat generalities; it was only rarely that he employed such stereotypes of expression. The true poet always senses the true tone; he does not have to strive to attain it. He seldom resorts to the exaggerated or "literary" poeticism; he uses the natural inflection instead of the false inflation. The strained attitude, the over-emotional pitch, the elocutionary quaver—all these result not only from the wrong way of reading, but from the wrong way of learning. The best authors write as inspired men talk—and the best poetry is the best conversation, a conversation which, though often colloquial, lifts itself and its hearers. First-hand observation is evidenced not only by the revelation of reality—the essence of meaning—but by alertness, flavor, and, above all, clarity in phrasing.

In fleeing from the hackneyed, threadbare subjects, however, some poets have gone to the opposite extreme of meaninglessness. The famous anecdote of Browning, who remarked that when he wrote a certain poem, "God and I knew what it meant, but now only God knows," might apply to several poets today. Seeking originality, the determinedly "advanced" poet often discovers nothing more original than strain and confusion.

The true poet instinctively knows what to avoid. He shuns the artificial image, the prettifying phrase; he discards the merely decorative word which has been used so often that it has lost all power of suggestion; he distrusts the grandiose expression, the pompous word which comes so easily to the pen and which comes probably from something he has read rather than from something he has experienced. He strives for the exact word, it is true, but he knows his striving must not become a search for the odd and bizarre epithet only because it is uncommon. He realizes that the natural "difference"—the thing which distinguishes one man's features and gestures from another's—is to be cultivated, but not freakishness for the sake of being different. "Poetry," Keats wrote in a letter which is as eloquent as many of his poems, "should surprise by a fine excess and not by singularity. It should strike the reader as a wording of his own highest thoughts and appear almost a remembrance. . . . The rise, the progress, the setting of imagery should, like the sun, *come natural to him,* shine over him and set soberly, although in magnificence, leaving him in the luxury of twilight. . . . If poetry comes not as naturally as the leaves to a tree, it had better not come at all."

The faults of expression vary in both directions from the norm—excesses of careless rhythm and rhyme and excesses of over-mechanized poetry. Examples of the former can be found in almost all amateur writing, and in much by the leading poets. Swinburne is an ever-present example of the latter fault. So great was his love of insistent rhythm and constant alliteration that he often allowed the devices to determine, or obscure, the meanings of his poems. A. C. Hilton scored this fault ruthlessly in "The Swinburnian Octopus":

Oh, breast that 'twere rapture to writhe on!
  Oh, arms 'twere delicious to feel
Clinging close with the crush of the python
  When she maketh her murderous meal!
In thy eight-fold embraces enfolden
  Let our empty existence escape;
Give us death that is glorious and golden,
  Crushed all out of shape!

Parody, this example should make clear, is one of the subtlest yet most effective forms of criticism; by making a careful study of the parodies of a poem or a poet, one can soon discover the major faults, magnified to ridicule. No essay could expose the faults of Longfellow's "Hiawatha" more vividly than the following brief parody:

THE MODERN HIAWATHA

He killed the noble Mudjokivis.
Of the skin he made him mittens,
Made them with the fur side inside,
Made them with the skin side outside;
He, to get the warm side inside,
Put the inside skin side outside;
He, to get the cold side outside,
Put the warm side fur side inside.
That's why he put the fur side inside,

Why he put the skin side outside,
Why he turned them inside outside.
—*Anonymous*

Readers are at times inclined to accept the judgments of others concerning the merits of a poem, never attempting to experiment for themselves. An ingenious way of discovering whether or not the true can be told from the false, the good from the bad, is to try to find the original verses among the following. Each group of three contains one genuine passage from an established poet together with two garbled versions—the originals being by Blake, Whitman, Cowley, Campion, and Yeats. The paraphrases do not appear in any particular order; the original verse sometimes appears as the first, sometimes as the second and sometimes as the last of the following groups. It should be instructive to separate the sentimental and the vulgar perversions, the exaggerated and the technically faulty, the absurdly prosaic and the hackneyed rhetorical, from the original and recognize why the other versions have failed to preserve the poets' intentions.

I

The countless gold of a merry heart,
  The rubies and pearls of a loving eye,
The indolent never can bring to the mart,
  Nor the cunning hoard up in his treasury.

✦

A cheerful heart is worth several tons of gold;
A loving glance drives the tears completely away.
It is things like these which cannot possibly be sold,
Though the buyer is more than willing to pay.

✦

Merry hearts can never be bought with filthy lucre,
  Nor is there a sale on loving eyes;
Contentment is something never put on sale—
            It comes as a prize.

II

O Missouri! you grand and glorious old river,
Rolling along full of mud and tree-trunks forever!
What a twinge you give my heart whenever I think of you!
I was born on your banks!
For that I give thanks!
My mother nursed me in a cabin there,
With all a mother's loving care!
My brother swam with me in your current!
You became part of me, you foster-parent!
I don't care at all for anything in life, not even for a minute,
If it hasn't got some of your spirit in it,
My good old Missouri!

✦

I live on the banks of the Missouri river.
I like its smell and I like the breeze from the prairies.

I don't care for any art that leaves them out.
But I don't blame others if they like things different.

✦

Others may praise what they like;
But I, from the banks of the running Missouri, praise nothing in art or aught else,
Till it has well inhaled the atmosphere of this river, also the western prairie-scent,
And exudes it all again.

III

Well, it certainly seems a pity,
But, somehow, I can't get used to the city.
Others may go into a perfect spasm
Of bliss, but I can't share their enthusiasm.
They can talk about the various joys
Of the metropolis, but to me it's nothing but noise.
Home of the burglar and political bandit,
It may seem honey and heaven to some. But I—I can't stand it.

✦

Well then, I now do plainly see
This busy world and I shall ne'er agree.
The very honey of all earthly joy
Does of all meats, the soonest cloy;
  And they, methinks, deserve my pity
Who for it can endure the stings,
The crowd and buzz and murmurings
  Of this great hive, the city!

✦

Some love the din where daily deeds are done,
  The ceaseless surf of streets where all dreams drown;
But there's short shrift for peace—the soul must shun
  The tortured testimony of the town.
Here in this maze of marts and murmurings,
  The clamorous cries will cloy and droop and die.
Give me a spot where sober Silence sings
  And bid the brash and busy world go by!

IV

Now bitter Boreas, blowing with might and main,
Calls up the clouds, speeds the tempestuous storms,
Shakes every chimney, slashes streets with sleet,
Lengthens the life of the horrendous hours;
While, indoors, music and wine-laden mirth
Endeavor to assuage the cruel cold—
And all this proves 'tis winter.

✦

In winter, nights are very long,
The cheerful days have gone.
The clouds are thick and gray,
Heavy with mist and rain,
That never seem to go away.
The chimney puffs and smokes
And life's no idle joke.
In winter, things are most forlorn
Unless there's wine and song.

✦

Now winter nights enlarge
  The number of their hours,
And clouds their storms discharge
  Upon the airy towers.
Let now the chimneys blaze
  And cups o'erflow with wine;
Let well-tuned words amaze
  With harmony divine.

V

The trees are in their autumn beauty,
The woodland paths are dry,
Under the October twilight the water
Mirrors a still sky;
Upon the brimming water among the stones
Are nine and fifty swans.

✦

I love fall-colored trees,
The road's dry melodies,
The water's evening glass,
Mirroring clouds that pass—
But my heart seems to break
When swans light on the lake.

✦

O Beauty, thou art bountiful! The trees
In autumn gold declare thy wondrous spell;
The ever-verdant glade, the bosky dell,
The azure sky, the incense-bearing breeze
Are all enchanted through thy magicries—
Even the driest woodland path can tell
Thy touch; October twilight knows it well
When dusk is loud with unseen melodies.

Now, Beauty, rise to thy majestic end,
As on the margin of the turquoise shore
The swans, like alabaster songs, descend
And the heart cries that it can bear no more.
    Yet, breathless though it is, 'tis not enough—
    What use is Beauty if there be not Love!

For a further testing of ability to select the original version of a poem from its perversions the reader is referred to Allen Abbott and M. R. Trabue's *Exercises in Judging Poetry* (Teachers College, Columbia University), a work which is as amusing as it is rewarding.

SUGGESTIONS FOR ADDITIONAL READING

CRITICAL PARODIES

A. Stodart Walker, *The Moxford Book of English Verse*
J. C. Squire, *Apes and Parrots: An Anthology*
J. C. Squire, *Tricks of the Trade*
J. C. Squire, *Imaginary Speeches*
Louis Untermeyer, *Collected Parodies*
A. S. Martin, *On Parody*
Owen Seaman, *The Battle of the Bays*
Carolyn Wells, *A Parody Anthology*
George Kitchin, *A Survey of Burlesque and Parody in English*

HUMOROUS CRITICISM

Hilaire Belloc, *Caliban's Guide to Letters*
Olga Katzin, *Peeps at Parnassus*
Louis Untermeyer, *Heavens*

20

THE READING OF POETRY

I

THE ACT of creation, whatever form it may take, is a private act. While he is painting or composing or fitting words to his emotions, the artist is concerned with nothing but his necessity to express; it is only when the work is completed that there is the urge to communicate. The moment his canvas is exhibited, his symphony performed, or his poem printed, his immediate desire is to share with some audience the pleasure of his creation. This sharing is as deep-rooted an impulse as creation itself. No matter what the artist's work may be made to teach, no matter how it is interpreted, its main object is to increase enjoyment.

In the case of poetry the sharing of enjoyment is made easier by the physical basis of rhythm. The first contact is not through the mind, not even through the ear—though that is almost immediate—but through the pulse. As an earlier chapter declared, we breathe rhythmically; our lives are regulated by night and day, light and darkness, by the pulse, the progress of seasons, by small or great rhythms. Until poetry is spoiled by being made a "word-study" or a problem in mathematical scansion, it is instinctively relished by children. The jingles of Mother Goose are instinctively appreciated by the child long before he understands them; the infant responds to poetry before he turns to prose.

With growth and experience the contact becomes less immediate. Once beyond the intuitive stage of enjoyment, poetry demands a closer attention; it demands a union of faculties; for its complete enjoyment it requires a sensitive ear, a quick eye, and a mind tuned to awareness. The poet has written under the spell of intense emotional and mental excitement. He has been seized by the fervor of an idea, the force of an incident, the power of a mood, and there has been conceived in him this living thing, this order out of chaos —a poem. His feelings and his craft have combined—his emotion has concentrated into an idea, his idea has found words—and a new thing has been created.

It should be understood that there are, generally speaking, two ways of approaching poetry: the experiential, the recognition of subject matter, and the purely intuitional. Some poets can best be known one way, some another. Such poets as Blake and, in our own day, Léonie Adams have to be known through intuition on the part of the reader; a *rapport* with such poets can only be established by an immediate entering into the states of their emotions.

The reader must not only react to this act of creation, he must share its intensity. He must understand something of the emotional disturbance and the process by which the inner turmoil is shaped into order. He must learn to perceive, beneath the thought which lies at the core of the poem, the illuminating phrase, the suggestive sound, the highly selective epithet. He must appreciate not only the significant details, but the implications of the poem—for a poem does not merely make a statement, it stimulates the imagination to move beyond the borders of the fact. He should, for a complete sharing, learn to recognize the pattern or form on which the poem is built. It is by such awareness that the poet lives again in his creation; the author is revivified with every sensitive reader.

All we have ever felt or thought is at the command of a poem, and the more we bring to it the richer return we carry away. No great poem ever grows stale no matter how often it is alertly read; it yields fresh beauties with each re-reading. It is only when we read it carelessly or superficially that we miss the thrill of rediscovery, the combination of the strange and the familiar. The great poem, vibrant with life, is never boring; it is we, too easily tired, who become bored.

This can be established by an examination of the most familiar of poems, if the re-reading is done with keen perception and fresh awareness.

> It is an ancient Mariner,
> And he stoppeth one of three.
> "By thy long grey beard and glittering eye,
> Now wherefore stopp'st thou me?"

It is the reader who has been suddenly stopped and, thus arrested, almost resents being button-holed by the poet. Nevertheless he listens. The poet's appeal is immediate, dramatic, and irresistible. Thus Coleridge begins "The Rime of the Ancient Mariner" in the simplest terms, directly, and with a minimum of "literary" devices. By this method he seeks not only the reader's interest and consent, but his coöperation. Assured of it, the poet proceeds to his tale.

> The ship was cheered, the harbour cleared,
> Merrily did we drop
> Below the kirk, below the hill,
> Below the lighthouse top.

Still simply, Coleridge persuades the reader to embark, and the long journey begins with the reader no longer an onlooker but a participant in the adventure. The ship is blown to the south pole; everywhere ice cracks and growls; the albatross, bird of good omen, follows the ship; it is killed; a curse descends upon the ship. . . . By this time poet and reader stand shoulder to shoulder, intent upon the outcome, in a creative excitement to which every tense phrase contributes. The mere picture of suspense is unforgettable.

> Day after day, day after day,
> We stuck, nor breath nor motion;
> As idle as a painted ship
> Upon a painted ocean.

The sense of terror increases, the horror is elaborated.

The very deep did rot: O Christ!
That ever this should be!
Yea, slimy things did crawl with legs
Upon the slimy sea.

As the poem grows more intense the epithets tighten, the effects are increased by every device in the poet's power. Onomatopoeia is used startlingly:

And every soul, it passed me by,
Like the whizz of my cross-bow!

Repetition and alliteration emphasize the physical and spiritual loneliness:

Alone, alone, all, all alone,
Alone on a wide, wide sea!

Alliteration and onomatopoeia are combined to reënforce the uncanny events:

And the coming wind did roar more loud,
And the sails did sigh like sedge.

A change begins. The spell is broken, the ship moves. With action, the speed of the verse increases; the stanzas are sometimes five and six lines long; there is even one of nine lines. Internal rhyme, dramatic dialogue, ghostly overtones emphasize the weird events.

This seraph-band, each waved his hand;
It was a heavenly sight!
They stood as signals to the land,
Each one a lovely light.

Effect is piled on effect until nearly the end. Then contrast is uncannily employed. The climax is not keener excitement, but a great calm.

Farewell, farewell! but this I tell
To thee, thou Wedding-Guest!
He prayeth well, who loveth well
Both man and bird and beast.

From the casual and minute, the reader has reached the immense; he has been speeded through desperation and death, and, quietly, he has been brought back into life again. He has been the wedding-guest and the ancient mariner; the poet's adventure has been apprehended, shared, completed. And it is the reader who has made the completion. By means so simple and yet so subtle that he is scarcely conscious of them, the reader has ceased being merely a reader and has become the chief actor in the poem—has become, during the taking-on of this intense emotional identification, the poet himself.

II

This identification is more readily achieved and awareness of the poet's methods heightened if the poem is read aloud. Poetry is a verbal legerdemain in which the ear is quicker than the eye. The poem on the printed page is only half alive when it is not sounded; it needs all the oral values, every shade of music, every nuance of vowel and consonant. The eye may perceive the pattern made by couplets, but it is the ear that realizes their tight decision, due to the matched sounds coming in sharp succession, little hammer-blows of rhyme. The ear senses, even before the mind knows the rules, how the stanza becomes looser the further rhyme is spread apart, and how "suspended" or "imperfect" rhyme increases that looseness.

So with the length of lines. The reader, reading aloud, will soon realize that short lines are clenched and usually bright and hard, indicating speed and firmness; while long lines are more fluent and "open," giving the effect of leisure and relaxation. The ear will immediately appreciate why a conspicuously short line at the end of a stanza of long lines, or inserted in the midst of one, is an excellent way of arresting the attention.

All this can be attained on one condition: that the reader overcome what seems to be a resistance to reading aloud. Possibly the resistance is founded not so much on reticence as on fear, the fear of sounding foolish or affected. Most students have fallen into one of two bad reading-habits: (1) a false modesty in oral interpretation, which prevents entering into the spirit of the poem, and (2) a careless rapidity of reading, a superficial "skimming" which, unless it is required and done with dramatic concentration, ruins whatever is read. The art of oral reading has suffered from association with elaborate and stilted "elocution." Elocution induces a strained attitude and artificial interpretation; good reading should reveal the natural qualities as well as the subtle values of poetry. Both extremes of expression should be avoided. Rapid slurring and theatrical over-emphasizing are equally reprehensible; to minimize the sonority of a line is no worse than to exaggerate it.

Since most poetry conveys its effect through pictures, it is important that the reader clearly visualize as he reads. That the "inner eye" is as necessary as the outer one is a more than physical truth—especially in poetry. One who reads Browning's "My Last Duchess" should be able to see the completely self-satisfied Duke, the portrait on the wall, "looking as if she were alive" with the passionate innocence her husband unwittingly describes, even the Count's silent messenger intent upon arranging the dowry for the new bride. Without a mental picture of sculptured men in "mad pursuit," maidens loth, struggling to escape, pipes and timbrels playing their "unheard melodies," Keats's "Ode on a Grecian Urn" loses most of its meaning.

Before the reader can render ideas as well as images, he must get the thought of the poem clear in his own mind. This grasp of content can be conveyed only by the correct pronunciation and clear enunciation of the words, by proper breathing so that the pauses aid the phrasing, by the inflections of vocal pitch to show questioning or exclamation, by changes in tempo and by emphases of volume upon the important ideas. To point a climax gestures may sometimes be added, though they should not be overused. The most important fact is this: if the reader does not have the meaning of the poem clearly in mind and the desire to communicate that meaning to another, all the training in pronunciation, breath-control, inflection, and gesture will be of little avail;

if the ideas are firmly grasped, the other aids should come as a matter of course and taste.

If the poem is one which presents a human character engaged in any activity, the dramatic ability inherent in all of us comes into play. The ability of the reader to identify himself with the person speaking, and to experience all that he experiences, is shown in the character portrayal, pantomime, and voice-changes of speed and quality. Tennyson's "Rizpah," together with every other dramatic monologue, requires this dramatic instinct; Rossetti's "Sister Helen" calls for rapid changes of voice and manner; Chaucer's "Pardoner's Tale" can be made vivid only if the reciter keeps his mind constantly on the action.

The foregoing requirement implies the next: an ability to feel the emotions of the poet and to present them sincerely. An interpretation which puts a cynical twist into an idyllic love poem such as Spenser's "Epithalamion" is falsifying just as much as one which inserts laughter in the midst of an elegy like Shelley's "Adonais." But, it may be asked, what if the emotion seems strained, artificial, ludicrous? The reader must then try to give what the author intended, even though it may be mawkish sentimentality. If the reader has a choice, let him choose poems in which the emotions agree with his own. If he finds fault with the emotions expressed, let him make it plain by a prologue or after-word, not by deflecting the poem from its course.

A persistent fault in reading poetry is the reader's slavery to patterns and rhythms. Instead of absorbing them into his consciousness and then devoting himself to the interpretation of content, the reader too often allows the rhyme and meter to master him; he forgets all meaning in the musical stress of the rhythm and stops dead at the end of each line. Good poetry fits meter to phrasing and tempo to action. A good rule for the interpreter to follow is to keep a conversational ideal always in mind; the metrical harmony will usually take care of itself. The most musical poem can be ruined by a mechanical insistence upon rhythm.

Taste in every art is, to a great extent, a matter of cultivation. But certain bases of judgment have been established and the reader should be able to guide himself by these. The greater his sensitivity the greater will be his reward; in his re-creation he will approximate the creator. "To have great poets," said Whitman, "there must be great audiences, too."

A CONDENSED REFERENCE LIST

The following list is not an attempt to cover the entire field of English poetry. It is a condensed reference bibliography of only the more important books, and particularly those which have been used in the preparation of this work. It does not include the various volumes of original poetry by the poets mentioned in these chapters, but only books about poetry, collections, and works of an analytical nature. An asterisk (*) in front of a title means that the book is technical or recommended for advanced students. Wherever possible the publishers mentioned are those of the more accessible American editions. The arrangement is alphabetical.

GENERAL AND CRITICAL

About English Poetry. *G. F. Bradby.* Oxford University Press. 1929.

American Literature. *Percy H. Boynton.* Ginn and Company. 1923.

* American Poetry Since 1900. *Louis Untermeyer.* Henry Holt and Company. 1923.

An Approach to Poetry. *Phosphor Mallam.* Thos. Y. Crowell Co. 1930.

The Art of Poetry. *William Paton Ker.* Oxford University Press. 1923.

Aspects of Literature. *John Middleton Murry.* Alfred A. Knopf, Inc. 1920.

* Axel's Castle. (A series of essays on Yeats, Eliot, the modern symbolists; a study in the imaginative literature of 1870-1930.) *Edmund Wilson.* Charles Scribner's Sons. 1931.

* Biographia Literaria. *Samuel Taylor Coleridge.* Everyman's Library: E. P. Dutton & Company. 1908.

Common Sense About Poetry. *L. A. Strong.* Alfred A. Knopf, Inc. 1932.

Convention and Revolt in Poetry. (New edition.) *John Livingston Lowes.* Houghton Mifflin Company. 1930.

Countries of the Mind. *John Middleton Murry.* (Two volumes.) Oxford University Press. 1931.

Creative Poetry. *B. Roland Lewis.* Stanford University Press. 1932.

The Criticism of Literature. *Elizabeth Nitchie.* The Macmillan Company. 1928.

A Defense of Poetry. *Percy Bysshe Shelley.* Houghton Mifflin Company. 1921.

Discovering Poetry. *Elizabeth Drew.* W. W. Norton, Inc. 1933.

Enjoyment of Poetry. *Max Eastman.* Charles Scribner's Sons. 1914.

* The Essentials of Poetry. *William Allan Neilson.* Houghton Mifflin Company. 1912.

* Form in Modern Poetry. *Herbert Read.* London. 1932.

The Garment of Praise: *The Necessity for Poetry.* By *Eleanor Carroll Chilton* and *Herbert Agar.* Doubleday, Doran & Company. 1929.

An Introduction to Poetry. *Hubbell and Beaty.* The Macmillan Company. 1922.

The Kinds of Poetry. *John Erskine.* Duffield and Company. 1923.

* Language. *Edward Sapir.* Harcourt, Brace and Company. 1921.

Literary Criticism. *William Wordsworth.* (Edited with an Introduction by Nowell C. Smith.) Oxford University Press.

THE NAME AND NATURE OF POETRY. *A. E. Housman.* Macmillan Co. 1933.
THE NATURE OF ENGLISH POETRY: An Elementary Survey. *L. S. Harris.* London: J. M. Dent & Sons, Ltd. 1931.
A NEW APPROACH TO POETRY. By *Elsa Chapin* and *Russell Thomas.* Chicago: The University of Chicago Press. 1929.
* A NEW DEFENSE OF POETRY (in *Heart of Man and Other Papers*). *George E. Woodberry.* Harcourt, Brace and Company. 1920.
* A NEW STUDY OF ENGLISH POETRY (Twelve essays on such subjects as "Poetry and Rhythm," "Poetry and Education," and "British Ballads"). *Henry Newbolt.* E. P. Dutton & Company. 1919.
* ON ENGLISH POETRY ("Being an irregular approach to the psychology of the art, from evidence mainly subjective"). *Robert Graves.* Alfred A. Knopf, Inc. 1922.
* PATTERN AND VARIATIONS IN POETRY. *Chard Powers Smith.* Charles Scribner's Sons. 1932.
* PHASES OF ENGLISH POETRY. *Herbert Read.* Harcourt, Brace and Company. 1929.
THE POETIC MIND. *F. C. Prescott.* The Macmillan Co. 1922.
THE POETIC WAY OF RELEASE. *Bonaro Wilkinson.* Alfred A. Knopf, Inc. 1932.
POETRY AT PRESENT. *Charles Williams.* Oxford University Press. 1930.
POETRY: ITS MUSIC AND MEANING. *Lascelles Abercrombie.* Oxford University Press. 1933.
POPULAR HISTORY OF ENGLISH POETRY. *T. Earle Welby.* London: A. M. Philpot, Ltd. 1924.
* PRACTICAL CRITICISM. *I. A. Richards.* Harcourt, Brace and Company. 1929.
THE PRELUDE TO POETRY: *The English Poets in Defence and Praise of Their Art.* Edited by *Ernest Rhys.* Everyman's Library: E. P. Dutton & Company. 1927.
* PRINCIPLES OF LITERARY CRITICISM. *I. A. Richards.* Harcourt, Brace and Company. 1925.
* SCEPTICISMS: NOTES ON CONTEMPORARY POETRY. *Conrad Aiken.* Alfred A. Knopf, Inc. 1919.
* SCIENCE AND POETRY. *I. A. Richards.* W. W. Norton Company. 1926.
* SELECTED ESSAYS. *T. S. Eliot.* Harcourt, Brace and Company. 1932.
A STUDY OF POETRY. *Bliss Perry.* Houghton Mifflin Company. 1920.
STUDIES OF CONTEMPORARY POETRY. *Mary C. Sturgeon.* Dodd, Mead and Company. 1919.
THE STUDY OF LITERATURE. *Louise Dudley.* Houghton Mifflin Company. 1928.
* THE THEORY OF POETRY. *Lascelles Abercrombie.* Harcourt, Brace and Company. 1924.
THE USE OF POETRY. By *T. S. Eliot.* Cambridge: The Harvard University Press. 1933.
THE WAY OF THE MAKERS. *Marguerite Wilkinson.* The Macmillan Co. 1925.

ANTHOLOGIES

There seems to be no end to the compiling of anthologies, and this list makes no pretense to being a catalog. It ignores the special and sectional anthologies entirely and lists only the larger and more notable collections.

AN AMERICAN ANTHOLOGY (From 1787 to 1900). Edited by *Edmund Clarence Stedman.* Houghton Mifflin Company. 1900.
AMERICAN POETRY: 1671-1928. Edited by *Conrad Aiken.* The Modern Library. 1929.

American Poetry: From the Beginning to Whitman. Edited by *Louis Untermeyer*. Harcourt, Brace and Company. 1932.

An Anthology of Modern Verse (Devoted exclusively to recent English poets). Chosen by *A. Methuen*. Methuen and Company (London). 1921.

The City Day. Edited by *Eda Lou Walton*. The Ronald Press Company. 1929.

Come Hither. A collection of rhymes for all ages. Edited by *Walter de la Mare*. Alfred A. Knopf, Inc. 1923.

English Poetry (1660-1800). Edited by *R. S. Crane*. Harper & Brothers. 1932.

The Golden Treasury. Edited by *Francis Turner Palgrave*. (With additional poems.) Oxford University Press. 1914.

The Home Book of Verse. Edited by *Burton E. Stevenson*. Henry Holt and Company. 1918.

Lyric America (1630-1930). Edited by *Alfred Kreymborg*. Coward-McCann, Inc. 1930.

Modern American Poetry (Fourth revised edition). Edited by *Louis Untermeyer*. Harcourt, Brace and Company. 1930.

Modern British Poetry (Third revised edition). Edited by *Louis Untermeyer*. Harcourt, Brace and Company. 1930.

The New Poetry: An Anthology of Twentieth Century Verse in English. Edited by *Harriet Monroe* and *Alice Corbin Henderson*. The Macmillan Company. 1923. Enlarged edition. 1932.

The Oxford Book of Ballads. Edited by *"Q" (A. T. Quiller-Couch)*. Oxford University Press. 1910.

The Oxford Book of English Verse. Edited by *"Q" (A. T. Quiller-Couch)*. Oxford University Press. 1907.

The Oxford Book of Eighteenth Century Verse. Edited by *David Nichol Smith*. Oxford University Press. 1926.

The Oxford Book of Sixteenth Century Verse. Edited by *E. K. Chambers*. Oxford University Press. 1932.

The Oxford Book of Victorian Verse. Edited by *"Q" (A. T. Quiller-Couch)*. Oxford University Press. 1925.

Poetry of the Nineties. Edited by *Clarence E. Andrews* and *M. O. Percival*. Harcourt, Brace and Company. 1926.

Romantic and Victorian Poetry. Edited by *C. E. Andrews* and *M. O. Percival*. A. A. Adams & Company (Columbus, Ohio). 1924.

Twentieth Century Poetry. Edited by *John Drinkwater, Henry Seidel Canby* and *William Rose Benét*. Houghton Mifflin Company. 1930.

A Victorian Anthology (From 1837 to 1895). Edited by *Edmund Clarence Stedman*. Houghton Mifflin Company. 1895.

STUDIES OF METRE, PROSODY AND TECHNIQUE

* Ballades and Rondeaus, Sestinas, Villanelles, Etc. Selected by *Gleeson White*. The Walter Scott Publishing Company. 1900.

* Form and Style in Poetry. *William Paton Ker*. The Macmillan Company. 1928.

The Forms of Poetry. (A Pocket Dictionary of Verse.) *Louis Untermeyer*. Harcourt, Brace and Company. 1926.

* History in English Words. *Owen Barfield*. Doubleday, Doran & Company. 1918.

* A History of English Prosody. *George Saintsbury*. (Three volumes.) The Macmillan Company. 1924.

* Lyric Forms from France: Their History and Their Use. Edited by *Helen Louise Cohen*. Harcourt, Brace and Company. Revised edition. 1930.

* New Methods for the Study of Literature. *Edith Rickert*. U. of Chicago Press. 1927.

One Hundred and One Ballades. (*Contributions by Maurice Baring, Hilaire Belloc, E. C. Bentley, G. K. Chesterton, J. C. Squire and others.*) London: Cobden-Sanderson. 1931.

* The Physical Basis of Rime. *Henry Lanz*. Leland Stanford University Press. 1931.

* The Principles of English Versification. *Franklin P. Baum*. Harvard University Press. 1922.

* A Study in English Metrics. *Adelaide Crapsey*. Alfred A. Knopf, Inc. 1918.

* Words and Poetry. *George H. W. Rylands*. Payson and Clarke. 1928.

The Writing and Reading of Verse. *Clarence E. Andrews*. D. Appleton & Company. 1918.

BALLADS AND FOLK-SONGS

Album of Songs: A Collection of Twenty Favorite Compositions (with music). *Stephen C. Foster*. G. Schirmer & Sons.

American Ballads and Songs. Collected by *Professor Louise Pound*. Charles Scribner's Sons. 1922.

American-English Folk Songs (with music). Collected in the Southern Appalachians. *Cecil J. Sharp*. G. Schirmer. 1918.

The American Songbag (with music). Edited by *Carl Sandburg*. Harcourt, Brace and Company.

The Ballad Book. Edited by *William Allingham*.

Ballads and Lyrics of Love. Edited by *Frank Sidgwick*. F. A. Stokes Company. 1908.

The Book of American Negro Poetry. Edited by *James Weldon Johnson*. Harcourt, Brace and Company. Revised edition. 1931.

Broad-Sheet Ballads: A Collection of Irish Popular Songs. With an Introduction by *Padraic Colum*. Baltimore: Norman Remington Company. 1914.

Cowboy Lore. By *Jules Verne Allen*. San Antonio, Texas: Naylor Printing Company. 1933.

Cowboy Songs and Frontier Ballads. Compiled by *John A. Lomax*. The Macmillan Company. 1921.

English and Scottish Popular Ballads. *Francis James Child*. Edited from his collection by *George Lyman Kittredge* and *Helen Child Sargent*. Houghton Mifflin Company. 1904.

Folk-Songs of the Kentucky Mountains (with music). *Loraine Wyman* and *Howard Brockway*. Oliver Ditson Company. 1920.

Folk-Songs of the South. Edited by *John Harrington Cox*. Harvard University Press. 1925.

Frankie and Johnny (Thirteen versions and a play). *John Huston*. A. and C. Boni. 1930.

Frontier Ballads. Heard and gathered by *Charles J. Finger*. Doubleday, Page and Company. 1927.

The Hobo's Hornbook (with music). *George Milburn*. Ives Washburn. 1930.

Kentucky Mountain Songs and Lonesome Tunes (with music). *Loraine Wyman* and *Howard Brockway*. Ditson and Company.

Legendary Ballads. Edited by *Frank Sidgwick*. F. A. Stokes Company. 1908.

MODERN STREET BALLADS. Collected, with an Introduction, by *John Ashton*. London: Chatto & Windus. 1888.

ON THE HISTORY OF BALLADS. *William Paton Ker*. Oxford University Press. 1910.

THE OXFORD BOOK OF BALLADS. Edited by *"Q" (A. T. Quiller-Couch)*. Oxford University Press. 1910.

OZARK MOUNTAIN FOLKS. By *Vance Randolph*. New York: The Vanguard Press. 1932.

PERCY'S RELIQUES OR RELIQUES OF ANCIENT ENGLISH POETRY. *Thomas Percy, Lord Bishop of Dromore*. Everyman's Library: E. P. Dutton & Company. 1906.

POETIC ORIGINS AND THE BALLAD. *Louise Pound*. The Macmillan Company. 1921.

THE POPULAR BALLAD. *Francis B. Gummere*. Houghton Mifflin Company. 1907.

POPULAR BRITISH BALLADS: ANCIENT AND MODERN. (Four volumes.) Chosen by *R. Brimley Johnson*. London: J. M. Dent & Company. 1894.

SONGS AND BALLADS OF THE MAINE LUMBERJACKS. *Roland Gray Palmer*. Harvard University Press. 1924.

SOUTH CAROLINA BALLADS. Collected and Edited by *Reed Smith*. Cambridge: Harvard University Press. 1928.

TRADITIONAL BALLADS OF VIRGINIA. Edited by *Arthur Kyle Davis, Jr*. Cambridge: Harvard University Press. 1929.

VERMONT FOLK-SONGS AND BALLADS. Edited by *Helen Hartness Flanders* and *George Brown*. Brattleboro: Stephen Daye Press. 1932.

WEEP SOME MORE, MY LADY. (A Companion Volume to READ 'EM AND WEEP.) *Sigmund Spaeth*. Doubleday, Page and Company. 1927.

LIGHT VERSE

The collections of light verse are almost as numerous as the usual type of anthology. Only a few of the more representative collections are listed.

AMERICAN FAMILIAR VERSE. Edited by *Brander Matthews*. Longmans, Green and Company.

THE LITTLE BOOK OF LIGHT VERSE. Edited by *Anthony C. Deane*. Dodd, Mead and Company.

THE LITTLE BOOK OF SOCIETY VERSE. Compiled by *Claude Moore Fuess* and *Harold Crawford Stearns*. Houghton Mifflin Company.

LYRA ELEGANTIARUM. Edited by *Frederick Locker-Lampson*. Ward, Lock and Company (London).

A TREASURY OF HUMOROUS POETRY. Edited by *Frederick Lawrence Knowles*. Dana Estes and Company.

A PARODY ANTHOLOGY. Collected by *Carolyn Wells*. Charles Scribner's Sons.

PATRICIAN RHYMES: *A Résumé of American Society Verse*. Edited by Clinton Scollard and Jessie B. Rittenhouse. Boston: Houghton Mifflin Company. 1932.

VERS DE SOCIÉTÉ. Edited by *Charles H. Jones*. Henry Holt and Company.

A VERS DE SOCIÉTÉ ANTHOLOGY. Collected by *Carolyn Wells*. Charles Scribner's Sons. 1907.

A WHIMSEY ANTHOLOGY. Collected by *Carolyn Wells*. Charles Scribner's Sons.

THE LYRIC

The best discussions as well as the most comprehensive analyses of the English lyric are to be found in:

ENGLISH LYRICAL POETRY. *Edward B. Reed.* Yale University Press. 1912.
* LYRIC POETRY. (From the earliest Norman melodies to the literary lyrics of the late Victorians.) *Ernest Rhys.* E. P. Dutton and Company. 1913.
THE LYRIC. *John Drinkwater.* George H. Doran Company. 1916.

There are several collections of purely lyrical verses, the best being:

EARLY ENGLISH LYRICS. Edited by *E. K. Chambers* and *F. Sidgwick.* London: Sidgwick & Jackson. 1926.
ENGLISH LYRICAL POETRY (1500-1700). Edited by *Frederic Ives Carpenter.* Charles Scribner's Sons.
SELECTIONS FROM MODERN POETS. Made by *J. C. Squire.* Martin Secker (London). 1921.
SHORTER LYRICS OF THE TWENTIETH CENTURY: 1900-1922. Selected by *W. H. Davies.* The Poetry Bookshop (London). 1923.
SHORTER MODERN POEMS: 1900-1931. Edited by *David Morton.* Harper & Brothers. 1932.

THE SONNET

The most thorough consideration as well as the best historical survey of the sonnet is:

THE ENGLISH SONNET. *T. W. H. Crossland.* Dodd, Mead and Company. 1917.

There are three general compilations which are excellent in themselves and especially interesting as comparative collections; the first covers the field from Henry Howard, Earl of Surrey (1517-1547), to the New England poets; the second is devoted entirely to the poets of the Nineteenth Century.

THE BOOK OF THE SONNET. (Two volumes.) Edited by *Leigh Hunt* and *S. Adams Lee.* Roberts Brothers.
SONNETS OF THIS CENTURY. (With a critical introduction on the sonnet.) *William Sharp.*
THE GOLDEN BOOK OF ENGLISH SONNETS. Selected by *William Robertson.* Harrap & Company (London). 1913.

THE EPIC

THE EPIC. *Lascelles Abercrombie.* G. H. Doran & Co.
ENGLISH EPIC AND HEROIC POETRY. Professor *W. MacNeile Dixon, M.A.* J. M. Dent and Sons (London). 1911.
EPIC AND ROMANCE. *William Paton Ker.* The Macmillan Company. 1908.
THE HEROIC AGE. *H. M. Chadwick.* Cambridge University Press. 1924.
THE OLDEST ENGLISH EPIC. *Francis B. Gummere.* The Macmillan Company. 1922.

FREE VERSE

The best discussion of free verse occurs in two volumes, both of them rather technical, presenting two almost opposed points of view.

* THE RHYTHM OF PROSE. *William Morrison Patterson.* Columbia University Press.
* TENDENCIES IN MODERN AMERICAN POETRY. *Amy Lowell.* Houghton Mifflin Company. 1921.

INDEXES

INDEX OF AUTHORS, TITLES, AND SUBJECTS

Poets who are represented by complete poems or considerable sections are indicated in capitals; critics, prose writers, and poets referred to with only fragmentary quotation are indicated in Roman. Titles of poems quoted in full or considerable part are in italics; titles referred to with only fragmentary quotation are in quotation marks. After each poet's name, the first numbers indicate the pages upon which the poet's name is mentioned or his poetry discussed; the numbers after the titles of poems by the poet indicate where the poem can be found; the titles of poems by each poet are arranged under his name in alphabetical order.

Subjects and terms defined are in Roman.

INDEX OF FIRST LINES